OCR Ant
for Classic
AS and A Level

The following titles are available from Bloomsbury for the OCR prescribed texts in Latin and Greek for examination June 2019 to June 2021

Apuleius *Metamorphoses* V: **A Selection** with introduction, notes and vocabulary
by Stuart R. Thomson

Cicero *Philippic* II: **A Selection**, with introduction, notes and vocabulary
by Christopher Tanfield

Ovid *Amores* II: **A Selection**, with introduction, notes and vocabulary
by Alfred Artley

Horace *Odes*: **A Selection**, with introduction, notes and vocabulary
by John Godwin

Horace *Satires*: **A Selection**, with introduction, notes and vocabulary
by John Godwin

Tacitus *Histories* IV: **A Selection**, with introduction by Ellen C. O'Gorman
and notes and vocabulary by Benedict Gravell

Virgil *Aeneid* XI: **A Selection**, with introduction, notes and vocabulary
by Ashley Carter

OCR Anthology for Classical Greek AS and A-level, covering the prescribed texts by Aristophanes, Euripides, Herodotus, Homer, Plato and Xenophon, with introduction, notes and vocabulary by Stephen Anderson, Rob Colborn, Neil Croally, Charlie Paterson, Chris Tudor and Claire Webster

Supplementary resources for these volumes can be found at
www.bloomsbury.com/OCR-editions-2019-2021

Please type the URL into your web browser and follow the instructions to access the Companion Website. If you experience any problems, please contact Bloomsbury at contact@bloomsbury.com

OCR Anthology for Classical Greek

AS and A Level: 2019–2021

Selections from

Herodotus, *Histories*, Book 7

Plato, *Phaedo*

Xenophon, *Anabasis*, Book 4

Homer, *Iliad* 9 and 18

Euripides, *Medea*

Aristophanes, *Peace*

With introduction, commentary notes and vocabulary by
*Stephen Anderson, Rob Colborn, Neil Croally, Charlie Paterson,
Chris Tudor and Claire Webster*

BLOOMSBURY ACADEMIC
LONDON · NEW YORK · OXFORD · NEW DELHI · SYDNEY

BLOOMSBURY ACADEMIC
Bloomsbury Publishing Plc
50 Bedford Square, London, WC1B 3DP, UK

BLOOMSBURY, BLOOMSBURY ACADEMIC and the Diana logo are trademarks of
Bloomsbury Publishing Plc

First published in Great Britain 2018
Reprinted 2019 (twice)

ISBN: PB: 978-1-3500-1260-8
         ePDF: 978-1-3500-1262-2
        eBook: 978-1-3500-1261-5

Typeset by Integra Software Services Pvt. Ltd.
Printed and bound in Great Britain

To find out more about our authors and books visit www.bloomsbury.com
and sign up for our newsletters.

CONTENTS

General Preface   vii

Herodotus, *Histories*, Book 7: 5–10, 34–35, 38–39, 45–52, 101–105   1

Introduction   3
Text   17
Commentary Notes   29
Vocabulary   61

Plato, *Phaedo* 62c9 to 67e6 and 69e6 to 75c5   71

Introduction   73
Text   93
Commentary Notes   107
Vocabulary   167

Xenophon, *Anabasis*, Book 4: 7–8   177

Introduction   179
Text   191
Commentary Notes   197
Vocabulary   211

Homer, *Iliad* 18: 1–38, 50–238 and *Iliad* 9: 182–431   221

Introduction   223
Text *Iliad* 18   253
Commentary Notes *Iliad* 18   259
Vocabulary *Iliad* 18   285
Text *Iliad* 9   296
Commentary Notes *Iliad* 9   303
Vocabulary *Iliad* 9   329

Euripides, *Medea*: 214–270, 271–356, 364–409, 663–758, 869–905, 1019–1055, 1136–1230 341

Introduction 343
Text 357
Commentary Notes 373
Vocabulary 407

Aristophanes, *Peace*: 1–10, 13–61, 180–336 421

Introduction 423
Text 443
Commentary Notes 453
Vocabulary 487

GENERAL PREFACE

The text and notes found in this volume are designed to guide any student who has mastered Greek up to GCSE level and wishes to read these selections in the original.

The editions are, however, particularly designed to support students who are reading the set texts in preparation for OCR's AS and A-Level Greek examination from June 2019 to 2021. (Please note this volume uses AS to refer indiscriminately to AS and the first year of A Level, i.e. Group 1.)

Herodotus, *Histories*
Introduction, commentary notes and vocabulary by Claire Webster
AS: Book 7: 5–10
A Level: Book 7: 34–35, 38–39, 45–52, 101–105

Plato, *Phaedo*
Introduction, commentary notes and vocabulary by Rob Colborn
AS: 62c9 to 67e6
A Level: 69e6 to 75c5

Xenophon, *Anabasis*
Introduction, commentary notes and vocabulary by Stephen Anderson
A Level: Book 4: 7–8

Homer, *Iliad*
Introduction, commentary notes and vocabulary by Chris Tudor
AS: Book 18: 1–38, 50–238
A Level: Book 9: 182–431

Euripides, *Medea*
Introduction, commentary notes and vocabulary by Neil Croally
AS: 271–356, 663–758, 869–905
A Level: 214–270, 364–409, 1019–1055, 1136–1230

Aristophanes, *Peace*
Introduction, commentary notes and vocabulary by Charlie Paterson
A Level: 1–10, 13–61, 180–336

Each edition contains a detailed introduction to the context of the ancient work. The notes aim to help students bridge the gap between GCSE and AS or A-Level Greek, and focus therefore on the harder points of grammar, word order and idiom. At the end of each edition is a full vocabulary list for all the words contained in the prescribed sections, with words in OCR's Defined Vocabulary List for AS-Level Greek flagged by means of an asterisk.

Herodotus, *Histories*

Introduction, Commentary Notes and
Vocabulary by Claire Webster

AS: Book 7: 5–10

A Level: Book 7:
34–35, 38–39, 45–52, 101–105

Introduction

The author and his work

Information about the life of Herodotus is scant. He himself tells us that he came from Halicarnassus (now Bodrum in Turkey), a Greek colony on the southwest coast of Asia Minor under the rule of the Persian empire. Ancient sources add that he came from a leading family and was related to an epic poet called Panyassis. The tradition stated that he was driven into exile for opposing a tyrant of Halicarnassus called Lygdamis, and opposition to tyranny certainly marks his work throughout. There are no precise dates for his life, but deducing from his writing we can guess that he was born some time in the 480s BC and lived into the 420s, since he refers to events in the Peloponnesian War, which began in 431. He travelled widely, apparently as far as Elephantine in Egypt, and certainly spent some time in Athens before becoming a citizen of the city of Thurii in Magna Graecia.

In the introduction (known as a 'proem') to his great work, Herodotus writes:

Ἡροδότου Ἁλικαρνησσέος ἱστορίης ἀπόδεξις ἥδε, ὡς μήτε τὰ γενόμενα ἐξ ἀνθρώπων τῷ χρόνῳ ἐξίτηλα γένηται, μήτε ἔργα μεγάλα τε καὶ θωμαστά, τὰ μὲν Ἕλλησι τὰ δὲ βαρβάροισι ἀποδεχθέντα, ἀκλεᾶ γένηται, τά τε ἄλλα καὶ δι᾽ ἣν αἰτίην ἐπολέμησαν ἀλλήλοισι. (*Histories* 1.1)

This is the setting forth of the inquiry of Herodotus of Halicarnassus, so that the things done by men might not fade away with time, and so that the great and marvellous deeds, some displayed by the Greeks, some by the barbarians, might not lose their renown, with regard to both other matters and to the reason why they went to war with each other.

The key word here is ἱστορίη: 'inquiry'. Herodotus grew up in an environment in which the scientific appraisal of natural phenomena was flowering. The scientists and thinkers whom we know as the pre-Socratic philosophers, and whom Aristotle termed the φυσικοί, who came from Ionia and Magna Graecia (Greek colonies in what is now Turkey and parts of Italy and Sicily), were thinking about how the world works and wondering about man's relation to it in the century before Herodotus' birth and during his lifetime. Thinkers such as Heraclitus and Anaximander of Ephesus, Thales and Anaximenes of Miletus, and Parmenides and Zeno of Elea questioned assumptions and the evidence of the senses while speculating on such questions as what the universe is made from, whether there is one god or many gods and what form any divine being might take. It is from this milieu of fervent innovation that Herodotus' work springs. The pre-Socratics, when they wrote (and only fragments survive), seem to have written almost exclusively in verse, and indeed verse seems to have been the natural medium for any kind of elevated writing in the early history of written Greek. Herodotus' immediate predecessors as writers of prose were the so-called *logographoi* or *logopoioi*, whose work again only exists now in fragments. These writers compiled genealogical, ethnographic and geographical material, often casting their writings in terms of a voyage describing both the topography of the area visited, and the customs and characteristics of the people encountered. Herodotus mentions one of these, Hecataeus of Miletus, who wrote two works, one a geographical treatise, the Περίοδος γῆς ('Journey round the Earth'), and the other a book of mythical geneaologies. Works such as these, and other technical treatises, were quite different from an undertaking with the scope of Herodotus' *Histories*, and it is right to regard Herodotus as a radical and innovative writer. John Herington says that 'Herodotus' *Histories* … stands at the frontier where two eras meet: the era in which poetry and legend were the prime media for the interpretation of our world, and the era of prose, of history, of rational enquiry generally'.

In the proem, Herodotus states that he is concerned to record both τὰ γενόμενα and ἔργα μεγάλα τε καὶ θωμαστά. We can presume that the latter means heroic deeds in war, as Herodotus' aim is that they might not become ἀκλεᾶ: this word, with its echo of the Homeric concept of kleos, places us in the context of epic heroism and the memorializing of the deeds of the heroes in song. There is a real sense in which Herodotus is seeking to emulate the author of the *Iliad* and the *Odyssey* in prose: in seeking to explain the causes of a war between Greek and barbarian, as Homer had the Trojan War, and in relating the exploits of the participants in that war. τὰ γενόμενα, then, can be taken to mean achievements of other kinds, including technical and architectural feats. These, coupled with the final stated intention of ascertaining why the Greeks and the barbarians came to war with one another, give us the blueprint for the extraordinary work that follows, combining as it does geographical, ethnographical and religious detail with political and military accounts and technical descriptions of a varied nature.

The work as we possess it is divided into nine books, not a division made by Herodotus himself, but by later editors. The first three books deal with the rise of the Persian empire, as Herodotus explores the circumstances that led to conflict between Persia and Greece; the second three cover the reign of Darius and his unsuccessful attempt to conquer Greece in 490, as well as the revolt of the Ionian Greeks (those Greeks living in colonies on the coast of Asia Minor) against Persian power; and the final three tell the story of Darius' son Xerxes' unsuccessful invasion of Greece in 480. Herodotus fills this bald-sounding outline, however, with myriad details of all sorts: nothing that might interest the reader is omitted, whether it be the treatment of crocodiles in Egypt or the sort of stories that make Herodotus such rich pickings for beginners' Greek books ('Arion and the Dolphin', 'Polycrates and the Ring', 'How Egyptians avoided Gnats'). He describes phenomena that will make the reader gasp – Xerxes' army was so big that it drank the rivers dry – and gives such detailed instructions for how to construct a bridge across the Hellespont or how the Scythians scalp their enemies that we could follow them ourselves should we so wish.

As has been stated, Herodotus' writing reveals him to be broadly pro-democracy, at least as it was practised in Athens, although he allows Megabyzus in the constitutional debate in Book 3 to point out the weaknesses of 'mob rule':

ὁμίλου γὰϱ ἀχϱηίου οὐδέν ἐστι ἀξυνετώτεϱον οὐδὲ ὑβϱιστότεϱον

Nothing is more foolish and violent than a useless mob.

On the other hand, as might be expected of someone with his background, he is a persistent critic of tyranny and records the cruelty of despots on both sides of the Greek/Persian divide. In Book 7, this means the apparently capricious punishments inflicted by Xerxes on those who displease him, notably the story of Pythius who asks that one of his sons might be left behind to care for him in his old age. Xerxes becomes enraged at the request and has Pythius' son cut in half, forcing the army to march between his remains.

Herodotus' religious beliefs inform his world view consistently and form a constant thread of motivation and explanation running through the narrative. Certain things are just taken for granted: the terrible crimes of the great will be suitably punished; hubris (excessive pride, especially involving defiance of the gods) will be followed by nemesis (retributive justice). So when Xerxes has dared to flog and throw chains into the Hellespont, which is in Greek terms a god, it is only right and to be expected that he should be punished by the failure of his enterprise. Nemesis may, terrifyingly, be delayed by generations, as it is for Croesus, who is told by the oracle that his defeat and the fall of Sardis are punishment for the long-distant murder of Candaules by Gyges. The gods are jealous and will resent any mortal's extraordinary prosperity: this is the basis of the story of the 'unfriending' of Polycrates, tyrant of Samos, by Amasis of Egypt, although there are other more rational explanations for the severing of their alliance. Finally, man, and even god, is always at the mercy of Fate, which can sometimes be delayed but never completely avoided: Apollo explains to Croesus that he would have liked to save Sardis because of all the offerings Croesus has made to him, and indeed he has delayed the destruction of the city as long as he can, but in the end even he cannot override the diktats of Fate. In all this, we can see Herodotus' work again as growing from the epic tradition, as we remember episodes such as the death of Sarpedon in *Iliad* 16, when Zeus wishes that he could save his mortal son and has to be reminded by Hera that he may on no account do such a thing.

Portents, dreams and oracles feature strongly in Herodotus' narrative as divine signs that reveal the truth and should never be dismissed or taken lightly. He explicitly states when discussing the apparently accurate oracle of Bacis before the battle of Salamis, 'As I view such occurrences and consider the clear statement of Bacis, I neither venture myself to say anything to contradict oracles, nor do I allow others to do so.' In Book 7 he relates that as the army finished crossing the Hellespont, a mare gave birth to a hare and comments that Xerxes 'took no account of it, although it was easy to interpret', the meaning being that Xerxes would cross into Greece proudly, but later come fleeing back, running for his life.

Dreams for Herodotus are not simply images or stories conjured by the mind of the sleeper, but physical manifestations sent by the gods, and a story in Book 7 shows the central role which he believes they take in explaining people's actions. In this episode, Xerxes has held a debate with the Persian nobles and decided to launch the invasion of Greece. Later on in the evening, privately, he changes his mind, but then sees a dream in which a man appears to him and advises him to stick to the original plan. Deciding to ignore the dream, he recalls the assembly and tells them the expedition is off, but the following night the man appears again and tells him that if he doesn't launch the expedition, he will fall from power. Xerxes, in a panic, summons his uncle Artabanus, who had advised against the invasion, and induces him very much against his will to dress up in the king's clothes and sleep in his bed to see whether the dream will appear to him too. Artabanus proffers rational explanations and excuses, but Xerxes makes him go through with the plan. He sees the dream, which threatens to burn his eyes with hot irons for his attempt to divert what is inevitable. Artabanus, forced to admit that the expedition seems to be divine will, withdraws his opposition.

Discussing this story, GEM de Ste Croix in his seminal article on Herodotus says 'if I had to recommend one single passage to illustrate Herodotus' religious outlook it would be this'. As de Ste Croix points out, the supernatural intervention provides the final link in the chain of causation for the invasion: all the human motives have been set out in the preceding chapters, and now the dream performs its function in preventing Xerxes from changing his mind.

Herodotus had a mixed reputation in antiquity: famously, Cicero combined calling him the 'father of history' (*pater historiae*) with a remark that in his work there were 'countless tall tales' (*innumerabiles fabulae*). Plutarch wrote a work entitled *de malignitate Herodoti* (*On the malice of Herodotus*), in which he complained that Herodotus showed excessive sympathy for barbarians, unfair favouritism towards Athens, gross unfairness towards other Greek cities such as Corinth and a general lack of truthfulness. The titles of other lost works, *On Herodotus' thefts*, *On Herodotus' lies* and *Against Herodotus*, all show that there was a significant group of critics who found Herodotus' work deeply problematic. In later times, too, he has suffered, mostly by comparison with his successor Thucydides. Those who have promoted Thucydides over Herodotus have tended to concentrate on what is seen as Herodotus' less scientific or rigorous historical method. Whereas Herodotus chose to conduct research into the events of the past, Thucydides rejected such investigation as impossible, with a probable rebuke of Herodotus implied (τὰ γὰρ πρὸ αὐτῶν καὶ τὰ ἔτι παλαίτερα σαφῶς μὲν εὑρεῖν διὰ χρόνου πλῆθος ἀδύνατα ἦν: 'the character of the events which preceded, whether immediately or in more remote antiquity, owing to the lapse of time, cannot be made out with certainty'). He chose instead to concentrate on writing about contemporary events, an approach followed by later ancient historians, who either wrote about the present, as Thucydides had done, or reinterpreted the works of earlier writers without conducting any new research. Herodotus tells us that he has written down what people told him, τὰ λεγόμενα, without deciding for the reader which he thinks is the 'correct' version.

By contrast, Thucydides decides for us which account he finds preferable and excises the other versions. While this may make Herodotus seem undiscerning, it can be an informative and useful approach, since it records the prejudices and rumours of the time, and thus has a historical function beyond the establishment of the 'facts'. By researching and presenting all the available versions of a story without judgement, Herodotus allows us as readers to decide for ourselves which is the most credible, possibly in the light of later events or information to which Herodotus did not have access. As a result, he might in fact be regarded as *more* scientific than his successor, who has suppressed information that might in the end have had a decisive bearing on our interpretation.

Crucial for our understanding of Herodotus' historical method are the four words he uses himself to describe how he composed his work. They are ὄψις ('sight'), γνώμη ('judgement'), ἱστορίη ('inquiry') and ἀκοή ('hearsay'). To elaborate, these tell us that as far as possible Herodotus went and saw for himself the sites of the events he is writing about (ὄψις); he used his own judgement to evaluate what he saw and heard (γνώμη); he conducted his own research by talking to people and finding out as much as it was possible to ascertain (ἱστορίη); and finally, when all those methods were exhausted, he had to rely on other people's stories (ἀκοή).

Aristotle called Herodotus ὁ μυθολόγος, 'the romancer', and we can presume that Thucydides is getting in another dig at his predecessor when he rejects τὸ μυθῶδες, the storytelling or legendary element, in his work. So the patronizing judgement of later generations has tended to be that Herodotus, while making a laudable attempt at starting up the practice of history, was really not all that good: not concerned enough with accuracy, too ready to believe what people told him, too credulous of supernatural interventions, not single-minded enough, too ready to go off on digressions. This is, I think, to miss the point in more than one important way.

To begin with his ancient admirers: Dionysius of Halicarnassus wrote 'If we take up his book, we are filled with admiration till the last syllable and always seek for more', praising his fellow-townsman for choosing a better subject, writing a better beginning and end, including more interesting material and arranging it better, and writing more vivid and graceful prose than Thucydides. The readability of Herodotus is undeniable: the sheer variety of his subject matter and the enthusiasm of his treatment of it make sure that this is the case. We also make a mistake in comparing Herodotus with Thucydides without acknowledging that his background and aims are very different. Herodotus should be seen as growing out of a poetic tradition. He actually mentions a large number of poets by name in his work (Homer, Hesiod, Archilochus, Anacreon, Sappho, Alcaeus, Simonides, Pindar, Aeschylus), as against a single prose writer, Hecataeus. He has a poet's overview of the way in which the individual fits into the wider scheme of human life. In his world, it is from poetry that authority comes: the poetic utterances of the oracles, particularly the Delphic oracle, so often quoted by Herodotus, were taken as judgements in disputes between cities (as reported in Thucydides 1.28). The tragedies of the Athenian playwrights also exert clear influence over his writing: he mentions Phrynichus and Aeschylus, and a reading of Book 7 reveals that he must surely have been familiar with the latter's *Persians*. On a wider scale, the preoccupations of tragedy – curses, dreams, oracles, hubris, nemesis – also inform his view of the events he describes. This is most clearly the case in the story of Croesus and the fall of Sardis, and the tale of

Adrastus and his son Atys, which might almost be a prose retelling of an actual play, so closely does it follow the form and conventions of the genre.

If Thucydides' aim is, as he states, to record the greatest war that has ever happened or will ever happen, in order that man might learn from it not to make the same mistakes again, Herodotus has a less immediately functional approach to his work. By looking at the events of the past, and contemplating the characters of the protagonists, Herodotus takes a long view of the lessons of history. He is not teaching us to avoid the same mistakes as our ancestors: history itself proves that this is impossible. But he enables us better to understand our state as humans and the conditions of our happiness. On numerous occasions throughout the work, characters meditate upon or come to an understanding of this: Croesus on the funeral pyre in *Histories* 1.86 realizes the truth of the words spoken to him years before by Solon, and in turn causes Cyrus to reflect on the mutability of human fortune. In 7.46, Xerxes bursts into tears when reviewing his vast forces and explains the reason for his outburst to his uncle Artabanus:

ἐσῆλθε γάρ με λογισάμενον κατοικτεῖραι ὡς βραχὺς εἴη ὁ πᾶς ἀνθρώπινος βίος, εἰ τούτων γε ἐόντων τοσούτων οὐδεὶς ἐς ἑκατοστὸν ἔτος περιέσται

For when I thought about it pity struck me for the brevity of the whole life of man, since of these men who number so many, no-one will survive a hundred years from now.

When it comes to the third stated aim of the proem, to record why the Greeks and the barbarians, which is to say the Persians, came to war with each other, we can learn much from the debate about whether or not to launch the invasion which Herodotus puts in Book 7. As Immerwahr, quoted by Grethlein, says of this scene: 'Its real importance lies not in the discussion of the advisability of the Greek campaign, but in the description of Xerxes' motives and the summary of Persian historical ambitions in general. In a sense, then, the scene gives a complete description of the causes of the Persian Wars.' By having Xerxes stress the obligation he feels to live up to the achievements of his ancestors, as well as cite the more immediate casus belli (an act or situation that provokes or justifies a war) of the burning of Sardis and the defeat at Marathon, Herodotus makes both the long- and short-term causes clear. The tenor of the whole work, too, sets up an unbridgeable divide between the Greek and Persian worlds and outlooks, although Herodotus has some admiration for the Persians. While he does not hesitate to point out the unpredictable despotic behaviour of Xerxes, he also tells stories that illustrate his humanity and kindness (e.g. when he sends Artabanus away with full honours to administer affairs in Susa 7.52). On the one hand, the portrayal of his mercurial character seems at times typical of what we expect of the stereotypical capricious and whimsical despot, but Herodotus' portrait of Xerxes is rather more rounded than that. He is fickle and headstrong, but he is capable of listening to his advisers, and of genuine deep feeling. While acknowledging the problems that one-man rule brings, Herodotus admires the strength that a unified command gives to the Persians, as well as the apparently unswerving loyalty of the king's staff. He makes it clear, however, that fear of the monarch hampers real discussion: in his account of the debate mentioned above, he tells us that only

Artabanus is bold enough, because of his age and status as Xerxes' uncle, to disagree with him. All the other nobles, although ostensibly summoned to give their advice, do not dare do so. The clearest statement of the ideological gulf between the two sides comes in the speech of the exiled Spartan king Demaratus in Book 7. The total inability of Xerxes to understand why men might be prepared to sacrifice their lives for a belief or ideal without the need for compulsion speaks volumes.

The prescribed text: an overview

Book 7 begins with an explanation of Xerxes' accession to the throne: his father, Darius, enraged by the defeat at Marathon and vowing to avenge the Persians, planned an expedition against Greece and sent messengers across his empire requisitioning troops and supplies from various cities throughout Asia. So vast was the undertaking, since the demands made were even greater than for the Marathon campaign, that, Herodotus tells us, it took three whole years. Further, in the fourth year, the Egyptians, who had been subdued by Darius' predecessor Cambyses, staged a rebellion.

Herodotus explains that it was the Persian custom for a king setting out on an expedition to appoint his successor prior to departure, presumably to ensure a swift and easy continuance of his line should he fail to return. In Darius' case, the succession was not clear-cut – he had had three sons by his first wife, and a further four by his second wife, Atossa, after he had succeeded to the kingship. So the eldest of his sons, Artobazanes, claimed the throne on the grounds of absolute seniority, while the eldest of the sons born to Darius and Atossa, Xerxes, staked his claim on the fact that Atossa was the daughter of Cyrus the Great. The deciding argument is presented here as being provided by Demaratus, the deposed king of Sparta, in self-imposed exile in Persia. He introduces the Spartan concept of porphyrogeniture, which is to say that a son born to a ruling king outranks any born before he ascended the throne, the very system which had led to Demaratus' own overthrow. The intervention by Demaratus introduces something of a theme of the book, showing the Persian king taking advice from wise counsellors, and indeed Demaratus himself appears again many chapters (and many years) later, lauding Spartan bravery and obedience to the laws in conversation with Xerxes.

One year into the Egyptian rebellion, Darius died and the kingdom passed to Xerxes. Herodotus tells us that Xerxes had no great enthusiasm for a campaign against Greece, but came under the sway of his cousin Mardonius, who, we are told, wielded 'a greater influence over him than any other Persian'. Mardonius has appeared in Book 6 of the *Histories* in command of a Persian force sent to punish the Athenians in the aftermath of the Ionian revolt of 492. He was last mentioned when Darius relieved him of his command after the catastrophic destruction of the fleet rounding the coast near Mount Athos, which Herodotus tells us saw the loss of 300 ships and some 2,000 men. His reappearance here marks his return to favour under the new regime and he is pivotal in persuading Xerxes to launch the expedition. The campaign of 480 saw some considerable success for Mardonius; he was made governor of the conquered parts of Greece and sacked the city of Athens. When the

Athenians rejected his offer of a truce, Mardonius led the Persians to meet them at Plataea and was killed in the ensuing battle, the final act in the 480 invasion.

Mardonius is shown as a persistent and persuasive character: he urges Xerxes to stage the campaign not only to punish the Athenians but also to win renown for himself and warn other states not to consider attacking his territory. He adds compelling detail about the beauty and fertility of Europe and combines this with flattery: 'What mortal save the King deserves to have it as his own?' Herodotus' opinion is that Mardonius is motivated by his own daredevil character and his ambition to be made governor of Greece: an ambition which, as mentioned above, is satisfied, if only in the short term.

The Egyptian rebellion is duly crushed, and the preparations for the expedition against Athens are under way when Herodotus describes a meeting called by Xerxes of 'the foremost noblemen in Persia' so that he can keep them informed of his plans and garner their opinions. Herodotus presents this meeting in terms of a formal debate with set-piece speeches from the participants. Xerxes speaks first, laying out his intentions to bridge the Hellespont, take revenge upon the Athenians and, in the process, conquer what amounts to the whole world.

Mardonius' speech follows, supporting Xerxes' plans, and moreover presenting the Greeks as negligible in battle.

At this point, Herodotus says that all the other Persians lacked the courage to voice an opinion against the proposal. Only Xerxes' uncle, Artabanus, dared to speak, emboldened by his age and close family relationship to the king.

Artabanus is presented throughout the prescribed text as an extremely cautious elder statesman, learned through experience, and steeped in proverbial wisdom. He provides a contrast to both the reckless and ambitious Mardonius and at times vacillating and uncertain Xerxes. His speech here recalls the defeats and disasters suffered by previous campaigns (which have been brushed over by Mardonius), points out that he had cautioned Darius against the expedition which ended in failure, and advises Xerxes not to run unnecessary risks.

Herodotus presents Xerxes as prey to external influences both human and divine, as well as to his own mutable character: Mardonius sways him in favour of the expedition, and he treats Artabanus' caution with rage, but when left alone as darkness falls, he falls victim to uncertainty and changes his mind. In his sleep he sees a dream vision advising him to stick to his decided course of action, but dismisses it and summons the Persians the next day to tell them that he has decided against the campaign after all. There follows a dramatic series of events included by Herodotus to show the part played by the divine in human affairs: the dream appears again, and throws Xerxes into such a panic that he summons Artabanus and requires him to dress up in the king's clothes in the hope that he will see the dream as well. Initially very reluctant, Artabanus is eventually persuaded to comply with Xerxes' plan, apparently believing that the dream will not be foolish enough to fall for the deception. He is duly terrified when the dream does appear, and rebukes him for his part in changing Xerxes' mind, and he rushes to advise the king to resume preparations, since it is clearly divine will that the expedition be launched. This view is apparently then further supported by another vision in which Xerxes sees himself with his head crowned with olive, the shoots of which envelop the earth. The Magi interpret this to mean that the whole earth, and all its people, will become Xerxes' slaves.

Herodotus spends the next part of the book describing some of the preparations for the campaign, emphasizing that this was the greatest army ever mustered, taking four years to amass, and drinking all but the greatest rivers dry as it passed. We are told that Xerxes had a canal dug across the Athos peninsula, in an attempt to avert any possible repeat of the naval losses suffered by Darius. Herodotus' opinion is that the king was partially motivated in this undertaking by the desire to reinforce his own magnificence, since it would have been possible to haul the ships over the isthmus rather than digging this canal, which he tells us was wide enough for two triremes to pass one another rowing.

As Xerxes passes through the city of Celaenae, he meets a hugely wealthy individual called Pythius, who not only treats the army with lavish hospitality, but offers the whole of his movable fortune to the war effort. Xerxes is shown by Herodotus to be amazed by Pythius' great wealth and genuinely moved by his generosity, granting him a formal title of friendship and magnanimously making a present to him of the fortune he offered, with extra money added.

The two episodes which follow appear to highlight the terrifyingly capricious nature of Xerxes' character. First, the pontoon bridge which has been built across the Hellespont is destroyed by a storm, throwing Xerxes into a passionate rage. Not only does he order the sea whipped and abused, he has the engineers responsible for building the bridges beheaded. Then, as the army sets off from Sardis after wintering there, the same Pythius who a few chapters earlier was treated with such generosity and open-heartedness by Xerxes presumes upon his official friendship with the king by begging him to allow the eldest of his four sons to stay behind to look after him in his old age. Xerxes is grossly offended and in retribution has Pythius' son hacked into two pieces which are placed on opposite sides of the road for the army to march between.

The army proceeds on its march, drinking the River Scamander dry and pausing at Priam's citadel, where Xerxes makes a sacrifice to Athena of Ilium and the Magi offer libations to the heroes. Herodotus tells us that the night after these rituals, a great terror seized the army. He offers no explanation, but perhaps we are supposed to think that the terror is a warning from the gods not to proceed. It certainly adds a feeling of doubt and uncertainty to the account.

Reaching Abydos, Xerxes holds a review of the forces at his disposal from a specially-built white stone dais. He is moved to tears and, when questioned by Artabanus, explains that he is musing on the fleeting nature of human life. Artabanus responds with a reminder that there are worse sufferings than the brevity of life – indeed, life is often so terrible that death comes as a release. In this moment of quiet reflection, Xerxes asks Artabanus whether, had it not been for the dream, he would have changed his mind about the expedition, and Artabanus confesses that he is full of anxiety about the outcome. He cryptically says that he regards 'the two greatest things in existence' as Xerxes' bitterest enemies. Xerxes is presented as taking things rather literally, and presumes that his uncle is talking about his army and fleet. Artabanus explains that his real meaning was that the sea and the land were Xerxes' enemies, because the fleet is so huge that no harbour exists large enough to hold it, while the army will starve because the land will be unable to support it.

Continuing the representation of him in this episode as reasonable and reflective, Herodotus shows Xerxes responding in measured tones, advising Artabanus to lay aside his overcautious and anxious approach. Xerxes observes that the Persian empire would not have reached its present extent had his predecessors not taken risks. He tells Artabanus that the campaign will be brought to such a swift and successful conclusion that the army won't have time to starve.

In his final intervention, Artabanus offers Xerxes one last piece of advice, which is that he should not lead the Ionian Greeks in war against their mother city of Athens. They are, he says, unnecessary to the success of the campaign; it is criminal to expect them to enslave their mother city; and the strong likelihood is that they will in fact go over to the other side and attempt to secure Athens' liberty. The calm and self-confident Xerxes of this exchange remains unmoved. He reassures Artabanus that the worth of the Ionians is not only unimpeachable but also reinforced by the fact that they have left their wives and children behind in Persian territory. The exchange concludes with Artabanus being sent back to Susa to keep Xerxes' rule safe in his absence.

Once Artabanus has gone, Xerxes summons the most eminent Persians to make a preliminary sacrifice, and then the great crossing of the Hellespont begins.

There follows an extensive and lavish description by Herodotus of the different contingents of the army and the various accoutrements and clothing by which they are distinguished one from another, followed by a catalogue of the fleet. Covering some 39 chapters, this excursus emphasizes the size and diversity of the forces amassed, and the detailed descriptions enhance the exoticism and glamour of the account.

Once the crossing has been completed, Xerxes conducts a review of the whole army and fleet, riding in a chariot between the ranks and sailing between the prows of the ships. This complete, he sends for Demaratus, the same Spartan exile whom we encountered right at the start of the book offering advice on the succession. In self-confident mood, buoyed by the sight of his vast array of armed forces, Xerxes asks Demaratus whether, speaking as a Greek, he really thinks that the Greeks will be able to withstand the Persian onslaught, and encourages him to speak the truth.

Demaratus, confining his answer to the Lacedaemonians, asserts that, even if the whole of the rest of Greece were to join forces with the Persians, the Lacedaemonians would never relent or consent to be enslaved. Xerxes greets Demaratus' claims with incredulity: surely his claim that a thousand Lacedaemonians would be prepared to stand against his combined forces is laughable? The idea that they would make such a stand, especially without a single, fearsome leader set over them, or someone whipping them into battle, is unthinkable.

Demaratus acknowledges his debt to the Persians, Darius in particular, who took him in following his exile from Sparta. He nonetheless renews his claim that the Spartans are inferior to none, subject as they are to the law of their land, which forbids them to turn tail in battle. Xerxes takes the whole matter light-heartedly and sends Demaratus away affectionately.

The speeches

Thucydides famously says of the speeches in his history:

χαλεπὸν τὴν ἀκρίβειαν αὐτὴν τῶν λεχθέντων διαμνημονεῦσαι ἦν ἐμοί τε ὧν αὐτὸς ἤκουσα καὶ τοῖς ἄλλοθέν ποθεν ἐμοὶ ἀπαγγέλλουσιν· ὡς δ᾽ ἂν ἐδόκουν ἐμοὶ ἕκαστοι περὶ τῶν αἰεὶ παρόντων τὰ δέοντα μάλιστ᾽ εἰπεῖν, ἐχομένῳ ὅτι ἐγγύτατα τῆς ξυμπάσης γνώμης τῶν ἀληθῶς λεχθέντων, οὕτως εἴρηται

I have found it difficult to retain a memory of the precise words which I had heard spoken; and so it was with those who brought me reports. But I have made the persons say what it seemed to me most opportune for them to say in view of each situation; at the same time, I have adhered as closely as possible to the general sense of what was actually said. (1.22)

In other words, Thucydides admits here that he had to make up the speeches, even those he heard himself, because he couldn't remember them properly, or didn't know what had been said. But he has put into the mouths of his protagonists words that we might assume to be the sort of thing someone would say in that situation.

Herodotus makes no comment about his speeches, although clearly they too must be 'made up', since how, for example, could anyone possibly know what Xerxes and Artabanus said to one another in private? Herodotus' speeches are mostly different from Thucydides' in being conversational rather than rhetorical and natural-sounding utterances rather than set pieces. To quote Jebb, '... the author seldom speaks when there is a fair pretext for making the characters speak': frequent and natural use of direct speech enlivens the narrative, an important consideration when one remembers that the first audience of the *Histories* would have been listening to the work read, not reading it themselves. Herodotus' growth out of the epic tradition and familiarity with tragedy make it natural for him to fill his work with the words of the actors who take part in it. It is no surprise that he does not feel the need to excuse or explain his practice, since it is for him the natural way to proceed.

Exceptions to the non-rhetorical rule include the debate on constitutions in Book 3 and the deliberations before the launch of the expedition in Book 7: in both of these cases, the speeches are more carefully honed and elaborated. Such speeches mark crucial turning points in the narrative, as well as dramatizing real-life dilemmas and revealing the characters of the speakers. We inevitably also suspect that Herodotus uses his speeches as one way of transmitting his own views and must admit at times that the words he places into the mouths of his speakers, particularly the prescient advice of Artabanus in the debate in Book 7, owe too much to hindsight or encapsulate ideas that are 'too Greek' to issue from the mouth of a fifth-century Persian.

The Graeco-Persian Wars

The origins of the conflict between Greece and Persia can be traced to Cyrus' conquest of the Greek cities of Ionia in 547 and the appointment of tyrants (local rulers answerable to the Great King) to rule over them. At the instigation of Aristagoras, tyrant of Miletus, the Ionian Greeks revolted against Persian rule in 499 and were not finally defeated until the battle of Lade in 494, by which time Athens and Eretria had joined forces with the colonists and helped them capture and burn the Persian regional capital of Sardis. This caused the Persian king Darius to swear vengeance upon the Athenians and Eretrians: Herodotus reports that he required a slave to say 'remember Athens' to him as he served him each meal.

The first Persian invasion of Greece was led by Mardonius in 492: he re-subjugated Thrace and conquered Macedon, but although he says in the speech in Book 7 that his expedition proved Persian superiority, Herodotus' account makes clear that the storm which struck the ships as they rounded Mount Athos was truly disastrous.

The second of Darius' attempts, under the command of Datis and Artaphrenes, took place in 490 and again enjoyed some success before decisive defeat at the Battle of Marathon, a humiliation cited by Xerxes in Book 7 as one of the reasons to go to war again.

The death of Darius in 486 meant that responsibility for continuing the campaign fell to his son Xerxes, and the preparations for his expedition in 480 form the focus of this set text. The victory at the narrow pass of Thermopylae, when the entire Persian army was held up by a force of 300 Spartans, who, Herodotus tells us, only suffered defeat because of treachery, allowed the Persians to reach and burn Athens. Decisive naval victory for the Greeks at the battle of Salamis, however, followed by victory for the combined Greek land forces at Plataea once again put an end to Persian hopes of conquest in Greece.

It is worth pointing out that although the victory over the Persians attained iconic status in Greece, the defeat suffered by Xerxes was most likely not viewed as so significant in Persia. Certainly it did not bring Xerxes' reign to an end: he continued to rule Persia for another fifteen years, continuing with ambitious building projects begun by Darius at Susa and Persepolis. He was ultimately assassinated in a palace intrigue by the commander of the royal bodyguard.

Herodotus' language

A brief glance at a page of the text will be sufficient to show that the language of Herodotus is distinct from the Greek written in Classical Athens with which we are most familiar. Herodotus, coming from Halicarnassus, wrote Ionic Greek, although the forms of words in the manuscripts that we have of the *Histories* differ widely between and even within the different copies. Clearly many corrections and alterations have been added by copyists, either changing original forms to Attic or restoring or inventing Ionic forms. In the case of the latter, we don't have enough original Ionic to check the veracity of the suggested emendations. For a very short and usable discussion of Herodotean dialect, refer to pages 228–9 of the *Oxford Grammar of Classical Greek* by James Morwood. For those interested in pursuing the topic at greater depth, A.M. Bowie's introduction to *Herodotus Histories Book VIII* in Cambridge Greek and Latin Classics, 2007 is excellent, and *Stein's Summary of the Dialect of Herodotus* (Heinrich Stein, 1880) is exhaustive and very easily accessible for free via the internet.

The list below gives some of the main features that you will notice and should look out for. Many of these examples are taken from the set text prescription.

ἀμ before β and π instead of ἀνα

κ for π in all adjectives and adverbs formed on the stem πο: κοῖος, ὁκοῖος, κόσος, κότερος, κότε, κού for ποῖος, etc.

κ for χ: δέκομαι for δέχομαι, οὐκί for οὐχί

Shifting or lack of aspiration: ἐνθαῦτα for ἐνταῦθα, ἐνθεῦτεν for ἐντεῦθεν, ἀπιγμένοι for ἀφιγμένοι

Shortening: γίνομαι for γίγνομαι, γινώσκω for γιγνώσκω

η for α: προθυμίη, θεήσομαι, ναυηγός, νεηνίης, νηός, θώρηξ, φλυηρέειν, τριήκοντα, στρατιήη, ἀδελφεῆς

ε for ει: κρέσσων, μέζων, πλέων, δέξαι, ἐδέχθην, and in the feminines of adjectives such as θῆλυς θήλεα and ταχύς ταχέα

Lack of contraction: νόος for νοῦς, γένεος for γένους, πλήρεες for πλήρεις, ποιέειν for ποιεῖν, ἐποιέετο for ἐποιεῖτο, πολεμέειν for πολεμεῖν, στρατηλάτεε for στρατηλατεῖ

Genitive singular masculine ending is -εω instead of -ου: Ξέρξεω for Ξέρξου

Genitive plural ending is -εων instead of -ων: μοιρέων for μοιρῶν

Dative plural endings are -ῃσι instead of -αις and -οισι instead of -οις: ἡμέρῃσι for ἡμέραις, λόγοισι for λόγοις.

Words like πόλις keep the iota: πόλιος for πόλεως, πόλι for πόλει

ἐμέο for ἐμοῦ, σέο for σοῦ

ὅστις has genitive s. ὅτευ, dative s. ὅτεωι, genitive pl. ὅτεων, dative pl. ὅτεοισι

In verbs, the augment is sometimes missing: ἀμειβόμην for ἠμειβόμην

-μι verbs sometimes conjugate like contracted verbs: e.g. τιθεῖς for τίθης, τιθεῖσι for τιθέασι

In εἰμί an initial epsilon is often preserved: ἐὼν for ὤν, παρεὼν for παρών

-αται, -ατο for -νται, -ντο: ἀπίκαται for ἀφίκονται

Also: ὦν for οὖν, ἰθέως for εὐθύς, μιν = αὐτον, αὐτήν; σφεας often = αὐτούς; εἶπα for εἶπον, εἶπας for εἰπών

Further reading

Asheri, David et al. Introduction to *A Commentary on Herodotus Books I-IV* (OUP, 2007).
Gould, John. *Herodotus* (Bloomsbury, 2000).
Marincola, John. *Greek Historians* (Greece and Rome New Surveys in the Classics No. 31, CUP, 2008).
de Selincourt, Aubrey. *The World of Herodotus* (North Point Press, 1982).
de Ste Croix, G.E.M. *Herodotus*. Greece and Rome Vol 24, No 2 (October 1977).
Thomas, Rosalind. *Herodotus in Context* (CUP, 2002).
Usher, Stephen. *The Historians of Greece and Rome* (Hamilton, 1969).

Tom Holland's 2013 translation for Penguin is vigorous and readable, with an excellent introduction and notes.

Text

Chapters 1–4: News of the defeat of the Persians at the Battle of Marathon makes King Darius eager to launch an expedition against Greece. Three years are spent raising troops, but in the fourth year the province of Egypt revolts. Darius wishes to appoint his successor before setting out on campaign, but there are rival claims to the throne from his sons Artobazanes and Xerxes. The exiled Spartan king Demaratus intervenes and decides the dispute in favour of Xerxes. One year into the Egyptian rebellion, Darius dies and Xerxes becomes king.

5

ἀποθανόντος δὲ Δαρείου ἡ βασιληίη ἀνεχώρησε ἐς τὸν παῖδα τὸν ἐκείνου 1
Ξέρξην. ὁ τοίνυν Ξέρξης ἐπὶ μὲν τὴν Ἑλλάδα οὐδαμῶς πρόθυμος ἦν κατ᾽
ἀρχὰς στρατεύεσθαι, ἐπὶ δὲ Αἴγυπτον ἐποιέετο στρατιῆς ἄγερσιν. παρεὼν δὲ
καὶ δυνάμενος παρ᾽ αὐτῷ μέγιστον Περσέων Μαρδόνιος ὁ Γωβρύεω, ὃς ἦν
Ξέρξῃ μὲν ἀνεψιός, Δαρείου δὲ ἀδελφεῆς παῖς, τοιούτου λόγου εἴχετο, λέγων·
"δέσποτα, οὐκ οἰκός ἐστι Ἀθηναίους ἐργασαμένους πολλὰ δὴ κακὰ Πέρσας 2
μὴ οὐ δοῦναι δίκας τῶν ἐποίησαν. ἀλλ᾽ εἰ τὸ μὲν νῦν ταῦτα πρήσσοις τά περ
ἐν χερσὶ ἔχεις· ἡμερώσας δὲ Αἴγυπτον τὴν ἐξυβρίσασαν στρατηλάτεε ἐπὶ
τὰς Ἀθήνας, ἵνα λόγος τέ σε ἔχῃ πρὸς ἀνθρώπων ἀγαθός καί τις ὕστερον
φυλάσσηται ἐπὶ γῆν τὴν σὴν στρατεύεσθαι." οὗτος μέν οἱ ὁ λόγος ἦν τιμωρός, 3
τούτου δὲ τοῦ λόγου παρενθήκην ποιεέσκετο τήνδε, ὡς ἡ Εὐρώπη περικαλλὴς
εἴη χώρη καὶ δένδρεα παντοῖα φέρει τὰ ἥμερα ἀρετήν τε ἄκρη, βασιλέϊ τε
μούνῳ θνητῶν ἀξίη ἐκτῆσθαι.

6

ταῦτα δὲ ἔλεγε οἷα νεωτέρων ἔργων ἐπιθυμητὴς ἐὼν καὶ θέλων αὐτὸς τῆς 1
Ἑλλάδος ὕπαρχος εἶναι. χρόνῳ δὲ κατεργάσατό τε καὶ ἀνέπεισε Ξέρξην
ὥστε ποιεῖν ταῦτα· συνέλαβε γὰρ καὶ ἄλλα οἱ σύμμαχα γενόμενα ἐς τὸ

πείθεσθαι Ξέρξην. τοῦτο μὲν ἀπὸ τῆς Θεσσαλίης παρὰ τῶν Ἀλευαδέων 2
ἀπιγμένοι ἄγγελοι ἐπεκαλέοντο βασιλέα πᾶσαν προθυμίην παρεχόμενοι
ἐπὶ τὴν Ἑλλάδα· (οἱ δὲ Ἀλευάδαι οὗτοι ἦσαν Θεσσαλίης βασιλέες), τοῦτο δὲ
Πεισιστρατιδέων οἱ ἀναβεβηκότες ἐς Σοῦσα, τῶν τε αὐτῶν λόγων ἐχόμενοι τῶν
καὶ οἱ Ἀλευάδαι, καὶ δή τι πρὸς τούτοισι ἔτι πλέον προσωρέγοντό οἱ. ἔχοντες 3
<δ'> Ὀνομάκριτον, ἄνδρα Ἀθηναῖον χρησμολόγον τε καὶ διαθέτην χρησμῶν
τῶν Μουσαίου, ἀναβεβήκεσαν, τὴν ἔχθρην προκαταλυσάμενοι· ἐξηλάσθη γὰρ
ὑπὸ Ἱππάρχου τοῦ Πεισιστράτου ὁ Ὀνομάκριτος ἐξ Ἀθηνέων, ἐπ᾽ αὐτοφώρῳ
ἁλοὺς ὑπὸ Λάσου τοῦ Ἑρμιονέος ἐμποιέων ἐς τὰ Μουσαίου χρησμόν ὡς αἱ
ἐπὶ Λήμνῳ ἐπικείμεναι νῆσοι ἀφανιζοίατο κατὰ τῆς θαλάσσης. διὸ ἐξήλασέ 4
μιν ὁ Ἵππαρχος, πρότερον χρεώμενος τὰ μάλιστα. τότε δὲ συναναβὰς ὅκως
ἀπίκοιτο ἐς ὄψιν τὴν βασιλέος, λεγόντων τῶν Πεισιστρατιδέων περὶ αὐτοῦ
σεμνοὺς λόγους κατέλεγε τῶν χρησμῶν· εἰ μέν τι ἐνέοι σφάλμα φέρον τῷ
βαρβάρῳ, τῶν μὲν ἔλεγε οὐδέν, ὁ δὲ τὰ εὐτυχέστατα ἐκλεγόμενος ἔλεγε, τόν
τε Ἑλλήσποντον ὡς ζευχθῆναι χρεὸν εἴη ὑπ᾽ ἀνδρὸς Πέρσεω, τήν τε ἔλασιν
ἐξηγεόμενος. οὗτός τε δὴ χρησμῳδέων προσεφέρετο, καὶ οἵ τε Πεισιστρατίδαι 5
καὶ οἱ Ἀλευάδαι γνώμας ἀποδεικνύμενοι.

7

ὡς δὲ ἀνεγνώσθη Ξέρξης στρατεύεσθαι ἐπὶ τὴν Ἑλλάδα, ἐνθαῦτα δευτέρῳ 1
μὲν ἔτεϊ μετὰ τὸν θάνατον τὸν Δαρείου πρῶτα στρατιὴν ποιέεται ἐπὶ τοὺς
ἀπεστεῶτας. τούτους μέν νυν καταστρεψάμενος καὶ Αἴγυπτον πᾶσαν
πολλὸν δουλοτέρην ποιήσας ἢ ἐπὶ Δαρείου ἦν, ἐπιτρέπει Ἀχαιμένεϊ, ἀδελφεῷ
μὲν ἑωυτοῦ, Δαρείου δὲ παιδί. Ἀχαιμένεα μέν νυν ἐπιτροπεύοντα Αἰγύπτου
χρόνῳ μετέπειτα ἐφόνευσε Ἰνάρως ὁ Ψαμμητίχου ἀνὴρ Λίβυς.

8

Ξέρξης δὲ μετὰ Αἰγύπτου ἅλωσιν ὡς ἔμελλε ἐς χεῖρας ἄξεσθαι τὸ στράτευμα 1
τὸ ἐπὶ τὰς Ἀθήνας, σύλλογον ἐπίκλητον Περσέων τῶν ἀρίστων ἐποιέετο,
ἵνα γνώμας τε πύθηταί σφεων καὶ αὐτὸς ἐν πᾶσι εἴπῃ τὰ θέλει. ὡς δὲ
συνελέχθησαν, ἔλεγε Ξέρξης τάδε·

8A

"ἄνδρες Πέρσαι, οὔτ᾽ αὐτὸς κατηγήσομαι νόμον τόνδε ἐν ὑμῖν τιθείς 1
παραδεξάμενός τε αὐτῷ χρήσομαι. ὡς γὰρ ἐγὼ πυνθάνομαι τῶν πρεσβυτέρων,
οὐδαμά κω ἠτρεμίσαμεν, ἐπείτε παρελάβομεν τὴν ἡγεμονίην τήνδε παρὰ
Μήδων, Κύρου κατελόντος Ἀστυάγεα· ἀλλὰ θεός τε οὕτω ἄγει καὶ αὐτοῖσι
ἡμῖν πολλὰ ἐπέπουσι συμφέρεται ἐπὶ τὸ ἄμεινον. τὰ μέν νυν Κῦρός τε καὶ
Καμβύσης πατήρ τε <ὁ> ἐμὸς Δαρεῖος κατεργάσαντο καὶ προσεκτήσαντο
ἔθνεα, ἐπισταμένοισι εὖ οὐκ ἄν τις λέγοι. ἐγὼ δὲ ἐπείτε παρέλαβον τὸν 2
θρόνον τοῦτον, ἐφρόντιζον ὅκως μὴ λείψομαι τῶν πρότερον γενομένων

ἐν τιμῇ τῇδε μηδὲ ἐλάσσω προσκτήσομαι δύναμιν Πέρσῃσι· φροντίζων δὲ εὑρίσκω ἅμα μὲν κῦδος ἡμῖν προσγινόμενον χώρην τε τῆς νῦν ἐκτήμεθα οὐκ ἐλάσσονα οὐδὲ φλαυροτέρην παμφορωτέρην δέ, ἅμα δὲ τιμωρίην τε καὶ τίσιν γινομένην. διὸ ὑμέας νῦν ἐγὼ συνέλεξα, ἵνα τὸ νοέω πρήσσειν ὑπερθέωμαι ὑμῖν.

8B

μέλλω ζεύξας τὸν Ἑλλήσποντον ἐλᾶν στρατὸν διὰ τῆς Εὐρώπης ἐπὶ τὴν 1
Ἑλλάδα, ἵνα Ἀθηναίους τιμωρήσωμαι ὅσα δὴ πεποιήκασι Πέρσας τε καὶ
πατέρα τὸν ἐμόν. ὡρᾶτε μέν νυν καὶ Δαρεῖον ἰθύοντα στρατεύεσθαι ἐπὶ τοὺς 2
ἄνδρας τούτους. ἀλλ᾿ ὃ μὲν τετελεύτηκε καὶ οὐκ ἐξεγένετό οἱ τιμωρήσασθαι·
ἐγὼ δὲ ὑπέρ τε ἐκείνου καὶ τῶν ἄλλων Περσέων οὐ πρότερον παύσομαι πρὶν
ἢ ἕλω τε καὶ πυρώσω τὰς Ἀθήνας, οἵ γε ἐμὲ καὶ πατέρα τὸν ἐμὸν ὑπῆρξαν
ἄδικα ποιεῦντες. πρῶτα μὲν ἐς Σάρδις ἐλθόντες ἅμα Ἀρισταγόρῃ τῷ Μιλησίῳ, 3
δούλῳ δὲ ἡμετέρῳ, ἀπικόμενοι ἐνέπρησαν τά τε ἄλσεα καὶ τὰ ἱρά· δεύτερα δὲ
ἡμέας οἷα ἔρξαν ἐς τὴν σφετέρην ἀποβάντας, ὅτε Δᾶτίς τε καὶ Ἀρταφρένης
ἐστρατήγεον, τὰ ἐπίστασθέ κου πάντες.

8C

τούτων μέντοι εἵνεκα ἀνάρτημαι ἐπ᾿ αὐτοὺς στρατεύεσθαι, ἀγαθὰ δὲ ἐν 1
αὐτοῖσι τοσάδε ἀνευρίσκω λογιζόμενος· εἰ τούτους τε καὶ τοὺς τούτοισι
πλησιοχώρους καταστρεψόμεθα, οἳ Πέλοπος τοῦ Φρυγὸς νέμονται χώρην,
γῆν τὴν Περσίδα ἀποδέξομεν τῷ Διὸς αἰθέρι ὁμουρέουσαν. οὐ γὰρ δὴ 2
χώρην γε οὐδεμίαν κατόψεται ἥλιος ὅμουρέουσαν τῇ ἡμετέρῃ, ἀλλὰ σφεας
πάσας ἐγὼ ἅμα ὑμῖν μίαν χώρην θήσω, διὰ πάσης διεξελθὼν τῆς Εὐρώπης.
πυνθάνομαι γὰρ ὧδε ἔχειν, οὔτε τινὰ πόλιν ἀνδρῶν οὐδεμίαν οὔτε ἔθνος 3
οὐδὲν ἀνθρώπων ὑπολείπεσθαι, τὸ ἡμῖν οἷόν τε ἔσται ἐλθεῖν ἐς μάχην,
τούτων τῶν κατέλεξα ὑπεξαραιρημένων. οὕτω οἵ τε ἡμῖν αἴτιοι ἕξουσι
δούλιον ζυγὸν οἵ τε ἀναίτιοι.

8D

ὑμεῖς δ᾿ ἂν μοι τάδε ποιέοντες χαρίζοισθε. ἐπεὰν ὑμῖν σημήνω τὸν χρόνον 1
ἐς τὸν ἥκειν δεῖ, προθύμως πάντα τινὰ ὑμέων χρήσει παρεῖναι· ὃς ἂν δὲ
ἔχων ἥκῃ παρεσκευασμένον στρατὸν κάλλιστα, δώσω οἱ δῶρα τὰ τιμιώτατα
νομίζεται εἶναι ἐν ἡμετέρου. ποιητέα μέν νυν ταῦτα ἐστὶ οὕτω· ἵνα δὲ μὴ 2
ἰδιοβουλέειν ὑμῖν δοκέω, τίθημι τὸ πρῆγμα ἐς μέσον, γνώμην κελεύων ὑμέων
τὸν βουλόμενον ἀποφαίνεσθαι." ταῦτα εἴπας ἐπαύετο.

9

μετ᾿ αὐτὸν δὲ Μαρδόνιος ἔλεγε· "ὦ δέσποτα, οὐ μοῦνον εἷς τῶν γενομένων 1
Περσέων ἄριστος, ἀλλὰ καὶ τῶν ἐσομένων, ὃς τά τε ἄλλα λέγων ἐπίκεο

ἄριστα καὶ ἀληθέστατα καὶ Ἴωνας τοὺς ἐν τῇ Εὐρώπῃ κατοικημένους οὐκ
ἐάσεις καταγελάσαι ἡμῖν ἐόντας ἀναξίους. καὶ γὰρ δεινὸν ἂν εἴη πρῆγμα, 2
εἰ Σάκας μὲν καὶ Ἰνδοὺς καὶ Αἰθίοπάς τε καὶ Ἀσσυρίους ἄλλα τε ἔθνεα
πολλὰ καὶ μεγάλα ἀδικήσαντα Πέρσας οὐδέν, ἀλλὰ δύναμιν προσκτᾶσθαι
βουλόμενοι, καταστρεψάμενοι δούλους ἔχομεν, Ἕλληνας δὲ ὑπάρξαντας
ἀδικίης οὐ τιμωρησόμεθα·

9A

τί δείσαντες; κοίην πλήθεος συστροφήν; κοίην δὲ χρημάτων δύναμιν; τῶν 1
ἐπιστάμεθα μὲν τὴν μάχην, ἐπιστάμεθα δὲ τὴν δύναμιν ἐοῦσαν ἀσθενέα·
ἔχομεν δὲ αὐτῶν παῖδας καταστρεψάμενοι, τούτους οἳ ἐν τῇ ἡμετέρῃ
κατοικημένοι Ἴωνές τε καὶ Αἰολέες καὶ Δωριέες καλέονται. ἐπειρήθην δὲ 2
καὶ αὐτὸς ἤδη ἐπελαύνων ἐπὶ τοὺς ἄνδρας τούτους ὑπὸ πατρὸς τοῦ σοῦ
κελευσθείς, καί μοι μέχρι Μακεδονίης ἐλάσαντι καὶ ὀλίγον ἀπολιπόντι ἐς
αὐτὰς Ἀθήνας ἀπικέσθαι οὐδεὶς ἠντιώθη ἐς μάχην.

9B

καίτοι γε ἐώθασι Ἕλληνες, ὡς πυνθάνομαι, ἀβουλότατα πολέμους ἵστασθαι 1
ὑπό τε ἀγνωμοσύνης καὶ σκαιότητος. ἐπεὰν γὰρ ἀλλήλοισι πόλεμον
προείπωσι, ἐξευρόντες τὸ κάλλιστον χωρίον καὶ λειότατον, ἐς τοῦτο κατιόντες
μάχονται, ὥστε σὺν κακῷ μεγάλῳ οἱ νικῶντες ἀπαλλάσσονται· περὶ δὲ τῶν
ἑσσουμένων οὐδὲ λέγω ἀρχήν, ἐξώλεες γὰρ δὴ γίνονται. τοὺς χρῆν, ἐόντας 2
ὁμογλώσσους, κήρυξί τε διαχρεωμένους καὶ ἀγγέλοισι καταλαμβάνειν τὰς
διαφορὰς καὶ παντὶ μᾶλλον ἢ μάχῃσι· εἰ δὲ πάντως ἔδεε πολεμέειν πρὸς
ἀλλήλους, ἐξευρίσκειν χρῆν τῇ ἑκάτεροι εἰσὶ δυσχειρωτότατοι καὶ ταύτῃ
πειρᾶν. τρόπῳ τοίνυν οὐ χρηστῷ Ἕλληνες διαχρεώμενοι ἐμέο ἐλάσαντος
μέχρι Μακεδονίης γῆς οὐκ ἦλθον ἐς τούτου λόγον ὥστε μάχεσθαι.

9C

σοὶ δὲ δὴ μέλλει τίς, ὦ βασιλεῦ, ἀντιώσεσθαι πόλεμον προφέρων, ἄγοντι καὶ 1
πλῆθος τὸ ἐκ τῆς Ἀσίης καὶ νέας τὰς ἁπάσας; ὡς μὲν ἐγὼ δοκέω, οὐκ ἐς τοῦτο
θάρσεος ἀνήκει τὰ Ἑλλήνων πρήγματα· εἰ δὲ ἄρα ἔγωγε ψευσθείην γνώμῃ
καὶ ἐκεῖνοι ἐπαρθέντες ἀβουλίῃ ἔλθοιεν ἡμῖν ἐς μάχην, μάθοιεν ἂν ὡς εἰμὲν
ἀνθρώπων ἄριστοι τὰ πολέμια. ἔστω δ᾽ ὦν μηδὲν ἀπείρητον· αὐτόματον γὰρ
οὐδέν, ἀλλ᾽ ἀπὸ πείρης πάντα ἀνθρώποισι φιλέει γίνεσθαι."

10

Μαρδόνιος μὲν τοσαῦτα ἐπιλεήνας τὴν Ξέρξεω γνώμην ἐπέπαυτο· σιωπώντων 1
δὲ τῶν ἄλλων Περσέων καὶ οὐ τολμώντων γνώμην ἀποδείκνυσθαι ἀντίην τῇ
προκειμένῃ, Ἀρτάβανος ὁ Ὑστάσπεος, πάτρως ἐὼν Ξέρξῃ, τῷ δὴ καὶ πίσυνος
ἐὼν ἔλεγε τάδε·

10A

"ὦ βασιλεῦ, μὴ λεχθεισέων μὲν γνωμέων ἀντιέων ἀλλήλῃσι οὐκ ἔστι τὴν 1
ἀμείνω αἱρεόμενον ἑλέσθαι, ἀλλὰ δεῖ τῇ εἰρημένῃ χρᾶσθαι, λεχθεισέων δὲ
ἔστι, ὥσπερ τὸν χρυσὸν τὸν ἀκήρατον αὐτὸν μὲν ἐπ᾽ ἑωυτοῦ οὐ διαγινώσκομεν,
ἐπεὰν δὲ παρατρίψωμεν ἄλλῳ χρυσῷ, διαγινώσκομεν τὸν ἀμείνω. ἐγὼ δὲ 2
καὶ πατρὶ τῷ σῷ, ἀδελφεῷ δὲ ἐμῷ, Δαρείῳ ἠγόρευον μὴ στρατεύεσθαι ἐπὶ
Σκύθας, ἄνδρας οὐδαμόθι γῆς ἄστυ νέμοντας. ὁ δὲ ἐλπίζων Σκύθας τοὺς
νομάδας καταστρέψεσθαι ἐμοί τε οὐκ ἐπείθετο, στρατευσάμενός τε πολλοὺς
καὶ ἀγαθοὺς τῆς στρατιῆς ἀποβαλὼν ἀπῆλθε. σὺ δέ, ὦ βασιλεῦ, μέλλεις ἐπ᾽ 3
ἄνδρας στρατεύεσθαι πολλὸν ἔτι ἀμείνονας ἢ Σκύθας, οἳ κατὰ θάλασσάν
τε ἄριστοι καὶ κατὰ γῆν λέγονται εἶναι. τὸ δὲ αὐτοῖσι ἔνεστι δεινόν, ἐμὲ σοὶ
δίκαιον ἐστὶ φράζειν.

10B

ζεύξας φῂς τὸν Ἑλλήσποντον ἐλᾶν στρατὸν διὰ τῆς Εὐρώπης ἐς τὴν Ἑλλάδα. 1
καὶ δὴ καὶ συνήνεικέ ἤτοι κατὰ γῆν ἢ καὶ κατὰ θάλασσαν ἑσσωθῆναι, ἢ καὶ κατ᾽
ἀμφότερα· οἱ γὰρ ἄνδρες λέγονται εἶναι ἄλκιμοι, πάρεστι δὲ καὶ σταθμώσασθαι,
εἰ στρατιήν γε τοσαύτην σὺν Δάτι καὶ Ἀρταφρένεϊ ἐλθοῦσαν ἐς τὴν Ἀττικὴν
χώρην μοῦνοι Ἀθηναῖοι διέφθειραν. οὐκ ὦν ἀμφοτέρῃ σφι ἐχώρησε· ἀλλ᾽ ἢν 2
τῇσι νηυσὶ ἐμβάλωσι καὶ νικήσαντες ναυμαχίῃ πλέωσι ἐς τὸν Ἑλλήσποντον καὶ
ἔπειτα λύσωσι τὴν γέφυραν, τοῦτο δή, βασιλεῦ, γίνεται δεινόν.

10C

ἐγὼ δὲ οὐδεμιῇ σοφίῃ οἰκηίῃ αὐτὸς ταῦτα συμβάλλομαι, ἀλλ᾽ οἷον κοτὲ ἡμέας 1
ὀλίγου ἐδέησε καταλαβεῖν πάθος, ὅτε πατὴρ <ὁ> σὸς ζεύξας Βόσπορον τὸν
Θρηίκιον, γεφυρώσας δὲ ποταμὸν Ἴστρον διέβη ἐπὶ Σκύθας. τότε παντοῖοι
ἐγένοντο Σκύθαι δεόμενοι Ἰώνων λῦσαι τὸν πόρον, τοῖσι ἐπετέτραπτο ἡ
φυλακὴ τῶν γεφυρέων τοῦ Ἴστρου. καὶ τότε γε Ἱστιαῖος ὁ Μιλήτου τύραννος 2
εἰ ἐπέσπετο τῶν ἄλλων τυράννων τῇ γνώμῃ μηδὲ ἠντιώθη, διέργαστο ἂν τὰ
Περσέων πρήγματα. καίτοι καὶ λόγῳ ἀκοῦσαι δεινόν, ἐπ᾽ ἀνδρί γε ἑνὶ πάντα
τὰ βασιλέος πρήγματα γεγενῆσθαι.

10D

σὺ ὦν μὴ βούλευ ἐς κίνδυνον μηδένα τοιοῦτον ἀπικέσθαι μηδεμιῆς ἀνάγκης 1
ἐούσης, ἀλλὰ ἐμοὶ πείθευ· νῦν μὲν τὸν σύλλογον τόνδε διάλυσον· αὖτις δέ,
ὅταν τοι δοκῇ, προσκεψάμενος ἐπὶ σεωυτοῦ προαγόρευε τά τοι δοκέει εἶναι
ἄριστα. τὸ γὰρ εὖ βουλεύεσθαι κέρδος μέγιστον εὑρίσκω ἐόν· εἰ γὰρ καὶ 2
ἐναντιωθῆναί τι θέλει, βεβούλευται μὲν οὐδὲν ἧσσον εὖ, ἕσσωται δὲ ὑπὸ τῆς
τύχης τὸ βούλευμα· ὁ δὲ βουλευσάμενος αἰσχρῶς, εἴ οἱ ἡ τύχη ἐπίσποιτο,
εὕρημα εὕρηκε, ἧσσον δὲ οὐδέν οἱ κακῶς βεβούλευται.

AS

10E

ὁρᾷς τὰ ὑπερέχοντα ζῷα ὡς κεραυνοῖ ὁ θεὸς οὐδὲ ἐᾷ φαντάζεσθαι, τὰ δὲ 1
σμικρὰ οὐδέν μιν κνίζει· ὁρᾷς δὲ ὡς ἐς οἰκήματα τὰ μέγιστα αἰεὶ καὶ δένδρεα
τὰ τοιαῦτα ἀποσκήπτει τὰ βέλεα· φιλέει γὰρ ὁ θεὸς τὰ ὑπερέχοντα πάντα
κολούειν. οὕτω δὲ καὶ στρατὸς πολλὸς ὑπὸ ὀλίγου διαφθείρεται κατὰ τοιόνδε·
ἐπεάν σφι ὁ θεὸς φθονήσας φόβον ἐμβάλῃ ἢ βροντήν, δι' ὦν ἐφθάρησαν
ἀναξίως ἑωυτῶν. οὐ γὰρ ἐᾷ φρονέειν μέγα ὁ θεὸς ἄλλον ἢ ἑωυτόν.

10F

ἐπειχθῆναι μέν νυν πᾶν πρῆγμα τίκτει σφάλματα, ἐκ τῶν ζημίαι μεγάλαι 1
φιλέουσι γίνεσθαι· ἐν δὲ τῷ ἐπισχεῖν ἔνεστι ἀγαθά, εἰ μὴ παραυτίκα δοκέοντα
εἶναι, ἀλλ' ἀνὰ χρόνον ἐξεύροι τις ἄν.

10G

σοὶ μὲν δὴ ταῦτα, ὦ βασιλεῦ, συμβουλεύω· σὺ δέ, ὦ παῖ Γωβρύεω Μαρδόνιε, 1
παῦσαι λέγων λόγους ματαίους περὶ Ἑλλήνων οὐκ ἐόντων ἀξίων φλαύρως
ἀκούειν. Ἕλληνας γὰρ διαβάλλων ἐπαίρεις αὐτὸν βασιλέα στρατεύεσθαι·
αὐτοῦ δὲ τούτου εἵνεκα δοκέεις μοι πᾶσαν προθυμίην ἐκτείνειν. μή νυν οὕτω
γένηται. διαβολὴ γὰρ ἐστὶ δεινότατον, ἐν τῇ δύο μὲν εἰσὶ οἱ ἀδικέοντες, εἷς δὲ 2
ὁ ἀδικεόμενος. ὁ μὲν γὰρ διαβάλλων ἀδικέει οὐ παρεόντος κατηγορέων, ὁ δὲ
ἀδικέει ἀναπειθόμενος πρὶν ἢ ἀτρεκέως ἐκμάθῃ· ὁ δὲ δὴ ἀπεὼν τοῦ λόγου
τάδε ἐν αὐτοῖσι ἀδικέεται, διαβληθείς τε ὑπὸ τοῦ ἑτέρου καὶ νομισθεὶς πρὸς
τοῦ ἑτέρου κακὸς εἶναι.

10H

ἀλλ' εἰ δὴ δεῖ γε πάντως ἐπὶ τοὺς ἄνδρας τούτους στρατεύεσθαι, φέρε, 1
βασιλεὺς μὲν αὐτὸς ἐν ἤθεσι τοῖσι Περσέων μενέτω, ἡμέων δὲ ἀμφοτέρων
παραβαλλομένων τὰ τέκνα στρατηλάτεε αὐτὸς σὺ ἐπιλεξάμενός τε ἄνδρας
τοὺς ἐθέλεις καὶ λαβὼν στρατιὴν ὁκόσην τινὰ βούλεαι. καὶ ἢν μὲν τῇ σὺ λέγεις 2
ἀναβαίνῃ βασιλέϊ τὰ πρήγματα, κτεινέσθων οἱ ἐμοὶ παῖδες, πρὸς δὲ αὐτοῖσι
καὶ ἐγώ· ἢν δὲ τῇ ἐγὼ προλέγω, οἱ σοὶ ταῦτα πασχόντων, σὺν δέ σφι καὶ σύ,
ἢν ἀπονοστήσῃς. εἰ δὲ ταῦτα μὲν ὑποδύνειν οὐκ ἐθελήσεις, σὺ δὲ πάντως 3
στράτευμα ἀνάξεις ἐπὶ τὴν Ἑλλάδα, ἀκούσεσθαι τινὰ φημὶ τῶν αὐτοῦ τῇδε
ὑπολειπομένων Μαρδόνιον, μέγα τι κακὸν ἐξεργασάμενον Πέρσας, ὑπὸ
κυνῶν τε καὶ ὀρνίθων διαφορεύμενον ἤ κου ἐν γῇ τῇ Ἀθηναίων ἢ σέ γε ἐν τῇ
Λακεδαιμονίων, εἰ μὴ ἄρα καὶ πρότερον κατ' ὁδόν, γνόντα ἐπ' οἵους ἄνδρας
ἀναγινώσκεις στρατεύεσθαι βασιλέα."

Chapters 11–33: A recurring dream persuades Xerxes to proceed with the invasion.
Preparation for war takes four years, and then the expeditionary force sets off from
Cappodocia to Sardis.

34

ἐς ταύτην ὦν τὴν ἀκτὴν ἐξ Ἀβύδου ὁρμώμενοι ἐγεφύρουν τοῖσι προσέκειτο, 1
τὴν μὲν λευκολίνου Φοίνικες, τὴν δὲ βυβλίνην Αἰγύπτιοι. ἔστι δὲ ἑπτὰ στάδιοι
ἐξ Ἀβύδου ἐς τὴν ἀπαντίον. καὶ δὴ ἐζευγμένου τοῦ πόρου ἐπιγενόμενος
χειμὼν μέγας συνέκοψέ τε ἐκεῖνα πάντα καὶ διέλυσε.

35

ὡς δ᾽ ἐπύθετο Ξέρξης, δεινὰ ποιεύμενος τὸν Ἑλλήσποντον ἐκέλευσε τριηκοσίας 1
ἐπικέσθαι μάστιγι πληγὰς καὶ κατεῖναι ἐς τὸ πέλαγος πεδέων ζεῦγος. ἤδη δὲ
ἤκουσα ὡς καὶ στιγέας ἅμα τούτοισι ἀπέπεμψε στίζοντας τὸν Ἑλλήσποντον.
ἐνετέλλετο δὲ ὦν ῥαπίζοντας λέγειν βάρβαρά τε καὶ ἀτάσθαλα· "ὦ πικρὸν 2
ὕδωρ, δεσπότης τοι δίκην ἐπιτιθεῖ τήνδε, ὅτι μιν ἠδίκησας οὐδὲν πρὸς ἐκείνου
ἄδικον παθόν. καὶ βασιλεὺς μὲν Ξέρξης διαβήσεταί σε, ἤν τε σύ γε βούλῃ ἤν
τε μή· σοὶ δὲ κατὰ δίκην ἄρα οὐδεὶς ἀνθρώπων θύει ὡς ἐόντι καὶ θολερῷ καὶ
ἁλμυρῷ ποταμῷ." τήν τε δὴ θάλασσαν ἐνετέλλετο τούτοισι ζημιοῦν καὶ τῶν 3
ἐπεστεώτων τῇ ζεύξι τοῦ Ἑλλησπόντου ἀποταμεῖν τὰς κεφαλάς.

Chapters 36–7: Herodotus gives a detailed description of the construction of the
replacement pontoon bridges over the Hellespont. The army winters at Sardis. Just
as it sets off in the spring for Abydos, there is an eclipse of the sun, which the Magi
interpret as predicting the abandonment by the Greeks of their cities.

38

ὡς δ᾽ ἐξήλαυνε τὴν στρατιήν, Πύθιος ὁ Λυδὸς καταρρωδήσας τὸ ἐκ τοῦ 1
οὐρανοῦ φάσμα ἐπαρθείς τε τοῖσι δωρήμασι ἐλθὼν παρὰ Ξέρξην ἔλεγε τάδε·
"ὦ δέσποτα, χρηίσας ἄν τι σεῦ βουλοίμην τυχεῖν, τὸ σοὶ μὲν ἐλαφρὸν τυγχάνει
ἐὸν ὑπουργῆσαι, ἐμοὶ δὲ μέγα γενόμενον." Ξέρξης δὲ πᾶν μᾶλλον δοκέων μιν 2
χρηίσειν ἢ τὸ ἐδεήθη, ἔφη τε ὑπουργήσειν καὶ δὴ ἀγορεύειν ἐκέλευε ὅτευ δέοιτο.
ὁ δὲ ἐπείτε ταῦτα ἤκουσε, ἔλεγε θαρσήσας τάδε· "ὦ δέσποτα, τυγχάνουσί μοι
παῖδες ἐόντες πέντε, καὶ σφεας καταλαμβάνει πάντας ἅμα σοὶ στρατεύεσθαι
ἐπὶ τὴν Ἑλλάδα. σὺ δέ, ὦ βασιλεῦ, ἐμὲ ἐς τόδε ἡλικίης ἥκοντα οἰκτίρας τῶν μοι 3
παίδων ἕνα παράλυσον τῆς στρατιῆς τὸν πρεσβύτατον, ἵνα αὐτοῦ τε ἐμεῦ καὶ
τῶν χρημάτων ᾖ μελεδωνός. τοὺς δὲ τέσσερας ἄγευ ἅμα σεωυτῷ καὶ πρήξας
τὰ νοέεις νοστήσειας ὀπίσω."

39

κάρτα τε ἐθυμώθη ὁ Ξέρξης καὶ ἀμείβετο τοῖσιδε. "ὦ κακὲ ἄνθρωπε, σὺ 1
ἐτόλμησας ἐμεῦ στρατευομένου αὐτοῦ ἐπὶ τὴν Ἑλλάδα καὶ ἄγοντος παῖδας
ἐμοὺς καὶ ἀδελφεοὺς καὶ οἰκηίους καὶ φίλους μνήσασθαι περὶ σέο παιδός,

A
Level

ἐὼν ἐμὸς δοῦλος, τὸν χρῆν πανοικίῃ αὐτῇ τῇ γυναικὶ συνέπεσθαι; εὖ νυν τόδ᾽
ἐξεπίστασο, ὡς ἐν τοῖσι ὠσὶ τῶν ἀνθρώπων οἰκέει ὁ θυμός, ὃς χρηστὰ μὲν
ἀκούσας τέρψιος ἐμπιπλεῖ τὸ σῶμα, ὑπεναντία δὲ τούτοισι ἀκούσας ἀνοιδέει.
ὅτε μέν νυν χρηστὰ ποιήσας ἕτερα τοιαῦτα ἐπηγγέλλεο, εὐεργεσίῃσι βασιλέα 2
οὐ καυχήσεαι ὑπερβαλέσθαι· ἐπείτε δὲ ἐς τὸ ἀναιδέστερον ἐτράπευ, τὴν
μὲν ἀξίην οὐ λάμψεαι, ἐλάσσω δὲ τῆς ἀξίης. σὲ μὲν γὰρ καὶ τοὺς τέσσερας
τῶν παίδων ῥύεται τὰ ξείνια· τοῦ δὲ ἑνός, τοῦ περιέχεαι μάλιστα, τῇ ψυχῇ
ζημιώσεαι." ὡς δὲ ταῦτα ὑπεκρίνατο, αὐτίκα ἐκέλευε τοῖσι προσετέτακτο 3
ταῦτα πρήσσειν, τῶν Πυθίου παίδων ἐξευρόντας τὸν πρεσβύτατον μέσον
διαταμεῖν, διαταμόντας δὲ τὰ ἡμίτομα διαθεῖναι τὸ μὲν ἐπὶ δεξιὰ τῆς ὁδοῦ, τὸ
δ᾽ ἐπ᾽ ἀριστερά, καὶ ταύτῃ διεξιέναι τὸν στρατόν.

*Chapters 40–4: Herodotus describes the army's departure from Sardis and its
progress through Lydia and Mysia. The army drinks the river Scamander dry, and
Xerxes visits the citadel of Troy. Arriving at Abydos, Xerxes has a dais of white stone
built from which to review his forces.*

45

ὡς δὲ ὥρα πάντα μὲν τὸν Ἑλλήσποντον ὑπὸ τῶν νεῶν ἀποκεκρυμμένον, 1
πάσας δὲ τὰς ἀκτὰς καὶ τὰ Ἀβυδηνῶν πεδία ἐπίπλεα ἀνθρώπων, ἐνθαῦτα ὁ
Ξέρξης ἑωυτὸν ἐμακάρισε, μετὰ δὲ τοῦτο ἐδάκρυσε.

46

μαθὼν δέ μιν Ἀρτάβανος ὁ πάτρως, ὃς τὸ πρῶτον γνώμην ἀπεδέξατο 1
ἐλευθέρως οὐ συμβουλεύων Ξέρξῃ στρατεύεσθαι ἐπὶ τὴν Ἑλλάδα, οὗτος
ὡνὴρ φρασθεὶς Ξέρξην δακρύσαντα εἴρετο τάδε· "ὦ βασιλεῦ, ὡς πολλὸν
ἀλλήλων κεχωρισμένα ἐργάσαο νῦν τε καὶ ὀλίγῳ πρότερον· μακαρίσας
γὰρ σεωυτὸν δακρύεις." ὁ δὲ εἶπε· "ἐσῆλθε γάρ με λογισάμενον κατοικτῖραι 2
ὡς βραχὺς εἴη ὁ πᾶς ἀνθρώπινος βίος, εἰ τούτων γε ἐόντων τοσούτων
οὐδεὶς ἐς ἑκατοστὸν ἔτος περιέσται." ὁ δὲ ἀμείβετο λέγων· "ἕτερα τούτου
παρὰ τὴν ζόην πεπόνθαμεν οἰκτρότερα. ἐν γὰρ οὕτω βραχέϊ βίῳ οὐδεὶς 3
οὕτως ἄνθρωπος ἐὼν εὐδαίμων πέφυκε, οὔτε τούτων οὔτε τῶν ἄλλων, τῷ
οὐ παραστήσεται πολλάκις καὶ οὐκὶ ἅπαξ τεθνάναι βούλεσθαι μᾶλλον ἢ
ζώειν. αἵ τε γὰρ συμφοραὶ προσπίπτουσαι καὶ αἱ νοῦσοι συνταράσσουσαι
καὶ βραχὺν ἐόντα μακρὸν δοκέειν εἶναι ποιεῦσι τὸν βίον. οὕτως ὁ μὲν 4
θάνατος μοχθηρῆς ἐούσης τῆς ζόης καταφυγὴ αἱρετωτάτη τῷ ἀνθρώπῳ
γέγονε, ὁ δὲ θεὸς γλυκὺν γεύσας τὸν αἰῶνα φθονερὸς ἐν αὐτῷ εὑρίσκεται
ἐών."

47

Ξέρξης δὲ ἀμείβετο λέγων· "Ἀρτάβανε, βιοτῆς μέν νυν ἀνθρωπηΐης πέρι, 1
ἐούσης τοιαύτης οἵην περ σὺ διαιρέαι εἶναι, παυσώμεθα, μηδὲ κακῶν
μεμνώμεθα χρηστὰ ἔχοντες πρήγματα ἐν χερσί· φράσον δέ μοι τόδε· εἴ τοι

ἡ ὄψις τοῦ ἐνυπνίου μὴ ἐναργὴς οὕτω ἐφάνη, εἶχες ἂν τὴν ἀρχαίην γνώμην, οὐκ ἐῶν με στρατεύεσθαι ἐπὶ τὴν Ἑλλάδα, ἢ μετέστης ἄν; φέρε τοῦτό μοι ἀτρεκέως εἰπέ." ὁ δὲ ἀμείβετο λέγων· "ὦ βασιλεῦ, ὄψις μὲν ἡ ἐπιφανεῖσα 2 τοῦ ὀνείρου, ὡς βουλόμεθα ἀμφότεροι, τελευτήσειε· ἐγὼ δ᾿ ἔτι καὶ ἐς τόδε δείματος εἰμὶ ὑπόπλεος οὐδ᾿ ἐντὸς ἐμεωυτοῦ, ἄλλα τε πολλὰ ἐπιλεγόμενος καὶ δὴ καὶ ὁρῶν τοι δύο τὰ μέγιστα πάντων ἐόντα πολεμιώτατα."

48

Ξέρξης δὲ πρὸς ταῦτα ἀμείβετο τοῖσιδε· Δαιμόνιε ἀνδρῶν, κοῖα ταῦτα δύο 1 λέγεις εἶναι μοι πολεμιώτατα; κότερά τοι ὁ πεζὸς μεμπτὸς κατὰ πλῆθός ἐστι, καὶ τὸ Ἑλληνικὸν στράτευμα φαίνεται πολλαπλήσιον ἔσεσθαι τοῦ ἡμετέρου, ἢ τὸ ναυτικὸν τὸ ἡμέτερον λείψεσθαι τοῦ ἐκείνων, ἢ καὶ συναμφότερα ταῦτα; εἰ γάρ τοι ταύτῃ φαίνεται ἐνδεέστερα εἶναι τὰ ἡμέτερα πρήγματα, στρατοῦ ἂν ἄλλου τις τὴν ταχίστην ἄγερσιν ποιοῖτο.

49

ὁ δ᾿ ἀμείβετο λέγων· "ὦ βασιλεῦ, οὔτε στρατὸν τοῦτον, ὅστις γε σύνεσιν 1 ἔχει, μέμφοιτ᾿ ἂν οὔτε τῶν νεῶν τὸ πλῆθος· ἢν δὲ πλεῦνας συλλέξῃς, τὰ δύο τοι τὰ λέγω πολλῷ ἔτι πολεμιώτερα γίνεται. τὰ δὲ δύο ταῦτα ἐστὶ γῆ τε καὶ θάλασσα. οὔτε γὰρ τῆς θαλάσσης ἐστὶ λιμὴν τοσοῦτος οὐδαμόθι, ὡς 2 ἐγὼ εἰκάζω, ὅστις ἐγειρομένου χειμῶνος δεξάμενός σευ τοῦτο τὸ ναυτικὸν φερέγγυος ἔσται διασῶσαι τὰς νέας. καίτοι οὐκὶ ἕνα αὐτὸν δεῖ εἶναι τὸν λιμένα, ἀλλὰ παρὰ πᾶσαν τὴν ἤπειρον παρ᾿ ἣν δὴ κομίζεαι. οὔκων ὢν 3 δὴ ἐόντων τοι λιμένων ὑποδεξίων, μάθε ὅτι αἱ συμφοραὶ τῶν ἀνθρώπων ἄρχουσι καὶ οὐκὶ ὥνθρωποι τῶν συμφορέων. καὶ δὴ τῶν δύο τοι τοῦ ἑτέρου εἰρημένου τὸ ἕτερον ἔρχομαι ἐρέων. γῆ δὲ πολεμίη τῇδέ τοι κατίσταται· εἰ 4 θέλει τοι μηδὲν ἀντίξοον καταστῆναι, τοσούτῳ τοι γίνεται πολεμιωτέρη ὅσῳ ἂν προβαίνῃς ἑκαστέρω, τὸ πρόσω αἰεὶ κλεπτόμενος· εὐπρηξίης δὲ οὐκ ἔστι ἀνθρώποισι οὐδεμία πληθώρη. καὶ δή τοι, ὡς οὐδενὸς ἐναντιευμένου, λέγω 5 τὴν χώρην πλεῦνα ἐν πλέονι χρόνῳ γινομένην λιμὸν τέξεσθαι. ἀνὴρ δὲ οὕτω ἂν εἴη ἄριστος, εἰ βουλευόμενος μὲν ἀρρωδέοι, πᾶν ἐπιλεγόμενος πείσεσθαι χρῆμα, ἐν δὲ τῷ ἔργῳ θρασὺς εἴη."

50

ἀμείβεται Ξέρξης τοῖσιδε· "Ἀρτάβανε, οἰκότως μὲν σύ γε τούτων ἕκαστα 1 διαιρέαι, ἀτὰρ μήτε πάντα φοβέο μήτε πᾶν ὁμοίως ἐπιλέγεο. εἰ γὰρ δὴ βούλοιο ἐπὶ τῷ αἰεὶ ἐπεσφερομένῳ πρήγματι τὸ πᾶν ὁμοίως ἐπιλέγεσθαι, ποιήσειας ἂν οὐδαμὰ οὐδέν· κρέσσον δὲ πάντα θαρσέοντα ἥμισυ τῶν δεινῶν πάσχειν μᾶλλον ἢ πᾶν χρῆμα προδειμαίνοντα μηδαμὰ μηδὲν παθεῖν. εἰ 2 δὲ ἐρίζων πρὸς πᾶν τὸ λεγόμενον μὴ τὸ βέβαιον ἀποδέξεις, σφάλλεσθαι ὀφείλεις ἐν αὐτοῖσι ὁμοίως καὶ ὁ ὑπεναντία τούτοισι λέξας. τοῦτο μέν νυν ἐπ᾿ ἴσης ἔχει· εἰδέναι δὲ ἄνθρωπον ἐόντα κῶς χρὴ τὸ βέβαιον; δοκέω μὲν οὐδαμῶς. τοῖσι τοίνυν βουλομένοισι ποιέειν ὡς τὸ ἐπίπαν φιλέει γίνεσθαι τὰ

κέρδεα, τοῖσι δὲ ἐπιλεγομένοισί τε πάντα καὶ ὀκνέουσι οὐ μάλα ἐθέλει. ὁρᾷς 3
τὰ Περσέων πρήγματα ἐς ὃ δυνάμιος προκεχώρηκε. εἰ τοίνυν ἐκεῖνοι οἱ πρὸ
ἐμεῦ γενόμενοι βασιλέες γνώμῃσι ἐχρέωντο ὁμοίῃσι καὶ σύ, ἢ μὴ χρεώμενοι
γνώμῃσι τοιαύτῃσι ἄλλους συμβούλους εἶχον τοιούτους, οὐκ ἄν κοτε εἶδες
αὐτὰ ἐς τοῦτο προελθόντα· νῦν δὲ κινδύνους ἀναρριπτέοντες ἐς τοῦτο
σφέα προηγάγοντο. μεγάλα γὰρ πρήγματα μεγάλοισι κινδύνοισι ἐθέλει
καταιρέεσθαι. ἡμεῖς τοίνυν ὁμοιεύμενοι ἐκείνοισι ὥρην τε τοῦ ἔτεος καλλίστην 4
πορευόμεθα καὶ καταστρεψάμενοι πᾶσαν τὴν Εὐρώπην νοστήσομεν ὀπίσω,
οὔτε λιμῷ ἐντυχόντες οὐδαμόθι οὔτε ἄλλο ἄχαρι οὐδὲν παθόντες. τοῦτο
μὲν γὰρ αὐτοὶ πολλὴν φορβὴν φερόμενοι πορευόμεθα, τοῦτο δέ, τῶν ἄν κου
ἐπιβέωμεν γῆν καὶ ἔθνος, τούτων τὸν σῖτον ἕξομεν· ἐπ᾽ ἀροτῆρας δὲ καὶ οὐ
νομάδας στρατευόμεθα ἄνδρας."

51

λέγει Ἀρτάβανος μετὰ ταῦτα· "ὦ βασιλεῦ, ἐπείτε ἀρρωδέειν οὐδὲν ἐᾷς 1
πρῆγμα, σὺ δέ μευ συμβουλίην ἔνδεξαι· ἀναγκαίως γὰρ ἔχει περὶ πολλῶν
πρηγμάτων πλεῦνα λόγον ἐκτεῖναι. Κῦρος ὁ Καμβύσεω Ἰωνίην πᾶσαν
πλὴν Ἀθηναίων κατεστρέψατο δασμοφόρον εἶναι Πέρσῃσι. τούτους ὦν τοὺς 2
ἄνδρας συμβουλεύω τοι μηδεμιῇ μηχανῇ ἄγειν ἐπὶ τοὺς πατέρας· καὶ γὰρ
ἄνευ τούτων οἷοί τε εἰμὲν τῶν ἐχθρῶν κατυπέρτεροι γίνεσθαι. ἢ γὰρ σφέας,
ἢν ἕπωνται, δεῖ ἀδικωτάτους γίνεσθαι καταδουλουμένους τὴν μητρόπολιν, ἢ
δικαιοτάτους συνελευθεροῦντας. ἀδικώτατοι μέν νυν γινόμενοι οὐδὲν κέρδος 3
μέγα ἡμῖν προσβάλλουσι, δικαιότατοι δὲ γινόμενοι οἷοί τε δηλήσασθαι
μεγάλως τὴν σὴν στρατιὴν γίνονται. ἐς θυμὸν ὦν βάλευ καὶ τὸ παλαιὸν ἔπος
ὡς εὖ εἴρηται, τὸ μὴ ἅμα ἀρχῇ πᾶν τέλος καταφαίνεσθαι."

52

ἀμείβεται πρὸς ταῦτα Ξέρξης· "Ἀρτάβανε, τῶν ἀπεφήναο γνωμέων 1
σφάλλεαι κατὰ ταύτην δὴ μάλιστα, ὃς Ἴωνας φοβέαι μὴ μεταβάλωσι, τῶν
ἔχομεν γνῶμα μέγιστον, τῶν σύ τε μάρτυς γίνεαι καὶ οἱ συστρατευσάμενοι
Δαρείῳ ἄλλοι ἐπὶ Σκύθας, ὅτι ἐπὶ τούτοισι ἡ πᾶσα Περσικὴ στρατιὴ ἐγένετο
διαφθεῖραι καὶ περιποιῆσαι· οἱ δὲ δικαιοσύνην καὶ πιστότητα ἐνέδωκαν, ἄχαρι
δὲ οὐδέν. πάρεξ δὲ τούτου, ἐν τῇ ἡμετέρῃ καταλιπόντας τέκνα καὶ γυναῖκας 2
καὶ χρήματα οὐδ᾽ ἐπιλέγεσθαι χρὴ νεώτερόν τι ποιήσειν. οὕτω μηδὲ τοῦτο
φοβέο, ἀλλὰ θυμὸν ἔχων ἀγαθὸν σῷζε οἶκόν τε τὸν ἐμὸν καὶ τυραννίδα τὴν
ἐμήν· σοὶ γὰρ ἐγὼ μούνῳ ἐκ πάντων σκῆπτρα τὰ ἐμὰ ἐπιτρέπω."

Chapters 53–100: After sending Artabanus away to Susa, Xerxes exhorts the leading Persians to pursue the war vigorously. They prepare sacrifices and the crossing of the Hellespont begins. It takes seven days and seven nights. Meanwhile, the fleet sails towards Cape Sarpedon. At Doriscos, Xerxes decides to hold a review of all his forces. Chapters 61–100 comprise a description of the various contingents of the land and naval forces.

**A
Level**

101

ὡς δὲ καὶ ταύτας διεξέπλωσε καὶ ἐξέβη ἐκ τῆς νεός, μετεπέμψατο Δημάρητον 1
τὸν Ἀρίστωνος συστρατευόμενον αὐτῷ ἐπὶ τὴν Ἑλλάδα, καλέσας δ᾽ αὐτὸν
εἴρετο τάδε· "Δημάρητε, νῦν μοι σὲ ἡδύ τι ἐστὶ εἰρέσθαι τὰ θέλω. σὺ εἶς Ἕλλην
τε, καὶ ὡς ἐγὼ πυνθάνομαι σεῦ τε καὶ τῶν ἄλλων Ἑλλήνων τῶν ἐμοὶ ἐς
λόγους ἀπικνεομένων, πόλιος οὔτ᾽ ἐλαχίστης οὔτ᾽ ἀσθενεστάτης. νῦν ὦν μοι 2
τόδε φράσον, εἰ Ἕλληνες ὑπομενέουσι χεῖρας ἐμοὶ ἀνταειρόμενοι. οὐ γάρ, ὡς
ἐγὼ δοκέω, οὐδ᾽ εἰ πάντες Ἕλληνες καὶ οἱ λοιποὶ οἱ πρὸς ἑσπέρης οἰκέοντες
ἄνθρωποι συλλεχθείησαν, οὐκ ἀξιόμαχοί εἰσι ἐμὲ ἐπιόντα ὑπομεῖναι, μὴ
ἐόντες ἄρθμιοι. ἐθέλω μέντοι καὶ τὸ ἀπὸ σεῦ, ὁκοῖόν τι λέγεις περὶ αὐτῶν, 3
πυθέσθαι." ὁ μὲν ταῦτα εἰρώτα, ὁ δὲ ὑπολαβὼν ἔφη· "βασιλεῦ, κότερα ἀληθείῃ
χρήσωμαι πρὸς σὲ ἢ ἡδονῇ;" ὁ δέ μιν ἀληθείῃ χρήσασθαι ἐκέλευε, φὰς οὐδέν
οἱ ἀηδέστερον ἔσεσθαι ἢ πρότερον ἦν.

102

ὡς δὲ ταῦτα ἤκουσε Δημάρητος, ἔλεγε τάδε· "βασιλεῦ, ἐπειδὴ ἀληθείῃ 1
διαχρήσασθαι πάντως κελεύεις ταῦτα λέγοντα τὰ μὴ ψευδόμενός τις
ὕστερον ὑπὸ σεῦ ἁλώσεται, τῇ Ἑλλάδι πενίη μὲν αἰεί κοτε σύντροφος ἐστί,
ἀρετὴ δὲ ἔπακτος ἐστί, ἀπό τε σοφίης κατεργασμένη καὶ νόμου ἰσχυροῦ·
τῇ διαχρεωμένῃ ἡ Ἑλλὰς τήν τε πενίην ἀπαμύνεται καὶ τὴν δεσποσύνην. 2
αἰνέω μέν νυν πάντας Ἕλληνας τοὺς περὶ ἐκείνους τοὺς Δωρικοὺς χώρους
οἰκημένους, ἔρχομαι δὲ λέξων οὐ περὶ πάντων τούσδε τοὺς λόγους, ἀλλὰ περὶ
Λακεδαιμονίων μούνων, πρῶτα μὲν ὅτι οὐκ ἔστι ὅκως κοτὲ σοὺς δέξονται
λόγους δουλοσύνην φέροντας τῇ Ἑλλάδι, αὖτις δὲ ὡς ἀντιώσονταί τοι ἐς μάχην
καὶ ἢν οἱ ἄλλοι Ἕλληνες πάντες τὰ σὰ φρονέωσι. ἀριθμοῦ δὲ πέρι, μή πύθῃ 3
ὅσοι τινές ἐόντες ταῦτα ποιέειν οἷοί τε εἰσί· ἤν τε γὰρ τύχωσι ἐξεστρατευμένοι
χίλιοι, οὗτοι μαχήσονταί τοι, ἤν τε ἐλάσσονες τούτων, ἤν τε καὶ πλεῦνες."

103

ταῦτα ἀκούσας Ξέρξης γελάσας ἔφη· "Δημάρητε, οἷον ἐφθέγξαο ἔπος, ἄνδρας 1
χιλίους στρατιῇ τοσῇδε μαχήσεσθαι. ἄγε, εἰπέ μοι, σὺ φῂς τούτων τῶν ἀνδρῶν
βασιλεὺς αὐτὸς γενέσθαι. σὺ ὦν ἐθελήσεις αὐτίκα μάλα πρὸς ἄνδρας δέκα
μάχεσθαι; καίτοι εἰ τὸ πολιτικὸν ὑμῖν πᾶν ἐστι τοιοῦτον οἷον σὺ διαιρέεις, σέ
γε τὸν κείνων βασιλέα πρέπει πρὸς τὸ διπλήσιον ἀντιτάσσεσθαι κατὰ νόμους
τοὺς ὑμετέρους. εἰ γὰρ κείνων ἕκαστος δέκα ἀνδρῶν τῆς στρατιῆς τῆς ἐμῆς 2
ἀντάξιος ἐστί, σὲ δέ γε δίζημαι εἴκοσι εἶναι ἀντάξιον· καὶ οὕτω μὲν ὀρθοῖτ᾽ ἂν
ὁ λόγος ὁ παρὰ σεῦ εἰρημένος· εἰ δὲ τοιοῦτοί τε ἐόντες καὶ μεγάθεα τοσοῦτοι,
ὅσοι σύ τε καὶ οἱ παρ᾽ ἐμὲ φοιτῶσι Ἑλλήνων ἐς λόγους, αὐχέετε τοσοῦτον, ὅρα
μὴ μάτην κόμπος ὁ λόγος οὗτος εἰρημένος ᾖ. ἐπεὶ φέρε ἴδω παντὶ τῷ οἰκότι· 3
κῶς ἂν δυναίατο χίλιοι ἢ καὶ μύριοι ἢ καὶ πεντακισμύριοι, ἐόντες γε ἐλεύθεροι
πάντες ὁμοίως καὶ μὴ ὑπ᾽ ἑνὸς ἀρχόμενοι, στρατῷ τοσῷδε ἀντιστῆναι; ἐπεὶ
τοι πλεῦνες περὶ ἕνα ἕκαστον γινόμεθα ἢ χίλιοι, ἐόντων ἐκείνων πέντε
χιλιάδων. ὑπὸ μὲν γὰρ ἑνὸς ἀρχόμενοι κατὰ τρόπον τὸν ἡμέτερον γενοίατ᾽ 4

A Level

ἂν δειμαίνοντες τοῦτον καὶ παρὰ τὴν ἑωυτῶν φύσιν ἀμείνονες καὶ ἴοιεν
ἀναγκαζόμενοι μάστιγι ἐς πλεῦνας ἐλάσσονες ἐόντες· ἀνειμένοι δὲ ἐς τὸ
ἐλεύθερον οὐκ ἂν ποιέοιεν τούτων οὐδέτερα. δοκέω δὲ ἔγωγε καὶ ἀνισωθέντας
πλήθεϊ χαλεπῶς ἂν Ἕλληνας Πέρσῃσι μούνοισι μάχεσθαι. ἀλλὰ παρ᾽ ἡμῖν 5
μέν μούνοισι τοῦτο ἐστὶ τὸ σὺ λέγεις, ἔστι γε μέντοι οὐ πολλὸν ἀλλὰ σπάνιον·
εἰσὶ γὰρ Περσέων τῶν ἐμῶν αἰχμοφόρων οἳ ἐθελήσουσι Ἑλλήνων ἀνδράσι
τρισὶ ὁμοῦ μάχεσθαι· τῶν σὺ ἐὼν ἄπειρος πολλὰ φλυηρέεις."

104

πρὸς ταῦτα Δημάρητος λέγει· "ὦ βασιλεῦ, ἀρχῆθεν ἠπιστάμην ὅτι ἀληθείῃ 1
χρεώμενος οὐ φίλα τοι ἐρέω· σὺ δὲ ἐπεὶ ἠνάγκασας λέγειν τῶν λόγων τοὺς
ἀληθεστάτους, ἔλεγον τὰ κατήκοντα Σπαρτιήτῃσι. καίτοι ὡς ἐγὼ τυγχάνω 2
τὰ νῦν τάδε ἐστοργὼς ἐκείνους, αὐτὸς μάλιστα ἐξεπίστεαι, οἵ με τιμήν τε καὶ
γέρεα ἀπελόμενοι πατρώϊα ἄπολίν τε καὶ φυγάδα πεποιήκασι, πατὴρ δὲ <ὁ>
σὸς ὑποδεξάμενος βίον τέ μοι καὶ οἶκον ἔδωκε. οὐκ ἂν οἰκός ἐστι ἄνδρα τὸν
σώφρονα εὐνοίην φαινομένην διωθέεσθαι, ἀλλὰ στέργειν μάλιστα. ἐγὼ δὲ ὁ 3
οὔτε δέκα ἀνδράσι ὑπίσχομαι οἷός τε εἶναι μάχεσθαι οὔτε δυοῖσι, ἑκών τε εἶναι
οὐδ᾽ ἂν μουνομαχέοιμι. εἰ δὲ ἀναγκαίη εἴη ἢ μέγας τις ὁ ἐποτρύνων ἀγών,
μαχοίμην ἂν πάντων ἥδιστα ἑνὶ τούτων τῶν ἀνδρῶν οἳ Ἑλλήνων ἕκαστος
φησὶ τριῶν ἄξιος εἶναι. ὡς δὲ καὶ Λακεδαιμόνιοι κατὰ μὲν ἕνα μαχόμενοι 4
οὐδαμῶν εἰσι κακίονες ἀνδρῶν, ἀλέες δὲ ἄριστοι ἀνδρῶν ἁπάντων. ἐλεύθεροι
γὰρ ἐόντες οὐ πάντα ἐλεύθεροί εἰσι· ἔπεστι γάρ σφι δεσπότης νόμος, τὸν
ὑποδειμαίνουσι πολλῷ ἔτι μᾶλλον ἢ οἱ σοὶ σέ. ποιεῦσι γῶν τὰ ἂν ἐκεῖνος 5
ἀνώγῃ· ἀνώγει δὲ τὠυτὸ αἰεί, οὐκ ἐῶν φεύγειν οὐδὲν πλῆθος ἀνθρώπων ἐκ
μάχης, ἀλλὰ μένοντας ἐν τῇ τάξι ἐπικρατέειν ἢ ἀπόλλυσθαι. σοὶ δὲ εἰ φαίνομαι
ταῦτα λέγων φλυηρέειν, ἀλλὰ σιγᾶν θέλω τὸ λοιπόν· νῦν τε ἀναγκασθεὶς
ἔλεξα. γένοιτο μέντοι κατὰ νόον τοι, βασιλεῦ."

105

ὁ μὲν δὴ ταῦτα ἀμείψατο, Ξέρξης δὲ ἐς γέλωτά τε ἔτρεψε καὶ οὐκ ἐποιήσατο 1
ὀργὴν οὐδεμίαν, ἀλλ᾽ ἠπίως αὐτὸν ἀπεπέμψατο. τούτῳ δὲ ἐς λόγους ἐλθὼν
Ξέρξης καὶ ὕπαρχον ἐν τῷ Δορίσκῳ τούτῳ καταστήσας Μασκάμην τὸν
Μεγαδόστεω, τὸν δὲ ὑπὸ Δαρείου σταθέντα καταπαύσας, ἐξήλαυνε τὸν
στρατὸν διὰ τῆς Θρηίκης ἐπὶ τὴν Ἑλλάδα.

Commentary Notes

Preliminary notes

Rather than attempt to pick out individual examples as they occur, I refer the reader to the section 'Herodotus' language' in the introduction, which clarifies the quirks of dialect encountered.

The abbreviation cf. is used throughout. Standing for Latin *confer* (although this is forgotten now and the abbreviation has simply entered standard usage) this means 'compare' and is used to draw the reader's attention to other passages similar to or casting light on the one being discussed.

Chapters 1–4: News of the defeat of the Persians at the Battle of Marathon makes King Darius eager to launch an expedition against Greece. Three years are spent raising troops, but in the fourth year the province of Egypt revolts. Darius wishes to appoint his successor before setting out on campaign, but there are rival claims to the throne from his sons Artobazanes and Xerxes. The exiled Spartan king Demaratus intervenes and decides the dispute in favour of Xerxes. One year into the Egyptian rebellion, Darius dies and Xerxes becomes king.

7.5.1

ἀνεχώρησε: the verb, which literally means to go backwards, is used when the succession comes back or reverts to the person seen as the rightful heir.

Ξέρξην: Xerxes was Darius I's son by his wife Atossa, the daughter of Cyrus the Great. The rival claimant was Artobazanes, the eldest of all Darius' children, born before his father attained the throne. Herodotus has explained through the speech of the Spartan Demaratus in 7.3 that the fact that his father was already king when he was born, while only a private citizen when Artobazanes was born, was a decisive factor in the choice of Xerxes as heir. Demaratus himself had fallen foul of this system of succession (known as porphyrogeniture: 'born to the purple') when he was deposed as co-king of Sparta by Cleomenes. Despite the prime role given to Demaratus here by Herodotus, Xerxes' descent from Cyrus was in fact possibly more significant, as it ensured that succession remained within the Achaemenid family.

ἐπὶ δὲ Αἴγυπτον: to quell the rebellion against the Persian rule initiated by Cambyses, as described by Herodotus in Book 3.

δυνάμενος παρ᾽ αὐτῷ μέγιστον Περσέων: 'who had the most influence with him of all the Persians'.

Μαρδόνιος ὁ Γοβρύεω: Mardonius the son of Gobryas. In Book 3 of the *Histories*, Herodotus tells the story of the conspiracy that deposed 'Smerdis' (also known as Gaumata) and put Darius on the throne. Gobryas was one of the six conspirators, and Mardonius his son by Darius' sister. Darius appointed Mardonius a general but after his fleet was destroyed rounding Mount Athos he was relieved of his command, as described by Herodotus in 6.94. This episode marks his return to favour with Xerxes. The Athenian tragedian Aeschylus, in his play *Persians*, puts a speech into the mouth of Xerxes' mother, Atossa, attributing his decision to invade Greece to the advice of 'evil men': Mardonius is clearly meant to be the chief of these.

7.5.2

Δέσποτα: 'Master', 'Lord': to an Athenian, this form of address would sound servile and characteristic of Eastern tyrannical rule.

τῶν ἐποίησαν: 'for the things which they have done': an example of relative attraction, the phenomenon in Greek whereby a relative pronoun is 'attracted' from its proper case into the case of its antecedent, especially from the accusative into the genitive (as here), or dative. The demonstrative pronoun to whose case the relative is attracted is usually omitted, as is the case in this example.

εἰ τὸ μὲν νῦν ταῦτα πρήσσοις τά περ ἐν χερσὶ ἔχεις: the use of εἰ + optative here, that is, the first part (protasis) of a conditional without the second part (apodosis) expressed, has the force of a mild imperative: 'by all means for the time being do the things you have on hand'. English has a similar idiom whereby someone might say 'If you'd like to take a seat …' implying an omitted apodosis ('… the Doctor will see you in a few minutes') but meaning simply 'Please take a seat'.

λόγος τέ σε ἔχῃ πρὸς ἀνθρώπων ἀγαθός: note that we need to transpose the subject and object in translating this phrase to make better English sense, so not 'a fine reputation will have you' but 'you will have a fine reputation'. Mardonius offers additional motivation for Xerxes to attack Athens aside from the revenge he has already outlined: first that it will enhance Xerxes' worldwide reputation, then that others will think twice before they attack Persia.

7.5.3

οὗτος μέν οἱ ὁ λόγος: 'this argument of his'. οἱ is the dative relative pronoun, used possessively.

ἡ Εὐρώπη περικαλλὴς εἴη χώρη: Mardonius adds to his speech urging vengeance alluring facts about the beauty and fruitfulness of Europe in order to induce Xerxes to invade.

δένδρεα παντοῖα φέρει τὰ ἥμερα: 'all kinds of fruit-bearing trees', so not just olives, although these were the chief economic crop in ancient Athens. We see

AS

in 7.31 how fond Xerxes is of trees, so this is a telling detail for Mardonius to include in his argument.

ἀρετήν τε ἄκρη: the accusative of respect: 'the pinnacle as regards excellence'.

βασιλέϊ τε μούνῳ θνητῶν ἀξίη ἐκτῆσθαι: Mardonius' speech ends on a note of flattery: of all mortals, only the king deserves to possess such a land.

7.6.1

νεωτέρων ἔργων: 'novel enterprises' or 'adventures': Herodotus suggests that Mardonius is at least partly motivated simply by his own thrill-seeking nature.

θέλων αὐτὸς τῆς Ἑλλάδος ὕπαρχος εἶναι: Mardonius' other motivation is personal advancement. He wishes, Herodotus says, to become the governor of Greece; the position is that of satrap, Persian provincial ruler, with supreme power in his region, but ultimately answerable to the Great King.

χρόνῳ δὲ κατεργάσατό: the combination of these two words, χρόνῳ meaning 'finally' and κατεργάσατό 'he worked away at' or 'he achieved by working', effectively conveys the idea that Mardonius kept on at Xerxes until he got his way.

οἱ σύμμαχα: 'helpful to him'.

ἐς τὸ πείθεσθαι: the article + infinitive makes a verbal noun (gerund) in Greek, so 'for the persuading of', but it can be translated 'for persuading'.

7.6.2

τοῦτο μὲν ... τοῦτο δὲ: picking up and explaining ἄλλα from the previous sentence.

τῶν Ἀλευαδέων: a Thessalian noble family who claimed descent from a mythical character called Aleuas, who had been given the gift of prophecy by a serpent. Herodotus' classification of them as 'kings' is generally regarded as rather loose. They are mentioned in a couple more places in Herodotus – in 7.172 the other Thessalians are portrayed as fed up with the Aleuadae's political manoeuvrings.

Πεισιστρατιδέων: the Peisistratidae were the family of Athenian tyrants, named for their patriarch Peisistratus. Peisistratus' son Hippias had ruled Athens at the end of the sixth century BC and, following his exile, had taken refuge in Persia, leading Darius to Marathon in the invasion of 490 BC.

Σοῦσα: this great ancient city of Susa had been captured by Cyrus the Great and had become one of four capital cities of the Achaemenid empire.

7.6.3

Ὀνομάκριτον ... Μουσαίου: Onomacritus was a compiler of oracles, or chresmologue. As Herodotus explains here, he had been hired by Peisistratus to compile the oracles of Musaeus, a legendary figure closely associated with Orpheus, but had fallen out of favour and been expelled by Hipparchus when caught forging the oracles. The traveller and geographer Pausanias says, 'I have read verses in which Musaeus receives from the North Wind the gift of flight, but, in my opinion, Onomacritus wrote them, and there are no certainly genuine works of Musaeus except a hymn to Demeter written for the Lycomidae' (Pausanias 1.22.7).

AS

Λάσου τοῦ Ἑρμιονέος: Lasus of Hermione was a lyric poet. Hipparchus was known as a sponsor and patron of poetry. The detail that Lasus exposed Onomacritus might give a small insight into the vying for position typical of the tyrannical court.

αἱ ἐπὶ Λήμνῳ ἐπικείμεναι νῆσοι ἀφανιζοίατο κατὰ τῆς θαλάσσης: not as outlandish as it might sound at first, since in a region of submarine volcanic activity islands do appear and disappear. The disappearance of the island of Chryse, one of those described by Herodotus here, is mentioned by Pausanias: 'No long sail from Lemnos was once an island Chryse, where, it is said, Philoctetes met with his accident from the water-snake. But the waves utterly overwhelmed it, and Chryse sank and disappeared in the depths' (Pausanias 8.33.4).

7.6.4

πρότερον χρεώμενος: the participle has a concessive force; 'although he had formerly relied on him'.

τὰ μάλιστα: = 'to the greatest extent', 'above all', 'particularly'.

σφάλμα φέρον: 'portending defeat/disaster'.

τῶν μὲν ἔλεγε οὐδέν: this highlights one of the problems of placing faith in soothsayers: the desire to please leads to suppression of unfavourable or unpalatable oracles.

τόν τε Ἑλλήσποντον: the Hellespont is the strait today called the Dardanelles. Separating Asia from Europe and allowing access from the Black Sea to the Mediterranean, it has been an area of military and economic significance since ancient times.

ζευχθῆναι: the verb literally means 'to join together under a yoke' (as farm animals) so comes to mean to 'yoke' two banks of a river together, in other words to bridge the river.

χρεὸν: 'that which is necessary', 'fate'.

7.6.5

οὗτός τε δὴ χρησμῳδέων προσεφέρετο, καὶ οἵ τε Πεισιστρατίδαι καὶ οἱ Ἀλευάδαι γνώμας ἀποδεικνύμενοι: this sentence gives a vivid idea of the number of influences and arguments surrounding and placing pressure upon Xerxes. The Peisistratids were the family of the Athenian tyrants Peisistratus and his sons and joint successors Hippias and Hipparchus, who ruled Athens from 546 to 510 BC. The Aleuadae were the ruling dynasty of Thessaly.

7.7.1

ὡς δὲ ἀνεγνώσθη: 'when he had been persuaded': the verb and its prominent placement make clear Herodotus' view that Xerxes has been brought to this decision by outside influences and not of his own volition.

ἐπὶ τοὺς ἀπεστεῶτας: Egypt had been under Persian rule since the 520s BC and archaeological evidence shows that Darius treated it as an important part of the empire, drafting laws and building a navigable waterway from the Nile to the Red Sea. Herodotus does not dwell on this rebellion, maintaining focus on the invasion of Greece.

δουλοτέρην: Herodotus makes it clear that the consequences of the rebellion for the Egyptians were negative. Whereas Darius had earned a reputation for religious tolerance, supporting the country's temples, Xerxes promoted Zoroastrianism over Egyptian religion and stopped funding Egyptian monuments. Moreover, he exacted more punishing tribute, most likely because of the requirements of the invasion of Greece he was planning.

Ἀχαιμένεϊ, ἀδελφεῷ μὲν ἑωυτοῦ: Achaemenes was Xerxes' full brother, here being made provincial governor, or satrap, of Egypt. (See note on 7.6.1 above for discussion of this role.) Inarus the Libyan led a rebellion in 460 BC with help from Athenian allies which inflicted considerable damage on the Persians before Inarus was finally defeated, taken to Susa and either crucified or impaled. Herodotus has already mentioned his death at 3.12, where he includes the detail that he himself, while visiting Egypt, inspected the skulls of those who had been killed by Inarus and his rebels and found that the Egyptian skulls were much tougher than the rather brittle Persian ones.

7.8.1

ἐπὶ τὰς Ἀθήνας: in the previous chapter, the expedition was described as ἐπὶ τὴν Ἑλλάδα. Clearly for the Persians the initial focus was on the Athenians, since revenge for Marathon was the motivating factor, but for Herodotus and his readership, and indeed in terms of the actual war, the fight was against an unprecedentedly united Greek nation.

σύλλογον ἐπίκλητον: a council of Persian nobles summoned when there was an important decision to be made, to provide an at least notional check on the power of an absolute ruler. However, as Herodotus makes clear in describing a similar council in Book 9, fear could be an inhibiting factor: no-one dares to speak against the opinion of the king for fear of incurring his wrath. The Darius vase, found in Apulia in the late eighteenth century, shows in its central band of decoration a scene of Darius enthroned surrounded by just such a council of nobles, who are expressing fear and alarm at the news brought by a bearded messenger shown at Darius' feet.

7.8.A1

Xerxes opens the debate with a speech setting out his plan to invade Greece. With self-confidence he claims that in so acting he will merely be following the pattern set by his predecessors, all of whom sought to enlarge the scope of Persian rule. Further, he will be enacting a just revenge against the Athenians and in doing so taking up the cause left unfinished at his death by Darius. So reasonable, in fact, does much of it sound that it is hard to remember that it was written by a Greek. Herodotus' skill at putting the appropriate words into the mouths of his protagonists is remarkable. Some of what he says would perhaps, however, have sounded overweening to a Greek audience: his plans to bridge the Hellespont and bring the Persian empire to the edge of Zeus' realm would have smacked of hubristic over-confidence.

AS

οὔτ᾽ αὐτὸς κατηγήσομαι νόμον τόνδε ἐν ὑμῖν τιθείς, παραδεξάμενός τε αὐτῷ χρήσομαι: Xerxes points out that in seeking to add to the empire he is not behaving differently from his predecessors as king.

Ἀστυάγεα: Astyages was the last king of the Median empire, deposed by Cyrus the Great in 550 BC. The story of the rise of Cyrus is told by Herodotus in 1.95ff.

θεός ... ἄγει: The assertion of divine approbation would have struck an ancient reader as hubristic, borne out by numerous episodes in history and literature where characters who claim such approval of their schemes receive a decided comeuppance from the gods. cf. the speech Xenophon puts into his own mouth in *Anabasis* 6.3.18: 'And it may be that the god is guiding events in this way, he who wills that those who talked boastfully, as though possessed of superior wisdom, should be brought low, and that we, who always begin with the gods, should be set in a place of higher honour than those boasters.' Herodotus himself in Book 1 relates the story of Croesus of Lydia, who consulted the Delphic oracle before launching a campaign against Cyrus. The oracle told him that if he crossed his borders, he would destroy a great empire: certain that this meant the empire of Cyrus, Croesus proceeded confidently with the invasion, only to realize in defeat that the empire referred to was his own.

συμφέρεται ἐπὶ τὸ ἄμεινον: 'it turns out for the better'.

τὰ μέν νυν Κῦρός ... οὐκ ἄν τις λέγοι: the transposition of the clauses in this sentence adds emphasis to the actions of Cyrus, Cambyses and Darius.

7.8A.2

ὅκως μὴ λείψομαι τῶν πρότερον γενομένων: the verb in the passive has the meaning 'fall short of' 'be inferior to' and is followed by a genitive because of the necessary comparison implied.

In his *Persians*, Aeschylus shows Xerxes' mother Atossa speaking to the ghost of his father Darius. She ascribes similar motivation to him to that put into his own mouth by Herodotus: 'they kept telling him that, whereas you won plentiful treasure for your children by your spear, he, on his part, through lack of manly spirit, played the warrior at home and did not increase his father's wealth. Hearing such taunts many a time from evil counsellors, he planned this expedition and army against Hellas.' As mentioned in the introduction, Herodotus would have been familiar with the play, and his narrative accords with it closely.

κῦδος: heroic glory, as, for example, at Homer, *Iliad* 16.84, where Achilles is encouraging Patroclus, who is about to take the field on his behalf:

ὡς ἄν μοι τιμὴν μεγάλην καὶ κῦδος ἄρηαι

πρὸς πάντων Δαναῶν

'so that you might win me great honour and glory at the hands of all the Danaans'.

We of course derive our word 'kudos' directly from the Greek.

παμφορωτέρην: the fruitfulness of Greece is emphasized, as Xerxes echoes the earlier persuasive words of Mardonius at 7.5.3.

τιμωρίην τε καὶ τίσιν: the dual motivation of imperial acquisition and vengeance is again stressed.

AS

τὸ: 'that which'.

τὸ νοέω πρήσσειν: Xerxes seems to make it clear that his mind is already made up. Given his power and, as we later see, tendency to punish severely those who displease him, it is interesting to imagine the feelings of those noblemen invited to the 'consultation'.

7.8B.1

μέλλω ... πατέρα τὸν ἐμόν: the simplicity of this sentence makes the expedition sound easy to accomplish, and the concentration here on vengeance and filial piety rather than empire-building adds a moral righteousness to the tone that would be difficult to argue with.

7.8B.2

ἰθύοντα: the idea that Xerxes is taking up and continuing a cherished plan of Darius' adds validation to his scheme.

οἵ: picking up τὰς Ἀθήνας, but by extension referring to the people within rather than to the city itself.

ἄδικα ποιεῦντες: Darius' attempt to punish Athens for aiding the Ionian revolt culminated in defeat at the Battle of Marathon in 490 BC.

7.8B.3

ἅμα Ἀρισταγόρῃ τῷ Μιλησίῳ: Aristagoras was the tyrant of Miletus in the late sixth and early fifth century BC. In Book 5, Herodotus tells the story of his attempts to persuade the Spartans (unsuccessfully) and Athenians (successfully) to support the Ionian revolt by travelling to those cities carrying a map 'of the whole world' engraved upon bronze to support his arguments. In Book 5, Herodotus had told us that in fact Aristagoras himself did not accompany the expedition but stayed in Miletus and appointed two deputies to command it in his place. It adds to the drama to imagine him present in person.

οἷα ἔρξαν ... πάντες: the Battle of Marathon. Herodotus makes it seem as though the episode is too painful for Xerxes to refer to directly.

7.8C.1

τοὺς τούτοισι πλησιοχώρους ... οἳ Πέλοπος τοῦ Φρυγὸς νέμονται χώρην: in other words, the aim will be to conquer the Spartans as well as the Athenians.

τῷ Διὸς αἰθέρι ὁμουρέουσαν: to understand Xerxes' vision, we must visualize the heavens as an upturned bowl meeting the earth at the edges. Thus, if the Persians conquer Greece, their empire will encompass the whole known world and the Persian king will rule the earth as Zeus rules the heavens. Herodotus uses the familiar Greek name Zeus to refer to the god whom Xerxes would have called Ahura Mazda, the god of the Zoroastrian religion. cf 1.131: 'they call the whole circuit of heaven Zeus, and to him they sacrifice on the highest peaks of the mountains'.

Ahura Mazda was not represented in art during this period but it seems to have been the case that when on expedition the Persian king brought a chariot with him

AS

for the god, pulled by sacred white horses. Herodotus mentions in 1.189 an episode in which one of the sacred white horses bolts, although he does not specifically mention that the horses' job was to pull the chariot of Ahura Mazda. Xenophon mentions the chariot when describing a procession issuing from the royal palace: 'after them came a chariot sacred to Zeus; it was drawn by white horses and with a yoke of gold and wreathed with garlands' (Xenophon *Cyropaedia* 8).

7.8C.2

ἥλιος: as well as being a poetic mode of expression, this reference to the all-seeing sun reminds us that for the Persians the sun was an object of worship.

7.8C.3

οὔτε τινὰ πόλιν ἀνδρῶν οὐδεμίαν οὔτε ἔθνος οὐδὲν ἀνθρώπων: the repeated negatives drive home Xerxes' point.

οἵ τε ... αἴτιοι ... οἵ τε ἀναίτιοι: the blameworthy are the Athenians, upon whom vengeance will be wrought; the rest of the Greeks are innocent, but they will suffer along with the Athenians. The vengeance will take the form of slavery to the Persian empire.

δούλιον ζυγὸν: 'the yoke of slavery': we can think of this both literally, as physical shackles binding captured slaves together, and figuratively, as the servitude imposed by the Persian empire on the whole country. These words are and echo of Aeschylus' play *Persians*: ζυγὸν ἀμφιβαλεῖν δούλιον Ἑλλάδι (Aeschylus *Persians* 50). To Greek ears, Xerxes' speech would sound dangerously hubristic.

7.8D.1

ὑμεῖς δ᾽ ἄν μοι τάδε ποιέοντες χαρίζοισθε: presumably the alternative to being in the king's favour would be unthinkable: we will find out later in the book the possible punishments awaiting those who displeased Xerxes.

παρεσκευασμένον στρατὸν κάλλιστα: 'the best-equipped army' (κάλλιστα is neuter superlative adjective used to express superlative adverb). The offering of such rewards is one of the qualities admired by Xenophon in his encomium of the Spartan king Agesilaus.

ἐν ἡμετέρου: 'amongst us'.

7.8D.2

ποιητέα: the verbal adjective expressing obligation: 'these things must be done'.

ἰδιοβουλέειν: a rare verb meaning 'to follow one's own advice', that is, to do what one wants without consulting others.

τίθημι τὸ πρῆγμα ἐς μέσον: literally 'I place the matter into the middle' and hence open it up for discussion. This expression calls to mind the democratic and egalitarian practices of the polis, quite antithetical to the way decisions would be made in the court of a despot. Either Herodotus is unthinkingly making Xerxes speak like an Athenian, or he is pointedly showing that, whatever Xerxes might say, the discussion will not actually be open and frank, since, as he says in 7.10, most of those present are too terrified to speak against the proposal.

τὸν βουλόμενον: 'the one wishing', so 'whoever wishes'.

7.9.1

As the first speaker in this 'debate', Mardonius agrees sycophantically with Xerxes. He deals first with the question of revenge, pointing out that if it is justifiable to attack other peoples simply in order to enlarge the empire, then how much more necessary must it be to punish aggressors such as the Greeks. He goes on to dismiss the Greeks as credible foes in battle, adducing his own experience (but conveniently omitting to mention the failure of the campaign in which he was involved). Full of exclamation and rhetorical questioning, his speech is confident and daring.

Μαρδόνιος: see note on 7.5.1 above.

τῶν γενομένων Περσέων ἄριστος ἀλλὰ καὶ τῶν ἐσομένων: hyperbolic flattering language.

ἐπίκεο: 'you have hit the mark'.

Ἴωνας τοὺς ἐν τῇ Εὐρώπῃ κατοικημένους: it is characteristic of Persians to refer to all Greeks as 'Ionians'. Similarly, the Greeks are referred to in the Old Testament as Yawan, which is cognate with Ionian.

καταγελάσαι: the risk of being laughed at is always a potent argument for ancient Greeks. The Homeric heroes lived in horror of mockery. The story of Ajax, for example, shows us someone who would literally rather die than suffer the mockery of his fellow heroes. The avoidance of this fate is characteristic of other heroic figures throughout Greek literature. For Medea in Euripides' play, the risk of suffering mockery is a major deciding factor as she wonders whether to kill her children to avenge her treatment by Jason.

7.9.2

Σάκας μὲν καὶ Ἰνδοὺς καὶ Αἰθίοπάς τε καὶ Ἀσσυρίους: Mardonius is exaggerating in that only part of each of these nations was conquered by Persia. Herodotus makes it clear, for example, in Book 3, when outlining the provinces of the Persian empire, that the Persians did not conquer the whole of India, saying 'these particular Indians live far beyond the reach of the Persians ... nor were ever subjects of King Darius'. He also tells us that Cambyses conquered the Ethiopians 'who border Egypt'.

ἀλλα τε ἔθνεα πολλὰ καὶ μεγάλα: this vague reference enhances the rhetorical effect of Mardonius' claims about the Persian empire.

καταστρεψάμενοι δούλους ἔχομεν: a harsh but honest representation of the realities of Persian conquest.

ὑπάρξαντας: Mardonius places the blame with the Athenians for opening hostilities by supporting the Ionian revolt.

7.9A.1

τί δείσαντες; κοίην πλήθεος συστροφήν; κοίην δὲ χρημάτων δύναμιν;: the string of rhetorical questions suggesting in the minds of the listener the answers 'nothing', 'no', and 'no' adds to the persuasiveness of Mardonius' speech.

ἐπιστάμεθα ... ἐπιστάμεθα ... παῖδας: the repetition of ἐπιστάμεθα and the emphasis on the relationship between the Athenians and subject Greeks in the Persian empire both bolster Mardonius' point that fighting the

AS

Athenians should hold no surprises for the Persians, and that victory will be accomplished easily.

Ἴωνές τε καὶ Αἰολέες καὶ Δωριέες: 'Ionians and Aeolians and Dorians': names applied to three of the four ancient tribes (the fourth being the Achaeans) who made up the Greek nation. Mardonius is referring to those Greeks in Asia Minor under Persian rule. Herodotus himself came from Halicarnassus, one of the Dorian cities in what is modern-day Turkey.

7.9A.2

ἐπειρήθην δὲ καὶ αὐτὸς: a reference to the expedition described by Herodotus in Book 6, which resulted in the loss of the fleet off Mount Athos (see note on 7.5.1 above).

ὀλίγον ἀπολιπόντι ἐς αὐτὰς Ἀθήνας: 'nearly to Athens itself'.

7.9B.1

ἀβουλότατα πολέμους ἵστασθαι ὑπό τε ἀγνωμοσύνης καὶ σκαιότητος: Herodotus continues to place dismissive vocabulary into the mouth of Mardonius to make the Greek opposition seem negligible, enhancing the persuasiveness of his speech.

ἐπεὰν γὰρ ἀλλήλοισι πόλεμον προείπωσι ... μάχονται: a rather crude characterization of Greek methods of warfare, which incidentally ignores the previous defeat of the Persians. Obviously, it would not play into Mardonius' hands to draw attention to the fact that the Greeks, with their 'inferior' methods, had actually conquered the last invading army of Persians.

7.9B.2

τοὺς χρῆν, ἐόντας ὁμογλώσσους ... καὶ παντὶ μᾶλλον ἢ μάχῃσι: Herodotus here seems to be expressing his own ideas via the mouthpiece of Mardonius.

7.9C.1

σοὶ δὲ δὴ μέλλει ... ἁπάσας;: Mardonius' rhetorical question increases the effect of the peroration of his speech, and, when combined with the hyperbolic language of πλῆθος τὸ ἐκ τῆς Ἀσίης and νέας τὰς ἁπάσας, makes the Persians seem to be an indefatigable and invincible force.

εἰ δὲ ἄρα ... ἄριστοι τὰ πολέμια: these words add irony to the fact that Mardonius will go on to command the Persian forces defeated on land by the Greeks at Plataea in 479 BC.

ἔστω ... φιλέει γίνεσθαι: these inspiring words fit with what we have read already in chapter 6 about Mardonius' thrill-seeking nature, and sit less well with what Herodotus has told us in the same chapter about his motivation of personal advancement.

7.10.1

ἐπιλεήνας: the verb, with the root λεαίνω, literally means to smooth over, as of wood or similar. Here, used figuratively to apply to speech, it means to soften or make plausible.

σιωπώντων δὲ ... τῇ προκειμένῃ: Herodotus makes it clear that the silence of all the other Persians cannot necessarily be taken as consent. Herodotus' description of the 'debate' among the Persians, in which the king has already made his view clear, and many are too frightened to express an opinion, would have been in complete contrast with the experience of his Athenian audience, for whom free debate was a central part of democratic life.

Artabanus is the only one who dares to make a reply, protected as he is by his age and his status as Xerxes' uncle. His intervention is characterized by caution, the wisdom born of experience and a reliance on proverbs or philosophical aphorisms, providing an effective contrast with the rash and headstrong Mardonius. His speech is liberally laced with 'gnomic' utterances: short, pithy maxims encapsulating universal truths. He begins by highlighting the value of sharing opinions in open debate, likening the process to rubbing gold on a touchstone to assess its purity. He cautions strongly against dismissing the Greeks as a credible enemy in the way that Mardonius has done, and against taking any steps which carry too much risk. Emphasizing the importance of planning and forethought, he further warns against the hubristic actions that bring sure punishment from the gods, and against rushing into things. In a dramatic rhetorical flourish designed to show the strength of his feeling, Artabanus ends his speech by suggesting openly to Mardonius that they make a deal: each will offer his children as security for his side of the bargain. Mardonius will lead the campaign against Greece and if he wins, Artabanus' children will be put to death. If he loses, his children will die.

7.10A.1

μὴ λεχθεισέων μὲν γνωμέων ἀντιέων ἀλλήλῃσι: the arguing of both sides of an argument was a skill taught in Athens by the sophists, travelling professional (i.e. paid) teachers of rhetoric and philosophy. Artabanus' opening words highlight the value of a system where there is open debate of policy and decision-making.

ὥσπερ τὸν χρυσὸν ... τὸν ἀμείνω: Artabanus is here describing the ancient method of determining the purity of gold and its alloys by rubbing them (παρατρίβω) against a 'touchstone', a dark, fine-grained stone, upon which they made a mark: the colour of the mark revealed the relative purity of the metal. The analogy is vivid, and at the same time enables Artabanus to imply that both sides of the argument have great merit: it is simply a matter of determining which is superior.

7.10A.2

πατρὶ τῷ σῷ, ἀδελφεῷ δὲ ἐμῷ, Δαρείῳ: Artabanus emphasizes the familial relationship between himself and Xerxes.

ἠγόρευον μὴ στρατεύεσθαι ... ἀγαθοὺς τῆς στρατιῆς ἀποβαλὼν ἀπῆλθε: Artabanus establishes his credentials as an advisor who should be heeded by reference to an earlier episode (4.83) in which Darius ignored his advice not to attack the nomadic Scythians, with disastrous results. The story of the failed expedition is related in Herodotus 4.89–142.

AS

7.10A.3

ἀμείνονας ἢ Σκύθας, οἳ κατὰ θάλασσάν τε ἄριστοι καὶ κατὰ γῆν λέγονται εἶναι: Artabanus contradicts Mardonius' assurances that the Greek forces will be a negligible enemy.

7.10B.1

ζεύξας: the use of the verb ζεύγνυμι, to join under a yoke, emphasizes the physical nature of the bridging, which was done by means of a pontoon of linked boats, as well as the important figurative idea of the taming of nature.

κατὰ γῆν ἢ καὶ κατὰ θάλασσαν ἑσσωθῆναι, ἢ καὶ κατ' ἀμφότερα: Artabanus repeats this fear from a different point of view a few lines later. By repeatedly emphasizing the twofold nature of the approaching engagements, as well as the skill in both arenas of the enemy, he makes the undertaking seem rash and risky.

ἄλκιμοι: an epic-sounding word emphasizing the heroic bravery of the enemy.

μοῦνοι Ἀθηναῖοι: the Athenians themselves liked to represent this as the case (see Herodotus 9.27). However, Herodotus makes it clear in 6.108 and 111 that the Plataeans played a large part in the defeat of the Persians.

ἀλλ' ἢν τῇσι νηυσὶ ... λύσωσι τὴν γέφυραν: the danger of being cut off if they were defeated and the bridge destroyed before they could re-cross the Hellespont is spelled out.

7.10.C.1

οὐδεμιῇ σοφίῃ οἰκηίη: Artabanus again seeks to focus on his experience, which diverts attention from any possible imputation of animus or enmity towards Mardonius personally.

ποταμὸν Ἴστρον: the river known to us as the Danube.

παντοῖοι ἐγένοντο Σκύθαι δεόμενοι Ἰώνων λῦσαι τὸν πόρον: the local tyrants were left guarding the bridge and told to destroy it if Darius had not returned in 60 days: the story is related by Herodotus in 4.136–9.

7.10.C.2

Ἱστιαῖος ὁ Μιλήτου τύραννος: Histiaeus was one of the local rulers ('tyrants') who owed their position to Persian patronage. In the episode of the Danube crossing in Book 4, Miltiades, the Athenian tyrant of the Chersonese, speaks in favour of doing what the Scythians say and breaking the bridge. Histiaeus, however, reminds the assembled tyrants that they all owe their positions of power to the Persians and that if Darius is overthrown, they are unlikely to be able to continue to rule their respective cities 'for all the cities will choose democracy rather than despotism'. After this, Histiaeus became a trusted advisor of Darius, but met a grisly end when he was impaled and beheaded by Artaphernes after having been suspected of contributing to the Ionian revolt (6.30).

καίτοι καὶ λόγῳ ... πρήγματα γεγενῆσθαι: Artabanus draws attention to the risks of having to rely on allies who may ultimately prove disloyal.

7.10.D.1

μηδεμιῆς ἀνάγκης ἐούσης: Artabanus' view is completely opposite to the risk-seeking nature of Mardonius.

τὸν σύλλογον τόνδε διάλυσον: this seems sound advice given the apparently false nature of the 'debate'.

ὅταν τοι δοκέῃ, προσκεψάμενος ἐπὶ σεωυτοῦ προαγόρευε τά τοι δοκέει εἶναι ἄριστα: Artabanus' words here, with the repetitive τοι /σεωυτοῦ /τοι, encourage Xerxes to make up his own mind.

7.10.D.2

εὖ βουλεύεσθαι ... ὑπὸ τῆς τύχης: in this paragraph Artabanus stresses the importance of relying on reason to plan carefully, even if plans are subsequently thwarted by the action of chance.

βουλεύεσθαι ... βεβούλευται ... τὸ βούλευμα ... ὁ δὲ βουλευσάμενος ... βεβούλευται τε: the frequent repetition of these cognate words leaves the listener in no doubt as to what Artabanus is advocating.

εὕρημα εὕρηκε: the cognate words here reinforce the idea that this prize is one that is only won by chance.

7.10.E.1

ὡς κεραυνοῖ ὁ θεός: Artabanus' language takes on a dramatic epic quality. The verb is the same used by Hesiod in his *Theogony* when Zeus defeats the monstrous Typhoeus.

τὰ δὲ σμικρὰ οὐδέν μιν κνίζει: this view, familiar from, for example, the tragedies of Aeschylus, holds that the lives of the humble do not attract the attention of the gods.

ὁρᾷς: the repetition of the verb makes it seem as though Artabanus is describing a self-evident truth.

φιλέει γὰρ ὁ θεὸς τὰ ὑπερέχοντα πάντα κολούειν: Artabanus' role here is of wise elder adviser stating universal truths in an attempt to warn Xerxes away from the path of overweening ambition and hubris. He is like a one-man tragic chorus.

Cf. Aeschylus *Agamemnon* ll.375–80: 'The penalty for reckless crime is ruin when men breathe a spirit of pride above just measure, because their mansions teem with more abundance than is good for them. But let there be such wealth as brings no distress, enough to satisfy a sensible man.'

and ll.469–71:

'Glory in excess is fraught with peril; the lofty peak is struck by Zeus' thunderbolt. I choose prosperity unassailed by envy.'

ὁ θεὸς φθονήσας φόβον ἐμβάλῃ: Artabanus refers to the belief that panic in battle (the original Homeric meaning of the word φόβος) was induced by supernatural intervention, just as the voice of the god Pan was supposed to cause cattle to stampede. Note that the participle φθονήσας draws attention to the god's motivation, namely jealousy.

οὐ γὰρ ἐᾷ φρονέειν μέγα ὁ θεὸς ἄλλον ἢ ἑωυτόν: a typical gnomic utterance from Artabanus in his role as older and wiser giver of advice.

AS

7.10.F.1

ἐπειχθῆναι: the infinitive used as a verbal noun, or gerund = 'haste'.

φιλέουσι: used to mean 'usually' or 'are likely to'.

ἐν δὲ τῷ ἐπισχεῖν: another gerund, as ἐπειχθῆναι above, this time with the article: 'in waiting'.

παραυτίκα ... ἀνὰ χρόνον: Artabanus' approach is summed up in the contrast between seeking instant gratification and waiting for time to tell.

7.10.G.1

σοὶ μὲν δὴ ταῦτα, ὦ βασιλεῦ, συμβουλεύω: the role which Herodotus gives Artabanus here is to offer sage counsel which will then be disregarded by his hot-headed and hubristic nephew.

φλαύρως ἀκούειν: 'to be ill-spoken of'.

λόγους ματαίους ... φλαύρως ἀκούειν ... διαβάλλων: 'idle words ... to be spoken ill of ... slandering': Artabanus makes clear his view that Mardonius' characterization of the Greeks is ignorant and wide of the mark.

ἐπαείρεις αὐτὸν βασιλέα στρατεύεσθαι: this is indeed what Herodotus has shown happening in the earlier passage.

μή νυν οὕτω γένηται: the suddenly contrasting short sentence adds impact to the sentiment.

7.10.G.2

διαβολὴ γὰρ ἐστὶ δεινότατον: Herodotus continues to characterize Artabanus as a wise commentator on human affairs: he turns now to an exposition of the iniquities of slander, explaining the widespread negative impact of making false accusations. The one making the accusation and the one who believes it are both to blame, and the victim is wronged twice over in consequence.

ἀδικέοντες ... ἀδικεόμενος ... ἀδικέει ... ἀδικέει ... ἀδικέεται: the saturation of the passage with the verb ἀδικέω drives home to the audience that slander is wrong and injurious.

οὐ παρεόντος ... ἀπεών: Artabanus emphasizes the inability of those slandered in their absence (such as the Greeks in this instance) to defend themselves.

7.10.H.1

στρατηλάτεε αὐτὸς σὺ ἐπιλεξάμενός τε ἄνδρας τοὺς ἐθέλεις: this is in fact what eventually happens after the defeat at Salamis, when Xerxes returns home and Mardonius remains behind with a view to the eventual conquest of Greece.

7.10.H.2

κτεινέσθων οἱ ἐμοὶ παῖδες, πρὸς δὲ αὐτοῖσι καὶ ἐγώ: this offer is intended to show Artabanus' passionate belief in his point of view. Xerxes, however, is enraged and utterly rejects Artabanus' advice.

ἐμοὶ ... σοὶ: possessive datives: 'my sons ... and yours'.

κτεινέσθων ... πασχόντων: third person imperatives: 'let them be killed' and 'let them suffer'.

AS

The balance and contrast in these phrases draws attention to the bargain Artabanus is suggesting.

ἢν ἀπονοστήσῃς: 'if you return': the implication being that he won't. And, indeed, he doesn't.

7.10.H.3

ἀνάξεις: 'you will lead by sea'.

ὑπὸ κυνῶν τε καὶ ὀρνίθων διαφορεύμενον: leaving a corpse unburied to be devoured by dogs and birds was anathema to the Greeks and is a fate often threatened for each other by warriors in the *Iliad* before single combat. Herodotus makes Artabanus speak like a Greek, forgetting, or unaware, that this form of burial was, and is, usual in Zoroastrianism.

γνόντα ἐπ' οἵους ἄνδρας ἀναγινώσκεις στρατεύεσθαι βασιλέα: in Book 9, Herodotus shows Mardonius continuing to underestimate the opposition mounted by the Lacedaemonians, as well as showing a disregard for oracles. He was killed at the Battle of Plataea, after, Herodotus tells us, proving to be the most courageous individual among the Persians. According to Herodotus, the eventual site of his burial was a mystery.

Chapters 11–33: Xerxes changes his mind and decides not to invade, but then has a recurring dream which threatens ruin unless he invades Greece. Artabanus, forced by Xerxes to sleep in his bed, also has the same dream, and so the decision is taken to proceed with the invasion. Preparation for war takes four years, and then the expeditionary force sets off from Cappodocia to Sardis.

7.34

τὴν μὲν ... τὴν δ᾽ ἑτέρην: referring to two separate bridges. Xerxes bridged the narrow crossing between Abydus and Sestus, famous from mythology as the scene of the nightly swim of Leander to visit Hero, later emulated by Lord Byron.

λευκολίνου ... βυβλίνην: although it is not immediately clear from this description, the white flax and papyrus are not used to make the entire bridge, but, manufactured into rope, to tie together the boats used to form a pontoon bridge.

ἑπτὰ στάδιοι: the stadion, or stade, was an ancient Greek unit of measurement of distance. There does not seem to have been one clearly defined standard length for a stade, but various different measurements depending on region, varying from about 150 to 200 metres. The stadion race was the premier event at the ancient Olympic Games, the original track measuring approximately 190 metres.

χειμὼν μέγας: the storm that destroys the original bridges could be regarded as a divine warning, which Xerxes fails to heed.

7.35.1

τριηκοσίας ἐπικέσθαι μάστιγι πληγὰς καὶ κατεῖναι ἐς τὸ πέλαγος πεδέων ζεῦγος: one of the most famous episodes in Herodotus' description of Xerxes, this seems to confirm the view of the Persian king as a deranged despot. It is possible, however, that Herodotus misunderstood the scene and may have taken a figurative reference to binding or fettering the sea, referring to the building of bridges over it, too literally. Cf. Aeschylus' *Persians* 745ff.: 'for he conceived the hope that he could by shackles, as if it were a slave, restrain the current of the sacred Hellespont, the Bosporus, a stream divine; he set himself to fashion a roadway of a new type, and, by casting upon it hammer-wrought fetters, made a spacious causeway for his mighty host.'

Even if Xerxes did take such action, it is not necessarily as maniacal as it first seems. Plenty of ancient, and less ancient, legal codes allow for the punishment of animals and inanimate objects: Aristotle's *Athenaion Politeia* mentions that this was the case in Athens, and Pausanias includes a number of stories of, for example, statues being punished for accidentally causing death.

στίξοντας: branding was a customary punishment for runaway slaves, so seems appropriate for the recalcitrant, disobedient Hellespont, but it is really quite hard to see how this might have been achieved.

7.35.2

βάρβαρά τε καὶ ἀτάσθαλα: Herodotus seems genuinely outraged at the Persian king's sacrilegious treatment of a divine waterway.

A
Level

Ὦ πικρὸν ὕδωρ: the direct speech adds a moment of drama to the narrative.

βασιλεὺς μὲν Ξέρξης διαβήσεταί σε, ἤν τε σύ γε βούλῃ ἤν τε μή: further demonstration of Xerxes' hubris.

θολερῷ καὶ ἁλμυρῷ ποταμῷ: 'a turbid and briny river': the Hellespont is in fact not a river at all, although its long winding shape may give that impression. Addressing it in this manner demeans it further – not only does it not count as part of the sea, its muddy, salty waters make it useless as a river, which needs to be clear and pure to be a viable source of water. cf. the River Borysthenes, 4.53: πίνεσθαι τε ἥδιστος ἐστί, ῥέει τε καθαρὸς: 'it is very sweet to drink and flows pure'.

οὐδεὶς ἀνθρώπων θύει: unlike, for example, the River Strymon, to which the Magi did sacrifice.

7.35.3

ἀποταμεῖν τὰς κεφαλάς: in Book 9, Herodotus again shows Xerxes summarily executing those who have displeased him during the Battle of Salamis. Beheading, however, was not a dishonourable death for the Persians: mutilation by cutting off the nose and ears, as happens to Zopyrus in Book 3, seems a more likely humiliation for those incurring the king's displeasure.

Chapters 36–7: Herodotus gives a detailed description of the construction of the replacement pontoon bridges over the Hellespont. The army winters at Sardis. Just as it sets off in the spring for Abydos, there is an eclipse of the sun, which the Magi interpret as predicting the abandonment by the Greeks of their cities.

7.38.1

Πύθιος ὁ Λυδός: the same character who offered Xerxes his fortune in chapters 27–9: see the overview of the prescription in the introduction.

καταρρωδήσας τὸ ἐκ τοῦ οὐρανοῦ φάσμα: the eclipse of the sun has terrified Pythius, despite the positive interpretation placed upon it by the Magi.

ἐπαρθείς τε τοῖσι δωρήμασι,: 'raised up'; 'encouraged'; 'puffed up': the verb is often used in circumstances where the person is falsely encouraged or his pride is unfounded. Here Pythius is deluded into thinking that the formalized exchange of gifts and official friendship received in 7.29 entitle him to special treatment from the king. The same verb is used of Mardonius in 9.49.

7.38.2

τὸ σοὶ μὲν ἐλαφρὸν ... ἐμοὶ δὲ μέγα ...: τὸ here is an example of the use of the article to stand for a relative pronoun, 'which'. The contrast between σοὶ and ἐμοὶ and between ἐλαφρὸν and μέγα draws attention to the distance between Pythius and Xerxes: it seems a small favour to ask from one who has so much. Pythius is badly misjudging the situation, unfortunately.

θαρσήσας: Xerxes' apparently encouraging response emboldens Pythius to make his request.

7.38.3

ἐς τόδε ἡλικίης: Pythius is said in 7.27 to be the son of Atys, making him the grandson of Croesus. This would mean that he was 70 or 80 years old by this time, an advanced age.

A
Level

τὸν πρεσβύτατον: if Pythius is 70 or 80, his eldest son would himself not be especially young.

νοστήσειας: optative: 'may you return'.

7.39.1

κάρτα τε ἐθυμώθη: we are by now becoming used to Xerxes' extreme and unpredictable reactions. He is outraged to think that Pythius should dare to ask for special treatment when he himself is leading an army, which contains many of his own relatives and friends.

παῖδας ἐμοὺς καὶ ἀδελφεοὺς καὶ οἰκηίους καὶ φίλους: the polysyndetic list gives rhetorical emphasis to Xerxes' point: why should Pythius be given special treatment when Xerxes himself is risking so much personally?

ἐὼν ἐμὸς δοῦλος: a stark reminder of the realities of their relationship: see ἐπαερθείς above.

πανοικίη αὐτῇ τῇ γυναικὶ: αὐτῇ τῇ γυναικὶ seems superfluous, but again serves to emphasize Xerxes' complete control over his subjects: if he says bring your wife, you bring your wife.

ὡς ἐν τοῖσι ὠσὶ τῶν ἀνθρώπων οἰκέει ὁ θυμός: this has the sound of a well-known maxim or proverb.

ὃς χρηστὰ μὲν ἀκούσας τέρψιος ἐμπιπλεῖ τὸ σῶμα, ὑπεναντία δὲ τούτοισι ἀκούσας ἀνοιδέει: whether or not this is a proverbial truth, it certainly describes Xerxes' own behaviour.

7.39.2

ἐλάσσω δὲ τῆς ἀξίης: in view of the punishment Xerxes goes on to inflict, this claim to leniency seems rather hollow.

τὰ ξείνια: the ancient and powerful concept of *xenia*, familiar from Homer, whereby strangers are welcomed without question, and gifts exchanged, on the understanding that a reciprocal relationship pertains wherever civilized life exists.

τοῦ περιέχεαι μάλιστα: a peculiarly tyrannical twist: it shall be the son Pythius most especially desires to keep that he shall lose.

7.39.3

Herodotus tells a story in Book 4 about Darius exacting a similar punishment: the Persian Oeobazus, a father of three sons serving in Darius' army, asks that one be left behind. Darius tells him that in fact he will leave *all* his sons behind, but fails to mention that they will be left behind dead.

διαταμόντας ... διεξιέναι τὸν στρατόν: a peculiarly horrific image, and one that, given the size of Xerxes' army, seems on the face of it practically very difficult to achieve in anything other than a symbolic sense. There is, however, evidence that the cutting in half of a sacrificial victim, and the walking between the two halves, conferred a protection upon those who practised the ritual: cf. Jeremiah 34.18–19.

Some argue that the whole of this passage is merely legendary, but even if that is the case, it is worth considering why a legend of this sort might attach itself to Xerxes: clearly for Herodotus, such behaviour was consistent with what he believed to be the character of Xerxes, as well as being typical of Eastern despots.

διαταμεῖν, διαταμόντας δὲ τὰ ἡμίτομα διαθεῖναι τὸ μὲν ἐπὶ δεξιὰ τῆς ὁδοῦ, τὸ δ᾽ ἐπ᾽ ἀριστερά: the repetitive language here dwells on the true horror of the situation described. The juxtaposition of διαταμεῖν, διαταμόντας suggests the immediate carrying out of the order, while the echoed prefix on διαθεῖναι drives home that the two halves of the body are placed separately, further spelled out by τὸ μὲν ἐπὶ δεξιά, τὸ δ᾽ ἐπ᾽ ἀριστερά.

Chapters 40–4: Herodotus describes the organization of the army and the escort that surrounded the king. In front of Xerxes travelled the 'sacred chariot of Zeus [that is presumably Ahura Mazda]', followed by Xerxes himself in a chariot. Herodotus tells us that Xerxes sometimes swapped the chariot for a carriage. He describes the spearmen following behind Xerxes: some had golden or silver pomegranates instead of spikes on the butts of their spears; those immediately behind Xerxes had golden apples. Then came 10,000 cavalry and the rest of the army behind them. We are told the route of the army from Lydia; they encounter violent storms on the foothills of Mount Ida, resulting in a substantial number of casualties. The expedition arrives at, and drinks dry, the River Scamander. Xerxes visits the site of Ilium and makes sacrifices. Unspecified terror seizes the whole army during the night. Xerxes reaches Abydus and reviews the army from a dais of white stone. A sailing race is held.

7.45.1

ὁ Ξέρξης ἑωυτὸν ἐμακάρισε, μετὰ δὲ τοῦτο ἐδάκρυσε: Herodotus does not always include the article with Xerxes' name. The inclusion here draws additional attention to the king and his emotions. Contrast this scene with Darius' similar review in Book 4.85–8, where there is no such philosophical or emotional response. In part at least this reaction seems in keeping with Xerxes' volatile nature as portrayed by Herodotus.

7.46.1

Ἀρτάβανος ὁ πάτρως: Xerxes' uncle Artabanus is reintroduced as a convenient sounding board and contrast to the character of the king. We must surely regard this entire exchange as fantasy on the part of Herodotus, and moreover one perhaps inspired by theatrical performances or epic verse. The whole scene works well if envisaged as a staged dialogue, and the language used throughout falls within the poetic register.

οὐ συμβουλεύων: 'advising you not …' (rather than 'not advising you …').

μακαρίσας γὰρ σεωυτὸν δακρύεις: the near-exact repetition of the words from the end of the previous chapter sets up the theme of the exchange, as well as echoing the formulaic nature of epic poetry. The conversation is placed in the realm of poetry or drama rather than reality.

7.46.2

ὁ δὲ: the standard method of showing a change of subject: 'And he … (Xerxes …)'.

**A
Level**

ἐς ἑκατοστὸν ἔτος: 'a hundred years from now' rather than 'to his (each individual's) hundredth year'.

Ἕτερα τούτου … οἰκτρότερα: Artabanus suggests that there are worse things than death.

παρὰ τὴν ζόην: 'during life'.

7.46.3

τεθνάναι βούλεσθαι μᾶλλον ἢ ζώειν: Herodotus seems receptive to the possibility that death can provide a release and a blessing. In the story of Croesus and Solon in Book 1, Herodotus has Solon tell the story of Cleobis and Biton, two pious young men whose mother asked Hera to bestow on them the greatest blessing possible for the gods to grant, whereupon they fell asleep in the temple and never woke up. 'A divinely authored proof', says Herodotus, 'that it is better to be dead than alive'.

αἵ τε γὰρ συμφοραὶ … τὸν βίον: Herodotus has Artabanus strike a mournful tone: life is short, but then often so filled with suffering as to appear too long.

7.46.4

ὁ δὲ θεὸς γλυκὺν γεύσας τὸν αἰῶνα φθονερὸς ἐν αὐτῷ εὑρίσκεται ἐών: this seems a characteristically Greek view. Artabanus again here sounds like the chorus in a Greek tragedy, claiming that the gods spitefully allow humans a brief idea of how pleasant life could be before jealously snatching it away again. Commentators agree that this is not how a worshipper of Ahura Mazda, viewed as wholly benevolent, would have viewed human life.

7.47.1

Ξέρξης δὲ ἀμείβετο λέγων: 'Xerxes said in reply': another epic-sounding formulation. The epic/heroic/poetic sound of the passage is further enhanced by the inclusion of the poetic word βιοτῆς instead of the more usual prose βίος.

μηδὲ κακῶν μεμνώμεθα χρηστὰ ἔχοντες πρήγματα ἐν χερσί: Xerxes' mood swings again. From tears at the brevity and suffering of human life, he turns to rebuking Artabanus for sympathizing with his melancholy and urges instead a concentration on the short term.

εἴ τοι ἡ ὄψις τοῦ ἐνυπνίου μὴ ἐναργὴς οὕτω ἐφάνη: a reference to the dream which appeared first to Xerxes and subsequently to Artabanus. The story is told by Herodotus in 7.12–18 (see the overview in the introduction). Although Xerxes forced Artabanus to look for the vision at the time, here he is asking him to lay aside any thought of divine intervention and give an honest assessment of the expedition and its chances.

φέρε τοῦτό μοι ἀτρεκέως εἰπέ: as has been previously noted, only Artabanus' age and status allowed him to speak freely to Xerxes, and even then it must have taken courage.

7.47.2

ὁ δὲ ἀμείβετο λέγων: the heroic-sounding exchange, couched in formulaic epic style, continues.

τελευτήσειε: the optative expressing a wish for the future: 'would that …', 'may …'

**A
Level**

οὐδ' ἐντὸς ἐμεωυτοῦ: 'not within myself': we might say 'beside myself'.

ὁρῶν τοι δύο τὰ μέγιστα πάντων ἐόντα πολεμιώτατα: 'seeing that the two greatest things in existence are your bitterest enemies': Artabanus explains this initially cryptic utterance in response to Xerxes' questioning below.

7.48.1

Δαιμόνιε ἀνδρῶν: δαιμόνιος properly means 'belonging to a δαίμων' or spirit, therefore miraculous or marvellous. It is used as a polite greeting in Homer simply to mean 'good sir/lady', 'my good man/woman', with the qualifying ἀνδρῶν added later. It's possible that Xerxes is simply saying 'my dear man', but also that he means something more like 'you strange man'. Xerxes is completely puzzled by what Artabanus has said and fires a series of questions at him in an attempt to understand.

κότερά τοι ὁ πεζὸς ... συναμφότερα ταῦτα: the questions present Xerxes as only able to interpret Artabanus' words in prosaic, practical terms: does he mean that the Greek *army* will be bigger, or the Greek *navy*, or *both*?

7.49.1

ἢν δὲ πλεῦνας συλλέξῃς, τὰ δύο τοι τὰ λέγω πολλῷ ἔτι πολεμιώτερα γίνεται: in reassuring Xerxes that his forces are not too small, Artabanus hints that they may in fact be too large, and at least that there would be no advantage in making them any bigger.

τὰ δὲ δύο ταῦτα ἐστὶ γῆ τε καὶ θάλασσα: after the cryptic talk, Artabanus lays out simply and clearly what he is driving at: the two enemies he was referring to are the land and the sea.

7.49.2

οὔτε: the οὔτε is not picked up by another οὔτε but by καὶ δὴ in 7.49.3.

ἐγειρομένου χειμῶνος: the memory of the fleet lost rounding Mount Athos is the unspoken reference of this passage.

διασῶσαι: the intensifying δια- prefix adds to the notion of salvation.

οὐκὶ ἕνα ... ἀλλὰ παρὰ πᾶσαν τὴν ἤπειρον: this whole passage carries the implication that the fleet is already so large as to be a danger to the expedition rather than an advantage.

7.49.3

λιμὴν ... δεξάμενός ... λιμένων ὑποδεξίων: the polyptoton of λιμὴν and repetition of cognates of δέχομαι sow anxiety about the availability of harbours large enough to take in the whole fleet.

αἱ συμφοραὶ τῶν ἀνθρώπων ἄρχουσι καὶ οὐκὶ ὥνθρωποι τῶν συμφορέων: 'events rule men and not men events': clearly a proverbial, gnomic saying, carefully and chiastically expressed, further enhancing the representation of Artabanus as a purveyor of home truths and timeless wisdom.

καὶ δὴ τῶν δύο τοι τοῦ ἑτέρου εἰρημένου τὸ ἕτερον ἔρχομαι ἐρέων: this seems a long-winded way of saying that Artabanus is moving on to his second 'enemy'. The repetition of τοῦ ἑτέρου ... τὸ ἕτερον and ε/ϱ sounds adds a ponderous quality to the speech that demands attention.

A Level

7.49.4

εἰ θέλει ... προβαίνῃς ἑκαστέρω: Artabanus describes a paradoxical situation whereby the less an invading army is opposed by the enemy, the more the land itself becomes the enemy, as they continue to advance into the unknown at the risk of running out of supplies.

τὸ πρόσω αἰεὶ κλεπτόμενος: interpretations of this phrase vary according to whether κλεπτόμενος is taken to be passive or middle. So either 'being drawn on' or 'snatching after more'.

εὐπρηξίης δὲ οὐκ ἔστι ἀνθρώποισι οὐδεμία πληθώρη: another truism from Artabanus: 'men can never have enough success'.

7.49.5

οὐδενὸς ἐναντιευμένου: Artabanus reintroduces the paradox mentioned above; it is the very fact that no-one opposes conquest that makes it dangerous, because it allows the invading army to overreach itself.

χώρην πλεῦνα ἐν πλέονι χρόνῳ: a pleasing chiastic arrangement of words, enhanced by the repeated consonantal sounds, emphasizing the key considerations of the acquisition of a lot of land over much time.

λιμὸν: Artabanus is taking the bleakest view of the possible outcomes.

ἀνὴρ δὲ οὕτω ἂν εἴη ἄριστος ...: Herodotus puts another piece of proverbial wisdom into Artabanus' mouth: caution in planning and looking for every eventuality leads to boldness in action when the time finally comes.

βουλευόμενος ... ἐν δὲ τῷ ἔργῳ; ἀρρωδέοι ... θρασὺς: the contrasting pairings of words between planning and action, and fear and boldness, give the speech a rhetorical flourish to finish with.

Artabanus is proved right in the long term: Xerxes' navy is severely damaged by storms (7.188 and 8.12) and after the defeat at Salamis the retreating army is forced to eat grass, leaves and tree bark (8.115.2–3). Herodotus, with the benefit of hindsight, is able to create in Artabanus a tragic prophet of doom, whose words, however wise, are fated to be ignored. The string of maxims which Herodotus makes him utter enhances the effect noticed earlier of the one-man tragic chorus or Cassandra/Teiresias-type figure, only proved right after the event.

7.50.1

Herodotus continues to present the philosophical, measured and reflective side of Xerxes in his reply, as well as giving him reasonable and persuasive answers to Artabanus' concerns. The overall thrust of Xerxes' argument, counter to Artabanus' anxious consideration of every possible negative eventuality, is that it is better to make a bold and daring attempt than to waste away imagining the worst. As evidence, he adduces the expansion of the Persian empire, a success enjoyed by his predecessors because of their willingness to risk all. More practically, and optimistically, he argues that the army won't be in Europe long enough to starve: not only will they take sufficient supplies with them, they confidently expect to have access to the crops grown by those they are going to subdue.

**A
Level**

οἰκότως: a measured term acknowledging the good sense of what Artabanus has said.

ἀτὰρ: a stronger alternative for δέ to answer the μέν.

μήτε πάντα φοβέο μήτε πᾶν ὁμοίως ἐπιλέγεο: the repeated μήτε and imperative verbs show Xerxes' emphatic rejection of his uncle's point of view on this occasion.

εἰ γὰρ δὴ βούλοιο ἐπὶ τῷ αἰεὶ ἐπεσφερομένῳ πρήγματι τὸ πᾶν ὁμοίως ἐπιλέγεσθαι, ποιήσειας ἂν οὐδαμὰ οὐδέν: a direct rebuttal of Artabanus' comment in the previous chapter that the best kind of man is he who feels alarm at the thought of everything that might go wrong. Xerxes' view is that if you spend all your time thinking about possible eventualities, you'll never do anything at all, a point emphasized by the repeated negatives at the end of this sentence.

κρέσσον δὲ πάντα θαρσέοντα ἥμισυ τῶν δεινῶν πάσχειν μᾶλλον ἢ πᾶν χρῆμα προδειμαίνοντα μηδαμὰ μηδὲν παθεῖν: 'it is better to approach everything boldly and suffer half of what you fear than to fear everything and never suffer anything': Xerxes shows that he can match Artabanus cliché for cliché. The repetitious μηδαμὰ μηδὲν directly echoes the οὐδαμὰ οὐδέν above, helping to reinforce Xerxes' argument that nothing ventured is nothing gained.

7.50.2

ἐρίξων: the verb, connected with ἔρις, strife, is used of wrangling or verbal disputation. Xerxes is characterizing his uncle here as one who has negative arguments to offer against everything others say, but nothing positive to offer in return.

σφάλλεσθαι: a vivid verb that can mean to be physically thrown off one's feet as well as, as here, to be foiled in an argument. One senses that Herodotus wishes to portray Xerxes as rather enjoying playing the devil-may-care hero to his staid, overly cautious uncle.

τοῖσι τοίνυν βουλομένοισι ποιέειν ὡς τὸ ἐπίπαν φιλέει γίνεσθαι τὰ κέρδεα, τοῖσι δὲ ἐπιλεγομένοισί τε πάντα καὶ ὀκνέουσι οὐ μάλα ἐθέλει: Xerxes is amassing his own collection of maxims to support his side of the argument: this could be loosely translated as 'he who dares wins'.

ἐθέλει: this use of ἐθέλει means to be naturally disposed, wont or accustomed.

Xerxes' claim, unlike Artabanus', is not supported by the account. The successful military actions carried out by Xerxes' predecessors were endorsed by his advisers, but Croesus, Cyrus, Cambyses and Darius might not have been defeated if they had listened to those cautioning them.

7.50.3

τὰ Περσέων πρήγματα: 'Persian affairs': almost just = 'Persia'.

ἐς ὃ δυνάμιος: 'To what of power', that is, 'to what power' or 'to what position of power'. Notice the characteristic Greek formulation whereby the subject of the subordinate clause is made the object of the main verb. 'You see Persian affairs, to what power they have come', meaning, 'You see to what position of power Persia has come'.

A
Level

γνώμῃσι ἐχρέωντο ... εἶχον τοιούτους: Xerxes makes what seems perhaps to be a rather pointed distinction between holding opinions like Artabanus', and not holding such opinions oneself, but having advisers who do. His argument is that if his predecessors had listened to advisers cautioning them in the way that Artabanus is attempting to caution him, they would never have achieved the successes they enjoyed.

κινδύνους ἀναρριπτέοντες: the metaphor is taken from playing dice.

μεγάλα γὰρ πρήγματα μεγάλοισι κινδύνοισι ἐθέλει καταιρέεσθαι: for the use of ἐθέλει, see 7.50.2 above. καταιρέεσθαι is passive of καθαιρέω, to take down, meaning 'to achieve', 'to win as a reward or prize'. Xerxes is proving that he is a match for Artabanus when it comes to finding proverbs to support his enterprise. Many of them sound familiar even to modern ears.

7.50.4

πᾶσαν τὴν Εὐρώπην: Xerxes is seeming to become more confident as he speaks – the object of the expedition is here stated as the conquest of the whole of Europe, as previously favoured by Mardonius.

οὔτε λιμῷ ἐντυχόντες οὐδαμόθι οὔτε ἄλλο ἄχαρι οὐδὲν παθόντες: the repetition of negatives serves effectively to reject all Artabanus' objections.

ἐπ᾽ ἀροτῆρας δὲ καὶ οὐ νομάδας στρατευόμεθα ἄνδρας: Xerxes dismisses Artabanus' fear of famine by pointing out that they will be conquering cultivated land so will be able to feed the army from the crops: the reference to nomads seems to be a direct reference to the disastrous Scythian campaign of Darius, brought forward as an argument against the expedition by Artabanus in 7.10.

7.51.1

σὺ δέ μευ συμβουλίην ἔνδεξαι: the δέ here imparts a special emphasis to this part of the sentence, rather than changing the subject as is often the case.

περὶ πολλῶν πρηγμάτων πλεῦνα: the alliteration helps stress the momentous nature of the deliberations.

Ἰωνίην: an ethnographic rather than geographic term.

πλὴν Ἀθηναίων: Athens claimed to be the mother-city of the Ionian race.

7.51.2

ἢ γὰρ σφέας, ἢν ἔπωνται, δεῖ ἀδικωτάτους γίνεσθαι καταδουλουμένους τὴν μητρόπολιν, ἢ δικαιοτάτους συνελευθεροῦντας: Artabanus cautions against involving the Ionian Greeks in the campaign, since it will strain their possibly doubtful loyalty to their Persian overlords. Artabanus appears to acknowledge the justice of the Ionians' case in not wishing to fight against Athens and speaks here like an Athenian, indeed exactly like the letter Herodotus tells us was written by Themistocles to the Ionian Greeks (8.22): 'Men of Ionia. What you are doing by making war against the land of your ancestors and enslaving Greece is a criminal act.'

7.51.3

ἀδικωτάτους ... καταδουλουμένους ... δικαιοτάτους συνελευθεροῦντας. ἀδικώτατοι ... οὐδὲν κέρδος μέγα ... δικαιότατοι ... δηλήσασθαι

A Level

μεγάλως ...: the balance and contrast here neatly encapsulate the paradox. If the Ionians behave unjustly (towards Athens by helping the Persians) they won't be much help to the Persians anyway; if they behave justly (towards Athens by seeking to liberate her from potential Persian domination) they might cause the Persian army a lot of trouble.

τὸ παλαιὸν ἔπος ὡς εὖ εἴρηται: Artabanus rounds off the exchange by openly acknowledging his debt to ancient proverbial wisdom and closing his speech with another saying: τὸ μὴ ἅμα ἀρχῇ πᾶν τέλος καταφαίνεσθαι: 'the end is not revealed completely at the beginning'. For Artabanus, at least as characterized by Herodotus, these sayings transmit universal truths, learned through long experience. Inconveniently for him, it is characteristic of proverbs that one can always find a contradictory example, something that Xerxes uses to his advantage in this conversation.

7.52.1

τῶν ἀπεφήναο γνωμέων σφάλλεαι: clearly if Artabanus was hoping to clinch the argument with his fears about the loyalty of the Ionians, he was mistaken. Xerxes is at a peak of self-confidence and seems to have an answer for every anxiety.

δικαιοσύνην καὶ πιστότητα ἐνέδωκαν, ἄχαρι δὲ οὐδέν: Xerxes' argument is on shaky ground. Herodotus has already explained in 7.10 how close the Persian army came to disaster in the episode of Histiaeus and the bridge over the Danube. Perhaps Herodotus puts this trusting speech into the mouth of Xerxes to show his naivety as a new king not yet embittered by experience.

7.52.2

τέκνα καὶ γυναῖκας καὶ χρήματα: the fact that the Ionians have left behind children, wives and possessions suggests more strongly than anything else that they plan to remain loyal.

νεώτερόν τι: literally 'something newer/rather new', but the standard way of expressing 'rebellion' or 'revolution'.

σῶζε οἶκόν τε τὸν ἐμὸν καὶ τυραννίδα τὴν ἐμήν· σοὶ γὰρ ἐγὼ μούνῳ ἐκ πάντων σκῆπτρα τὰ ἐμὰ ἐπιτρέπω: Artabanus is despatched to Susa to mind affairs while the king is away. This is a dramatic and public conferring by Xerxes of the powers of regent, using poetic language (σκῆπτρα). Xerxes emphasizes his hold on power by the repetition of τὸν ἐμὸν ... τὴν ἐμήν ... τὰ ἐμὰ but entrusts all to his uncle. We can imagine our fantasy stage scene concluding with a flourish at this point, with the physical handing over perhaps of the sceptre as a concrete symbol of Artabanus' status.

This exchange, culminating in the Xerxes' honourable despatch of Artabanus, seems to mark a new stage in the king's self-confidence: he is not cowed by his uncle, but neither does he petulantly fly into a rage. Instead, he is reasonable, if bolder than the older man, and knows his own mind. The sending of Artabanus back to Susa seems to mark the moment at which Xerxes no longer feels the need of advice or guidance from his elders.

A
Level

Chapters 53–100: After sending Artabanus away to Susa, Xerxes exhorts the leading Persians to pursue the war vigorously. They prepare sacrifices and the crossing of the Hellespont begins. It takes seven days and seven nights. Meanwhile the fleet sails towards Cape Sarpedon. At Doriscos, Xerxes decides to hold a review of all his forces. Chapters 61–100 comprise a description of the various contingents of the land and naval forces. As chapter 101 begins, Xerxes has just completed a review of the army and the navy, riding in his chariot between the ranks of the soldiers and sailing in a boat between the ships' prows and the shore.

7.101.1

Δημάρητον τὸν Ἀρίστωνος: this is the same Demaratus was mentioned in 7.3, where he was offering advice on the succession. See the overview of the prescribed texts in the introduction. Herodotus once again introduces him as a trusted adviser, setting up the exchange between him and Xerxes to reveal the king's ultimate ignorance of the enemy he is planning to attack.

πόλιος οὔτ' ἐλαχίστης οὔτ' ἀσθενεστάτης: this is Sparta, and the Persians have learned the hard way that it is not to be underestimated. In 7.133, Herodotus explains that when Darius sent heralds to demand the earth and water that betokened surrender, the heralds were thrown into a pit and a well and told to get the earth and water from there. Xerxes, following the review of his vast armament, is portrayed by Herodotus as being in confident mood, yet with residual doubt, summoning the Spartan Demaratus in order to get him to admit that the Persian army is now invincible, even by his fearsome former countrymen.

Herodotus repeatedly emphasizes the proud freedom of the Spartans: in 7.135, the Persian governor Hydarnes entertains two nobly born Spartiates who are on their way to offer themselves as sacrificial tribute in recompense for the murdered heralds and asks them why the Lacedaemonians spurn the king's friendship. They reply proudly: 'Hydarnes, this advice you are giving us is not balanced; part of it rests on experience, part on ignorance. For you know very well how to be a slave, but you have not had experience of freedom.'

7.101.2

εἰ Ἕλληνες ὑπομενέουσι χεῖρας ἐμοὶ ἀνταειρόμενοι: Xerxes asks this question and immediately provides his own answer: οὐ γάρ, ὡς ἐγὼ δοκέω.

οὐ ... οὐδ' ... οὐκ: the repeated negatives give the effect of Xerxes trying to convince himself that what he says is true.

μὴ ἐόντες ἄρθμιοι: the participle here is used to express a conditional: 'unless they are united'. In fact, the Greeks weren't united, as Herodotus points out at 7.138: 'No matter that the Greeks themselves had long been aware of this, there was a complete lack of consensus as to how they should respond.' However, they still manage to defeat Xerxes.

7.101.3

βασιλεῦ, κότερα ἀληθείῃ χρήσωμαι πρὸς σὲ ἢ ἡδονῇ;: a nice Laconic response and one which bears out Herodotus' characterization of the Spartans as fearless and proud.

A Level

ὁ δέ μιν ἀληθείῃ χρήσασθαι ἐκέλευε: Xerxes, echoing Demaratus' words directly, demands the truth, but we see as the conversation unfolds that he doesn't like what he hears.

7.102.1

ἐπειδὴ ἀληθείῃ διαχρήσασθαι πάντως κελεύεις …: the word ἀληθείῃ is picked up and thrown between the two speakers like a ball. Demaratus is talking here about the current situation, but Herodotus has already mentioned when discussing Persian customs in 1.138: 'The worst offence of all that a man can commit, they think, is to tell a lie …'. The Behistun inscription in which Darius records the events of his reign sets him up in opposition to 'The Lie' and urges future kings to punish anyone who is a 'Lie-follower'.

σύντροφος: 'congenital'. Contrasted with ἔπακτος (acquired) in the balancing phrase: poverty (πενίη) is endemic, but courage (ἀρετὴ) is acquired. This is achieved through σοφίης … καὶ νόμου ἰσχυροῦ 'wisdom and tough law'. Thucydides expresses a similar idea at 1.123: πάτριον γὰρ ὑμῖν ἐκ τῶν πόνων τὰς ἀρετὰς κτᾶσθαι. Demaratus outlines the conditions through which Spartans have attained their legendary bravery, and which were maintained purposely under the system of Spartan education. The sentence comes full circle, with the claim that this acquired ἀρετὴ is used to ward off both poverty and tyranny. There is perhaps a slight paradox in this claim, since at the beginning of the sentence poverty has been described as endemic, but the sentence is rhetorically neat.

καὶ τὴν δεσποσύνην: the καὶ and the placement at the end of the sentence draw attention to this phrase, which must be regarded as pointed when used in conversation with the King of Persia.

7.102.2

αἰνέω μέν νυν: Herodotus puts into Demaratus' mouth a eulogy of the Spartans. It is hard to think of Demaratus here as a disgruntled deposed king in the court of an enemy power, such is the admiration and affection he feels for his native land and people. The circumstances of his own life do not appear to have dimmed his ardour for Spartan values: his experiences of living under Persian kings have perhaps, if anything, strengthened his admiration for the tough regime under which he grew up. If we presume, as we must, that the Demaratus we see here and the words he speaks are a Herodotean construct, written with the benefit of hindsight, then Herodotus creates this scene to highlight Xerxes' ultimate ignorance about the country he plans to conquer, as well as to laud the Spartan bravery that contributed to his defeat.

πρῶτα μὲν … αὖτις δὲ: Demaratus constructs his speech carefully, marshalling his points in praise of the Spartans.

ἀντιώσονταί τοι ἐς μάχην: the whole of this section of the text is imbued with Herodotus' retrospective knowledge of the Battle of Thermopylae, which took place in August 480. The bravery of the 300 Spartans who held the narrow pass of Thermopylae against the vast Persian host achieved an instantaneous legendary status which persists to this day. Famous details of the story endure in the memory: the astonishment of the Persian spy who observed the Spartans

A
Level

coolly combing their long hair before the battle; the Laconic reply of Dieneces when he was warned that the Persians were so numerous their arrows would blot out the sun ('... then we can fight them in the shade'); the epitaph for the Spartan dead ('Report to the people of Lacedaemon, stranger, that here, obedient to their orders, we lie'). Herodotus obviously cannot refer to the battle openly, since when the conversation described here takes place it has yet to occur (he tells the story in 7.201 and following), but it clearly strongly influences what he writes about the Spartans.

7.102.3

ἀριθμοῦ δὲ πέρι, μή πύθη ὅσοι ...: Xerxes has been obsessed with the size of his expedition, holding fast to the belief that numerical superiority must lead to victory. cf. his conversation with Artabanus above at 7.48. Demaratus, however, makes it clear that numbers to Spartans are just that.

οὗτοι μαχήσονταί τοι, ἤν τε ἐλάσσονες τούτων ἤν τε καὶ πλεῦνες: again we think of Thermopylae, where the Persians were fabulously numerous, and the Spartans famously numbered only 300.

7.103.1

γελάσας: Xerxes' response is marked by incredulity and a persistent inability to see conflict as anything other than a simple numbers game.

διπλήσιον: the reference to the king having to fight twice as many men as the ordinary Spartan alludes to the fact that the kings, as Herodotus tells us at 6.57, were given a double portion of food at feasts. The words given to Xerxes by Herodotus suggest that he has spent time talking to Demaratus about the customs of Sparta, but that he is here wrongly extrapolating from one situation to another, creating a sort of reductio ad absurdum in which, because the kings were given a double portion of food, they had to have or do twice over whatever any other Spartan had or did in any circumstance. Once again, Herodotus presents Xerxes as rather literal-minded and convinced that numerical superiority is key.

7.103.2

κόμπος: a din or clash, coming to mean as here 'a boast'.

7.103.3

ἐόντες γε ἐλεύθεροι πάντες ὁμοίως καὶ μὴ ὑπ᾽ ἑνὸς ἀρχόμενοι: in the discussion about constitutions in Book 3, Darius speaks in favour of rule by one individual: 'A single individual who cannot be improved upon is self-evidently the best – for the judgement of such a man can be deployed in the governance of his people, without his ever being criticised' (3.82).

χίλιοι ... μύριοι ... πεντακισμύριοι, ... ἑνὸς ... ἕνα ... χίλιοι, ... πέντε χιλιάδων: the concentration of numbers in this short passage is remarkable. We have already observed Xerxes' general obsession with numbers. It begins to sound here rather as though, as with the repeated negatives noted above at 7.101.2, doubt is creeping in and he is attempting to convince himself as well as his audience that his numerical superiority really will count in the final analysis.

7.103.4

δειμαίνοντες τοῦτον: Xerxes' view that a strong leader might inspire his troops to achieve better things is underpinned by the belief that this has to come about through fear. This is certainly the principle upon which the Persian empire has achieved success and he is unable to conceive of another. Indeed it is fair to say that the Spartans whose freedom is so vaunted by Demaratus were themselves operating in fear, as he himself goes on to explain in the next chapter, although it is fear not of an individual but of the law and customs of their land.

ἀναγκαζόμενοι μάστιγι: Herodotus has already told us in 7.56 that the Persian soldiers were lashed forwards by commanders with whips to encourage them to cross the pontoons over the Hellespont, and again at 7.223 he records that the army was whipped forward at the Battle of Thermopylae. To a Greek audience, this detail would only serve to emphasize the cultural difference between them and the Persians; for Greeks, only slaves were whipped. The insertion of this phrase here shows Xerxes' total lack of understanding of the Spartan patriotism and courage that Demaratus is describing.

ἀνειμένοι δὲ ἐς τὸ ἐλεύθερον οὐκ ἂν ποιέοιεν τούτων οὐδέτερα: Xerxes' view of human nature is pessimistic and diametrically opposed to Demaratus'.

7.103.5

ἀλλὰ παρ᾽ ἡμῖν ... τοῦτο ἐστὶ τὸ σὺ λέγεις: Xerxes has worked himself into petulant-sounding outrage at Demaratus' claims for the Spartans.

εἰσὶ γὰρ Περσέων τῶν ἐμῶν αἰχμοφόρων οἳ ἐθελήσουσι Ἑλλήνων ἀνδράσι τρισὶ ὁμοῦ μάχεσθαι: this begins to sound like childish boast-trading.

φλυηρέεις: 'you are talking nonsense': a highly dismissive word to finish this speech with.

By the end of this speech, as is illustrated by the three quotations above, Herodotus has shown us Xerxes at his childish worst: gone for the moment is the reasonable and reflective interlocutor of the exchanges with Artabanus. Insecurity, a longing to believe that the system he knows is the correct and only successful one, the need to convince himself that his army is the greatest the world has ever seen and will carry success before it, and a deep-seated fear that this might not prove to be the case all help to explain his tone here.

7.104.1

ἀρχῆθεν ἠπιστάμην ὅτι ἀληθείη χρεώμενος οὐ φίλα τοι ἐρέω: Demaratus continues to sound unflappable and wise, throwing the word ἀληθείη back at Xerxes one last time: he'd known all along that the truth would be unpalatable to a king seeking the flattery and obsequious agreement he has come to expect.

τὰ κατήκοντα Σπαρτιήτῃσι: 'how things stand with the Spartans'.

7.104.2

οἵ με τιμήν τε καὶ γέρεα ἀπελόμενοι πατρώϊα ἄπολίν τε καὶ φυγάδα πεποιήκασι: Herodotus explains how this came about in 6.61. Demaratus was said to have slandered Cleomenes in his absence, and Cleomenes on his return plotted to depose him.

A
Level

οὐκ ἂν οἰκός ... στέργειν μάλιστα: Demaratus makes his gratitude and loyalty clear, using conventional, gnomic language.

7.104.3

εἰ δὲ ἀναγκαίη εἴη: this seems a slightly dangerous thing to say: knowing Xerxes, we might expect him to make exactly such a demand as this on a whim, especially in the kind of petulant mood he is displaying in this passage.

7.104.4

ὡς δὲ καὶ Λακεδαιμόνιοι κατὰ μὲν ἕνα μαχόμενοι οὐδαμῶν εἰσι κακίονες ἀνδρῶν, ἀλέες δὲ ἄριστοι ἀνδρῶν ἁπάντων: the Spartans' reputation for bravery was pre-eminent. In Thucydides Book 6, Nicias says 'military honour is the be-all and end-all of their existence' and Xenophon's *Constitution of the Spartans* explains the terrible outcome for anyone branded a coward in Sparta, concluding, 'I don't wonder that where such a load of dishonour burdens the coward death seems preferable instead of a dishonoured and shameful life.' (9.6) The balance and contrast of this sentence (κατὰ μὲν ἕνα ... ἀλέες; κακίονες ... ἄριστοι; οὐδαμῶν ... ἀνδρῶν ... ἀνδρῶν ἁπάντων) together with the assonance in the last clause, focus the audience's attention on this, the key point of Demaratus' speech.

ἐλεύθεροι γὰρ ἐόντες οὐ πάντα ἐλεύθεροι εἰσί· ἔπεστι γάρ σφι δεσπότης νόμος: νόμος here means not just law but custom, habit and tradition. The use of the word δεσπότης is pointed: the Spartans might regard νόμος as their δεσπότης, but the word means something rather different to Demaratus from what it would mean to a Persian under Xerxes. For Demaratus, there is a fundamental difference between a society in which everyone is subject to the same mutually agreed laws and customs, even when the penalties for breaking those laws are severe and terrifying, and one in which the people are at the whim of a single leader who may be capricious or cruel. For Demaratus, the fundamental freedom which he claims for the Spartans seems to consist in freedom from rule by an individual, or indeed another state, since personal freedom was clearly heavily curtailed. A Spartan would certainly be a stranger to the sort of personal and political freedom enjoyed by some members of Athenian society.

τὸν ὑποδειμαίνουσι πολλῷ ἔτι μᾶλλον ἢ οἱ σοὶ σέ: there is something thrilling for the audience in Herodotus' portrayal of Demaratus' boldness in telling Xerxes some plain truths.

ποιεῦσι γῶν τὰ ἂν ἐκεῖνος ἀνώγῃ· ἀνώγει δὲ τὠυτὸ αἰεί, οὐκ ἐῶν φεύγειν οὐδὲν πλῆθος ἀνθρώπων ἐκ μάχης, ἀλλὰ μένοντας ἐν τῇ τάξι ἐπικρατέειν ἢ ἀπόλλυσθαι: this explanation hints at the famous supposed parting cry of Spartan mothers to their sons as recorded by Plutarch, 'Come back with your shield or on it'. This, together with what Xenophon has to say about those convicted of cowardice (discussed above), makes it clear that desertion from battle was regarded as a terrible crime by the Spartans. We should not interpret this as an addiction to senseless self-sacrifice, however: evidence shows that the sort of treatment of cowards described by Xenophon was reserved for those who had deserted when the rest of their contingent had stood firm. It is clear that an agreed retreat by the whole contingent was perfectly acceptable in circumstances where no military advantage would accrue from continuing to hold out. For example, the Spartans at Thermopylae only learned that they had been outflanked on the third morning of the battle, at which point the most important concern was to create time for the rest of the Greek forces to withdraw to continue the defence of Greece: the last stand of the 300 is not a futile heroic gesture but a considered strategic plan. By contrast, the 120 Spartans who surrendered to the Athenians on the island of Sphacteria in 425 BC during the Peloponnesian War did so with the full approval of the Spartan leadership to prevent unnecessary casualties. Sparta worked hard for the return of these captives and although they were demoted from full citizenship for a period, they were later fully reinstated.

σοὶ δὲ εἰ φαίνομαι ταῦτα λέγων φλυηρέειν, ἀλλὰ σιγᾶν θέλω τὸ λοιπόν· νῦν τε ἀναγκασθεὶς ἔλεξα: Demaratus replies bluntly to Xerxes' accusation that he is talking nonsense, picking up the same verb (φλυηρέειν) employed by the king at the end of his preceding speech, and reminding him that he has spoken frankly because he was required by Xerxes to do so.

γένοιτο μέντοι κατὰ νόον τοι, βασιλεῦ: 'But may your wish be fulfilled, King'. Demaratus concludes with one of the formulaic wishes for the ruler's well-being or success which pepper the speech of the subjects of absolute rulers ('Oh king, may you live forever …'). He is assuring Xerxes that he realizes that his moment of freedom to speak truth to power is over.

7.105.1

Ξέρξης δὲ ἐς γέλωτά τε ἔτρεψε καὶ οὐκ ἐποιήσατο ὀργὴν οὐδεμίαν, ἀλλ' ἠπίως αὐτὸν ἀπεπέμψατο: as we have seen from other episodes, given Xerxes' unpredictable character, this could very easily have turned out differently. Either Demaratus has shown great skill in averting the possible wrath of the king by the reassertion of his inferior status noted above or Xerxes is so far from being able to understand Demaratus' ideological standpoint that he is able to dismiss what he says as laughably unimportant.

ὕπαρχον ἐν τῷ Δορίσκῳ: Doriscus was last mentioned in 7.59 as being the place where Xerxes held a review of his troops. It is both the name of a region in Thrace and of the royal fortress built there by Darius. Mascames is being appointed at least as commander of the garrison installed in the fort, and probably also as satrap of the region. (In the next chapter, after the end of the set text prescription, Herodotus tells us that Mascames was greatly admired by Xerxes, especially because he was never deposed by the Greeks and continued successfully to defend Doriscus. As a mark of his regard, Xerxes sent Mascames yearly gifts, and his son, Artaxerxes, continued to reward Mascames' heirs.)

τὸν δὲ ὑπὸ Δαρείου σταθέντα καταπαύσας: Xerxes replaces the former incumbent with his own man. The periphrasis here perhaps suggests that Herodotus was unable to find out the name of Darius' appointee.

A
Level

Vocabulary

An asterisk * denotes a word in OCR's Defined Vocabulary List for AS.

ἀβουλία, -ας, ἡ	ill-advisedness, thoughtlessness
ἄβουλος, ον	ill-advised
Ἄβυδος, -ου, ἡ	Abydos
*ἀγαθός, -ή, -όν	good
*ἄγγελος, ου, ὁ	messenger, envoy
ἄγερσις, εως, ἡ	gathering, mustering
ἀγνωμοσύνη, -ης, ἡ	want of sense, folly
ἀγορεύω	to speak in the assembly, advise
*ἄγω, fut. inf. ἄξεσθαι	to bring, lead to get
ἀδελφεός, -εοῦ, ὁ	brother
*ἀδελφή, -ης, ἡ	sister
*ἀδικέω	to do wrong
*ἄδικος, -όν	wrong, unjust
*Ἀθηναῖος, -α, -ον	Athenian
Αἰγύπτιος, -η, ον	Egyptian
Αἴγυπτος, -ου, ἡ	Egypt
αἰθήρ, έρος, ἡ	heaven
Αἰθίοψ, -οπος, ὁ	Ethiopian
αἰνέω	to praise
Αἰολεύς, -έως, ὁ	Aeolian
*αἱρέομαι, aor. inf. ἑλέσθαι	to choose
αἱρετός	to be chosen, desirable
*αἱρέω, 1st aor. subj. ἕλω	to take, seize
αἰσχρῶς	badly, shamefully
*αἴτιος, -α, ον	responsible, guilty
αἰών, -ῶνος, ὁ	life
ἀκήρατος, ον	pure
*ἀκούω + acc. of sound, gen of person	to hear
ἄκρη, -ης, ἡ	summit
*ἀκτή, -ῆς, ἡ	headland, promontory
Ἀλευάδαι, -ῶν, οἱ	the Aleuadai
ἀλήθεια, -ας, ἡ	truth
*ἀληθής, -ές ἀληθέστατος, -η, ον	true, clear most true, most clear
ἁλίσκομαι, aor. part. ἁλούς	to be captured
ἄλκιμος, -ον	brave, valiant
*ἀλλήλους, -ῶν	one another
ἁλμυρός, -ά, όν	briny, salty (of the sea)
ἄλσος, -εος, τό	grove
ἅλωσις, -εως, ἡ	capture
ἀμείβομαι	to reply
ἀμείνων	better
ἄμεινον	the better

*ἀμφότερος, -α, -ον	both
ἀναβαίνω	come up
*ἀναγιγνώσκω	to persuade, induce
*ἀναγκάζω	to force, compel
*ἀνάγκη, -ης, ἡ	necessity
ἀνάγω	to lead up
ἀνάξιος, -ον	unworthy
ἀναπείθω	to persuade
ἀναρτέομαι	to be ready, prepared
*ἀναχωρέω	to revert
ἀνευρίσκω	to find, discover
ἀνεψιός, -οῦ, ὁ	cousin
ἀνήκω	to have come up to
*ἀνήρ, ἀνδρός, ὁ	man
ἀνθρώπειος, -α, -ον	human
ἀνθρώπινος, -η, -ον	of man, human
*ἄνθρωπος, -ου, ὁ	man
ἀνοιδέω	to swell up
ἀντίξοος, -ον	opposed to, adverse
ἀντιόομαι	to resist, oppose
ἀντίος, -ία, -ίον	against
ἀντιτάσσω	to set opposite to, range against
*ἄξιος, -ία, -ιον	worthy
ἀπαλλάσσω	to get off, escape
ἀπαμύνω	to keep off, ward off
ἀπαντίον	opposite
ἅπαξ	once
ἄπειμι	to be absent
ἀπείρητος, -ον	untried
ἀπέρχομαι	to go away, retreat
ἀποβαίνω	to disembark
ἀποβάλλω	to throw away, lose
ἀποδείκνυμι	to point out, make known, make, render
*ἀποθνήσκω	to die, be killed
ἀποκρύπτω	to cover, hide
ἀπολιμπάνω	to leave
ἀπονοστέω	to return
ἀποτέμνω	to cut off
ἀποφαίνω	to reveal
*ἀρετή, -ῆς, ἡ	goodness, excellence
Ἀρτάβανος, -ου, ὁ	Artabanos
Ἀρταφρένης, -ους, ὁ	Artaphrenes
ἀρχαῖος, -α, -ον	old
Ἀρισταγόρας, -ου, ὁ	Aristagoras
ἄριστος, -η, -ον	best, noblest
Ἀρίστων, -ωνος, ὁ	Ariston
ἀρρωδέω	to dread, shrink from
*ἀρχή, -ῆς, ἡ κατ᾽ ἀρχάς	beginning; in the beginning, at first
ἀρχῆθεν	from the beginning
*ἄρχω	to rule, command
*ἀσθενής, -ές	weak
Ἀσσύριοι, -ῶν, οἱ	Assyrians
*ἄστυ, -εως, τό	town
Ἀστυάγης, -ους, ὁ	Astyages
ἀτάσθαλος, -ον	wicked, presumptuous, insolent
ἀτρεκής, -ές	strict, precise, exact, true
ἀτρεμίζω	keep quiet
Ἀττική, -ῆς, ἡ	Attica
αὐτόματος, -η, -ον	acting of one's own will
αὐτόφωρος, -ον	self-detected, in the act, red-handed
ἀφανίζω	to make unseen, hide
ἀφεστήξω	to stand away, rebel
*ἀφικνέομαι, perf. part. ἀπιγμένοι	to arrive
Ἀχαιμένης, -ους, ὁ	Achaemenes
ἄχαρις, ἄχαρι	grievous
*βάρβαρος, -ον	barbarian, outlandish, barbarous
*βασιλεύς, -έως, ὁ	king
βασιληίη, ῆς, ἡ	kingdom, rule
βέλος, -εος, τό	missile
*βίος, -ου, ὁ	life

βιοτή, -ῆς, ἡ	life	διαβάλλω	to slander, falsely accuse
Βόσπορος, -ου, ὁ	the Bosphorus	διαβολή, -ῆς, ἡ	slander, false accusation
βούλευμα, -ατος, τό	plan, resolution	διαγιγνώσκω	to distinguish, know one from the other
*βουλεύω	to take counsel, deliberate		
*βούλομαι	to wish, be willing	διαθέτης, -ου, ὁ	one who sets in order
βραχύς, -εῖα, ύ	short	διαιρέω	to define
βροντή, -ῆς, ἡ	thunder	διαλύω	to destroy, dissolve
βύβλινος, -η, -ον	made of papyrus	διασῴζω	to save and preserve
*γελάω	to laugh, smile	*διαφθείρω	to destroy
γέλως, -ωτος, ὁ	laughter	διαφορά, -ᾶς	difference, dispute
γεύω	to give a taste	διαφορέω	to spread about, tear apart
*γέφυρα, -ας, ἡ	bridge		
γεφυρόω	to make a bridge over	διαχράομαι	to make use of
*γῆ, -ῆς, ἡ	land	*δίδωμι fut. δώσω	to give
*γίγνομαι	to happen	διεκπλέω	to sail out through
*γιγνώσκω	to learn, get to know	διεξέρχομαι	to pass through
γλυκύς, -εῖα, ύ	sweet	διεργάζομαι	to make an end of, destroy
*γνώμη, -ης, ἡ	opinion		
*γυνή, -αικός, ἡ	wife	*δίκαιος, -α, -ον	right, just
δαιμόνιος, -α, -ον	divine, miraculous	*δικαιοσύνη, -ης, ἡ	justice
*δακρύω	weep, shed tears	*δίκην διδόναι	to pay the penalty, make amends
Δαρεῖος, -ου, ὁ	Darius		
δασμοφόρος, -ον	bringing tribute	διό	because of which
Δᾶτις, -ιδος, ὁ	Datis	διπλάσιος, -α, ον	double
*δεῖ	there is need, it is necessary	*δοκέω	to seem
		Δορίσκος, -ου, ὁ	Doriscos
δείδω	to fear	δούλιος, -α, -ον	servile, of slavery
δεῖμα, -ατος, τό	fear	*δοῦλος, -ου, ὁ	slave
δεινός, -ή, -όν	strange, terrible	δουλοσύνη, -ης, ἡ	slavery
*δέκα	ten	δουλότερος, -α, -ον	more enslaved
δένδρεον, -ου, τό	tree	*δύναμαι	to be strong enough, be able, be powerful
*δέομαι	to ask for, beg		
δεσποσύνη, -ης, ἡ	absolute rule, tyranny	*δύναμις, -εως, ἡ	power
*δεσπότης, -ου, ὁ	master, lord	*δύο	two
*δεύτερος, -α, -ον	second	δυσχείρωτος, -ον	hard to subdue
δέω	to lack	δώρημα, -ατος, τό	gift
Δημάρητος, -ου, ὁ	Demaratus	Δωριεύς, -εως, ὁ	Dorian
*διαβαίνω	to cross	*δῶρον, -ου, τό	gift
		*ἐάω	to allow

ἐγείρω	to raise
*ἐθέλω	to want, be willing
*ἔθνος, -εος, τό	tribe, people
εἰκάζω	to guess
εἴωθα	to be accustomed, be wont
*εἰμί	to be
εἵνεκα	on account of
*εἶπον (aor. of λέγω)	I said
εἰρημένος	having been spoken
*εἷς, μία, ἕν	one
ἑκαστέρω	farther
ἑκατοστός, -ή, όν	hundredth
ἐκβαίνω	to step out of, disembark
ἐκγίγνεται	(impersonal) it is granted
ἐκλέγω	to pick
ἐκμανθάνω	to learn thoroughly
ἐκτείνω	to be eager for
ἔλασις, -εως, ἡ	expedition
ἐλάσσων	less
*ἐλαύνω	to drive, set in motion, lead
ἐλαφρός, -ά, -όν	light, trivial
ἐλάχιστος, -η, -ον	smallest, least
*ἐλεύθερος, -α, -ν	free
*Ἑλλάς, -άδος, ἡ	Greece
Ἑλλήσποντος, -ου, ὁ	Hellespont
*ἐλπίζω	to hope
ἐμβάλλω	to attack, throw in
ἐμπίμπρημι	to burn
ἐμπίπλημι	to fill
ἐμποιέω	to put in, insert, interpolate
ἐναντιόομαι	to oppose
ἐναργής, -ές	visible, palpable
ἐνδεής, -ές	wanting, lacking
ἔνειμι, 3rd s. opt. ἐνέοι	to be in
ἐνθαῦτα = *ἐνταῦθα	then, next
ἐντέλλω	to command
ἐνύπνιον, -ου, τό	dream
ἐξελαύνω	to drive out
ἐξεπίσταμαι	to know thoroughly, understand well
ἐξεργάζομαι	to bring to completion
ἐξηγέομαι	to explain, describe
ἐξευρίσκω	to find, discover
ἐξυβρίζω	to behave insolently
ἐξώλης, -ες	utterly destroyed
ἐπαίρω	to lift up and set on, incite
ἐπακτός, -όν	acquired
ἐπεάν	whenever
ἐπείγω	to press hard, hurry
ἐπεισφέρω	to bring in
ἐπείτε	since
ἐπελαύνω	to march against
ἐπιγίγνομαι	to come after
ἐπιθυμητής, -οῖ, ὁ	one who desires, longs for
ἐπικαλέω	to summon
ἐπίκειμαι	to lie upon, lie near
ἐπίκλητος, -ον	specially summoned
ἐπιλεαίνω	to smooth over
ἐπιλέγω	to pick, cite
ἐπίπλεος, -έη, έον	full of
*ἐπίσταμαι	to know, understand
ἐπίσχω	to hold back
*ἐπιτρέπω	to turn over, hand over
ἐπιτροπεύω	to be an administrator
ἐπιφαίνω	to display
ἔπος, -εος, τό	word
*ἑπτά	seven
*ἐργάζομαι	to work, commit
*ἔργον, -ου, τό	deed, action
ἔρδω	to do
*ἔρχομαι	to go

*ἔτος, -ους, -τό	year	*θάνατος, -ου, ὁ	death
*εὖ	well	θαρσέω	to be of good courage
*εὐδαίμων, -ον	fortunate, blessed	*θεός, -οῦ, ὁ	god
εὐπρηξίη, -ης, ἡ	success	Θεσσαλία	Thessaly
εὕρημα, -ατος, τό	discovery	θνήσκω	to die
Εὐρώπη, -ης, ἡ	Europe	θνητός, -ή, -όν	mortal
εὐτυχέστατος, -η, -ον	most auspicious	θολερός, -ά, -όν	muddy, foul, turbid
		θράσος, -εος, τό	courage, boldness
ἐφέπω	to be busy with enterprises	*θρασύς, -εῖα, ὑ	bold
ἐφίστημι	to be placed in authority	Θρῆϊξ, -κος, ὁ	Thracian
ἔχθρη, -ης, ἡ	enmity, hatred	θρόνος, -ου, ὁ	throne
*ἔχω	to have, bear, carry	θυμός, -οῦ, ὁ	spirit
ζεύγνυμι	to yoke, join opposite banks by bridges	θυμόω	to make angry, provoke
		*θύω	to sacrifice
ζεῦγος, -εος, τό	pair	ἰδιοβουλέω	to follow one's own counsel, take one's own way
*Ζεύς, Διός, ὁ	Zeus		
ζημία, -ας, ἡ	loss, damage	ἰθύω	to be eager, strive
ζημιόω	to be punished	Ἰνάρως, -ω, ὁ	Inaros (a river)
ζωή, -ῆς, ἡ	life	*ἵστημι	to set up, wage
ζυγόν, -ου, τό	yoke (a wooden crosspiece fastened over the necks of two animals and attached to a plough or cart)	Ἰστιαῖος, -ου, ὁ	Histiaeus
		Ἴστρος, -ου, ὁ	Ister (a river)
		Ἰνδός, -ή, -όν	Indian
		Ἵππαρχος, -ου, ὁ	Hipparchos
ζῷον, -ου, τό	creature	ἱρός, -ή, -όν	holy; as noun: holy place, temple
ζώω = *ζάω	to live		
ἡγεμονία, -ας, ἡ	leadership, sovereignty	*ἰσχυρός, -ά, -όν	strong
*ἡδύς, -εῖα, ὑ	pleasant	Ἴων, -ωνος, ὁ	Ionian
ἦθος, -εος, τό	accustomed place	καθαιρέω	to take down, depose
ἡμερόω	to make tame	καθηγέομαι	to bring in
*ἥκω	to have come, be present	καθίημι	to throw into
ἥλιος, -ου, ὁ	the sun	καθοράω	to look down upon
ἥμερος, -α, -ον	tame; of plants: cultivated, fruit-bearing	κακόν, -ου, τό	evil, suffering
		*κακός, -ή, -όν	bad, evil
ἥμισυς, -εια, -υ	half	*καλέω	to call, summon
*ἤπειρος, -ου, ἡ	mainland	*καλός, -ή, -όν	fair
ἤπιος, -α, -ον	kind, pleasant	Καμβύσης, -ου, ὁ	Cambyses
ἡσσάομαι	to be beaten	καταγελάω	to laugh at
ἤτοι	surely, in truth	καταλαμβάνω	to put an end to, seize, lay hold of
*θάλασσα, -ης, ἡ	the sea		

καταλέγω	to recount	*λόγος, -ου, ὁ	word, speech
καταπαύω	to put an end to, stop, depose	Λυδός, -ου, ὁ	Lydian
		*λύω	to take apart, destroy
καταρρωδέω	to fear, dread	μακαρίζω	to bless, think blessed
καταστρέφω	to subdue, trample	Μακεδονίη, -ης, ἡ	Macedonia
καταφυγή, -ῆς, ἡ	place of refuge	*μακρός, -ά, -όν	long
κάτειμι	to go down	*μάλιστα	very much, especially
κατεργάζομαι	to achieve, work on	*μᾶλλον	rather
κατηγορέω	to accuse, speak against	Μαρδόνιος, -ου, ὁ	Mardonios
κατήκοντα, τὰ	circumstances	μάρτυς, -υρος, ὁ, ἡ	witness
κατοικέω	to settle in, colonize	Μασκάμης, ὁ	Mascames
κατοικτείρω	to have mercy, pity	μάστιξ, -ιγος, ὁ	whip
κελεύω	to urge, order	μάταιος, -α, -ον	vain, empty, idle
κεραυνόω	to strike with thunderbolts	*μάχη, -ης, ὁ	battle
		*μάχομαι	to fight
κέρδος, -εος, τό	gain, profit	Μεγαδόστης, ὁ	Megadostes
κεφαλή, -ῆς, ἡ	head	*μέγας, μεγάλη, μέγα	big, great
*κῆρυξ, -υκος, ὁ	herald		
*κίνδυνος, -ου, ὁ	danger	μεθίστημι	to change, change one's mind
*κλέπτω	to steal		
κνίζω	to chafe, annoy	*μέλλω	to be about to, be going to
κοῖος, -η, -ον = *ποῖος	what sort of		
κολούω	to punish	μέμφομαι μεμπτός	to blame, find fault blameworthy, at fault
*κομίζω	to carry (passive: to travel)		
		*μένω	to remain, wait
κου	doubtless	*μέσος, -η, -ον	middle
*κτάομαι	to obtain, get for oneself	μεταβάλλω	to change sides
κτείνω	to kill, slay	*μεταπέμπομαι	to send for
κῦδος, -εος, τό	glory, renown	μετέπειτα	afterwards
κύων, κυνός, ὁ, ἡ	dog	*μέχρι	as far as
κω	yet	*μηδείς, μηδεμία, μηδέν	not one
*λέγω	to say, speak		
λεῖος, -α, -ον	smooth	Μῆδος, -ου, ὁ	Mede
*λείπω + gen.	to be inferior to	Μιλήσιος, -α, -ον	Milesian
λευκόλινον, -ου, τό	flax	Μίλητος, -ου, ἡ	Miletos
Λίβυς, -υος, ὁ	Libyan	μιμνήσκω	to remind, + gen. = mention
*λιμήν, -ένος, ὁ	harbour		
λιμός, -οῦ, ὁ	hunger	*μοῦνος, -η, -ον	alone, only
λογίζομαι	to reckon	μοχθηρός, -ά, -όν	wretched, miserable

*ναυμαχίη, -ης, ἡ	sea-battle
*ναῦς, νεώς, ἡ	ship
*ναυτικόν, -ου, τό	fleet
νέμω	to possess, dwell in
νεώτερος, -α, -ον	newer
*νῆσος, -ου, ἡ	island
*νικάω	to conquer
νοέω	to intend
νομάς, -αδος, ὁ, ἡ	nomad
*νομίζω	to think, consider
*νόμος, -ου, ὁ	law
*νοῦσος, -ου, ἡ	sickness, disease
Ξέρξης, -ου, ὁ	Xerxes
οἰκεῖος, -α, -ον	of one's own
οἴκημα, -ατος, τό	house, dwelling, building
οἰκώς, οἰκυῖα, οἰκός	reasonable
οἰκτρός, -ά, -όν	pitiable
ὁκόσος, -α, -ον	as great, as many
ὅκως = ὅπως	as, in such a manner, how
*ὀλίγος, -η, -ον	little, small
ὁμόγλωσσος, -ον	speaking the same language
ὁμουρέω	to border on
ὅμουρος, -ον	having the same borders as
ὄνειρος, -ου, ὁ	dream
Ὀνομάκριτος, -ου, ὁ	Onomacritos
*ὁράω	to see
*ὀργή, -ῆς, ἡ	anger
ὁρμάομαι	to set out, begin
ὄρνις, ὄρνιθος, ὁ	bird
οὐδαμά	never
οὐδαμόθι	nowhere
*οὐδαμῶς	in no way
οὐδείς, οὐδεμία, οὐδέν	no one, nothing
*οὐρανός, -ου, ὁ	heaven
ὄψις, -εως, ἡ	sight, presence, vision
πάθος, -ου, ὁ	suffering, disaster
*παῖς, παιδός, ὁ, ἡ	child
πάμφορος, -ον	productive, fertile
πανοικία, -ας, ἡ	whole household
παντοῖος, -α, -ον	of all sorts
πάντως	in every way
παρά + gen.	from
παραβάλλω	to risk the life of
παραδέχομαι	to receive, inherit
παραλαμβάνω	to receive from
*παρασκευάζω	to prepare
παρατρίβω	to rub beside
παραυτίκα	at once
*πάρειμι	to be present
παρενθήκη	in addition
*παρέχω	to hand over
παρίστημι	to occur to
*πάσχω	to suffer, be treated
*πατήρ, πατρός, ὁ	father
πάτρως, -ωος, ὁ	uncle
*παύομαι	to cease
*παύω	to stop
πέδη, -ης, ἡ	fetter, shackle, manacle, chain
*πέδιον, -ου, τό	plain
*πεζός, -ή, όν	on foot (in m. as noun: infantry)
*πείθω	to persuade
πεῖρα, -ας, ἡ	to attempt, trying
πειράω	to make an attempt, try
Πεισιστρατίδαι, -ῶν, οἱ	the Peisistratids
Πεισίστρατος, -ου, ὁ	Peisistratos
πέλαγος, -εος, τό	sea
Πέλοψ, -οπος, ὁ	Pelops
πενίη, -ης, ἡ	poverty
πέρ	particle adding force
περίειμι	to be around, survive

περικαλλής, -ές	very beautiful
περιποιέω	to keep safe, preserve
*Πέρσης, -ου, ὁ	Persian
πικρός, -ά, -όν	bitter
πιστότης, -ητος, ἡ	good faith
πίσυνος, -ον	trusting on, relying on
πλείων, -ον	more
πλέω	to sail
πληγή, -ῆς, ἡ	blow, stroke
*πλῆθος, -εος, τό	great number
πληθώρη, -ης, ἡ	satiety, fullness
πλησιόχωρος, -ον	neighbouring, adjacent, bordering on
*ποιέω	to make
*πολέμιος, -α, -ον	of war, hostile, at enmity
*πόλεμος, -ου, ὁ	war
*πόλις, -εως, ἡ	city
πολιτικός, -ή, όν	civic, state
*πολλάκις	often
πολλαπλήσιος, -η, ον	many times greater than
*πολύς, πολλή, πολύ	much, pl. many
πόρος, -ου, ὁ	crossing, route, way through, passage
*ποταμός, -ου, ὁ	river
*πράσσω	to do
Πρέπει	it is fitting
πρεσβύτερος, -α, -ον	elder
πρῆγμα, -ατος, τό	deed, matter
*πρίν	before
προαγορεύω	to proclaim
προβαίνω	to advance
προδειμαίνω	to fear beforehand
προεῖπον (aor. w. no present)	to declare, proclaim
προθυμιη, -ης, ἡ	readiness, willingness, eagerness
*πρόθυμος, ον	willing, eager,
προθύμως	readily, willingly
προκαταλύω	to reconcile
πρόκειμαι	to be set before one
προλέγω	to foretell
προσγίγνομαι	to be added, accrue
πρόσκειμαι	to be placed
προσκτάομαι	to gain, get
προσορέγομαι	to urge
προσπίπτω	to fall upon
προσφέρω	to bring to bear
πρόσω	forwards, onwards
πρότερον	formerly, before
προφέρω	to bring forward
πρῶτα	first of all
Πύθιος, -ου, ὁ	Pythios
*πυνθάνομαι	to learn
πυρόω	to burn
ῥαπίζω	to thrash, whip
Σάκαι, -ῶν, οἱ	Sacae
Σάρδεις, -εων, αἱ	Sardis
σεμνός, -ή, -όν	revered, holy
σημαίνω	to indicate, give a sign
σιωπάω	to be quiet, be silent
σκαιότης, -ητος, ἡ	ineptitude
σκέπτομαι	to look, consider
σμικρός, -ά, -όν	small, unimportant
Σοῦσα,-ῶν, τά	Susa
*σοφίη, -ης, ἡ	wisdom
Σπαρτιάτης, -ου, ὁ	a Spartan
*στάδιον, -ου, τό	stade
σταθμόομαι	to judge, form an estimate
στιγεύς, -έως, ὁ	brander
στίζω	to brand
*στράτευμα, -ατος, τό	expedition
*στρατεύω	to march with an army, advance
στρατηγέω	to be general
στρατηλατέω	to lead an army into the field

*στρατιή, -ῆς, ἡ	army
*στρατός, -ου, ὁ	army
συγκόπτω	to cut down, break down
συλλαμβάνω	to gather together, contribute
*συλλέγω	to gather
σύλλογος, -ου, ὁ	meeting, assembly
συμβάλλομαι	to conjecture
*συμβουλεύω	to advise, counsel
*σύμμαχος, -ον	allied, in league
συμφέρω	to contribute, turn out
*συμφορή, -ῆς, ἡ	misfortune
συναμφότεροι	both together
συναναβαίνω	to go up with
συνέπομαι	to follow along with, accompany
σύνεσις, -εως, ἡ	wit, intelligence
συνταράσσω	to throw into confusion
σύντροφος, -ον	habitual, familiar, endemic
συστρατεύω	to march together with
συστροφή, -ῆς, ἡ	density, mass
σφάλλω	to baffle, passive be mistaken
σφάλμα, -ατος, τό	failure, defeat
*σῶμα, -ατος, τό	body
*ταχύς, -εῖα, -ύ	fast, quick
*τέκνον, -ου, τό	child
*τελευτάω	to die, bring to an end, accomplish
τέρψις, -εως, ἡ	joy, enjoyment, delight
*τίθημι	to establish
τίκτω	to engender, give birth to
τοίνυν	therefore
*τολμάω	to dare
*τρέπω	to turn
τριακόσιοι, ῶν, οἱ	three hundred
*τιμή, -ῆς, ἡ	esteem, honour
τιμιώτατος, -η, -ον	most highly valued
τιμωρέω	to exact vengeance
τίσις, -εως, ἡ	retribution
*τρόπος, -ου, ὁ	way
*τυγχάνω + gen.	to meet with, get
τύραννος, -ου, ὁ	tyrant
*τύχη, -ης, ἡ	chance
*ὕδωρ, -ατος, τό	water
ὕπαρχος, -ου, ὁ	governor, lieutenant
ὑπάρχω	to take the initiative in doing
ὑπερέχω	to be prominent
ὑπερτίθημι	to communicate
ὑποδέξιος, -α, -ον	able to receive
ὑποδύνω	to submit
ὑπολείπω	to leave remaining
ὑπεναντίος, -α, -ον	opposite
ὑπεξαιρέω	to take away, remove
*ὑπέρ + gen.	on behalf of
ὑπόπλεος, -ον	full of
ὑπουργέω	to render service
Ὑστάσπης, -ου, ὁ	Hystaspes (river)
*ὕστερος, -α, -ον	later
φαντάζομαι	to be on display
φάσμα, -ατος, τό	apparition, phantom
φερέγγυος, -ον	providing a guarantee
*φέρω	to carry, bear
φθέγγομαι	to talk about, mention
φθείρω	to destroy
φθονερός, -ά, -όν	envious, jealous
*φθονέω	to grudge, bear ill will
*φιλέω	to love, be wont
*φίλος, -η, -ον	dear, welcome
φλαῦρος, -α, -ον	paltry, worse
φλαύρως ἀκούειν	to be spoken ill of
*φοβέομαι	to fear
*φόβος, -ου, ὁ	panic, flight born of panic
Φοῖνιξ, -ικός, ὁ	a Phoenician
*φονεύω	to murder, kill
φράζω	to point out

φρονέω	to be minded, think	χρή fut. χρήσει	it is necessary
φροντίζω	to consider, reflect	χρησμόλογος, -ον	uttering oracles
Φρύξ, -υγός, ὁ	a Phrygian	χρησμός, -ου, ὁ	oracle
φυλακή, -ῆς, ἡ	the job of guarding	χρησμῳδέω	to deliver oracles, prophesy
*φυλάσσω	to keep guard, guard against	χρηστός, -ή, -όν	useful, good
φύω	to bring forth, be born	*χρόνος, -ου, ὁ	time
χαρίζω	to gratify, please	*χρυσός, -οῦ, ὁ	gold
*χειμών, -ῶνος, ὁ	storm	*χωρέω	to advance, succeed
*χείρ, χειρός, ἡ	hand	*χώρη, -ης, ἡ	country, place
χίλιοι, -αι, -α	thousand	χωρίζω	to divide
*χράομαι + dat.	to consult, use	*χωρίον, -ου, τό	place
χρεόν	that which is necessary, fated	Ψαμμητίχος, -ου, ὁ	Psammetichos
*χρήματα, -ῶν, τά	money, wealth	ψεύδω	to lie

Plato, *Phaedo*

Introduction, Commentary Notes and
Vocabulary by Rob Colborn

AS: 62c9 to 67e6

A Level: 69e6 to 75c5

Introduction

Philosophy in action

The *Phaedo* offers a portrait of a man in the last three or four hours of his life and ends with his execution. The man, Socrates, does not choose to enjoy a final meal, spend time consoling his family or seek any distraction from what is ahead. Instead, he chooses to engage in philosophical argument with his friends, explaining why he is not afraid of death, but is sure in his hope of a better life beyond the present one. This is no lecture: although the others feel sorry for their friend in his plight, they do not shrink from challenging his arguments. What we have in the *Phaedo* is, rather, a live discussion. Arguments are put forth, picked apart, rejected and refined and progress is made. We watch a man work hard to justify as best he can the cheerful approach he is taking to his own death, ready to accept that the efforts may end in failure. As readers, we cannot help but join the conversation, find our own faults with the arguments and work through the same problems ourselves.

Whichever of the prescriptions you read, you will find in it a mix of moving drama, extraordinary prose and satisfyingly tough philosophy in action. All of it makes for provocative reading: do not expect to agree with it all, or any of it, but expect the challenge of exploring the arguments to be no less rewarding for it.

Socrates, Plato and Plato's Socrates

How real a picture the *Phaedo* gives of the actual historical Socrates cannot be known. It is not until the Roman era that writers start taking a serious interest in the lives of philosophers and writing biographies of them. By then Socrates had been dead for some centuries, and the stories told about him had attained a generous coating of myth. Even the detailed portraits offered by his contemporaries Plato and Xenophon, who both knew him personally, and the satirical sketch of the comic playwright Aristophanes in *The Clouds*, differ wildly from each other. Few nowadays would see the *Phaedo*'s main aim as providing a historical document of the real Socrates' final hours; but that such a view held sway well into the twentieth century attests to the convincingly lifelike portrayal of Socrates in this work.

We can indeed enjoy the *Phaedo*'s Socrates, on his own terms, for the wonderfully lively and compelling character he is. But any reading of the *Phaedo* is made the richer for an understanding of what the real Socrates was like, and how he comes across in Plato's other works. What follows is an outline of the man as he emerges from the evidence. I offer directions to more detailed accounts in the 'Further reading' section of this introduction, and after that a timeline including the most important known dates of his life.

The historical Socrates

Socrates was an old man, aged about 70, when he died in 399 BC, which puts his year of birth around 469. He lived through several enormous political changes in his native Athens. During his boyhood, the threat of Persia waned and Athens grew into the leading imperial power of the Mediterranean. Later came three decades of conflict with Sparta and an eventual defeat in the Peloponnesian War (431–404).

When Sparta insisted on the establishment of an oligarchy in Athens in 404, most of the leading democrats went into exile. Socrates, however, chose to stay in Athens, reflecting what he saw as an apolitical stance. This can have earned him little favour in the eyes of the democrats, who returned to eject the oligarchy (the so-called Thirty Tyrants) and reinstate democracy the following year. During these years of political unease, Socrates' friendship with members of the Thirty must have added to the suspicion that he was against democracy, stoking the hostility that led the people of Athens to convict Socrates and sentence him to death in 399.

In fact, the little we do hear about Socrates' political activity shows him standing up against the oligarchs and defending proper democratic procedure. During the Thirty's murderous purges of dissenters, Socrates was ordered to arrest a democratic general, Leon of Salamis, for execution, but refused to let them bloody his hands. Fortunately for Socrates, the rule of the Thirty was overthrown before they could punish him for his dissent. In 406, Socrates stood in the way of another miscarriage of justice, this time against the angry citizen body, who were clamouring for a joint and summary execution of Athens' general, blaming them for not recovering the bodies of those lost at sea in the Battle of Arginusae. Socrates' unsuccessful attempt to prevent an illegal joint trial must have earned him some enemies, who saw his defence of due legal process as an act of defiance against the people's will.

When Socrates is taken to court in 399, however, neither of the two charges against him is overtly political. In one of his earliest surviving works, Plato records the charges as follows (*Apology* 24b):

(i) of not believing in (οὐ νομίζοντα) the same gods the state believes in, but in other novel 'divinities' (δαιμόνια); and

(ii) of corrupting (διαφθείροντα) the young men of Athens.

That work, the *Apology*, is Plato's reconstruction of Socrates' speech in his own defence (ἀπολογία in Greek) against the two charges and a perfect introduction to Socrates' personality. A brief survey of his responses to the charges will fill in many of the remaining gaps in our picture of the historical Socrates.

In answer to the first, Socrates insists that his prosecutors confused his thoughts on the gods with those of another celebrity intellectual, Anaxagoras of Clazomenae (*Apology* 26c–e). Anaxagoras had, some decades earlier, been kicked out of Athens for his supposedly irreligious views, which offered naturalistic explanations for many supposedly divine phenomena (considering the Sun and Moon, for instance, to be not gods but bits of rock). Why, then, was Socrates supposed to share these beliefs? As Plato has him explain, the blame lay with Aristophanes' comic parody of the new wave of intellectuals – philosophers and so-called sophists – who had flocked to Athens in the mid fifth century. In his play *The Clouds*, Aristophanes applies the name 'Socrates' to a character who is really a mashup of various types of intellectual. 'Socrates' runs an expensive educational establishment called the Φροντιστήριον ('Thinkstitute'), where he conducts various absurd experiments. More insidiously, Aristophanes has his 'Socrates' offer naturalistic explanations for the way the world works, denying the gods their traditional role in the natural order. That he chose the name 'Socrates' for his character is understandable: the real man was a famous eccentric, a celebrity his audience were bound to recognize more readily than Anaxagoras, who had died some years before the staging of *The Clouds* in 423. Still, *The Clouds*, which saw a second wave of popularity after Aristophanes redrafted it around 420–417, is probably the greatest exposure most Athenians had had to Socrates. Many will have seen him conversing with friends and fans in Athens' main public spaces, but few will have stopped to hear whether he was, in fact, spreading irreligious teachings. Such people were surely predisposed to find him guilty of not believing in their gods.

Whether Socrates was guilty of believing in other novel divinities (δαιμόνια καίνα) is left rather more unclear. As Plato has him admit in the *Apology*, he had sometimes received a sign from a tutelary δαιμόνιον, telling him not to follow a certain course of action (40a–c). This unorthodox belief is unlikely to have warranted a trial on its own, for the Athenians were relatively accepting of differences in religious opinion, so long as people joined in with the rites and sacrifices expected of them – practices on which Socrates was outspokenly keen. His belief in a personal δαιμόνιον, however, one that granted him powers of divination, was bound to provoke envy from some and fuel the suspicions of others.

The second charge, that of 'corrupting' or 'spoiling' the youth (διαφθείροντα τοὺς νέους), is directed more at Socrates' self-conduct than at his beliefs. Socrates would spend much of his free time in conversation with friends and strangers alike, many of whom were young Athenian men, drawn to the older Socrates by his colourful persona and quick sense of humour. It was surely entertaining to observe him winding up pompous intellectuals with his 'irony' (εἰρωνεία), or feigning of naivety and ignorance. Just as attractive, presumably, was the opportunity of meeting his many famous friends, including the controversial aristocrat Alcibiades. To judge from the earlier works of Plato, conversation with Socrates would be an electrifying thing to observe, but could be a crushing experience for those involved: he would engage his interlocutors in a process of ἔλεγχος ('cross-examination'), asking their opinion on a philosophical question such as the nature of justice, and gradually leading them, through a series of questions, to the realization that the belief they had once been so confident in was really false. This he saw as a great service, ridding people of misconceptions that were surely harmful. For, in the famous words of the *Apology*, 'the unexamined life is not worth living for a human' (38a). Yet the state of perplexity in which he would leave his interlocutors, called ἀπορία (literally 'not being able to see a way out of a problem'), is not one that many of us would find pleasant. The negative reaction that the ἔλεγχος would provoke is exemplified nowhere better than in the *Apology*: we see Socrates engage his prosecutor Meletus in this very kind of conversation and subject him to public embarrassment, a daring and perhaps arrogant strategy that makes it rather easier to see why the opinion of his jurors was so ready to turn against him.

The Socratic Method

For Socrates, engaging in philosophy meant having conversations, working towards a better understanding of a topic by arguing the matter out loud. While giving one's opinion on a question is generally quite easy, constructive debate of this kind takes practice and skill; and for this reason Plato has Socrates call it ἡ διαλεκτική (i.e. τεχνή), or the skill of dialectic, an adjective formed from the verb διαλέγομαι 'I converse with'. If philosophy for Socrates is a kind of conversation, it is no surprise that he never wrote any philosophical works – or anything, for that matter, until his incarceration. Socrates also placed great emphasis on his own ignorance. When the Delphic oracle proclaims that there is nobody wiser than Socrates, he takes it upon himself to prove it wrong. After engaging various apparently wise people in conversation (and making plenty of enemies in the process), Socrates comes to realize the one thing that makes him a little bit wiser than others: he knows the limits of his own ignorance (*Apology* 21d: 'whatever I do not know, I do not even suppose I know'). For this reason, Socrates refused to be called a teacher – he did not pass on wisdom to others as one might imagine a teacher doing, but simply helped others to see that they did not know quite as much as they thought they did.

It was not Socrates' teachings, then, that landed him in trouble, but his modus operandi. For the method of ἔλεγχος could not only be annoying for those whose ignorance it revealed but could also be seen as a danger to the moral fabric of society, as people began to question their core values and the fundamentals of their world view. Unsurprisingly, perhaps, the ἔλεγχος also became a craze among the young (*Apology* 23c), driven by the twin aims of philosophical zeal and a desire to annoy their elders. These imitators, few of whom can have become very adept at the ἔλεγχος, only helped to spread the moral panic. For all who saw shared Athenian values as the glue of society, it must really have seemed that Socrates was a damaging influence on the youth.

If Socrates' interests were more in line with the other intellectuals of his day, focusing on natural sciences, rhetoric, literature and so on, the panic would surely have been less. But for Socrates, what mattered most were moral questions and the well-being of one's 'soul', to use his term (*Apology* 30b: on the term 'soul' and what this means for Socrates in the *Phaedo*, see further below). This is the real aim of philosophy. We can get closer to it only through self-examination and the pursuit of 'wisdom' – that is, the knowledge of what virtue, justice and other such morally significant values really are.

Ordinarily, those sentenced to death by an Athenian jury would not have to wait long for their punishment. According to the *Phaedo*, however, Socrates' trial happened to coincide with a period of enforced ritual purity in Athenian religion, during which no executions could take place. Socrates had, then, to spend an extended stint in Athens' small state prison, near the Agora. Prisoners were free to receive visitors (as we see Socrates doing in the *Phaedo*) and for those who were sentenced to death, it seems generally to have been possible to leave, on the understanding that they would then go into exile. That Socrates chooses instead to take the hemlock and end his life is yet another example of his adherence to Athenian law, unswerving to the very end.

Plato and his 'Socrates'

If the historical Socrates is hard to make out behind the evidence, Plato is almost impossible. Aside from the late biographical tradition, our other main source, a set of autobiographical letters attributed to Plato are of spurious (or at least dubious) authenticity. Plato turns up only once in his own works, and even then it is only a cameo appearance at the trial of Socrates. He never appears as a participant in any of his dialogues – not even the *Phaedo*, where his absence during Socrates' last hours is attributed to illness (*Phaedo* 59b; one explanation for his absence, real or otherwise, is offered in the overview later in this introduction). It is from his works, however, that we can deduce the most about Plato's intellectual development and his relationship with Socrates.

Born sometime in the 420s BC, Plato was a good forty years younger than Socrates. While the late biographical tradition calls him either the student or the follower of the older man, the picture that emerges from the Seventh Letter (of dubious authenticity but earlier date) is more of a family friend. Indeed, Plato's uncle and great uncle Charmides and Critias, two of the Thirty Tyrants, were close friends of Socrates and figure prominently in the dialogues. Whether as one of the young men who flocked to Socrates, or simply through his family connections, Plato is bound to have seen much of Socrates during his youth. It is clear from his writings that he knew the man and his quirks well, and could give a faithful portrayal of his philosophical habits. That they were intimate friends is clear from the opening of the *Phaedo*, where the eponymous Phaedo, listing those present at the death of Socrates, feels he must give a reason for the absence of Plato (59b). Above all, however, the sensitivity and pathos with which Plato describes his friend's death, years after the event, reveal his genuine and lasting affection for the man.

Plato's intellectual debt to Socrates is clearest in his earlier works. Their detailed reconstructions of the ἔλεγχος show that Plato has mastered that technique far better than the young copycats described in the *Apology*. The debt is clearest, though, in the dialogue form that most of Plato's works take. Like Socrates, Plato seems to see conversation – dialectic – as the true means of philosophy and tries to capture (or recreate) the process of philosophy in action by writing conversations rather than treatises. A clear effort is made to make the discussions as plausible and immersive as possible: while the other great master of Attic prose, Thucydides, has all his characters deliver speeches in basically the same fashion, Plato takes every opportunity to bring his interlocutors to life by careful characterization in their spoken style and through a rich use of conversational idiom. He takes clear care, too, to find the ideal setting for each conversation, so that the characters' surroundings, company and recent experiences can offer them interesting and apposite prompts. He is, in short, a master dramatist.

Plato is not unaware of the shortcomings of written dialogues in contrast with live conversation, issues he explores in his dialogue the *Phaedrus*. As we read, we may have our own thoughts and questions to contribute to the conversation, but the text is 'mute' and cannot reply (*Phaedrus* 275e). Still, reading a written dialogue has all the benefits of witnessing the dialectic of others, letting us watch the participants explore and develop their arguments in real time and pause as often as we need to appraise them in our own time.

Plato does not tell us the order in which he composed his works. Carefully analysing the evolutions in his style (a practice called stylometry), scholars have striven to arrange his surviving works into a rough chronology. While many details remain disputed, most agree on a loose grouping into three periods: early, middle and late. The grouping reveals that Plato did not deal with the events in Socrates' life in chronological order: in fact, the *Apology* is among his earliest writing, and he went on to produce several more works after the *Phaedo*, in which Socrates dies.

We can, however, trace an evolution in the ideas and practices of his Socrates over time. In the earliest dialogues, Socrates spends most of his time engaged in his method of ἔλεγχος ('cross-examination') and leaves his interlocutors in a state of ἀπορία. We would still expect no less from the historical Socrates. Over time, however, Socrates spends less and less time picking apart other's beliefs and grows more inclined to put forward views of his own. His range of interests grows beyond the moral and into metaphysics; in the late *Timaeus* he even strays into cosmology, despite claiming elsewhere to have abandoned natural science in his youth (*Phaedo* 96a). It seems, then, that Plato is using Socrates more and more as a vehicle for his own philosophical explorations and feeling a dwindling obligation to keep his portrait true to the Socrates of history. In his early works, Plato was not yet using Socrates as a mouthpiece for his own views – for, of course, the Socrates of those dialogues does not put any forth. But from the middle period on, this is increasingly his role.

Stylometry places the *Phaedo* firmly in Plato's middle period, rather later than the *Apology* (perhaps by some decades) and a little before his best-known work, the *Republic*. Plato had recognized that he could only tell the story of Socrates' final hours only once and saved this dramatic setting for a time when he wished to devote a dialogue to the topics of death and the afterlife. While the *Phaedo* may paint a fairly accurate picture of the events of that evening, many of the ideas put forward by Socrates during his final conversations must be Plato's own. There are the usual giveaways one would expect in a middle-period work: its ideas are (i) absent from the earlier dialogues, (ii) stray beyond the historical Socrates' areas of interest and (iii) lack the tentativeness with which he presented ideas for discussion.

At the heart of the *Phaedo* lie two of Plato's most important contributions to philosophy, the Theory of Forms and the model of the human soul. In the *Phaedo* both appear in an early stage of development and go on to be critiqued and refined much in Plato's later dialogues, but are no less vital to this work's main arguments for the immortality of the soul. On account of their crucial role in the *Phaedo* and in Platonism at large, both deserve a little more exploration here, before we look at the *Phaedo* as a whole.

The Theory of Forms

Perhaps the most famous of all his contributions to metaphysics, the so-called Theory of Forms (εἴδη) or Ideas (ἰδέαι) is subject to constant refinement in Plato's later works, but all its iterations have the following outline in common.

The things we see in the world around us cannot be said really to *be* (or exist) in the strict sense of the word, since they are always in some state of change: as Plato puts it, they are 'becoming' (γίγνονται) rather than being. The things that really exist, by contrast, are unchanging and eternal. To this category belong the Forms, non-physical exemplars or patterns in nature (παραδείγματα) of the things we see in the world around us, and that we are reminded of when we see those things. In some dialogues we hear about forms of objects, such as tables and chairs: there is, outside our world, a Form of Table to which all the tables in our world conform. And if we know that Form, we will be able to say whether any given object is or is not a table. In the early-to-middle dialogue the *Cratylus*, Socrates says that when a craftsman begins to make a weaver's shuttle, it is precisely the Form of Shuttle that he brings to mind. It is knowing this Form well, then, that allows him to perform his craft.

Elsewhere, we hear of forms corresponding to what we might call properties, such as a Form of Largeness, which all large things in our world resemble in some way. We know an object we see to be large because we know the Form of Largeness and see that the object resembles that form. Likewise, we know that something is small because we see that it resembles the Form of Smallness. Things in the world, however, are often both large and small at the same time: a cat is large in relation to a mouse, but small compared with a cow. The Forms, by contrast, are entirely free of this so-called 'compresence of opposites'. The Form of Largeness is understood to be itself large and nothing but large, regardless of any point of comparison: that is, the Form of Largeness exemplifies itself. This is understandable, since for Plato, to know the Form of Largeness and to know what 'large' is are one and the same thing. It does, however, provide some problems. For instance, the Form of Largeness surely cannot be large in the way that a blue whale is large, since forms are non-physical entities. The resultant problem for the theory is explored in the later dialogue the *Parmenides* (the famous 'Third Man Argument' of 132a–b).

The Theory of Forms allows Plato to make headway on many different problems of philosophy. It gives us a way of explaining how we know what largeness is, even though we have never had anything pointed out to us that is exclusively large, and not also small when set in comparison with something even larger. It allows us to explain, too, how you and I both know what tables are, even though our personal experiences of tables may have been very different. Lastly, the Forms offer a handy, if simplistic, account of causation: for Plato, the Form of Hot is what ultimately causes my lunch to be hot, even if I might prefer to name the microwave as a more specific cause.

In the *Phaedo*, Plato is not yet using the words εἶδος ('form'), ἰδέα ('idea', a synonym) or παράδειγμα as technical terms, the discussions of properties in the abstract, such as 'the just itself' (i.e. that which is just and only just), reveal that he is talking about the same thing. In the commentary, I have avoided the term 'form' all the same, to avoid anachronism. For, given Plato's readiness to challenge and overhaul his own ideas, we must take care not to read any later thoughts about the forms back into the *Phaedo*.

Plato on the soul

Readers familiar with Homer will know that in the worlds of the *Iliad* and *Odyssey*, a certain part of a person lives on in Hades, the underworld, after their death. Homer calls this thing a ψυχή, which we translate as 'soul'. It is ghostlike and insubstantial, but still has the identifiable shape of the person it belonged to. In Greek, the word ψυχή has two other familiar senses, 'life' (i.e. that which distinguishes living things from dead) and 'mind', the seat of the intellect and emotions (hence our modern derivation, 'psychology'). Any speaker of Greek would agree that a living person has ψυχή, even though they might disagree on the question of what exactly it is. We therefore cannot dismiss that question just because the corresponding English term 'soul' is no longer much used outside religious circles. We will find it to be a harder one to answer than meets the eye.

In the *Phaedo*, the interlocutors approach the question in an open-minded way, using the Homeric associations of the term ψυχή only as a springboard for discussion. The term allows the interlocutors to suggest a simple definition of death: the separation of the ψυχή from the body. This does the job, since death is the point beyond which the body no longer shows any signs of life, feeling or cognition. Nor does the definition assume that the ψυχή is an actual thing in its own right: for later on, the interlocutors are happy to consider the possibility that the soul is something more like the tuning of a lyre, which cannot exist apart from the instrument. It is, in short, perfectly possible for Greeks to use the term ψυχή without committing themselves to the belief that it is anything more than a property of living things. In this respect, it is very different to our own term 'soul'. Henceforth and in the commentary, I use the term 'soul' as a translation for ψυχή, since that is the convention in Platonic scholarship. Readers must try not to let their own associations with word colour their reading, and know that this is generally less awkward than using the Greek term instead.

While it is hard to imagine Socrates' final conversations involving anything like the Theory of Forms (he would surely have seen that kind of metaphysical enquiry as lying outside the remit of his knowledge and his interests), it is easier to see him speculating what, if anything, would happen to his soul after death. Indeed, if Plato's *Apology* does accurately represent Socrates' defence speech, he may already have indulged in some such speculation at his trial. At the end of the *Apology*, Socrates presents the court with two possibilities: either being dead is a kind of sleep, and a dead person feels nothing more after death, or, as many think, the soul passes from this world to another place (40c–d). For him, both outcomes are attractive, for we all enjoy a good night's sleep; and if he should end up in the company of those who died before him, he can look forward to meeting and performing the ἔλεγχος on Odysseus, Sisyphus and countless other famous people (41b–c).

By contrast, the Socrates of the *Phaedo* is far more confident in his opinions on the soul. He is unshakeable in his faith that it will outlast his body and end up in the company of other good men and, indeed, gods. This is quite a way away from the non-committal Socrates of the *Apology*, but we might expect as much from a middle-period dialogue, as Plato begins to explore the nature of the soul himself through the medium of his interlocutors.

Several key ideas emerge from the *Phaedo*. The soul is indestructible and cannot die, a view the interlocutors feel to be conclusively proven at the end of the dialogue. It has much in common with the Forms, and is even said to be 'akin' to them: the soul, like the Forms, is incorporeal and invisible, and can only be grasped by the mind. Like the Forms it is also a true cause, not of largeness or tables but of life. It must, they agree, also be incomposite, that is, not divisible into parts.

Why do people behave the way they do, and not simply pursue wisdom? In the *Phaedo*, it is suggested that an average person's soul is not entirely rational or irrational, but somewhere in the middle. The irrationality is the result of the soul's contamination with the body, whose needs and desires it must service while the two are joined together. Anyone wishing to come closer to being rational must bow as little as possible to the body's demands. But to be fully free of its contamination only becomes possible when one dies, and then only after a life devoted to purifying the soul of its influence. Anyone who achieves this goal, suggests Socrates, can look forward to joining the gods and enjoying the pursuit of wisdom in the company of other truly philosophical souls. Others will find themselves reincarnated as animals, the species matching the nature of their souls (the greedy and merciless, for instance, may become wolves). The theory thus offers a side benefit of explaining the characteristics of different animals.

Plato offers a radically different picture of the soul in later dialogues. In the *Republic* and the *Phaedrus*, the soul is seen as having three parts that must be reconciled. Book 4 of the *Republic* offers the clearest description: the first part (the smallest) is the seat of rational thought, one the seat of the emotions and one responsible for the appetites of the body. A soul can be called 'just' only if it allows the rational part to rule the others (*Republic* 4.439d–e). In the *Phaedrus*, Socrates offers the allegory of a charioteer, who representing the rational part of the soul. His chariot is led by two horses: on the right is a white one of noble stock, representing the higher-minded side of emotional impulse (such as moral outrage), and on the left a far wilder dark horse, representing the less noble urges. The charioteer's job is to keep both horses running in the same direction, towards wisdom (*Phaedrus* 253c–254e). The appeal of a tripartite model for the soul is that it can explain why a person might behave rationally at one moment and impetuously or lustfully at another. It also explains why many people have a tendency towards one or other kind of drive: they are allowing the part of the soul responsible to rule the others.

Plato, of course, does not explain the move from the *Phaedo*'s idea of the soul to the tripartite models of the *Republic* and *Phaedrus* – we must puzzle out his reasons for ourselves. One way in which the tripartite models improve on the *Phaedo*'s is in their accounting for emotions. It is easy enough to see how irrational appetites might arise from the body's contamination of the soul, since these are usually associated with the needs of the body. When hunger distracts me from my work, it is easy to blame the body. But when I feel anger at an unjust act against a stranger, it is difficult to see on the *Phaedo*'s model where that comes from: it is not a purely rational response, so impossible for a totally pure soul, but what needs of the body could it be seen to meet? The tripartite models recognize, too, that not all irrational drives are to the detriment of the soul, at least while it is paired with a body. What is damaging is an imbalance of power away from the rational element.

The *Phaedo*: an overview

The dramatic setting for the *Phaedo* is in the city of Phlius, not quite 20 miles west of Corinth in the Peloponnese. There we see the eponymous Phaedo recounting to his friend Echecrates the final hours and execution of Socrates, at which Phaedo had been present. Although most of the dialogue is taken up with Phaedo's account, he pauses on occasion to reflect with Echecrates on what is happening in his story (88c–89b, 102a–b). The conversations between Phaedo and Echecrates are, however, much more than a framing device. By having Phaedo relay the final hours of Socrates at second hand, Plato is able to provide bits of narrative description that would otherwise have been impossible: for Plato, like all ancient dramatists, never includes stage directions. Phaedo's most important is to describe the events that follow Socrates' last conversations, as he takes the hemlock and meets his end.

His other job is to explain why Plato is not telling the events in his own voice. As Phaedo tells Echecrates, Plato was absent on Socrates' final evening because he was ill (59b). Do we believe him? Was it in fact the historical Phaedo who told Plato everything that happened in the prison that night? These things cannot be known. But we can be sure that Plato wants us to reflect on the impossibility of Phaedo remembering the whole evening's conversation. Phaedo has only one lapse of memory in the whole dialogue, forgetting which of the company raised a certain objection (103a). What the person said, however, is relayed verbatim. With this one unlikely lapse, I suspect Plato wishes to flag up the artificiality of the dialogue, and remind us that, despite centring on the real Socrates' preoccupation with the well-being of the soul, the conversations of the *Phaedo* are ultimately Plato's fiction.

Plato weaves various themes into the framing conversation and those relayed by Phaedo. These two elements of the work are united, first of all, by the common theme of religious purification. Socrates, we learn, had to wait for his execution because his trial fell at a time when, by Athenian religion, any execution would make the city unclean (see below). True or not, this foreshadows Socrates' belief that the main task of philosophers during their lifetime is the κάθαρσις, or cleansing, of their souls from the toxic influences of the body (see 64e6 and 69c–d, with commentary). A second recurrent theme is the religiosity of Socrates. One of the charges of which his jury had convicted him was not recognizing the same gods as Athens (see p. 74 above), and in the *Phaedo* Plato often seems to be trying to vindicate Socrates of this charge. On several occasions he shows a special devotion to Apollo, composing a hymn to him (60d) and likening himself the swan, who sings its death-song to that god (84c). It is surely no coincidence that the god in whose honour Athens is keeping itself ritually clean at the time of his trial is also Apollo (58b–c). Finally, Socrates' last words are to ask Crito to pay a cockerel he owes to Asclepius, god of healing and son of Apollo (118a). Plato, perhaps still smarting from the unjust condemnation of his friend, ends the *Phaedo* with this reminder of how wrong the accusers were.

A key part of the *Phaedo*'s drama is a tug of war between Socrates, keen to show his friends that he has every reason to look forward to death, and his friends, who cannot fight the very human urge to console the condemned man. The friends keep getting this wrong. For instance, shortly before Socrates takes the hemlock, Crito asks how he wants to be buried. Socrates chides his friend for confusing Socrates with his dead body, adding that they would be lucky to catch him (115c). Simmias, earlier on, admits he is hesitant to find fault with Socrates' argument and upset him at this difficult time, forgetting that Socrates is in fact in a good mood (84c–85b). It is indeed often hard to tell how persuaded Socrates' friends are by his arguments, and tempting at times to see them as going along with him out of pity or respect. We are left wondering how much Phaedo himself has bought into them: for despite his the traces of good cheer in his voice at the beginning of the dialogue (58e–59a), Plato has him end with such an emotionally charged description of Socrates' death. And in the scene's final detail ('Crito closed his mouth and eyes', 118a), is Phaedo not committing the same error that Crito had made earlier? These are all welcome provocations to us, as the readers, to chew over the arguments and see how much of them we ourselves are convinced by.

A word, finally, is needed on the convention for referring to parts of the text – for many readers will have noticed that the section numbering of the Phaedo begins not at 1 but 57. For centuries Platonists have followed the page numbering used by the Swiss scholar H. Stephanus in his 1578 edition of Plato's complete works. In the reference 'Phaedo 57a1', the first number refers to the page of Stephanus' edition while the letter tells you the section of that page (each is divided into five sections, a–e). The second number, on the other hand, refers to the line as it is printed in John Burnet's *Oxford Classical Texts* edition. The same line numbering has been followed by most scholars since Burnet, a convention followed in this book.

The main characters

Phaedo of Elis appears only here in all of Plato. In fact, the only other sources to mention him are the third-century AD biographer of philosophers, Diogenes Laertius and Aulus Gellius a century before that. Some of what Diogenes says has a ring of falsehood to it, sounding like a fantasy based on the *Phaedo* – for instance, that he was taken as a prisoner of war by the Athenians, sold into sex-slavery and then ransomed by Crito and Alcibiades at Socrates' request (Diogenes Laertius 2.105). He seems to have been a philosopher of at least some importance, however, for he is derided along with various other thinkers in a fragment by the satirist Timon of Phlius (fr. 28: 'I don't care ... for Phaedo, whoever he is').

Echecrates of Phlius is another figure about whom little information survives. It is clear from the *Phaedo* that he is a philosopher with Pythagorean leanings, a detail corroborated by Aristoxenus in the generation after Plato. By having a known Pythagorean as one of his interlocutors, Plato sets an appropriate tone for a discussion of the ethics of suicide and of reincarnation, topics that loom large in Pythagorean doctrine.

Simmias and Cebes are two Thebans who, according to Plato's *Crito* (45b), have come to Athens with money to help Socrates escape from prison. While some scholars assume them to be Pythagoreans, this is far from clear: all we hear in the *Phaedo* is that they had once listened to Philolaus, a famous Pythagorean, on his visit to Thebes (61d), though they cannot remember what he had to say on the ethics of suicide. What emerges from the dialogue is that they are both well-informed philosophers, the former very ready to agree and the latter a little more sceptical.

Crito is a wealthy Athenian friend of Socrates, from his home deme (district) of Alopeke and of about the same age (*Apology* 33e). Roughly the same age as Socrates, Crito turns up in various Socratic works of Xenophon and Plato, including the eponymous dialogue cited above. Despite the claims of Diogenes Laertius, Crito does not come across as a philosopher but a successful farmer who married into an aristocratic family and remained lifelong friends with Socrates. In the *Phaedo*, he is shown to be a practically minded man, concerned more with taking care of Socrates than with the philosophical discussions.

57a–59c: Opening conversation

Echecrates, learning that Phaedo was present on Socrates' final evening, asks Phaedo to describe his final conversations – for Phaedo is the first person to come to Phlius from Athens since then. Echecrates had heard, however, about the delay between trial and execution. Phaedo explains that on the day before the trial, the ship sent yearly to Delos, to commemorate the safe return of Theseus from Crete, had been crowned and sent on its way, in accordance with an ancient vow made by the Athenians to Apollo. No executions could be performed until the ship had returned to Athens. Phaedo describes his feelings that evening, 'a mixture of pleasure and pain combined' (59a), but not pity. He lists the various people present, mentioning Plato's absence on grounds of illness. According to Phaedo, Socrates' friends had been in the habit of visiting him every day and spending the day in philosophical discussion. On that day that had come especially early, as they had heard that the ship was back from Delos.

60a–61b: Socrates introduced

Phaedo describes how, on entering, they found Socrates' wife Xanthippe with their little son, bidding him an impassioned farewell. Socrates merely asks for her to be taken home. He reflects on how pleasure and pain rarely visit a person together, but one tends to follow the other. Socrates tells Cebes how he had been instructed in a dream to 'make art and practise it'. Previously he had taken this to mean that he should perform philosophy, a very high art form. While in prison, however, he had interpreted it as an instruction to write poetry, so had written a hymn to Apollo and set some of Aesop's fables to verse.

61b–63a: A philosopher should look forward to death, though suicide is wrong

Socrates gives Cebes a message to pass on to his poet and philosopher friend Euenus: he is setting off today, and if he has any sense, Euenus will follow him as soon as possible, since true philosophers will look forward to death. Cebes is shocked, but Socrates reassures him that he is not advising him to take his own life. He asks Simmias and Cebes if they had ever heard the Pythagorean Philolaus give his reasons why suicide is wrong during his stay in Thebes. (Given the Pythagoreans' belief in reincarnation, their opinions on the matter are surely of interest.) They do not recall what Philolaus said. They agree on the view, based loosely on that of the mystery religions (62b), that humans are the possessions of the gods and they look after us. In that case it would be wrong to die before the gods wish it and make it unavoidable – as they now have to Socrates.

63b–69e: Socrates defends the view that a philosopher should look forward to death

Cebes is keen to hear how Socrates can reconcile this belief, that we should not wish to leave the stewardship of the gods, with his evident keenness to die. Socrates takes this as an invitation to give another defence speech (ἀπολογία), and hopes that this time he can do a better job of persuading the jury – that is, his friends – than he did at his actual trial. Before he begins his defence, Crito relays the advice of the executioner that Socrates should not get too animated, otherwise he will need extra doses of the poison. (Prisoners who chose to be executed by hemlock had to pay for it themselves, and it did not come cheap.) Socrates explains that that would be fine by him.

He opens his defence with the provocative claim that philosophers do nothing but 'practise dying and being dead' (64a). He gets Simmias to agree that death can be defined as the separation of the soul from the body, and that philosophers are not much bothered with the concerns of the body (such as food, clothes and sex) and care more for the soul. They agree that philosophers have most success in achieving their aims when the body is allowed to distract them as little as possible, either with its needs or with perceptions from the sense-organs. They agree that we only come to know the things that have real existence (i.e. the Forms, though they are not called that here) through thinking alone, and that our sense-organs are of no help in that endeavour. In fact, they are unreliable and only hold us back. Philosophers, then, should strive to separate themselves as far as they can from the body – something that can only be achieved fully when they die. That being the case, they are bound to look forward to death rather than resent it and will spend their lives getting their souls ready for that moment.

Philosophers are therefore very different from ordinary people, who tend to prioritize the concerns of the body ahead of the pursuit of wisdom (which for Plato amounts to knowing the things that really exist). They differ, too, in that for them, the virtues of courage and moderation are genuine products of wisdom: they do not fear death or give in to the body's temptations simply because they know that ridding themselves of the body is in their interests. Normal people, on the other hand, only have an inferior kind of courage, motivated by a fear of something worse, and an inferior kind of moderation, holding off from some pleasures so they can pursue others. Socrates has striven throughout his life to belong to the group of true philosophers and will soon find out whether his efforts have been successful. On that note he ends his defence speech.

69e–78b: The 'Cyclical Argument' for immortality and the argument from the Theory of Recollection

As Cebes points out, everything Socrates has said assumes that the soul is not destroyed at death but will live on, which goes against what most people think (70a). Socrates will need to show not just that the soul survives death but that it retains its intelligence, contrary to the Homeric view (see commentary on 70a5). The first two arguments for immortality address each of these two concerns in turn.

As a starting point, Socrates cites the ancient idea of reincarnation that the souls of the dead become the souls of the living, just as the living become the dead. He then leads Cebes through the following argument in favour of that view: all things that are larger must previously have been smaller, and vice versa. This is the case for all such opposites. Between any such pair, there are two 'processes of becoming' – for example, becoming bigger and becoming smaller – going in both directions. The opposite states of sleeping and being awake have between them processes we call falling asleep and waking up. Likewise, being dead and being alive must also have two processes between them: dying and, balancing that, coming back to life. If these did not balance each other out, then the world would run out of souls. Since that plainly has not happened, the living must be coming back to life after being dead, and vice versa. Compelled by the argument's logic, Cebes accepts its conclusion. We, however, might ask why all pairs of opposites should conform to this pattern. Being young and being old, for instance, are opposites of a similar sort, but we would not so willingly say that there are two balanced processes of becoming between them, only growing old. Socrates, it seems, has had to pull the wool over Cebes' eyes here. Luckily for them both, Socrates will offer strong arguments later on.

Cebes is reminded of a theory of Socrates' that may be of relevance to their present enquiries. According to this theory, all of what we call learning is really recollection of things we had come to know in a previous state of existence. This argument, which had first appeared in Plato's *Meno*, runs as follows. Socrates meets a slave boy, who does not know how to work out the area of a square. By a series of well-chosen (or, we might say, leading) questions, he leads the slave boy to solve the problem and arrive at a rule for other squares. The slave boy has not had any of this told to him directly, but has been led to reveal it himself through Socrates' questions. For Socrates, this shows that he really had the knowledge in him all along, and is not learning it but simply recollecting it (see *Meno* 81a–86b).

This alone is not enough, however, to show that the soul remains intelligent when parted from its body and answer that part of Cebes' question. Socrates therefore gives a fuller version of the theory, running roughly as follows. It is possible to be reminded of one thing by the sight or sound of another thing. For instance, I might be reminded by a guitarist just by seeing her guitar, even if she herself is not there. The same is true of the things that have real existence (i.e. the Forms, though again they are not named as such here). If I see two Lego bricks of the same size and shape, they remind me of equality (i.e. the Form of Equal). I have never seen equality itself, or perceived it by any other sense. So I must have known about it beforehand; otherwise I could not be said to be reminded of it. If I did not come to know it through the senses, it must have happened before I was born. Our souls, therefore, must have existed (and possessed intelligence) before we were born.

As Simmias points out, this only shows that our souls existed before birth, not after death. Socrates suggests that the argument could work in tandem with the one before it (the Cyclical Argument) to prove that the soul is immortal.

78b–80c: The 'Affinity (or Kinship) Argument' for immortality

Unsatisfied, perhaps, with the previous arguments – the first of which had indeed involved some sleight of hand – Socrates offers a new one. He observes that a distinction can be made between the things in the world we perceive with our senses and the set of things that really exist (the Forms), which we can grasp only with our minds. The former is subject to constant change; the things in it die or break apart and are themselves made up of parts. By contrast, the things that really exist are unchanging, undying and incomposite. The soul, he observes, is surely akin to the latter, since it is invisible; the body, on the other hand, clearly belongs to the first group, since it is visible and dies. If the soul belongs to the latter group, it must also be undying – presuming, at least, that it has been suitably prepared by a life spent in philosophy.

80c–84b: Reincarnation

Socrates offers a hypothesis on what will happen to the souls after death. He thinks it likely that the purified souls of philosophers will ascend to the realm of the gods. Everyone else's will drift about like the shades of the dead in Homer until they are reincarnated as animals in accordance with their natures: the greedy and bloodthirsty will become wolves or birds of prey, while more orderly (but not philosophical) souls will be ants or bees.

84c–85b: Socrates' swan song

Simmias and Cebes are reluctant to voice their concerns with what Socrates has just said. Socrates picks up on this, and they admit that they did not want to upset him in his time of difficulty. Socrates reminds them that he is in good spirits: he is like the swan, a fellow devotee of Apollo that sings its most beautiful song just before it dies, and is likewise filled with prophecy and joy as he approaches his own death.

85b–95a: Simmias and Cebes offer their opinions; Socrates refutes them

What if, asks Simmias, the soul is really like the harmonious tuning of a lyre – invisible and akin the divine (Harmonia, whose name means harmony or tuning, is a goddess)? Why should it not be destroyed along with the body, then, just as the destruction of the musical instrument means the destruction of its tuning too?

Cebes, too, gives an objection of his own: what if the soul is like a weaver, who makes himself a new cloak every time the previous one is worn out? He will keep replacing his cloaks while he lives, but will one day die, and his final cloak after a time will disintegrate. Perhaps it is the same for the soul: it will produce a new body for itself every time the last one dies, but this process might be finite, with the soul one day dying itself. If that is the case, we should be afraid that the death we are about to die is our last.

Echecrates, who has been listening silently to Phaedo up to this point, now interrupts him, and the two briefly discuss how difficult these objections must have been for Socrates to fend off. Returning to his narrative, Phaedo tells how Socrates warned those present not to become haters of arguments ('misologues'). For just as people come to be misanthropes after just a few bad experiences with other people, so it would be easy to slip into misology just because a few arguments in which you had placed your hopes later turn out to be unsound.

Taking on Simmias' objection first, Socrates explains that the soul cannot be a harmony. For wickedness is a form of disharmony, and if all souls are harmonious then they must all be free of wickedness, which is false. What is more, it is clear that some parts of the soul (the purely rational) are in opposition to others (those contaminated with the desires of the body). Since opposition is a form of disharmony, the soul cannot be a harmony.

The response to Cebes' objection will come in the form of the Final Argument (see below).

95a–102a: Socrates describes his intellectual development

Socrates explains how he came to scorn the natural science so beloved by Anaxagoras and other early philosophers. He had hoped to find in them a true explanation of the causes of things, but found that their accounts of causation were never any good. In time, he came to see that the true causes of things were the Forms: something is beautiful precisely because the (Form of) Beautiful makes them beautiful (100d). An appeal to the Forms is, he says, the safest answer on questions of causation.

102a–107b: The 'Final Argument'
for the immortality of the soul

Simmias, Cebes and all those in Socrates' company agree with his method of explaining causation, and this in turn prompts Echecrates and Phaedo to voice their agreement too. Using this method, Socrates now turns to his final argument, which boils down to the observation that the soul is ultimately the cause of life (and so rather like a Form of Life). It runs as follows. For any pair of opposites A and B, A cannot become B without ceasing to be A. This is true of opposite properties (e.g. 'hot' and 'cold'), and something similar is true, too, of things that have those opposed properties (e.g. fire and snow): snow cannot become hot without ceasing to be snow. The soul can be said always to bring life with it, since everything that is alive has a soul. Therefore, a soul cannot have the property 'dead' without ceasing to be a soul. Since that which cannot become dead cannot be destroyed, the soul must be indestructible – that is, immortal.

We might well object to the claim that what cannot become dead cannot be destroyed. Objects that were not alive to begin with, such as the book you are holding, seem an obvious counterexample. Simmias suspects that some objections to the argument will come to him later, but Socrates reassures him that the argument will be able to withstand them once they have clarified its hypotheses.

107c–115a: Socrates' myth of the afterlife and the true earth

Since the soul is immortal, there must be a whole story to be discovered as to where it goes when it dies, where it dwells between its incarnations and how this fits in with our wider understanding of the way the world works. Socrates accordingly offers a possible account (μῦθος) of all this, describing the journey of the souls to Hades, the topography of the underworld and the rewards and punishments of the good philosophers and the bad non-philosophers. Socrates points out that what matters are not whether the details of the myth are literally true, but that we are happy to accept that something along such lines is true. The tale, then, can serve as a charm against the fear of death, which will spur us on in our quest to become good philosophers in our present lives.

115b–118a: The final scene

To summarize this moving episode would risk lessening its effect. All serious students should read and appreciate it on its own terms. They will find in it much to reflect upon.

Further reading

The *Apology* is an ideal starting point for further exploration of Plato. It is a wonderful work of prose in its own right, but also paints in colourful but faithful detail the character of Socrates, which is so important to Plato's works of all periods. The *Meno* is a sensible second port of call, a transitional work between the early and middle periods, in which we can watch Socrates apply the ἔλεγχος in discussion on his home turf of ethics, and witness an earlier argument for the Theory of Recollection. Thereafter, readers are advised just to follow their noses and try works on topics that interest them. Detailed summaries of numerous dialogues can be found on the Stanford Encyclopedia of Philosophy (plato.stanford.edu) and the Internet Encyclopedia of Philosophy (iep.utm.edu).

For an accessible but in-depth introduction to each of the dialogues, the best starting point is Peter Adamson's recent book *Classical Philosophy* (Oxford 2014). The book offers wide-ranging coverage of Ancient Greek Philosophy from its very beginnings and an excellent discussion of the evidence problems for Socrates – all vital background for the study of Plato. The book's contents are based almost to the letter on Adamson's series of podcasts, all of which are free to download at historyofphilosophy.net.

Those wishing to delve deeper into the *Phaedo* have a wealth of resources to assist their journey. Among the translations, Hugh Tredennick's wonderfully clear and idiomatic translation is the most widely available, in his Penguin Classics edition

The Last Days of Socrates, which also includes his translation of the *Apology*. David Gallop offers another very modern and readable translation in his *Plato: Phaedo* (Oxford 1975), accompanied by a detailed philosophical commentary. Lastly, Reginald Hackforth's translation (Cambridge 1955) is recommended for its helpful division of the work into more manageable segments of a few pages, each with a summary and piece of lucid philosophical analysis. Many will find this the most accessible point of entry, even if the English is at times rather dated.

Among the texts and commentaries on the Greek, John Burnet's 1911 edition deserves a special mention, as his Greek text (printed also in the *Oxford Classical Texts* series) has been the foundation for all subsequent editions of the text, including the one printed in this book. I would encourage any reader of the *Phaedo* to peruse at least the introduction to Burnet's edition, where he defends courageously the view that the *Phaedo* is an accurate account of Socrates' final conversations. The view is presently out of fashion, but Burnet puts it as well as it can be put. The commentary that I have found most helpful in preparing my own, however, is C.J. Rowe's in the Cambridge 'green-and-yellow' series (Cambridge 1993). Though demanding in its detail, Rowe's commentary is a great help on both linguistic and philosophical points for those wishing to read beyond the prescriptions.

Lastly, David Bostock's *Plato's Phaedo* offers a fantastic philosophical exploration of the whole dialogue, in very accessible English, as well as a fine discussion of the historical Socrates. The ideas are as tricky as ever, and the content is no easy read as Bostock plays rival interpretations offagainst each other. But anyone who wants to dig deeper into the arguments in the prescription they have read, or those of any part of the *Phaedo*, should enjoy taking on Bostock.

Timeline

c. 469	birth of Socrates
431	beginning of the Peloponnesian War between Athens and Sparta
428/7	birth of Plato (according to the biographer Diogenes Laertius)
423	first staging of Aristophanes' *Clouds*
420–417	Aristophanes redrafts the *Clouds*
406	Battle of Arginusae and the execution of the Athenian generals
404	end of the Peloponnesian War and overthrow of the democracy
403	restoration of the democracy
399	trial and execution of Socrates
c. 398	Bostock's suggested date for the *Apology*
c. 388	Plato visits Sicily and stays with Dionysius I of Syracuse
c. 384	Bostock's suggested date for the *Phaedo*
348/7	death of Plato (according to Diogenes)

Rough chronology of Plato's works

Few of Plato's works can be assigned a date with any confidence. They are therefore listed separately here, in the conventional groupings of early, middle and late. Within each group, the ordering given below (taken from Bostock, p. 2) is rather less certain than the groupings themselves.

Early
  Apology
  Crito
  Ion
  Hippias minor
  Euthyphro
  Lysis
  Laches
  Charmides
  Hippias major
  Meno
  Euthydemus
  Protagoras
  Gorgias

Early or middle
  Cratylus

Middle
  Phaedo
  Symposium
  Republic
  Phaedrus

Middle or late
  Timaeus
  Critias

Late
  Parmenides
  Theaetetus
  Sophist
  Statesman
  Philebus
  Laws

Text

ἀλλ᾽ εἰκός, ἔφη ὁ Κέβης, τοῦτό γε φαίνεται. ὁ μέντοι   62c9
νυνδὴ ἔλεγες, τὸ τοὺς φιλοσόφους ῥᾳδίως ἂν ἐθέλειν
ἀποθνήσκειν, ἔοικεν τοῦτο, ὦ Σώκρατες, ἀτόπῳ, εἴπερ ὃ   62d
νυνδὴ ἐλέγομεν εὐλόγως ἔχει, τὸ θεόν τε εἶναι τὸν ἐπιμελούμενον
ἡμῶν καὶ ἡμᾶς ἐκείνου κτήματα εἶναι. τὸ γὰρ μὴ
ἀγανακτεῖν τοὺς φρονιμωτάτους ἐκ ταύτης τῆς θεραπείας
ἀπιόντας, ἐν ᾗ ἐπιστατοῦσιν αὐτῶν οἵπερ ἄριστοί εἰσιν τῶν   5
ὄντων ἐπιστάται, θεοί, οὐκ ἔχει λόγον· οὐ γάρ που αὐτός γε
αὑτοῦ οἴεται ἄμεινον ἐπιμελήσεσθαι ἐλεύθερος γενόμενος.
ἀλλ᾽ ἀνόητος μὲν ἄνθρωπος τάχ᾽ ἂν οἰηθείη ταῦτα, φευκτέον
εἶναι ἀπὸ τοῦ δεσπότου, καὶ οὐκ ἂν λογίζοιτο ὅτι οὐ δεῖ ἀπό   62e
γε τοῦ ἀγαθοῦ φεύγειν ἀλλ᾽ ὅτι μάλιστα παραμένειν, διὸ
ἀλογίστως ἂν φεύγοι· ὁ δὲ νοῦν ἔχων ἐπιθυμοῖ που ἂν ἀεὶ
εἶναι παρὰ τῷ αὑτοῦ βελτίονι. καίτοι οὕτως, ὦ Σώκρατες,
τοὐναντίον εἶναι εἰκὸς ἢ ὃ νυνδὴ ἐλέγετο· τοὺς μὲν γὰρ   5
φρονίμους ἀγανακτεῖν ἀποθνήσκοντας πρέπει, τοὺς δὲ ἄφρονας
χαίρειν.

ἀκούσας οὖν ὁ Σωκράτης ἡσθῆναί τέ μοι ἔδοξε τῇ τοῦ
Κέβητος πραγματείᾳ, καὶ ἐπιβλέψας εἰς ἡμᾶς, ἀεί τοι,   63a
ἔφη, ὁ Κέβης λόγους τινὰς ἀνερευνᾷ, καὶ οὐ πάνυ εὐθέως
ἐθέλει πείθεσθαι ὅτι ἄν τις εἴπῃ.

καὶ ὁ Σιμμίας, ἀλλὰ μήν, ἔφη, ὦ Σώκρατες, νῦν γέ μοι
δοκεῖ τι καὶ αὐτῷ λέγειν Κέβης· τί γὰρ ἂν βουλόμενοι   5
ἄνδρες σοφοὶ ὡς ἀληθῶς δεσπότας ἀμείνους αὐτῶν φεύγοιεν
καὶ ῥᾳδίως ἀπαλλάττοιντο αὐτῶν; καί μοι δοκεῖ Κέβης εἰς
σὲ τείνειν τὸν λόγον, ὅτι οὕτω ῥᾳδίως φέρεις καὶ ἡμᾶς

ἀπολείπων καὶ ἄρχοντας ἀγαθούς, ὡς αὐτὸς ὁμολογεῖς, θεούς.

δίκαια, ἔφη, λέγετε· οἶμαι γὰρ ὑμᾶς λέγειν ὅτι χρή με   **63b**
πρὸς ταῦτα ἀπολογήσασθαι ὥσπερ ἐν δικαστηρίῳ.

πάνυ μὲν οὖν, ἔφη ὁ Σιμμίας.

φέρε δή, ἦ δ᾽ ὅς, πειραθῶ πιθανώτερον πρὸς ὑμᾶς ἀπολογήσασθαι
ἢ πρὸς τοὺς δικαστάς. ἐγὼ γάρ, ἔφη, ὦ Σιμμία τε   **5**
καὶ Κέβης, εἰ μὲν μὴ ᾤμην ἥξειν πρῶτον μὲν παρὰ
θεοὺς ἄλλους σοφούς τε καὶ ἀγαθούς, ἔπειτα καὶ παρ᾽
ἀνθρώπους τετελευτηκότας ἀμείνους τῶν ἐνθάδε, ἠδίκουν
ἂν οὐκ ἀγανακτῶν τῷ θανάτῳ· νῦν δὲ εὖ ἴστε ὅτι παρ᾽
ἄνδρας τε ἐλπίζω ἀφίξεσθαι ἀγαθούς – καὶ τοῦτο μὲν οὐκ ἂν   **63c**
πάνυ διισχυρισαίμην – ὅτι μέντοι παρὰ θεοὺς δεσπότας πάνυ
ἀγαθοὺς ἥξειν, εὖ ἴστε ὅτι εἴπερ τι ἄλλο τῶν τοιούτων
διισχυρισαίμην ἂν καὶ τοῦτο. ὥστε διὰ ταῦτα οὐχ ὁμοίως
ἀγανακτῶ, ἀλλ᾽ εὐελπίς εἰμι εἶναί τι τοῖς τετελευτηκόσι καί,   **5**
ὥσπερ γε καὶ πάλαι λέγεται, πολὺ ἄμεινον τοῖς ἀγαθοῖς ἢ
τοῖς κακοῖς.

τί οὖν, ἔφη ὁ Σιμμίας, ὦ Σώκρατες; αὐτὸς ἔχων τὴν
διάνοιαν ταύτην ἐν νῷ ἔχεις ἀπιέναι, ἢ κἂν ἡμῖν μεταδοίης;
κοινὸν γὰρ δὴ ἔμοιγε δοκεῖ καὶ ἡμῖν εἶναι ἀγαθὸν τοῦτο, καὶ   **63d**
ἅμα σοι ἡ ἀπολογία ἔσται, ἐὰν ἅπερ λέγεις ἡμᾶς πείσῃς.

ἀλλὰ πειράσομαι, ἔφη. πρῶτον δὲ Κρίτωνα τόνδε
σκεψώμεθα τί ἐστιν ὃ βούλεσθαί μοι δοκεῖ πάλαι εἰπεῖν.

τί δέ, ὦ Σώκρατες, ἔφη ὁ Κρίτων, ἄλλο γε ἢ πάλαι   **5**
μοι λέγει ὁ μέλλων σοι δώσειν τὸ φάρμακον ὅτι χρή σοι
φράζειν ὡς ἐλάχιστα διαλέγεσθαι; φησὶ γὰρ θερμαίνεσθαι
μᾶλλον διαλεγομένους, δεῖν δὲ οὐδὲν τοιοῦτον προσφέρειν
τῷ φαρμάκῳ· εἰ δὲ μή, ἐνίοτε ἀναγκάζεσθαι καὶ δὶς καὶ τρὶς   **63e**
πίνειν τούς τι τοιοῦτον ποιοῦντας.

καὶ ὁ Σωκράτης, ἔα, ἔφη, χαίρειν αὐτόν· ἀλλὰ μόνον
τὸ ἑαυτοῦ παρασκευαζέτω ὡς καὶ δὶς δώσων, ἐὰν δὲ δέῃ,
καὶ τρίς.   **5**

ἀλλὰ σχεδὸν μέν τι ἤδη, ἔφη ὁ Κρίτων· ἀλλά μοι πάλαι
πράγματα παρέχει.

ἔα αὐτόν, ἔφη. ἀλλ᾽ ὑμῖν δὴ τοῖς δικασταῖς βούλομαι
ἤδη τὸν λόγον ἀποδοῦναι, ὥς μοι φαίνεται εἰκότως ἀνὴρ τῷ
ὄντι ἐν φιλοσοφίᾳ διατρίψας τὸν βίον θαρρεῖν μέλλων   **10**
ἀποθανεῖσθαι καὶ εὐελπις εἶναι ἐκεῖ μέγιστα οἴσεσθαι ἀγαθὰ   **64a**
ἐπειδὰν τελευτήσῃ. πῶς ἂν οὖν δὴ τοῦθ᾽ οὕτως ἔχοι, ὦ
Σιμμία τε καὶ Κέβης, ἐγὼ πειράσομαι φράσαι.

AS

κινδυνεύουσι γὰρ ὅσοι τυγχάνουσιν ὀρθῶς ἁπτόμενοι
φιλοσοφίας λεληθέναι τοὺς ἄλλους ὅτι οὐδὲν ἄλλο αὐτοὶ   5
ἐπιτηδεύουσιν ἢ ἀποθνήσκειν τε καὶ τεθνάναι. εἰ οὖν τοῦτο
ἀληθές, ἄτοπον δήπου ἂν εἴη προθυμεῖσθαι μὲν ἐν παντὶ τῷ
βίῳ μηδὲν ἄλλο ἢ τοῦτο, ἥκοντος δὲ δὴ αὐτοῦ ἀγανακτεῖν
ὃ πάλαι προυθυμοῦντό τε καὶ ἐπετήδευον.

και ὁ Σιμμίας γελάσας, νὴ τὸν Δία, ἔφη, ὦ Σώκρατες,   10
οὐ πάνυ γέ με νυνδὴ γελασείοντα ἐποίησας γελάσαι. οἶμαι   64b
γὰρ ἂν τοὺς πολλοὺς αὐτὸ τοῦτο ἀκούσαντας δοκεῖν εὖ πάνυ
εἰρῆσθαι εἰς τοὺς φιλοσοφοῦντας – καὶ συμφάναι ἂν τοὺς μὲν
παρ᾽ ἡμῖν ἀνθρώπους καὶ πάνυ – ὅτι τῷ ὄντι οἱ φιλοσοφοῦντες
θανατῶσι, καὶ σφᾶς γε οὐ λελήθασιν ὅτι ἄξιοί εἰσιν   5
τοῦτο πάσχειν.

καὶ ἀληθῆ γ᾽ ἂν λέγοιεν, ὦ Σιμμία, πλήν γε τοῦ σφᾶς
μὴ λεληθέναι. λέληθεν γὰρ αὐτοὺς ᾗ τε θανατῶσι καὶ ᾗ ἄξιοί
εἰσιν θανάτου καὶ οἵου θανάτου οἱ ὡς ἀληθῶς φιλόσοφοι.
εἴπωμεν γάρ, ἔφη, πρὸς ἡμᾶς αὐτούς, χαίρειν εἰπόντες ἐκείνοις·   64c
ἡγούμεθά τι τὸν θάνατον εἶναι;

πάνυ γε, ἔφη ὑπολαβὼν ὁ Σιμμίας.

ἆρα μὴ ἄλλο τι ἢ τὴν τῆς ψυχῆς ἀπὸ τοῦ σώματος
ἀπαλλαγήν; καὶ εἶναι τοῦτο τὸ τεθνάναι, χωρὶς μὲν ἀπὸ τῆς   5
ψυχῆς ἀπαλλαγὲν αὐτὸ καθ᾽ αὑτὸ τὸ σῶμα γεγονέναι, χωρὶς
δὲ τὴν ψυχὴν ἀπὸ τοῦ σώματος ἀπαλλαγεῖσαν αὐτὴν καθ᾽
αὑτὴν εἶναι; ἆρα μὴ ἄλλο τι ᾖ ὁ θάνατος ἢ τοῦτο;

οὔκ, ἀλλὰ τοῦτο, ἔφη.

σκέψαι δή, ὠγαθέ, ἐὰν ἄρα καὶ σοὶ συνδοκῇ ἅπερ ἐμοί·   10
ἐκ γὰρ τούτων μᾶλλον οἶμαι ἡμᾶς εἴσεσθαι περὶ ὧν σκοποῦμεν.   64d
φαίνεταί σοι φιλοσόφου ἀνδρὸς εἶναι ἐσπουδακέναι
περὶ τὰς ἡδονὰς καλουμένας τὰς τοιάσδε, οἷον σιτίων τε
καὶ ποτῶν;

ἥκιστα, ὦ Σώκρατες, ἔφη ὁ Σιμμίας.   5
τί δὲ τὰς τῶν ἀφροδισίων;
οὐδαμῶς.
τί δὲ τὰς ἄλλας τὰς περὶ τὸ σῶμα θεραπείας; δοκεῖ σοι
ἐντίμους ἡγεῖσθαι ὁ τοιοῦτος; οἷον ἱματίων διαφερόντων
κτήσεις καὶ ὑποδημάτων καὶ τοὺς ἄλλους καλλωπισμοὺς   10
τοὺς περὶ τὸ σῶμα πότερον τιμᾶν δοκεῖ σοι ἢ ἀτιμάζειν,
καθ᾽ ὅσον μὴ πολλὴ ἀνάγκη μετέχειν αὐτῶν;   64e
ἀτιμάζειν ἔμοιγε δοκεῖ, ἔφη, ὅ γε ὡς ἀληθῶς
φιλόσοφος.

οὐκοῦν ὅλως δοκεῖ σοι, ἔφη, ἡ τοῦ τοιούτου πραγματεία
οὐ περὶ τὸ σῶμα εἶναι, ἀλλὰ καθ᾽ ὅσον δύναται   5
    ἀφεστάναι αὐτοῦ, πρὸς δὲ τὴν ψυχὴν τετράφθαι;
    ἔμοιγε.
    ἆρ᾽ οὖν πρῶτον μὲν ἐν τοῖς τοιούτοις δῆλός ἐστιν ὁ
φιλόσοφος ἀπολύων ὅτι μάλιστα τὴν ψυχὴν ἀπὸ τῆς τοῦ   65a
σώματος κοινωνίας διαφερόντως τῶν ἄλλων ἀνθρώπων;
    φαίνεται.
    καὶ δοκεῖ γέ που, ὦ Σιμμία, τοῖς πολλοῖς ἀνθρώποις
ᾧ μηδὲν ἡδὺ τῶν τοιούτων μηδὲ μετέχει αὐτῶν οὐκ ἄξιον
εἶναι ζῆν, ἀλλ᾽ ἐγγύς τι τείνειν τοῦ τεθνάναι ὁ μηδὲν φροντίζων
τῶν ἡδονῶν αἳ διὰ τοῦ σώματός εἰσιν.
    πάνυ μὲν οὖν ἀληθῆ λέγεις.
    τί δὲ δὴ περὶ αὐτὴν τὴν τῆς φρονήσεως κτῆσιν; πότερον
ἐμπόδιον τὸ σῶμα ἢ οὔ, ἐάν τις αὐτὸ ἐν τῇ ζητήσει   10
κοινωνὸν συμπαραλαμβάνῃ; οἷον τὸ τοιόνδε λέγω· ἆρα ἔχει   65b
ἀλήθειάν τινα ὄψις τε καὶ ἀκοὴ τοῖς ἀνθρώποις, ἢ τά γε
τοιαῦτα καὶ οἱ ποιηταὶ ἡμῖν ἀεὶ θρυλοῦσιν, ὅτι οὔτ᾽ ἀκούομεν
ἀκριβὲς οὐδὲν οὔτε ὁρῶμεν; καίτοι εἰ αὗται τῶν περὶ τὸ
σῶμα αἰσθήσεων μὴ ἀκριβεῖς εἰσιν μηδὲ σαφεῖς, σχολῇ   5
αἵ γε ἄλλαι· πᾶσαι γάρ που τούτων φαυλότεραί εἰσιν. ἢ
σοὶ οὐ δοκοῦσιν;
    πάνυ μὲν οὖν, ἔφη.
    πότε οὖν, ἦ δ᾽ ὅς, ἡ ψυχὴ τῆς ἀληθείας ἅπτεται; ὅταν
μὲν γὰρ μετὰ τοῦ σώματος ἐπιχειρῇ τι σκοπεῖν, δῆλον ὅτι   10
τότε ἐξαπατᾶται ὑπ᾽ αὐτοῦ.
    ἀληθῆ λέγεις.   65c
    ἆρ᾽ οὖν οὐκ ἐν τῷ λογίζεσθαι εἴπερ που ἄλλοθι κατάδηλον
αὐτῇ γίγνεταί τι τῶν ὄντων;
    ναί.
    λογίζεται δέ γέ που τότε κάλλιστα, ὅταν αὐτὴν τούτων   5
μηδὲν παραλυπῇ, μήτε ἀκοὴ μήτε ὄψις μήτε ἀλγηδὼν μηδέ
τις ἡδονή, ἀλλ᾽ ὅτι μάλιστα αὐτὴ καθ᾽ αὑτὴν γίγνηται ἐῶσα
χαίρειν τὸ σῶμα, καὶ καθ᾽ ὅσον δύναται μὴ κοινωνοῦσα
αὐτῷ μηδ᾽ ἁπτομένη ὀρέγηται τοῦ ὄντος.
    ἔστι ταῦτα.   10
    οὐκοῦν καὶ ἐνταῦθα ἡ τοῦ φιλοσόφου ψυχὴ μάλιστα
ἀτιμάζει τὸ σῶμα καὶ φεύγει ἀπ᾽ αὐτοῦ, ζητεῖ δὲ αὐτὴ καθ᾽ 65d
αὑτὴν γίγνεσθαι;
    φαίνεται.

τί δὲ δὴ τὰ τοιάδε, ὦ Σιμμία; φαμέν τι εἶναι δίκαιον
αὐτὸ ἢ οὐδέν;   5

   φαμὲν μέντοι νὴ Δία.
   καὶ αὖ καλόν γέ τι καὶ ἀγαθόν;
   πῶς δ᾽ οὔ;
   ἤδη οὖν πώποτέ τι τῶν τοιούτων τοῖς ὀφθαλμοῖς εἶδες;
   οὐδαμῶς, ἦ δ᾽ ὅς.   10

ἀλλ᾽ ἄλλη τινὶ αἰσθήσει τῶν διὰ τοῦ σώματος ἐφήψω
αὐτῶν; λέγω δὲ περὶ πάντων, οἷον μεγέθους πέρι, ὑγιείας,
ἰσχύος, καὶ τῶν ἄλλων ἑνὶ λόγῳ ἁπάντων τῆς οὐσίας ὃ
τυγχάνει ἕκαστον ὄν· ἆρα διὰ τοῦ σώματος αὐτῶν τὸ   65e
ἀληθέστατον θεωρεῖται, ἢ ὧδε ἔχει· ὃς ἂν μάλιστα ἡμῶν
καὶ ἀκριβέστατα παρασκευάσηται αὐτὸ ἕκαστον διανοηθῆναι
περὶ οὗ σκοπεῖ, οὗτος ἂν ἐγγύτατα ἴοι τοῦ γνῶναι ἕκαστον;
   πάνυ μὲν οὖν.   5

ἆρ᾽ οὖν ἐκεῖνος ἂν τοῦτο ποιήσειεν καθαρώτατα ὅστις
ὅτι μάλιστα αὐτῇ τῇ διανοίᾳ ἴοι ἐφ᾽ ἕκαστον, μήτε τιν᾽
ὄψιν παρατιθέμενος ἐν τῷ διανοεῖσθαι μήτε τινὰ ἄλλην
αἴσθησιν ἐφέλκων μηδεμίαν μετὰ τοῦ λογισμοῦ, ἀλλ᾽ αὐτῇ   66a
καθ᾽ αὑτὴν εἰλικρινεῖ τῇ διανοίᾳ χρώμενος αὐτὸ καθ᾽ αὑτὸ εἰλικρινὲς
ἕκαστον ἐπιχειροῖ θηρεύειν τῶν ὄντων, ἀπαλλαγεὶς
ὅτι μάλιστα ὀφθαλμῶν τε καὶ ὤτων καὶ ὡς ἔπος εἰπεῖν σύμπαντος
τοῦ σώματος, ὡς ταράττοντος καὶ οὐκ ἐῶντος   5
τὴν ψυχὴν κτήσασθαι ἀλήθειάν τε καὶ φρόνησιν ὅταν κοινωνῇ;
ἆρ᾽ οὐχ οὗτός ἐστιν, ὦ Σιμμία, εἴπερ τις καὶ ἄλλος ὁ
τευξόμενος τοῦ ὄντος;
   ὑπερφυῶς, ἔφη ὁ Σιμμίας, ὡς ἀληθῆ λέγεις, ὦ
Σώκρατες.   10

   οὐκοῦν ἀνάγκη, ἔφη, ἐκ πάντων τούτων παρίστασθαι   66b
δόξαν τοιάνδε τινὰ τοῖς γνησίως φιλοσόφοις, ὥστε καὶ πρὸς
ἀλλήλους τοιαῦτα ἄττα λέγειν, ὅτι 'κινδυνεύει τοι ὥσπερ
ἀτραπός τις ἐκφέρειν ἡμᾶς μετὰ τοῦ λόγου ἐν τῇ σκέψει,
ὅτι, ἕως ἂν τὸ σῶμα ἔχωμεν καὶ συμπεφυρμένη ᾖ ἡμῶν ἡ   5
ψυχὴ μετὰ τοιούτου κακοῦ, οὐ μή ποτε κτησώμεθα ἱκανῶς
οὗ ἐπιθυμοῦμεν· φαμὲν δὲ τοῦτο εἶναι τὸ ἀληθές. μυρίας
μὲν γὰρ ἡμῖν ἀσχολίας παρέχει τὸ σῶμα διὰ τὴν ἀναγκαίαν
τροφήν· ἔτι δέ, ἄν τινες νόσοι προσπέσωσιν, ἐμποδίζουσιν   66c
ἡμῶν τὴν τοῦ ὄντος θήραν. ἐρώτων δὲ καὶ ἐπιθυμιῶν καὶ
φόβων καὶ εἰδώλων παντοδαπῶν καὶ φλυαρίας ἐμπίμπλησιν
ἡμᾶς πολλῆς, ὥστε τὸ λεγόμενον ὡς ἀληθῶς τῷ ὄντι ὑπ᾽

αὐτοῦ οὐδὲ φρονῆσαι ἡμῖν ἐγγίγνεται οὐδέποτε οὐδέν. καὶ   5
γὰρ πολέμους καὶ στάσεις καὶ μάχας οὐδὲν ἄλλο παρέχει ἢ
τὸ σῶμα καὶ αἱ τούτου ἐπιθυμίαι. διὰ γὰρ τὴν τῶν χρημάτων
κτῆσιν πάντες οἱ πόλεμοι γίγνονται, τὰ δὲ χρήματα
ἀναγκαζόμεθα κτᾶσθαι διὰ τὸ σῶμα, δουλεύοντες τῇ τούτου   66d
θεραπείᾳ· καὶ ἐκ τούτου ἀσχολίαν ἄγομεν φιλοσοφίας πέρι
διὰ πάντα ταῦτα. τὸ δ᾽ ἔσχατον πάντων ὅτι, ἐάν τις
ἡμῖν καὶ σχολὴ γένηται ἀπ᾽ αὐτοῦ καὶ τραπώμεθα πρὸς τὸ
σκοπεῖν τι, ἐν ταῖς ζητήσεσιν αὖ πανταχοῦ παραπῖπτον   5
θόρυβον παρέχει καὶ ταραχὴν καὶ ἐκπλήττει, ὥστε μὴ
δύνασθαι ὑπ᾽ αὐτοῦ καθορᾶν τἀληθές. ἀλλὰ τῷ ὄντι ἡμῖν
δέδεικται ὅτι, εἰ μέλλομέν ποτε καθαρῶς τι εἴσεσθαι,
ἀπαλλακτέον αὐτοῦ καὶ αὐτῇ τῇ ψυχῇ θεατέον αὐτὰ τὰ   66e
πράγματα· καὶ τότε, ὡς ἔοικεν, ἡμῖν ἔσται οὗ ἐπιθυμοῦμέν τε
καί φαμεν ἐρασταὶ εἶναι, φρονήσεως, ἐπειδὰν τελευτήσωμεν,
ὡς ὁ λόγος σημαίνει, ζῶσιν δὲ οὔ. εἰ γὰρ μὴ οἷόν τε
μετὰ τοῦ σώματος μηδὲν καθαρῶς γνῶναι, δυοῖν θάτερον,   5
ἢ οὐδαμοῦ ἔστιν κτήσασθαι τὸ εἰδέναι ἢ τελευτήσασιν· τότε
γὰρ αὐτὴ καθ᾽ αὑτὴν ἡ ψυχὴ ἔσται χωρὶς τοῦ σώματος,   67a
πρότερον δ᾽ οὔ. καὶ ἐν ᾧ ἂν ζῶμεν, οὕτως, ὡς ἔοικεν,
ἐγγυτάτω ἐσόμεθα τοῦ εἰδέναι, ἐὰν ὅτι μάλιστα μηδὲν
ὁμιλῶμεν τῷ σώματι μηδὲ κοινωνῶμεν, ὅτι μὴ πᾶσα ἀνάγκη,
μηδὲ ἀναπιμπλώμεθα τῆς τούτου φύσεως, ἀλλὰ καθαρεύωμεν   5
ἀπ᾽ αὐτοῦ, ἕως ἂν ὁ θεὸς αὐτὸς ἀπολύσῃ ἡμᾶς· καὶ οὕτω μὲν
καθαροὶ ἀπαλλαττόμενοι τῆς τοῦ σώματος ἀφροσύνης, ὡς τὸ
εἰκὸς μετὰ τοιούτων τε ἐσόμεθα καὶ γνωσόμεθα δι᾽ ἡμῶν
αὐτῶν πᾶν τὸ εἰλικρινές, τοῦτο δ᾽ ἐστὶν ἴσως τὸ ἀληθές·   67b
μὴ καθαρῷ γὰρ καθαροῦ ἐφάπτεσθαι μὴ οὐ θεμιτὸν ᾖ᾽.
τοιαῦτα οἶμαι, ὦ Σιμμία, ἀναγκαῖον εἶναι πρὸς ἀλλήλους
λέγειν τε καὶ δοξάζειν πάντας τοὺς ὀρθῶς φιλομαθεῖς. ἢ οὐ
δοκεῖ σοι οὕτως;   5

    παντός γε μᾶλλον, ὦ Σώκρατες.

    οὐκοῦν, ἔφη ὁ Σωκράτης, εἰ ταῦτα ἀληθῆ, ὦ ἑταῖρε,
πολλὴ ἐλπὶς ἀφικομένῳ οἷ ἐγὼ πορεύομαι, ἐκεῖ ἱκανῶς,
εἴπερ που ἄλλοθι, κτήσασθαι τοῦτο οὗ ἕνεκα ἡ πολλὴ
πραγματεία ἡμῖν ἐν τῷ παρελθόντι βίῳ γέγονεν, ὥστε ἥ γε   10
ἀποδημία ἡ νῦν μοι προστεταγμένη μετὰ ἀγαθῆς ἐλπίδος   67c
γίγνεται καὶ ἄλλῳ ἀνδρὶ ὃς ἡγεῖταί οἱ παρεσκευάσθαι τὴν
διάνοιαν ὥσπερ κεκαθαρμένην.

    πάνυ μὲν οὖν, ἔφη ὁ Σιμμίας.

κάθαρσις δὲ εἶναι ἆρα οὐ τοῦτο συμβαίνει, ὅπερ πάλαι   5
ἐν τῷ λόγῳ λέγεται, τὸ χωρίζειν ὅτι μάλιστα ἀπὸ τοῦ
σώματος τὴν ψυχὴν καὶ ἐθίσαι αὐτὴν καθ᾽ αὑτὴν πανταχόθεν
ἐκ τοῦ σώματος συναγείρεσθαί τε καὶ ἁθροΐζεσθαι,
καὶ οἰκεῖν κατὰ τὸ δυνατὸν καὶ ἐν τῷ νῦν παρόντι καὶ ἐν τῷ
ἔπειτα μόνην καθ᾽ αὑτήν, ἐκλυομένην ὥσπερ ἐκ δεσμῶν ἐκ   67d
τοῦ σώματος;

    πάνυ μὲν οὖν, ἔφη.

    οὐκοῦν τοῦτό γε θάνατος ὀνομάζεται, λύσις καὶ χωρισμὸς
ψυχῆς ἀπὸ σώματος;   5

    παντάπασί γε, ἦ δ᾽ ὅς.

    λύειν δέ γε αὐτήν, ὥς φαμεν, προθυμοῦνται ἀεὶ μάλιστα
καὶ μόνοι οἱ φιλοσοφοῦντες ὀρθῶς, καὶ τὸ μελέτημα αὐτὸ
τοῦτό ἐστιν τῶν φιλοσόφων, λύσις καὶ χωρισμὸς ψυχῆς
ἀπὸ σώματος· ἢ οὔ;   10

    φαίνεται.

    οὐκοῦν, ὅπερ ἐν ἀρχῇ ἔλεγον, γελοῖον ἂν εἴη ἄνδρα
παρασκευάζονθ᾽ ἑαυτὸν ἐν τῷ βίῳ ὅτι ἐγγυτάτω ὄντα τοῦ   67e
τεθνάναι οὕτω ζῆν, κἄπειθ᾽ ἥκοντος αὐτῷ τούτου ἀγανακτεῖν;

    γελοῖον· πῶς δ᾽ οὔ;

    τῷ ὄντι ἄρα, ἔφη, ὦ Σιμμία, οἱ ὀρθῶς φιλοσοφοῦντες
ἀποθνῄσκειν μελετῶσι, καὶ τὸ τεθνάναι ἥκιστα αὐτοῖς   5
ἀνθρώπων φοβερόν.

On the content of the intervening passage (67e6–69e5), see p. 136 of the commentary.

εἰπόντος δὴ τοῦ Σωκράτους ταῦτα, ὑπολαβὼν ὁ Κέβης   **69e6**
ἔφη· ὦ Σώκρατες, τὰ μὲν ἄλλα ἔμοιγε δοκεῖ καλῶς λέγεσθαι,
τὰ δὲ περὶ τῆς ψυχῆς πολλὴν ἀπιστίαν παρέχει τοῖς ἀνθρώποις   **70a**
μή, ἐπειδὰν ἀπαλλαγῇ τοῦ σώματος, οὐδαμοῦ ἔτι ᾖ, ἀλλ᾽ ἐκείνη
τῇ ἡμέρᾳ διαφθείρηταί τε καὶ ἀπολλύηται ᾗ ἂν ὁ ἄνθρωπος ἀποθνῄσκῃ,
εὐθὺς ἀπαλλαττομένη τοῦ σώματος, καὶ ἐκβαίνουσα
ὥσπερ πνεῦμα ἢ καπνὸς διασκεδασθεῖσα οἴχηται διαπτομένη   **5**
καὶ οὐδὲν ἔτι οὐδαμοῦ ᾖ. ἐπεί, εἴπερ εἴη που αὐτὴ καθ᾽
αὑτὴν συνηθροισμένη καὶ ἀπηλλαγμένη τούτων τῶν κακῶν
ὧν σὺ νυνδὴ διῆλθες, πολλὴ ἂν εἴη ἐλπὶς καὶ καλή, ὦ
Σώκρατες, ὡς ἀληθῆ ἐστιν ἃ σὺ λέγεις· ἀλλὰ τοῦτο δὴ   **70b**
ἴσως οὐκ ὀλίγης παραμυθίας δεῖται καὶ πίστεως, ὡς ἔστι τε
ψυχὴ ἀποθανόντος τοῦ ἀνθρώπου καί τινα δύναμιν ἔχει καὶ
φρόνησιν.

ἀληθῆ, ἔφη, λέγεις, ὁ Σωκράτης, ὦ Κέβης· ἀλλὰ τί δὴ   **5**
ποιῶμεν; ἢ περὶ αὐτῶν τούτων βούλει διαμυθολογῶμεν, εἴτε
εἰκὸς οὕτως ἔχειν εἴτε μή;

ἐγὼ γοῦν, ἔφη ὁ Κέβης, ἡδέως ἂν ἀκούσαιμι ἥντινα
δόξαν ἔχεις περὶ αὐτῶν.

οὔκουν γ᾽ ἂν οἶμαι, ἦ δ᾽ ὃς ὁ Σωκράτης, εἰπεῖν τινα νῦν   **10**
ἀκούσαντα, οὐδ᾽ εἰ κωμῳδοποιὸς εἴη, ὡς ἀδολεσχῶ καὶ οὐ   **70c**
περὶ προσηκόντων τοὺς λόγους ποιοῦμαι. εἰ οὖν δοκεῖ, χρὴ
διασκοπεῖσθαι.

σκεψώμεθα δὲ αὐτὸ τῇδέ πη, εἴτ᾽ ἄρα ἐν Ἅιδου εἰσὶν αἱ
ψυχαὶ τελευτησάντων τῶν ἀνθρώπων εἴτε καὶ οὔ. παλαιὸς   **5**
μὲν οὖν ἔστι τις λόγος οὗ μεμνήμεθα, ὡς εἰσὶν ἐνθένδε
ἀφικόμεναι ἐκεῖ, καὶ πάλιν γε δεῦρο ἀφικνοῦνται καὶ γίγνονται
ἐκ τῶν τεθνεώτων· καὶ εἰ τοῦθ᾽ οὕτως ἔχει, πάλιν
γίγνεσθαι ἐκ τῶν ἀποθανόντων τοὺς ζῶντας, ἄλλο τι ἢ εἶεν
ἂν αἱ ψυχαὶ ἡμῶν ἐκεῖ; οὐ γὰρ ἂν που πάλιν ἐγίγνοντο μὴ   **70d**
οὖσαι, καὶ τοῦτο ἱκανὸν τεκμήριον τοῦ ταῦτ᾽ εἶναι, εἰ τῷ
ὄντι φανερὸν γίγνοιτο ὅτι οὐδαμόθεν ἄλλοθεν γίγνονται οἱ
ζῶντες ἢ ἐκ τῶν τεθνεώτων· εἰ δὲ μὴ ἔστι τοῦτο, ἄλλου ἂν
τοῦ δέοι λόγου.   **5**

πάνυ μὲν οὖν, ἔφη ὁ Κέβης.

μὴ τοίνυν κατ᾽ ἀνθρώπων, ἦ δ᾽ ὅς, σκόπει μόνον τοῦτο,
εἰ βούλει ῥᾷον μαθεῖν, ἀλλὰ καὶ κατὰ ζῴων πάντων καὶ
φυτῶν, καὶ συλλήβδην ὅσαπερ ἔχει γένεσιν περὶ πάντων
ἴδωμεν ἆρ᾽ οὑτωσὶ γίγνεται πάντα, οὐκ ἄλλοθεν ἢ ἐκ τῶν   **70e**
ἐναντίων τὰ ἐναντία, ὅσοις τυγχάνει ὂν τοιοῦτόν τι, οἷον τὸ

καλὸν τῷ αἰσχρῷ ἐναντίον που καὶ δίκαιον ἀδίκῳ, καὶ ἄλλα
δὴ μυρία οὕτως ἔχει. τοῦτο οὖν σκεψώμεθα, ἆρα ἀναγκαῖον
ὅσοις ἔστι τι ἐναντίον, μηδαμόθεν ἄλλοθεν αὐτὸ γίγνεσθαι   5
ἢ ἐκ τοῦ αὐτῷ ἐναντίου. οἷον ὅταν μεῖζόν τι γίγνηται,
ἀνάγκη που ἐξ ἐλάττονος ὄντος πρότερον ἔπειτα μεῖζον
γίγνεσθαι;
    ναί.
    οὐκοῦν κἂν ἔλαττον γίγνηται, ἐκ μείζονος ὄντος πρότερον   10
ὕστερον ἔλαττον γενήσεται;   71a
        ἔστιν οὕτω, ἔφη.
        καὶ μὴν ἐξ ἰσχυροτέρου γε τὸ ἀσθενέστερον καὶ ἐκ βραδυτέρου
τὸ θᾶττον;
        πάνυ γε.   5
        τί δέ; ἄν τι χεῖρον γίγνηται, οὐκ ἐξ ἀμείνονος, καὶ ἂν
δικαιότερον, ἐξ ἀδικωτέρου;
        πῶς γὰρ οὔ;
        ἱκανῶς οὖν, ἔφη, ἔχομεν τοῦτο, ὅτι πάντα οὕτω γίγνεται,
ἐξ ἐναντίων τὰ ἐναντία πράγματα;   10
        πάνυ γε.
        τί δ᾽ αὖ; ἔστι τι καὶ τοιόνδε ἐν αὐτοῖς, οἷον μεταξὺ
ἀμφοτέρων πάντων τῶν ἐναντίων δυοῖν ὄντοιν δύο γενέσεις,
ἀπὸ μὲν τοῦ ἑτέρου ἐπὶ τὸ ἕτερον, ἀπὸ δ᾽ αὖ τοῦ ἑτέρου   71b
πάλιν ἐπὶ τὸ ἕτερον· μείζονος μὲν πράγματος καὶ ἐλάττονος
μεταξὺ αὔξησις καὶ φθίσις, καὶ καλοῦμεν οὕτω τὸ μὲν αὐξάνεσθαι,
τὸ δὲ φθίνειν;
        ναί, ἔφη.   5
οὐκοῦν καὶ διακρίνεσθαι καὶ συγκρίνεσθαι, καὶ ψύχεσθαι
καὶ θερμαίνεσθαι, καὶ πάντα οὕτω, κἂν εἰ μὴ χρώμεθα τοῖς
ὀνόμασιν ἐνιαχοῦ, ἀλλ᾽ ἔργῳ γοῦν πανταχοῦ οὕτως ἔχειν
ἀναγκαῖον, γίγνεσθαί τε αὐτὰ ἐξ ἀλλήλων γένεσίν τε εἶναι
ἑκατέρου εἰς ἄλληλα;   10
        πάνυ μὲν οὖν, ἦ δ᾽ ὅς.
        τί οὖν; ἔφη, τῷ ζῆν ἐστί τι ἐναντίον, ὥσπερ τῷ   71c
ἐγρηγορέναι τὸ καθεύδειν;
        πάνυ μὲν οὖν, ἔφη.
        τί;
        τὸ τεθνάναι, ἔφη.   5
        οὐκοῦν ἐξ ἀλλήλων τε γίγνεται ταῦτα, εἴπερ ἐναντία
ἐστιν, καὶ αἱ γενέσεις εἰσὶν αὐτοῖν μεταξὺ δύο δυοῖν ὄντοιν;
        πῶς γὰρ οὔ;
        τὴν μὲν τοίνυν ἑτέραν συζυγίαν ὧν νυνδὴ ἔλεγον ἐγώ
σοι, ἔφη, ἐρῶ, ὁ Σωκράτης, καὶ αὐτὴν καὶ τὰς γενέσεις· σὺ   10

A
Level

δέ μοι τὴν ἑτέραν. λέγω δὲ τὸ μὲν καθεύδειν, τὸ δὲ ἐγρηγορέναι,
καὶ ἐκ τοῦ καθεύδειν τὸ ἐγρηγορέναι γίγνεσθαι καὶ
ἐκ τοῦ ἐγρηγορέναι τὸ καθεύδειν, καὶ τὰς γενέσεις αὐτοῖν   71d
τὴν μὲν καταδαρθάνειν εἶναι, τὴν δ᾽ ἀνεγείρεσθαι. ἱκανῶς
σοι, ἔφη, ἢ οὔ;
    πάνυ μὲν οὖν.
    λέγε δή μοι καὶ σύ, ἔφη, οὕτω περὶ ζωῆς καὶ θανάτου.   5
οὐκ ἐναντίον μὲν φὴς τῷ ζῆν τὸ τεθνάναι εἶναι;
    ἔγωγε.
    γίγνεσθαι δὲ ἐξ ἀλλήλων;
    ναί.
    ἐξ οὖν τοῦ ζῶντος τί τὸ γιγνόμενον;   10
    τὸ τεθνηκός, ἔφη.
    τί δέ, ἦ δ᾽ ὅς, ἐκ τοῦ τεθνεῶτος;
    ἀναγκαῖον, ἔφη, ὁμολογεῖν ὅτι τὸ ζῶν.
    ἐκ τῶν τεθνεώτων ἄρα, ὦ Κέβης, τὰ ζῶντά τε καὶ οἱ
ζῶντες γίγνονται;   15
    φαίνεται, ἔφη.   71e
    εἰσὶν ἄρα, ἔφη, αἱ ψυχαὶ ἡμῶν ἐν Ἅιδου.
    ἔοικεν.
    οὐκοῦν καὶ τοῖν γενεσέοιν τοῖν περὶ ταῦτα ἥ γ᾽ ἑτέρα
σαφὴς οὖσα τυγχάνει; τὸ γὰρ ἀποθνήσκειν σαφὲς δήπου,   5
ἢ οὔ;
    πάνυ μὲν οὖν, ἔφη.
    πῶς οὖν, ἦ δ᾽ ὅς, ποιήσομεν; οὐκ ἀνταποδώσομεν τὴν
ἐναντίαν γένεσιν, ἀλλὰ ταύτῃ χωλὴ ἔσται ἡ φύσις; ἢ ἀνάγκη
ἀποδοῦναι τῷ ἀποθνήσκειν ἐναντίαν τινὰ γένεσιν;   10
    πάντως που, ἔφη.
    τίνα ταύτην;
    τὸ ἀναβιώσκεσθαι.
    οὐκοῦν, ἦ δ᾽ ὅς, εἴπερ ἔστι τὸ ἀναβιώσκεσθαι, ἐκ τῶν
τεθνεώτων ἂν εἴη γένεσις εἰς τοὺς ζῶντας αὕτη, τὸ   72a
ἀναβιώσκεσθαι;
    πάνυ γε.
    ὁμολογεῖται ἄρα ἡμῖν καὶ ταύτῃ τοὺς ζῶντας ἐκ τῶν
τεθνεώτων γεγονέναι οὐδὲν ἧττον ἢ τοὺς τεθνεῶτας ἐκ τῶν   5
ζώντων, τούτου δὲ ὄντος ἱκανόν που ἐδόκει τεκμήριον εἶναι
ὅτι ἀναγκαῖον τὰς τῶν τεθνεώτων ψυχὰς εἶναί που, ὅθεν δὴ
πάλιν γίγνεσθαι.
    δοκεῖ μοι, ἔφη, ὦ Σώκρατες, ἐκ τῶν ὡμολογημένων
ἀναγκαῖον οὕτως ἔχειν.   10
    ἰδὲ τοίνυν οὕτως, ἔφη, ὦ Κέβης, ὅτι οὐδ᾽ ἀδίκως

A
Level

ὡμολογήκαμεν, ὡς ἐμοὶ δοκεῖ. εἰ γὰρ μὴ ἀεὶ ἀνταποδιδοίη τὰ
ἕτερα τοῖς ἑτέροις γιγνόμενα, ὡσπερεὶ κύκλῳ περιιόντα, ἀλλ᾽   **72b**
εὐθεῖά τις εἴη ἡ γένεσις ἐκ τοῦ ἑτέρου μόνον εἰς τὸ καταντικρὺ
καὶ μὴ ἀνακάμπτοι πάλιν ἐπὶ τὸ ἕτερον μηδὲ καμπὴν
ποιοῖτο, οἶσθ᾽ ὅτι πάντα τελευτῶντα τὸ αὐτὸ σχῆμα ἂν σχοίη
καὶ τὸ αὐτὸ πάθος ἂν πάθοι καὶ παύσαιτο γιγνόμενα;   **5**
  πῶς λέγεις; ἔφη.
  οὐδὲν χαλεπόν, ἦ δ᾽ ὅς, ἐννοῆσαι ὃ λέγω· ἀλλ᾽ οἷον εἰ
τὸ καταδαρθάνειν μὲν εἴη, τὸ δ᾽ ἀνεγείρεσθαι μὴ ἀνταποδιδοίη
γιγνόμενον ἐκ τοῦ καθεύδοντος, οἶσθ᾽ ὅτι τελευτῶντα πάντ᾽
<ἂν> λῆρον τὸν Ἐνδυμίωνα ἀποδείξειεν καὶ οὐδαμοῦ ἂν   **72c**
φαίνοιτο διὰ τὸ καὶ τἆλλα πάντα ταὐτὸν ἐκείνῳ πεπονθέναι,
καθεύδειν. κἂν εἰ συγκρίνοιτο μὲν πάντα, διακρίνοιτο δὲ
μή, ταχὺ ἂν τὸ τοῦ Ἀναξαγόρου γεγονὸς εἴη, ‘ὁμοῦ πάντα
χρήματα᾽. ὡσαύτως δέ, ὦ φίλε Κέβης, καὶ εἰ ἀποθνῄσκοι   **5**
μὲν πάντα ὅσα τοῦ ζῆν μεταλάβοι, ἐπειδὴ δὲ ἀποθάνοι,
μένοι ἐν τούτῳ τῷ σχήματι τὰ τεθνεῶτα καὶ μὴ πάλιν
ἀναβιώσκοιτο, ἆρ᾽ οὐ πολλὴ ἀνάγκη τελευτῶντα πάντα
τεθνάναι καὶ μηδὲν ζῆν; εἰ γὰρ ἐκ μὲν τῶν ἄλλων τὰ   **72d**
ζῶντα γίγνοιτο, τὰ δὲ ζῶντα θνῄσκοι, τίς μηχανὴ μὴ οὐχὶ
πάντα καταναλωθῆναι εἰς τὸ τεθνάναι;
  οὐδὲ μία μοι δοκεῖ, ἔφη ὁ Κέβης, ὦ Σώκρατες, ἀλλά μοι
δοκεῖς παντάπασιν ἀληθῆ λέγειν.   **5**
  ἔστιν γάρ, ἔφη, ὦ Κέβης, ὡς ἐμοὶ δοκεῖ, παντὸς μᾶλλον
οὕτω, καὶ ἡμεῖς αὐτὰ ταῦτα οὐκ ἐξαπατώμενοι ὁμολογοῦμεν,
ἀλλ᾽ ἔστι τῷ ὄντι καὶ τὸ ἀναβιώσκεσθαι καὶ ἐκ τῶν τεθνεώτων
τοὺς ζῶντας γίγνεσθαι καὶ τὰς τῶν τεθνεώτων ψυχὰς
εἶναι καὶ ταῖς μέν γε ἀγαθαῖς ἄμεινον εἶναι, ταῖς δὲ κακαῖς   **72e**
κάκιον.
  καὶ μήν, ἔφη ὁ Κέβης ὑπολαβών, καὶ κατ᾽ ἐκεῖνόν γε
τὸν λόγον, ὦ Σώκρατες, εἰ ἀληθής ἐστιν, ὃν σὺ εἴωθας
θαμὰ λέγειν, ὅτι ἡμῖν ἡ μάθησις οὐκ ἄλλο τι ἢ ἀνάμνησις   **5**
τυγχάνει οὖσα, καὶ κατὰ τοῦτον ἀνάγκη που ἡμᾶς ἐν προτέρῳ
τινὶ χρόνῳ μεμαθηκέναι ἃ νῦν ἀναμιμνῃσκόμεθα. τοῦτο δὲ
ἀδύνατον, εἰ μὴ ἦν που ἡμῖν ἡ ψυχὴ πρὶν ἐν τῷδε τῷ   **73a**
ἀνθρωπίνῳ εἴδει γενέσθαι· ὥστε καὶ ταύτῃ ἀθάνατον ἡ ψυχή τι
ἔοικεν εἶναι.
  ἀλλά, ὦ Κέβης, ἔφη ὁ Σιμμίας ὑπολαβών, ποῖαι τούτων
αἱ ἀποδείξεις; ὑπόμνησόν με· οὐ γὰρ σφόδρα ἐν τῷ παρόντι   **5**
μέμνημαι.
  ἑνὶ μὲν λόγῳ, ἔφη ὁ Κέβης, καλλίστῳ, ὅτι ἐρωτώμενοι
οἱ ἄνθρωποι, ἐάν τις καλῶς ἐρωτᾷ, αὐτοὶ λέγουσιν πάντα ᾗ

A
Level

ἔχει – καίτοι εἰ μὴ ἐτύγχανεν αὐτοῖς ἐπιστήμη ἐνοῦσα καὶ
ὀρθὸς λόγος, οὐκ ἂν οἷοί τ᾽ ἦσαν τοῦτο ποιῆσαι – ἔπειτα   10
ἐάν τις ἐπὶ τὰ διαγράμματα ἄγῃ ἢ ἄλλο τι τῶν τοιούτων,   73b
ἐνταῦθα σαφέστατα κατηγορεῖ ὅτι τοῦτο οὕτως ἔχει.

   εἰ δὲ μὴ ταύτῃ γε, ἔφη, πείθῃ, ὦ Σιμμία, ὁ Σωκράτης,
σκέψαι ἂν τῇδέ πῃ σοι σκοπουμένῳ συνδόξῃ. ἀπιστεῖς γὰρ
δὴ πῶς ἡ καλουμένη μάθησις ἀνάμνησίς ἐστιν;   5

   ἀπιστῶ μέν σοι ἔγωγε, ἦ δ᾽ ὃς ὁ Σιμμίας, οὔ, αὐτὸ δὲ
τοῦτο, ἔφη, δέομαι παθεῖν περὶ οὗ ὁ λόγος, ἀναμνησθῆναι.
καὶ σχεδόν γε ἐξ ὧν Κέβης ἐπεχείρησε λέγειν ἤδη μέμνημαι
καὶ πείθομαι· οὐδὲν μεντἂν ἧττον ἀκούοιμι νῦν πῇ σὺ
ἐπεχείρησας λέγειν.   10

   τῇδ᾽ ἔγωγε, ἦ δ᾽ ὅς. ὁμολογοῦμεν γὰρ δήπου, εἴ τίς τι   73c
ἀναμνησθήσεται, δεῖν αὐτὸν τοῦτο πρότερόν ποτε ἐπίστασθαι.

   πάνυ γ᾽, ἔφη.

   ἆρ᾽ οὖν καὶ τόδε ὁμολογοῦμεν, ὅταν ἐπιστήμη παραγίγνηται
τρόπῳ τοιούτῳ, ἀνάμνησιν εἶναι; λέγω δὲ τίνα   5
τρόπον; τόνδε. ἐάν τίς τι ἕτερον ἢ ἰδὼν ἢ ἀκούσας ἤ τινα
ἄλλην αἴσθησιν λαβὼν μὴ μόνον ἐκεῖνο γνῷ, ἀλλὰ καὶ
ἕτερον ἐννοήσῃ οὗ μὴ ἡ αὐτὴ ἐπιστήμη ἀλλ᾽ ἄλλη, ἆρα
οὐχὶ τοῦτο δικαίως λέγομεν ὅτι ἀνεμνήσθη, οὗ τὴν ἔννοιαν
ἔλαβεν;   73d

   πῶς λέγεις;

   οἷον τὰ τοιάδε· ἄλλη που ἐπιστήμη ἀνθρώπου καὶ λύρας.

   πῶς γὰρ οὔ;

   οὐκοῦν οἶσθα ὅτι οἱ ἐρασταί, ὅταν ἴδωσιν λύραν ἢ ἱμάτιον   5
ἢ ἄλλο τι οἷς τὰ παιδικὰ αὐτῶν εἴωθε χρῆσθαι, πάσχουσι
τοῦτο· ἔγνωσάν τε τὴν λύραν καὶ ἐν τῇ διανοίᾳ ἔλαβον τὸ
εἶδος τοῦ παιδὸς οὗ ἦν ἡ λύρα; τοῦτο δέ ἐστιν ἀνάμνησις·
ὥσπερ γε καὶ Σιμμίαν τις ἰδὼν πολλάκις Κέβητος ἀνεμνήσθη,
καὶ ἄλλα που μυρία τοιαῦτ᾽ ἂν εἴη.   10

   μυρία μέντοι νὴ Δία, ἔφη ὁ Σιμμίας.

   οὐκοῦν, ἦ δ᾽ ὅς, τὸ τοιοῦτον ἀνάμνησίς τίς ἐστι; μάλιστα   73e
μέντοι ὅταν τις τοῦτο πάθῃ περὶ ἐκεῖνα ἃ ὑπὸ χρόνου καὶ τοῦ
μὴ ἐπισκοπεῖν ἤδη ἐπελέληστο;

   πάνυ μὲν οὖν, ἔφη.

   τί δέ; ἦ δ᾽ ὅς· ἔστιν ἵππον γεγραμμένον ἰδόντα καὶ   5
λύραν γεγραμμένην ἀνθρώπου ἀναμνησθῆναι, καὶ Σιμμίαν
ἰδόντα γεγραμμένον Κέβητος ἀναμνησθῆναι;

   πάνυ γε.

   οὐκοῦν καὶ Σιμμίαν ἰδόντα γεγραμμένον αὐτοῦ Σιμμίου
ἀναμνησθῆναι;   10

**A
Level**

ἔστι μέντοι, ἔφη.   **74a**

ἆρ᾽ οὖν οὐ κατὰ πάντα ταῦτα συμβαίνει τὴν ἀνάμνησιν
εἶναι μὲν ἀφ᾽ ὁμοίων, εἶναι δὲ καὶ ἀπὸ ἀνομοίων;

συμβαίνει.

ἀλλ᾽ ὅταν γε ἀπὸ τῶν ὁμοίων ἀναμιμνῄσκηταί τίς τι, ἆρ᾽   **5**
οὐκ ἀναγκαῖον τόδε προσπάσχειν, ἐννοεῖν εἴτε τι ἐλλείπει
τοῦτο κατὰ τὴν ὁμοιότητα εἴτε μὴ ἐκείνου οὗ ἀνεμνήσθη;

ἀνάγκη, ἔφη.

σκόπει δή, ἦ δ᾽ ὅς, εἰ ταῦτα οὕτως ἔχει. φαμέν πού τι
εἶναι ἴσον, οὐ ξύλον λέγω ξύλῳ οὐδὲ λίθον λίθῳ οὐδ᾽ ἄλλο   **10**
τῶν τοιούτων οὐδέν, ἀλλὰ παρὰ ταῦτα πάντα ἕτερόν τι, αὐτὸ
τὸ ἴσον· φῶμέν τι εἶναι ἢ μηδέν;

φῶμεν μέντοι νὴ Δί᾽, ἔφη ὁ Σιμμίας, θαυμαστῶς γε.   **74b**

ἦ καὶ ἐπιστάμεθα αὐτὸ ὃ ἔστιν;

πάνυ γε, ἦ δ᾽ ὅς.

πόθεν λαβόντες αὐτοῦ τὴν ἐπιστήμην; ἆρ᾽ οὐκ ἐξ ὧν
νυνδὴ ἐλέγομεν, ἢ ξύλα ἢ λίθους ἢ ἄλλα ἄττα ἰδόντες   **5**
ἴσα, ἐκ τούτων ἐκεῖνο ἐνενοήσαμεν, ἕτερον ὂν τούτων; ἢ
οὐχ ἕτερόν σοι φαίνεται; σκόπει δὲ καὶ τῇδε. ἆρ᾽ οὐ λίθοι μὲν
ἴσοι καὶ ξύλα ἐνίοτε ταὐτὰ ὄντα τῷ μὲν ἴσα φαίνεται,
τῷ δ᾽ οὔ;

πάνυ μὲν οὖν.   **10**

τί δέ; αὐτὰ τὰ ἴσα ἔστιν ὅτε ἄνισά σοι ἐφάνη, ἢ ἡ ἰσότης   **74c**
ἀνισότης;

οὐδεπώποτέ γε, ὦ Σώκρατες.

οὐ ταὐτὸν ἄρα ἐστίν, ἦ δ᾽ ὅς, ταῦτά τε τὰ ἴσα καὶ αὐτὸ
τὸ ἴσον.   **5**

οὐδαμῶς μοι φαίνεται, ὦ Σώκρατες.

ἀλλὰ μὴν ἐκ τούτων γ᾽, ἔφη, τῶν ἴσων, ἑτέρων ὄντων
ἐκείνου τοῦ ἴσου, ὅμως αὐτοῦ τὴν ἐπιστήμην ἐννενόηκάς τε
καὶ εἴληφας;

ἀληθέστατα, ἔφη, λέγεις.   **10**

οὐκοῦν ἢ ὁμοίου ὄντος τούτοις ἢ ἀνομοίου;

πάνυ γε.

διαφέρει δέ γε, ἦ δ᾽ ὅς, οὐδέν· ἕως ἂν ἄλλο ἰδὼν ἀπὸ
ταύτης τῆς ὄψεως ἄλλο ἐννοήσῃς, εἴτε ὅμοιον εἴτε ἀνόμοιον,   **74d**
ἀναγκαῖον, ἔφη, αὐτὸ ἀνάμνησιν γεγονέναι.

πάνυ μὲν οὖν.

τί δέ; ἦ δ᾽ ὅς· ἦ πάσχομέν τι τοιοῦτον περὶ τὰ ἐν τοῖς
ξύλοις τε καὶ οἷς νυνδὴ ἐλέγομεν τοῖς ἴσοις; ἆρα φαίνεται   **5**
ἡμῖν οὕτως ἴσα εἶναι ὥσπερ αὐτὸ τὸ ὃ ἔστιν, ἢ ἐνδεῖ τι
ἐκείνου τῷ τοιοῦτον εἶναι οἷον τὸ ἴσον, ἢ οὐδέν;

**A
Level**

καὶ πολύ γε, ἔφη, ἐνδεῖ.

οὐκοῦν ὁμολογοῦμεν, ὅταν τίς τι ἰδὼν ἐννοήσῃ ὅτι
βούλεται μὲν τοῦτο ὃ νῦν ἐγὼ ὁρῶ εἶναι οἶον ἄλλο τι τῶν ὄντων,   10
ἐνδεῖ δὲ καὶ οὐ δύναται τοιοῦτον εἶναι ἴσον οἶον ἐκεῖνο, ἀλλ᾽   74e
ἔστιν φαυλότερον, ἀναγκαῖόν που τὸν τοῦτο ἐννοοῦντα τυχεῖν
προειδότα ἐκεῖνο ᾧ φησιν αὐτὸ προσεοικέναι μέν, ἐνδεεστέρως δὲ
ἔχειν;

    ἀνάγκη.   5

τί οὖν; τὸ τοιοῦτον πεπόνθαμεν καὶ ἡμεῖς ἢ οὔ περί τε
τὰ ἴσα καὶ αὐτὸ τὸ ἴσον;

    παντάπασί γε.

ἀναγκαῖον ἄρα ἡμᾶς προειδέναι τὸ ἴσον πρὸ ἐκείνου τοῦ
χρόνου ὅτε τὸ πρῶτον ἰδόντες τὰ ἴσα ἐνενοήσαμεν ὅτι   75a
ὀρέγεται μὲν πάντα ταῦτα εἶναι οἶον τὸ ἴσον, ἔχει δὲ
ἐνδεεστέρως.

    ἔστι ταῦτα.

ἀλλὰ μὴν καὶ τόδε ὁμολογοῦμεν, μὴ ἄλλοθεν αὐτὸ   5
ἐννενοηκέναι μηδὲ δυνατὸν εἶναι ἐννοῆσαι ἀλλ᾽ ἢ ἐκ τοῦ ἰδεῖν
ἢ ἅψασθαι ἢ ἔκ τινος ἄλλης τῶν αἰσθήσεων· ταὐτὸν δὲ
πάντα ταῦτα λέγω.

    ταὐτὸν γὰρ ἔστιν, ὦ Σώκρατες, πρός γε ὃ βούλεται
    δηλῶσαι ὁ λόγος.   10

ἀλλὰ μὲν δὴ ἔκ γε τῶν αἰσθήσεων δεῖ ἐννοῆσαι ὅτι
πάντα τὰ ἐν ταῖς αἰσθήσεσιν ἐκείνου τε ὀρέγεται τοῦ ὃ   75b
ἔστιν ἴσον, καὶ αὐτοῦ ἐνδεέστερά ἐστιν· ἢ πῶς λέγομεν;

    οὕτως.

πρὸ τοῦ ἄρα ἄρξασθαι ἡμᾶς ὁρᾶν καὶ ἀκούειν καὶ τἆλλα
αἰσθάνεσθαι τυχεῖν ἔδει που εἰληφότας ἐπιστήμην αὐτοῦ   5
τοῦ ἴσου ὅτι ἔστιν, εἰ ἐμέλλομεν τὰ ἐκ τῶν αἰσθήσεων
ἴσα ἐκεῖσε ἀνοίσειν, ὅτι προθυμεῖται μὲν πάντα τοιαῦτ᾽ εἶναι οἶον
ἐκεῖνο, ἔστιν δὲ αὐτοῦ φαυλότερα.

    ἀνάγκη ἐκ τῶν προειρημένων, ὦ Σώκρατες.

οὐκοῦν γενόμενοι εὐθὺς ἑωρῶμέν τε καὶ ἠκούομεν καὶ τὰς   10
ἄλλας αἰσθήσεις εἴχομεν;

    πάνυ γε.

ἔδει δέ γε, φαμέν, πρὸ τούτων τὴν τοῦ ἴσου ἐπιστήμην   75c
εἰληφέναι;

    ναί.

πρὶν γενέσθαι ἄρα, ὡς ἔοικεν, ἀνάγκη ἡμῖν αὐτὴν
εἰληφέναι;   5

**A
Level**

Commentary Notes

62c9–63b1 – a true philosopher will look forward to death

Cebes and Simmias are surprised at Socrates' suggestion that a philosopher should be content to die. They had just been discussing how it would be wrong to kill oneself, because we mortals are the property of the gods, and they are good masters. If dying would mean leaving the care of such masters, Cebes wonders, how can a wise person look forward to death?

62c9

ἀλλ' εἰκός ... τοῦτό γε φαίνεται: 'this, at least, seems plausible'. Socrates has just concluded that it is wrong to kill oneself, and one must wait until the gods make death unavoidable, as it is now for him (c7–8). Frequently in prose dialogue, ἀλλά does not introduce an objection but shows that the speaker (Cebes here) concurs with an opinion just voiced.

62c10–d1

τὸ τοὺς φιλοσόφους ῥᾳδίως ἂν ἐθέλειν ἀποθνῄσκειν: 'that philosophers would readily be willing to die'. As an alternative to an indirect statement with ὅτι, Plato often uses τό with an acc. + inf. The phrase here is in apposition to the relative clause ὃ ... νυνδὴ ἔλεγες 'what you were saying just now'.

ἔοικεν τοῦτο ... ἀτόπῳ: 'this seems strange'. ἔοικα 'I resemble' has a dative object (hence ἀτόπῳ, which is delayed for emphasis).

62d2

εὐλόγως ἔχει: 'is reasonable, makes sense'. ἔχω + adverb is equivalent to εἰμί + adjective.

62d2–3

'That it is a god who looks after us and that we are his possessions'. Cebes is repeating the reasons previously discussed why suicide is wrong. ἐπιμελέομαι 'I take care of' takes a genitive object, in this case, ἡμῶν. Note the chiastic arrangement of the sentence.

62d3–5

τὸ ... μὴ ἀγανακτεῖν ... ἐκ ταύτης τῆς θεραπείας ἀπιόντας: a long articular infinitive (gerund) and the subject of ἔχει below: 'not to be displeased on leaving this care is not reasonable' (i.e. the care given to the living by the god).

τοὺς φρονιμωτάτους: 'those who are very wise'. In Plato, φρόνιμος and σόφος are equivalent.

62d5–6

οἵπερ ἄριστοί εἰσιν τῶν ὄντων ἐπιστάται: 'who are the very best overseers of all' (lit. 'of the ones that are'). -περ, added to the relative or to εἰ 'if', emphasizes more precisely the thing or condition in question (so οἵπερ = 'the very ones who').

θεοί is in apposition to the relative clause.

62d6–7

οὐ γάρ που αὐτός ... αὑτοῦ οἴεται ἄμεινον ἐπιμελήσεσθαι: 'I don't suppose each thinks he will take better care of himself.' The subject has shifted from plural to singular.

που as a particle serves to temper the assertiveness of a sentence and hence is best translated with 'I suppose' or the like. αὑτοῦ is a contraction of ἑαυτοῦ, the gen. obj. of the fut. ἐπιμελήσεσθαι.

62d8–e1

ἀνόητος ... ἄνθρωπος: 'a foolish individual'. ἄνθρωπος often conveys a touch of contempt.

τάχ᾽ ἄν 'perhaps' is followed by two potential optatives here, οἰηθείη and λογίζοιτο (with ἄν repeated), 'could think', 'could reason'.

φευκτέον εἶναι ἀπὸ τοῦ δεσπότου: 'that he must run away from his master', an acc. + inf. in apposition to ταῦτα. Plato here uses the neuter impersonal use of the gerundive φευκτέος 'needing to be fled' (from φεύγω) and leaves out the dat. of agent.

62e1–2

οὐ δεῖ ... ἀπὸ ... τοῦ ἀγαθοῦ φεύγειν: 'he must not run away from the good (master)'. οὐ δεῖ means 'it is necessary that ... not' (compare οὐ φημί 'I deny').

ὅτι μάλιστα: 'as much as possible'. Like ὡς, ὅτι with superlative means 'as X as possible'.

62e3

ἀλογίστως ἄν φεύγοι: 'it would be irrational to flee'.

ὁ δὲ νοῦν ἔχων: 'anyone with sense'.

AS

62e4

παρὰ τῷ αὐτοῦ βελτίονι: 'with one better than himself'.

62e5

τοὐναντίον ... ἢ ὃ νυνδὴ ἐλέγετο: 'the opposite (τὸ ἐναντίον) to what was just now being said'. As in its usual sense ('than'), ἤ here articulates a contrast.

62e5–7

πρέπει = 'it is fitting for ... to ...', with accusative of the person and infinitive. Here imagined attitudes of the wise and foolish towards dying are contrasted clearly, (i) with μέν and δέ and (ii) their positions at the sentence's start and end, framing the participle they share (ἀποθνῄσκοντας, 'when they are dying').

62e7–63a1

ὁ Σωκράτης ἡσθῆναί τέ μοι ἔδοξε: this brief observation from the narrator (Phaedo) is one of a handful of reminders that the conversation is being relayed to us at second hand.

63a1–2

ἀεί τοι ... Κέβης λόγους τινὰς ἀνερευνᾷ: 'See how Cebes is always examining some argument or other'. The main job of the particle τοι is to bring to the listener's attention something important that the speaker thinks has gone unnoticed. It is accordingly common in philosophical dialogues.

ὁ Κέβης: One way Plato distinguishes direct speech from the narrative is in his use of the article before names, omitting it in the former and using it in the latter. For this reason many scholars join Burnet in bracketing the article here, despite most manuscripts having one.

63a2–3

οὐ πάνυ εὐθέως ἐθέλει πείθεσθαι ὅτι ἄν τις εἴπῃ: 'he is not at all keen to believe straightaway whatever someone is saying'. The ὅτι-clause is indefinite (hence ἄν + subjunctive).

63a4–5

ἀλλὰ μὴν νῦν γέ: 'And indeed, on this occasion at least' (i.e. 'for once').

μοι δοκεῖ τι καὶ αὐτῷ λέγειν Κέβης: 'Cebes seems – even to me – to be onto something.' Simmias feigns surprise at his friend's good point, lending a touch of humour. μοι καὶ αὐτῷ, to me myself also, with the intensive pronoun.

63a5–7

τί ... ἂν βουλόμενοι ... φεύγοιεν: 'Why would they willingly flee'.

σοφοὶ ὡς ἀληθῶς: 'truly wise'. (The ὡς is best left untranslated.)

ἀμείνους αὐτῶν: 'better than themselves'. ἀμείνους is m. acc. pl., an alternative contract form of ἀμείνονες/ἀμείνονας. αὐτῶν = ἑαυτῶν.

ἀπαλλάττοιντο: reflexive middle, 'rid themselves'. ἀπαλλάττω and its cognate ἀπαλλαγή 'deliverance, escape' are key terms in the following discussion and like their English meanings have connotations of an improvement in condition. The optative is potential, supply ἄν from earlier.

63a7–8

δοκεῖ εἰς ... σὲ τείνειν τὸν λόγον: 'he seems to be aiming his argument at you': for as Cebes and Simmias have spotted, Socrates himself is facing death, and the prospect of leaving the care of the gods, in good cheer. The metaphor of aiming, as of a bow and arrow (which one must draw (τείνω) to shoot), is poignantly witty: Cebes is challenging Socrates' acceptance of death by placing him, as it were, in his crosshairs.

63a8–9

οὕτω ῥᾳδίως φέρεις ... ἀπολείπων: 'you are taking your departure so lightly'.

63b1–67e6 – Socrates' 'second apology'

Socrates now defends himself against the charge of inconsistency that Cebes and Simmias have levelled against him. He presents his belief that a better existence and the care of other gods await a good man after death. Socrates argues at length that for a true philosopher, the whole of life is a preparation for this better existence, and that the goals of philosophy can really be attained only then. Recalling his famous defence speech (recorded in Plato's *Apology*) before the Athenian jury that condemned him to death, Socrates promises to deliver this defence of his views in the form of a second defence speech (ἀπολογία), this time with his friends as the jury.

63b1

δίκαια ... λέγετε: 'what you're saying is just' – a pun, as he is about to call upon his friends to serve as a jury (63b4–5).

63b1–2

Socrates infers that Cebes and Simmias are asking him to answer their questions as a defendant in a court of law (ὥσπερ ἐν δικαστηρίῳ). Socrates is really putting this idea in their mouths; but the interlocutors are happy to run with it and join in the pretence of a second trial.

πρὸς ταῦτα ἀπολογήσασθαι: 'to defend myself against these (charges)'.

63b3

πάνυ μὲν οὖν: 'yes indeed', or the like. The phrase is a common response of agreement in Platonic dialogue.

63b4–5

Socrates promises to try to defend himself more convincingly than he did in his actual trial, which ended with his death sentence. The irony is that he is now speaking in defence of his own willingness to die.

φέρε δή: 'come on, then'. The phrase usually introduces some sort of exhortation.

ἦ δ' ὅς: 'he said', a common idiom for marking direct speech in a dialogue. 3rd sg. impf. ἠμί and demonstrative ὅς to change speakers.

πειραθῶ: 'let me try', a hortative subjunctive.

63b5–9

Socrates expects that on death, he will find himself in the care of other wise and good gods, and of people 'better than those here' (ἀμείνους τῶν ἐνθάδε, b8). This is a direct enough response to his friends' questions and starkly unsentimental at the prospect of their separation.

εἰ μὲν μὴ ᾤμην ἥξειν ... ἠδίκουν ἄν: one long present closed conditional. This first μέν is answered by the δέ at b9.

πρῶτον μέν is answered not by any δέ but by ἔπειτα καί: 'first into the company of other wise and good gods, and then ...'.

θεοὺς ἄλλους: Socrates leaves their identity vague, but we may presume them to be the chthonic gods (those of the underworld).

ἀνθρώπους τετελευτηκότας: 'people who are now dead' may best capture the sense of the perfect participle here (from τελευτάω, 'I die'). The Greek perfect is used when the author wishes to highlight the state that someone (or something) is now in, as a result of a past event. At the end of the *Apology*, Socrates had already described his excitement at the prospect of meeting and discussing famous dead Greeks, including Homer, Hesiod and various mythical mortals (*Apology* 41a6).

ἠδίκουν ἂν οὐκ ἀγανακτῶν: 'I would be unjust in that I am not aggrieved'. The negative οὐκ affirms that he is not in fact aggrieved (as against μή, which lends a conditional force to a participle). ἠδίκουν continues the imagery of the courtroom.

63b9–c4

Plato's Socrates is not in the habit of giving his opinions dogmatically, preferring to lead others to see the flaws in their own. Here, however, he must defend his own attitude towards death, something he cannot do without voicing some opinion. There is a touch of ironic, self-referential humour in his use of assertive language (εὖ ἴστε ὅτι, twice) amid his general tentativeness (ἐλπίζω) on whether he will gain the company of good masters and of other good men after death. Of the two, he feels more sure of getting the former, but does not say why.

παρ' ἄνδρας τε ἐλπίζω ἀφίξεσθαι ἀγαθούς: 'I hope I shall arrive in the company of good men.'

καὶ τοῦτο μὲν οὐκ ἂν πάνυ διισχυρισαίμην: 'and I would not assert this first thing (τοῦτο μέν) with full certainty'. The clause is balanced against the final clause of the sentence (διισχυρισαίμην ἂν καὶ τοῦτο), with τοῦτο μέν in the first answered by καὶ τοῦτο at the sentence's end. The contrast is illustrated further by the chiastic word order across the two clauses.

ὅτι μέντοι ... ἥξειν: the syntax requires a finite verb, and we should assume an ellipsis of a second ἐλπίζω ('however, that <I hope> I will come').

AS

εἴπερ τι ἄλλο τῶν τοιούτων: 'if (I will affirm) anything on such matters', i.e. on what he can expect after death.

63c4–5

ὥστε ... εὐελπίς εἰμι: the indicative after ὥστε is more rhetorically forceful than an infinitive, stressing the reality of the result.

εἶναί τι τοῖς τετελευτηκόσι: an indirect statement, 'that there is something (i.e., in store) for those who have died' – that is, some sort of afterlife.

63c6–7

ὥσπερ ... πάλαι λέγεται: 'as has long been said'. The present tense here stresses that it is still now being said. Socrates is hopeful that the afterlife will be 'better for the good than the bad'. Belief in reward and punishment in the afterlife was not a question all Greek agreed upon, but mythology furnishes enough examples of it for Socrates' claim here to hold good.

63c8–d3

Simmias jovially presses Socrates to explain his beliefs about the afterlife, saying that if he can persuade them, the explanation will serve as his real defence speech (σοι ἡ ἀπολογία ἔσται, d1).

63c8–9

τί οὖν ... ὦ Σώκρατες: the British idiom 'Hang on' may best capture the sense of Simmias' question. The 'what then' is inferential and is often used with impatient questions.

αὐτὸς ἔχων τὴν διάνοιαν ταύτην: 'keeping this thought to yourself'.

ἐν νῷ ἔχεις: 'have in mind', i.e. 'intend'.

ἢ κἂν ἡμῖν μεταδοίης: a potential optative, with ἄν, used to make a polite request ('or might you share it with us too?'). κἂν is a crasis of καί and ἄν. μεταδοίης is the 2sg. aor. opt. act. of μεταδίδωμι, 'I share'. Note the chiastic contrast between holding back and sharing.

63d1

κοινὸν ... καὶ ἡμῖν ἀγαθὸν: 'something we too could benefit from having in common'.

63d3

ἀλλὰ πειράσομαι: 'indeed I shall try'. For ἀλλὰ see 62c9 n.

63d3–e8

Socrates pauses his ἀπολογία to hear his friend Crito, who has a message from the executioner: if Socrates allows himself to get too animated, it will reduce the efficacy of the poison and he will need to take further doses. This brief episode lets us see that Plato's Socrates is no hypocrite: he really does not fear death, dismissing the warning in a carefree and cheerful manner. It is a moving scene. There is especial poignancy in the revelation that Crito had been waiting for some time, torn between his keenness to spare his friend considerable pain and his reluctance to interrupt the discussion.

63d3

Κρίτωνα τόνδε: 'Crito here'.

63d4

ὃ βούλεσθαί ... δοκεῖ πάλαι εἰπεῖν: 'that he has for a long while seemed to want to say'. On πάλαι with a present verb, see c6–7 n. The adverb need not mean 'in times of yore' but is also used of the relatively recent past.

63d5

τί δέ ... ἄλλο γε ἤ: properly a question ('What else but that ...?'), but better rendered as 'simply that ...'. Here it expresses some surprised and precedes a follow-up question.

63d6–7

χρή σοι φράζειν ὡς ἐλάχιστα διαλέγεσθαι: 'you should converse as little as possible'. In contrast with δεῖ, χρή is used to express a moral obligation. This is, then, kindly advice from the executioner.

63d7–9

φησὶ γὰρ θερμαίνεσθαι ... μᾶλλον διαλεγομένους: 'he says that people who talk rather a lot grow warm'. φησὶ here introduces a run of indirect statements, lasting until 63e2.

δεῖν δὲ οὐδὲν τοιοῦτον προσφέρειν τῷ φαρμάκῳ: 'and that one must not add anything of this kind to the drug'. For to do so would interfere with its function. τοιοῦτον here must refer to any such complicating behaviour. προσφέρω 'I add' takes a dative, after the fashion of uncompounded πρός + dat. 'in addition to'.

63e1–2

Crito continues to report the executioner's speech with accusative + infinitive.

εἰ δὲ μή: i.e. if this advice is not heeded, 'otherwise'.

63e3–4

ἔα ... χαίρειν αὐτόν: 'never mind about him', literally 'let him say goodbye'. χαίρειν ἐάω and χαίρειν λέγω, both 'I say goodbye to', are used of banishing thoughts from one's mind. The choice of expression lends some black humour, however, as Socrates knows they will see the executioner again soon enough.

τὸ ἑαυτοῦ παρασκευαζέτω: 'let him sort out his own equipment'. παρασκευαζέτω is a 3sg. active imperative.

ὡς ... δώσων: ὡς with future participle, expressing purpose.

63e6

σχεδὸν μέν τι ἤδη: 'I should have known' (lit. 'I almost knew something'). The μέν here has no corresponding δέ, though one might take ἀλλά in the next sentence as serving the same purpose.

AS

63e6–7

πάλαι πράγματα παρέχει: 'he has been bothering me for some time'.

63e8

ἔα αὐτόν: not 'let him', but an abbreviation of ἔα αὐτόν χαίρειν (see 63e3–4 n.).

63e8–9

ἀλλ' ... δή: 'but now'. The particle δή serves not just to emphasize the preceding word, but often marks a transition to a new topic. Socrates now resumes his prior discussion where he left off.

ὑμῖν ... τοῖς δικασταῖς: in apposition, 'to you as my jurors'.

βούλομαι ἤδη τὸν λόγον ἀποδοῦναι: 'I want now to give the account that is due'. ἀποδίδωμι is used of giving or returning something owed.

ὡς here introduces the topic of the λόγος, rather than the λόγος itself – that a man who has spent his life engaged in philosophy can expect to win great rewards when he dies.

63e9–10

φαίνεται εἰκότως ... θαρρεῖν: 'seems to have good reason to be confident'. θαρρέω has no single-word equivalent in English, but is used as an opposite to φοβέομαι.

ἀνὴρ ... διατρίψας τὸν βίον: 'a man who has spent his life'. διατρίβω 'I rub' is used metaphorically to mean 'I spend time'.

τῷ ὄντι: 'in reality', an adverbial idiom common in Plato's early and middle works.

63e10–64a1

μέλλων ἀποθανεῖσθαι: μέλλω + fut. inf. means 'I am about to', 'I intend to' or less often, 'I hesitate to'. Only the first of these senses really works here; but in working this out, the reader is forced to reflect on the attitude of the person described.

εὔελπις εἶναι: the phrase (again at 64a1) lends opportunity for variety alongside ἐλπίζειν, but also the added connotations of the adjective εὔελπις, which means both 'helpful' and 'cheerful'.

οἴσεσθαι: fut. inf. from φέρω, which in the middle has the sense 'I win'.

64a2

ἐπειδὰν τελευτήσῃ: an indefinite, reflecting our uncertainty about when any person is going to die. As the indefinite often also suggests a repeated event ('whenever he dies') the phrase acts as a forward reference to the doctrine of reincarnation that Socrates will later espouse (77a–d).

πῶς ἂν ... οὕτως ἔχοι: 'how this might be the case', an indirect question with potential optative (ἂν ... ἔχοι). On οὕτως ἔχειν see 62d2 n.

64a4–6

Socrates introduces the idea that those who practise philosophy are really 'in the business of dying and being dead'. What exactly this means and why Socrates thinks it are the focus of the rest of his ἀπολογία.

AS

κινδυνεύουσι ... λεληθέναι τοὺς ἄλλους ὅτι: 'it may be that other people are unaware that they ...'. It is often better to render λανθάνω 'I escape the notice of (acc.)' with the subject and object reversed ('[acc.] does not notice'). The negation of its perfect '[acc.] has not noticed/is unaware' is often used as a substitute for οἶδα. κινδυνεύουσι 'they run the risk of' (i.e. 'it is possible that they') is an ironic understatement here: there is surely no chance that anyone, Socrates excepted, has ever thought (let alone noticed) that philosophers are mostly concerned with dying and being dead.

ὅσοι: usually best rendered with 'all those who'.

τοὺς ἄλλους: 'the other people', i.e. 'everyone else'.

οὐδὲν ἄλλο ... ἢ: 'nothing other than', i.e. 'exclusively'.

ἐπιτηδεύουσιν: this verb means 'practise' not in the sense of developing a skill but as in applying it (as in 'I practise medicine'), i.e. making it one's business.

ἀποθνῄσκειν τε καὶ τεθνάναι: both infinitives are objects of ἐπιτηδεύουσιν. Philosophers are busying themselves with the process of dying (present infinitive) and the condition of being dead (perfect infinitive). As Socrates will explain, true philosophers want to get as close as possible to this state, so they may be best prepared for it when it comes.

64a7–9

If this is really the business of philosophers, they will surely not be aggrieved when the time comes to die.

64a7

δήπου: 'surely'. Though originally the particle expressed some doubt (as a compound of που 'I suppose'), Socrates uses it with a touch of irony to state strong claims.

64a8

ἥκοντος δὲ δὴ αὐτοῦ: genitive absolute, 'but when it has finally (δή) come' (i.e. death).

64a10

ὁ Σιμμίας γελάσας: Simmias' laughter creates a dramatic change in the tone. It is a hint that Socrates' good mood may be proving infectious.

64b1

οὐ πάνυ γε ... γελασείοντα: 'though not at all in the mood for laughing'. Verbs ending in -σείω belong to a class called desideratives, which express actions their subject wants to do.

64b2

ἄν: belongs with δοκεῖν, in an indirect statement after οἶμαι: 'I think most people (τοὺς πολλοὺς) ... would think'. δοκέω here is in its personal sense, 'I think'.

64b2–3

εὖ πάνυ εἰρῆσθαι εἰς τοὺς φιλοσοφοῦντας: another indirect statement, dependent on δοκεῖν: 'that this is spot on about those who do philosophy'.

εἰρῆσθαι is an impersonal perfect passive from λέγω and is followed by ὅτι at b4, after a parenthesis.

64b3–4

συμφάναι ἂν τοὺς μὲν παρ᾽ ἡμῖν ἀνθρώπους καὶ πάνυ: 'people where we come from (παρ᾽ ἡμῖν) would very much agree': another indirect statement dependent on οἶμαι (b1). It is this joke that has made Simmias laugh: he and Cebes are from Thebes, whose citizens were stereotyped as disinclined to intellectual activity and rather slow-witted. Thebans, he quips, would readily see philosophers as having a deathwish – something for which Socrates offers a good precedent. Besides, philosophers (as Socrates presents them) have no interest in any of the pleasures typically associated with a good life. In making their lives hardly lives at all, they are, in that sense too, closer to being dead.

ἀνθρώπους: the noun often has a faintly derogatory sense, as (presumably) here. Compare the similar English use of 'individual' and 'person'.

64b4

οἱ φιλοσοφοῦντες: those who do philosophy, i.e. philosophers. By using the participle rather than the noun φιλόσοφος, Plato keeps our attention on what they do, and not just what they are labelled as being. Plato will vary this expression several times in the *Phaedo*.

θανατῶσι: θανατάω can mean either 'I wish to die' or simply 'I am going to die'.

64b5–6

σφᾶς γε οὐ λελήθασιν: 'they are well aware'. On λανθάνω rendered thus, see 64a4–6 n. Simmias is merely relaying what he thinks the Thebans would say, and not implying that he feels the same way (as 'are aware' might imply). σφεῖς (acc. σφᾶς, gen. σφῶν, dat. σφίσι) is a 3 pl. pronoun common in prose and verse of most kinds.

ἄξιοί εἰσιν τοῦτο πάσχειν: 'they deserve to suffer this'. The joke is presumably that philosophers are a nuisance to those who do not share their inclinations (such as the stereotypical Theban philistine).

64b7–8

πλήν γε τοῦ σφᾶς ... μὴ λεληθέναι: 'except, that is, the bit about them being aware'.

64b8–9

The imaginary Thebans, Socrates says, do not know in what way philosophers are ready for death, how it is they deserve death or the sort of death they deserve. He himself will directly address only the first of these questions before he dies.

ᾗ: adverbial, 'in what way'.

οἵου θανάτου: 'of what sort of death [they are worthy]'.

64c1

εἴπωμεν ... πρὸς ἡμᾶς αὐτούς: εἴπωμεν is a hortative subjunctive, 'let us speak amongst ourselves'.

χαίρειν εἰπόντες: see 63e3–4 n.

64c2–9

Having dismissed the imaginary Thebans, Socrates feels ready to the more serious philosophical business of his ἀπολογία. He and Simmias begin by defining death as the total separation of the soul from the body, and vice versa. What exactly Socrates means by 'the soul' is left open for now: this will be addressed at 69e–70b.

64c2

ἡγούμεθά τι τὸν θάνατον εἶναι: 'do we think there is such a thing as death?' It is Socrates' standard practice to get his interlocutors to agree on some fundamental points at the beginning of a discussion.

64c4–5

ἆρα μὴ ἄλλο τι ἤ: 'surely it (i.e. death) is nothing other than'. ἆρα μή introduces a yes/no question that assumes the answer 'no'. Socrates will give Simmias only one option to assent to.

τὴν ... ἀπαλλαγήν: see 63a5–7 n.

καὶ εἶναι τοῦτο τὸ τεθνάναι: 'and that the state of having died is this'. Socrates continues to speak in acc. + inf. indirect statements, following ἡγούμεθά (c2). The perfect infinitive emphasizes that he is asking about the state of being dead (or having died), rather than the event (aorist) or the process (present).

64c5–8

In the form of an inviting question, Socrates suggests that to be dead equates to the body coming to be 'by itself, separated from the soul' and the soul being 'by itself, separated from the body'. The two requirements really entail each other; giving both merely serves to drive the point home that the two must become utterly separate.

ἀπαλλαγὲν ... ἀπαλλαγεῖσαν: both aor. past. participles from ἀπαλλάττω (on which see, 63a5–7 n.).

αὐτὸ καθ᾽ αὑτὸ: 'by itself on its own'. αὐτό = ἑαυτό, i.e. the very thing in its essence and 'unmixed' (this will be important later). Key philosophical vocabulary. Plato often combines an intensive (αὐτός) and reflexive (ἑαυτοῦ) to denote separation. The phrase is already pleonastic, as αὐτός alone often means 'by oneself'. But along with χωρὶς 'separately' and ἀπὸ τῆς ψυχῆς ἀπαλλαγὲν 'separated from the soul', the phrase is even more emphatically pleonastic.

64c8

ἆρα μὴ ἄλλο τι ἢ ὁ θάνατος ἢ τοῦτο: 'death can't be anything other than this, can it?' ἆρα μή expects the answer 'no', while the subjunctive ἢ after μή adds a note of caution to the assertion.

AS

64c10

σκέψαι δή: 'consider this, then': an object must be supplied for the imperative.

ὠγαθέ: an affectionate crasis of ὦ and the vocative ἀγαθέ.

ἐὰν ἄρα καὶ σοὶ συνδοκῇ ἅπερ ἐμοί: 'in case, after all (ἄρα), you too will share my view'. This is not an indirect question (which would require εἰ with indicative) nor an open condition, but a distinct use of εἰ/ἐάν used to present the motive for the action in the main clause ('in case', 'in the hope that'): Smyth § 2354.

ἅπερ ἐμοί: we must assume the previous verb again (συνδοκῇ) in ellipsis. On ἅπερ, see 62d5–6 n.

64d1

μᾶλλον οἶμαι ἡμᾶς εἴσεσθαι περὶ ὧν σκοποῦμεν: 'I think we will gain knowledge about the things we are looking into'. μᾶλλον modifies εἴσεσθαι (future infinitive of οἶδα). The case of the relative ὧν should strictly be accusative, given its role in its clause as the direct object of σκοποῦμεν, but with no antecedent for the preposition περί to govern, it is dragged by the preposition περί into the genitive case, a common phenomenon called the attraction of the relative.

64d2

φιλοσόφου ἀνδρὸς εἶναι: εἰμί + gen. means 'belong to', or better here, 'be characteristic of'.

64d2–3

ἐσπουδακέναι περί: 'to busy themselves with', the perfect infinitive (of σπουδάζω) implying established and lasting behaviour. This infinitive phrase is the subject of the sentence.

τὰς ἡδονὰς καλουμένας τὰς τοιάσδε: 'the so-called pleasures, such as the following'. τοιόσδε ('such as this'), like ὅδε ('this') and ὧδε ('thus'), tends to point ahead to what it refers. καλουμένας suggests that they are not 'true' pleasures (at least not to a philosopher).

64d2–3

οἷον σιτίων καὶ ποτῶν: 'for example, [the pleasures] of food and drink'. Plato often uses adverbial οἷον to introduce a set of one or more examples.

64d5

ἥκιστα: like the Latin *minime*, this superlative adverb can simply mean 'no', as here. It may surprise us that Simmias is so ready to join Socrates in denying the true philosopher any share in bodily pleasures. It is easy to see that philosophers should not overindulge in these, but why they should not enjoy them even in moderation is never explained.

64d6

τί δὲ τὰς τῶν ἀφροδισίων: 'what about those (the pleasures) of sex?'.

AS

64d7

οὐδαμῶς: 'no way'. From now on, Phaedo will only sometimes include a phrase meaning 'he said', leaving it to us to deduce when one speaker takes over from another. With Simmias rarely saying more than brief phrases of assent in this passage, this poses little difficulty to the reader.

64d8

τὰς περὶ τὸ σῶμα θεραπείας: 'the other attendances to bodily needs'.

64d9

ἐντίμους: 'of value', f. acc. pl. agreeing with θεραπείας. Being a compound, ἔντιμος is a two-termination adjective (its m. and f. endings are the same).

ὁ τοιοῦτος: 'someone of this sort', i.e. a philosopher.

64d9–10

οἷον ἱματίων διαφερόντων κτήσεις καὶ ὑποδημάτων: 'for example, the owning of fancy clothes and shoes'. The base meaning of διαφέρω is 'I differ', but it has the extended sense 'I excel' (compare the English 'distinguished'). A philosopher need not go naked or unshod, but will take no pleasure in owning finery. The sentence's main verb (δοκεῖ) is delayed until d11.

64d11

πότερον τιμᾶν δοκεῖ σοι ἢ ἀτιμάζειν: πότερον ... ἢ articulate a direct question with two alternatives ('do you think he values them or holds them in no regard?') ἀτιμάζω implies rather stronger disapproval than just οὐ τιμάω.

64e1

καθ' ὅσον μὴ πολλὴ ἀνάγκη μετέχειν αὐτῶν: 'insofar as there is not a great necessity to take part in them', i.e. beyond what is absolutely necessary. ἐστι is omitted as obvious. αὐτῶν refers back to the θεραπείας of d8.

μετέχειν : Key philosophical vocabulary. Plato often uses this verb to describe the relationship between an object and a form. For example, the number three is odd because three participates in or shares in (μετέχει) the form oddness. The nature of the participation of objects with forms is a subject of scholarly debate.

64e2

ἀτιμάζειν ἔμοιγε δοκεῖ: it may surprise us that Simmias is so ready to join Socrates in denying the true philosopher any share in things that bring the body pleasure beyond what is necessary for survival. It is easy to see that philosophers should not overindulge in these, but why they should not enjoy them even in moderation is never explained.

64e4–6

Socrates now casts the philosopher as one who concerns himself as much as possible with the soul and as little as possible with the body.

AS

64e4

οὐκοῦν ... δοκεῖ σοι: 'don't you think ...?' οὐκοῦν, accentuated thus, introduces a question inviting the answer 'yes'.

ἡ τοῦ τοιούτου πραγματεία: 'the business of someone like this'. πραγματεία here has a different sense from that at 63a1 (diligent effort).

64e5

καθ᾽ ὅσον δύναται: 'as much as it can'.

64e6

ἀφεστάναι αὐτοῦ, πρὸς δὲ τὴν ψυχὴν τετράφθαι: 'to stand apart from it (the body), and to have turned himself to face the soul'. This is the first of many occasions in the dialogue in which mental activity is expressed through markedly physical metaphors. The incongruity presses the reader to think through the distinction between the mental and the bodily. Both ἀφεστάναι (intransitive, from ἀφίστημι) and τετράφθαι (reflexive middle, from τρέπω) are perfect infinitives with present force.

64e8–65a2

ἆρ᾽ ... δῆλός ἐστιν ὁ φιλόσοφος ἀπολύων: 'is it clear that the philosopher frees'. δῆλός ἐστι is typically followed by a dependent participle. ἀπολύω is rich in appropriate connotations, meaning not just 'set free' but 'acquit' (of a legal charge), 'ransom' (both active and middle) and 'pay off' (of a debt of mortgage).

ὅτι μάλιστα: 'as much as possible', as often when ὅτι is followed by a superlative see 62e1–2 n.

διαφερόντως: here 'to a greater degree than', though originally 'differently from' (see 64d9–10 n.), followed by a genitive of separation.

65a3

φαίνεται: 'evidently', assuming ἀπολύων (a1) as its complement. While φαίνομαι with the infinitive means 'I appear' (and may or may not be), with a participle the verb has the stronger sense 'I am clearly'.

65a4–7

Socrates presumes, not without plausibility, that the ascetic life of his true philosopher would not strike most people as much of a life.

δοκεῖ γέ που ... τοῖς πολλοῖς ἀνθρώποις ... οὐκ ἄξιον εἶναι ζῆν: 'I suppose at least most people think it is not worth it to be alive.'

65a5

ᾧ μηδὲν ἡδὺ τῶν τοιούτων: '[someone] for whom there is nothing pleasurable in such things'. It is common in Greek for the antecedent of a relative clause to be left out. (It is this that creates the need for attraction of the relative: see 64d1 n.)

μηδὲ μετέχει αὐτῶν: the subject now changes to the referent of ᾧ, 'and does not partake of them'.

AS

65a6

ἀλλ᾽ ἐγγύς τι τείνειν τοῦ τεθνάναι: we must supply δοκεῖ again, this time with ὁ μηδὲν φροντίζων ('the one who thinks nothing of') as its subject. ἐγγύς τι τείνειν 'to skirt rather close to' is an ironically dynamic metaphor drawn from the domain of horse- and chariot-racing. τοῦ τεθνάναι is genitive after ἐγγύς. The perfect infinitive again serves to pinpoint a state (being dead), rather than the event or process of dying. Hackforth's translation 'to have one foot in the grave' captures the sense well.

65a7

τῶν ἡδονῶν αἱ διὰ τοῦ σώματός εἰσιν: i.e. those which are had by means of the body: διά with the genitive can mean 'through' in the sense of instrument or manner, as well as of time or space.

65a9–c1

Socrates advances an idea that will be central to his following argument, that the bodily senses are of no help in our acquisition of knowledge, but without exception hinder it. That Simmias needs no persuading on the matter may shock us. This is not because the senses were generally held in so little regard at the time. Rather, Plato must be keen to have Socrates plough on through his main argument with as little interruption as is necessary.

65a9

φρονήσεως: a synonym of σοφία ('wisdom, learning') in Plato, and hence the prime goal of all philosophical endeavour.

65a10

ἐμπόδιον τὸ σῶμα: 'the body is in the way', i.e. a hindrance. Taken literally, ἐμπόδιος ('at one's feet') is neatly paradoxical – for how can one's body lie at one's feet when the feet are part of it? In processing the phrase, the reader is prompted to reflect further on the relationship between body and soul.

65a10–b1

ἐάν τις αὐτὸ ἐν τῇ ζητήσει κοινωνὸν συμπαραλαμβάνῃ: 'if someone should bring it (i.e. the body) along with them as a companion in their search [for wisdom]'. The description makes sense only if we identify our true selves as being our souls alone, and not body and soul together. Socrates is encouraging us to take precisely this perspective, a vital step if we are to sympathize with the arguments ahead.

οἷον τὸ τοιόνδε λέγω: 'I mean something along the following lines.' οἷον is adverbial and τὸ τοιόνδε the direct object of λέγω.

65b2–3

τά γε τοιαῦτα καὶ οἱ ποιηταὶ ἀεὶ θρυλοῦσιν: 'are the poets too not always going on about such things (τὰ τοιαῦτα)'? The ungenerous verb θρυλέω 'babble' is ironic here, as their opinion chimes with Socrates' own.

AS

65b3–4

οὔτ' ἀκούομεν ἀκριβὲς οὐδὲν οὔτε ὁρῶμεν: one surviving line of the comic playwright and philosopher Epicharmus comes close to the sentiment: νοῦς ὁρῇ καὶ νοῦς ἀκούει· τἆλλα κωφὰ καὶ τυφλά ('the mind sees and the mind hears; all other [organs] are deaf and blind', Diels-Kranz 23 B 2). Plato often has Socrates quote lines of poetry directly, and it may be that these words are a rough paraphrase of a specific line (the iambic/trochaic character of, e.g. οὐδὲν οὔθ' ὁρῶμεν may hint at the metre).

65b4–5

αὗται τῶν περὶ τὸ σῶμα αἰσθήσεων: 'these of the body's senses', i.e. sight and sound. περί here has the same sense as διά at a7.

65b5

σχολῇ: 'hardly' (lit. 'with leisure').

65b9

τῆς ἀληθείας ἅπτεται: 'takes hold of' or 'grasps' the truth. Unlike the comparable English 'grasp', which is a dead metaphor (i.e. one so common that it is hardly treated as one in conversation), the Greek ἅπτομαι makes for a more striking bodily metaphor for mental activity. Like many middle verbs of grasping (e.g. λαμβάνομαι), ἅπτομαι takes a genitive.

65b9–10

ὅταν ... ἐπιχειρῇ τι σκοπεῖν: 'whenever it (the soul) tries to examine something'. The indefinite construction adds an important emphasis: there is never any situation in which the bodily senses grant us access to knowledge.

65b11

ἐξαπατᾶται: 'is deceived, seduced'. The metaphor adds a touch of the sinister, underscoring the harmful influence of the body on the soul.

65c1

We may again feel surprise at Simmias' readiness to deny the senses any role in apprehending truth, and simply must not want to interrupt Socrates' flow. (See 65a9–c1 n.)

65c2

ἆρ' ... οὐκ: in contrast to ἆρα μή, ἆρα οὐκ introduces a direct question expecting the answer 'yes'.

ἐν τῷ λογίζεσθαι: 'in the activity of reasoning'. λογίζομαι and its noun λογισμός are used both of mathematical calculation and of other forms of pure thinking.

εἴπερ που ἄλλοθι: 'if anywhere else at all'. On -περ see 62d5–6. που here is not the particle ('I suppose') but the indefinite correlative ('somewhere') of the question-word ποῦ; ('where?').

AS

65c2–3

κατάδηλον αὐτῇ γίγνεταί τι τῶν ὄντων: 'a part of reality comes to be manifest to it (the soul)'. In Plato, τὰ ὄντα – literally 'the things that are (or exist)' – and its singular τὸ ὄν serve to mean 'reality' and 'the truth' (compare τῷ ὄντι: see 63e9–10 n.). Note the κατά- used for emphasis.

65c5–9

One might then assume that the soul does its best pure thinking (λογίζεται κάλλιστα) when the body presents no distracting sense or sensation, and the soul can be as separate from it as possible.

65c6

παραλυπῇ: 'troubles it besides'. The verb expresses a grievance or distraction on top of some other issue – here, presumably, the effort of thinking.

65c6–7

μηδέ τις ἡδονή: 'and not even any pleasure'. μηδέ/οὐδέ, which like καί can have a further adverbial force ('not even'), here highlights pleasure as a surprising final component in the list of distractions. On reflection, however, Socrates' audience will recall that he had begun his argument by showing how little philosophers will care for most sources of bodily pleasure (64d2–3).

65c7–8

ἐῶσα χαίρειν τὸ σῶμα: 'saying goodbye to the body'. Socrates has used similar phrases shortly before (63e3: see n.) of dismissing his executioner and the imagined worldly Thebans (64c1); the echo here helps us see the link between leaving his earthly state and engaging purely in philosophy.

65c8–9

μὴ κοινωνοῦσα αὐτῷ μηδ' ἁπτομένη: 'not having it (the body) as its partner and not fastening itself to it'. Taken at face value, the second participle already suggests that the philosopher's soul should ideally be no longer even connected with the body – a state which Simmias and Socrates had already agreed on to be death (64c4–9).

65c9

ὀρέγηται τοῦ ὄντος: 'reaches out after reality', another metaphor, an action of the body used to describe the activity of the soul.

65c10

ἔστι ταῦτα: 'this is true'. Plato often uses εἶναι in a so-called 'veridical' sense ('to be true'), as well as the existential ('to be real'). Many arguments in his works hinge on the intersection of these senses.

AS

65d3

φαίνεται: the strength of Simmias' assent is ambiguous: whether his reply means 'so it seems' or 'obviously' would depend on whether an infinitive or participle is assumed to depend upon it (see 65a3 n.).

65d4–e5

Socrates and Simmias agree that certain things exist that we do not know through the senses, and for which only reasoning is of any use. It is to this category that the main interests of the philosophers belong, such as justice, beauty and goodness. Although Greek has its own abstract nouns for such things, Plato avoids them here, to encourage us to reflect with more care on the aspects of reality he wishes to pinpoint. This produces Greek that is difficult to translate, but that a thoughtful modern reader should still find easy enough to follow. On the passage's relation to Plato's later Theory of Forms, see introduction, pp. 79–80.

65d4–5

τί δὲ δὴ τὰ τοιάδε: 'what, then, about things such as the following?'

φαμέν τι εἶναι δίκαιον αὐτὸ ἢ οὐδέν: 'do we say there exists something that is itself right, or is there no such thing?' In other words, is there something that is right *and nothing else* – i.e. rightness (or justice) itself?

65d6

φαμὲν μέντοι νὴ Δία: 'indeed we do, by Zeus'. The particle μέντοι often adds emphasis to a word repeated as the answer to a yes/no question, as here. By now the reader is used to Simmias' ready assent even on questions which to them may raise an eyebrow. Here, however, we should note that the claim Socrates is suggesting sounds especially convincing to a speaker of Greek, who is more used than us to using adjectives in lieu of nouns (e.g. τὸ δίκαιον).

65d7

καὶ αὖ καλόν γέ τι καὶ ἀγαθόν: 'and again, [is there] something [that is in itself] beautiful, and [something that is in itself] good?' The Greek is elliptical, but the sense is clear.

65d9

ἤδη οὖν πώποτέ τι τῶν τοιούτων τοῖς ὀφθαλμοῖς εἶδες: 'well now, have you ever seen any of these with your eyes?' Socrates' pleonasm makes it clear that ὁράω is meant literally: he is asking Simmias why he is ready to assent to there being such things as the beautiful and the good even though he has never actually seen them.

65d11–12

ἄλλη τινὶ αἰσθήσει ... ἐφήψω αὐτῶν: 'have you laid hold of them (i.e. such things) using any other sense?' ἐφήψω is 2sg. aor. mid. of ἐφάπτομαι, which expresses a slightly more forceful action than the uncompounded verb.

65d12–e4

Socrates now asks if the same is not true of such things as size, health, strength and everything else that counts as 'real'. We might think we understand something like size based on sensory information; but Socrates is talking not about big and small things but about size itself, divorced from the objects that exemplify it. For Socrates, the only things that deserve to be called 'real' are such things as size itself, health itself and so on: on this outlook, see introduction, pp. 79–80.

65d12

λέγω δὲ περὶ πάντων, οἷον μεγέθους πέρι: 'I'm talking about everything – about size, for example'. μέγεθος is strictly speaking 'bigness', the property of things that are big (in English we would say that small things have size, but they do not μέγεθος). As its accent reveals, πέρι is postpositional, governing μεγέθους (contrast the prepositional form περί, with accent on the second syllable). Though postpositional, the following string of genitives (ὑγιείας ... ἁπάντων) also depend on πέρι.

65d13

τῶν ἄλλων ἑνὶ λόγῳ ἁπάντων τῆς οὐσίας: 'in short, [about] the reality of every single other thing'. ἑνὶ λόγῳ does not quite match the English idiom 'in a word' (λόγος generally is not used of a single word), but really means 'in one short utterance'. ἅπας is a somewhat more emphatic form of πᾶς 'all, every'. Plato's first readers might expect οὐσία to mean 'property' (its more usual sense) rather than 'reality', as here. But, as an abstract noun derived from a participle stem of εἰμί, it must have appealed to Plato as a fitting synonym for τὰ ὄντα.

65d13–e1

ὃ τυγχάνει ἕκαστον ὄν: 'what each thing is'. The clause is added, presumably, to clarify Plato's more philosophically technical use of οὐσία (see previous n.).
As the LSJ points out, τυγχάνω often 'cannot be translated at all', especially with a participle of εἰμί. In such instances, τυγχάνω seems nonetheless to stress that the action of the participle really happens or happened ('I actually am').

65e1–2

αὐτῶν τὸ ἀληθέστατον θεωρεῖται: 'the full truth of them is beheld' (Hackforth). θεωρέω is used variously of spectators at events, of people contemplating and of people theorizing. In all cases the verb communicates some lasting effort.
ἢ ὧδε ἔχει: 'or is it as follows'. On the construction, see 62d2 n. Since the first option (that we learn about such things through the body's senses) is plainly wrong in Socrates' eyes, we know that what follows will be his real opinion.

65e2–3

ὃς ἂν ἡμῶν παρασκευάσηται: 'whichever of us has prepared himself'. The verb is a reflexive middle.
μάλιστα ... καὶ ἀκριβέστατα αὐτὸ ἕκαστον διανοηθῆναι: the adverbs modify the infinitive, and not παρασκευάσηται: 'to think especially and most precisely of each thing by itself' (αὐτό). διανοηθῆναι is passive in form but middle in

meaning ('to think of, have in mind'). It will be worthwhile to note the various superlatives used in this passage.

65e4

περὶ οὗ σκοπεῖ: '(each thing) he is investigating about'. On the attraction of the relative, see 64d1 n.

οὗτος ἂν ἐγγύτατα ἴοι τοῦ γνῶναι ἕκαστον: 'this person would come closest to knowing each thing': for Socrates will go on to claim that we must be utterly rid of the body, i.e. dead, to actually get there.

ἴοι is 3sg. pres. opt. act. of εἶμι 'I shall go', a metaphor more strikingly physical in the Greek than in the English, where it is commonplace. γνῶναι is the aor. act. infinitive ('to have come to know' = to know). The repetition of ἕκαστον stresses that the person would come close to gaining knowledge of specific things, rather than being more generally knowledgeable.

65e6

καθαρώτατα: 'most purely'. The adverb, rich in religious connotations of ritual cleansing, may strike the first-time reader as a surprising choice here, with no precedent so far in the dialogue. However, the idea of purity, and in particular the importance of the soul's purity from the body, will loom large over the following discussion (69c–d: see introduction, pp. 80–82).

65e6–7

ὅστις ὅτι μάλιστα αὐτῇ τῇ διανοίᾳ ἴοι ἐφ' ἕκαστον: 'whoever approaches each thing as far as possible through thought alone' (αὐτῇ, '(by) itself'). ὅστις introduces an indefinite construction with optative (ἴοι) and no ἄν, as the main verb (ποιήσειεν), though optative too, is still in a historic tense. διανοίᾳ is dat. of means.

65e–66a1

μήτε τιν' ὄψιν παρατιθέμενος: 'neither serving oneself a side helping of sight' may capture the whimsical sense of παρατίθεμαι, a verb whose principal use is of food.

ἐν τῷ διανοεῖσθαι: 'while he has [it] in mind', with ἐν here expressing either time or condition.

μήτε ἄλλην αἴσθησιν ἐφέλκων μηδεμίαν: 'nor dragging along behind him any other sense'. The metaphor captures perfectly the impediment that Socrates sees the body's senses to be.

μετὰ τοῦ λογισμοῦ: 'along with his reasoning'.

65a2–3

ἀλλ' ἕκαστον ἐπιχειροῖ θηρεύειν τῶν ὄντων: the indefinite construction after ὅστις (65e6) continues: 'but attempts to hunt each of the things that exist'. ἐπιχειρέω and θηρεύω are more ironically physical metaphors for striving after incorporeal things: the former is really 'I try my hand (χείρ) at' and the latter used of hunting wild beasts (θῆρες).

εἰλικρινεῖ τῇ διανοίᾳ χρώμενος: 'using undiluted thought'. χράομαι 'I use' is followed by a dative. εἰλικρινής originally is 'pure' as in 'unmixed', without the religious connotations of καθαρός.

65a3–5

ἀπαλλαγεὶς ... ὡς ἔπος εἰπεῖν σύμπαντος τοῦ σώματος: 'having been set free from ... almost the entire body'. ὡς ἔπος εἰπεῖν 'so to speak' is used to discourage the reader from taking a statement too literally (e.g. οὐδεὶς ὡς ἔπος εἰπεῖν = 'almost nobody'). Here the phrase reminds us that Socrates is talking about philosophers who are still alive – since being fully set free from the body would mean being dead (64c4–9).

65a5–6

ὡς ταράττοντος καὶ οὐκ ἐῶντος τὴν ψυχήν: ὡς here is causal, and both participles haveτὴν ψυχὴν as object: 'since [the body] confuses and does not allow the soul ...'.

65a7–8

ἀρ' οὐχ οὗτός ἐστιν ... εἴπερ τις ἄλλος ὁ τευξόμενος τοῦ ὄντος: 'surely this is the man who will hit upon what is real, if anyone [will]'. With a genitive object, τυγχάνω means 'I light upon', 'meet' or 'obtain', all of which work here. τευξόμενος is its future participle (always middle). On τοῦ ὄντος, see 65c2–3 n.

66b1–67b4 – the testimony of the True Philosophers

Socrates now summarizes all he has said about the obstacles humans face in obtaining knowledge during their lifetime. He does this in the voice of some imaginary true philosophers, who describe in first person their plight as they labour under their cruel master, the body. It is a colourful and forceful piece of rhetoric which aside from its role as summary serves two purposes: it will be the strongest piece of evidence in Socrates' ἀπολογία for why any good philosopher, himself included, can expect to be much better off when he is dead and free of the body. In this respect his True Philosophers recall the witnesses that litigants at trial in Athens would invoke in support of their cases. The philosophers also offer Socrates a mouthpiece through which he may speak with uncharacteristic assertiveness: for while his preferred method is to explore arguments by questioning others (the elenchus: see introduction, p. 76), his fictional philosophers are free to speak as they wish.

66b1–2

ἀνάγκη ... τοῖς γνησίως φιλοσόφοις: 'it is necessary for those who are genuinely philosophers'. The original sense of γνήσιος, an adjective cognate with γένος, is 'born within wedlock, legitimate'. Note Plato's variation of phrase for those who 'truly' philosophize.

AS

ἐκ πάντων τούτων: 'from [i.e. based on] all this, it is necessary ...'.

παρίστασθαι δόξαν τοιάνδε τινά: 'to bring forward some opinion such as the following'. παρίσταμαι (transitive middle) is used in a legal context to mean 'bring forward', of witnesses and of other evidence.

66b2–3

ὥστε καὶ πρὸς ἀλλήλους τοιαῦτα ἄττα λέγειν: 'so that they say some such things, to each other too'. ἄττα is an alternate for τινά. The vagueness of τοιάνδε τινὰ (b2) and τοιαῦτα ἄττα (b3) makes it clear that the direct speech that follows is a product of Socrates' imagination.

66b3–5

κινδυνεύει ... ἐκφέρειν ἡμᾶς ... ὅτι: the subject of this complex clause is ὅτι 'that'. It is therefore simplest to reverse passive and active in our translation thus: 'it seems likely that, as if by some path, we are being led by the opinion that ...'.

ὥσπερ ἀτραπός τις: the point of the simile is presumably that the opinion they are about to give follows directly from what comes before. That the path of the simile is 'leading us out' (ἐκφέρειν) calls to mind the state of perplexity or ἀπορία (lit. 'having no way out') that Socrates' conversations often leave people in. In contrast to having no way, the True Philosophers follow a clear path.

66b5

συμπεφυρμένη ᾖ: perfect passive subjunctive of συμφυράω 'I mix (or knead) up with'. This state of the soul is opposite to its being εἰλικρινής or καθαρός. In this particular metaphor it is striking that the soul almost takes on a physical existence.

τοιούτου κακοῦ: 'such a base thing', i.e. the body.

66b6

οὐ μή ποτε κτησώμεθα: 'we will never acquire'. οὐ μή with an aorist subjunctive expresses an especially forceful denial.

66b7

φαμὲν δὲ τοῦτο εἶναι τὸ ἀληθές: Socrates is plainly relishing the opportunity to speak forthrightly, or at least to create as strong a contrast as possible with his usual manner.

66b7–8

μυρίας ... ἀσχολίας: 'countless jobs to do'. An ἀσχολία is any distraction from σχολή, leisure time within which one may pursue philosophy. Note the continued exaggeration; μυρίας is in effect here another superlative.

66b8–c1

διὰ τὴν ἀναγκαίαν τροφήν: Socrates had told us that a philosopher will scorn bodily attendances beyond those that are absolutely necessary: every living person must eat, drink and sleep, for instance. The suggestion here, however, is that even these basic requirements get in the way of philosophy.

66c1

ἄν τινες νόσοι προσπέσωσιν: 'if ever some diseases befall us', protasis of an indefinite present condition (ἄν here is a contraction of ἐάν).

ἐμποδίζουσιν ἡμῶν ... τὴν θήραν: 'they get in the way of our hunt'. Socrates has used both metaphors in his own speech: see 65a10 and 66a2–3 nn.

66c2–4

ἐρώτων ... καὶ φλυαρίας ἐμπίμπλησιν ἡμᾶς πολλῆς: 'it [the body] fills us with desires ... and a great deal of foolishness'. πίμπλημι and its compounds are followed by an accusative (the thing filled) and a genitive (that with which it is filled). ἔρωτες need not be, but are generally, sexual desires – hence the inclusion of ἐπιθυμίαι (appetites more generally) in the list too. ἡμᾶς here must refer to the philosophers' souls only.

εἰδώλων παντοδαπῶν: 'all sorts of images', or 'fantasies'. Given Socrates' hostility even to the sense of sight, these are presumably recollections of things we have seen that distract us from our pure reasoning.

66c4–5

ὥστε ... οὐδὲ φρονῆσαι ἡμῖν ἐγγίγνεται οὐδέποτε οὐδέν: 'so that it is not even (οὐδέ) possible for us to think about anything ever'. The multiple negatives drive home the point. The indicative after ὥστε, too, emphasizes the reality of the result. Emphatic positioning of οὐδέποτε οὐδέν.

τὸ λεγόμενον: 'as is said', an accusative of respect. The words do not match up with any known saying, and it may just be a humorous fancy of Socrates' to pretend that philosophers were going around saying that they can never ever get any thinking done.

ὡς ἀληθῶς τῷ ὄντι: emphatic, 'really truly'.

66c5–7

The grammatical subject he is the phrase οὐδὲν ἄλλο ... ἢ τὸ σῶμα καὶ αἱ τούτου ἐπιθυμίαι ('nothing other than the body and its desires').

στάσεις: conflicts between factions, generally within city-states, i.e. civil strife. Readers familiar with the *Republic* may be reminded here of the analogy in that work between the city-state and its rulers and the body and the soul.

66c7–d2

The luxury of speaking through the True Philosophers lets Socrates advance some potentially controversial claims without challenge: that all wars come from a desire for money, and that we need money for the care of our bodies.

66d1–2

δουλεύοντες τῇ τούτου θεραπείᾳ: 'being slaves to the care of this thing', an image Plato has been saving for this rhetorically climactic point.

AS

66d2

ἀσχολίαν ἄγομεν φιλοσοφίας πέρι: 'we have no time for philosophy'. πέρι is postpositional (see 65d12 n.).

66d3

τὸ δ᾽ ἔσχατον πάντων: 'and the worst thing of all [is]'.

66d3–4

ἐάν τις ἡμῖν καὶ σχολὴ γένηται ἀπ᾽ αὐτοῦ: 'if we do ever get some rest from it', protasis of a present indefinite conditional. καί is adverbial, emphasizing σχολή γένηται ('if we *do* ever get some rest ...').

66d4–5

καὶ τραπώμεθα πρὸς τὸ σκοπεῖν τι: 'and apply ourselves to the examination of something'. τραπώμεθα is an intransitive middle aorist subjunctive from τρέπω, 'I turn'.

66d5–6

αὖ πανταχοῦ παραπῖπτον: 'turning up afresh at every point'. παραπίπτω is literally 'fall in one's way' and by extension 'turn up unexpected'. Either is strikingly paradoxical when used of one's own body. (τὸ σῶμα) παραπῖπτον: (the body) getting in the way ...; nom. sg. neut. part. modifies σῶμα.

θόρυβον παρέχει καὶ ταραχὴν καὶ ἐκπλήττει: the body bothers presents our souls with various distractions. In classical Greek a θόρυβος is generally a loud noise or din – an example of a distraction to which most readers will relate. ταραχή can be 'disorder' either of the body (especially of the bowels) or of the mind. Take note of the arrangement of the καὶ ... καὶ ...

66d7

καθορᾶν τἀληθές: the metaphor of sight has an ironic ring, given Socrates' recent discrediting of all the body's senses.

66d7–8

ἡμῖν δέδεικται: 'it has been shown' (i.e. is clear) 'to us'. δέδεικται is a perfect passive from δείκνυμι.

66d8

εἰ μέλλομέν ποτε καθαρῶς τι εἴσεσθαι: 'if we intend ever to know anything purely', i.e. to know it as a thing itself distinct from others, the kind of knowledge discussed at 65d4–66a8. μέλλω is as usual followed by a future infinitive (εἴσεσθαι = fut. inf. of οἶδα). ποτε as an enclitic (i.e. unaccented) means 'ever'. καθαρῶς will be used several times in this passage, in different forms.

66e1

ἀπαλλακτέον αὐτοῦ καὶ αὐτῇ τῇ ψυχῇ θεατέον: two impersonal uses of gerundives from ἀπαλλάσσω and θεάομαι. The former is followed by a

AS

genitive of separation αὐτοῦ ('from it'). The dative αὐτῇ τῇ ψυχῇ expresses the agent of θεατέον (i.e. 'the soul [by] itself must contemplate').

66e2

ἡμῖν ἔσται: possessive dative, 'we will have'.

66e2–3

οὗ ... φαμεν ἐρασταὶ εἶναι: 'of which we claim to be lovers'. Like the English, the Greek ἐραστής often implies a specifically sexual desire. The connotation adds a touch of irony: for the True Philosophers, of course, scorn such desires of the body.

ἐπειδὰν τελευτήσωμεν: indefinite because the speakers do not know when they will die.

66e4

ζῶσιν δὲ οὔ: the dat. pl. follows on from ἡμῖν ἔσται (e2): 'we will not have it while we live'.

66e4–5

εἰ γὰρ μὴ οἷόν τε ... μηδὲν καθαρῶς γνῶναι: 'For if it is possible to know nothing purely ...'. The verb is impersonal, with ἐστι omitted after τε.

66e5

δυοῖν θάτερον: 'one or other of two things [is true]'. θάτερον = τὸ ἕτερον, by a crasis of the article with an earlier form of the adjective, ἅτερος (hence its vowel). δυοῖν is the genitive/dative form of δύο, a word that is naturally dual. Note particularly the exclusive options which Socrates presents; since people will be unlikely to accept the first option, then they must agree to the second.

66e6

ἔστιν κτήσασθαι τὸ εἰδέναι: 'nowhere is it possible to get hold of knowledge'. Much like ἔξεστι, the uncompounded ἔστι with a dative and infinitive may mean 'it is possible for (dat.) to (inf.)'. τὸ εἰδέναι is really 'the state of knowing', an articular infinitive of οἶδα.

ἢ οὐδαμοῦ ... ἢ τελευτήσασιν: '[it is possible] either nowhere or for those who have died', i.e. only the dead stand a chance of actually knowing anything.

67a2–6

According to the True Philosophers, during life we can still come as close as possible to knowing something, by freeing and cleansing ourselves of the body. Philosophers, whose goal is actual knowledge and not a near miss, may not be satisfied merely by coming close. But, Socrates will suggest, this cleansing and freeing is all just practice for being dead, when we can really learn (c5–10).

67a2

ἐν ᾧ ἂν ζῶμεν: 'while we are alive', indefinite because one does not know the length of one's life while it is happening.

AS

67a3

ἐγγυτάτω: an alternative superlative of the adverb ἐγγύς. But, as it modifies ἐσόμεθα here, we must take it adjectivally ('we will be nearest').

67a4

ὅτι μὴ πᾶσα ἀνάγκη: 'except when entirely necessary', a slightly stronger version of καθ᾽ ὅσον μὴ πολλὴ ἀνάγκη at 64e1.

67a5

μηδὲ ἀναπιμπλώμεθα τῆς τούτου φύσεως: 'and do not infect ourselves with its nature'. This medical sense of ἀναπίμπλημι (really 'I fill up') seems appropriate here, given the True Philosophers' attitude towards the body. On the genitive, see 66c2–4 n. φύσις can mean 'nature' in the sense of something's character, temperament or (of animals) instincts. All of these make good sense here.

67a6

ἕως ἂν ὁ θεὸς αὐτὸς ἀπολύσῃ ἡμᾶς: 'until the god himself sets us free', i.e. allows us to die. There is no reason to see ὁ θεός as suggesting that the True Philosophers are monotheists; it makes better sense to take the singular as meaning 'the god responsible' (so Rowe). Plato often has his characters switch seamlessly between plural and singular when speaking of gods.

67a6–b2

The Philosophers expect to be in like-minded company after death – that is, the company of others who too have become pure. For, they explain, 'it is not right for someone who is impure to lay hold of what is pure'. On this note the speech of the Philosophers ends.

67a6–7

οὕτω μὲν καθαροὶ ἀπαλλαττόμενοι τῆς τοῦ σώματος ἀφροσύνης: 'being thus pure as we escape the thoughtlessness of the body'. Note the present tense of the participle. The μέν here has no corresponding δέ, but looks forward to b2, where the opposite situation (that of being impure) is presented.

67a7–8

ὡς τὸ εἰκός: 'as seems likely', the first trace of uncertainty in a hitherto assertive speech.

67a8–b1

γνωσόμεθα δι᾽ ἡμῶν αὐτῶν πᾶν τὸ εἰλικρινές: 'we will know the whole pure thing through our own selves', that is, through our souls, without the intermediary of any sense or teacher.

67b1

τοῦτο δ᾽ ἐστὶν ἴσως τὸ ἀληθές: the Philosophers' strongest admission of uncertainty yet, but with good reason: they of course cannot know if what they

AS

have advanced is true until they are dead. The job of ἴσως (really 'we suppose' here) is to mark that the view presented is just the opinion of the speaker.

67b2

μὴ καθαρῷ γὰρ καθαροῦ ἐφάπτεσθαι: 'for [someone] impure to grasp hold of [something] pure'. Note the juxtaposition.

μὴ οὐ θεμιτὸν ᾖ: 'it is not right'. μὴ οὐ ... ᾖ is really a negative fear-clause with the verb omitted. It is an idiom Plato uses often to make a modest assertion.

67b6

παντός γε μᾶλλον: 'yes, more than anything'. The particle γε confirms that Simmias is answering in the affirmative.

67b7–e6 – why philosophers are really practising for death

In the True Philosophers' arguments Socrates finds much cause for hope, for himself and for anyone else who believes they have purified their thoughts. Socrates now offers definitions of purification and of death. Finding them both to involve roughly the same thing, the separation and freeing of the soul from the body, he concludes that what philosophers are really doing is practising dying and being dead.

67b8–9

πολλὴ ἐλπὶς ἀφικομένῳ οἷ ἐγὼ πορεύομαι ... ἱκανῶς ... κτήσασθαι: '(there is) much hope for someone who has arrived where I am travelling, that he will adequately possess'. ἐλπὶς here introduces an indirect statement ('hope that ...'). An aorist infinitive is common in indirect statements of hope, instead of a future infinitive. οἷ is the relative (subordinating) form of ποῖ; 'to where?' Socrates may be speaking generally about the experience of a certain type of people when they die, it is striking that he still has his own death very much in mind.

67b9–10

τοῦτο οὗ ἕνεκα ἡ πολλὴ πραγματεία ἡμῖν ... γέγονεν: 'the thing that has been our main occupation'.

67b10

ἐν τῷ παρελθόντι βίῳ: 'in the life we have lived'. παρέρχομαι is a common verb for time's passage. παρελθόντι is aorist, and elicits some pathos, that his life is now over.

67b10–c2

ὥστε ... γίγνεται: an indicative in a result clause emphasizes the reality of the result and thus Socrates' hopeful attitude.

AS

ἥ ... ἀποδημία ἥ νῦν μοι προστεταγμένη: 'the journey abroad that has been
prescribed for me now'. ἀποδημία, really meaning a stretch of time away
from one's δῆμος, is a poignant euphemism for death, not least given Socrates'
reluctance to leave Athens to avoid execution. However, just as speaking of 'time
away' in English implies a return, ἀποδημία may hint already at the doctrine of
reincarnation that Socrates later advances (77a–d).

67c2–3

ὃς ἡγεῖταί οἱ παρεσκευάσθαι τὴν διάνοιαν: 'who thinks that his mind has been
prepared'. οἱ = αὐτῷ, a dative of possession ('his'). παρεσκευάσθαι is a perfect
passive infinitive of παρασκευάζω.

ὥσπερ κεκαθαρμένην: 'as if it has been purified'. As Socrates will go on to explain,
it is only on its way to being purified: that will require the full separation of soul
from body (c5–7).

67c5

κάθαρσις ... εἶναι ἆρα οὐ τοῦτο συμβαίνει: 'it then follows (συμβαίνει),
doesn't it, that purification is this?' Philosophical authors often use συμβαίνω
to express that a conclusion logically follows from something already said.

67c5–6

ὅπερ πάλαι ἐν τῷ λόγῳ λέγεται: Socrates is not claiming that he has already
discussed κάθαρσις explicitly (he has not), but that κάθαρσις is something he
and Simmias have already discussed: the separation, as far as possible, of the
soul from the body (c6–7).

67c6–9

τὸ χωρίζειν ... καὶ ἐθίσαι: a single articular infinitive phrase. The infinitives that
follow all depend on ἐθίσαι.

67c7–8

κάθαρσις involves 'the accustoming of the soul to gather together and assemble
(συναγείρεσθαί τε καὶ ἀθροίζεσθαι) itself on its own out of every part of
the body (πανταχόθεν ἐκ τοῦ σώματος)'. Socrates here offers slightly more
illumination on the nature of the soul: for most humans, we conclude, it is
spread throughout the body and the philosopher must strive to concentrate it in
such a way that there are no bits of body amid the soul. As ἐθίσαι suggests, this
is a matter of habit for the soul and must come with practice.

συναγείρεσθαί τε καὶ ἀθροίζεσθαι: synonyms, the pleonasm drawing our focus
onto this new detail, that the soul must gather itself together out of every part
of the body. Plato, often when speaking metaphorically, will often use several
synonyms to help convey his meaning.

67c8–d1

καὶ οἰκεῖν κατὰ τὸ δυνατὸν ... μόνην καθ᾽ αὑτήν: 'and to live as much as
it can ... on its own'. What is important is the continued effort the soul must

make to do without the body: this is all part of 'practising dying and being dead' (e1–2).

καὶ ἐν τῷ νῦν παρόντι καὶ ἐν τῷ ἔπειτα: 'at the present time and in future': it is to be a lasting effort.

67d1–2

ἐκλυομένην ... ἐκ τοῦ σώματος: 'being freed from the body'. The present participle, which could also be read as middle ('freeing itself'), stresses the ongoing process of freeing, which must continue until the individual dies. The analogy of prison-chains (δεσμῶν) is particularly poignant in Socrates' current circumstances.

67d4

λύσις καὶ χωρισμὸς: emphatic near-synonyms, but with λύσις adding the optimistic connotation of an escape to something better (echoing 67d1).

67d7–8

μάλιστα καὶ μόνοι: this freeing of the soul is something true philosophers desire especially keenly (μάλιστα), and they alone (μόνοι). For everyone else, this sounds like no life at all (65a6).

67d8–9

τὸ μελέτημα αὐτὸ τοῦτό ἐστιν τῶν φιλοσόφων: 'and this is the very thing the philosophers practise'. μελέτημα and its cognate verb μελετάω (e5) refer to the practising of some activity with the aim of improving one's proficiency in it: contrast ἐπιτηδεύουσι at 64a6 (see n.).

67d11

φαίνεται: a less enthusiastic response from Simmias; but perhaps the preceding points had already made it abundantly clear that this λύσις καὶ χωρισμός will take repeated and sustained effort (practice).

67d12

ὅπερ ἐν ἀρχῇ ἔλεγον: Socrates had indeed made the same point at 64a6–9, in similar terms.

67d12–e2

γελοῖον ἂν εἴη: introduces an acc. + inf. indirect statement (ἄνδρα ... ἀγανακτεῖν), but most simply translated, 'It would be ridiculous if ...'.

ὅτι ἐγγυτάτω ὄντα τοῦ τεθνάναι: 'being as close as possible to being dead', that is, with his soul as separate as possible from the body. All degrees of ἐγγύς are followed by a genitive.

κἄπειθ᾽ ἥκοντος ... τούτου: 'and then, when this has come' (i.e. death). κἄπειτα is a crasis of καί and ἔπειτα.

67e3

πῶς δ᾽ οὔ: 'how could it not be?'

AS

67e7–69e5 – Socrates ends his ἀπολογία

Socrates draws his defence speech to a close (see 63b1–67e6 n.), having proved to
his satisfaction that he is right to welcome his approaching death in good cheer.
Death, he says, allows philosophers finally to get what they have worked towards
all their lives: escape from the distractions and confusions of their bodies, which
hamper their pursuit of wisdom in this life. On this view, philosophers will see
death as the release they have prepared for all their lives. Anyone who dreads
death cannot be a philosopher but must be a 'lover of the body', since they must
place a higher value on it than on wisdom.

For Socrates, wisdom is worth pursuing beyond all else: without it, all other supposed
virtues ring hollow. He argues that bravery (say) – or what passes for bravery
among most people – is really a product of fear. The philosopher, however, can
be truly brave: he knows death is not to be feared but welcomed.

69e6–70c3 – Cebes' question: How can we know that the soul can survive death?

Cebes applauds Socrates' speech, but wonders why his friend is so sure that a person's soul is not immediately annihilated at the moment of death, as many think.

69e6–7

ὑπολαβὼν ... ἔφη: 'he said in reply'. ὑπολαμβάνω 'I reply' is really a metaphor ('I take up [role of person speaking]'), hence the aorist participle here.

69e7–70a1

τὰ μὲν ἄλλα ... τὰ δὲ περὶ τῆς ψυχῆς: Cebes uses a μέν/δέ contrast to isolate the part needing further discussion in what Socrates has said. τὰ μὲν ἄλλα ('most of what you say' – lit. 'everything else') tells us to expect an exception: τὰ δὲ περὶ τῆς ψυχῆς ('the stuff about the soul, on the other hand').

ἔμοιγε: 'to me, at least', setting up a contrast with τοῖς ἀνθρώποις (70a1).

δοκεῖ καλῶς λέγεσθαι: 'seems to be well put', i.e. convincing. δοκεῖ here is not impersonal, but has τὰ ἄλλα as its subject. The infinitive is present, reflecting the lasting importance of what Socrates has said.

70a1–2

πολλὴν ἀπιστίαν παρέχει ... μή ... οὐδαμοῦ ἔτι ᾖ: 'causes much doubt that it [the soul] will not exist anywhere anymore'. μή here introduces a series of fear-clauses, with verbs in the subjunctive as usual (ᾖ, διαφθείρηταί, ἀπολλύηται, οἴχηται). The word prompting the fear-construction is ἀπιστίαν, which should thus be taken as connoting some worry on top of the disbelief. ᾖ (3sg. pres. subj.) is an example of the 'existential' use of εἰμί ('I exist, am real') common in philosophical texts.

ἐπειδὰν ἀπαλλαγῇ τοῦ σώματος: an indefinite temporal clause (here ἐπειδάν + subjunctive), because one's time of death is unknown ('when'). It need not imply belief in reincarnation ('whenever'), the possibility of which is currently being called into question.

70a3

διαφθείρηταί τε καὶ ἀπολλύηται: present subjunctives, after μή (see a1–2 n.). The words are synonyms, the pleonasm for emphasis.

ἡμέρα ... ᾖ ἂν ὁ ἄνθρωπος ἀποθνήσκῃ: 'the day ... on which the person dies', again indefinite (see a1–2n.) with ἄν + subjunctive.

70a3–4

ἐκβαίνουσα ... διασκεδασθεῖσα ... διαπτομένη: the three participles, in asyndeton, describe the soul's departure and dissolution. διασκεδασθεῖσα is an aorist passive participle from διασκεδάννυμι 'I scatter abroad'. διαπτομένη is an aorist middle participle from διαπέτομαι 'I fly off'.

οἴχηται: subjunctive after μή (see a1–2 n.). οἴχομαι 'I have gone' is present with perfect sense. There is some wordplay here: for like the English 'departed', the verb has the secondary meaning 'I have died'.

A Level

70a5

ὥσπερ πνεῦμα ἢ καπνός: echoes a Homeric simile of the soul to smoke (*Iliad* 23.100). In the same passage, the souls of the dead are said to be mere images lacking any real intelligence (*Iliad* 23.103–104: compare b3–4 below).

70a6

οὐδὲν ἔτι οὐδαμοῦ ἦ: closely echoes a2, but with an adverbial οὐδέν ('not at all') for further emphasis.

70a6–8

εἴπερ εἴη που ... πολλὴ ἂν εἴη ἐλπίς: 'if indeed it were to be anywhere ... there would be a great hope'. The future remote conditional suggests some scepticism on Cebes' part. που is not 'I suppose' but the indefinite correlative of ποῦ; 'where?'. -περ ('indeed' here) is added to εἰ or a relative to pinpoint more precisely the condition or thing in question (e.g. ἅπερ 'the very things which'; compare ὥσπερ 'just as').

αὐτὴ καθ᾽ αὑτήν: 'on its own, by itself'. On this recurrent phrase, see 64c5–8 n.

συνηθροισμένη καὶ ἀπηλλαγμένη: perfect middle participles of συναθροίζω 'I gather' and ἀπαλλάττω 'I release'.

70a8

ὧν σὺ νυνδὴ διῆλθες: '[the evils] which you have just now described'. In Plato διέρχομαι, 'I go through' is generally a metaphor for recounting or describing in sequence.

καλή: the hope would be 'fine' as in well justified (much like καλῶς at 69a7).

70b1

ἀληθῆ ἐστιν: 'they are true', with neuter pl. subject taking a singular verb as usual.

70b2

οὐκ ὀλίγης παραμυθίας δεῖται καὶ πίστεως: 'much reassurance and proof is needed'. δεῖται 'there is a need of' is impersonal and followed by the genitive.

70b2–3

ὡς ἔστι τε ψυχὴ: existential ἔστι (see 70a1–2 n.), 'that the soul exists'. Plato often omits the article before ψυχή, with no change to the meaning.

ἀποθανόντος τοῦ ἀνθρώπου: better taken as a genitive absolute than a possessive genitive: Socrates and his friends do not speak of someone who has died as still being an ἄνθρωπος (as the latter would imply).

70b3–4

τινα δύναμιν ἔχει καὶ φρόνησιν: the hopes Socrates had expressed of a better future after death (62c9–69e5) hinge on the soul having 'some power and intelligence' after death. Cebes is cutting to the chase.

**A
Level**

70b5–6

τί δὴ ποιῶμεν: a deliberative subjunctive: 'what are we to do, then?'

70b6

βούλει διαμυθολογῶμεν: 'do you want us to talk through [whether X or Y]'. Occasionally a deliberative subjunctive occurs after βούλομαι in a direct question; the result is really a combination of two ('do you want …?' and 'shall we talk through …?' As a 2nd sg. middle-passive ending, -ει is far commoner in later classical Greek than -ῃ.

70b6–7

εἴτε … εἴτε: 'whether … or' in indirect questions (much like πότερον … ἤ).

εἰκὸς οὕτως ἔχειν: '[it is] likely that this is the case'. εἰκός (generally with ἔστι omitted as understood) introduces an acc. + inf. indirect statement. ἔχω + adverb is equivalent to εἰμί + adjective.

70b8–9

ἐγὼ γοῦν … ἡδέως ἂν ἀκούσαιμι: 'Well I for one would be pleased to hear'. The potential optative with ἄν is used for polite requests: it is really the apodosis of a future remote conditional, with the protasis ('if you should be so kind', or the like), omitted as obvious. γοῦν is a crasis of γε and οὖν and roughly equivalent to γε.

ἥντινα δόξαν ἔχεις: an indirect question – hence ἥντινα, the indirect question form of τίνα (f. acc. sg.).

70b10

οὔκουν γ᾽ ἂν οἶμαι … εἰπεῖν τινα: 'I don't think anyone would say'. ἄν here belongs with εἰπεῖν in the indirect statement.

70c1

οὐδ᾽ εἰ κωμῳδοποιὸς εἴη: 'not even if he were a comedy-writer'. Aristophanes, in his comedy the *Clouds*, grossly misrepresents Socrates and his practices for humorous effect, and has the character Strepsiades call him and his followers ἀδόλεσχοι ('nonsense-talkers', *Clouds* 1485). Another comic playwright, Eupolis, has him called ἀδόλεσχης (a cognate meaning the same). Elsewhere Plato has Socrates plausibly imply that the *Clouds* had a great part in turning the Athenian public against him (*Apology* 19b–c), giving the joke here a sinister edge.

ἀδολεσχῶ: 'I talk rubbish', a verb formed from ἀδόλεσχος/ἀδόλεσχης (see previous n.) and so a direct nod to the comedians.

70c1–2

οὐ περὶ προσηκόντων: Socrates cannot be accused of talking 'about things that don't concern' him, as is soon to die and keen to know the fate of his soul. προσήκει is commonly impersonal ('it concerns').

A Level

70c2–3

εἰ … δοκεῖ: 'if you agree', with the pronoun understood.

χρὴ διασκοπεῖσθαι: 'we ought to look into it thoroughly', with a middle infinitive, as they would be doing so for their own benefit.

70c4–72e1 – the first argument for the soul's immortality: The cycle of opposites

For any two pairs of opposite conditions such as 'bigger' and 'smaller', or 'awake' and 'asleep', the one must come from the other. For something can only be bigger if it was hitherto smaller. In any such pair, there are two processes of 'coming to be', one going in each direction (e.g. from bigger to smaller, and from smaller to bigger). Socrates argues that the same must be true of the opposites 'living' and 'dead': if there is a process one way (from being alive to being dead – i.e. dying), there must be one going the other – coming back to life.

Readers who find the argument frustrating or plainly erroneous must remember that it is just a first approach to the challenge of proving the soul's immortality. Later in the dialogue, Socrates and his friends will try other avenues and find them more profitable. This argument and its successor, the argument from recollection (72e3–77a5), must also be read and appraised as a pair: for as Socrates says himself, only together do they serve as a proof for the soul's immortality (77c–e).

70c4

σκεψώμεθα: hortative subjunctive, 'let us examine'. As with an imperative, the aorist is for aspect: they are to examine the matter once, now, rather than as a general principle of behaviour (present).

αὐτὸ: i.e. the matter at hand.

τῇδέ πη: 'in some way (πη) such as the following (τῇδέ)'. πη is the indefinite correlative of the question-word πῇ; 'in what way?'. Like τῇδε here, demonstratives in -δε generally point ahead to what is coming next.

70c4–5

εἴτ᾽ ἄρα … εἴτε καὶ: 'whether … or …', an indirect question following σκεψώμεθα. After εἴτε, ἄρα (not to be confused with the closed question-marker ἆρα) and καί are really untranslatable, but serve to mark the question as a genuinely open one with no bias either way.

ἐν Ἅιδου: 'in [the house] of Hades'. Socrates does not mean literally the Hades of classical myth, but is using the name as a shorthand for the dwelling place of dead souls, wherever and whatever that may be. He will put forth his own take on the myths of the afterlife and the underworld at the end of the *Phaedo* (107c–115a).

τελευτησάντων τῶν ἀνθρώπων: genitive absolute again, rather than possessive (see b2–3 n.).

**A
Level**

70c5–6

παλαιὸς ... ἔστι τις λόγος: the 'ancient legend' (or 'hypothesis') in question is that of reincarnation (παλιγγενεσία). In Plato's *Meno* (81a–c) the doctrine is credited to various priests, priestesses and 'inspired poets'. Such a tale is told, for instance, by the lyric poet Pindar (*Olympian* 2.56–80).

οὗ μεμνήμεθα: 'which we recall'. μέμνημαι 'I remember' is a reflexive middle perfect of μιμνήσκω 'I remind', with present sense. It takes a genitive object.

ὡς: 'that', introducing the παλαιὸς λόγος.

70c6–7

εἰσὶν ... ἐκεῖ: existential, 'they exist there'.

70c7–8

πάλιν ... γίγνονται: 'they are born again'. Based on πάλιν γίγνεσθαι at c8–9, it seems best to take πάλιν with γίγνονται here too. γίγνομαι can mean 'I am born' as well as 'become' (compare its cognate γένος).

ἐκ τῶν τεθνεώτων: 'from the dead'. τεθνεώς is a perfect participle from (ἀπο) θνήσκω 'I die'.

70c8–9

πάλιν γίγνεσθαι ... τοὺς ζῶντας: 'that the living are born again', an acc. + inf. indirect statement after οὕτως ἔχει.

70c9–d1

ἄλλο τι ἤ: '[would] anything else [be the case] than [that]'; i.e. 'surely ...?'

εἶεν ἂν αἱ ψυχαὶ ἡμῶν ἐκεῖ: 'our souls would exist there', a remote-conditional apodosis, despite the open-conditional protasis εἰ τοῦθ᾽ οὕτως ἔχει. This is because a second, counterfactual protasis is implied ('and if we were dead').

70d1–2

μὴ οὖσαι: 'if they did not exist'. When negated with μή and not οὐ, participles take on a conditional force.

70d2

τοῦτο ἱκανὸν τεκμήριον τοῦ ταῦτ᾽ εἶναι: 'this [is] sufficient evidence of [the fact] that these things are true'. As an alternative to an indirect statement with ὅτι, Plato often uses τό with an acc. + inf. εἶναι here is in a 'veridical' sense ('to be true'), a use common in Plato alongside the existential ('to be real').

70d2–3

τῷ ὄντι: 'in reality', an adverbial idiom common in Plato's early and middle works. Plato regularly uses τὸ ὄν in other cases, as well as the plural τὰ ὄντα, to mean 'reality' and 'the truth'.

70d3

οὐδαμόθεν ἄλλοθεν ... ἤ: 'from nowhere else than'.

**A
Level**

70d4–5

The form of the sentence is a present open conditional, with a present indicative in the protasis (εἰ-clause) but with a potential optative with ἄν in the apodosis (main clause). In conditionals of this type, the potential optative serves to suggest that the speaker is making an inference (Smyth § 2300e): 'if X, then I presume Y'.

εἰ δὲ μὴ ἔστι τοῦτο: ἔστι is veridical ('is true').

ἄλλου ἄν του δέοι λόγου: 'we would need another argument'. The impersonal δεῖ with a genitive means 'there is need of'. του here is not the article (τοῦ) but an alternative to τινός.

70d6

πάνυ μὲν οὖν: 'yes indeed', or the like. The phrase is a common response of agreement in Platonic dialogue.

70d7

κατ᾽ ἀνθρώπων: 'in relation to human beings'.

ἦ δ᾽ ὅς: 'he said', a common phrase for marking direct speech in a dialogue.

70d9

συλλήβδην: an adverb formed from συλλαμβάνω ('I take together'), meaning either 'collectively' or 'in short'. Either sense works here.

ὅσαπερ ἔχει γένεσιν: 'all those things that have generation'. The relative ὅσαπερ is neuter to match its most recent antecedent φυτῶν ('plants'). On the addition of -περ, see 70a5 n. The noun γένεσις is awkward to translate, and its sense may best be captured by 'coming into being'.

70e1

ἴδωμεν ἄρ᾽: hortative subjunctive ('let's see'), with ἄρα introducing an indirect yes/no question ('whether …') instead of the far commoner εἰ.

οὑτωσὶ γίγνεται πάντα: 'everything comes into being in this very way'. The suffix -ι on οὕτως can be added to all demonstratives for emphasis.

70e1–2

οὐκ ἄλλοθεν ἢ ἐκ τῶν ἐναντίων τὰ ἐναντία: 'opposites [coming into being] from nowhere but from their opposites'.

ὅσοις τυγχάνει ὂν τοιοῦτόν τι: 'all those that happen to have something like that'. ὅσοις here is possessive dative. The clause clarifies that what Socrates will say will pertain to any two things that are opposite to each other.

οἷον: '[as,] for example'. The adverbial οἷον ('for example') is a common Platonic idiom.

70e2–3

τὸ καλὸν τῷ αἰσχρῷ ἐναντίον που: 'the beautiful, I suppose, [is] opposite to the ugly'. Alternatively, καλός and αἰσχρός can be taken in their other opposite senses, 'honourable' and 'shameful'.

**A
Level**

70e4

τοῦτο ... σκεψώμεθα, ἆρα: see 70e1 n.

70e4–5

ἀναγκαῖον ... αὐτὸ γίγνεσθαι: '[it is] necessary for it to come into being'.

ὅσοις ἔστι τι ἐναντίον: another dative of possession with ἔστι.

70e6

ὅταν μεῖζόν τι γίγνηται: indefinite, 'whenever something becomes bigger'.

70e7

ἀνάγκη: as with ἀναγκαῖον (e4), ἔστι must be supplied.

ἐξ ἐλάττονος ὄντος πρότερον: something must become bigger (μεῖζον) 'from [itself] being formerly smaller'. It is still the same 'something', just a different size.

70e10–71a

Socrates is keen to show, by this example, that the process of becoming between opposites goes both ways.

70e10

οὐκοῦν introduces a question inviting the answer 'yes' and can therefore often be translated just as 'surely'. It has a secondary role, however, which is to mark that the sentence as a logical consequence of what has come before. In such cases, it is better to translate οὐκοῦν as 'therefore' and treat the question as a statement.

κἂν ἔλαττον γίγνηται: κἂν is a crasis of καὶ εἀν 'if, too', introducing a future open condition.

71a2

ἔστιν οὕτω: 'that's right'.

71a3–4

To avoid unnecessary repetition, the verb (presumably γίγνεται) is omitted as understood.

καὶ μὴν: 'and then', marking the speaker's keenness to get on to what he has to say next. The particle γε here works with it in tandem, focusing attention further on that example.

71a6

θᾶττον: neuter singular comparative of ταχύς.

71a8

πῶς γὰρ οὔ: 'how could it not be?'

71a9

ἱκανῶς ... ἔχομεν τοῦτο: 'we are satisfied with this' (lit. 'have it sufficiently').

A Level

71a9
πράγματα means 'things' of either an abstract or concrete nature.

71a12–b4
Socrates gets Cebes to agree that for any pair of opposites A and B, there are two
   processes of becoming (γενέσεις) between them, which allow something that is
   A to become B and vice versa.

71a12
τί δ' αὖ: 'what about this, next?'

71a12–b1
ἔστι τι καὶ τοιόνδε ἐν αὐτοῖς, οἷον ... δύο γενέσεις: is there also something like
   this in them [i.e. opposites]: something such as two processes of coming into
   being?'.
μεταξὺ ἀμφοτέρων πάντων τῶν ἐναντίων: the processes are 'between both of
   all opposites'.
δυοῖν ὄντοιν: genitive, agreeing with ἀμφοτέρων ('[between] both, being two').
   δυοῖν and ὄντοιν are in the dual number, for which -οιν is the genitive/dative
   ending in the second- and third declensions.

71b2–3
μείζονος μὲν πράγματος καὶ ἐλάττονος μεταξὺ: μεταξύ ('between') takes the
   genitive and here governs the words preceding it: 'between a greater thing and a
   smaller one [there is] growth and decay'.

71b3–4
καλοῦμεν ... τὸ μὲν αὐξάνεσθαι τὸ δὲ φθίνειν: 'we call the one thing (τὸ μὲν)
   "growing" and the other (τὸ δὲ) "decaying"'. With αὔξησις and φθίσις both
   being feminine, we might expect the articles to be the same. Instead, they have
   taken on the neuter gender of the infinitives. The articular infinitive in the present
   tense is a clear and convenient way of denoting processes, and one Socrates will
   take much advantage of in the ensuing lines.

71b6–9
οὐκοῦν καὶ διακρίνεσθαι καὶ συγκρίνεσθαι ... καὶ πάντα οὕτω: 'And
   therefore there is also separating and combining ... and all such things'. The
   entire sentence is punctuated as a question owing to the initial οὐκοῦν (on
   which see, 70e10 n.).

71b7–8
κἂν εἰ μὴ χρώμεθα τοῖς ὀνόμασιν ἐνιαχοῦ: 'even if we don't use their names
   in some cases'. That is, the same is true for pairs of opposites for which our
   language lacks terms. κἂν here is a crasis of καὶ and ἄν (not ἐὰν as at 70e10),
   even though ἄν properly belongs within the protasis (εἰ-clause).

**A
Level**

71b8–9

ἀλλ' ἔργῳ γοῦν: 'still, in actual fact'. This phrase introduces the apodosis to κἂν εἰ in the previous line, and so ἀλλά must be left untranslated. The adverbial ἔργῳ is often found alongside the contrasting λόγῳ 'in word' (i.e. allegedly).

πανταχοῦ οὕτως ἔχειν ἀναγκαῖον: 'it is necessary that they (i.e. pairs of opposites) are like this everywhere'.

γίγνεσθαί τε αὐτὰ ... γένεσίν τε εἶναι: these two acc. + inf. phrases follow on from οὕτως: '[they are like this everywhere]: they come into being from each other ...'.

71b10

ἑκατέρου εἰς ἄλληλα: 'from each of the two into the other'. The reciprocal pronoun ἄλληλα ('each other') is naturally plural despite the sense requiring a singular.

71c1–2

Socrates leads Cebes to agree on the pivotal point for his argument: that living and being dead are pairs of the kind just described.

τί οὖν: 'what about this, then?'

ζῆν: present infinitive of ζάω 'I live'.

τῷ ἐγρηγορέναι: 'being awake'. ἐγρηγορέναι is the intransitive perfect infinitive of ἐγείρω 'I awaken' and is accordingly used with the present sense 'to be awake'. The articular infinitive in the perfect tense offers a convenient way to form nouns denoting states or conditions.

71c5

τεθνάναι is the perfect infinitive of (ἀπο) θνήσκω and so means 'to have died' or 'to be dead'. The latter sense is better here, as Cebes is naming the opposite state to being alive.

71c6

εἴπερ: 'if indeed': see 70a6–8 n.

71c7

αἱ γενέσεις εἰσὶν αὐτοῖν μεταξὺ δύο δυοῖν ὄντοιν: 'there are two processes of becoming between the two [states]'. δύο agrees with γένεσις, and the duals αὐτοῖν ... δυοῖν ὄντοιν are genitive after μεταξύ. The hyperbaton here mirrors the interrelation of the two.

71c9–d5

Socrates returns in more depth to the examples of being awake and sleeping, and invites Cebes to give him in turn an analogous account of life and death.

71c9

συζυγίαν: 'pair'. The original sense of the word is of animals joined together with a yoke, such as horses or oxen.

A
Level

ὧν νυνδὴ ἔλεγον ἐγώ: 'of the ones which I was saying just now'. The case of the relative pronoun here is determined not by its role in the clause; instead it takes on the case the antecedent would have had if there had been one (a phenomenon called the attraction of the relative).

71c9–10

ἐγώ σοι, ἔφη, ἐρῶ, ὁ Σωκράτης: '"I shall tell you" said Socrates'. The interleaved word-order (ABAB) is a pattern of which Plato is fond.

καὶ αὐτὴν καὶ τὰς γενέσεις: expands on τὴν συζυγίαν: '[I shall name for you] both [the pair] itself and its processes'.

71c11

λέγω here has as its objects both simple noun phrases (τὸ μὲν καθεύδειν, τὸ δὲ ἐγρηγορέναι) and indirect statements (ἐκ τοῦ καθεύδειν τὸ ἐγρηγορέναι γίγνεσθαι …) and must be translated in different ways for each. I suggest 'I am talking about' for the former and 'I say that' for the latter.

71d2

τὴν μὲν καταδαρθάνειν εἶναι, τὴν δ' ἀνεγείρεσθαι: 'the one [process] is falling asleep, the other waking up'. The acc. sg. γένεσιν is assumed, hence the feminine article. Again, the use of present infinitives makes clear that he is talking of processes and not events (aorist) or states (perfect).

71d2–3

ἱκανῶς σοι: 'is that enough for you?', assuming ἔχει (see 70b6–7 n.).

71c5

λέγε δή μοι καὶ σύ: the particle δή is common after imperatives, where it conveys some added sense of exhortation such as 'come, now' in English. καί here is adverbial ('you too').

71d8–9

γίγνεσθαι δὲ ἐξ ἀλλήλων: 'and [do you say that] they come into being from each other?' That Cebes is so ready to agree (ναί) may shock us: for our experience can bear witness to only one of the processes, that between living and being dead. He is compelled to do so, however, by a premise he has already agreed on, that between pairs of opposites there are processes of becoming in both directions.

71d10

ἐξ … τοῦ ζῶντος τί τὸ γιγνόμενον: 'what is the thing that comes into being from that which is living?' Socrates moves from articular infinitives (which express processes and states) to articles with participles, which allow him to talk about the things that exemplify the states and processes ('that which is X-ing').

A Level

71d11

τὸ τεθνηκός: 'that which is dead'. Plato uses two different perfect active participles of (ἀπο)θνῄσκω in the passage, τεθνηκώς and τεθνεώς.

71d13

ἀναγκαῖον ... ὁμολογεῖν ὅτι τὸ ζῶν: 'it is necessary to agree that it is that which is living'. Rowe detects a trace of reluctance in Cebes' agreement here and in his next few replies (φαίνεται and ἔοικεν), in contrast to the more confident πάνυ μὲν οὖν and πῶς γὰρ οὔ of before. Cebes, it seems, is now beginning to question the premises he had been led to agree with.

71d14–15

τὰ ζῶντά τε καὶ οἱ ζῶντες: i.e. non-human living things (φυτόν and ζῷον are both neuter) and humans (οἱ ζῶντες), the main focus of the argument. Both groups together comprise the broader category τὸ ζῶν 'that which is alive'.

71e1

φαίνεται: while this can mean 'clearly' (assuming a dependent participle), it is better to take it as 'it seems' (assuming a dependent infinitive) here, given Cebes' less confident responses at d13 and e3.

71e2

ἐν Ἅιδου: see 70c4–5 n.

71e4

τοῖν γενεσέοιν τοῖν περὶ ταῦτα: 'of the two processes of becoming concerning these things', i.e. concerning that which is alive and that which is dead. τοῖν γενεσέοιν is genitive dual.

71e5

σαφὴς οὖσα τυγχάνει: 'is actually visible'. Especially with a participle of εἰμί, τυγχάνω is often used to stress the reality of the action of the participle ('I really am'). σαφής here means clear as in 'visible, obvious' – our experience confirms that dying (τὸ ἀποθνῄσκειν) is real.

δήπου: 'surely, presumably'. Though originally the particle expressed some doubt (as a compound of που 'I suppose'), Socrates uses it with a touch of irony to state strong claims.

71e8–10

Picking up, perhaps, on the doubt in Cebes' voice, Socrates loads his next questions with persuasive emotional appeal.

οὐκ ἀνταποδώσομεν: 'shall we not grant, as is due ...?', i.e. as is required for maintaining balance. Though ἀνταποδίδωμι is used more often later in the *Phaedo* of arriving at a balance, its primary sense is of repaying a debt. The verb hints, then, at a moral obligation to posit a second process alongside dying.

**A
Level**

ταύτῃ χωλὴ ἔσται ἡ φύσις: 'will we make Nature lame in this respect?' The
future ἔσται 'will be', instead of present ἔστι, implies that it is in their power to
decide the matter, and that to answer 'yes' would be an act of cruelty. ταύτῃ is
adverbial, a demonstrative correlative to ᾗ 'in which way, how' (73a8) and πῃ
(70c4).

φύσις: on top of the senses listed in 67a5 n., φύσις can mean Nature in the sense
of the entirely of creation.

71e11
πάντως που: Cebes' response betrays further traces of doubt.

71e12
τίνα ταύτην: accusative, as if continuing the acc. + inf. construction after ἀνάγκη
(e9).

71e13
τὸ ἀναβιώσκεσθαι: 'coming back to life'. The word may well be Plato's own
coinage. Since they are talking about a process of coming to be from τὸ
τεθνηκός, which can just as readily mean 'that which has died', as 'that which
is dead', it makes sense that Cebes calls that process not just 'coming to life' but
'coming back to life'.

71e14–72a2
On the form of this conditional, see 70d4–5 n.
εἴπερ ἔστι τὸ ἀναβιώσκεσθαι: ἔστι is existential.
ἂν εἴη γένεσις … αὕτη, τὸ ἀναβιώσκεσθαι: 'it – coming back to life – would be
this process of becoming'. This second τὸ ἀναβιώσκεσθαι is really redundant,
simply clarifying what is understood as the subject of εἴη.
ἐκ τῶν τεθνεώτων … εἰς τοὺς ζῶντας: 'from the dead into the living', i.e. dead
people (hence the masculine participles) into living ones.

72a4
ὁμολογεῖται ἄρα ἡμῖν: ἡμῖν is a dative of relation: 'as far as we're concerned,
then (ἄρα), it is agreed'. What follows is an acc. + inf. indirect statement.
καὶ ταύτῃ: 'in this way, too'. Both words are adverbial (see 71e8–10 n.).

72a5
γεγονέναι: 'have come into being', perfect infinitive of γίγνομαι.

72a6
τούτου δὲ ὄντος: 'with this being the case' (taking ὄντος as veridical).
που: 'I suppose' in a6, but 'somewhere' in a7.

72a7–8
ἀναγκαῖον: '[it is] necessary', introducing an acc. + inf. indirect statement.

ὅθεν δὴ πάλιν γίγνεσθαι: δή marks out ὅθεν as picking up που (a7): 'the place, that is, from which they come back into being', i.e. are born again.

72a9–10

Cebes recognizes that the conclusion follows from the premises they agreed on, but voices no discernible enthusiasm at the revelation.

ἐκ τῶν ὡμολογημένων: 'from the things we have agreed upon'. The participle is a perfect passive.

72a11–d3

Socrates argues that without a corresponding process in the other direction, the process from living to being dead could not go on for long. For within a finite universe, the stock of souls from which new life could arise would eventually be exhausted.

72a11–12

οὐδ᾽ ἀδίκως ὡμολογήκαμεν: 'we are not wrong to have agreed, either'. Like καί, οὐδέ/μηδέ can play an adverbial role ('not even', 'not … either'). The perfect ὡμολογήκαμεν picks up on Cebes' ὡμολογημένων and invites us to read these as words of encouragement to Cebes, who may well be doubting their conclusion (see 71d13 n.).

72a12–b1

εἰ … μὴ ἀεὶ ἀνταποδιδοίη τὰ ἕτερα τοῖς ἑτέροις γιγνόμενα: 'if one lot' (i.e. either the dead or the living) 'did not always achieve a balance with the others when coming into being'. ἀποδίδωμι is here used in its intransitive sense, 'I correspond with, achieve balance'. Its subject here is τὰ ἕτερα 'the one group' (in both singular and plural, ἕτερος is used to contrast between two things or groups). The future remote form of the conditional lends some persuasive power to Socrates' words, warranted or not: for in this pair of opposites there really is only one process of coming to be – from being alive to being dead.

ὡσπερεὶ κύκλῳ περιιόντα: 'just as if [they are] going around in a cycle'. The simile's intended point of reference is probably not a circle as in the shape (also κύκλος) but a recurrent cycle of events such as the orbit of the heavenly bodies or the cycle of the seasons (both also called κύκλοι). Though ὡσπερεί is properly a compound of ὥσπερ and εἰ, it can be followed by a participle or noun just as readily as a full clause.

72b2

εὐθεῖά τις εἴη ἡ γένεσις: 'the process of coming to be were a straight one', that is, in a single direction.

ἐκ τοῦ ἑτέρου μόνον εἰς τὸ καταντικρὺ: both are neuter in keeping with τὸ τεθνεώς and τὸ ζῶν, to which they refer.

72b3

καὶ μὴ ἀνακάμπτοι πάλιν … μηδὲ καμπὴν ποιοῖτο: 'and does not bend back round again, nor makes a turn back'. The pleonasm draws our full attention to

A
Level

the metaphor, of a runner, horse or chariot rounding the turning-post (καμπή) of a racecourse.

72b4

οἶσθ' ὅτι: Socrates packages the apodosis of the conditional as a question: 'do you realise that …?' To render οἶσθα here as 'know' does not capture the spirit in which the question is put and something more like the above is needed.

πάντα τελευτῶντα τὸ αὐτὸ σχῆμα ἂν σχοίη: 'everything would end up having the same form'. Plato has frequently used τελευτάω to mean 'I die' so far in the *Phaedo*. Here its participle must mean rather 'being at the end' (i.e. 'finally') but the connotations from its other sense make for a good pun. σχοίη is a 3sg. aor. opt. act. of ἔχω. Some wordplay is surely intended with σχῆμα, a cognate, as with πάθος and πάθοι (see next n.).

72b5

τὸ αὐτὸ πάθος ἂν πάθοι: 'would come to be in the same state'. πάσχω, like Latin *patior*, need not imply suffering, but can simply mean 'I have something happen to me', 'I am come to be in a certain state'. πάθος is used accordingly to refer to that state.

παύσαιτο γιγνόμενα: παύομαι with a participle means 'I cease from X-ing'.

72b7–c2

Socrates takes the example of 'going to sleep' and 'waking up' to show that such processes must all be bidirectional. For if there was no 'waking up', we would all be permanently asleep.

72b7

οὐδὲν χαλεπόν … ἐννοῆσαι: '[it is] not at all difficult to get your head around'. οὐδέν is adverbial.

οἷον: 'for example'.

72b7–8

εἰ τὸ καταδαρθάνειν … εἴη: although Cebes and Socrates have already agreed that there is such a thing as going to sleep (71d2–4), the optative εἴη is still needed here, as the protasis, as a whole, is future remote.

72b8

ἀνταποδιδοίη: 'achieve a balance', the intransitive sense again of ἀποδίδωμι (see 72a12–b1 n.).

72b9

οἶσθ' ὅτι: again a question ('do you realise …?') as at 72b4.

τελευτῶντα: 'in the end' (see 72b4 n.).

72b9–c1

πάντ' <ἂν>: the manuscripts transmit πάντα, but we should join Bekker in emending the text to include ἄν, a requisite for the apodosis of a future remote

A Level

conditional. With another ἄν shortly after, it is easy to imagine a scribe omitting the first (a so-called 'haplography'), perhaps assuming the word to have been accidentally repeated by an earlier copyist (a 'dittography').

<ἄν> λῆρον τὸν Ἐνδυμίωνα ἀποδείξειεν: '[in the end everything] would show up Endymion as nothing special'. The mythological shepherd Endymion, lover of the moon-goddess Selene, is famous for sleeping eternally. (Zeus had put him in this state as a double-edged favour to Selene, so he would never grow old.) Without that one claim to fame, Endymion would be λῆρος ('rubbish'). ἀποδείξειεν is 3sg. aor. act. opt. of ἀποδείκνυμι 'I show X to be Y'.

72c1–2

οὐδαμοῦ ἂν φαίνοιτο: 'he would be nowhere to be seen', i.e. would not stand out at all. The idiom (οὐδαμοῦ φαίνομαι) was used commonly in the context of horse racing, where it meant to finish in a low position. Connotations of the racecourse are humorously inapposite in a discussion of the inert Endymion.

διὰ τὸ καὶ τἆλλα πάντα ταὐτὸν ἐκείνῳ πεπονθέναι: 'because all the other things would have undergone the same thing as him too'. On the articular construction, see 70d2 n. τἆλλα and ταὐτὸν are, respectively, τὰ ἄλλα and τὸ αὐτόν with crasis. πεπονθέναι is the perf. act. inf. of πάσχω.

72c3

καθεύδειν: in apposition to, and explaining, ταὐτὸν.

72c3–5

As a second example, Socrates points out that matter, if it only ever combined and never separated, would eventually end up in one big lump. This he calls 'all things in the same place' (ὁμοῦ πάντα χρήματα), a phrase borrowed from Anaxagoras. There is a poignant touch to the mention of this philosopher-scientist, a generation older than Socrates: in Plato's *Apology*, Socrates had ascribed the charge of impiety against him to rumours that he shared some of Anaxagoras' more impious views ('that the sun is stone and the moon is earth', rather than gods: *Apology* 26d).

κἂν εἰ: see 71b7–8 n.

ταχὺ ἂν τὸ τοῦ Ἀναξαγόρου γεγονὸς εἴη: 'soon, what Anaxagoras describes would have become a reality'.

ὁμοῦ πάντα χρήματα: 'all things in the same place'. For Anaxagoras, this is the original indiscriminate state of the universe's matter, before it took shape to form the world as we know it.

72c5

ὡσαύτως: 'in the same way', the adverbial equivalent of ὁ αὐτός.

καὶ εἰ: 'if, too', not 'even if'.

72c6

πάντα ὅσα τοῦ ζῆν μεταλάβοι: 'everything that has got a share of life'. Though we would expect an indicative verb here, μεταλάβοι has been assimilated into the optative to match ἀποθνήσκοι (c5). The meaning is unaffected.

A
Level

ἐπειδὴ δὲ ἀποθάνοι: likewise, what would normally be an indefinite clause with the subjunctive (ἐπειδὰν δὲ ἀποθάνῃ) has also been assimilated into the optative.

72c6

μένοι ἐν τούτῳ τῷ σχήματι τὰ τεθνεῶτα: 'dead things would stay in this form', i.e. being dead.

72c8

ἆρ᾽ οὐ πολλὴ ἀνάγκη: both the verb (εἴη) and the required ἄν are omitted as obvious: 'wouldn't it be greatly necessary [that]'.

72d1

τεθνάναι καὶ μηδὲν ζῆν: 'be (i.e. remain) dead and not one of them live'.

72d1–2

εἰ ... ἐκ μὲν τῶν ἄλλων τὰ ζῶντα γίγνοιτο: 'if living things come into being from something else', that is, than the dead. ἐκ τῶν ἄλλων means literally 'from the rest of things' and therefore 'any other source'.

τὰ δὲ ζῶντα θνῇσκοι: 'but the living things die', which in the scenario means they cannot be the source of new living things.

72d2–3

τίς μηχανὴ μὴ οὐχὶ πάντα καταναλωθῆναι εἰς τὸ τεθνάναι: 'what contrivance could prevent everything being used up on dying?' After a negated verb of preventing, Greek uses μή οὐ and an infinitive to express what is being prevented. Here the verb is omitted, and the added negative οὐχί (a variant of οὐ) justified by the negative answer expected by this rhetorical question. καταναλωθῆναι is the aorist passive infinitive of καταναλίσκω, 'I use up, spend lavishly'. In Greek one spends money εἴς τι (on something), hence εἰς τὸ τεθνάναι.

72d4

οὐδὲ μία μοι δοκεῖ: 'I don't think there can be one at all' (i.e. contrivance). οὐδὲ μία is a more emphatic form of the feminine οὐδεμία. The difference in pronunciation between the two is revealed by the accented or unaccented ε.

72d6–7

ἔστιν ... παντὸς μᾶλλον οὕτω: 'it is like this more than anything'.

αὐτὰ ταῦτα ὁμολογοῦμεν: ὁμολογέω can be used with a direct object ('I agree on').

72d8

ἔστι τῷ ὄντι καὶ τὸ ἀναβιώσκεσθαι: 'coming back to life really does exist'. The καί is the first in a run of three, linking three units in polysyndeton.

72e1–2

καὶ ταῖς ... κάκιον: Burnet is surely right to bracket these words, which bear no relation to the argument just presented. A very similar phrase occurs at 63c6, where it is much more suited to the context. It is likely an interpolation from a Christian-era copyist who felt that Socrates has not said enough on the different fates of the good and the bad in the afterlife.

72e3–77a5 – the second argument for immortality: The theory of recollection

Cebes reminds everyone of Socrates' theory of recollection, according to which everything we learn during life we are really just remembering. For how else could people be brought, by questioning alone, to say true things on issues they had previously been ignorant of? (For more on the theory, see Introduction, pp. 79–80.) Socrates and his friends discuss the theory and conclude that it would be impossible unless our souls existed before birth.

72e3

καὶ μὴν ... γε: see 71a3–4 n. Here, the phrase communicates Cebes' enthusiasm to share the connection he has spotted between the cycle of opposites and the theory of recollection.

ὑπολαβών: see 69e6–7 n.

72e4

εἰ ἀληθής ἐστιν: i.e. if its conclusions are right.

72e4–5

εἴωθας θαμὰ λέγειν: 'you are often saying'. εἴωθα 'I am accustomed to' is a perfect with present sense. Socrates does in fact discuss his theory of recollection in two other Platonic dialogues, the *Phaedrus* and, more famously, the *Meno* (see introduction, pp. 86–87).

οὐκ ἄλλο τι ἤ: 'nothing other than'.

72e6

τυγχάνει οὖσα: see 71e5 n.

κατὰ τοῦτον: i.e. τὸν λόγον.

72e6–7

ἀνάγκη που ἡμᾶς ... μεμαθηκέναι: 'I suppose we must have learned'.

ἃ νῦν ἀναμιμνησκόμεθα: 'which we now recall'. ἀναμιμνήσκομαι is always strictly passive ('I am reminded'), but can also be middle in meaning – that is, not imply some other agent ('I recall'). It is used thus throughout this part of the *Phaedo*.

A Level

73a1

εἰ μὴ ἦν που ἡμῖν ἡ ψυχὴ: 'if our soul did not exist (ἦν) somewhere (που)', a present closed conditional.

73a2

ταύτῃ: 'in this way' (see 71e8–10 n.).

ἀθάνατον ... τι: 'something immortal'. As Cebes has put it so far, recollection hardly requires the soul to be immortal, but just to have existed and acquired knowledge before birth.

73a4–5

ποῖαι τούτων αἱ ἀποδείξεις: 'what are the proofs of this like?' ποῖαι 'what sort?' requests a rough gist.

73a5–6

ὑπόμνησόν: 2sg. aor. act. imperative of ὑπομιμνήσκω 'I remind'.

οὐ γὰρ σφόδρα ... μέμνημαι: 'I don't remember [it] too well'. Simmias' lapse of memory permits not just a joke but also an opportunity to review briefly the argument for recollection, as presented in the *Meno*.

ἐν τῷ παρόντι: 'at present'.

73a7

ἑνὶ μὲν λόγῳ ... καλλίστῳ: [it is proved] 'by one outstanding argument'.

ἐρωτώμενοι: passive, 'being asked questions'.

73a8

ἐάν τις καλῶς ἐρωτᾷ: 'if someone is asking them properly'. Not all questions can lead to recollection (what we would call discovery), only those that guide the person towards the right answer.

73a8–9

πάντα ᾗ ἔχει: 'everything as it is', i.e. they can say things that are true that they previously could not. ᾗ is a relative used adverbially ('in which way': see 71e8–10 n.), and so ἔχω alongside it means 'I am'.

73a9

εἰ μὴ ἐτύγχανεν αὐτοῖς ἐπιστήμη ἐνοῦσα: 'if there wasn't really knowledge in them'. On τυγχάνω in this sense, see 71e5 n.

73b1

ἐάν τις ἐπὶ τὰ διαγράμματα ἄγῃ: we must infer an αὐτοὺς as the object.

73b2

σαφέστατα κατηγορεῖ: 'it proves very clearly'. As present κατηγορεῖ shows, the conditional is not a future, but a generalizing present: the ἐάν + subjunctive of the protasis are indefinite ('if ever ...').

73b3

εἰ δὲ μὴ ταύτῃ ... πείθῃ: the verb is a 2sg. present passive, not middle. ταύτῃ is adverbial 'in this way'.

73b4

σκέψαι ἄν ... σοι ... συνδόξῃ: 'consider if you agree'. σκέψαι is 2sg. aor. mid. imperative of σκέπτομαι, and ἄν here = ἐάν.

τῇδέ πή: see 70c4 n.

73b5

καλουμένη: i.e. 'so-called'.

73b6

ἀπιστῶ ... ἔγωγε ... οὔ: the verb is promoted to mark Simmias' words as a direct response to Socrates' (ἀπιστεῖς, b4) and the negative held back for emphasis. ἔγωγε 'I at least' hints that Socrates must go into more detail if others are to share Simmias' faith in the theory.

73b6–7

αὐτὸ δὲ τοῦτο ... δέομαι παθεῖν ... ἀναμνησθῆναι: 'I need to experience this very thing, [namely] to be reminded' (or 'recall'). On the sense of πάσχω, see 72b5 n.

περὶ οὗ ὁ λόγος: ἔστι must be assumed.

73b8

ἐξ ὧν Κέβης ἐπεχείρησε λέγειν: the relative is attracted into the genitive after ἐξ (see 71c9 n.). In saying that Cebes has only 'tried' ἐπεχείρησε to state the case, Simmias may intend a dig at his friend, who had felt his summary of recollection had proved the immortality of the soul (73a2 n.).

73b9

πείθομαι: again passive, not middle.

οὐδὲν μεντἂν ἧττον ἀκούοιμι: a potential optative with ἄν can express a polite request (μεντἂν is a crasis of μέντοι and ἄν). οὐδὲν ἧττον is adverbial here and means 'nonetheless' (lit. 'nothing less').

πῇ: 'how' – accented, and hence a question-word here.

73b10

ἐπεχείρησας λέγειν: 'you put your hand to stating it'. The verb is aorist because Socrates has already tackled the question in his own mind at this point, not to mention previous conversations (72e4–5). ἐπιχειρέω is in a slightly different sense here ('undertake, set to work at') to at b8 ('try, attempt').

73c1–2

ὁμολογοῦμεν ... δεῖν αὐτόν: the verb introduces an indirect statement: 'we agree ... that he must'.

**A
Level**

εἴ τίς τι ἀναμνησθήσεται: a future indicative in a conditional's protasis stresses that the consequences described in the main clause (ὁμολογοῦμεν …) are unavoidable if the condition is met. It is a rhetorically powerful choice here.

πρότερόν ποτε: 'at some earlier time'.

73c4–d11

Socrates and Simmias agree that it is possible to be reminded of something or someone by the perception of something else entirely: someone spotting Simmias, for instance, might thus be prompted to remember Cebes too.

73c4

τόδε ὁμολογοῦμεν: τόδε is the direct object ('we agree on this') and stands in apposition to the indirect statement that follows ὁμολογοῦμεν.

παραγίγνηται: 'comes to [someone]'.

73c5–6

λέγω δὲ τίνα τρόπον; τόνδε: Socrates asks himself 'in what way do I mean?', and answers, 'The following [way]'. τίνα τρόπον and τόνδε are adverbial accusatives.

73c6–7

τι ἕτερον: 'some one thing', with ἕτερον corresponding with ἕτερον again at c8 ('another thing').

τινα ἄλλην αἴσθησιν λαβών: 'having perceived it some other way' (lit. 'having taken some other perception').

73c7–8

μὴ μόνον ἐκεῖνο γνῷ, ἀλλὰ καὶ ἕτερον ἐννοήσῃ: 'not only recognises that thing, but also thinks of another'. ἐκεῖνο refers back to τι ἕτερον at c6. γνῷ is 3sg. root aor. subj. of γιγνώσκω.

οὗ μὴ ἡ αὐτὴ ἐπιστήμη ἀλλ᾽ ἄλλη: 'of which [there is] not the same knowledge but another'. Socrates is envisaging two things where someone can know the one but not the other. For example, someone might know Simmias but have never met Cebes. Odd and even, however, would not count, since nobody can understand what one is without understanding the other.

73c8–9

ἆρα οὐχὶ … δικαίως λέγομεν: 'are we not right to say'. ἆρα οὐχὶ introduces a closed question expecting the answer 'yes' (οὐχί is a variant of οὐ).

τοῦτο: looks forward to the ὅτι-clause, so is better left untranslated.

73d2

πῶς λέγεις: 'how do you mean?'

73d3

ἄλλη που ἐπιστήμη ἀνθρώπου καὶ λύρας: 'the knowledge of a person is, I suppose, different from the knowledge of his lyre'.

73d4

οἱ ἐρασταί: 'lovers'. The article shows that Socrates is speaking of lovers in general.

73d6

τὰ παιδικὰ: the n. pl. of the adjective παιδικός 'of a child' is used as a noun to refer to a lover's 'beloved' or 'darling'. (For Athenians, this is usually a young male, hence the word's origin.) Here it is best taken as a true plural ('boyfriends'), to match οἱ ἐρασταί (d4).

πάσχουσι: 'they experience'.

73d7

ἔγνωσάν ... ἔλαβον: the aorist tense is used to mark that these are commonly occurring actions, or general truths, that may well be familiar from one's experience (the so-called gnomic aorist).

ἐν τῇ διανοίᾳ: 'in the process of thinking', i.e. about the object.

73d7–8

ἔλαβον τὸ εἶδος τοῦ παιδὸς: 'grasped the mental image (εἶδος) of the boy'.

οὗ ἦν ἡ λύρα: 'to whom the lyre belongs'. ἦν should be translated as present: it is only imperfect in keeping with the (gnomic) aorists ἔγνωσάν and ἔλαβον.

73d10

ἄλλα ... μυρία τοιαῦτ᾽ ἂν εἴη: a potential optative phrase, 'there would be countless other such examples'.

73d11

μυρία μέντοι νὴ Δία: 'countless indeed, by Zeus'. μέντοι here does not have its usual adversative sense (as at e2), but instead marks a strong agreement. (Compare the English 'but of course!')

73e1

οὐκοῦν ... τὸ τοιοῦτον ἀνάμνησίς τίς ἐστι: 'is this sort of thing a case of recollection, then?'

73e1–2

μάλιστα μέντοι ὅταν: 'however, [isn't recollection] more especially when ...'. Socrates is pointing out that what they have been discussing is not ἀνάμνησις in the most usual sense of the word, which is more often the remembering of something one has forgotten.

τοῦτο πάθῃ: i.e. recollects.

73e2–3

ὑπὸ χρόνου καὶ τοῦ μὴ ἐπισκοπεῖν: 'through time and inattention'.

ἐπελέληστο: 3sg. pluperfect of ἐπιλανθάνομαι 'I forget'. The verb can take a genitive or (as here) accusative object.

A
Level

73e5
τί δέ: 'what about this?', heralding a forward move in the discussion (as at 71a12).
ἔστιν: 'is it possible?' Uncompounded ἔστι functions in this sense much like ἔξεστιν,
    but is followed by an accusative (rather than a dative) and infinitive.
ἵππον γεγραμμένον: i.e. a drawing or painting of a horse.
ἰδόντα: 'someone having seen'.

73e9–10
ἔστιν in the sense 'it is possible' (e5) must be supplied again here.

73e9
αὐτοῦ Σιμμίου: 'the actual Simmias', as opposed to an image of him.

74a1
ἔστι μέντοι: see 73e1–2 and e5 nn.

74a2
ἆρ᾽ ... οὐ κατὰ πάντα ταῦτα συμβαίνει: 'does it not follow (συμβαίνει) from
    all this?' Philosophical authors often use συμβαίνω to express that a conclusion
    logically follows from something already said. It is typically followed by an acc.
    + inf. indirect statement.

74a2–3
εἶναι μὲν ἀφ᾽ ὁμοίων, εἶναι δὲ καὶ ἀπὸ ἀνομοίων: recollection 'exists from
    things that are alike, but it also exists from things that are unalike'. We are
    reminded of A by an image of A (i.e. something 'alike') but can also be reminded
    of A by something different altogether (B).

74a6
τόδε προσπάσχειν: 'to experience the following thing as well'. προς with a dative
    means 'in addition to', and this is the sense of prefix here. τόδε looks forward to
    the infinitive ἐννοεῖν, which stands in apposition to it ('[namely,] having in mind').

74a9
σκόπει: 2sg. pres. act. imperative of σκοπέω.

74a9–12
φαμέν πού τι εἶναι ἴσον ... αὐτὸ τὸ ἴσον: 'we say, I suppose, that there is
    something that is equal', that is, not examples of things in the world that might
    be called equal (like two identical copies of this book), but 'the equal itself'. In
    his wording, Plato invites us to recall the earlier discussion of abstract things
    that exist and that we know, but not through the senses (65d4–e5: see n.). These
    are what Plato will go on to call Forms (see introduction, pp. 79–80).
οὐ ξύλον λέγω ξύλῳ ... οὐδ᾽ ἄλλο τῶν τοιούτων οὐδέν: the examples make it
    clear that Socrates is not talking about equality between objects we perceive in
    the world.
παρὰ ταῦτα πάντα ἕτερόν τι: 'but something else over and above all these'.

A
Level

74a12

φῶμέν τι εἶναι ἢ μηδέν: φῶμέν, 1pl. pres. subjunctive of φημί, is deliberative ('should we say that it is something [i.e. exists] or nothing?'), which accounts also for μηδέν instead of οὐδέν.

74b1

φῶμέν: in typical Greek fashion, Simmias says 'yes' by repeating the verb of the question. Here the 'yes' is further reinforced by μέντοι νὴ Δί(α) (on which see, 73d11 n.).

θαυμαστῶς γε: a further expression of approval, showing that Simmias' enthusiasm has grown since his otherwise similar approbation at 73d11. We cannot translate the words literally ('marvellously indeed') and still capture this sense: something like 'without a doubt' comes closer.

74b2

ἦ καὶ ἐπιστάμεθα αὐτὸ ὃ ἔστιν: 'and do we know what it, by itself, is?' Given Plato's tendency to omit the antecedent of a relative clause, we should treat αὐτό here as emphatic, in the sense ('by itself'), as used in the earlier discussion of abstract 'things by themselves' (64d4–e5; see 64c5 n.). ἦ is not 'or' (ἤ, as at c6), but a particle, used as here to mark a yes/no question or to introduce a confident statement.

74b3

Having already agreed at 65d that similar abstract 'things by themselves' exists, Simmias is understandably ready to go along with Socrates again here. See also 65d6 n.

74b4

πόθεν λαβόντες αὐτοῦ τὴν ἐπιστήμην: 'having got the knowledge of it from where?' There is no main verb because ἐπιστάμεθα (b2) is assumed again as obvious.

74b4–6

This complex sentence must be broken down into its components before sense can be made of it. These are as follows.

ἆρ᾽ οὐκ ... ἐκ τούτων ἐκεῖνο ἐνενοήσαμεν: the main clause, 'do we not come to have that thing (i.e. τὸ ἴσον) in mind from these'. τούτων ('these') refer to the equal-looking objects we see in the world (see next n. but one). ἐνενοήσαμεν is a gnomic aorist (see 73d7 n.).

ἐξ ὧν ... ἐλέγομεν: the case of the relative has been attracted into the genitive by ἐξ, even though its role in its clause should demand an accusative ('attraction of the relative').

ἢ ξύλα ἢ λίθους ἢ ἄλλα ἄττα ἰδόντες ἴσα: 'when we see equal pieces of wood or equal blocks of stone or some other equal things'. (ἄττα here is a variant of τινά.) Such things may be 'equal' insofar as they look identical and/or have the same weight, value, size, purpose, and so on. Materials such as pieces of wood and blocks of stone (λίθοι) offer a good example, since, as common building materials these are usually cut to precise measurements, so as to differ as little as possible from each other.

ἕτεϱον ὂν τούτων: 'since it (ἐκεινό) is different from these things', i.e. equal pieces of wood and blocks of stones, etc.

74b7

τῇδε: see 70c4 n.

74b7–9

The interpretation of this sentence is hotly disputed among Platonic scholars. The two main options are presented below, and readers must choose which they prefer. More in-depth discussion can be found in all the works in the 'Further reading' section of the introduction (pp. 89–90).

ἐνίοτε: 'sometimes' must modify φαίνεται, not ὄντα.

ταὐτὰ ὄντα: 'though being the same', i.e. as each other. They are not the actual same piece of wood or stone, but just resemble each other in every other way. ταὐτά is a crasis of τὰ αὐτά. Although they agree with both a neuter (ξύλα) and a masculine (λίθοι), these words are neuter because that is the gender of the more recent of the two.

τῷ μὲν ἴσα φαίνεται τῷ δ᾽ οὔ: the pieces of wood or stone 'seem equal to X (τῷ μὲν) but not to Y (τῷ δ᾽)'. The reader must decide whether X and Y refer to:

(a) observers, one who sees the objects as equal and one who doesn't; or

(b) other *things*, one that looks equal to the objects and one that doesn't.

Both have the same consequence: that unlike 'the equal itself', things in the world are not purely equal. On (a), people disagree on whether objects are equal because they only remind us of 'the equal itself', and people's recollections are triggered by different things. On (b), the issue is that objects can be simultaneously both equal and unequal: one can be equal to another, but unequal to a third. This is not true of 'the equal itself', which, Socrates says, cannot ever be unequal to anything (c1–6).

74c1–2

τί δέ: see 73e5 n.

αὐτὰ τὰ ἴσα ἔστιν ὅτε ἄνισά σοι ἐφάνη: interpretation is again controversial, but Simmias' immediate confident response ('never!', c3) suggests reading the question in the following way, as a no-brainer: 'did the things that are equal in themselves (αὐτὰ) at times seem unequal to you?' Socrates is asking whether Simmias has ever perceived something that is equal in and of itself as being also unequal. At this stage he is leaving open the question of how many things really belong to that category, but it will soon become clear that it is only one, 'the equal itself'.

ἔστιν ὅτε: 'sometimes', an adverbial phrase offering an alternative to ἐνίοτε (b8).

ἢ ἡ ἰσότης ἀνισότης: 'or has equality [sometimes seemed to you to be] inequality?' The detail further encourages reading the whole question as a no-brainer.

**A
Level**

74c3

οὐδεπώποτέ γε: 'never yet!'

74c4–5

οὐ ταὐτὸν ἄρα ἐστίν: '[they] are not the same, then'. Note the crasis in ταὐτὸν.
αὐτὸ τὸ ἴσον: see 74a9–12 n.

74c7–10

Socrates and Simmias agree that we have (re)gained our knowledge of the equal itself via the equal things (such as equal pieces of wood) that we have seen in the world (ἐκ τούτων ... τῶν ἴσων).

ἑτέρων ὄντων ἐκείνου τοῦ ἴσου: 'though different from that [one] equal', i.e. the equal itself. ἐκείνου τοῦ ἴσου is a genitive of separation ('from').

αὐτοῦ τὴν ἐπιστήμην ἐννενόηκάς τε καὶ εἴληφας: 'you have come to have in mind and got hold of the knowledge of it' (i.e. of the equal itself). ἐννενόηκάς and εἴληφας are 2sg. perfect actives of ἐννοέω and λαμβάνω, respectively. These two verbs were earlier used to express the key activities involved in recollection (73e4–9).

74c11

οὐκοῦν ἢ ὁμοίου ὄντος τούτοις ἢ ἀνομοίου: the words continue Socrates' previous sentence, as a yes/no question: 'it [i.e. the equal itself] being either similar or dissimilar to them?' The point of the question is to pave the way for Socrates' next remark, that it doesn't matter whether what reminds us of the equal itself is similar or dissimilar to it (c13). For as they had agreed before, one can be reminded of something (e.g. Simmias) either by a likeness of it (a painting of Simmias) or something different entirely (Cebes).

74c13–15

διαφέρει ... οὐδέν: 'it makes no difference'.
ἕως ἂν: indefinite, 'so long as'.
ἄλλο ἰδὼν ... ἄλλο ἐννοήσῃς: 'seeing one thing, you come to think of another'.
ἀπὸ ταύτης τῆς ὄψεως: i.e. as a result of seeing the first thing.
ἀναγκαῖον ... αὐτὸ ἀνάμνησιν γεγονέναι: 'the process in question (αὐτὸ) must have been recollection'.

74d4–8

Socrates and Simmias return to the examples of equal pieces of wood (and the like) and conclude that they appear equal to us in a way that falls short of the equal itself.

74d4

ἢ πάσχομέν τι τοιοῦτον: 'do we experience something like this', referring to what follows.

74d5

οἷς νυνδὴ ἐλέγομεν: the relative is attracted into the dative to show it follows on from ἐν (d4).

A Level

74d5–6

ἆρα φαίνεται ἡμῖν οὕτως ἴσα εἶναι: οὕτως looks forward to ὥσπερ. The verb
is singular because the subject is neuter plural.

ὥσπερ αὐτὸ τὸ ὃ ἔστιν: 'just as the [thing] which is [equal] itself'. The formulation
is convoluted, but Plato's readers are now familiar enough with the idea of 'the
X itself' to recognize it here, even with the 'X' omitted.

74d6–7

ἢ ἐνδεῖ τι ἐκείνου ... ἢ οὐδέν: 'do they fall short of that [i.e. the equal itself] in
some way, or not at all?' ἐνδέω 'I fall short of' is followed by a genitive. τι and
οὐδέν are accusatives of respect (adverbial).

τῷ τοιοῦτον εἶναι οἷον τὸ ἴσον: an articular infinitive phrase and dative of
relation. Socrates asks whether they fall short 'in being like (τοιοῦτον ... οἷον)
the equal'.

74d8

πολύ: adverbial.

74d9–75c5

Socrates enters the final stretch of his account of recollection. To understand it, we
must recall that in his view, only certain things really exist: these exclude the
objects we see in the world, but include 'the just itself', 'the equal itself', and so
on – what he later calls the Forms (see introduction, pp. 79–80). Suppose I see
an object (O) in the world, and it reminds me of one of the things that really
exist (F); for when I see O, I notice that it resembles F but falls short of it in some
way. That I am reminded of F means, by definition, that I already know F. Yet I
have never perceived F through the senses (65d4–e5), only things that reminded
me of F. I must, then, recall F from before I started perceiving things – that is,
before I was born.

74d9

ὅταν τίς τι ἰδὼν ἐννοήσῃ ὅτι: 'whenever someone sees a thing and thinks to
himself, ...'. Despite the ὅτι, what follows must be treated as a direct statement,
as the first person ὁρῶ (d10) reveals.

74d10

βούλεται μὲν ... εἶναι οἷον ἄλλο τι τῶν ὄντων: 'aspires to be like some other
real thing' (lit. 'of the things that exist'). βούλεται μὲν looks forward to ἐνδεῖ
δὲ (74e1).

τοῦτο ὃ νῦν ἐγὼ ὁρῶ: the subject of βούλεται: 'this thing which I now see'.

74e1

οὐ δύναται τοιοῦτον εἶναι οἷον ἐκεῖνο: it cannot be of the same sort as that
thing', that is, it is only a pale imitation of the thing that really exists.

74e1–2

ἀλλ' ἔστιν φαυλότερον: 'but is inferior to it'. After this the ὅτι-clause ends.

**A
Level**

74e2–3

ἀναγκαῖόν ... τὸν τοῦτο ἐννοοῦντα τυχεῖν προειδότα: 'the person thinking this must really have known from before'. On this sense of τυγχάνω, see 71e5n. προειδότα is the acc. sg. pres. act. participle of πρόοιδα 'I know in advance'.

ἐκεῖνο ᾧ φησιν αὐτὸ προσεοικέναι μέν, ἐνδεεστέρως δὲ ἔχειν: 'that which he says it is similar to, but falls short of'. προσεοικέναι is the infinitive of προσέοικα 'I resemble' (+ dative), which like its uncompounded form is perfect in form but present in meaning. On ἔχω with an adverb, see 70b6–7.

74e6

τὸ τοιοῦτον πεπόνθαμεν: 'we have experienced the same thing'. πεπόνθαμεν is a perfect from πάσχω.

74e9

προειδέναι: infinitive of πρόοιδα.

75a2

ὀρέγεται ... πάντα ταῦτα εἶναι οἷον τὸ ἴσον: 'all these things were striving (lit. "reaching") to be like the equal'. ὀρέγεται, like βούλεται (74d10), adds a touch of personification to the account of how objects in the world relate to the things-themselves (or Forms) they identify.

75a5–6

μὴ ἄλλοθεν αὐτὸ ἐννενοηκέναι ... ἀλλ' ἤ: indirect statement in apposition to τόδε, 'that we haven't come to think of it from anywhere ... except'.

75a6–7

ἐκ τοῦ ἰδεῖν ἢ ἅψασθαι: 'from seeing or touching it', really two articular infinitives, but sharing one article.

75a7–8

ταὐτὸν δὲ πάντα ταῦτα λέγω: 'I count all these [as] the same'. That is, the same is true of all the senses, not just vision, which Socrates has been referring to most.

75a9–10

πρός γε ὃ βούλεται δηλῶσαι ὁ λόγος: 'for what the argument seeks to show'.

75b1–2

ἐκείνου τε ὀρέγεται τοῦ ὃ ἔστιν ἴσον: 'strives for that thing which the equal is'. On τὸ ὃ ἔστιν (ἴσον), see 74d5–6n.

75b2

ἢ πῶς λέγομεν: better translated with a future: 'or how shall we put it?'

75b4–5

πρὸ τοῦ ... ἄρξασθαι ἡμᾶς ὁρᾶν καὶ ἀκούειν: articular infinitive with dependent infinitives, 'before we began to see and hear'.

A
Level

καὶ τἆλλα αἰσθάνεσθαι: 'and to perceive by the other [senses]'. τἆλλα is an accusative of respect.

75b5–6

τυχεῖν ἔδει ... εἰληφότας ἐπιστήμην: 'we must really have got hold of knowledge'. εἰληφότας is the acc. masc. pl. of the perf. act. participle of λαμβάνω.

ἐπιστήμην αὐτοῦ τοῦ ἴσου ὅτι ἔστιν: 'knowledge of what the equal itself is'. It is common in Greek for what ought to be the subject of a subordinate clause to come ahead of it, with the case appropriately changed. This is called anticipation or prolepsis. ὅτι is the indirect-question form of τί; 'what', often printed as ὅ τι to distinguish it from other uses of ὅτι.

75b6–7

εἰ ἐμέλλομεν τὰ ἐκ τῶν αἰσθήσεων ἴσα ἐκεῖσε ἀνοίσειν: we would need to know what the equal itself is 'if we were going to refer the equal things [we recognise] from our perceptions to it'.

τὰ ἐκ τῶν αἰσθήσεων ἴσα: i.e. the objects we perceive to be equal.

ἀνοίσειν: future infinitive of ἀναφέρω, 'I bring back' or, metaphorically, 'I refer'.

75b7

ὅτι: causal ('because').

προθυμεῖται: 'are eager', another personifying metaphor for the way in which objects relate to the things-themselves (or Forms) they resemble.

75b8

ἔστιν δὲ αὐτοῦ φαυλότερα: 'but they are inferior to it' (i.e. αὐτὸ τὸ ἴσον, looking back to ἐκεῖνο just before). αὐτοῦ is a genitive of comparison.

75b9

προειρημένων: perfect passive participle of προλέγω 'I say before'.

75b10

γενόμενοι εὐθὺς ἑωρῶμέν: 'we began to see straight away after we were born'. ἑώρων is the imperfect of ὁράω. On this sense of γίγνομαι, see 70c7–8 n.

75c2

εἰληφέναι: perfect active infinitive of λαμβάνω.

75c6–77c5: the end of the argument from recollection. Socrates leads Simmias through the line of reasoning detailed below.

Just as we knew the equal itself before we were born, we must also possess 'pieces of knowledge' of all the other things we identify as having real existence: the good itself, the just itself and anything else we call 'the X itself'. What we call learning, then, is really the recovery of pieces of knowledge that we had once had, but were made to forget at the moment at birth. For we certainly don't have them as newborns. And it seems implausible, they agree, that we received the knowledge at birth and then immediately forgot it afterwards. We must, then, have got it before birth. If the

A Level

objects of knowledge really exist (and Simmias happily concurs that they do), so too our souls must have existed and come to know them before birth.

Simmias refers Socrates back to Cebes' original question (69e6–70c3), whether our souls outlast our bodies or are destroyed when we die. For until we have answered that, we cannot yet be sure of the soul's immortality, just that it existed before birth. For Socrates' response to the problem (which lies beyond the limit of the prescription), see introduction, pp. 80–82.

A
Level

Vocabulary

An asterisk * denotes a word in OCR's Defined Vocabulary List for AS.

* ἀγαθός -ή -όν	good, virtuous	ἄλλοθεν	from another place
ἀγανακτέω	be annoyed, aggrieved, angry	ἄλλοθι	elsewhere
* ἄγω	lead	* ἄλλος, -η, -ο	other
* ἀδικέω	wrong, act unjustly	ἀλογίστως	irrationally, without reason
* ἄδικος, -η, -ον	unjust, wrong	* ἅμα	at once; (+ dat.) together with
ἀδολεσχέω	talk nonsense	* ἀμείνων, -ον (m./f. acc. pl. ἀμείνους)	better (comp. of ἀγαθός)
ἀδύνατος, -η, -ον	impossible		
* ἀεί	always	* ἀμφότερος, -α, -ον	both (of two)
ἀθάνατος, -ον	immortal		
ἀθροίζω	gather	* ἄν	(hypothetical or indefinite particle; or a contraction of ἐάν)
Ἅιδου	(the house) of Hades		
* αἰσθάνομαι	perceive		
αἴσθησις, -εως, ἡ	perception	ἀναβιώσκομαι	come back to life
* αἰσχρός, -ή, -όν	shameful	* ἀναγκάζω	compel
ἀκοή, -ῆς, ἡ	hearing	ἀναγκαῖος, -α, -ον	necessary
* ἀκούω	hear, listen		
ἀκριβής, -ές	accurate	* ἀνάγκη, -ῆς, ἡ	necessity
ἀλγηδών, -όνος, ἡ	pain	ἀνακάμπτω	bend back; return
		ἀναμιμνήσκω	remind; (mid.) recall
ἀλήθεια, -ας, ἡ	truth	ἀνάμνησις, -εως, ἡ	recollection
* ἀληθής, -ές	true		
* ἀλλά	but	ἀναπίμπλημι	fill up, fill full
ἄλλη	elsewhere; to another place	ἀνεγείρω	rouse, wake up
		ἀνερευνάω	search out, investigate
* ἀλλήλους, -ας, -α	each other	* ἀνήρ, ἀνδρός, ὁ	man

ἀνθρώπινος, -η, -ον   human

* ἄνθρωπος, -ου, ὁ/ἡ   person, man, human

ἄνισος, -ον   unequal

ἀνισότης, -τητος, ἡ   inequality

ἀνόητος, -ον   foolish

ἀνοίσειν   fut. act. inf. of ἀναφέρω, 'I refer'

ἀνόμοιος, -ον   unlike, dissimilar

ἀνταποδίδωμι   give back, repay; assign as a balance; make to correspond

* ἄξιος, -α, -ον   worthy, fit

ἀπαλλαγείς   aor. pass. part. of ἀπαλλάττω

ἀπαλλαγή, -ῆς, ἡ   release, relief, separation

ἀπαλλακτέον   one must release

ἀπαλλάττω   set free, release; (mid./pass.) escape, be released

* ἅπας, ἅπασα, ἅπαν   all, the whole, every

ἄπειμι   depart

ἀπιστέω   disbelieve, distrust

ἀπιστία, -ας, ἡ   disbelief, distrust

* ἀπό + gen.   from, away from

ἀπόδειξις, -εως, ἡ   demonstration, proof

ἀποδημία, -ας, ἡ   time abroad, journey, exile

ἀποδίδωμι   give back, pay what is due

* ἀποθνήσκω, fut. ἀποθανοῦμαι, aor. ἀπέθανον, perf. τέθνηκα   die

ἀπολείπω   leave behind

ἀπόλλυμι   destroy, kill; (intr. mid.) die

* ἀπολογέομαι   speak in one's own defence

ἀπολογία, -ας, ἡ   defence-speech

ἀπολύω   release, set free, undo

ἅπτω   fasten; (mid.) grasp

ἄρα   after all, then

* ἆρα   (introduces a yes/no question)

* ἄριστός, -ή, -όν   best, very good (superl. of ἀγαθός)

* ἀρχή, -ῆς, ἡ   beginning

* ἄρχομαι   begin

* ἄρχων, -οντος, ὁ   ruler

* ἀσθενής, -ές   weak

ἀσχολία, -ας, ἡ   lack of leisure

ἀτιμάζω   dishonour

ἄτοπος, -ον   strange

ἀτραπός, -οῦ, ὁ   path, shortcut

ἄττα   = τινά (see τις, τι)

* αὖ   again; moreover; in turn

αὐξάνομαι   grow, increase

αὔξησις, -εως, ἡ   growth, increase

αὐτὸ   contraction of ἑαυτό

* αὐτός, -ή, -ό   (emphatic adjective) -self; (pronoun in oblique cases) him, her, it, them

* ὁ αὐτός   the same

αὐτοῦ   just here, just there

ἀφεστάναι   intransitive perf. inf. of ἀφίσταμαι 'stand apart'

* ἀφικνέομαι   arrive

ἀφροδίσια, -ων, τά   sexual pleasures

ἀφροσύνη, -ης, ἡ   foolishness

ἄφρων, -ον   foolish, senseless

βελτίων, -ον   better

* βίος, -ου, ὁ   life

* βούλομαι   wish, want

* βραδύς, -εῖα, -ύ   slow

* γάρ   for

* γε   at any rate

* γράφω   write

* γελάω   laugh

γελασείω   be inclined to laugh

γελοῖος, -α, -ον   ludicrous, funny

γένεσις, -εως, ἡ   coming into being, origin, becoming

* γίγνομαι   become, happen, come to be

γνησίως	genuinely	δικαστήριον -ου, τό	law-court
* γιγνώσκω	get to know, find out, realize	δικαστής, -οῦ, ὁ	juror
* γοῦν	at least, at any rate	διό	for which reason (= δι’ ὅ)
* δέ	but, and	δίς	twice
* δεῖ	it is necessary	* δοκέω	think, have an opinion; intend; seem
* δείκνυμι	show	* δόξα, -ας, ἡ	opinion, judgement; glory
* δέομαι	be lacking, need; ask for	δοξάζω	think, suppose
* δεσμός, -οῦ, ὁ	bond, chain	* δουλεύω	be a slave
* δεσπότης, -ου, ὁ	master	* δύναμαι	be able
* δεῦρο	here	* δύναμις, -εως, ἡ	power
* δή	indeed	* δυνατός, -ή, -όν	able, capable
* δῆλός, -ή, -όν	clear	* δύο, gen./dat. δυοῖν	two
* δηλόω	show, make clear		
δήπου	I presume; perhaps; surely not?	* ἐάν	if (future open conditional)
* διά + acc.	on account of	* ἑαυτόν -ήν -ό	himself, herself, itself (reflexive)
* διά + gen.	through	* ἐάω	allow; χαίρειν ἐάω = ‘say goodbye’
διαγράμμα, -ατος, τό	(mathematical) diagram	ἐγγίγνομαι	happen in, be born in, come to be in
διακρίνω	separate, distinguish		
* διαλέγομαι	discuss, converse	* ἐγγύς (superl. adv. either ἐγγύτατα or ἐγγυτάτω)	near (+ gen.)
διαμυθολογέω	converse, express in speech		
διανοέω/ διανοέομαι	have in mind, intend; think of	ἐγείρω	rouse, wake up
διανοία, -ας, ἡ	thought, intention, understanding	ἐγρηγορέναι	perf. intr. act. inf. of ἐγείρω ‘I wake up’
διαπέτομαι, aor. part. διαπτόμενος	fly away, vanish	* ἐγώ	I
		* ἔγωγε	I for one
διασκεδάννυμι	scatter	* ἐθέλω	want
διασκοπέω	examine thoroughly	ἐθίζω	accustom
διατρίβω	spend time; wear away	* εἰ	If
διαφερόντως	to a greater degree	εἶδος, -ους, τό	appearance, form, shape
διαφέρω	excel; differ	εἴδωλον, -ου, τό	image, phantom
* διαφθείρω	destroy	εἶεν	well then
* δίδωμι, fut. δώσω	give	* εἰκός	(it is) likely, reasonable (strictly a participle of ἔοικα)
διέρχομαι, aor. διῆλθον	go through		
διΐσχυρίζομαι	affirm strongly	εἰκότως	reasonably
* δίκαιος, -η, -ον	just	εἰλικρινέω	purify

εἰλικρινής, -ές | pure

* εἰμί | be

* εἰμι, pres. part. ἰών, inf. ἰέναι) | (will) go

εἴπερ | if, precisely if

* εἰρῆσθαι | perf. pass. inf. of λέγω

* εἰς (+ acc.) | into

* εἷς, μία, ἕν | one

* εἴτε | either, or

εἴωθα | be accustomed

* ἐκ (+ gen.) | out of

* ἕκαστος, -η, -ον | each

* ἑκάτερος, -α, -ον | each of two

ἐκβαίνω | go out

* ἐκεῖ | there

* ἐκεῖνος, -η, -ο | that

* ἐκεῖσε | to that place

ἐκλύω | release, free

ἐκπλήττω | shock, amaze, astound

ἐκφέρω | carry out

ἐλάττων, -ον | smaller, less

ἐλάχιστος, -η, -ον | least, very little

* ἐλεύθερος, -α, -ον | free

ἐλλείπω | leave in, leave behind, leave out

* ἐλπίζω | hope

ἐλπίς, -ίδος, ἡ | hope

ἐμπίμπλημι | fill up

ἐμποδίζω | get in the way, hinder

ἐμπόδιος, -α, -ον | in the way

* ἐν (+ dat.) | in

* ἐναντίος, -α, -ον | opposite

ἐνδεής, -ές | lacking

ἐνδέω | fall short, be lacking

ἔνειμι | be in

* ἕνεκα (+ gen.) | on account of

* ἐνθάδε | to here, to there

* ἐνθένδε | from here, from there

ἐνιαχοῦ | in some places, in some cases

ἐνίοτε | sometimes

* ἐννοέω | have in mind, think about, consider

ἔννοια, -ας, ἡ | thought, intent, notion

* ἐνταῦθα | here, there

ἔντιμος, -ον | honoured, valued

* ἐξ (+ gen.) | out of

* ἐξαπατάω | deceive

ἔοικα | seem, seem likely; resemble (+ dat.)

* ἐπεί | when, since

* ἐπειδάν | whenever (= ἐπειδή + ἄν)

* ἔπειτα | then

ἐπελέληστο | 3sg. perf. mid./pass. of ἐπιλανθάνομαι 'forget'

ἐπεχειρέω | put one's hand to, try

* ἐπί (+ acc.) | to, towards, onto, for the sake of

* ἐπί (+ dat.) | on, at, for, for the sake of

ἐπιβλέπω | look upon

ἐπιθυμέω | desire, be eager

ἐπιθυμία, -ας, ἡ | desire

ἐπιλανθάνομαι | forget (+ gen.)

ἐπιμελέομαι | care for, take care of

ἐπισκοπέω | look upon, observe, inspect

* ἐπίσταμαι | know

ἐπιστατέω | be in charge of, take care of

ἐπιστάτης, -ου, ὁ | overseer, person in charge

ἐπιστήμη -ης, ἡ | knowledge

ἐπιτηδεύω | make something one's business, take care to do, practise

* ἔπος -ους, τό | word

ἐραστής, -οῦ, ὁ | lover

* ἔργον, -ου, τό | deed, work, task

* ἐρωτάω | ask

* ἔσχατος, -η, -ον | last, final; worst

* ἑταῖρος, -ου, ὁ | friend, companion

* ἕτερος, -η, -ον	one, the other (of two)	θάτερον	= τὸ ἕτερον (crasis)
* ἔτι	still	* θάττων, -ον	quicker (comparative of ταχύς)
* εὖ	well		
εὔελπις, -ι	in good hope	θαυμαστῶς	wonderfully
* εὐθύς, -εῖα, -ύ (adv. εὐθέως)	straight	θεατέον	one must see (θεάομαι)
		θεμιτός, -ή, -όν	lawful, permitted
εὐλόγως	reasonably	* θεός, -οῦ, ὁ	god
ἐφάπτομαι	grasp (+ gen.)	θεραπεία, -ας, ἡ	care
ἐφέλκω	drag to	θερμαίνω	heat up
* ἔχω	have	θεωρέω	consider, contemplate
* ἔχω + adverb	be	θήρα, -ας, ἡ	hunt
* ἕως	while, until	θηρεύω	hunt
* ζάω, inf. ζῆν	live	θνήσκω, fut. Θανοῦμαι, aor. ἔθανον, perf. τέθνηκα	die
* ζητέω	seek		
ζήτησις, -εως, ἡ	search		
ζωή, -ῆς, ἡ	life	θόρυβος, -ου, ὁ	din
ζῷον, -ου, τό	animal, living thing	θρυλέω	babble, keep saying
* ἤ	or; either … or	* ἱκανός, -ή, -όν	sufficient
* ἤ	than	ἱμάτιον, - ου, τό	cloak
ἤ	(introduces question)	* ἵππος, -ου, ὁ	horse
* ἦ δ' ὅς	he said	* ἴσος, -η, -ον	equal, balanced
* ἡγέομαι	lead, think	ἰσότης, -τητος, ἡ	equality
* ἡδέως	gladly	ἰσχύς, -ύος, ἡ	strength
* ἤδη	already, now, furthermore	* ἰσχυρός, -ά, -όν	strong
* ἥδομαι	be glad, take pleasure in	* ἴσως	perhaps; equally
ἡδονή, -ῆς, ἡ	pleasure	καθαρεύω	be clean, pure
* ἡδύς, -εῖα, -ύ	pleasant, sweet	καθαρός, -ή, -όν	clean, pure
* ἥκιστα	least, very little	κάθαρσις, -εως, ἡ	cleansing, purification
* ἥκω	have come	* καθεύδω	sleep
* ἡμεῖς	we	καθοράω	observe, perceive; look down on
* ἡμέρα, -ας, ἡ	day		
* ἦν	imperfect from εἰμί; crasis of ἐάν	* καί	and, also, too, even
		* καίτοι	and yet
ἥσσων -ον	less, weaker, worse	* κακός, -ή, -όν	bad, evil
θαμὰ	often	* καλέω	call
* θάνατος, -ου, ὁ	death	καλλωπισμός, -οῦ, ὁ	ornamentation, beautification
θανατάω	desire to die		
* θαρρέω	take courage	* καλός, -ή, -όν	fine, good, beautiful
		καμπή, -ῆς, ἡ	bend, turn; turning post

* κἄν	crasis of (a) καί and ἔαν or (b) καί and ἄν		μάθησις, -εως, ἡ	the act of learning
καπνός, -οῦ, ὁ	smoke		* μάλιστα	especially, very much
* κατά (+ acc.)	according to, in accordance with, along, down		* μᾶλλον	more
			* μανθάνω	I learn
κατά (+ gen.)	concerning; against		* μάχη, -ης, ἡ	battle
καταδαρθάνω	fall asleep		* μέγας, μεγάλη, μέγα, superl. μεγίστος	large
κατάδηλος, -η, -ον	visible, clear			
καταναλίσκω, aor. pass. κατανηλώθην	use up, spend, lavish		μέγεθος, -ους, τό	largeness, size
			μελετάω	practise
			μελέτημα, -ατος, τό	practice
καταντικρύ	right opposite; τό καταντικρύ, 'the very opposite'		* μέλλω	intend, be about to; hesitate
* κατηγορέω	accuse, allege		* μέμνημαι	remember (perf. mid. of μιμνήσκω)
* κινδυνεύω	run the risk, be likely to		* μέν ... δέ	on the one hand ... on the other (articulates a contrast)
* κοινός, -ή, -όν	common, shared, mutual			
κοινωνέω	have in common; be in partnership			
			* μέντοι	however
κοινωνία, -ας, ἡ	partnership, communion		* μένω	remain, stay
κοινωνός, -οῦ, ὁ	companion, partner		* μετά + acc.	after
* κτάομαι	obtain		* μετά + gen.	with
* κτῆμα, -ατος, τά	possession, property		μεταδίδωμι	give part of, give a share of
κτῆσις, -εως, ἡ	possession, acquisition		μεταλαμβάνω	get a share of, partake of
κύκλος, -ου, ὁ	circle		μεταξύ + gen.	between
κωμῳδοποιός, -οῦ, ὁ	comedy-writer		μετέχω	have a share in, partake of
			* μή	not
* λαμβάνω	take, get		μηδαμόθεν	from no place
* λανθάνω, perf. λέληθα	escape one's notice		* μηδέ	and not
			* μηδείς, μηδεμία, μηδέν	nothing
* λέγω	say, speak, mention, tell			
λῆρος, -ου, ὁ	rubbish, nonsense		μήν	truly, indeed
* λίθος, -ου, ὁ	stone		* μήτε	neither, nor
λογίζομαι	calculate, reckon		* μηχανή, -ῆς, ἡ	contrivance, device; way, means
λογισμός, -οῦ, ὁ	reckoning, calculation, reasoning			
			μιμνήσκω	remind
* λόγος, -ου, ὁ	speech, argument, story, something said		* μόνος, -η, -ον	only, alone
			μυρίοι, -αι, -α	countless; 10,000
λύρα, -ας, ἡ	lyre		* ναί	yes
λύσις, -εως, ἡ	release, deliverance		νή (+ acc.)	by
* λύω	release, set free			

* νόσος, -ου, ἡ	disease	* ὅταν	whenever
* νοῦς, -οῦ, ὁ	mind	* ὅτε	when
* νῦν	now	* ὅτι	because (or from ὅστις)
νυνδή	just now	* οὐ	not
ξύλον, -ου, τό	(piece of) wood	* οὗ	where
* ὅδε, ἥδε, τόδε	this, the following	οὐδαμόθεν	from nowhere
* ὅθεν	whence, from where	* οὐδαμοῦ	nowhere
* οἷ	to where	* οὐδαμῶς	not at all
* οἶδα	know	* οὐδὲ	and not, nor; not even
* οἰκέω	live, dwell	* οὐδείς, οὐδεμία, οὐδέν	no, nobody, nothing
οἶμαι	think		
* οἷον	for example, such as	* οὐδέποτε	never
* οἷός τ' εἰμι	be able	οὐδεπώποτε	never yet
* οἷος, -α, -ον	of what sort	* οὐκοῦν	surely; therefore
οἴχομαι	go, be gone; be dead	* οὔκουν	certainly not, I don't think
* ὀλίγος, -η, -ον	few, little	* οὖν	therefore, so
ὅλως	wholly	οὖς, ὠτός, τό	ear
ὁμιλέω	be in company with; speak with	οὐσία, -ας, ἡ	being, existence; essence, substance
* ὅμοιος, -α, -ον	similar	* οὔτε	neither, nor
ὁμοιότης, -τητος, ἡ	similarity	* οὗτος, αὕτη, τοῦτο	this
* ὁμολογέω	agree	* οὕτω(ς)	thus, in this way; so
ὁμοῦ	together, in the same place	οὑτωσί	in this very way
* ὅμως	nevertheless	* ὀφθαλμός, -οῦ, ὁ	eye
* ὄνομα, -ματος, τό	name	ὄψις, -εως, ἡ	eyesight, vision
ὀνομάζω	call	πάθος, -ους, τό	experience, suffering, emotion
* ὁράω	see	παιδικά, -ῶν, τά	beloved (pl. for sg.)
ὀρέγω	reach, stretch; (med.) reach for, grasp	* παῖς, παιδός, ὁ/ἡ	child, boy, girl
* ὀρθός, -ή, -όν	upright, straight; correct	* πάλαι	long ago, some time ago; a while ago
* ὅς, ἥ, ὅ	who, which (relative pronoun)	* παλαιός, -ή, -όν	old, of old
ὅσαπερ	all the very things which (= ὅσα + περ)	* πάλιν	back, again
		παντάπασι	all in all, wholly
* ὅσος, ὅσα, ὅσον	as much as; (pl.) as many as, all those which	πανταχόθεν	from all quarters, from everywhere
ὅσπερ, ἥπερ, ὅπερ	the very one(s) which	πανταχοῦ	everywhere
* ὅστις, ἥτις, ὅτι	who (indirect pronoun), whoever (indefinite)	παντοδαπός, -ή, -όν	of every kind

πάντως	entirely
πάνυ	very
* παρά + acc.	beside, near, with
* παρά + dat.	by the side of, in the presence of
παραγίγνομαι	be beside, be at hand
παραλυπέω	trouble, grieve besides
παραμένω	stay near
παραμυθία, -ας, ἡ	encouragement, gentle persuasion
παραπίπτω	fall in one's way
* παρασκευάζω	prepare
παρατίθημι	place beside
* πάρειμι	be present
παρέρχομαι	pass by, arrive at
* παρέχω	provide, offer
παρίσταμαι	stand beside
* πᾶς, πᾶσα, πᾶν	all, whole, every
* πάσχω, aor. ἔπαθον, perf. πέπονθα	suffer, experience
* παύω	stop; (mid.) cease
* πείθομαι	obey; believe, trust
* πειράομαι	try, attempt
* περί + acc./gen.	about, concerning
περίειμι	go around
πῇ	in what way? How?
πιθανός, -ή, -όν	trustworthy, plausible, persuasive
* πίνω	drink
πίστις, -εως, ἡ	trust, belief
* πλήν + gen.	except
πνεῦμα, -ματος, τό	breath, spirit
πόθεν	from where
* ποιέω	do, make
* ποῖος, -α, -ον	of what sort?
* πόλεμος, -ου, ὁ	war
* πολλάκις	often

* πολύς, πολλή, πολύ	much; (pl.) many
* πορεύομαι	make a journey, march
* ποτε	once, at some time
* πότερον	(introduces a question with two options)
ποτόν, -οῦ, τό	drink
* που	I suppose (particle)
που	somewhere (indefinite)
* πρᾶγμα, -ατος, τό	business, thing, matter
πραγματεία, -ας, ἡ	occupation, business, diligent effort
πρέπει	it is fitting
* πρίν	before
* πρό + gen.	before, in front of
προειδέναι	inf. of πρόοιδα 'know in advance'
προειρημένων	perf. mid. part. from προλέγω 'say beforehand'
προθυμέομαι	be eager
προλέγω	say beforehand
πρόοιδα	know in advance
* πρός + acc.	towards, to, regarding
προσέοικα	seem fit; resemble (+ dat.)
προσήκω	be fitting
προσπάσχω	experience, suffer in addition
προσπίπτω, aor. προσέπεσον	befall, encounter; attack
προστάττω	put in place, appoint, assign
προστεταγμένη	perf. mid. part. from προστάττω
προσφέρω	add
* πρότερος, -η, -ον	former, previous
* πρῶτον	first (adv.)
πώποτε	ever
* πῶς	how?
πη	in some way, somehow
* ῥᾴδιος, -α, -ον, comp. ῥᾴων, -ον	easy, light

* σαφής, -ές	clear	* τιμάω	honour, value
* σημαίνω	show	* τις, τι	a certain, someone, something
σιτίον, -ου, τό	food, grain		
σκέπτομαι	examine, consider	* τίς, τί	who? which? what?
* σκοπέω	inspect, examine	* τοι	look now
* σοφός, -ή, -όν	wise	τοίνυν	well then
σπουδάζω	be busy, serious; hurry	τοιόσδε, -άδε, -όνδε	such as this
στάσις, -εως, ή	faction-fighting, civil strife	* τοιοῦτος, -αύτη, -οῦτο	of such a kind, such
* σύ	you (sg.)		
συγκρίνω	combine	* τότε	then
συζυγία, -ας, ή	coupling, joining together	* τρέπομαι, aor. ἐτραπόμην	turn oneself
συλλήβδην	taken together (adv.)		
συμβαίνει	it happens	τρέφω	nourish, rear, cause to grow
συμπαραλαμβάνω	take along with one	τρίς	three times
σύμπας, -πασα, -παν	all together, at once	* τρόπος, -ου, ό	way
		τροφή, -ῆς, ή	food, nourishment, nurture
σύμφημι	agree	* τυγχάνω, aor. ἔτυχον, fut. τεύξομαι	encounter (+ dat.); happen to, really be (+ part.)
συμφύρω	mix up with, knead up with		
συναγείρω	gather, collect		
συναθροίζω	gather, collect	ὑγιεία, -ας, ή	health
συνδοκεῖ (+ dat.)	seem good also	* ὑμεῖς	you (pl.)
* σφεῖς	they	ὑπερφυῶς	enormously
* σφόδρα	very	* ὑπὸ (+ gen.)	under, by, at the hands of
* σχεδόν	almost	ὑποδημάτα, -ων, τό	sandals, shoes
σχῆμα -ατος, τό	shape, form, figure		
σχολή, -ῆς, ή	leisure, ease, free time	ὑπολαμβάνω	take up; reply
σχολῇ	hardly (adv.)	ὑπομιμνήσκω	remind, mention
* σῶμα, -ατος, τό	body	* ὕστερος, -α, -ον	later
* ταράττω	disturb, trouble, put in disorder	* φαίνομαι	appear, seem
		φανερός, -ή, -όν	clear, visible
ταραχή, -ῆς, ή	disturbance, disorder	φάρμακον, -ου, τό	drug
ταύτη	in this way (adv.)		
ταὐτόν	= τὸ αὐτόν (crasis)	φαῦλος, -η, -ον	petty, bad, feeble
* τάχ᾽ ἄν	perhaps	φέρε	come!
* ταχύς, -εῖα, -ύ	quick	* φέρω, fut. οἴσω	carry; (mid.) win
τείνω	stretch; direct	* φεύγω	flee
τεκμήριον, -ου, τό	proof	* φημί	say
		φθίνω	decay, waste away
* τελευτάω	die, finish, come to an end	φθίσις, -εως, ή	wasting away, decay

φιλομαθής, ές	fond of learning	* χείρων, -ον	worse
* φίλος, -η, -ον	dear, pleasing	* χρή	it is necessary
φιλοσοφέω	be a philosopher, love wisdom	* χρήματα, -ων, τά	money
		* χράομαι (+ dat.)	use
φιλοσοφία, -ας, ἡ	philosophy	* χρόνος, -ου, ὁ	time
φίλοσοφος, -ου, ὁ	philosopher, lover of wisdom	χωλός, -ή, -όν	lame, limping; defective
φλυαρία, -ας, ἡ	nonsense, rubbish	χωρίζω	separate, divide
φοβερός, -ή, -όν	frightening	χωρίς (+ gen.)	apart from, without
* φόβος, -ου, ὁ	fear	χωρισμός, -οῦ, ὁ	separation
φράζω	speak, say, tell	ψύχω	make cool, cold
φρονέω	have understanding, be wise, think	ψυχή, -ης, ἡ	life, soul, spirit, mind
		* ὧδε	thus, in the following way
φρόνησις, -εως, ἡ	wisdom, thought, knowledge	* ὡς	as, how, that, since
φρόνιμος, -η, -ον	sensible, prudent, wise	* ὡς + future participle	in order to
φροντίζω	consider, care, be thoughtful, worry	* ὡς + superlative	as … as possible
		ὡσαύτως	in this very way
φύσις -εως, ἡ	nature, character; origin, birth	* ὥσπερ	just as, just as if
		ὡσπερεί	just as if
φυτόν, -οῦ, τό	plant	* ὥστε	with the result that
* χαίρω	rejoice, enjoy; greet; say goodbye (χαίρειν ἐάω)	ὤτων	see οὖς
* χαλεπός, -ή, -όν	difficult, harsh, painful		

Xenophon, *Anabasis*

Introduction, Commentary Notes and
Vocabulary by Stephen Anderson

A Level: Book 4: 7–8

Introduction

Xenophon's life

Xenophon, son of Gryllus, an Athenian, was born at some time around 430 BC. His family came from the deme of Erchia, a country district a little to the north-east of Athens, and must have been reasonably wealthy – certainly wealthy enough to provide the young Xenophon with a horse, so that at the age of 20 he could enlist in the cavalry – but there is no indication that it played any active role in the politics of the day.

In the dangerous climate of the early years of the Peloponnesian War (431–404 BC), it is likely that Gryllus and his family sought safety inside the city walls. Certainly Xenophon received his education in Athens, and in the course of it associated with, and was heavily influenced by, the philosopher Socrates. A story related by Diogenes Laertius tells how Socrates met the young Xenophon in a narrow alley, and blocking his path asked him where one might buy various goods. When Xenophon answered, he asked again where men could become honourable and virtuous. This time Xenophon had no answer, and Socrates said, 'Follow me and learn'.

After some experience fighting in the cavalry in various campaigns during the closing years of the Peloponnesian War, Xenophon returned to Athens, and at this stage may have begun to flex his muscles as a writer. He was still in Athens during the rule of the Thirty Tyrants (404–403 BC), the tyrannical government imposed by Sparta after Athens' defeat in the Peloponnesian War, and it is likely that, given his oligarchic sympathies, he played some part in fighting in the cavalry against the exiled democrats.

Although protected by an amnesty after the restoration of democracy in 403, Xenophon must now have found life in Athens rather uncomfortable. His big break came in 401 BC. At the invitation of his Boeotian friend Proxenus, he joined the mercenary forces enlisted by Cyrus the Younger in a campaign against his elder brother, Artaxerxes II, king of Persia. This ill-fated expedition, and the subsequent retreat of the Greeks under his own leadership, Xenophon was later to immortalize in his most famous work, the *Anabasis*, or 'March Up-Country'.

Mercenary soldiers, it is worth saying, were never in short supply in the Greek world: there was almost always a war somewhere, there was no shortage of men for whom a love of adventure, poverty or poor home circumstances made professional soldiering an attractive proposition and, even when military service was seen as a duty in one's home state, there were plenty of tyrants and foreign potentates ready to pay for such support. Cyrus was able to raise more than ten thousand Greeks for his attempt on his brother's kingdom, including not only specialist Cretan archers and Rhodian slingers, but also considerable contingents of Spartans, Athenians, Arcadians, Achaeans, Boeotians and Thessalians.

At the end of the expedition, after some ultimately unsatisfactory service with Seuthes, king of Thrace, Xenophon eventually, in 399 BC, handed over the remnant of the 'Cyreans' to the Spartans, to help with their campaign to protect the Greek cities of Asia Minor against Persian aggression. He himself stayed with them and served successively under each of Thibron, Dercylidas and King Agesilaus.

In 394, Agesilaus was recalled to deal with rebellion on the part of Sparta's allies. Xenophon came with him and fought alongside him at Coronea against Athens and Boeotia. This act of treachery led to his formal exile from Athens, unless, as some hold, this had already happened earlier, as a result either of his joining Cyrus' expedition in the first place or of his continuing opposition to Artaxerxes.

Whatever, he was comfortably settled by the Spartans on a country estate at Scillus, near Olympia in Elis (see *Anab.*5.3.5 ff.), acting as Spartan *proxenos* in that area, and for the next twenty years or so enjoying country life and writing his books.

After the Battle of Leuctra (371 BC) Sparta lost her position as the pre-eminent state in Greece. Elis accordingly reclaimed the estate at Scillus, and Xenophon and his family were obliged to retire to Corinth. There, in all likelihood, despite the revocation of his banishment from Athens in *c.* 368, he stayed for the rest of his life, eventually dying in or around 354. It is recorded that his two sons fought for Athens at Mantinea in 362, Gryllus, the elder of them, dying in the course of the battle.

Xenophon's works

Although his fame in antiquity was greatest as a philosopher and leader of mercenary soldiers, Xenophon can, with some justification, be counted a pretty prolific writer. All the works we know of, some fourteen of them, still survive, though we have only a vague sense of their relative chronologies. They may conveniently be divided into three loose categories: first, historical or quasi-historical narratives, secondly Socratic texts and thirdly a more miscellaneous group, itself containing *inter alia* a collection of technical treatises on subjects closely reflecting the author's own interests and experience.

The historical narrative group contains (i) the *Hellenica*, a seven-book history of Greece from 411 to 362 BC, not in essence a single work, but rather a series of instalments eventually published together; (ii) the *Anabasis*, Xenophon's account of Cyrus the Younger's doomed campaign against his brother, King Artaxerxes II of Persia, and of the retreat of the Ten Thousand Greeks after the battle of Cunaxa;

and (iii) the rather different *Cyropaedia*, a pseudo-historical account of the career of Cyrus the Great, founder of the Achaemenid Persian empire.

Even though his grasp of philosophy may never have been the strongest, Xenophon's early association with Socrates, whom he greatly admired, is responsible for some four of his works: in the *Apology* he gives his own account of Socrates' defence speech at his trial in Athens in 399 BC, a poor second, it has to be admitted, to Plato's speech of the same name; the *Memorabilia* provides us with four books of reminiscences of Socrates, largely imaginary conversations which describe the philosopher's character and some of his views; the *Symposium* recalls the discourse, both witty and serious, at an imaginary banquet at the House of Callias in *c*. 421 BC; and in the *Oeconomicus*, possibly the best of the Socratic works, the subject at issue is household and estate management, presented in the form of a dialogue between Socrates and two interlocutors. The second of these, Ischomachus, may well represent Xenophon himself.

In the third group, then, the treatise *On Horsemanship* offers equestrian training, the *Hipparchicus* deals with the duties of a cavalry commander, the *Cynegeticus* gives advice on hunting with hounds, and *Ways and Means* suggests practical ways of increasing public resources through commercial and industrial enterprises; whilst the *Constitution of the Spartans* provides an uncritical account of the system of government in Sparta, the *Hieron* consists of a dialogue between Hieron of Syracuse and the poet Simonides of Ceos, comparing the lot of the tyrant with that of the private citizen, and the *Agesilaus* gives us an encomium of the Spartan king with whom Xenophon served and whom he much admired.

A number of common factors can be seen to pervade the whole of Xenophon's *oeuvre*, most significantly (i) the close relationship between the author's writings and his own personal experience, (ii) a strong didactic thread particularly as regards matters of leadership and military skill, and (iii) an entirely conventional brand of morality, founded on an unquestioning belief in the gods and in the importance of omens and sacrifices: Xenophon is at his happiest, whether as leader, as teacher or as writer, when he is confident that he is acting, to use his own phrase, σὺν τοῖς θεοῖς.

The *Anabasis*

The *Anabasis* is easily the most famous of Xenophon's works, thanks, in no small part, to its popularity as a school text: generations of schoolchildren have been alternatively delighted or bored rigid by its tales of soldiers advancing so many parasangs towards uninhabited villages, or by the analysis of how hard it was, when supplies ran short in the Arabian desert, to catch an ostrich for the pot, compared with the relative ease of outmanoeuvring a bustard. Its seven books constitute the first extended autobiographical work in ancient literature and the earliest military memoir in history. They recount the events of 401–399 BC, telling how Cyrus, the younger son of Darius II of Persia, led an army of Greek mercenary soldiers against his brother, King Artaxerxes, and how, after Cyrus' defeat and death at the Battle of Cunaxa, Xenophon led his men back to the fringes of the Greek world through the mountainous deserts of Armenia.

The work's date of composition remains uncertain; various theories have been advanced, but some time in the course of the 360s seems the most likely. And there were other accounts too of the same expedition: certainly we know of one by another of the Greek commanders, Sophaenetus of Stymphalus, and Xenophon himself (*Hell.* 3.1.2) tells us that the story was written up by one Themistogenes of Syracuse, though it is usually assumed that this is merely a pseudonym used by the author himself, perhaps so that he could present a rosy picture of his own role with minimal embarrassment.

Xenophon's aim in writing the *Anabasis* may have been to tell his side of a controversial story, and, with an apparently objective, third-person account, to defend himself against criticisms of his leadership; he may have been trying to manipulate the Athenians who had exiled him, or the Spartans after their awkward dealings with the Ten Thousand on their arrival at Byzantium; or again he may have been trying to illustrate the overall weakness of the Persians as an encouragement to the Greeks to mount a panhellenic attack upon them. All these motives have been claimed, and all are possible: we cannot be sure. What is definite, however, is that we have in the *Anabasis* Xenophon's own fresh, interesting and eminently readable account of an exciting adventure in which he himself took part: that is at least as important as any other more hypothetical consideration.

General summary

Book 1

After the death of King Darius and the accession of Artaxerxes, Cyrus gathers his army at Sardis and sets out ostensibly against the Pisidians, but in reality against his brother. At Thapsacus, on the River Euphrates, he reveals his true goal, and the Ten Thousand continue their march across the Arabian Desert. The traitor Orontas is captured and put to death and battle is eventually joined with the forces of Artaxerxes at Cunaxa. Cyrus is killed, the king plunders his brother's camp and the Greeks repulse a Persian attack.

Book 2

On learning of Cyrus' death, the Ten Thousand refuse to surrender to Artaxerxes and join forces with Ariaeus, Cyrus' second-in-command. When a truce is suggested, the Greeks agree terms with Tissaphernes, the king's envoy. However, after the retreat has begun, Ariaeus joins forces with Tissaphernes, and as suspicion grows between Greeks and Persians, Clearchus, now the *de facto* leader of the mercenaries, has what he considers a successful meeting with Tissaphernes. He is then invited a second time, with four other Greek commanders. All are seized and put to death, and the book ends with obituary notices for all five, Clearchus of Sparta, Proxenus of Boeotia, Meno of Thessaly, Agias of Arcadia and Socrates of Achaea.

Book 3

After initial despair in the Greek camp, Xenophon emerges as leader, and when new generals have been elected, the Ten Thousand resume their retreat, under attack from

Persian cavalry and archers. Marching past Larisa and Mespila, still skirmishing with Persian troops they reach the hills, and when eventually caught between the River Tigris and difficult high ground, they decide not to try to cross the river on animal skins, as has been suggested, but rather to head into the Carduchian mountains.

Book 4

As the Greeks enter the mountains, the Carduchians abandon their villages and attack them from higher ground. The Ten Thousand, however, do eventually reach the plain on the other side and cross the River Centrites. They then continue their march, dealing with Tiribazus, governor of western Armenia, suffering hardship as they pass through the snow, facing opposition from troublesome locals and finally arriving at Gymnias, from where a guide leads them to a sight of the sea. After appropriate jubilation they move on, and eventually come to Trapezus on the shores of the Black Sea. Here they hold sacrifices and celebratory games.

[For a detailed summary of the A Level prescription, Anab, 4.5–8, see below.]

Book 5

Chirisophus now leaves to fetch ships, and the Ten Thousand proceed to Cerasus – and it is at this point that Xenophon gives us a fascinating flash-forward to his later life at Scillus. Then, resuming his story, he tells how the Greeks continue on their way and come to Cotyora; here they receive envoys from Sinope who advise them to complete their journey by sea. Xenophon briefly thinks of staying behind and founding a colony; he also defends himself against various allegations of misconduct which are brought against him.

Book 6

The Ten Thousand elect Chirisophus as supreme commander and sail to Heraclea. Here the Arcadians and Achaeans split from the rest of the army and the whole force marches or sails on in three separate groups. They are reunited, however, at Calpe Harbour, where there is trouble over supplies and some fighting with the cavalry of Pharnabazus, the local Persian satrap. Meanwhile Cleander, the Spartan governor of Byzantium, has arrived to bring help; but when a mini-riot breaks out among the men, he threatens to leave and to direct all Greek cities to refuse them assistance or shelter. Still, he is eventually placated and the Ten Thousand proceed on their way through Bithynia and arrive at Chrysopolis in Chalcedonia.

Book 7

When the Ten Thousand cross to Byzantium they are ordered out of the city. The Spartan admiral Anaxibius wants to take them back to Asia, but they decide to join up with Seuthes, king of Thrace. This doesn't turn out well, as there are disputes over pay and Xenophon himself is charged with having received bribes. Eventually, the

Spartans offer to employ the army, and sailing over to Lampsacus they make their way to Pergamum where they join the Spartan general Thibron.

Prescribed text: *Anabasis* 4.5–6 (English), 7–8 (Greek)

As well as containing the most famous and iconic scene in the whole *Anabasis* (the sighting of the sea), these four chapters give us useful examples of many of the main themes which pervade the whole work. In particular a spotlight is shone on Xenophon's own qualities as a leader – his resourcefulness, strategic ability and his care for his men; and also on the types of problem which the Ten Thousand regularly have to surmount in the course of their long march – bad weather (snow), difficult terrain (rivers and mountains) and hostile local tribes (Chalybians, Taochians, Phasians, Macronians and Colchians). Again and again, from whatever difficulties appear in his path, Xenophon manages to emerge triumphant.

Book 4, Chapter 5

Determined to evade Tiribazus and his hostile attacks, the Greeks advance through heavy snow and wade across the River Euphrates. They continue their march across a plain covered with thick snow, making a sacrifice to the wind, in the hope that this will alleviate the weather conditions, and obliged to deal with those suffering from *bulimia*, not the modern eating disorder of the same name, but rather an extreme hunger that caused faintness, particularly prevalent in cold weather. Chirisophus at the head of the marching column, reaches a village and is able to spend the night there, but Xenophon and most of the army are forced to bivouac without fire or food.

　　On the next day they all meet up at the village where Chirisophus had spent the night, and separate divisions of the army are allotted to different villages. The underground dwellings of the village where Xenophon ends up, and whose headman promises to be their guide, are described in considerable detail.

　　The next day Xenophon and the village headman go for a meeting with Chirisophus. The Greeks discover that they are in Armenia. Xenophon then returns with the headman to his village and gives him a horse to be fattened up and sacrificed to the Sun God.

Book 4, Chapter 6

Some seven days later the Ten Thousand continue on their march with Chirisophus in the van and the village headman as guide. On the third day Chirisophus gets angry and strikes the headman; he then runs away the following night, but leaves behind his son, who had accompanied them.

　　After a week's further march the Greeks come to and cross the River Phasis, and two days later they arrive at a mountain pass held by a force of Chalybians, Taochians and Phasians. Chirisophus, Cleanor and Xenophon joke with each other about whether Spartans or Athenians are the better thieves. Xenophon's suggestion, that they seize the heights of the pass by night, meets with approval and is adopted with pleasing success: after only minor fighting on the next day, the enemy turn tail and flee, and the Greeks march down the other side to the plain where they find well-stocked villages, able to supply all their needs.

Book 4, Chapter 7

The Greeks arrive at a Taochian stronghold. As supplies are running low, they need to take this, but are currently prevented by the enemy rolling down huge stones and rocks upon them. Xenophon realizes that they can easily take the place if they can trick the enemy into using up all their rocks. This they do, helped by rivalry among some of the soldiers, and the hilltop is duly taken. Rather than submit to capture, the Taochians hurl themselves down from the clifftops.

The Ten Thousand then pass through the country of the Chalybians and crossing the River Harpasus march through Scythenian territory. On their arrival at the city of Gymnias, the local ruler sends them a guide who promises in five days to bring them within sight of the sea.

The Greeks are overjoyed by their sight of the sea from Mount Theches. Crying θάλαττα θάλαττα, they embrace one another in tears, build a cairn to mark the spot and send off their guide, suitably rewarded for his services.

Book 4, Chapter 8

While passing through Macronian territory, the Greeks arrive at a river crossing where a crowd of hostile locals blocks the way on the opposite bank. Still, a former slave who can speak their language negotiates successfully with them, and with their help the Greeks cross the river and advance to the Colchian border.

There the Colchians are drawn up against them on a mountain range. Xenophon's plan now is that the Ten Thousand should advance on the enemy not in horizontal lines, but in vertical columns. This stratagem is successful, and the enemy are put to flight.

After scaling the mountain, the Greeks encamp in some villages where they encounter some poisonous honey. No one, however, dies, and after a march of two more days they eventually reach the sea at the city of Trapezus. Here sacrifices are made and athletic competitions are held to the great enjoyment of all.

Greece and Persia

The Achaemenid empire of Persia was one of the greatest and most important in the ancient world. It had been founded through the amalgamation of two earlier kingdoms, Media and Persia, by Cyrus the Great in 559 BC; its capital was at Susa, and it consisted of some twenty provinces, each under the control of its own governor or satrap. The satraps, then, were answerable to the king himself; and he kept watch over all their activities through his own agents, each known as 'the King's Eye': Pseudartabas in Aristophanes' *Acharnians* is a richly comic example. There was a highly developed network of roads stretching out in all directions from

Susa, and a complex communications system, involving riders with fresh horses at various stages along the way, enabled the easy dissemination of information from the centre.

Existing side by side with this was the Greek world with its independent city-states, each with its own fighting force, and all regarding their Persian neighbours as βάρβαροι, non-Greek speakers of unintelligible gibberish. Relations between the two were never easy, certainly never completely friendly, but never entirely in conflict either. Hostilities were at their peak during the two so-called Persian Wars, in 490 and 480–479 BC. Even then, however, there were Greek cities, both in Asia Minor and on the mainland, which supported the Persian side; and the single most important architect of the Persian defeat at Salamis, the Athenian Themistocles, was able to end his days in a position of great honour in the retinue of Artaxerxes I, with whom he had sought refuge from his political enemies in Greece.

After 479, Persian policy was largely directed towards encouraging Greek cities to fight with one another, so ensuring that they remained as weak as possible: at the close of the Peloponnesian War Persia helped Sparta build a fleet with which it could oppose Athens; but when Sparta in turn became more powerful, the Persians then helped the Athenians rebuild their navy to be a match for their Peloponnesian opponents. Indeed, it was against the meddlesome interference of Persia with the Greek cities of Asia Minor that the Spartans were actively campaigning when, at Pergamum, Xenophon handed over to Thibron the remnant of the Ten Thousand Cyreans in 399 BC.

Xenophon's language

Xenophon has long been famous for the straightforward, clear and elegant quality of his Greek. An Athenian, he wrote in Attic, but, because of his long absence from Athens, in a brand of Attic less akin to the pure dialect of Plato or the orators, and more influenced by both the usage and vocabulary of other parts of Greece.

His narrative style has a liveliness and fluency greatly admired by the critics of all ages. He achieves this in a number of readily identifiable ways:

(i)   by avoiding a complex periodic structure, but rather writing in a sequence of simple sentences with parallel coordinate clauses;

(ii) by the regular use of direct speech;

(iii) by varying the tenses he uses, and in particular by pinpointing important moments by use of the historic present; cf. 4.7.24 – καὶ ἀναβὰς ἐφ᾽ ἵππον … παρεβοήθει· καὶ τάχα δὴ <u>ἀκούουσι</u> βοώντων τῶν στρατιωτῶν θάλαττα θάλαττα …;

(iv) by inventive word order, in particular by promoting finite verbs to an early position in their sentences, so that the action in question is given greater prominence; cf. 4.8.4 – ἔνθα δὴ <u>προσέρχεται</u> Ξενοφῶντι τῶν πελταστῶν ἀνὴρ Ἀθήνησι φάσκων δεδουλευκέναι (also a significant historic present);

(v)   by the occasional omission of a verbal form; cf. 4.7.3 – τὸ γὰρ χωρίον αἱρετέον, where ἐστί is left out, or 4.8.20 – ἀλλ᾽ οἱ μὲν ὀλίγον

ἐδηδοκότες σφόδρα μεθύουσιν ἐῴκεσαν, οἱ δὲ πολὺ μαινομένοις,
οἱ δὲ καὶ ἀποθνῄσκουσιν, where ἐδηδοκότες must be understood with
πολύ, and ἐῴκεσαν with both μαινομένοις and ἀποθνῄσκουσιν.

On the whole Xenophon avoids writing in a markedly rhetorical way. Still, various
devices are common to all or virtually all Greek prose authors, and Xenophon is no
exception. A few examples from the prescribed portion of text are:

(i)   anaphora: repetition, particularly of the same word in a significant
      position; cf. 4.8.19 – ἐν <u>πολλαῖς</u> κώμαις καὶ τἀπιτήδεια <u>πολλὰ</u>
      ἐχούσαις ;
(ii) polyptoton: the close repetition of the same word in different grammatical
      forms; cf. 4.8.19 – ἀλλὰ φυγῇ <u>ἄλλος</u> <u>ἄλλῃ</u> ἐτράπετο ;
(iii) balance, often with μὲν ... δέ: cf. 4.8.2 – ἦν δὲ οὗτος δασὺς δένδρεσι
      <u>παχέσι μὲν οὔ</u>, <u>πυκνοῖς δέ</u> ; 4.8.9 – καὶ <u>τὸ μὲν πρῶτον</u> οἱ Ἕλληνες ...
      <u>ἔπειτα δὲ</u> ἔδοξε τοῖς στρατηγοῖς ; 4.8.17 – οἱ μὲν ἐπὶ τὸ δεξιὸν οἱ δὲ
      ἐπὶ τὸ εὐώνυμον διεσπάσθησαν ;
(iv) hyperbaton, where emphasis is created by a disturbance of normal word
      order; cf. 4.7.1 – <u>χωρία</u> γὰρ ᾤκουν <u>ἰσχυρὰ</u> οἱ Τάοχοι ;
(v)   use of particles: though not all are found in the prescribed passage,
      Xenophon is particularly fond of δή, καὶ ... δή, τε καί and μέντοι; cf.
      4.7.4 – ἐνταῦθα δὴ κοινῇ ἐβουλεύοντο ; the first two of these, especially
      by putting the words around them in higher profile, serve to pinpoint
      important moments in the story ;
(vi) asyndeton (the omission of connecting particles and conjunctions):
      cf. 4.7.18 – ἐκ τούτων οἱ Ἕλληνες ἀφίκοντο (at the beginning of a
      sentence) and at the start of the next sentence, ἐντεῦθεν ἐπορεύθησαν
      διὰ Σκυθηνῶν. We might have expected – ἐκ <u>δὲ</u> τούτων οἱ Ἕλληνες
      ἀφίκοντο and <u>καὶ</u> ἐντεῦθεν ἐπορεύθησαν διὰ Σκυθηνῶν. Here the
      effect is to add urgency and rapidity to the narrative.

A few of Xenophon's usages are at odds with the normal Attic practice. Not all are
exemplified in the prescribed passage, but they are included here for the sake of
completeness:

(i)   ὡς and ὡς ἄν in place of ὅπως and ὅπως ἄν introducing purpose clauses
      and after verbs of precaution;
(ii) a fondness for the optative which makes him more likely than other
      writers to use it when he might have had the more vivid indicative
      or subjunctive: cf. 4.7.19 – ἡγεμόνα πέμπει, ὅπως διὰ τῆς ἑαυτῶν
      πολεμίας χώρας <u>ἄγοι</u> αὐτούς, where especially after the historic present
      he might have had the subjunctive ἄγῃ ; 4.8.4 – λέγων ὅτι <u>γιγνώσκοι</u>
      τὴν φωνὴν τῶν ἀνθρώπων, where another writer might well have had a
      present indicative in the indirect statement.
(iii) ὡς in place of ὥστε + infinitive or indicative in consecutive clauses;
(iv) some prepositional usages: σύν + dative instead of μετά + genitive;
      cf. 4.8.16 – καὶ Χειρίσοφος μὲν καὶ Ξενοφῶν καὶ οἱ <u>σὺν αὐτοῖς</u>
      πελτασταὶ ...; ἀνά and ἀμφί which are rarely found in Attic authors;

cf. 4.8.21 – ἀμφὶ δὲ τὴν αὐτήν πως ὥραν; and ἐκ, παρά and πρός + genitive with passive verbs (Attic usually has ὑπό);

(v)   words and forms not usually found in Attic prose; cf. 4.7.16 – ὅσον ξυήλην Λακωνικήν ('a Laconian dagger'); 4.8.5 – ἀντιτετάχαται (Ionic for ἀντιτεταγμένοι εἰσίν).

Further reading

Texts, editions and translations

Antrich, J. and Usher, S. *Xenophon, The Persian Expedition* (BCP, 1978).

*Brownson, C.L. revised Dillery, J. *Xenophon: Anabasis* (Loeb, Harvard University Press, 1998).

Marchant, E.C. *Xenophontis Opera Omnia, Tomus III, Expeditio Cyri* (Oxford, OCT, 1904).

Mather, M.W. and Hewitt, J.W. *Xenophon's Anabasis, Books I–IV* (University of Oklahoma Press, 1962).

*Warner, R. *Xenophon: The Persian Expedition* (Penguin, 1972).

*Waterfield, R. *Xenophon: The Expedition of Cyrus* (Oxford, Oxford World's Classics, 2005).

*= translation

Xenophon

Anderson, J.K. *Xenophon* (London, Duckworth, 1974).

Flower, M.A. (ed.) *The Cambridge Companion to Xenophon* (Cambridge, Cambridge University Press, 2017).

Gray, V.J. (ed.) *Oxford Readings in Classical Studies: Xenophon* (Oxford, Oxford University Press, 2010).

The *Anabasis*

Cawkwell, G.L. 'Introduction', in *Xenophon: The Persian Expedition*, trans. R Warner (Penguin, 1972).

Lane Fox, R. (ed.) *The Long March: Xenophon and the Ten Thousand* (New Haven, Yale University Press, 2004).

Parker, R.C.T. 'One Man's Piety: The Religious Dimension of the *Anabasis*', in R. Lane Fox (ed.), *The Long March* (New Haven, Yale University Press, 2004).

Rood, T.C.B. *The Sea! The Sea! The Shout of the Ten Thousand in the Modern Imagination* (London, Duckworth, 2004).

Rood, T.C.B. 'Introduction', in *Xenophon: The Expedition of Cyrus*, trans. R. Waterfield (Oxford, Oxford University Press, 2005).

Waterfield, R. *Xenophon's Retreat: Greece, Persia and the End of the Golden Age* (London, WCIN, 2006).

Mercenary soldiers

Parke, H.W. *Greek Mercenary Soldiers: From the Earliest Times to the Battle of Ipsus* (Oxford, Clarendon Press, 1933).

Roy, J. 'The Ambitions of a Mercenary', in R. Lane Fox (ed.), *The Long March* (New Haven, Yale University Press, 2004).

Persia

Brosius, M. (trans. and ed.) *The Persian Empire from Cyrus II to Artaxerxes I* (London, LACTOR 16, 2000).

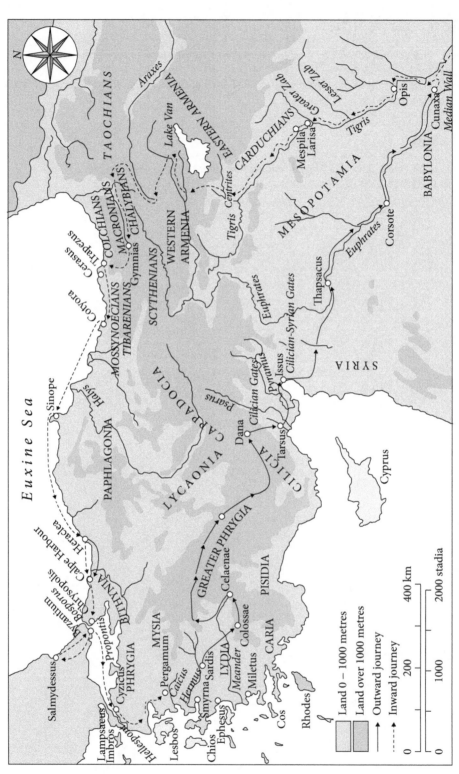

Map *The route taken by Xenophon and the Ten Thousand through Persia*

Text

7

ἐκ δὲ τούτων ἐπορεύθησαν εἰς Τάοχους σταθμοὺς πέντε παρασάγγας τριάκοντα· καὶ τὰ ἐπιτήδεια ἐπέλειπε· χωρία γὰρ ᾤκουν ἰσχυρὰ οἱ Τάοχοι, ἐν οἷς καὶ τὰ ἐπιτήδεια ἅπαντα εἶχον ἀνακεκομισμένοι. ἐπεὶ δ᾿ ἀφίκοντο πρὸς χωρίον ὃ πόλιν μὲν οὐκ εἶχεν οὐδ᾿ οἰκίας - 2 συνεληλυθότες δ᾿ ἦσαν αὐτόσε καὶ ἄνδρες καὶ γυναῖκες καὶ κτήνη πολλά - Χειρίσοφος μὲν οὖν πρὸς τοῦτο προσέβαλλεν εὐθὺς ἥκων· ἐπειδὴ δὲ ἡ πρώτη τάξις ἀπέκαμεν, ἄλλη προσῄει καὶ αὖθις ἄλλη· οὐ γὰρ ἦν ἀθρόοις περιστῆναι, ἀλλ᾿ ἀπότομον ἦν κύκλῳ. ἐπειδὴ δὲ 3 Ξενοφῶν ἦλθε σὺν τοῖς ὀπισθοφύλαξι καὶ πελτασταῖς καὶ ὁπλίταις, ἐνταῦθα δὴ λέγει Χειρίσοφος· "εἰς καλὸν ἥκετε· τὸ γὰρ χωρίον αἱρετέον· τῇ γὰρ στρατιᾷ οὐκ ἔστι τὰ ἐπιτήδεια, εἰ μὴ ληψόμεθα τὸ χωρίον." ἐνταῦθα δὴ κοινῇ ἐβουλεύοντο· καὶ τοῦ Ξενοφῶντος ἐρωτῶντος τί τὸ 4 κωλῦον εἴη εἰσελθεῖν, εἶπεν ὁ Χειρίσοφος· "μία αὕτη πάροδός ἐστιν ἣν ὁρᾷς· ὅταν δέ τις ταύτῃ πειρᾶται παριέναι, κυλίνδουσι λίθους ὑπὲρ ταύτης τῆς ὑπερεχούσης πέτρας· ὃς δ᾿ ἂν καταληφθῇ, οὕτω διατίθεται." ἅμα δ᾿ ἔδειξε συντετριμμένους ἀνθρώπους καὶ σκέλη καὶ πλευράς. "ἢν 5 δὲ τοὺς λίθους ἀναλώσωσιν," ἔφη ὁ Ξενοφῶν, "ἄλλο τι ἢ οὐδὲν κωλύει παριέναι; οὐ γὰρ δὴ ἐκ τοῦ ἐναντίου ὁρῶμεν εἰ μὴ ὀλίγους τούτους ἀνθρώπους, καὶ τούτων δύο ἢ τρεῖς ὡπλισμένους. τὸ δὲ χωρίον, 6 ὡς καὶ σὺ ὁρᾷς, σχεδὸν τρία ἡμίπλεθρά ἐστιν ὃ δεῖ βαλλομένους διελθεῖν· τούτου δὲ ὅσον πλέθρον δασὺ πίτυσι διαλειπούσαις μεγάλαις, ἀνθ᾿ ὧν ἑστηκότες ἄνδρες τί ἂν πάσχοιεν ἢ ὑπὸ τῶν φερομένων λίθων ἢ ὑπὸ τῶν κυλινδομένων; τὸ λοιπὸν οὖν γίγνεται ὡς ἡμίπλεθρον, ὃ δεῖ ὅταν λωφήσωσιν οἱ λίθοι παραδραμεῖν." "ἀλλὰ εὐθύς," ἔφη ὁ Χειρίσοφος, 7

"ἐπειδὰν ἀρξώμεθα εἰς τὸ δασὺ προσιέναι, φέρονται οἱ λίθοι πολλοί."
"αὐτὸ ἄν," ἔφη, "τὸ δέον εἴη· θᾶττον γὰρ ἀναλώσουσι τοὺς λίθους. ἀλλὰ
πορευώμεθα ἔνθεν ἡμῖν μικρόν τι παραδραμεῖν ἔσται, ἢν δυνώμεθα,
καὶ ἀπελθεῖν ῥᾴδιον, ἢν βουλώμεθα."

ἐντεῦθεν ἐπορεύοντο Χειρίσοφος καὶ Ξενοφῶν καὶ Καλλίμαχος 8
Παρράσιος λοχαγός· τούτου γὰρ ἡ ἡγεμονία ἦν τῶν ὀπισθοφυλάκων
λοχαγῶν ἐκείνῃ τῇ ἡμέρᾳ· οἱ δὲ ἄλλοι λοχαγοὶ ἔμενον ἐν τῷ ἀσφαλεῖ.
μετὰ τοῦτο οὖν ἀπῆλθον ὑπὸ τὰ δένδρα ἄνθρωποι ὡς ἑβδομήκοντα,
οὐχ ἁθρόοι ἀλλὰ καθ᾽ ἕνα, ἕκαστος φυλαττόμενος ὡς ἐδύνατο.
Ἀγασίας δὲ ὁ Στυμφάλιος καὶ Ἀριστώνυμος Μεθυδριεύς, καὶ οὗτοι 9
τῶν ὀπισθοφυλάκων λοχαγοὶ ὄντες, καὶ ἄλλοι δέ, ἐφέστασαν ἔξω
τῶν δένδρων· οὐ γὰρ ἦν ἀσφαλῶς ἐν τοῖς δένδροις ἑστάναι
πλέον ἢ τὸν ἕνα λόχον. ἔνθα δὴ Καλλίμαχος μηχανᾶταί τι· προύτρεχεν 10
ἀπὸ τοῦ δένδρου ὑφ᾽ ᾧ ἦν αὐτὸς δύο ἢ τρία βήματα· ἐπειδὴ δὲ οἱ λίθοι
φέροιντο, ἀνέχαζεν εὐπετῶς· ἐφ᾽ ἑκάστης δὲ τῆς προδρομῆς πλέον ἢ
δέκα ἅμαξαι πετρῶν ἀνηλίσκοντο. ὁ δὲ Ἀγασίας ὡς ὁρᾷ τὸν Καλλίμαχον 11
ἃ ἐποίει τὸ στράτευμα πᾶν θεώμενον, δείσας μὴ οὐ πρῶτος παραδράμῃ
εἰς τὸ χωρίον, οὐδὲ τὸν Ἀριστώνυμον πλησίον ὄντα παρακαλέσας οὐδὲ
Εὐρύλοχον τὸν Λουσιέα, ἑταίρους ὄντας, οὐδὲ ἄλλον οὐδένα χωρεῖ
αὐτός, καὶ παρέρχεται πάντας. ὁ δὲ Καλλίμαχος ὡς ὁρᾷ αὐτὸν παριόντα, 12
ἐπιλαμβάνεται αὐτοῦ τῆς ἴτυος· ἐν δὲ τούτῳ παραθεῖ αὐτοὺς
Ἀριστώνυμος Μεθυδριεύς, καὶ μετὰ τοῦτον Εὐρύλοχος Λουσιεύς· πάντες
γὰρ οὗτοι ἀντεποιοῦντο ἀρετῆς καὶ διηγωνίζοντο πρὸς ἀλλήλους· καὶ
οὕτως ἐρίζοντες αἱροῦσι τὸ χωρίον. ὡς γὰρ ἅπαξ εἰσέδραμον, οὐδεὶς
πέτρος ἄνωθεν ἠνέχθη. ἐνταῦθα δὴ δεινὸν ἦν θέαμα. αἱ γὰρ γυναῖκες 13
ῥίπτουσαι τὰ παιδία εἶτα ἑαυτὰς ἐπικατερρίπτουν, καὶ οἱ ἄνδρες
ὡσαύτως. ἐνταῦθα δὴ καὶ Αἰνείας Στυμφάλιος λοχαγὸς ἰδών τινα
θέοντα ὡς ῥίψοντα ἑαυτὸν στολὴν ἔχοντα καλὴν ἐπιλαμβάνεται ὡς
κωλύσων· ὁ δὲ αὐτὸν ἐπισπᾶται, καὶ ἀμφότεροι ᾤχοντο κατὰ τῶν 14
πετρῶν φερόμενοι καὶ ἀπέθανον. ἐντεῦθεν ἄνθρωποι μὲν πάνυ ὀλίγοι
ἐλήφθησαν, βόες δὲ καὶ ὄνοι πολλοὶ καὶ πρόβατα.

ἐντεῦθεν ἐπορεύθησαν διὰ Χαλύβων σταθμοὺς ἑπτὰ παρασάγγας 15
πεντήκοντα. οὗτοι ἦσαν ὧν διῆλθον ἀλκιμώτατοι, καὶ εἰς χεῖρας ἦσαν.
εἶχον δὲ θώρακας λινοῦς μέχρι τοῦ ἤτρου, ἀντὶ δὲ τῶν πτερύγων
σπάρτα πυκνὰ ἐστραμμένα. εἶχον δὲ καὶ κνημῖδας καὶ κράνη καὶ παρὰ 16
τὴν ζώνην μαχαίριον ὅσον ξυήλην Λακωνικήν, ᾧ ἔσφαττον ὧν κρατεῖν
δύναιντο, καὶ ἀποτεμόντες ἂν τὰς κεφαλὰς ἔχοντες ἐπορεύοντο, καὶ
ᾖδον καὶ ἐχόρευον ὁπότε οἱ πολέμιοι αὐτοὺς ὄψεσθαι ἔμελλον. εἶχον

δὲ καὶ δόρυ ὡς πεντεκαίδεκα πήχεων μίαν λόγχην ἔχον. οὗτοι ἐνέμενον 17
ἐν τοῖς πολίσμασιν· ἐπεὶ δὲ παρέλθοιεν οἱ Ἕλληνες, εἵποντο ἀεὶ
μαχούμενοι. ᾤκουν δὲ ἐν τοῖς ὀχυροῖς, καὶ τὰ ἐπιτήδεια ἐν τούτοις
ἀνακεκομισμένοι ἦσαν· ὥστε μηδὲν λαμβάνειν αὐτόθεν τοὺς Ἕλληνας,
ἀλλὰ διετράφησαν τοῖς κτήνεσιν ἃ ἐκ τῶν Τάοχων ἔλαβον. ἐκ τούτων 18
οἱ Ἕλληνες ἀφίκοντο ἐπὶ Ἅρπασον ποταμόν, εὖρος τεττάρων πλέθρων.
ἐντεῦθεν ἐπορεύθησαν διὰ Σκυθηνῶν σταθμοὺς τέτταρας παρασάγγας
εἴκοσι διὰ πεδίου εἰς κώμας· ἐν αἷς ἔμειναν ἡμέρας τρεῖς καὶ ἐπεσιτίσαντο.

ἐντεῦθεν διῆλθον σταθμοὺς τέτταρας παρασάγγας εἴκοσι πρὸς πόλιν 19
μεγάλην καὶ εὐδαίμονα καὶ οἰκουμένην ἣ ἐκαλεῖτο Γυμνιάς. ἐκ ταύτης ὁ
τῆς χώρας ἄρχων τοῖς Ἕλλησιν ἡγεμόνα πέμπει, ὅπως διὰ τῆς ἑαυτῶν
πολεμίας χώρας ἄγοι αὐτούς. ἐλθὼν δ᾽ ἐκεῖνος λέγει ὅτι ἄξει αὐτοὺς 20
πέντε ἡμερῶν εἰς χωρίον ὅθεν ὄψονται θάλατταν· εἰ δὲ μή, τεθνάναι
ἐπηγγείλατο. καὶ ἡγούμενος ἐπειδὴ ἐνέβαλλεν εἰς τὴν πολεμίαν,
παρεκελεύετο αἴθειν καὶ φθείρειν τὴν χώραν· ᾧ καὶ δῆλον ἐγένετο ὅτι
τούτου ἕνεκα ἔλθοι, οὐ τῆς τῶν Ἑλλήνων εὐνοίας.

καὶ ἀφικνοῦνται ἐπὶ τὸ ὄρος τῇ πέμπτῃ ἡμέρᾳ· ὄνομα δὲ τῷ ὄρει ἦν 21
Θήχης. ἐπεὶ δὲ οἱ πρῶτοι ἐγένοντο ἐπὶ τοῦ ὄρους καὶ κατεῖδον τὴν
θάλατταν, κραυγὴ πολλὴ ἐγένετο. ἀκούσας δὲ ὁ Ξενοφῶν καὶ οἱ 22
ὀπισθοφύλακες ᾠήθησαν ἔμπροσθεν ἄλλους ἐπιτίθεσθαι πολεμίους·
εἵποντο γὰρ καὶ ὄπισθεν ἐκ τῆς καιομένης χώρας, καὶ αὐτῶν οἱ
ὀπισθοφύλακες ἀπέκτεινάν τέ τινας καὶ ἐζώγρησαν ἐνέδραν
ποιησάμενοι, καὶ γέρρα ἔλαβον δασειῶν βοῶν ὠμοβόεια ἀμφὶ τὰ
εἴκοσιν. ἐπειδὴ δὲ βοὴ πλείων τε ἐγίγνετο καὶ ἐγγύτερον καὶ οἱ ἀεὶ 23
ἐπιόντες ἔθεον δρόμῳ ἐπὶ τοὺς ἀεὶ βοῶντας καὶ πολλῷ μεῖζον ἐγίγνετο
ἡ βοὴ ὅσῳ δὴ πλείους ἐγίγνοντο, ἐδόκει δὴ μεῖζόν τι εἶναι τῷ Ξενοφῶντι,
καὶ ἀναβὰς ἐφ᾽ ἵππον καὶ Λύκιον καὶ τοὺς ἱππέας ἀναλαβὼν 24
παρεβοήθει· καὶ τάχα δὴ ἀκούουσι βοώντων τῶν στρατιωτῶν
"θάλαττα θάλαττα" καὶ παρεγγυώντων. ἔνθα δὴ ἔθεον πάντες καὶ οἱ
ὀπισθοφύλακες, καὶ τὰ ὑποζύγια ἠλαύνετο καὶ οἱ ἵπποι. ἐπεὶ δὲ 25
ἀφίκοντο πάντες ἐπὶ τὸ ἄκρον, ἐνταῦθα δὴ περιέβαλλον ἀλλήλους καὶ
στρατηγοὺς καὶ λοχαγοὺς δακρύοντες. καὶ ἐξαπίνης ὅτου δὴ
παρεγγυήσαντος οἱ στρατιῶται φέρουσι λίθους καὶ ποιοῦσι κολωνὸν
μέγαν. ἐνταῦθα ἀνετίθεσαν δερμάτων πλῆθος ὠμοβοείων καὶ βακτηρίας 26
καὶ τὰ αἰχμάλωτα γέρρα, καὶ ὁ ἡγεμὼν αὐτός τε κατέτεμνε τὰ γέρρα καὶ
τοῖς ἄλλοις διεκελεύετο. μετὰ ταῦτα τὸν ἡγεμόνα οἱ Ἕλληνες 27
ἀποπέμπουσι δῶρα δόντες ἀπὸ κοινοῦ ἵππον καὶ φιάλην ἀργυρᾶν καὶ
σκευὴν Περσικὴν καὶ δαρεικοὺς δέκα· ᾔτει δὲ μάλιστα τοὺς δακτυλίους,

καὶ ἔλαβε πολλοὺς παρὰ τῶν στρατιωτῶν. κώμην δὲ δείξας αὐτοῖς οὗ σκηνήσουσι καὶ τὴν ὁδὸν ἣν πορεύσονται εἰς Μάκρωνας, ἐπεὶ ἑσπέρα ἐγένετο, ᾤχετο τῆς νυκτὸς ἀπιών.

8

ἐντεῦθεν δ᾽ ἐπορεύθησαν οἱ Ἕλληνες διὰ Μακρώνων σταθμοὺς τρεῖς παρασάγγας δέκα. τῇ πρώτῃ δὲ ἡμέρᾳ ἀφίκοντο ἐπὶ τὸν ποταμὸν ὃς ὥριζε τὴν τῶν Μακρώνων καὶ τὴν τῶν Σκυθηνῶν. εἶχον δ᾽ ὑπὲρ δεξιῶν 2 χωρίον οἷον χαλεπώτατον καὶ ἐξ ἀριστερᾶς ἄλλον ποταμόν, εἰς ὃν ἐνέβαλλεν ὁ ὁρίζων, δι᾽ οὗ ἔδει διαβῆναι. ἦν δὲ οὗτος δασὺς δένδρεσι παχέσι μὲν οὔ, πυκνοῖς δέ. ταῦτ᾽ ἐπεὶ προσῆλθον οἱ Ἕλληνες ἔκοπτον, σπεύδοντες ἐκ τοῦ χωρίου ὡς τάχιστα ἐξελθεῖν. οἱ δὲ Μάκρωνες ἔχοντες 3 γέρρα καὶ λόγχας καὶ τριχίνους χιτῶνας κατ᾽ ἀντιπέραν τῆς διαβάσεως παρατεταγμένοι ἦσαν καὶ ἀλλήλοις διεκελεύοντο καὶ λίθους εἰς τὸν ποταμὸν ἔρριπτον· ἐξικνοῦντο γὰρ οὒ οὐδ᾽ ἔβλαπτον οὐδέν.

ἔνθα δὴ προσέρχεται Ξενοφῶντι τῶν πελταστῶν ἀνὴρ Ἀθήνησι φάσκων 4 δεδουλευκέναι, λέγων ὅτι γιγνώσκοι τὴν φωνὴν τῶν ἀνθρώπων. "καὶ οἶμαι," ἔφη, "ἐμὴν ταύτην πατρίδα εἶναι· καὶ εἰ μή τι κωλύει, ἐθέλω αὐτοῖς διαλεχθῆναι." "ἀλλ᾽ οὐδὲν κωλύει," ἔφη, "ἀλλὰ διαλέγου καὶ μάθε πρῶτον 5 τίνες εἰσίν." οἱ δ᾽ εἶπον ἐρωτήσαντος ὅτι Μάκρωνες. "ἐρῶτα τοίνυν," ἔφη, "αὐτοὺς τί ἀντιτέτακται καὶ χρῄζουσιν ἡμῖν πολέμιοι εἶναι." οἱ δ᾽ 6 ἀπεκρίναντο "ὅτι καὶ ὑμεῖς ἐπὶ τὴν ἡμετέραν χώραν ἔρχεσθε." λέγειν ἐκέλευον οἱ στρατηγοὶ ὅτι οὐ κακῶς γε ποιήσοντες, ἀλλὰ βασιλεῖ πολεμήσαντες ἀπερχόμεθα εἰς τὴν Ἑλλάδα, καὶ ἐπὶ θάλατταν βουλόμεθα ἀφικέσθαι. ἠρώτων ἐκεῖνοι εἰ δοῖεν ἂν τούτων τὰ πιστά. οἱ δ᾽ 7 ἔφασαν καὶ δοῦναι καὶ λαβεῖν ἐθέλειν. ἐντεῦθεν διδόασιν οἱ Μάκρωνες βαρβαρικὴν λόγχην τοῖς Ἕλλησιν, οἱ δὲ Ἕλληνες ἐκείνοις Ἑλληνικήν· ταῦτα γὰρ ἔφασαν πιστὰ εἶναι· θεοὺς δ᾽ ἐπεμαρτύραντο ἀμφότεροι.

μετὰ δὲ τὰ πιστὰ εὐθὺς οἱ Μάκρωνες τὰ δένδρα συνεξέκοπτον τήν τε 8 ὁδὸν ὡδοποίουν ὡς διαβιβάσοντες ἐν μέσοις ἀναμεμιγμένοι τοῖς Ἕλλησι, καὶ ἀγορὰν οἵαν ἐδύναντο παρεῖχον, καὶ παρήγαγον ἐν τρισὶν ἡμέραις ἕως ἐπὶ τὰ Κόλχων ὅρια κατέστησαν τοὺς Ἕλληνας. ἐνταῦθα ἦν ὄρος 9 μέγα, προσβατὸν δέ· καὶ ἐπὶ τούτου οἱ Κόλχοι παρατεταγμένοι ἦσαν. καὶ τὸ μὲν πρῶτον οἱ Ἕλληνες ἀντιπαρετάξαντο φάλαγγα, ὡς οὕτως ἄξοντες πρὸς τὸ ὄρος· ἔπειτα δὲ ἔδοξε τοῖς στρατηγοῖς βουλεύσασθαι συλλεγεῖσιν ὅπως ὡς κάλλιστα ἀγωνιοῦνται. ἔλεξεν οὖν Ξενοφῶν ὅτι 10 δοκοίη παύσαντας τὴν φάλαγγα λόχους ὀρθίους ποιῆσαι· "ἡ μὲν γὰρ φάλαγξ διασπασθήσεται εὐθύς· τῇ μὲν γὰρ ἄνοδον τῇ δὲ εὔοδον

εὑρήσομεν τὸ ὄρος· καὶ εὐθὺς τοῦτο ἀθυμίαν ποιήσει ὅταν τεταγμένοι
εἰς φάλαγγα ταύτην διεσπασμένην ὁρῶσιν. ἔπειτα ἢν μὲν ἐπὶ πολλῶν 11
τεταγμένοι προσάγωμεν, περιττεύσουσιν ἡμῶν οἱ πολέμιοι καὶ τοῖς
περιττοῖς χρήσονται ὅ τι ἂν βούλωνται· ἐὰν δὲ ἐπ᾽ ὀλίγων τεταγμένοι
ὦμεν, οὐδὲν ἂν εἴη θαυμαστὸν εἰ διακοπείη ἡμῶν ἡ φάλαγξ ὑπὸ ἀθρόων
καὶ βελῶν καὶ ἀνθρώπων πολλῶν ἐμπεσόντων· εἰ δέ πη τοῦτο ἔσται, τῇ
ὅλῃ φάλαγγι κακὸν ἔσται. ἀλλά μοι δοκεῖ ὀρθίους τοὺς λόχους 12
ποιησαμένους τοσοῦτον χωρίον κατασχεῖν διαλιπόντας τοῖς λόχοις
ὅσον ἔξω τοὺς ἐσχάτους λόχους γενέσθαι τῶν πολεμίων κεράτων· καὶ
οὕτως ἐσόμεθα τῆς τε τῶν πολεμίων φάλαγγος ἔξω οἱ ἔσχατοι λόχοι, καὶ
ὀρθίους ἄγοντες οἱ κράτιστοι ἡμῶν πρῶτοι προσίασιν, ᾗ τε ἂν εὔοδον ᾖ,
ταύτῃ ἕκαστος ἄξει ὁ λόχος. καὶ εἴς τε τὸ διαλεῖπον οὐ ῥᾴδιον ἔσται τοῖς 13
πολεμίοις εἰσελθεῖν ἔνθεν καὶ ἔνθεν λόχων ὄντων, διακόψαι τε οὐ
ῥᾴδιον ἔσται λόχον ὄρθιον προσιόντα. ἄν τέ τις πιέζηται τῶν λόχων,
ὁ πλησίον βοηθήσει. ἤν τε εἷς πη δυνηθῇ τῶν λόχων ἐπὶ τὸ ἄκρον
ἀναβῆναι, οὐδεὶς μηκέτι μείνῃ τῶν πολεμίων.” ταῦτα ἔδοξε, καὶ ἐποίουν 14
ὀρθίους τοὺς λόχους. Ξενοφῶν δὲ ἀπιὼν ἐπὶ τὸ εὐώνυμον ἀπὸ τοῦ
δεξιοῦ ἔλεγε τοῖς στρατιώταις· “ἄνδρες, οὗτοί εἰσιν οὓς ὁρᾶτε μόνοι ἔτι
ἡμῖν ἐμποδὼν τὸ μὴ ἤδη εἶναι ἔνθα πάλαι σπεύδομεν· τούτους, ἤν πως
δυνώμεθα, καὶ ὠμοὺς δεῖ καταφαγεῖν.”

ἐπεὶ δ᾽ ἐν ταῖς χώραις ἕκαστοι ἐγένοντο καὶ τοὺς λόχους ὀρθίους 15
ἐποιήσαντο, ἐγένοντο μὲν λόχοι τῶν ὁπλιτῶν ἀμφὶ τοὺς ὀγδοήκοντα, ὁ
δὲ λόχος ἕκαστος σχεδὸν εἰς τοὺς ἑκατόν· τοὺς δὲ πελταστὰς καὶ τοὺς
τοξότας τριχῇ ἐποιήσαντο, τοὺς μὲν τοῦ εὐωνύμου ἔξω, τοὺς δὲ τοῦ
δεξιοῦ, τοὺς δὲ κατὰ μέσον, σχεδὸν ἑξακοσίους ἑκάστους. ἐκ τούτου 16
παρηγγύησαν οἱ στρατηγοὶ εὔχεσθαι· εὐξάμενοι δὲ καὶ παιανίσαντες
ἐπορεύοντο. καὶ Χειρίσοφος μὲν καὶ Ξενοφῶν καὶ οἱ σὺν αὐτοῖς
πελτασταὶ τῆς τῶν πολεμίων φάλαγγος ἔξω γενόμενοι ἐπορεύοντο· οἱ 17
δὲ πολέμιοι ὡς εἶδον αὐτούς, ἀντιπαραθέοντες οἱ μὲν ἐπὶ τὸ δεξιὸν οἱ
δὲ ἐπὶ τὸ εὐώνυμον διεσπάσθησαν, καὶ πολὺ τῆς αὑτῶν φάλαγγος
ἐν τῷ μέσῳ κενὸν ἐποίησαν. οἱ δὲ κατὰ τὸ Ἀρκαδικὸν πελτασταί, ὧν 18
ἦρχεν Αἰσχίνης ὁ Ἀκαρνάν, νομίσαντες φεύγειν ἀνακραγόντες ἔθεον·
καὶ οὗτοι πρῶτοι ἐπὶ τὸ ὄρος ἀναβαίνουσι· συνεφείπετο δὲ αὐτοῖς καὶ
τὸ Ἀρκαδικὸν ὁπλιτικόν, ὧν ἦρχε Κλεάνωρ ὁ Ὀρχομένιος. οἱ δὲ 19
πολέμιοι, ὡς ἤρξαντο θεῖν, οὐκέτι ἔστησαν, ἀλλὰ φυγῇ ἄλλος ἄλλῃ
ἐτράπετο. οἱ δὲ Ἕλληνες ἀναβάντες ἐστρατοπεδεύοντο ἐν πολλαῖς
κώμαις καὶ τἀπιτήδεια πολλὰ ἐχούσαις. καὶ τὰ μὲν ἄλλα οὐδὲν ὅ τι καὶ 20
ἐθαύμασαν· τὰ δὲ σμήνη πολλὰ ἦν αὐτόθι, καὶ τῶν κηρίων ὅσοι ἔφαγον
τῶν στρατιωτῶν πάντες ἄφρονές τε ἐγίγνοντο καὶ ἤμουν καὶ κάτω

διεχώρει αὐτοῖς καὶ ὀρθὸς οὐδεὶς ἐδύνατο ἵστασθαι, ἀλλ᾿ οἱ μὲν ὀλίγον
ἐδηδοκότες σφόδρα μεθύουσιν ἐῴκεσαν, οἱ δὲ πολὺ μαινομένοις, οἱ δὲ
καὶ ἀποθνῄσκουσιν. ἔκειντο δὲ οὕτω πολλοὶ ὥσπερ τροπῆς γεγενημένης, 21
καὶ πολλὴ ἦν ἀθυμία. τῇ δ᾿ ὑστεραίᾳ ἀπέθανε μὲν οὐδείς, ἀμφὶ δὲ
τὴν αὐτήν πως ὥραν ἀνεφρόνουν· τρίτῃ δὲ καὶ τετάρτῃ ἀνίσταντο ὥσπερ
ἐκ φαρμακοποσίας.

ἐντεῦθεν δ᾿ ἐπορεύθησαν δύο σταθμοὺς παρασάγγας ἑπτά, καὶ ἦλθον ἐπὶ 22
θάλατταν εἰς Τραπεζοῦντα πόλιν Ἑλληνίδα οἰκουμένην ἐν τῷ Εὐξείνῳ Πόντῳ,
Σινωπέων ἀποικίαν, ἐν τῇ Κόλχων χώρᾳ. ἐνταῦθα ἔμειναν ἡμέρας ἀμφὶ τὰς
τριάκοντα ἐν ταῖς τῶν Κόλχων κώμαις· κἀντεῦθεν ὁρμώμενοι ἐλήϊζοντο τὴν 23
Κολχίδα. ἀγορὰν δὲ παρεῖχον τῷ στρατοπέδῳ Τραπεζούντιοι, καὶ ἐδέξαντό τε
τοὺς Ἕλληνας καὶ ξένια ἔδοσαν βοῦς καὶ ἄλφιτα καὶ οἶνον. συνδιεπράττοντο 24
δὲ καὶ ὑπὲρ τῶν πλησίον Κόλχων τῶν ἐν τῷ πεδίῳ μάλιστα οἰκούντων, καὶ
ξένια καὶ παρ᾿ ἐκείνων ἦλθον βόες. μετὰ δὲ τοῦτο τὴν θυσίαν ἣν ηὔξαντο 25
παρεσκευάζοντο· ἦλθον δ᾿ αὐτοῖς ἱκανοὶ βόες ἀποθῦσαι τῷ Διὶ τῷ σωτῆρι
καὶ τῷ Ἡρακλεῖ ἡγεμόσυνα καὶ τοῖς ἄλλοις θεοῖς ἃ ηὔξαντο. ἐποίησαν δὲ
καὶ ἀγῶνα γυμνικὸν ἐν τῷ ὄρει ἔνθαπερ ἐσκήνουν. εἵλοντο δὲ Δρακόντιον
Σπαρτιάτην, ὃς ἔφυγε παῖς ἔτι ὢν οἴκοθεν, παῖδα ἄκων κατακανὼν ξυήλῃ
πατάξας, δρόμου τ᾿ ἐπιμεληθῆναι καὶ τοῦ ἀγῶνος προστατῆσαι. ἐπειδὴ δὲ ἡ 26
θυσία ἐγένετο, τὰ δέρματα παρέδοσαν τῷ Δρακοντίῳ, καὶ ἡγεῖσθαι ἐκέλευον
ὅπου τὸν δρόμον πεποιηκὼς εἴη. ὁ δὲ δείξας οὗπερ ἑστηκότες ἐτύγχανον
"οὗτος ὁ λόφος," ἔφη, "κάλλιστος τρέχειν ὅπου ἄν τις βούληται." "πῶς
οὖν," ἔφασαν, "δυνήσονται παλαίειν ἐν σκληρῷ καὶ δασεῖ οὕτως;" ὁ δ᾿ εἶπε·
"μᾶλλόν τι ἀνιάσεται ὁ καταπεσών." ἠγωνίζοντο δὲ παῖδες μὲν στάδιον τῶν 27
αἰχμαλώτων οἱ πλεῖστοι, δόλιχον δὲ Κρῆτες πλείους ἢ ἑξήκοντα ἔθεον, πάλην
δὲ καὶ πυγμὴν καὶ παγκράτιον ἕτεροι, καὶ καλὴ θέα ἐγένετο· πολλοὶ γὰρ
κατέβησαν καὶ ἅτε θεωμένων τῶν ἑταίρων πολλὴ φιλονικία ἐγίγνετο. ἔθεον 28
δὲ καὶ ἵπποι καὶ ἔδει αὐτοὺς κατὰ τοῦ πρανοῦς ἐλάσαντας ἐν τῇ θαλάττῃ
ἀποστρέψαντας πάλιν πρὸς τὸν βωμὸν ἄγειν. καὶ κάτω μὲν οἱ πολλοὶ
ἐκαλινδοῦντο· ἄνω δὲ πρὸς τὸ ἰσχυρῶς ὄρθιον μόλις βάδην ἐπορεύοντο οἱ
ἵπποι· ἔνθα πολλὴ κραυγὴ καὶ γέλως καὶ παρακέλευσις ἐγίγνετο.

Commentary Notes

Chapter 7

7.1–7.7

The Greeks arrive at a stronghold of the Taochians. Supplies are running low, so they need to take this, but there are difficulties. Xenophon and Chirisophus discuss tactics.

7.1

ἐκ δὲ τούτων: 'after this', i.e. the capture of the mountain pass related at the end of the previous chapter.

εἰς Ταόχους: 'into (the territory of) the Taochians', a largely Ionic usage. The Taochians were a tribe living near the south-eastern shore of the Black Sea.

σταθμοὺς πέντε: an accusative of extent of space = 'five days' march'. σταθμός properly means 'a stopping place' and then comes to be used of the distance between each nightly stop, i.e. 'a day's march'.

παρασάγγας τριάκοντα: another accusative of extent of space = '(a distance of) thirty parasangs'. The parasang was a Persian unit of measurement denoting two hours' travel, an average of three miles; but the distance was dependent on the nature of the terrain and the speed of the travellers. It is likely that here we are talking about a distance of some 60 miles rather than the 90 which we might expect.

χωρία ... ἰσχυρά: 'strongholds'. Notice that the natural word order (i.e. χωρία γὰρ ἰσχυρὰ ᾤκουν ...) has been disturbed here by hyperbaton: see introduction, p. 187, first note iv). The effect is to put emphasis on the strength of these positions.

καί: 'also', i.e. as well as themselves.

ἀνακεκομισμένοι: perf. part. mid. of ἀνακομίζω, lit. 'having carried up for themselves, having stored up'. The whole relative clause (ἐν οἷς ... ἀνακεκομισμένοι) can be translated: 'in which they kept stored up all their provisions also'.

7.2

ἀφίκοντο: the subject is 'the Greeks'.

συνεληλυθότες δ' ἦσαν αὐτόσε: 'but there were gathered there'. συνεληλυθότες is the nom. masc. pl. of συνεληλυθώς, perfect participle of συνέρχομαι; this combination of perfect participle with ἦσαν (imperfect of εἰμί) is the equivalent of a pluperfect (συνεληλύθεσαν), but with an emphasis on the result rather than on the act.

Χειρίσοφος: 'Chirisophus', a Spartan general, originally sent by his government to help Cyrus, and now, with Xenophon, one of the main leaders of the Greek army.

μὲν οὖν: resumes the main thought after the parenthesis; best omitted in translation.

προσέβαλλεν: 'began to attack', an inceptive imperfect.

εὐθὺς ἥκων: 'immediately on his arrival'.

τάξις: 'detachment' or 'division'.

προσῄει: third pers. sing. of the imperfect of προσέρχομαι.

οὐ γὰρ ... περιστῆναι: 'for it was impossible for a continuous line (lit. 'them [sc. αὐτοῖς] all together) to surround it'. Note that ἦν here = ἐξῆν ('it was possible').

κύκλῳ: lit. = 'in a circle' = 'all around'.

7.3

σὺν τοῖς ὀπισθοφύλαξι ... ὁπλίταις: note that Xenophon regularly uses σύν + dative as an alternative to μετά + genitive: see introduction, p. 187, second note iv).

εἰς καλόν: 'at just the right moment', a colloquial usage.

αἱρετέον: passive verbal adjective expressing obligation from αἱρέω; ἐστίν is understood.

εἰ μή: used here with fut. indicative, instead of ἐὰν μή + subjunctive, in a future open condition expressing a warning.

7.4

ἐνταῦθα δή: note the lack of the usual connecting particle at the beginning of this sentence. This asyndeton (see introduction, p. 187, note vi) is a regular feature of Xenophon's writing. Students should keep a careful watch for it; it usually serves to speed up the narrative. But it will not be commented on every time it occurs.

κοινῇ: 'in common', 'together'.

τί τὸ κωλῦον εἴη εἰσελθεῖν: 'what it was that was preventing them from entering'; the neuter of the present participle is here used with the article as a noun ('the thing preventing'), 'them' is left unexpressed and the infinitive εἰσελθεῖν is the regular construction after κωλύω.

μία αὕτη πάροδός ἐστιν: 'there is (just) this one approach route'. The fortress was on a hill which was precipitous all the way round, and whose only approach was made impassable by men rolling down rocks and boulders.

ταύτῃ: 'this way'.

ὑπέρ: + gen. = (here) 'down over'.

ὃς δ' ἄν: here for the more common ὅστις ἄν = 'and whoever'.

οὕτω διατίθεται: lit. 'is treated thus' = 'ends up like this'; as the next words make clear, Chirisophus is pointing at some victims while saying this.

συντετριμμένους ... πλευράς: 'men with both legs and ribs crushed'. σκέλη and πλευράς are both accusatives of respect (lit. 'men crushed with respect to both legs and ribs').

7.5

Ἤν: = ἐάν.

ἄλλο τι ἤ: used to introduce a question which expects the listener to agree. The whole phrase, ἄλλο τι ἢ οὐδὲν κωλύει, means 'there is nothing, is there, to hinder'.

οὐ ... δὴ ... εἰ μή: 'nothing at all except'.

ἐκ τοῦ ἐναντίου: 'opposite', 'on the other side'.

δύο ἢ τρεῖς: '(only) two or three'.

7.6

χωρίον: (here) 'distance'.

καὶ σύ: 'you also'.

σχεδὸν τρία ἡμίπλεθρα: a plethron measures about 100 ft (approx. 30.5 m); so 'nearly three half-plethra', as here, is a distance of approximately 150 ft (45.75 m).

ὃ δεῖ βαλλομένους διελθεῖν: understand ἡμᾶς with βαλλομένους = 'which we must cross under fire'.

ὅσον πλέθρον: 'as much as a plethron'.

δασύ: understand ἐστί.

διαλειπούσαις: 'with space between them'.

ἀνθ' ὧν ἑστηκότες ἄνδρες: the participle is conditional; = 'and if men were to stand behind them'.

ὑπὸ τῶν φερομένων λίθων: 'from the flying (lit. 'being borne') stones'. We might have expected a Dative of Instrument here, but ὑπό + gen. is sometimes used of things, especially if destructive, as well as of people.

γίγνεται ὡς ἡμίπλεθρον: 'comes to' (lit. 'becomes') about (ὡς) a half-plethron, i.e. about 50 ft (approx. 15.25 m).

7.7

τὸ δασύ: 'the wooded area'.

Αὐτὸ ... εἴη: = 'the very thing we'd want'.

ἔνθεν: '(to a point) from where'.

μικρόν τι: 'just a small distance'.

ἤν: = ἐάν (both times).

ῥάδιον: ἔσται is understood.

7.8–7.14

Rivalry among the soldiers helps the Greeks take the Taochian stronghold. There is then a horrible sight to behold.

7.8

ἐπορεύοντο: 'began to advance'.

Παρράσιος: 'of Parrhasia', a district in south-west Arcadia.

τούτου … τῇ ἡμέρᾳ: we can deduce from this that the captains of the rearguard, and presumably also of the vanguard, took it in turns, a day at a time, to lead their divisions.

ἐν τῷ ἀσφαλεῖ: i.e. 'in safety'.

καθ᾽ ἕνα: 'one by one'.

φυλαττόμενος ὡς ἐδύνατο: 'protecting himself as best he could'; note this reflexive use of the middle.

7.9

Στυμφάλιος: of Stymphalus, a town in Arcadia.

Μεθυδριεύς: of Methydrium, a town in central Arcadia.

καὶ οὗτοι … ὄντες: 'who also were' (lit. 'these too being').

καὶ ἄλλοι δέ: 'and some others too'.

ἐφέστασαν: 3 pl. plup. (intrans.) of ἐφίστημι = 'took up positions'.

οὐ γὰρ ἦν: = οὐ γὰρ ἐξῆν.

πλέον ἢ τὸν ἕνα λόχον: 'that more than the one company', i.e. that of Callimachus. The whole phrase is subject of the infinitive ἑστάναι.

7.10

μηχανᾶται: historic present, the first in a series in this passage, cf. ὁρᾷ, χωρεῖ, παρέρχεται (7.11) and ὁρᾷ, ἐπιλαμβάνεται, παραθεῖ and αἱροῦσι (7.12). The effect each time is to highlight the action of the verb as the story progresses (see introduction, p. 186, note iii).

ἐπειδὴ … φέροιντο: 'whenever … began to fly'; note the indefinite construction after ἐπειδή.

ἐφ᾽: 'at'.

7.11

τὸν Καλλίμαχον … θεώμενον: 'the whole army watching what Callimachus was doing'. The subject of the indirect question, Callimachus, is extracted from it and made the object of the introductory verb, θεώμενον.

τὸ χωρίον: 'the enemy position'.

πλησίον ὄντα: 'though he was close by'; the participle, as in ἑταίρους ὄντας later in the sentence, is concessive.

Λουσιέα: 'of Lusi' (in northern Arcadia).

χωρεῖ αὐτός: 'set off on his own'.

7.12

μετὰ τοῦτον: 'after him'; note that τοῦτον is masculine.

ἀντεποιοῦντο ἀρετῆς: 'were rivals in valour'.

ὡς γὰρ ἅπαξ εἰσέδραμον: 'once they had run in' (lit. 'when they had once run in').

ἄνωθεν ἠνέχθη: 'flew down (lit. 'was borne') from above'.

7.13

ὡς ῥίψοντα: both this future participle with ὡς and ὡς κωλύσων later in the sentence are used to express purpose.

στολὴν ἔχοντα καλήν: 'wearing a beautiful garment'. Aeneas seems to have been more concerned to save the robe than the man.

7.14

ὁ δέ: 'but he', i.e. the man with the beautiful robe; αὐτόν is Aeneas.

ᾤχοντο κατὰ τῶν πετρῶν φερόμενοι: 'went flying down the cliffs' (lit. 'were gone being carried down the cliffs').

7.15–7.18

The Greeks pass through the country of the warlike Chalybians, cross the River Harpasus and then march through the territory of the Scythenians.

7.15

διὰ Χαλύβων: 'through (the land of) the Chalybians'; cf. εἰς Ταόχους (7.1).

ὧν διῆλθον: relative attraction = ἐκείνων οὓς διῆλθον.

εἰς χεῖρας ἦσαν: 'they fought at close quarters'.

ἀντὶ δὲ τῶν πτερύγων: 'and instead of flaps'. In normal Greek hoplite armour πτέρυγες (lit. 'wings') were flaps, of either leather or felt, which hung from the lower edge of the θώραξ to protect the hips and groin.

σπάρτα πυκνὰ ἐστραμμένα: 'thick twisted cords'; these formed a sort of fringe, taking the place of the πτέρυγες on a Greek θώραξ, but are unlikely to have offered much effective protection.

7.16

εἶχον δὲ καί: 'and they had also'; note that the next sentence starts with the very same words.

ὅσον ξυήλην Λακωνικήν: 'as long as a Spartan dagger'; a ξυήλη, not an Attic word, was a curved Spartan dagger.

ὧν: more relative attraction = ἐκείνους ὧν.

ἄν ... ἐπορεύοντο: 'would march on'. ἄν is used here with the imperfect indicative to denote customary action, things which the Chalybians regularly did; it is to be taken also with ἦδον and ἐχόρευον, i.e. 'they would sing and dance'.

μίαν λόγχην ἔχον: 'with (only) one point', a fact worth recording, as the normal Greek spear was pointed at both ends, so that it could be stuck upright in the ground.

7.17

ἐπεί: 'whenever', as the optative παρέλθοιεν shows.

μαχούμενοι: N.B. future = 'ready to fight'.

ἀνακεκομισμένοι ἦσαν: plup. mid. = 'they had stored away'.

7.18

ἐκ τούτων: 'from here' (lit. 'from these people'); note also that once again the lack of any connection speeds up the narrative.

Ἅρπασον ποταμόν: a definite identification is not possible, but it is likely that this is the Kara Su, the northern stretch of the Euphrates.

εὖρος τεττάρων πλέθρων: *c.* 400 ft (122 m).

παρασάγγας εἴκοσι: a distance of some 80 to 85 miles.

7.19–7.20

The Greeks come to Gymnias, where the local ruler sends them a guide who promises to bring them in five days within sight of the sea.

7.19

παρασάγγας εἴκοσι: cf. on 7.18.

Γυμνιάς: quite possibly the modern Bayburt, a city in north-eastern Turkey, approximately 50 miles south of the southern shores of the Black Sea.

ἐκ ταύτης ὁ τῆς χώρας ἄρχων: this simple transposition, suggested by Schneider, eliminates the textual problem noted in the OCT; = 'from this the local ruler'.

διὰ τῆς ἑαυτῶν πολεμίας χώρας: 'through territory at war with his own people' (lit. 'through their own hostile territory').

ἄγοι: note the use of the optative here, in a final (purpose) clause (after ὅπως) following an historic present (πέμπει). On Xenophon's liking for the optative, see introduction, p. 187, second note ii).

7.20

ὄψονται θάλατταν: important, as they hoped that arrival at the coast would mean an easy voyage home to Greece.

τεθνάναι ἐπηγγείλατο: 'he said he was ready to be put to death' (lit. 'he offered to be dead').

τὴν πολεμίαν: χώραν is understood.

παρεκελεύετο: the use of the imperfect is significant: the guide 'kept on exhorting' them.

ᾧ καὶ δῆλον ἐγένετο: 'and thereby it became clear' (lit. by which it also became clear').

ἔλθοι: this optative in an indirect statement, where he might have had an indicative, is in keeping with Xenophon's preference; see above on ἄγοι (7.19).

τῆς τῶν Ἑλλήνων εὐνοίας: 'goodwill towards the Greeks', an objective genitive. If the genitive were subjective, the phrase would mean 'the goodwill of the Greeks', i.e. towards others, clearly not the case here.

7.21–7.27

The Greeks are overjoyed at the sight of the sea. They build a cairn and the guide, suitably rewarded, takes his leave.

7.21

Θήχης: Theches, identified as Deveboynu Tepe, some thirty miles south of Trabzon (ancient Trapezus). In *Online News* of the Archaeological Institute of America (April 7, 1997), Norman Hammond reports that Timothy Mitford, the scholar who made the identification, found at the mountain-top 'no fleeting glimpse between the mountains, no view snatched from a precipitous track, but a stupendous vantage point where perhaps 400 men could stand and gaze down on the distant sea'.

7.22

ἄλλους ... πολεμίους: i.e. in addition to those in the rear, mentioned in the following sentence.

εἵποντο: the subject is 'enemies'.

ἐκ τῆς καιομένης χώρας: i.e. the Greeks are burning and plundering as they go, in compliance with the guide's request.

αὐτῶν: to be taken with τινάς later in the sentence.

ἀπέκτεινάν ... ἐζώγρησαν ... ἔλαβον: all these aorists are best translated as pluperfects.

γέρρα ... δασειῶν βοῶν ὠμοβόεια ... εἴκοσιν: 'about twenty wicker shields covered with raw, shaggy ox-hides' (Brownson).

7.23

ἔθεον δρόμῳ: 'started running at full speed'.

πολλῷ μείζων ... ἐγίγνοντο: 'the shout became much greater the more of them there were' (lit. 'by how much indeed they became more numerous'). Both πολλῷ and ὅσῳ are Datives of the Measure of Difference.

μεῖζόν τι: 'something quite important'.

7.24

Λύκιον: Lycius was commander of the Athenian cavalry.

τάχα δή: 'suddenly'.

βοώντων τῶν στρατιωτῶν: a genitive of the source of sound after ἀκούω.

παρεγγυώντων: i.e. as if it were a watchword or instruction from a commander.

πάντες καὶ οἱ ὀπισθοφύλακες: 'all the rearguard also'.

7.25

ὅτου δή: = τινός, ὅστις δὴ ἦν, i.e. 'someone or other'.

κολωνὸν μέγαν: as a trophy or shrine; its base, some 40 ft in diameter, can still be seen on Deveboynu Tepe (cf. note on 7.21).

7.26

τὰ αἰχμάλωτα γέρρα: 'the captured wicker shields'.

κατέτεμνε ... διεκελεύετο: presumably to prevent them being reused by enemies.

7.27

ἀπὸ κοινοῦ: 'from the common store'.

δαρεικοὺς δέκα: 'ten darics', gold coins introduced as regular currency in Persia by
     Darius I. Each was worth approximately 25 Athenian drachmae.
σκηνήσουσι ... πορεύσονται: both futures of purpose after the relatives οὗ and
     ἥν = 'a village to encamp in and the road to take for the land of the Macronians'.
τῆς νυκτός: presumably because he had to negotiate hostile terrain.

Chapter 8

8.1–8.3

At a river crossing the Greeks have some initial trouble with the Macronians.

8.1

διὰ Μακρώνων: 'through (the country of) the Macronians'. The Macronians were
     a tribe living close to the south-eastern shore of the Black Sea, near the city of
     Trapezus (modern Trabzon).
τὴν ... Σκυθηνῶν: χώραν is to be understood with τήν in both phrases. The
     Scythenians were yet another tribe in the same area.

8.2

ὑπὲρ δεξιῶν: = 'above them, on the right'.
χωρίον οἷον χαλεπώτατον: 'extremely difficult ground'; οἷον, like ὡς or ὅτι,
     strengthens the superlative.
ἐνέβαλλεν: ἐμβάλλω can be used intransitively of rivers, meaning, as here, 'to
     empty (into)'.
ὁ ὁρίζων: sc. ποταμός = 'the boundary stream'.
παχέσι μὲν οὔ, πυκνοῖς δέ: a neatly balanced pair of phrases; see introduction,
     page 187, first note iii); παχέσι = 'of large girth' (lit. 'stout, chunky').

8.3

κατ᾽ ἀντιπέραν: on the other side of (+ *gen.*)
εἰς τὸν ποταμόν: just a hint of sarcastic humour here. As Xenophon goes on to
     show, the Macronian efforts are far from effective, and they end up doing no
     more than throwing stones into the river.
ἐξικνοῦντο γὰρ οὔ: the subject is the stones = 'for they did not reach their mark'.
     Note that οὐ is accented, as here, at the end of a clause or sentence.

8.4–8.7

A slave who can speak their language negotiates successfully with the Macronians.

8.4

προσέρχεται: the verb's early position in the sentence gives some prominence to
     the action; see introduction, page 186, note iv).

γιγνώσκοι: 'he recognised'.

εἰ μή τι κωλύει: 'if there is no objection' (lit. 'unless something hinders it').

8.5

ἀλλ': 'Well', as often conversationally.

ἐρωτήσαντος: a one-word genitive absolute; understand αὐτοῦ.

ὅτι Μάκρωνες: understand εἰσίν or εἶεν.

τί: = διὰ τί.

ἀντιτετάχαται: Ionic third pers. pl. of the perfect passive of ἀντιτάσσω. In Attic
we should expect the more usual periphrastic form, ἀντιτεταγμένοι εἰσίν.

8.6

ὅτι ... ἀπερχόμεθα ... βουλόμεθα: despite the ὅτι, Xenophon writes here
essentially in direct speech, adding immediacy and pinpointing the importance
of what the Greeks are saying. In a real indirect statement we should expect
ἀπέρχονται and βούλονται. In translation omit ὅτι and render in direct speech
= 'The generals told him to say, "... we are going back to Greece and want to
reach the sea"'.

οὐ κακῶς γε ποιήσοντες: the future participle denotes purpose; = 'with no evil
intent'.

8.7

ἐκεῖνοι: i.e. the Macronians.

εἰ δοῖεν ἄν: an indirect question representing δοῖτε ἄν ('would you give?') in the
original direct speech.

τούτων τὰ πιστά: 'pledges to this effect' (lit. 'the usual [= τά] pledges of this').

οἱ δ': 'and they', i.e. the Greek generals.

διδόασιν: historic present.

ἔφασαν: the Macronians are the subject.

ἀμφότεροι: 'both parties'; note the emphatic position at the end.

8.8–8.14

With the Macronians' help the Greeks cross the river and advance to the Colchian
border. The Colchians are drawn up against them on a mountain range: Xenophon
gives his views on how to proceed.

8.8

τήν τε ὁδὸν ὡδοποίουν: the noun in this phrase is redundant, as the sense is
already present in the first part of the compound verb.

ὡς διαβιβάσοντες: a future participle of purpose = 'in order to get them across'.

ἀναμεμιγμένοι: perf. part. mid. and pass. of ἀναμίγνυμι.

ἀγορὰν οἵαν ἐδύναντο: 'the best market they could' (lit. 'a market such as they
were able').

Κόλχων: the Colchians are another tribe living close to the southern shore of the
Black Sea.

8.9

καὶ τὸ μὲν πρῶτον: contrasted with ἔπειτα δέ later in the section.

ἀντιπαρετάξαντο φάλαγγα: 'drew up their line in opposition'.

ὡς οὕτως ἄξοντες: another future participle of purpose = 'intending to advance in this formation'; note this intransitive use of ἄγω.

συλλεγεῖσιν: dat. pl. of aor. part. pass. of συλλέγω, agreeing with τοῖς στρατηγοῖς.

8.10

παύσαντας τὴν φάλαγγα: understand αὐτούς, i.e. 'that having broken up (lit. 'put an end to') the phalanx, they should ...'.

λόχους ὀρθίους ποιῆσαι: 'form companies in columns' (lit. 'straight companies').

ἡ μὲν γὰρ κτλ: Xenophon continues his remarks in direct speech.

τῇ μὲν ... τῇ δέ: 'in one place ... in another'. Note the balancing phrases, further highlighted by the contrasting adjectives ἄνοδον and εὔοδον.

ὅταν ... ὁρῶσιν: εἰς φάλαγγα belongs with τεταγμένοι, ταύτην with διεσπασμένην ὁρῶσιν, i.e. 'whenever drawn up in a phalanx they (i.e. the soldiers) see this broken up'.

8.11

ἤν: = ἐάν.

ἐπὶ πολλῶν: 'many deep'.

προσάγωμεν: 'advance towards (them)'.

χρήσονται ὅ τι ἂν βούλωνται: ' will make whatever use they like'.

ἐπ' ὀλίγων: '(just) a few deep'; cf. ἐπὶ πολλῶν.

ὑπὸ ... ἐμπεσόντων: ἀθρόων should be taken with ἐμπεσόντων, and πολλῶν with both βελῶν and ἀνθρώπων = 'by many missiles and many men falling upon it all together'.

8.12

ποιησαμένους: with ἡμᾶς, the understood subject of κατασχεῖν.

τοσοῦτον χωρίον κατασχεῖν: 'should cover as much ground'.

διαλιπόντας τοῖς λόχοις: 'by leaving spaces between (lit. 'with') the companies'.

ὅσον ... κεράτων: 'as will allow the outermost companies to get beyond the enemy wings'. ὅσον (correlative with, i.e. picking up the sense of, τοσοῦτον) is here followed by an accusative + infinitive (τοὺς ἐσχάτους λόχους γενέσθαι) and ἔξω is separated from its genitive (τῶν πολεμίων κεράτων), its early position some indication of how important Xenophon considered the outflanking of the enemy.

οἱ ἔσχατοι λόχοι: in apposition to 'we' in ἐσόμεθα.

ὀρθίους ἄγοντες: i.e. 'at the heads of columns'.

οἱ κράτιστοι ἡμῶν: it was the norm in a Greek force for the best men to be at the very front, so that they would be first to fight with the enemy.

ᾗ τε ἂν ... ταύτῃ: 'and wherever ... there'.

ἄξει: intransitive again, as at 8.9.

8.13

τὸ διαλεῖπον: 'the intervening space'.

ἔνθεν καὶ ἔνθεν: to be taken with the genitive absolute λόχων ὄντων = 'with companies on this side and on that'.

ἄν: = ἐάν.

ἤν: = ἐάν.

οὐδεὶς ... πολεμίων: 'none of the enemy will any longer remain'. οὐ μή + aorist subjunctive expresses an emphatic negative in the future.

8.14

ἀπὸ τοῦ δεξιοῦ: these words show that the council of war took place on the right wing of the battle line. Xenophon now returns to the left, the usual position for the rearguard once the phalanx is in formation.

τὸ μὴ ἤδη εἶναι: 'from now being'; note the regular redundant μή with an expression of preventing.

ἔνθα πάλαι σπεύδομεν: 'where we have long been eager (to be)'. Note this use of the present tense with πάλαι.

καὶ ὠμοὺς δεῖ καταφαγεῖν: 'we must eat quite raw', a proverbial expression which indicates the total annihilation of the enemy; cf. in English such expressions as 'make utter mincemeat of'.

8.15–8.21

Xenophon's stratagem is successful and the Colchians are put to flight. The Greeks encounter some toxic honey.

8.15

ἐν ταῖς χώραις: 'in position'.

ἕκαστοι: 'each group'.

ἀμφὶ τοὺς ὀγδοήκοντα: 'about eighty'.

σχεδὸν εἰς τοὺς ἑκατόν: '(numbered) close to a hundred'.

τριχῇ ἐποιήσαντο: 'they divided in three'.

τοῦ εὐωνύμου ἔξω: 'beyond the left wing', i.e. of the hoplites.

τοῦ δεξιοῦ: understand ἔξω from the previous phrase.

σχεδὸν ἑξακοσίους ἑκάστους: 'each division numbering almost six hundred'.

8.16

παρηγγύησαν: cf. on 7.24.

σὺν αὐτοῖς: Xenophon often uses σύν + dative where we might expect μετά + genitive.

τῆς τῶν πολεμίων ... ἐπορεύοντο: 'were making their way forward, outflanking (lit. 'having got outside') the enemy phalanx'.

8.17

οἱ μὲν ... τὸ εὐώνυμον: note the carefully balanced phrases with μέν and δέ.

κενὸν ἐποίησαν: 'they left empty'.

8.18

κατὰ τὸ Ἀρκαδικόν: 'in the Arcadian division'.

νομίσαντες φεύγειν: understand αὐτούς = 'thinking that they were fleeing'.

ὧν: note the plural relative pronoun with a singular antecedent (τὸ Ἀρκαδικὸν ὁπλιτικόν) which is collective.

8.19

ἤρξαντο: the Arcadians are the subject.

ἀλλὰ ... ἐτράπετο: 'but took to flight in various directions' (lit. 'another one in another direction'). Note the polyptoton in ἄλλος ἄλλη; see introduction, p. 187, second note ii).

ἀναβάντες: i.e. 'having got to the top'.

ἐν πολλαῖς ... ἐχούσαις: καί technically links πολλαῖς with ἐχούσαις, but a relative clause works better in translation = 'in many villages which had an abundance of provisions'.

8.20

τὰ μὲν ἄλλα: an accusative of respect = 'as for everything else'.

οὐδὲν ὅ τι καὶ ἐθαύμασαν: 'there was (ἦν is understood) nothing at which they were really surprised'.

τῶν κηρίων: partitive genitive, i.e. 'any of the honeycombs'.

πάντες ἄφρονες ... ἐγίγνοντο: the fragrant yellow flowers of the *rhododendron luteum*, sometimes incorrectly called *azalea pontica*, are the culprits here. This poisonous plant grows profusely in the area and will have provided a lot of the bees' food. Some 350 years later, local tribesman are said to have left out supplies of this 'mad honey' as a trap for Pompey's soldiers.

κάτω διεχώρει αὐτοῖς: i.e. 'suffered from diarrhoea'.

σφόδρα: with μεθύουσιν.

οἱ δὲ πολὺ ... ἀποθνήσκουσιν: ἐδηδοκότες is to be understood again with πολύ, and ἐῴκεσαν (from ἔοικα) with both μαινομένοις and ἀποθνήσκουσιν.

8.21

ἔκειντο δὲ οὕτω πολλοί: 'accordingly there were many lying (on the ground)'.
ὥσπερ: here with a genitive absolute.

ἀπέθανε: translate as pluperfect.

ἐκ φαρμακοποσίας: 'after taking medicine'.

8.22–8.28

The Greeks come to Trapezus. They make sacrifices and hold athletic competitions.

8.22

εἰς Τραπεζοῦντα: 'at Trapezus', the modern Trabzon (earlier known in English as Trebizond), an important Greek city on the southern shore of the Black Sea, euphemistically known to the Greeks as the Euxine (i.e. 'hospitable') Sea. Trapezus was a colony of Sinope, a Milesian colony also on the Black Sea.

8.23

κἀντεῦθεν ὁρμώμενοι: 'and using these as a base' (lit. 'setting out from there').

ξένια: in apposition with the objects, = 'as gifts of hospitality'; cf. the same thing in καὶ ξένια καὶ παρ᾽ ἐκείνων ἦλθον βόες (8.24).

8.24

συνδιεπράττοντο: i.e. they joined (with the Colchians) in negotiations (with the Greeks), presumably in order to protect the Colchians from further plundering.

τῶν ... μάλιστα οἰκούντων: 'who lived for the most part on the plain'.

καὶ παρ᾽ ἐκείνων: 'from them too'.

8.25

τὴν θυσίαν ἣν ηὔξαντο: i.e. when they had begun the retreat after the Battle of Cunaxa.

ἦλθον: translate as pluperfect.

ἀποθῦσαι ... ἡγεμόσυνα: 'to sacrifice to Zeus the Saviour and to Heracles thank offerings for guidance'.

Σπαρτιάτην: 'a Spartiate', a member of the Spartan ruling class.

ἔφυγε ... οἴκοθεν: 'had been exiled from home', as was normal for the avoidance of pollution, when someone, even accidentally, as here, had caused another's death. κατακανών: aor. part. act. of κατακαίνω, not an Attic word.

ξυήλῃ: cf. on 7.16.

8.26

τὰ δέρματα: i.e. of the sacrificial victims. These were entrusted to Dracontius presumably as prizes for the competitors in the games.

ὅπου: '(to the place) where'.

κάλλιστος τρέχειν: understand ἐστί = 'is the best for running'; τρέχειν is an epexegetic or explanatory infinitive.

ἐν σκληρῷ καὶ δασεῖ οὕτως: 'on hard, overgrown ground like this'.

μᾶλλόν τι: emphatic at the beginning of the sentence. The likelihood of competitors sustaining even serious physical harm was no obstacle in the organization of games like these.

8.27

ἠγωνίζοντο ... οἱ πλεῖστοι: 'boys competed in the stade-race, most of them belonging to prisoners'. The stade-race, approximately 200 yards (c. 183 m), was the regular short race in Greek athletics.

δόλιχον: anything between three and twelve circuits of the stadium.

πάλην: 'wrestling'; three throws were usually considered a win. Spraining an opponent's toes or fingers and throttling were considered all part of the fun.

πυγμήν: 'boxing'. As an equivalent of modern boxing gloves competitors wore strips of leather bound round the hands. These increased the force of the blow and could have nails and pieces of lead attached.

παγκράτιον: the 'pancratium', a vicious combination of wrestling and boxing. The sport had virtually no rules, and, as well as more normal techniques, regularly included such elements as kicking and choking. Only biting, eye-gouging and attacks on the genitals were forbidden. The pancratium was introduced to the Olympic Games in 648 BC and in 200 BC was extended to include boys as well as adults.

ἕτεροι: understand ἠγωνίζοντο again.

θέα: to be carefully distinguished from θεά.

κατέβησαν: i.e. 'entered the contest'.

8.28

αὐτούς: i.e. the riders.

κατὰ τοῦ πρανοῦς: 'down the slope'.

ἐλάσαντας ... ἀποστρέψαντας ... ἄγειν: understand τοὺς ἵππους as the object of all three verbs.

ἐν τῇ θαλάττῃ: i.e. 'on the shore', 'at the water's edge'.

πρὸς τὸν βωμόν: the altar where the sacrifices had been offered clearly served also as a starting post for the races.

κάτω: 'on the way down', followed by ἄνω = 'on the way up'.

πρὸς τὸ ἰσχυρῶς ὄρθιον: 'against the exceedingly steep slope'.

Vocabulary

While there is no Defined Vocabulary List for A Level, words in the OCR Defined Vocabulary List for AS are marked with * so that students can quickly see the vocabulary with which they should be particularly familiar.

Ἀγασίας -ου, m. — Agasias, a captain in the Greek army

*ἀγορά -ᾶς, f. — marketplace, market

*ἄγω — to lead, lead up; bring, carry; to lead the way, advance

*ἀγών -ῶνος, m. — contest, games; struggle

ἀγωνίζομαι — to contend, strive, fight

ᾄδω (imperf. ᾖδον) — to sing

*ἀεί — always

Ἀθήνησι — at Athens

ἀθρόος -α -ον — all together, close together, in a mass

ἀθυμία -ας, f. — despondency, despair

αἴθω — to burn

Αἰνείας -ου, m. — Aeneas, a captain in the Greek army

*αἱρέω — to take, capture, catch; mid. to choose

Αἰσχίνης -ου, m. — Aeschines, a leader of peltasts in the Greek army

*αἰτέω — to ask, ask for

*αἰχμάλωτος -ον — taken by the spear, captive; m. as noun prisoner

Ἀκαρνάν -ᾶνος, m. — an Acarnanian, someone from Acarnania (on the west coast of Greece)

*ἀκούω — to hear

*ἄκρος -α -ον — at the point, highest; neut. as noun summit; pl. heights

*ἄκων, ἄκουσα, ἄκον — unwilling(ly), unintentional(ly)

ἄλκιμος -ον — mighty, valiant, brave

*ἀλλά — but

ἀλλήλους -ας -α — one another, each other

ἄλλος -η -ο — other

ἄλφιτα, -ων, n. pl. — barley meal

*ἅμα — at the same time; + dat. at the same time as

ἅμαξα -ης, f. — waggon

*ἀμφί — + acc. round, about, on

*ἀμφότερος -α -ον — both; in pl. both parties

ἀναβαίνω — to go up; mount (a horse)

ἀνακομίζω — to carry up; mid. to carry up for oneself, store up

ἀνακράζω (aor. ἀνέκραγον) — to raise a shout

ἀναλαμβάνω — to take up, take along

ἀναλίσκω (fut. ἀναλώσω) — to use up, squander, waste

ἀναμίγνυμι — to mix up, mingle

ἀνατίθημι — to set up, dedicate

ἀναφρονέω — to come back to one's senses

ἀναχάζω — to retreat, draw back

*ἀνήρ, ἀνδρός, m. — man

*ἄνθρωπος -ου, m. — man, person, human being

ἀνιάω (fut. mid. as pass. ἀνιάσομαι) — to trouble, hurt

ἀνίστημι — *trans. tenses* to make get up; *intrans.* to stand up, get up

ἄνοδος -ον — impassable

*ἀντί — + *gen.* facing, opposite to; instead of

ἀντιπαραθέω — to run along to oppose

ἀντιπαρασ- κευάζομαι — to make preparations in turn

ἀντιπαρατάττομαι — to draw up against

ἀντιπέραν — over against, opposite

ἀντιποιέομαι — + *gen.* to be rivals in

ἀντιτάττω — to array against; *mid. or pass.* to array oneself against

ἄνω — up, upwards; above

ἄνωθεν — from above

ἅπαξ — once

*ἅπας, ἅπασα, ἅπαν — all together

ἀπέρχομαι — to go away, go back

*ἀποθνήσκω — to die; be killed

ἀποθύω — to sacrifice (what is due), pay a vow

ἀποικία -ας, f. — colony

ἀποκάμνω — to grow tired

*ἀποκρίνομαι — to answer, reply

*ἀποκτείνω — to kill, put to death

ἀποπέμπω — to send back, send away

ἀποστρέφω — to turn back, turn round

ἀποτέμνω — to cut off

ἀπότομος -ον — steep, precipitous

*ἀργυροῦς -ᾶ -οῦν — of silver, silver

*ἀρετή -ῆς, f. — excellence, valour; good service

*ἀριστερός -ά -όν — on the left

Ἀριστώνυμος -ου, m. — Aristonymus, a captain in the Greek army

Ἀρκαδικός -ή -όν — Arcadian

Ἅρπασος -ου, m. — Harpasus, a river in north-east Asia Minor

*ἄρχω — *act.* be first, rule, command; *act. & mid.* to begin (+ *gen.*)

*ἄρχων -οντος, m. — ruler, leader

*ἀσφαλής -ές — safe, secure

*αὖθις — again

αὐτόθεν — from there, thence

αὐτόθι — there

*αὐτός -ή -ό — him, her, it, them; himself, herself, etc.; ὁ αὐτός, etc. the same

αὐτόσε — to the very place, thither, there

*ἀφικνέομαι — to arrive

ἄφρων -ον — out of one's mind

βάδην — at a walk

βακτηρία -ας, f. — walking stick, stick

*βάλλω — to throw, pelt

βαρβαρικός -ή -όν — barbarian, foreign

*βασιλεύς -έως, m. — king (without an article when referring to the King of Persia)

βέλος -ους, n. — missile

βῆμα -ατος, n. — step

*βλάπτω — to harm, injure

*βοάω — to shout

*βοή -ῆς, f. — shout, cry

*βοηθέω — to come to the aid of (+ *dat.*); go to the rescue

*βουλεύω — to plan; usually mid. to take counsel, deliberate, plan

*βούλομαι — to wish, be willing

βοῦς, βοός, c. — ox, cow

*βωμός -οῦ, m. — altar

*γάϱ — for

γέλως -ωτος, m. — laughter

γέϱϱον -ου, n. — wicker shield

*γίγνομαι — to become, happen, be

*γιγνώσκω — to (get to) know, find out; understand

Γυμνιάς -άδος, f. — Gymnias, a city of the Scytheni, possibly the modern Bayburt

γυμνικός -ή -όν — athletic, gymnastic

*γυνή, γυναικός, f. — woman, wife

*δακϱύω — to weep

δακτύλιος -ου, m. — finger ring, ring

δαϱεικός -οῦ, m. — daric (a Persian gold coin)

δασύς -εῖα -ύ — thickly wooded, bushy; shaggy

*δέ — but, and

*δεῖ — it is necessary

δείδω (aor. ἔδεισα) — to fear, be afraid

*δείκνυμι — to show, point out

δέκα — ten

*δένδϱον -ου, n. — tree

*δεξιός -ά -όν — right, on the right hand

δέϱμα -ατος, n. — skin, hide

*δή — indeed

*δῆλος -η -ον — clear, evident

*διά — + gen. through, by means of

*διαβαίνω — to cross, go over

διάβασις -εως, f. — crossing

διαβιβάζω — to take across, transport

διαγωνίζομαι — to strive continually

διακελεύομαι — to urge on, encourage

διακόπτω — to cut to pieces, cut through

*διαλέγομαι — to speak with, converse with

διαλείπω — to leave an interval between, stand at intervals

διασπάω — to draw apart, separate

διατίθημι — to place apart, arrange; of persons to treat

διατϱέφω — to nourish thoroughly, support

διαχωϱέω — to go through

*δίδωμι (aor. part. δούς, δόντος) — to give

διέϱχομαι — to go through; of distance to cover

*δοκεῖ — it seems good

δόλιχος -ου, m. — long race

δόϱυ, δόϱατος, n. — spear, spear shaft

δουλεύω — to be a slave

Δϱακόντιος -ου, m. — Dracontius, a Spartan in the Greek army

*δϱόμος -ου, m. — running; race course; δϱόμῳ at a run

*δύναμαι — to be able

δύο, δυοῖν — two

*δῶϱον -ου, n. — gift

*ἑαυτόν -ήν -ό — himself, herself, itself; pl. themselves

ἑβδομήκοντα — seventy

*ἐγγύτεϱον — nearer

*ἐθέλω — to be willing, wish

*εἰ — if, whether

εἴκοσι — twenty

*εἰμί — to be

*εἰς — + acc. into, to; with numerals up to, about

εἷς, μία, ἕν — one

εἰσέϱχομαι — to go into, enter

εἰστϱέχω — to run into

εἶτα — then, next

*ἐκ — + gen. out of, from

*ἕκαστος -η -ον — each

ἑκατόν — a hundred

*ἐκεῖνος -η -ο — that; he, she, it, they

*ἐλαύνω — to drive; to ride

*Ἑλλάς -άδος, f. — Greece

*Ἕλλην -ηνος, m. — a Greek

Ἑλληνικός -ή -όν · Greek, Grecian

Ἑλληνίς -ίδος · *fem. adj.* Greek

ἐμβάλλω · + εἰς + *acc.* to invade; *of a river* to empty into

ἐμέω · to vomit

ἐμμένω · to stay in

ἐμός -ή -όν · my

ἐμπίπτω · to fall upon, attack

ἐμποδών · in the way, hindering

ἔμπροσθεν · before, in front

*ἐν · + *dat.* in, on, at, among

*ἐναντίος -α -ον · opposite, over against; opposed to, against

ἐνέδρα -ας, f. · ambush

*ἕνεκα · *usually after gen.* on account of, because of

*ἔνθα · where; there, then, thereupon

ἔνθαπερ · just where

ἔνθεν · from where, whence; to the place from which

ἐνθύμημα -ατος n. · idea

*ἐνταῦθα · there, thither; thereupon, then

*ἐντεῦθεν · from that place, thence; then, afterwards

ἑξακόσιοι -αι -α · six hundred

ἐξαπίνης · suddenly

ἐξέρχομαι · to come out, go out, escape

ἑξήκοντα · sixty

ἐξικνέομαι · to arrive at, reach (the mark)

ἔξω · outside; + *gen.* outside of, beyond, outflanking

ἔοικα · to be like, resemble

ἐπαγγέλλω · to notify, proclaim; *mid.* to promise, offer

*ἐπεί · when, after; since, as

*ἐπειδάν · when, whenever

*ἐπειδή · when; since

*ἐπί · + *gen.* on, upon; at; + *acc.* on upon, to, against

ἐπικαταρριπτέω · to throw down upon

ἐπιλαμβάνω · to seize upon; *mid.* to lay hold of, catch

ἐπιλείπω · to leave behind; *of things* to run out, fail

ἐπιμαρτύρομαι · to call to witness, invoke

ἐπιμέλομαι · to take care of, take charge of

ἐπισιτίζομαι · to lay in provisions

ἐπισπάω · to draw to, draw after; *mid.* to draw after oneself

ἐπιτήδειος -α -ον · suitable, fit, necessary; *n. pl. as noun* provisions, necessaries

ἐπιτίθεμαι · + *dat.* to attack, set upon

*ἕπομαι (imperf. εἱπόμην) · + *dat.* to follow

ἑπτά · seven

*ἔρχομαι · to come, go

*ἐρωτάω · to ask, enquire

*ἐσθίω (perf. ἐδήδοκα) · to eat

*ἑσπέρα -ας, f. · evening

*ἔσχατος -η -ον · furthest, last, outermost

*ἑταῖρος -ου, m. · companion, comrade

*ἕτερος -α -ον · the other (of two); another; *pl.* others

*εὐδαίμων -ον · happy, fortunate, prosperous

*εὐθύς · immediately, at once

εὔνοια -ας, f. · goodwill, friendly feeling

Εὔξεινος -ον · Euxine; *used as a proper name for* the Black Sea.

εὔοδος -ον · easy to travel, passable

εὐπετῶς · easily

*εὑρίσκω · to find, invent

εὖρος -ους, n. · width, breadth

Εὐρύλοχος -ου, m. · Eurylochus, an Arcadian in the Greek army

*εὔχομαι · to pray; to vow, promise

εὐώνυμος -ον · on the left

ἐφίστημι · *trans. tenses* to set over, put in command; *intrans.* to take a position

*ἔχω · to have, hold; *mid.* to hold on to

*ἕως	until, while, as long as	*ἵστημι (perf. infin. ἑστάναι)	trans. tenses to cause to stand, stop, set up; intrans. to stand, be stationed, stand one's ground
*Ζεύς, Διός, m.	Zeus		
ζωγρέω	to take alive		
ζώνη -ης, f.	belt, girdle	*ἰσχυρός -ά -όν	strong, powerful
*ἤ	or; than; ἤ … ἤ either … or	ἴτυς -υος, f.	edge, rim (of a shield)
ἡγεμονία -ας, f.	leadership, command	ἴχνος -ους, n.	track, footprint
ἡγεμόσυνα -ων, n. pl.	thank offerings for guidance	*καθίστημι	trans. tenses to set down, station, establish, appoint; intrans. to be established, take one's place, be stationed
*ἡγεμών -όνος, m.	leader, guide; commander		
*ἡγέομαι	to lead, guide	καθοράω	to look down at, see, observe, catch sight of
*ἥκω	to have come, to come, arrive		
*ἡμεῖς, ἡμῶν	we	*καί	and, also, even
*ἡμέρα -ας, f.	day	*καίω	to burn
*ἡμέτερος -α -ον	our	*κακός -ή -όν	bad, wicked
ἡμίπλεθρον -ου, n.	a half-plethron (c. 50 feet)	καλινδέομαι	to roll over and over
ἤν	= ἐάν	Καλλίμαχος -ου, m.	Callimachus, a captain in the Greek army
Ἡρακλῆς -έους, m.	Heracles	*καλέω	to call
ἦτρον -ου, n.	abdomen, belly	*καλός -ή -όν	beautiful, fine, handsome
*θάλαττα –ης, f.	sea	*κατά	+ acc. at, in, by, according to; + gen. down from, down over
θάττων	comparative of ταχύς		
*θαυμάζω	to wonder, be astonished; to admire, wonder at	καταβαίνω	to come down, go down; to enter a contest
θαυμαστός -ή -όν	wonderful, surprising	κατακαίνω	to kill
θέα -ας, f.	sight, spectacle	καταλαμβάνω	to capture, seize, occupy
θέαμα -ατος, n.	sight, spectacle	καταπίπτω	to fall down
*θεάομαι	to watch	κατατέμνω	to cut down, cut up, cut to pieces
*θεός -οῦ, m.	god	κατεσθίω (aor. κατέφαγον)	to eat up, gobble down
θέω	to run		
Θήχης -ου, m.	Theches, a mountain, possibly the modern Deveboynu Tepe	κατέχω (aor. infin. κατασχεῖν)	to hold down, restrain; hold, occupy; cover (a space)
-θνήσκω	to die, be killed	κάτω	down below
θυσία -ας, f.	sacrifice	*κεῖμαι	to lie
*θώραξ –ακος, m.	breastplate	*κελεύω	to order, command
*ἱκανός -ή -όν	sufficient, enough; able	*κενός -ή -όν	empty
*ἱππεύς -έως, m.	cavalryman; in pl. cavalry	*κέρας -ατος, n.	horn; wing (of an army)
		*κεφαλή -ῆς, f.	head
*ἵππος -ου, m.	horse	κηρίον -ου, n.	honeycomb

Κλεάνωρ -ορος, m. Cleanor, a general in the Greek army

κνημίς -ῖδος, f. greave

κοινῇ in common, together

*κοινός -ή -όν common, shared by all; ἀπὸ κοινοῦ from the common store

Κολχίς -ίδος, f. Colchis, a district along the eastern and south-eastern coast of the Black sea

Κόλχοι -ων, m. pl. Colchians, a tribe living near Trapezus

κολωνός -οῦ, m. mound (of stones), cairn

*κόπτω to cut down

κράνος -ους, n. helmet

*κρατέω to rule, hold sway over (+ *gen.*)

κράτιστος -η -ον best, strongest, bravest

κραυγή -ῆς, f. cry, shout, uproar

Κρής, Κρητός, m. a Cretan

κτῆνος -ους, n. piece of property, domestic animal; *pl.* cattle, livestock

*κύκλος -ου, m. circle, ring

κυλινδέω (or -ω) to roll, roll down

κωλύω to hinder, prevent

*κώμη -ης, f. village

Λακωνικός -ή -όν Laconian, Spartan

*λαμβάνω to catch, capture, take

*λέγω to say, speak, tell

λήζομαι to plunder, pillage

*λίθος -ου, m. stone

λινοῦς -ῆ -οῦν of linen

*λόγχη -ης, f. spear, spearhead

*λοιπός -ή -όν left, remaining

Λουσιεύς -έως a Lusian, someone from Lusi (in northern Arcadia)

λόφος -ου, m. hill, ridge

*λοχαγός -ου, m. captain

λόχος -ου, m. ambush; company

Λύκιος -ου, m. Lycius, a cavalry commander

λωφάω to abate, cease

μαίνομαι to be mad, insane

Μάκρωνες -ων, m. pl. Macronians

*μάλιστα most of all, especially

*μανθάνω to learn, find out

μαχαίριον -ου, n. knife

*μάχομαι to fight

*μέγας, μεγάλη, μέγα great, large

Μεθυδριεύς -έως a native of Methydrium, a small town in Arcadia

μεθύω to be drunk

μείζων -ον comparative of μέγας

*μέλλω to be about to, be going to

*μὲν... δέ on the one hand ... on the other

*μένω to remain

*μέσος -η -ον (in the) middle

*μετά + *acc.* after, next to

*μέχρι + *gen.* up to, as far as

*μή not

*μηδείς, μηδεμία, μηδέν no, no one, nobody; nothing

μηχανάομαι to contrive, devise

*μικρός -ά -όν small, little

*μόνος -η -ον alone, only

*νομίζω to think

*νύξ, νυκτός, f. night

ξένια -ων, n. pl. gifts of friendship

Ξενοφῶν -ῶντος, m. Xenophon, an Athenian, eventual leader of the Greek army, and author of the *Anabasis*

ξυήλη -ης, f. curved dagger

*ὁ, ἡ, τό the

ὀγδοήκοντα eighty

ὁδοποιέω to make a road

*ὁδός -οῦ, f. way, road

*ὅθεν whence, from where

*οἰκέω to live; live in, inhabit; pass. be inhabited, situated

*οἴκοθεν	from home
*οἶνος -ου, m.	wine
οἴομαι/οἶμαι (aor. ᾠήθην)	to think
οἴχομαι	to have gone, take one's leave
*ὀλίγος -η -ον	small, little; in pl. (a) few
ὅλος -η -ον	whole, entire, all
*ὄνομα -ατος, n.	name
ὄνος -ου, m.	ass, donkey
*ὄπισθεν	in the rear, from the rear, behind
*ὁπλίζω	to arm, equip
*ὁπλίτης -ου, m.	hoplite, heavy-armed infantryman
ὁπλιτικός -ή -όν	of a hoplite; neut. as noun hoplite division
ὁπότε	when, whenever
ὅπως	how; that, in order that
*ὁράω	to see
ὄρθιος -α -ον	straight up, steep; in column
*ὀρθός -ή -όν	straight, upright
ὅρια -ων, n. pl.	borders, boundaries
ὁρίζω	to separate, be the boundary between
*ὁρμάομαι (aor. ὡρμήθην)	to set out, start
*ὄρος -ους, n.	hill, mountain
Ὀρχομένιος -α -ον	Orchomenian, from Orchomenus (in Arcadia)
*ὅς, ἥ, ὅ	who, which
*ὅσος -η -ον	as much as; pl. as many as, all those who
*ὅστις, ἥτις, ὅ τι	whoever, whatever
*ὅταν	when, whenever
*οὐ	not
οὖ	where
*οὐδέ	and not, but not; not even
*οὖν	accordingly, therefore, then, so
*οὗτος, αὕτη, τοῦτο	this
*οὕτω(ς)	in this way, so, under these circumstances

ὀχυρός -ά -όν	strong
παγκράτιον -ου, n.	pancratium, all-round contest (a combination of boxing and wrestling)
παιανίζω	to sing a paean, sing a war song
παῖς, παιδός, c.	child
*πάλαι	long ago, long since
παλαίω	I wrestle
πάλη -ης, f.	wrestling
*πάλιν	back; again
πάνυ	very
*παρά	+ acc. by (the side of), beside; + gen. from
παραβοηθέω	to go to help, go to the rescue
παράγω	to lead along, lead on
*παραδίδωμι	to give up, hand over, surrender
παραθέω	to run past
παρακαλέω	to call to, summon, invite
παρακελεύομαι	to urge, advise, exhort
παρακέλευσις -εως, f.	encouragement, cheering
παρασάγγης -ου, m.	parasang (a Persian measure of distance denoting 2 hours' travel or approx. 3 miles)
*παρασκευάζω	to prepare; mid. to prepare (for oneself), provide
παρατάττω	to draw up side by side
παρατρέχω	to run over, run across
παρεγγυάω	to pass the word along
παρέρχομαι	to pass by, pass through, go along
*παρέχω	to furnish, provide, supply, offer
πάροδος -ου, m.	way past, approach route
Παρράσιος -α -ον	Parrhasian, from Parrhasia, a district in south-west Arcadia
*πᾶς, πᾶσα, πᾶν	all, the whole
*πάσχω	to suffer, be hurt, experience
πατάσσω	to strike
*πατρίς -ίδος, f.	native land
*παύω	to stop, put an end to; mid. to cease, desist

παχύς -εῖα -ύ thick, large

*πεδίον -ου, n. plain, level ground

*πελταστής -οῦ, m. a peltast, light-armed soldier

πέμπτος -η -ον fifth

*πέμπω to send

πέντε five

πεντεκαίδεκα fifteen

πεντήκοντα fifty

περιβάλλω to embrace

περιίστημι *transitive tenses* to set around; *intrans.* to stand around, surround

περιττεύω to be over and above, outflank

περιττός -ή -όν over and above, superfluous; οἱ περιττοί the outflanking troops

Περσικός -ή -όν Persian

πέτρα -ας, f. rock, cliff, boulder

πέτρος -ου, m. stone

πή in any way

πῆχυς -εως, m. cubit (*c.* 17½ inches or 444 mm)

*πιέζω to press, press hard

*πιστός -ή -όν faithful, trusty; πιστά pledges

πίτυς -υος, f. pine tree

πλέθρον -ου, n. a plethron (*c.* 100 feet or 30.5 m)

πλείων -ον comparative of πολύς

πλευρά -ᾶς, f. rib

πλησίον nearby

*ποιέω to do, make; κακῶς ποιεῖν to injure, maltreat

*πολεμέω to make war (upon + *dat.*)

*πολέμιος -α -ον hostile; m. pl. the enemy

*πόλις -εως, f. city, state

πόλισμα -ατος, n. town

*πολύς, πολλή, πολύ much, great, large; pl. many

πόντος -ου, m. sea

*πορεύομαι to go, proceed, march, travel

*ποταμός -οῦ, m. river

πρανής -οῦς steep

πρόβατον -ου, n. sheep

προδρομή -ῆς, f. running forward, sally

*πρός + *acc.* to, towards

προσάγω to lead towards, lead against; march against

*προσβάλλω to attack (+ *dat.*)

προσβατός -ή -όν accessible

προσέρχομαι to come *or* go to; to come up, approach

προστατέω to be manager of (+ *gen.*)

προτρέχω to run forward

*πρῶτος -η -ον first

πτέρυξ -υγος, f. wing; flap

πυγμή -ῆς, f. boxing

πυκνός -ή -όν close together, compact, solid

*πῶς how? in what way?

*ῥάδιος -α -ον easy

*ῥίπτω to throw, throw aside, hurl down

Σινωπεύς -έως, m. a Sinopean, a citizen of Sinope, a colony of Miletus on the southern shore of the Black Sea

σκέλος -ους, n. leg

σκευή -ῆς, f. dress, attire

σκηνέω to be encamped

σκηνόω to encamp

σκληρός -ά -όν hard, rough; neut. as noun rough ground

Σκυθηνοί -ῶν, m. pl. Scythenians, a tribe living near the south-eastern shore of the Black Sea

σμῆνος -ους, n. swarm of bees

Σπαρτιάτης -ου, m. a Spartan (citizen)

σπάρτον -ου, n. rope, cord

σπεύδω to hasten, be in a hurry

*στάδιον -ου, n. stade; stade-race

σταθμός -οῦ, m. halting place; day's march

στολή -ῆς, f.	robe
*στράτευμα -ατος, n.	army
*στρατηγός -οῦ, m.	general
*στρατιά -ᾶς, f.	army
*στρατιώτης -ου, m.	soldier
*στρατοπεδεύ ομαι	to encamp
στρέφω (perf. pass. ἔστραμμαι)	to turn, twist
Στυμφάλιος -α -ον	Stymphalian, from Stymphalus in north-eastern Arcadia
συλλέγω	to collect, gather, assemble
*σύν	+ dat. with
συνδιαπράττ ομαι	to join in negotiations
συνεκκόπτω	to help cut down
συνέρχομαι (perf. συνελήλυθα)	to come together, assemble
συνεφέπομαι	to follow after, accompany
συντρίβω (perf. pass. συντέτριμμαι)	to crush
σφάττω	to slaughter, kill
*σφόδρα	very, very much, exceedingly
*σχέδον	nearly, almost
σωτήρ -ῆρος, m.	saviour, deliverer
*τάξις -εως, f.	rank, line
Τάοχοι -ων, m. pl.	the Taochians, a tribe near the south-eastern shore of the Black Sea
*τάττω	to draw up, arrange
τάχα	quickly, forthwith
τεθνάναι	perf. infin. of θνήσκω
τέταρτος -η -ον	fourth
τέτταρες -α	four
τήμερον	today
*τίς, τί	who? what?

*τις, τι	someone, something; any one, anything; a certain
τοίνυν	therefore, then; well then
*τοξότης -ου, m.	archer
*τοσοῦτος -αύτη -οῦτο	so great; pl. so many
Τραπεζοῦς -οῦντος, f.	Trapezus (modern Trabzon)
τρεῖς, τρία	three
*τρέπω (aor. mid. ἐτραπόμην)	to turn
*τρέχω	to run
τριάκοντα	thirty
τρίτος -η -ον	third
τριχῇ	in three
*τρίχινος -η -ον	of hair, made of hair
τροπή -ῆς, f.	flight, rout
*τυγχάνω	to happen
*ὑμεῖς, ὑμων	you
*ὑπέρ	+ gen. over, down over, on behalf of
ὑπερέχω	to be above, project, overhang
*ὑπό	+ acc. under, at the foot of; + gen. by, from, at the hands of
ὑποζύγιον -ου, n.	pack animal
*ὑστεραῖος -α -ον	following, next; τῇ ὑστεραίᾳ on the next day
φάλαγξ -αγγος, f.	phalanx, line of battle
φαρμακοποσία -ας, f.	taking medicine
φάσκω	to assert; to allege, claim
*φέρω	to bear, bring, carry; pass. to be borne, be thrown, rush on
*φεύγω	to flee, run away
*φημί	to say, assert
φιάλη -ης, f.	cup
φιλονικία -ας, f.	rivalry
*φυγή -ῆς, f.	flight
*φυλάττω	to guard, keep guard, defend; mid. to be on one's guard, defend oneself
*φωνή -ῆς, f.	voice; language

*χαλεπός -ή -όν   hard, difficult

Χάλυβες -ων, m.   the Chalybes, a tribe on the
pl.   northern frontier of Armenia

*χείρ, χειρός, f.   hand; εἰς χεῖρας in, to hand-
to-hand conflict

Χειρίσοφος   Chirisophus, a Spartan general
-ου, m.   in Xenophon's army

χορεύω   to dance

*χράομαι   to use, make use of (+ *dat.*)

χρήζω   to need, desire

*χώρα -ας, f.   country, land; post, station

ὠμοβόειος -α -ον   of raw oxhide

ὠμός -ή -όν   raw

*ὥρα -ας, f.   hour

*ὡς   as, how; *with numerals* about

ὡσαύτως   in this same way, likewise

*ὥστε   so that

Homer, *Iliad*

Introduction, Commentary Notes and
Vocabulary by Chris Tudor

AS: Book 18: 1–38, 50–238

A Level: Book 9: 182–431

Introduction

Homer's *Iliad* is the earliest surviving work of ancient Greek literature – and must be ranked as one of its greatest. Composed in the second half of the eighth century BC, the poem centres on the tragic figure of Achilles, his wrath and its terrible consequences for those around him. Along the way, the poem engages with some of most fundamental questions of human existence: the relationship between man and the gods, man's purpose on earth and the meaning of human suffering. It is undeniably a poetic masterpiece.

The influence of the *Iliad* on Greek culture was colossal, determining much of later literature, thought and art. The tragedian Aeschylus described his own plays as 'mere slices from the great banquet of Homer', while Aristotle studied it in detail in his *Poetics*. Plato quoted the poem extensively in his *Republic*, while Alexander the Great was said to carry a copy of the poem with him wherever he went. In the history of Western literature, few works have enjoyed a similar status and influence.

The following sections are aimed at providing students with a simple and concise introduction to Homer's *Iliad*. We start with the story of the *Iliad*, before moving on to consider the origin, date and authorship of the poem, the metre of epic poetry, the use of formulae, type-scenes and story patterns, and the language and style of Homeric verse.

The mythic background of the *Iliad*

The *Iliad* describes a single episode in the tenth year of the Trojan War: the wrath of Achilles, his withdrawal from the fighting and its disastrous consequences for those around him. The story was a traditional one, and the poet could rely on his audience to be familiar both with its major characters (Achilles, Agamemnon, Hector, etc.) and with the events of the Trojan War itself. For the benefit of the modern reader, however, who may be less familiar with this material, there follows a detailed introduction to the mythic background to the Trojan War, up to the point where the *Iliad* starts.

The origins of the Trojan War could be traced back to the wedding of the goddess Thetis to the mortal Peleus. Invitations to the wedding had been extended to everyone except for the goddess Eris ('Strife'), a well-known mischief-maker who had been told to stay at home. Angered by the snub, Eris had come to the wedding anyway, leaving a golden apple in the middle of the wedding feast which she had labelled καλλίστῃ ('for the most beautiful woman'). This apple was claimed by three goddesses: Hera, Athena and Aphrodite. Unable to decide between themselves which of them was κάλλιστα ('the most beautiful'), they asked Zeus to make the decision for them. Zeus refused and sent them instead to the Trojan prince, Paris, who agreed to help. With Hermes as their guide, the three goddesses met on Mount Ida for what came to be known as the Judgement of Paris.

On the day of the Judgement itself, each of the goddesses offered Paris a gift related to her personal sphere of influence: Hera offered him kingship, Athena wisdom and success in war and Aphrodite the world's most beautiful woman: Helen of Sparta. After some consideration, Paris rejected Hera and Athena in favour of Aphrodite and Helen. Shortly afterwards, he made a trip to Sparta where he seduced Helen and smuggled her back to Troy. Helen's husband, Menelaus, furious at the theft of his wife, appealed to his brother, Agamemnon, to defend his honour and recover Helen. An army was mustered and the Greek forces set sail for Troy – and so began the Trojan War.

The first nine years of the war were inconclusive. Some of the key events in this period included the initial arrival of the Greeks at Troy, the loss of several Greek heroes (Protesilaus, Philoctetes, etc.), the attempt by Odysseus and Menelaus to settle the matter by negotiation and the Greek raids on towns in the surrounding area. While most of these events have little impact on the narrative of the *Iliad*, two incidents are of particular importance: first, the raid on Lyrnessus, in which Achilles captures the girl Briseïs; second, the raid on Thebe, in which Achilles captures the girl Chryseïs. It is shortly after the raid on Thebe and the capture of Chryseïs that the action of the *Iliad* begins.

The setting of the *Iliad*

There are three basic settings for the human action in the *Iliad*: the Greek encampment, the city of Troy and the plain in between the two. All of these are located in a region known as the Troad. Important geographical landmarks include Mount Ida, located about twenty miles southeast of the city of Troy, as well as two major rivers, the Scamander and the Simoeïs.

The Trojans are based in the city of Troy, otherwise known as Ilium (whence the name 'Iliad' = 'the song of Ilium'). The city is distinguished by its huge walls, said to have been built by Apollo and Poseidon, and the monumental Scaean gate, which provides the major entrance to the city. Other landmarks include the grand palace of Priam (the king of Troy) and the temple of Athena, which forms the highest point of the city.

The Greeks (always referred to as Argives, Achaeans or Danaans) are based in a military encampment on the coast, made up of several hundred Greek ships dragged up onto the beach. In Book 7, the Greeks construct a large rampart and a ditch to further protect their ships. The Greek army is comprised of forces from every part of Greece, and each contingent occupies a different part of the camp. Agamemnon, as commander-in-chief of the whole expedition, is located in the middle, while Achilles and Ajax, the two strongest warriors, are located at either end.

In between the Greek camp and the city of Ilium lies the plain of Troy, where (almost) all the fighting in the poem takes place.

The other key location is Olympus, the divine realm which provides the residence for most of the gods in the poem. It is in this realm that the gods can discuss how they might intervene in the affairs below, where they can receive and dispatch messengers, tend to any injuries they have sustained in the fighting or generally eat, drink and be merry.

A handful of gods do not live on Olympus. Hades is thought of as living in the Underworld with his consort Persephone, while Poseidon lives under the sea. The most important of the non-Olympian gods, however, is Achilles' mother Thetis, who lives in a submarine grotto with her father, Nereus, and with her several dozen sisters, known collectively as the Nereïds.

The story of the *Iliad*

The *Iliad* begins as all ancient epics do – by announcing its subject ('the wrath of Achilles', 1.1) and giving a brief overview of what will happen in the poem ('... which brought uncounted anguish on the Greeks', 1.2). This traditional opening is known as the proem, and it is here that we told that the wrath of Achilles will cause of deaths of 'countless heroes', whose bodies will 'provide a feast for the dogs and birds' (1.3-5).

After the proem, the narrative proper begins by describing a plague in the Greek camp. This has been sent by the god Apollo in revenge for the Greeks' treatment of his priest, Chryses. Chryses' daughter, Chryseïs, had recently been captured by the Greeks and her father had offered a ransom to the Greeks to get her back. When this request is refused by Agamemnon, Chryses prays to Apollo to punish Agamemnon's insolence.

After almost two weeks of plague, Achilles decides to call an assembly of the Greek leaders to discuss a solution to the problem, during which it is suggested that Agamemnon return Chryseïs to her father. Agamemnon reluctantly agrees to this, but demands another girl to replace the one he is losing. Achilles suggests waiting until a later raid, but Agamemnon instead demands that Achilles hand over *his* concubine, Briseïs. An argument breaks out, during which Achilles must be physically restrained from killing Agamemnon by the goddess Athena. After levelling vicious insults at the king, Achilles agrees to let Briseïs go, but announces his intention to withdraw from the fighting with immediate effect. Furthermore, he prays to his mother, Thetis, to ask Zeus to bring death and destruction to the Greeks in order that Agamemnon should recognize his mistake in insulting him so gravely. Zeus agrees to this with a solemn nod that shakes Mount Olympus to its very core (Book 1).

The poem continues with Agamemnon rallying the troops, followed by a long list of the various contingents fighting on the Greek or Trojan side known as the

Catalogue of Ships (Book 2). The sides approach one another, but before general fighting begins, a duel is arranged between Menelaus and Paris, with both sides swearing a 'great oath' that the duel will settle the war. The duel begins, which Menelaus dominates. When Menelaus is on the brink of killing Paris, however, the goddess Aphrodite spirits Paris away to the city of Troy, leaving Menelaus grasping at thin air. While Menelaus is trying to figure out what has happened, the Trojan archer Pandarus aims at him with his bow, hitting Menelaus and drawing blood. The Greeks are appalled that the Trojans have broken their 'great oath' and general hostilities begin (Books 3–5).

The champion warrior on the Trojan side is Paris' brother, Hector, who decides to find out where his brother has gone and goes to look for him in the city of Troy. While in Troy, he speaks with his wife, Andromache, who tries to persuade him not to go back out to fight, which he refuses. Hector finds Paris and the two return to the battlefield (Book 6). Another duel is arranged, this time between Hector and the Greek hero, Ajax, which ends in a draw and a handshake. Night falls, and the Greeks decide to reinforce their camp, building a wall and digging a ditch (Book 7). At sunrise, hostilities are resumed and the Trojans begin to gain the upper hand, pushing the Greek forces back towards their ships. Night falls again, and the Trojans decide to camp out in the plain, rather than returning to the city (Book 8).

The Greeks assemble to discuss how they can turn the tide of battle against the Trojans and agree to send an appeal to Achilles, who is still refusing to fight. Agamemnon in particular offers grand reparations to Achilles if he will return to the fighting and save the Greeks from the Trojan onslaught. The appeal is made by a delegation of three men – Odysseus, Phoenix and Ajax – each of whom try to persuade Achilles to return to battle. Achilles refuses, although his position does change from leaving immediately in the morning to waiting and seeing what will happen, and then to agreeing to fight if and when Hector reaches his ships (Book 9). There follows a short night-time mission, in which Odysseus and Diomedes capture and execute a Trojan spy (Book 10), before morning comes and fighting resumes again (Book 11).

Over the course of the next five books – and thanks in part to Zeus' continued support of the Trojans – the Trojans gain the upper hand, injuring several Greek heroes, smashing through the gates into the Greek encampment and setting fire to one of their ships (Books 11–15). At this point, Achilles' second-in-command, Patroclus, begs Achilles to be allowed into battle in order to push the Trojans back from the Greek ships. Achilles reluctantly agrees, lending Patroclus his weapons and armour for the job, but ordering him only to push the Trojans out of the Greek camp, and not to fight on beyond that. He prays to Zeus to protect his companion in battle, a prayer that Zeus refuses. Patroclus storms into battle and almost single-handedly pushes the Trojans into a mass retreat, killing the Lycian hero Sarpedon in the process. However, he ignores Achilles' advice and pushes on as far as the walls of Troy, where he is killed by Hector, who strips him of his (i.e. Achilles') armour (Book 16). There is furious fighting over Patroclus' body, and the Greeks are once again pushed back towards their camp (Book 17).

Achilles observes the retreat of the Greeks and fears that something terrible has happened to Patroclus. Almost immediately after this, the Greek hero Antilochus arrives to announce that Patroclus has been killed by Hector, sending Achilles into the depths of grief, despair and rage. Achilles announces to his mother, Thetis, that he will return to battle to kill Hector, even if this means that his own death must follow. Thetis reluctantly agrees to this, but Achilles cannot return to battle until he has a new suit of armour, which Thetis agrees to arrange for him. In the meantime, Achilles stands on the ramparts of the Greek camp and lets out an almighty war cry, pushing the Trojans back and allowing the Greeks to recover Patroclus' body. Night falls, bringing hostilities to an end. Meanwhile, Thetis visits the blacksmith god Hephaestus to ask him to construct a new set of armour for Achilles. The full set of armour, and especially the shield, is described in great detail (Book 18).

After a few formalities, including an apology from Agamemnon to Achilles and the delivery of the gifts that had been promised earlier (Book 19), Achilles returns to battle and devastates the Trojan forces (Books 20–21). With the Trojans in complete disarray, Hector decides to take a stand against Achilles outside the Scaean gate. In full view of the whole city, including his wife and parents, Hector is pursued three times round the city of Troy, before he is finally killed by Achilles. In his rage, Achilles ties Hector's body to the back of his chariot, dragging it in the dust back to the Greek camp (Book 22).

After a ceremonial funeral for Patroclus, which includes a whole programme of athletic events (Book 23), we are treated to the climactic moment of the poem: Priam's visit to Achilles in the middle of the night to ask for the body of his son back. After an extraordinary meeting between the two men, where they weep for those they have lost and reflect on the meaning of human suffering, Achilles releases Hector's body, which is brought back to the city of Troy. The three women in Hector's life lament for him, and the last lines of the poem describe the funeral of Hector (Book 24).

The origin, date and authorship of the *Iliad*

Ever since antiquity, there has been a debate about the origin, date and authorship of the *Iliad*. In this section, we trace some of the prevailing views about the composition of the poem, from the ancients' view that the *Iliad* was the work of a single, outstanding poet, through the ideas of the analysts in the nineteenth and twentieth centuries, to the theory of orality developed by Milman Parry and Albert Lord in the 1930s.

Homer

In antiquity, the *Iliad* was attributed to a single poet known as Homer. The earliest known reference to Homer is by the seventh-century poet Callinus, who claimed that Homer was the author of an epic poem known as the *Thebaid*. Just over a century later, Homer was already being written about as a poet of exceptional status and influence: the sixth-century poet Xenophanes (born *c.* 570 BC) wrote that 'everyone has learned in accordance with Homer', while for the philosopher Heraclitus (lived *c.* 500 BC) Homer was 'the wisest of the Greeks'.

Despite his status, the ancients seemed to have known very little about the basic facts of Homer's life, and opinions on when and where he lived, his parentage, his real name, the manner of his death, etc., varied widely. The most popular traditions described Homer as a native of the Ionian part of Asia Minor, from either the town of Smyrna or the island of Chios, though other traditions associated him with Rhodes, Athens, Argos, Salamis, Egypt and even Rome. Suggestions for *when* he lived were similarly diverse, with dates ranging from the fall of Troy itself (which the Greeks believed happened in *c.* 1200 BC) to the second half of the ninth century BC.

Nor could the ancients agree on Homer's poetic output. The fifth-century historian Herodotus, for example, records the tradition that Homer was the author not only of the *Iliad* and the *Odyssey* but also of the epic poems known as the *Epigoni* and the *Cypria*. A set of thirty-three hymns known as the Homeric Hymns were also ascribed to Homer, as were a number of less serious poems, including a poem called the *Margites*, which is mentioned by Aristotle in his *Politics*. As time went on, however, it seems that fewer and fewer of these works were considered genuinely Homeric. By the late Roman and early Byzantine periods (*c.* 300–400 AD), a consensus had arisen that the only genuine works of Homer were the *Iliad* and the *Odyssey*, a view that was to persist for the next fourteen hundred years.

Analysts and unitarians

By the seventeenth and eighteenth centuries, new doubts began to be raised over the authorship of the Homeric poems. In 1664, the French playwright and literary critic Abbé d'Aubignac declared that there was no such person as Homer, and that the Homeric poems were cobbled together from earlier oral poems. In 1713, the English scholar Richard Bentley construed a similar picture, suggesting that Homer was an oral poet who lived in the eleventh or tenth century BC whose songs were 'collected together in the form of an epic poem' some five hundred years later. By far the most influential book to be published, however, was that of Friedrich August Wolf, whose *Prolegomena ad Homerum* (1795) argued that the Homeric poems were composed orally in the tenth century BC in the form of short separate songs, but not written down and joined together until four hundred years later.

Wolf's work began a trend in Homeric scholarship that involved identifying which parts of the poem were older than others. The scholars who engaged in this kind of work came to be known as analysts, and the two basic models that emerged were known as the lay theory and the nucleus theory. The lay theory assumed that the *Iliad* was the result of a combination of several originally separate and independent short poems, while the nucleus theory claimed that the *Iliad* consisted of an original 'core' to which material had progressively been added. Certain assumptions, however, commanded broad agreement: first, the Homeric poems had been created over a period of several centuries; and second, they had been created from several smaller poems.

In contrast to the analysts stood a group of scholars known as the unitarians, who argued that the artistic unity of the poems proved that they were the work of a single creative mind, and not the result of the addition of material round an original core or the stitching together of several independent poems. The debate between the analysts and unitarians came to be known as the Homeric Question and provided one of the key focuses for Homeric scholarship throughout the nineteenth and twentieth centuries.

The theory of orality

In the 1930s, a new theory came to light, based on the fieldwork of two young American scholars, Milman Parry and Albert Lord. Working with oral poets (or *guslari*) in what was then Yugoslavia, Parry and Lord noticed several similarities between the kind of poetry produced by the *guslari* and that of Homer, particularly in its use of repeated phrases and expressions. Parry and Lord concluded that the *Iliad* must have begun life as an extemporaneously composed oral poem like the poems they were hearing in Yugoslavia, with oral poets drawing on set phrases and expressions, typical scenes and story patterns (known as formulae) to help them compose in performance.

While the theory of orality has proved compelling to many scholars, it is worth keeping in mind that Parry and Lord's fieldwork was designed to explain a single element in the Homeric poems – its repeated phrases and expressions. Indeed, it is important to note what while Parry and Lord's theory came to be known as the theory of orality, it did *not* introduce the idea that the Homeric poems were orally composed and transmitted (which had already been suggested by the Abbé d'Aubignac in 1664), but merely the idea that oral composition was responsible for the poem's otherwise inexplicable repetitiveness.

The debate over the origins of the *Iliad* – its authorship, the circumstances of its composition, etc. – is far from settled. One question that remains is whether the *Iliad* is an oral poem or merely an orally derived one For the *Iliad* to be a genuinely oral poem, it would have to represent a word-for-word transcription of an oral performance. Many scholars think that this is not the case. Rather, it is argued, the *Iliad* is a poem that has made extensive use of the repeated phrases and expressions that are characteristic of oral poetry, but has actually been composed with the aid of writing. It is, in other words, a poem formed in the oral tradition, an orally derived poem, but not itself an oral poem.

Neoanalysis

One of the more recent strands in Homeric scholarship is neoanalysis. This considers the relationship between the *Iliad* and the other poems of the so-called epic cycle, which told of other episodes within the Trojan War. Poems within the epic cycle included the *Cypria*, which dealt with the origins of the war, as well as the *Aethiopis, Little Iliad* and *Sack of Ilium*, all of which dealt with events after the *Iliad*. While none of these poems survive in full, we do have brief summaries of their contents as well as a handful of fragments where lines from the poem have been quoted by authors whose works *do* survive.

One relationship that has been of particular interest to the neoanalysts has been that between the *Iliad* and the lost epic known as the *Aethiopis*, the plots of which appear to have been extremely similar. In both epics, Achilles withdraws from battle based on a prophecy from his mother, but returns when a friend (Patroclus in the *Iliad*, Antilochus in the *Aethiopis*) is killed by a Trojan or Ethiopian champion (Hector in the *Iliad*, Memnon in the *Aethiopis*). Achilles manages to kill the person responsible for his friend's death, but knows that his own death must follow shortly afterwards. The *Iliad* ends with Achilles still alive, although his death has been repeatedly prophesied, while the *Aethiopis* depicts his death at the hands of Apollo and Paris, as well as his funeral.

It has been suggested that the poet of the *Iliad* transposed scenes from the *Aethiopis* into his own poem, putting them into contexts for which they were not primarily intended. We know, for example, that the *Aethiopis* contained a scene where Thetis and the Nereids mourned over the body of Achilles. In the *Iliad*, this becomes the strange scene in Book 18 where Thetis and the Nereids mourn over Achilles while he is still alive. Stranger still is the scene in Book 23 of the *Iliad* where the Greeks cannot get the funeral pyre of Patroclus to light because the winds are refusing to blow, but no explanation is given of why this might be the case. In the *Aethiopis*, however, the refusal of the winds to blow is explained by the fact the wind gods are mourning the death of their brother, Memnon, whom Achilles has just killed. Both scenes – the appearance of Thetis and the Nereids in Book 18 and the winds' refusal to blow in Book 23 – appear to fit much more comfortably into the narrative of the *Aethiopis* than the *Iliad*.

The rhythm of epic poetry: dactylic hexameter

Prosody

Unlike the poetry of English, which is based on patterns of stressed and unstressed syllables, Greek metre is based on patterns of long and short syllables. We use a '–' to indicate a long syllable, '∪' to indicate a short syllable and 'x' to indicate a syllable that may be long or short.

In order to scan Greek verse, it is necessary to know which syllables are long and which are short. In brief, a short syllable is one where a single short vowel (ε, o and short α, ι and υ) is followed by no more than one consonant; a long syllable is one containing either a long vowel (η, ω and long α, ι and υ) or a diphthong (e.g. ου, οι, αι), or a short vowel followed by two or more consonants, where ζ [zd], ξ [ks] and ψ [ps] count as double consonants. The scanning of a short vowel as long if it is followed by two consonants is known as lengthening by position.

There are a handful of exceptions to these basic rules of scansion.

First, a short vowel can be scanned short before two consonants if the consonants in question are a mute (e.g. π, β, φ, κ, γ, χ, τ, δ and θ) followed by a liquid (λ, μ, ν and ρ). Thus the combinations πρ, τρ, πλ, etc., do *not* lengthen the preceding syllable. Exception to the exception: the heaviest combinations of mutes and liquids (e.g. βλ, γλ, γν, γμ, δν, δμ) act like regular double consonants, i.e. they *do* lengthen the preceding syllable.

Second, a short vowel is sometimes lengthened even before a single consonant (usually δ, λ, μ, ν or σ), where the word was *originally* spelt with two consonants. This is almost always the case when a word *used* to be spelt with a digamma (ϝ). This was a letter that represented a 'w' sound, but which fell out of use before the Homeric poems could be written down. It nevertheless retained an impact on the scansion of certain words and expressions. The first syllable of καλά, for example, is long because the word originally contained a digamma after the λ, i.e. καλϝός.

Elision, hiatus, correption and synizesis

In most cases, short open vowels (i.e. not followed by a consonant) at the end of words will be elided if the following word begins with a vowel. In the fourth line of Book 18, for example (τὰ φρονέοντ᾽ ἀνὰ θυμὸν ἃ δὴ τετελεσμένα ἦεν), φρονέοντα is elided by ἀνὰ, leaving φρονέοντ᾽ ἀνὰ. Elision is *always* marked in Greek verse, unlike in Latin verse, where it is not.

Sometimes, elision does not happen when we expect it to, a phenomenon known as hiatus. Hiatus can occur when the short open vowel at the end of a word immediately precedes one of the main caesurae or diaereses (see below) in the line, or when the word that follows it begins with a vowel, but used to be spelt with a digamma. In the line Ἀτρεΐδη κύδιστε ἄναξ ἀνδρῶν Ἀγάμεμνον (9.96 = 164, 677, 697), for example, the reason κύδιστε does not elide with ἄναξ is because ἄναξ used to be spelt with a digamma, i.e. ϝάναξ.

A long vowel or diphthong followed by a word beginning with a vowel may be scanned as short. This is known as epic correption and is relatively common.

Finally, two vowels together within a word or in successive words may be treated as combining into a single, long syllable. This is known as synizesis and is relatively rare.

Metre

As we have already mentioned, the metre used in epic poetry is known as dactylic hexameter. This is a line made of six feet (or metra), each of which will either be a dactyl (long-short-short) or a spondee (long-long). The exception is the sixth foot, which is always made up of two syllables, the second of which may be either long or short. Thus, the line can be represented schematically as follows:

$$- \cup \cup \mid - \cup \cup \mid - \cup \cup \mid - \cup \cup \mid - \cup \cup \mid - \cup \cup$$

To demonstrate the variety of rhythms allowed by the dactylic hexameter line, here is the scansion of the first four lines of Book 18, which shows three different ways the hexameter line could scan (the second and fourth lines have the same rhythm):

$$- - \mid - - \mid - \cup \cup \mid - \cup \cup \mid - \cup \cup \mid - \cup$$

ὣς οἳ μὲν μάρναντο δέμας πυρὸς αἰθομένοιο,

$$- \cup \cup \mid - \cup \cup \mid - \cup \cup \mid - \cup \cup \mid - \cup \cup \mid - \cup$$

Ἀντίλοχος δ᾽ Ἀχιλῆϊ πόδας ταχὺς ἄγγελος ἦλθε.

− − | − ∪ ∪ | − ∪ ∪ | − − | − − | − −

τὸν δ᾽ εὗρε προπάροιθε νεῶν ὀρθοκραιράων

− ∪ ∪ | − ∪ ∪ | − ∪ ∪ | − ∪ ∪ | − ∪ ∪ | − ∪

τὰ φρονέοντ᾽ ἀνὰ θυμὸν ἃ δὴ τετελεσμένα ἦεν:

Caesurae, diaereses and cola

Beyond this basic metrical framework, almost every line in Homer has a word break (or caesura) near the middle of the line, usually after the first long syllable of the third foot (strong caesura) or after the first short syllable of the third foot (weak caesura), which divides the line into two unequal halves.

Each of these halves may contain a further word break. In the first half of the line, a break may appear (i) between the first and second feet, or (ii) after the first syllable of the second foot. In the second half of the line, a break may appear (i) after the first syllable of the first foot, or (ii) between the fourth and fifth feet. There are technical names for each of these breaks, though for now one only needs to distinguish between the breaks that come *within* feet, which are known as caesurae (singular: caesura), and those that come *between* feet, which are known as diaereses (singular: diaeresis).

In any case, the result of these various breaks is the division of the line into a total of up to four sections (or cola, from the Greek for 'limb', singular: colon), depending on exactly where each of the caesurae or diaereses fall:

1.	2.	3.	4.
− ∪ ∪	∪ ∪ −	∪ −	− ∪ ∪ − x
− ∪ ∪ −	∪ ∪ − ∪	∪ ∪ −	∪ ∪ − ∪ ∪ − x
	− ∪ ∪ −	∪ − ∪ ∪	
	− ∪ ∪ − ∪	∪ ∪ − ∪ ∪	

Analysing the line in terms of cola rather than feet is a much more intuitive way of understanding how the oral poet constructed his line. We note in particular that while certain metrical patterns can fit into multiple cola, others can only fit into one: the pattern short-long-short-short (∪ − ∪ ∪), for example, can only fit into the third colon, while long-long-short (− − ∪) can only fit into the second. The upshot of this is that whenever the poet wants to use a word or phrase that scans (e.g.) short-long-short-short, he knows straightaway that he will have to place it in the third colon, since this is the only place it will fit metrically.

Formulae

The tendency for the hexameter line to only accept certain metrical patterns in certain positions made it relatively difficult for the oral poet to compose verse extemporaneously. In order to help him do so, he memorized a vast number of metrically useful phrases and expressions that he could use as and when required. These stock phrases and expressions are referred to as formulae (singular: formula) and could be anything from a single word to a whole line, or even several lines.

Repeated verses and formular expressions

One type of formula is the repeated verse. These were stock lines that the poet could deploy whenever a particular situation arose. To take a simple example, there are four occasions in the *Iliad* when the narrative moves from a scene of general fighting to something taking place away from the battlefield. Rather than coming up with a new way to describe the change of scene each time, the poet makes use of exactly the same line on all four occasions: ὣς οἳ μὲν μάρναντο δέμας πυρὸς αἰθομένοιο ('and so they continued to fight like blazing fire').

Another type of formula is the formular expression. These had exactly the same function as repeated verses, but were shorter in length. Some of the most easily recognizable formular expressions are the noun-epithet combinations that are used to describe almost all the major characters in the poem, e.g. 'swift-footed Achilles' or 'Agamemnon, lord of men'. While the use of epithets throughout the poem can seem gratuitous, they are actually performing an important metrical function in extending the description of characters from the three or four syllables of their name (e.g. Ἀγαμέμνων, 'Agamemnon') to a much more useable length – five, six or seven syllables if the poet wanted to fill the final colon of the line (e.g. κρείων Ἀγαμέμνων, 'lord Agamemnon'), or eight or nine syllables if he wanted to fill the whole second half of the line (e.g. ἄναξ ἀνδρῶν Ἀγαμέμνων, 'Agamemnon, lord of men').

Noun-epithet combinations can be found throughout the poem, and not just for characters' names. Spears are 'long-shadowed' (δολιχόσκιον ἔγχος), ships are 'hollow' (νῆας ... γλαφυράς), destruction is 'sheer' (αἰπὺν ὄλεθρον), fate is 'black' (κῆρα μέλαιναν) and so on. In all of these cases, it is important to note that the role of the epithet is primarily metrical, not poetic: when the poet describes spears as 'long-shadowed' or the ships as 'hollow', for example, these descriptors appear only because the poet needed an expression to fit a particular metrical pattern.

Formular expressions exist for a whole range of different parts of speech, not just the noun-epithet combinations we have seen above. Thus we find formular expressions combining adverbs and verbs, conjunctions and verbs and so on. By far the most common formulae in the poem are those used to describe characters speaking to one another, though the oral poet seems to have memorized stock phrases and expressions for almost every commonly occurring action or situation in the poem, e.g. putting on armour, throwing a spear, falling on the ground, agonizing over what to do, weeping, preparing a meal, drinking wine, or offering a sacrifice.

Type-scenes

In addition to repeated actions and situations, the *Iliad* also contains entire scenes that recur several times throughout the poem. These are known as type-scenes and include things like the arrival and reception of a guest, the performance of a sacrifice, the preparation of a meal, the arming of a warrior and so on. The first person to study type-scenes in detail was the German scholar Walter Arend, who noted that type-scenes tended to be made up of a sequence of events which occurred in the same order every single time. In the case of a warrior arming himself, for example – something that happens four times in the *Iliad* – Arend noticed that the scene always began with a line or two of introduction, before describing (in order) the greaves and the breastplate, the sword, the shield, the helmet and the spear.

The use of type-scenes dominates the narrative of the *Iliad*. The scholar Mark Edwards has even gone so far as to say that the narrative of the *Iliad* 'is carried forward almost entirely by a succession of type-scenes, with only occasional use of short passages of description, similes, or apostrophes by the poet'. Indeed, one could analyse the beginning of Book 18 in terms of a succession of type-scenes: the arrival of a messenger (1–34), a scene of mourning (35–64), a divine visit (65–147), a battle scene (148–164), a divine visit (165–202) and so on.

While type-scenes provide the scaffolding for certain scenes in the poem, however, it is not the case that they are all absolutely identical. While the order of elements tended to remain constant, the poet could expand or contract any individual element however he liked, depending on its importance in the context. The type-scene of two warriors meeting on the battlefield, for example, could fill anything from a single line to several hundred lines, as in the case of the meeting of Achilles and Aeneas in Book 20.

The poet could also negate elements altogether. In Book 6, for example, the poet follows Hector as he goes to meet his wife, Andromache. Ordinarily, the type-scene that involves the arrival of a guest ends with the visitor meeting his host. In this case, however, Hector comes to his family home to find that no one is there, a striking negation of what the audience expected to hear next. In Book 16, similarly, we follow Patroclus as he puts on the armour of Achilles. It is the third such scene in the poem, all of which end with the warrior picking up either a single spear or a pair of spears. In this case, however, immediately after Patroclus picks up a pair of spears, the poet adds the detail that there was one spear that he was *not* able to pick up – 'the spear of the excellent Achilles … the huge, heavy, massive spear which no other Achaean could wield, but Achilles alone had the skill to handle' (16.140–3). The expectation that the warrior will complete his arming when he picks up his spear is emphatically denied in the case of Patroclus, and the implication is clear: Patroclus is not quite the warrior that Achilles wants him to be.

Story patterns

In the previous section, we thought about the use of type-scenes, recurring scenes in the poem such as the arrival and reception of a guest, where a sequence of elements tend to appear in the same order. In this section, we move on to story patterns, broader plot structures that underlie whole episodes in the poem.

One of the most fundamental story patterns in the *Iliad* is that which has been described by scholars as withdrawal, devastation and return. This is a pattern that involves the withdrawal of the hero from society, the subsequent catastrophic effects for that society and/or for the hero himself and a final return to society by the hero that restores peace, order and harmony. In some cases, the focus is not on the devastation of the society abandoned by the hero, but on the experience of the hero himself during his withdrawal, which often involves some kind of test, sometimes a symbolic death and a triumphant return to the society he has left behind.

In any case, it is clear to see how the pattern of withdrawal, devastation and return underpins the main storyline in the poem: Achilles withdraws from battle, the Greek army suffers catastrophic losses in his absence, before Achilles returns to battle and restores order by defeating Hector. At the same time, however, it is interesting to see just how often this basic story pattern recurs, either in part or in full, elsewhere in the poem.

In Book 9, for example, Phoenix attempts to convince Achilles to return to battle by telling him the myth of Meleager (9.524–605). In his story, Phoenix describes how Meleager and the Aetolians were defending their city against the Couretes, when Meleager decided to withdraw from the battle in wrath (550–572), just as Achilles had done (and was continuing to do) at Troy. The story continues with the detail that Meleager had rejected the Aetolians' offer of gifts to return to battle, and had ultimately been forced to return to battle only when his own house was under attack, at which point the gifts were no longer on offer (573–594). While Phoenix has clearly emphasized the similarities between Meleager's situation and Achilles' own for rhetorical effect, it nevertheless remains a repeat of the basic pattern of withdrawal, devastation, return.

We get glimpses of other withdrawals elsewhere in the poem, too. The removal of Paris from the battlefield by Aphrodite in Book 3 leads to a kind of withdrawal on his part for the next three books: he only returns to battle when Hector physically goes to get him in Book 6. Another withdrawal – more fleeting still – is that of Aeneas, who is seen skulking at the back of the fighting in Book 13. The reason for his withdrawal, the poet explains, is on the grounds of his anger at Priam, who has not shown him sufficient honour (13.459–61). No more details are provided, and Aeneas almost immediately returns to battle after some encouragement from Deiphobus, but it is a glimpse of another withdrawal, devastation, return story nonetheless.

While the withdrawal, devastation, return story pattern provides the narrative superstructure for the poem as a whole, the poet appears to make use of a number of other story patterns in individual episodes. Another story pattern that occurs frequently in the poem is that of the revenge killing. Within the main storyline, Patroclus kills Sarpedon, which leads Hector to kill Patroclus, which leads Achilles to kill Hector. But the same basic pattern can be seen in miniature throughout the poem (e.g. in Book 11, Agamemnon kills Iphidamas, which leads Coön to stab Agamemnon, which leads Agamemnon to kill Coön) while similar chains of revenge killings could be found in other episodes from the Trojan War, too (e.g. in the *Aethiopis*, Memnon kills Antilochus, which leads Achilles to kill Memnon, which leads Apollo and Paris to kill Achilles).

Story patterns are similar to type-scenes in that they provide a poet with a superstructure within which he can build his story. Whereas the type-scene only provides the superstructure for a particular action, however, the story pattern can provide the structure for the whole poem. Like type-scenes, story patterns can appear in a range of sizes: just as duels between warriors can be anything from two to two-hundred lines, so too do we see story-patterns recur in both highly condensed and highly expanded forms – from the ten-line withdrawal and return of Aeneas to the fifteen-thousand-line withdrawal and return of Achilles.

Creativity and innovation in oral poetry

The reliance on formulae, type-scenes and story patterns throughout the *Iliad* may seem to preclude any kind of creativity or innovation on the part of the poet. Is the *Iliad* anything more than a poetic 'paint-by-numbers', where the poet slots prefabricated blocks of poetry (formulae) into predetermined arrangements (type-scenes, story patterns)?

In some cases, it appears that the poet had very little control over what he could say. In Book 18, for example, the poet describes Achilles as 'swift-footed' despite the fact he spends most of the book sitting or lying on the floor. At one point, Achilles even refers to himself as a 'useless burden on the earth' (ἐτώσιον ἄχθος ἀρούρης, 18.104), less than ten lines after he has been described as 'swift-footed Achilles' (πόδας ὠκὺς Ἀχιλλεύς, 18.97).

If we look a little closer, however, we find that the poet manipulates formulae in creative and innovative ways throughout the poem. At the beginning of Book 18, for example, the poet describes the arrival of Antilochus at the huts of Achilles to deliver the news of Patroclus' death: Ἀντίλοχος δ᾽ Ἀχιλῆϊ πόδας ταχὺς ἄγγελος ἦλθε ('Swift-footed Antilochus came as a messenger to Achilles'). The line seems unremarkable at first glance, but when we look closer we realize it is not Achilles who is described as 'swift-footed', but Antilochus. It is a surprising reattribution of Achilles' traditional epithet, but entirely appropriate to the context: Achilles is sitting by the ships, while Antilochus has just run the entire length of the battlefield to deliver his message.

A few lines later, we find another adaptation of a standard formula when Antilochus addresses Achilles. The usual vocative formula for Achilles is ὦ Ἀχιλεῦ, Πηλῆος υἱέ, μέγα φέρτατ᾽ Ἀχαιῶν. Here, it is changed to the shorter ὦ μοι Πηλέος υἱὲ δαΐφρονος (18.18), which leads to a harsh enjambment between adjective and noun (λυγρῆς ... ἀγγελίης, 18.18-19). Again, the adaptation of the standard formula is entirely appropriate to the context: Antilochus is nervous and the delivery of his message is appropriately inelegant.

When it comes to type-scenes, too, we have already seen how the poet could negate individual aspects to add particular emphasis in specific contexts, e.g. Patroclus' emphatic *failure* to pick up Achilles' spear at the end of his arming scene in Book 16 or Achilles' emphatic *abstention* from food after the preparation of the meal in Book 19. These, too, represent creative and innovative departures from the traditional material.

Finally, the story of the *Iliad* may well have represented a radical departure from traditional stories about the Trojan War. It has been suggested, for example, that Homer was the first to introduce the tragic deaths of previously immortal heroes such as Heracles and the Dioscuri, that his presentation of Achilles in particular was markedly different from traditional stories in which he was simply an unstoppable killing machine and that his sympathetic presentation of Troy and the Trojans was untraditional, if not unprecedented.

The manipulation of traditional material was one the key ways in which oral poets demonstrated their creativity and ingenuity, and the *Iliad* is brimming with it. If the poem were genuinely an oral poem, the innovative manipulation of formulae and type-scenes that we find throughout may well indicate an oral poet of particular talent or expertise. If it were an orally derived poem, composed with the aid of writing, it may indicate the extent to which writing allowed a poet to introduce a level of creativity previously unattainable by oral means alone.

Translating Homer

Those coming to Homer for the first time may find translation difficult, not least because of the epic dialect. While most grammars provide an exhaustive list of *all* the differences between Attic and Homeric Greek, which can be overwhelming, this section outlines the differences that appear most often, and which it might be preferable to learn first of all.

Nouns

When it comes to nouns, Homer makes use of alternative endings across all declensions and cases. Many of these are fairly similar to their Attic equivalent, e.g. -αων or -εων instead of -ῶν in the genitive plural, though one should take particular notice of alternative endings for the genitive singular, which are quite different. These include -αο or -εω as alternatives to -ου in the first declension (e.g. Ἀτρείδαο and Ἀτρείδεω, instead of Ἀτρείδου, 'son of Atreus') and -οιο as an alternative to -ου for nouns of the second declension (e.g. πεδίοιο instead of πεδίου, 'the plain').

In addition to this, Homer alternates freely between -σ- and -σσ-, depending on what is required by the metre. ποσί and ποσσί (dat. pl. of πούς, 'foot') are equivalent, for example. The same doubling of the sigma can be found in adjectives, too, e.g. τόσσος and τόσος, μέσσος and μέσος.

Pronouns

Pronouns have a tendency to look quite different from their Attic equivalents, too. This includes the genitive singular, where potential endings include -εῖο, -εο, -εῦ and -εθεν, e.g. ἐμεῖο, ἐμέο ('me'), σεῖο, σέο ('you'), as well as the Ionic forms of common pronouns, e.g. ἄμμες, ἄμμε and ἄμμι, which are alternatives to ἡμεῖς, ἡμᾶς and ἡμῖν ('we', 'us').

Most importantly, it is important to note that what *looks like* the definite article in Attic Greek (ὁ, ἡ, τό) is (almost always) used not as a definite article, but a third person pronoun ('him, her, it'). In the line τόφϱά οἱ ἐγγύθεν ἦλθεν ἀγαυοῦ Νέστοϱος υἱὸς (18.17), for example, οἱ means '(to) him' and is governed by the phrase ἐγγύθεν ἦλθεν ('came close to', 'approached').

Verbs

When it comes to the verb, there are two things to look for. The first is that the aorist and imperfect tenses will often drop their augment: βάλον can appear instead of ἔβαλον, for example, or ἔμβαλε instead of ἐνέβαλε. The second is that verbs can be left uncontracted, i.e. one might find ἐϱέω instead of ἐϱῶ and so on.

Finally, it is worth noting that the infinitive can end in -εμεν, -μεναι or -ναι, which can make it look like a present participle, e.g. δόμεναι = δοῦναι, ἀκουέμεναι = ἀκούειν. In addition to this, ἔμεν, ἔμμεν and ἔμμεναι are all used as an alternative to the Attic εἶναι ('to be').

The dual

In Attic Greek, nouns, adjectives and verbs are usually one of two numbers: singular or plural: βαίνει ('he/she/it goes') indicates the movement of a single person, while βαίνουσῐ(ν) indicates the movement of several people and so on.

In Homer, however, there is a third number known as the dual, which can be used when the verb has exactly two people or things for its subject, or if a noun or adjective denotes two people or things. Thus, τὼ καλὼ ἀνθϱώπω = 'the *two* handsome men', βαίνετον = 'they *both* go'.

The dual is rare in Homer, though there are a string of them at the beginning of the set text in Book 9. The key endings to learn and recognize are (i) the third person endings for verbs in the past tense, which are -την (active) and -σθην (middle/passive), (ii) the third person pronouns, which are τώ (nominative and accusative) and τοῖν (genitive and dative) across all genders and (iii) the endings for nouns and adjectives in the second declension, which are -ω (nom./acc.) and -οιν (gen./dat.).

Like other past tense verbs in Homer, verbs in the dual can be left unaugmented, e.g. βάτην ('they both went', 9.182).

The structure of Homeric verse

One of the aspects of Homeric verse that makes it slightly easier to translate than other poetry is the relative simplicity of Homeric syntax. Because oral composition is greatly facilitated by lines that are self-contained units of thought, almost three quarters of the lines in Homer are grammatically complete by the end of the line. This way of structuring the poem gave the poet the freedom to elaborate or qualify a particular thought if he wanted to, or to move on to the next sentence if he did not. An example of this can be seen in the first six lines of the poem quoted below. These have been translated literally to retain the line structure of the original Greek:

μῆνιν ἄειδε, θεά, Πηληϊάδεω Ἀχιλῆος
οὐλομένην, ἣ μυρί᾽ Ἀχαιοῖς ἄλγε᾽ ἔθηκε,
πολλὰς δ᾽ ἰφθίμους ψυχὰς Ἄϊδι προΐαψεν
ἡρώων, αὐτοὺς δὲ ἑλώρια τεῦχε κύνεσσιν
οἰωνοῖσί τε πᾶσι, Διὸς δ᾽ ἐτελείετο βουλή,
ἐξ οὗ δὴ τὰ πρῶτα διαστήτην ἐρίσαντε
Ἀτρεΐδης τε ἄναξ ἀνδρῶν καὶ δῖος Ἀχιλλεύς.

Sing, goddess, of the anger of Achilles, son of Peleus
the accursed anger, which brought uncounted anguish on the Achaeans
and hurled down to Hades many mighty souls
of heroes, and which made their bodies the prey to dogs
and to all the birds, and the plan of Zeus was fulfilled,
from the time when the two men quarrelled and stood apart,
Atreus' son, the lord of men, and godlike Achilles.

1.1–6

As we can see, the sentence could end at the end of any of the six lines: the first line is a complete sentence, as are the first two lines, as are first three lines and so on. Despite the difficulties of the epic dialect, the structure of Homeric verse is much more straightforward than much of later Greek (and Latin) literature. Translation can be tackled line by line, rather than the much more diffuse, difficult syntax of writers like Thucydides and Cicero.

Language and style

Another important aspect of Homeric Greek is the language and style of the poem. In this section, we will discuss the Homeric dialect, before looking at several stylistic elements found within the poem: (1) hapax legomena; (2) similes; (3) ring composition; (4) end-stopping and enjambment; and (5) rhetorical devices.

The epic dialect

Ancient Greek had several literary dialects, which could differ from one another as much as Italian from Spanish. The three major dialects were Ionic, Aeolic and Doric, although there were subdialects of each of these. Attic Greek, the dialect with which students will likely be most familiar, was a subdialect of the Ionic dialect, for example.

Most literature was written in a single dialect: choral lyric tended to be written in Doric, while philosophy, oratory and history tended to be written in Attic. When we come to the language of Homer, however, we find that it is a combination of several dialects: it is primarily Ionic, but also features a great deal of Aeolic and some Attic.

The rationale for using such a mixed language was to give the poet the widest range of material for composition in performance. Having a larger number of options for filling particular material gaps was more important than maintaining dialectical purity. Thus the epic dialect allowed for both the Ionic and Aeolic words for 'we' (Ionic: ἡμεῖς, Aeolic: ἄμμες), which mean the same thing but are scanned differently. Other examples of where words from other dialects gave the poet the same words but in a different rhythm include the use of both προτί (Aeolic) and πρός (Ionic), κεν (Aeolic) and ἄν (Ionic) and of all three of μέν (Ionic), μάν (Aeolic) and μήν (Attic).

Sometimes, the Aeolic word was metrically identical to its Ionic equivalent, but allowed for rhythmic manipulation elsewhere in the line. Examples of this include the use of the Aeolic πτόλις and πτόλεμος alongside the Ionic πόλις and πόλεμος, where the double-consonant at the beginning of the Aeolic form ensured that the syllable that came before it would be scanned long.

The desire for metrical flexibility also manifests itself in nouns and verbs. The poet has no fewer than three options for the nominative plural of υἱός ('son') – υἱέες, υἱεῖς and υἷες – all of which scan differently, while we have already seen the range of grammatically equivalent but metrically different case endings available to the oral poet, such as the use of both -οιο and -ου in the genitive singular. The admission of both uncontracted verbs and artificially lengthened verbs (e.g. the additional ό in κομόωντες, 18.6, a phenomenon known as diectasis) also serves the same purpose.

Another aspect of facilitating composition in dactylic hexameter was the preservation of certain words and expressions even where they were already several centuries old. The phrase κλέος ἄφθιτον ('undying glory'), for example, is exactly equivalent to the Sanskrit *srávas áksitam* and has thus been dated to the second millennium BC. The phrase 'two-handled cup' (δέπας ἀμφικύπελλον) must date back to a similar period because two-handled cups seem to have been a product of the Mycenaean period (*c.* 1600–1100 BC) but not later. In some cases, the metrical usefulness of a word or expression resulted in its preservation even when the meaning of the word itself was lost. The word ἐριούνιος is often used in the *Iliad* as an epithet for Hermes (e.g. Ἑρμείας ἐριούνιος, 24.457), for example, although its meaning was unknown even to the Greeks.

Finally, many of the grammatical oddities of Homeric verse also appear to be of great antiquity, and we should assume that these too were preserved in the oral tradition in order to facilitate composition in dactylic hexameter. The separation of prepositional pre-verbs from their verbs (e.g. ἐν δ᾽ ἄρα νῶτον ἔθηκ᾽ at 9.207 = Attic ἐνέθηκε), for example, was archaic even by the Mycenaean period, as was the omission of the augment in past tense verbs, but both gave the poet more flexibility when it came to composing his line.

In general, the epic dialect should be seen as being optimized for composition in performance in dactylic hexameter. Anything that could be done to facilitate this process, e.g. the use of words and expressions from different dialects and periods or the ability to add vowels in the middle of words (diectasis) or remove augments or pre-verbs, was preserved in the oral tradition and helps to explain why the epic dialect has the characteristics that it does.

Hapax legomena

Given the reliance of the oral poet on formulaic lines and phrases, special attention must be paid to words that appear only once in the poem. These words are known by the Greek term *hapax legomenon* (plural: *hapax legomena* or *hapaxes*). According to the most recent count of *hapaxes* in Homer, there are 1,142 such words in the *Iliad*, or one every 13.7 verses.

Hapaxes are strongly linked to non-formulaic contexts, where the poet is describing something that does not happen often in the poem. Battle-scenes feature very few *hapaxes*, for example, because they happen frequently throughout the poem, and the poet will rarely throw in a completely new word when describing the same kind of event. A warrior will not suddenly produce a totally new kind of weapon, for example, or engage in a totally different set of actions. Consequently, the books with the fewest *hapaxes* are also those which are the most battle-heavy – Books 7, 8 and 17.

Where the poet moves into more 'unusual' subject matter, however, *hapaxes* are far more common. The seduction of Zeus by Hera in Book 14, for example, takes the poet into relatively uncharted territory and includes a large number of *hapaxes*. The same is true of the description of the Shield of Achilles in Book 18, where the poet describes the images that Hephaestus has depicted on its surface: various planets and stars, a domestic scene featuring a quarrel in a village square, various scenes of agriculture, viticulture and animal husbandry and so on. Almost none of this appears elsewhere in the poem, which is why we get so many *hapaxes*.

The character who uses *hapaxes* more than any other in the *Iliad* is Achilles, who uses a total of 80 (1 every 12.2 lines). Eighteen of these words are never used again in the entirety of Greek literature. His use of *hapaxes* has been seen as a sign of his eloquence, as well as of a character with a uniquely broad philosophical and emotional range.

Similes

A general rule in Homeric verse is that the more important something is, the more time the poet will spend on it. Earlier, we looked at the first six lines of the poem and saw how the structure of Homeric verse allowed for the poet to constantly expand his thoughts line after line by the use of qualifying adjectives, conjunctions or subordinate clauses. Before that, we discussed the use of type-scenes, which could also be greatly expanded if the poet wanted to pause on a moment of particular significance.

Another way that the poet can slow down the narrative, however, is through the use of similes. In Book 17, for example, the poet adds to the gravity of Menelaus' decision to leave the battlefield by including a simile: he retreats from the battle, we are told, 'like a great bearded lion driven from a farmstead by dogs' (17.109–10). If the poet wants to add great emphasis to the importance of a particular moment, he can use several similes in a row. In Book 2, for example, as the Greeks march into battle, the poet produces no fewer than five similes back to back: the Greeks' bronze armour gleams 'like annihilating fire', the various contingents of the Greek forces are 'like great flocks of flying birds' or 'great crowds of swarming flies', their leaders are like herdsman herding cattle, while Agamemnon himself is 'like the foremost of all the cattle'.

Similes can be very short, such as the description of the Greeks and Trojans fighting 'like blazing fire' (δέμας πυρὸς αἰθομένοιο, 18.1), but they can also be very long, expanding over several lines to describe a whole scene and potentially having several points of contact with the narrative proper. In Book 18, for example, we get the following simile to describe the magical fireball that Athena has conjured round Achilles' head:

> As when the smoke rises up from a city to reach the sky, from an island in the distance, where enemies are attacking and the inhabitants run the trial of hateful Ares all day long, fighting from their city: and then with the setting of the sun the light from the line of beacons blazes out, and the glare shoots up high for the neighbouring islanders to see, in the hope that they will come across in their ships to protect them from disaster – such was the light that blazed from Achilles' head up into the sky.
>
> 18.207–14

The primary point of contact between the narrative and the simile is the fire itself, which is like the 'signal-beacons' (πυρσοί, 211) of a city under siege. But there are other points of reference, too. The image of the besieged city clearly evokes Troy, while the besiegers are like the Greeks. Moreover, the detail that the combatants have been fighting 'all day long' (πανημέριοι, 209) reflects the full day's fighting between the Greeks and Trojans in the narrative proper, while the description of the setting sun (ἅμα δ᾽ ἠελίῳ καταδύντι, 210) will be matched by the (actual) setting of the sun just over thirty lines later (ἠέλιος μὲν ἔδυ, 241).

Two more points about similes. First, they tend to draw their imagery from the world that is pointedly *not* the world of warfare. The subjects for similes include weather and other natural phenomena (storms, floods, fires, etc.), hunting, herding and other animals (lions, boars, birds, etc.) and human technology (carpentry, weaving, etc.). One of the effects of this is to heighten the emotional impact of a scene by virtue of the contrast between the world of the simile and the world of the narrative. To take one example, consider the description of Gorgythion in Book 8, whose head droops down 'like a poppy in a garden, bent by the weight of its seed and the showers of spring' (8.306–8). The delicacy of the image of the poppy contrasts strongly with the brutality of Gorgythion's death, enhancing its emotional impact.

Second, it is important to note that similes can be used by both the narrator and his characters – although they are much less common in direct speech. As we might expect, the character who uses similes the most is Achilles (8 in total, 4 long and 4 short), and his doing so is just another sign of his emotional range and self-awareness. Of particular interest are those moments where Achilles uses similes to analyse his own situation, such as in Book 9, when he compares his situation in the Greek camp as being 'like a bird that brings back to her unfledged chicks every morsel she can find, and has to go without herself' (9.323–4).

Ring composition

Speeches in the *Iliad* – or parts of them – may follow a structural pattern that is known as ring composition. This is where the opening elements of a speech (A, B,

C) are mirrored by its closing elements but in reverse order (C', B', A'). One of the clearest examples of this is in Book 18, where Achilles announces he will return to battle to kill Hector:

> And now I shall go, to find the destroyer of that dear life, Hector – and I shall take my own death at whatever time Zeus and the other immortal gods wish to bring it on me. Even the mighty Heracles could not escape death, and he was the dearest of men to lord Zeus, son of Cronus: but fate conquered him, and the cruel enmity of Hera. So I too, if the same fate is there for me, will lie finished when I die. But now my wish is to win great glory ...
>
> 18.114–21

This is all clear enough, but note how the speech can be arranged into 'rings', where thoughts expressed at the beginning of a passage are answered later on in reverse order.

A And now I shall go, to find the destroyer of that death life, Hector

B And I shall take my own death at whatever time Zeus and the other immortal gods wish to bring it on me

C Even the mighty Heracles could not escape death ...

B' So I too, if the same fate is there for me, will lie finished when I die

A' But now I shall win great glory

Ring composition underlies the basic architecture in many of the speeches in the poem. It no doubt provided a useful organizing principle for the oral poet, as well as a sense of recognition, satisfaction and completion for his audience.

At times, however, characters will subtly change the point they are making when they come back to it a second time. In the speech of Achilles just mentioned, for example, we notice how the desire to kill Hector (A) is explicitly linked to his desire for glory when he returns to the point later in the speech (A'). Comparing and contrasting the 'rings' in a speech in this way can often give subtle pointers about the development of a character's thought.

End-stopping and enjambment

One of the most commonly used stylistic features in Homeric verse is the use of word position to lend special emphasis to a particular word or phrase. Two things that students should look out for are end-stopping (where the end of the line marks the end of a clause) and enjambment (where the clause runs over to the next line). There is clearly a kind of inevitability to this – lines will either be end-stopped or not end-stopped – so students should look for the repetition of end-stopped lines, or for words placed in what is known as the emphatic runover position, which is where the enjambment consists of a single word, followed immediately by a pause. In general, frequent end-stopping represents slowly spoken, calm, measured speech, whereas frequent emphatic runover words indicate high emotion, anger, bitterness, vehemence and so on.

Achilles' speech to Odysseus in Book 9 provides fertile ground for seeing this in action. In the first 22 lines of the speech (9.308–29), most of the lines are heavily end-stopped. In the 12 lines that follow, however, we get a series of words in the emphatic runover position. What the structure of these lines shows us is that Achilles begins his speech in a calm, measured way before increasingly losing his temper as he reflects on his treatment at the hands of Agamemnon.

In addition to this, we might note how end-stopped lines allow for greater than usual emphasis on the first word of the following line. This allows for certain words or ideas to be given particular emphasis, or for a series of points to be 'hammered home'. Again, we can turn to Achilles' speech to Odysseus in Book 9 for an example of how these two effects can be combined. In the lines quoted below, Achilles is explaining the difference between the kind of material goods that are on offer from Agamemnon (which can be bought back or stolen if they are given away or lost) and his own life (which cannot). The translation attempts to recreate the impact of the original Greek:

λῃϊστοὶ μὲν γάρ τε βόες καὶ ἴφια μῆλα,
κτητοὶ δὲ τρίποδές τε καὶ ἵππων ξανθὰ κάρηνα,
ἀνδρὸς δὲ ψυχὴ πάλιν ἐλθεῖν οὔτε λεϊστὴ
οὔθ᾽ ἑλετή, ἐπεὶ ἄρ κεν ἀμείψεται ἕρκος ὀδόντων.

Stealable are cattle and fertile flocks,
Winnable are tripods and chestnut horses,
A man's life, however, cannot be stolen back
nor caught, once it has passed the barrier of one's teeth.

9.406–9, my translation

The effect is quite hard to render in English because of the lack of elegant translations for the verbal adjectives λῃϊστοὶ, κτητοὶ and ἑλετή. In Greek, however, it makes for a thumping rhetorical tour de force, driven by the end-stopped lines and the placement of key terms at the beginning of the following line.

Rhetorical devices

The poet of the *Iliad* was highly attuned to the impact of rhetorical devices, and they are deployed carefully and knowingly throughout the poem. Rather than simply *identifying* different rhetorical devices, students should think about how they enact meaning. What is their impact? If a character uses a rhetorical device, what might this say about that character? How might we read the sentence differently if it had *not* included that particular rhetorical device?

Anaphora is the repetition of words at the beginning of two or more consecutive clauses. The repetition might be used for emphasis, with each clause building on the last, or it might invite comparison, in which case the anaphora may be accompanied by the particles μέν and δὲ. In Book 18, for example, we read the following lines:

τρὶς μέν μιν μετόπισθε ποδῶν λάβε φαίδιμος Ἕκτωρ
ἑλκέμεναι μεμαώς, μέγα δὲ Τρώεσσιν ὁμόκλα:
τρὶς δὲ δύ᾽ Αἴαντες θοῦριν ἐπιειμένοι ἀλκὴν
νεκροῦ ἀπεστυφέλιξαν.

Three times glorious Hector caught [Patroclus' body] by the feet from behind, intent on dragging it away, and shouted loud to the Trojans: **and three times** the two Aiantes, clothed in fighting spirit, battered him away from the corpse.

18.155–8

Here, the use of anaphora (τρὶς ... τρὶς, 18.155, 18.157) emphasizes just how close the fighting is over the body of Patroclus: the action of Hector is met by an equal and opposite reaction by the two Aiantes. The balance is further emphasized by the fact that this happens not just once, but 'three times'. But note also the difference in the length of the clauses: the description of Hector takes up two full lines, while that of the two Aiantes fills takes up just one and a half. Are we to conclude that the tide is turning ever so slightly in the Trojans' favour?

Asyndeton is the omission of one or more conjunctions. In the *Iliad*, it often indicates heightened emotions. One of the best examples of the impact of asyndeton can be seen in Book 18, when Antilochus announces the death of Patroclus:

ὤ μοι Πηλέος υἱὲ δαΐφρονος ἦ μάλα λυγρῆς
πεύσεαι ἀγγελίης, ἣ μὴ ὤφελλε γενέσθαι.
κεῖται Πάτροκλος, νέκυος δὲ δὴ ἀμφιμάχονται
γυμνοῦ: ἀτὰρ τά γε τεύχε᾽ ἔχει κορυθαίολος Ἕκτωρ.

Oh, son of warrior Peleus, there is terrible news for you to hear, which I wish had never happened. Patroclus lies dead, and they are fighting over his body. It is naked now – Hector of the glinting helmet has his armour.

18.18–21

We are to imagine Antilochus as a relatively young character. More importantly, he is delivering the worst news imaginable to the greatest hero in the Greek army, who is also notoriously volatile. No wonder he is nervous. The first sign of Antilochus' nerves come with the awkward enjambment of noun (ἀγγελίης) and adjective (λυγρῆς) in lines 18–19. Then come the words κεῖται Πάτροκλος ('Patroclus is dead', 18.20). This is abrupt in itself, but it is made more so by the lack of any kind of conjunction, which emphasizes the fact that Antilochus has blurted out his message, rather than delivering it in a calm, measured way.

Anacoluthon is the absence of the expected grammatical sequence. As with asyndeton, it can indicate moments of high emotion. But it can do more than that, too. Consider the following lines:

ὤ μοι ἐγὼ δειλή, ὤ μοι δυσαριστοτόκεια,
ἥ τ᾽ ἐπεὶ ἂρ τέκον υἱὸν ἀμύμονά τε κρατερόν τε
ἔξοχον ἡρώων: ὃ δ᾽ ἀνέδραμεν ἔρνεϊ ἶσος:

Oh, my misery! Oh, the pain of being mother to the best of men! Because I bore a son who was to be noble and strong, the greatest of heroes ... he shot up like a young sapling ...

18.54–6, lightly adapted from Hammond

The speaker here is Thetis, who is reflecting on the life of her son, Achilles, who is shortly to die. It is a highly emotional speech, as is shown by the opening ὤ μοι ('Alas!') followed by the extraordinary *hapax legomenon* δυσαριστοτόκεια (lit: 'unfortunate mother to a child who is the best'). The sentence also contains an example of anacoluthon, since the main clause to which ἐπεὶ ought to be subordinated never actually appears. Most translators actually ignore the anacoluthon altogether, translating as if the ἐπεὶ clause were subordinate to the vocatives in 18.54 or as if the word ἐπεὶ were not there at all. But the anacoluthon is important and should not be ignored. In terms of what it means, we might say simply that Thetis is 'emotional' and forgets to finish her sentence. But it might also be an indication of how her mind works: she begins by reflecting on her misfortunes as a mother to a doomed son, but the mention of the birth of her son (τέκον υἱὸν, 'I gave birth to a son', 18.55) leads her to ignore whatever it was that she was going to say and to reflect on Achilles' upbringing at more length. The use of anacoluthon provides a psychologically realistic account of how a grieving mother might actually think.

We can find another example of anacoluthon a little later in Book 18. This time, the speaker is Achilles, who is on the point of announcing he will return to battle. He starts by saying 'So now, since I shall not return to my dear native land, since I have not been a saving light to Patroclus ...' (νῦν δ᾽ ἐπεὶ οὐ νέομαί γε φίλην ἐς πατρίδα γαῖαν, οὐδέ τι Πατρόκλῳ γενόμην φάος, 18.101–2), and we expect him to say something like '... I shall return to battle and kill Hector.' But he doesn't say this. Instead, he spends the next eleven lines reflecting on the reasons for his withdrawal from battle and the damage it has done to his companions, his quarrel with Agamemnon and the nature of rivalry itself. It is the kind of flight of fancy in which Achilles often engages, and the anacoluthon provides a satisfying way of representing what might be described as Achilles' 'stream of consciousness'.

Paronomasia is a play on words. An example of this is the phrase κούρην δ᾽ οὐ γαμέω Ἀγαμέμνονος Ἀτρεΐδαο ('I will not marry the daughter of Agamemnon, son of Atreus', 9.388) which might represent a play on words between Ἀγαμέμνονος ('Agamemnon') and οὐ γαμέω ('I will not marry'). If so, it tells us something about the character of Achilles: despite the brusque start to his speech, the use of paronomasia here perhaps shows us that Achilles can be a little more rhetorical than he and the others give him credit for?

Appendix: Homeric Greek

The Homeric dialect has numerous differences from the Attic Greek that students will be most familiar with. The following section, while not exhaustive, lists some of the main features of the Homeric dialect. More extensive notes are provided where necessary in the line-by-line commentary.

Nouns

First declension

- For ᾱ, we always find η, regardless of where it appears in the word, e.g. χώρη = Att. χώρα, θύρη = Att. θύρα, νεηνίης = Att. νεανίας
- The nom. sing. of some masculines in -ης is shortened to ᾰ, e.g. ἱππότα = Att. ἱππότης, νεφεληγερέτα = Att. νεφεληγερέτης
- The gen. sing. of masculines ends in -αω or -εω, e.g. Ἀτρείδαο, Ἀτρείδεω = Att. Ἀτρείδου
- The gen. pl. of masculines ends in -άων or -έων, e.g. θεάων = Att. θεῶν, νυμφάων = Att. νυμφῶν
- The dat. pl. almost always ends in -ῃσι(ν) or -ῃς, e.g. πύλῃσιν = Att. πύλαις, but θεαῖς

Second declension

- The gen. sing. ends in -οιο as well as -ου, e.g. πεδίοιο and πεδίου
- The dat. pl. ends in -οισι as well as -οις, e.g. φύλλοισι and φύλλοις
- The gen. and dat. dual end in -οιϊν, so ἵπποιϊν, not ἵπποιν

Third declension

- The acc. sing ends in -ιν as well as -ιδα, e.g. γλαυκῶπιν and γλαυκώπιδα
- Endings in -ηα correspond to -εα, e.g. βασιλῆα = Att. βασιλέα
- Gen. sing. endings in -ηος and -ιος correspond to -εως, e.g. βασιλῆος = Att. βασιλέως, πόλιος = Att. πόλεως
- Acc. pl. endings in -ηας correspond to -εας, e.g. βασιλῆας = Att. βασιλέας
- Gen. pl. endings in -ηων correspond to -εων, e.g. βασιλήων = Att. βασιλέων
- The dat. pl. ends in -εσσι and -σι, e.g. πόδεσσι = Att. ποσί, ἔπεσσι = Att. ἔπεσι
- The gen. and dat. dual end in -οιιν, e.g. ποδοῖιν

Pronouns

ἐγώ, σύ, 'I', 'you'
- Gen. sing: ἐμεῖο, ἐμέο, ἐμεῦ, μευ, ἐμέθεν; so with σύ – σεῖο, σέο, etc.

ἕ, 'him'
- Gen. sing.: εἷο, ἕο, εὗ, ἕθεν = Attic: αὐτοῦ
- = Attic: αὐτῷ

ἡμεῖς, ὑμεῖς, 'we', 'you'
- Acc. pl.: ἡμέας, ἄμμε
- Gen. pl.: ἡμείων, ἡμέων
- Dat. pl.: ἄμμιν; so with ὑμεῖς

σφεῖς, 'they'
- Acc. pl.: σφε, σφέας, σφας
- Gen. pl.: σφείων, σφέων
- Dat. pl.: σφι, σφισί

τίς, 'who, what, which'
- Nom. sing.: τίς
- Acc. sing.: τίνα
- Gen. sing.: τέο, τεῦ
- Dat. sing.: τέῳ
- Gen. pl.: τέων

ὁ, ἡ, τό, 'he, she, it'
- In Homer, ὁ, ἡ, τό is used for the third person pronoun ('he, she, it'), not the definite article ('the')
- Nom. pl.: οἱ, αἱ, or τοί, ταί
- Dat. pl.: τοῖς, τοῖσι, τῆς, τῇσι as well as ταῖς

Verbs

Future

- Generally uncontracted, e.g. ἐρέω = Att. ἐρῶ, τελέω = Att. τελέσω

Present/Imperfect

- The endings -σκον and -σκόμην may be used to express repetition of the action, e.g. φύγεσκον = 'they kept on running away'

Aorist/Imperfect

- The augment may be omitted in both the aorist and imperfect tense, e.g. βάλον = Att. ἔβαλον, ἔμβαλε = Att. ἐνέβαλε
- Third person pl. of aorist passive may end in -εν instead of -ησαν, e.g. φόβηθεν = Att. ἐφοβήθησαν, ἔμιχθεν = Att. ἐμίχθησαν

Moods

Subjunctive

- Appears with a short vowel, e.g. ἴομεν = Att. ἴωμεν
- Second person singular middle ends in -ηαι or -εαι, e.g. εὔξεαι = Att. εὔξῃ
- Third person singular active ends in -σι, e.g. φορέῃσι = φορῇ
- Occasionally used in place of the future tense

Infinitive

- Appears with the endings -μεν, -μεναι and -ναι for -ειν and -ναι, e.g. δόμεναι = Att. δοῦναι, ἴμεν = Att. ἰέναι, ἀκουέμεν(αι) = Att. ἀκούειν
- ἔμεν, ἔμμεν and ἔμμεναι = Att. εἶναι

Contracted verbs

- Verbs in -άω can appear contracted, uncontracted or even expanded with the addition of a like-sounding, short vowel either side of the long vowel, e.g. ὁρόωντες = Att. ὁρῶντες
- Verbs in -έω are generally uncontracted, but sometimes form ει from εε or εει, η from εε or ευ from εο or εου
- Verbs in -όω are generally contracted

Particles

- ἄρα (also ἄρ, ῥά) = 'so, next'
- δή = 'indeed'

- ἦ = 'surely'
- πεϱ = 'just, even'
- τε = 'and', or to show a general remark
- τοι = 'I tell you', but may also = σοι ('to you, for you')

Further reading

All quotations in this introduction have been taken from Martin Hammond's prose translation of the *Iliad*, first published by Penguin in 1987, unless otherwise indicated. Where necessary, the names of characters have been changed to their more familiar Latin forms, e.g. 'Achilles' instead of 'Achilleus', 'Achaeans' instead of 'Achaians' and so on.

Short introductions

Barker, E. and Christensen, J. *Homer: A Beginner's Guide* (London, 2013).
Graziosi, B. *Homer* (Oxford, 2016).
Silk, M. *Homer: The Iliad* (Cambridge, 1987).

Texts and commentaries

Willcock, M.M. (ed.) *Homer, Iliad I–XII* (Bristol, 1984).
Willcock, M.M. (ed.) *Homer, Iliad XIII–XXIV* (Bristol, 1984).
Kirk, G.S. *The Iliad: A Commentary. Volume I: Books 1–4* (Cambridge, 1985).
Kirk, G.S. *The Iliad: A Commentary. Volume II: Books 5–8* (Cambridge, 1990).
Hainsworth, J.B. *The Iliad: A Commentary. Volume III: Books 9–12* (Cambridge, 1993).
Janko, R. *The Iliad: A Commentary. Volume IV: Books 13–16* (Cambridge, 1992).
Edwards, M. *The Iliad: A Commentary. Volume V: Books 17–20* (Cambridge, 1991).
Richardson, N. *The Iliad: A Commentary. Volume VI: Books 21–24* (Cambridge, 1993).
Griffin, J. *Homer Iliad IX* (Oxford, 1995).
Jones, P. *Homer's Iliad: A Commentary on Three Translations* (Bristol, 2003).

General studies

Cairns, D.L. (ed.) *Oxford Readings in Homer's Iliad* (Oxford, 2001).
Fowler, R. (ed.) *The Cambridge Companion to Homer* (Cambridge, 2004).
Griffin, J. *Homer on Life and Death* (Oxford, 1980).
Morris, I. and Powell, B. (eds.) *A New Companion to Homer* (Leiden, 1997).
Taplin, O. *Homeric Soundings* (Oxford, 1992).

Oral poetry and composition in performance

Bakker, E. *Pointing at the Past: From Formula to Performance in Homeric Poetics* (Cambridge, MA, 2005).

Lord, B. *The Singer of Tales* (Cambridge, MA, 1960).

Parry, M. *The Making of Homeric Verse: The Collected Papers of Milman Parry* (Oxford, 1971).

Type-scenes

Edwards, M. 'Convention and Individuality in *Iliad* 1', *Harvard Studies in Classical Philology* 84 (1980), pp. 1–28.

Neoanalysis

West, M. L. *The East Face of Helicon: West Asiatic Elements in Greek Poetry and Myth* (Oxford, 1997).

Story patterns

Propp, V. *Morphology of the Folktale* (Austin, 1968).

Nagler, M.N. *Spontaneity and Tradition: A Study in the Oral Art of Homer* (Berkeley and Los Angeles, 1974).

Heroes and heroism

Cairns, D. *Aidōs: The Psychology and Ethics of Honour and Shame in Ancient Greek Literature* (Oxford, 1993).

Nagy, G. *The Best of the Achaeans: Concepts of the Hero in Archaic Greek Poetry* (2nd edn. Baltimore, 1999).

Schein, S.L. *The Mortal Hero: An Introduction to Homer's Iliad* (London, 1984).

Acknowledgements

I would like to thank Dr Andrew Sillett (St Anne's College, Oxford), Mr Mathew Owen (Classics Department, Caterham School) and Revd Richard Smail for their encouragement and expertise in writing this introduction and commentary.

Text
Iliad 18

ὣς οἳ μὲν μάρναντο δέμας πυρὸς αἰθομένοιο,
Ἀντίλοχος δ᾽ Ἀχιλῆϊ πόδας ταχὺς ἄγγελος ἦλθε.
τὸν δ᾽ εὗρε προπάροιθε νεῶν ὀρθοκραιράων
τὰ φρονέοντ᾽ ἀνὰ θυμὸν ἃ δὴ τετελεσμένα ἦεν·
ὀχθήσας δ᾽ ἄρα εἶπε πρὸς ὃν μεγαλήτορα θυμόν·   5
ὤ μοι ἐγώ, τί τ᾽ ἄρ᾽ αὖτε κάρη κομόωντες Ἀχαιοὶ
νηυσὶν ἔπι κλονέονται ἀτυζόμενοι πεδίοιο;
μὴ δή μοι τελέσωσι θεοὶ κακὰ κήδεα θυμῷ,
ὥς ποτέ μοι μήτηρ διεπέφραδε καί μοι ἔειπε
Μυρμιδόνων τὸν ἄριστον ἔτι ζώοντος ἐμεῖο   10
χερσὶν ὕπο Τρώων λείψειν φάος ἠελίοιο.
ἦ μάλα δὴ τέθνηκε Μενοιτίου ἄλκιμος υἱὸς
σχέτλιος· ἦ τ᾽ ἐκέλευον ἀπωσάμενον δήϊον πῦρ
ἂψ ἐπὶ νῆας ἴμεν, μηδ᾽ Ἕκτορι ἶφι μάχεσθαι.
εἷος ὃ ταῦθ᾽ ὥρμαινε κατὰ φρένα καὶ κατὰ θυμόν,   15
τόφρά οἱ ἐγγύθεν ἦλθεν ἀγαυοῦ Νέστορος υἱὸς
δάκρυα θερμὰ χέων, φάτο δ᾽ ἀγγελίην ἀλεγεινήν·
ὤ μοι Πηλέος υἱὲ δαΐφρονος ἦ μάλα λυγρῆς
πεύσεαι ἀγγελίης, ἣ μὴ ὤφελλε γενέσθαι.
κεῖται Πάτροκλος, νέκυος δὲ δὴ ἀμφιμάχονται   20
γυμνοῦ· ἀτὰρ τά γε τεύχε᾽ ἔχει κορυθαίολος Ἕκτωρ.
ὣς φάτο, τὸν δ᾽ ἄχεος νεφέλη ἐκάλυψε μέλαινα·
ἀμφοτέρῃσι δὲ χερσὶν ἑλὼν κόνιν αἰθαλόεσσαν
χεύατο κὰκ κεφαλῆς, χαρίεν δ᾽ ᾔσχυνε πρόσωπον·
νεκταρέῳ δὲ χιτῶνι μέλαιν᾽ ἀμφίζανε τέφρη.   25
αὐτὸς δ᾽ ἐν κονίῃσι μέγας μεγαλωστὶ τανυσθεὶς

κεῖτο, φίλῃσι δὲ χερσὶ κόμην ᾔσχυνε δαΐζων.
δμῳαὶ δ᾽ ἃς Ἀχιλεὺς ληΐσσατο Πάτροκλός τε
θυμὸν ἀκηχέμεναι μεγάλ᾽ ἴαχον, ἐκ δὲ θύραζε
ἔδραμον ἀμφ᾽ Ἀχιλῆα δαΐφρονα, χερσὶ δὲ πᾶσαι   30
στήθεα πεπλήγοντο, λύθεν δ᾽ ὑπὸ γυῖα ἑκάστης.
Ἀντίλοχος δ᾽ ἑτέρωθεν ὀδύρετο δάκρυα λείβων
χεῖρας ἔχων Ἀχιλῆος: ὃ δ᾽ ἔστενε κυδάλιμον κῆρ:
δείδιε γὰρ μὴ λαιμὸν ἀπαμήσειε σιδήρῳ.
σμερδαλέον δ᾽ ᾤμωξεν: ἄκουσε δὲ πότνια μήτηρ   35
ἡμένη ἐν βένθεσσιν ἁλὸς παρὰ πατρὶ γέροντι,
κώκυσέν τ᾽ ἄρ᾽ ἔπειτα: θεαὶ δέ μιν ἀμφαγέροντο
πᾶσαι ὅσαι κατὰ βένθος ἁλὸς Νηρηΐδες ἦσαν.

39–49: The poet lists the names of the Nereids.

τῶν δὲ καὶ ἀργύφεον πλῆτο σπέος: αἳ δ᾽ ἅμα πᾶσαι   50
στήθεα πεπλήγοντο, Θέτις δ᾽ ἐξῆρχε γόοιο:
'κλῦτε κασίγνηται Νηρηΐδες, ὄφρ᾽ ἐῢ πᾶσαι
εἴδετ᾽ ἀκούουσαι ὅσ᾽ ἐμῷ ἔνι κήδεα θυμῷ.
ὤ μοι ἐγὼ δειλή, ὤ μοι δυσαριστοτόκεια,
ἥ τ᾽ ἐπεὶ ἂρ τέκον υἱὸν ἀμύμονά τε κρατερόν τε   55
ἔξοχον ἡρώων: ὃ δ᾽ ἀνέδραμεν ἔρνεϊ ἶσος:
τὸν μὲν ἐγὼ θρέψασα φυτὸν ὣς γουνῷ ἀλωῆς
νηυσὶν ἐπιπροέηκα κορωνίσιν Ἴλιον εἴσω
Τρωσὶ μαχησόμενον: τὸν δ᾽ οὐχ ὑποδέξομαι αὖτις
οἴκαδε νοστήσαντα δόμον Πηλήϊον εἴσω.   60
ὄφρα δέ μοι ζώει καὶ ὁρᾷ φάος ἠελίοιο
ἄχνυται, οὐδέ τί οἱ δύναμαι χραισμῆσαι ἰοῦσα.
ἀλλ᾽ εἶμ᾽, ὄφρα ἴδωμι φίλον τέκος, ἠδ᾽ ἐπακούσω
ὅττί μιν ἵκετο πένθος ἀπὸ πτολέμοιο μένοντα.
ὣς ἄρα φωνήσασα λίπε σπέος: αἳ δὲ σὺν αὐτῇ   65
δακρυόεσσαι ἴσαν, περὶ δέ σφισι κῦμα θαλάσσης
ῥήγνυτο: ταὶ δ᾽ ὅτε δὴ Τροίην ἐρίβωλον ἵκοντο
ἀκτὴν εἰσανέβαινον ἐπισχερώ, ἔνθα θαμειαὶ
Μυρμιδόνων εἴρυντο νέες ταχὺν ἀμφ᾽ Ἀχιλῆα.
τῷ δὲ βαρὺ στενάχοντι παρίστατο πότνια μήτηρ,   70
ὀξὺ δὲ κωκύσασα κάρη λάβε παιδὸς ἑοῖο,
καί ῥ᾽ ὀλοφυρομένη ἔπεα πτερόεντα προσηύδα:
'τέκνον τί κλαίεις; τί δέ σε φρένας ἵκετο πένθος;
ἐξαύδα, μὴ κεῦθε: τὰ μὲν δή τοι τετέλεσται
ἐκ Διός, ὡς ἄρα δὴ πρίν γ᾽ εὔχεο χεῖρας ἀνασχὼν   75

πάντας ἐπὶ πρύμνῃσιν ἀλήμεναι υἷας Ἀχαιῶν
σεῦ ἐπιδευομένους, παθέειν τ᾽ ἀεκήλια ἔργα.
τὴν δὲ βαρὺ στενάχων προσέφη πόδας ὠκὺς Ἀχιλλεύς·
'μῆτερ ἐμή, τὰ μὲν ἄρ μοι Ὀλύμπιος ἐξετέλεσσεν·
ἀλλὰ τί μοι τῶν ἦδος ἐπεὶ φίλος ὤλεθ᾽ ἑταῖρος   80
Πάτροκλος, τὸν ἐγὼ περὶ πάντων τῖον ἑταίρων
ἶσον ἐμῇ κεφαλῇ; τὸν ἀπώλεσα, τεύχεα δ᾽ Ἕκτωρ
δῃώσας ἀπέδυσε πελώρια θαῦμα ἰδέσθαι
καλά· τὰ μὲν Πηλῆϊ θεοὶ δόσαν ἀγλαὰ δῶρα
ἤματι τῷ ὅτε σε βροτοῦ ἀνέρος ἔμβαλον εὐνῇ.   85
αἴθ᾽ ὄφελες σὺ μὲν αὖθι μετ᾽ ἀθανάτῃς ἁλίῃσι
ναίειν, Πηλεὺς δὲ θνητὴν ἀγαγέσθαι ἄκοιτιν.
νῦν δ᾽ ἵνα καὶ σοὶ πένθος ἐνὶ φρεσὶ μυρίον εἴη
παιδὸς ἀποφθιμένοιο, τὸν οὐχ ὑποδέξεαι αὖτις
οἴκαδε νοστήσαντ᾽, ἐπεὶ οὐδ᾽ ἐμὲ θυμὸς ἄνωγε   90
ζώειν οὐδ᾽ ἄνδρεσσι μετέμμεναι, αἴ κε μὴ Ἕκτωρ
πρῶτος ἐμῷ ὑπὸ δουρὶ τυπεὶς ἀπὸ θυμὸν ὀλέσσῃ,
Πατρόκλοιο δ᾽ ἕλωρα Μενοιτιάδεω ἀποτίσῃ.
τὸν δ᾽ αὖτε προσέειπε Θέτις κατὰ δάκρυ χέουσα·
ὠκύμορος δή μοι τέκος ἔσσεαι, οἷ᾽ ἀγορεύεις·   95
αὐτίκα γάρ τοι ἔπειτα μεθ᾽ Ἕκτορα πότμος ἑτοῖμος.
τὴν δὲ μέγ᾽ ὀχθήσας προσέφη πόδας ὠκὺς Ἀχιλλεύς·
'αὐτίκα τεθναίην, ἐπεὶ οὐκ ἄρ᾽ ἔμελλον ἑταίρῳ
κτεινομένῳ ἐπαμῦναι· ὃ μὲν μάλα τηλόθι πάτρης
ἔφθιτ᾽, ἐμεῖο δὲ δῆσεν ἀρῆς ἀλκτῆρα γενέσθαι.   100
νῦν δ᾽ ἐπεὶ οὐ νέομαί γε φίλην ἐς πατρίδα γαῖαν,
οὐδέ τι Πατρόκλῳ γενόμην φάος οὐδ᾽ ἑτάροισι
τοῖς ἄλλοις, οἳ δὴ πολέες δάμεν Ἕκτορι δίῳ,
ἀλλ᾽ ἧμαι παρὰ νηυσὶν ἐτώσιον ἄχθος ἀρούρης,
τοῖος ἐὼν οἷος οὔ τις Ἀχαιῶν χαλκοχιτώνων   105
ἐν πολέμῳ· ἀγορῇ δέ τ᾽ ἀμείνονές εἰσι καὶ ἄλλοι.
ὡς ἔρις ἔκ τε θεῶν ἔκ τ᾽ ἀνθρώπων ἀπόλοιτο
καὶ χόλος, ὅς τ᾽ ἐφέηκε πολύφρονά περ χαλεπῆναι,
ὅς τε πολὺ γλυκίων μέλιτος καταλειβομένοιο
ἀνδρῶν ἐν στήθεσσιν ἀέξεται ἠΰτε καπνός·   110
ὡς ἐμὲ νῦν ἐχόλωσεν ἄναξ ἀνδρῶν Ἀγαμέμνων.
ἀλλὰ τὰ μὲν προτετύχθαι ἐάσομεν ἀχνύμενοί περ,
θυμὸν ἐνὶ στήθεσσι φίλον δαμάσαντες ἀνάγκῃ·
νῦν δ᾽ εἶμ᾽ ὄφρα φίλης κεφαλῆς ὀλετῆρα κιχείω
Ἕκτορα· κῆρα δ᾽ ἐγὼ τότε δέξομαι ὁππότε κεν δὴ   115
Ζεὺς ἐθέλῃ τελέσαι ἠδ᾽ ἀθάνατοι θεοὶ ἄλλοι.

οὐδὲ γὰρ οὐδὲ βίη Ἡρακλῆος φύγε κῆρα,
ὅς περ φίλτατος ἔσκε Διὶ Κρονίωνι ἄνακτι:
ἀλλά ἑ μοῖρα δάμασσε καὶ ἀργαλέος χόλος Ἥρης.
ὣς καὶ ἐγών, εἰ δή μοι ὁμοίη μοῖρα τέτυκται,   120
κείσομ᾽ ἐπεί κε θάνω: νῦν δὲ κλέος ἐσθλὸν ἀροίμην,
καί τινα Τρωϊάδων καὶ Δαρδανίδων βαθυκόλπων
ἀμφοτέρῃσιν χερσὶ παρειάων ἁπαλάων
δάκρυ᾽ ὀμορξαμένην ἁδινὸν στοναχῆσαι ἐφείην,
γνοῖεν δ᾽ ὡς δὴ δηρὸν ἐγὼ πολέμοιο πέπαυμαι: 125
μὴ δέ μ᾽ ἔρυκε μάχης φιλέουσά περ: οὐδέ με πείσεις.
τὸν δ᾽ ἠμείβετ᾽ ἔπειτα θεὰ Θέτις ἀργυρόπεζα:
῾ναὶ δὴ ταῦτά γε τέκνον ἐτήτυμον οὐ κακόν ἐστι
τειρομένοις ἑτάροισιν ἀμυνέμεν αἰπὺν ὄλεθρον.
ἀλλά τοι ἔντεα καλὰ μετὰ Τρώεσσιν ἔχονται   130
χάλκεα μαρμαίροντα: τὰ μὲν κορυθαίολος Ἕκτωρ
αὐτὸς ἔχων ὤμοισιν ἀγάλλεται: οὐδέ ἕ φημι
δηρὸν ἐπαγλαϊεῖσθαι, ἐπεὶ φόνος ἐγγύθεν αὐτῷ.
ἀλλὰ σὺ μὲν μή πω καταδύσεο μῶλον Ἄρηος
πρίν γ᾽ ἐμὲ δεῦρ᾽ ἐλθοῦσαν ἐν ὀφθαλμοῖσιν ἴδηαι: 135
ἠῶθεν γὰρ νεῦμαι ἅμ᾽ ἠελίῳ ἀνιόντι
τεύχεα καλὰ φέρουσα παρ᾽ Ἡφαίστοιο ἄνακτος.
ὣς ἄρα φωνήσασα πάλιν τράπεθ᾽ υἷος ἑοῖο,
καὶ στρεφθεῖσ᾽ ἁλίῃσι κασιγνήτῃσι μετηύδα:
ὑμεῖς μὲν νῦν δῦτε θαλάσσης εὐρέα κόλπον   140
ὀψόμεναί τε γέρονθ᾽ ἅλιον καὶ δώματα πατρός,
καί οἱ πάντ᾽ ἀγορεύσατ᾽: ἐγὼ δ᾽ ἐς μακρὸν Ὄλυμπον
εἶμι παρ᾽ Ἥφαιστον κλυτοτέχνην, αἴ κ᾽ ἐθέλῃσιν
υἱεῖ ἐμῷ δόμεναι κλυτὰ τεύχεα παμφανόωντα.
ὣς ἔφαθ᾽, αἳ δ᾽ ὑπὸ κῦμα θαλάσσης αὐτίκ᾽ ἔδυσαν: 145
ἣ δ᾽ αὖτ᾽ Οὔλυμπον δὲ θεὰ Θέτις ἀργυρόπεζα
ἤϊεν ὄφρα φίλῳ παιδὶ κλυτὰ τεύχε᾽ ἐνείκαι.
τὴν μὲν ἄρ᾽ Οὔλυμπον δὲ πόδες φέρον: αὐτὰρ Ἀχαιοὶ
θεσπεσίῳ ἀλαλητῷ ὑφ᾽ Ἕκτορος ἀνδροφόνοιο
φεύγοντες νῆάς τε καὶ Ἑλλήσποντον ἵκοντο.   150
οὐδέ κε Πάτροκλόν περ ἐϋκνήμιδες Ἀχαιοὶ
ἐκ βελέων ἐρύσαντο νέκυν θεράποντ᾽ Ἀχιλῆος:
αὖτις γὰρ δὴ τόν γε κίχον λαός τε καὶ ἵπποι
Ἕκτωρ τε Πριάμοιο πάϊς φλογὶ εἴκελος ἀλκήν.
τρὶς μέν μιν μετόπισθε ποδῶν λάβε φαίδιμος Ἕκτωρ   155
ἑλκέμεναι μεμαώς, μέγα δὲ Τρώεσσιν ὁμόκλα:
τρὶς δὲ δύ᾽ Αἴαντες θοῦριν ἐπιειμένοι ἀλκὴν

νεκροῦ ἀπεστυφέλιξαν· ὃ δ᾽ ἔμπεδον ἀλκὶ πεποιθὼς
ἄλλοτ᾽ ἐπαΐξασκε κατὰ μόθον, ἄλλοτε δ᾽ αὖτε
στάσκε μέγα ἰάχων· ὀπίσω δ᾽ οὐ χάζετο πάμπαν.   160
ὡς δ᾽ ἀπὸ σώματος οὔ τι λέοντ᾽ αἴθωνα δύνανται
ποιμένες ἄγραυλοι μέγα πεινάοντα δίεσθαι,
ὣς ῥα τὸν οὐκ ἐδύναντο δύω Αἴαντε κορυστὰ
Ἕκτορα Πριαμίδην ἀπὸ νεκροῦ δειδίξασθαι.
καί νύ κεν εἴρυσσέν τε καὶ ἄσπετον ἤρατο κῦδος,   165
εἰ μὴ Πηλεΐωνι ποδήνεμος ὠκέα Ἶρις
ἄγγελος ἦλθε θέουσ᾽ ἀπ᾽ Ὀλύμπου θωρήσσεσθαι
κρύβδα Διὸς ἄλλων τε θεῶν· πρὸ γὰρ ἧκέ μιν Ἥρη.
ἀγχοῦ δ᾽ ἱσταμένη ἔπεα πτερόεντα προσηύδα·
ὄρσεο Πηλεΐδη, πάντων ἐκπαγλότατ᾽ ἀνδρῶν·   170
Πατρόκλῳ ἐπάμυνον, οὗ εἵνεκα φύλοπις αἰνὴ
ἕστηκε πρὸ νεῶν· οἳ δ᾽ ἀλλήλους ὀλέκουσιν
οἳ μὲν ἀμυνόμενοι νέκυος πέρι τεθνηῶτος,
οἳ δὲ ἐρύσσασθαι ποτὶ Ἴλιον ἠνεμόεσσαν
Τρῶες ἐπιθύουσι· μάλιστα δὲ φαίδιμος Ἕκτωρ   175
ἑλκέμεναι μέμονεν· κεφαλὴν δέ ἑ θυμὸς ἄνωγε
πῆξαι ἀνὰ σκολόπεσσι ταμόνθ᾽ ἁπαλῆς ἀπὸ δειρῆς.
ἀλλ᾽ ἄνα μηδ᾽ ἔτι κεῖσο· σέβας δέ σε θυμὸν ἱκέσθω
Πάτροκλον Τρῳῇσι κυσὶν μέλπηθρα γενέσθαι·
σοὶ λώβη, αἴ κέν τι νέκυς ᾐσχυμμένος ἔλθῃ.   180
τὴν δ᾽ ἠμείβετ᾽ ἔπειτα ποδάρκης δῖος Ἀχιλλεύς·
Ἶρι θεὰ τίς γάρ σε θεῶν ἐμοὶ ἄγγελον ἧκε;
τὸν δ᾽ αὖτε προσέειπε ποδήνεμος ὠκέα Ἶρις·
Ἥρη με προέηκε Διὸς κυδρὴ παράκοιτις·
οὐδ᾽ οἶδε Κρονίδης ὑψίζυγος οὐδέ τις ἄλλος   185
ἀθανάτων, οἳ Ὄλυμπον ἀγάννιφον ἀμφινέμονται.
τὴν δ᾽ ἀπαμειβόμενος προσέφη πόδας ὠκὺς Ἀχιλλεύς·
πῶς τὰρ ἴω μετὰ μῶλον; ἔχουσι δὲ τεύχε᾽ ἐκεῖνοι·
μήτηρ δ᾽ οὔ με φίλη πρίν γ᾽ εἴα θωρήσσεσθαι
πρίν γ᾽ αὐτὴν ἐλθοῦσαν ἐν ὀφθαλμοῖσιν ἴδωμαι·   190
στεῦτο γὰρ Ἡφαίστοιο πάρ᾽ οἰσέμεν ἔντεα καλά.
ἄλλου δ᾽ οὔ τευ οἶδα τεῦ ἂν κλυτὰ τεύχεα δύω,
εἰ μὴ Αἴαντός γε σάκος Τελαμωνιάδαο.
ἀλλὰ καὶ αὐτὸς ὅ γ᾽ ἔλπομ᾽ ἐνὶ πρώτοισιν ὁμιλεῖ
ἔγχεϊ δηϊόων περὶ Πατρόκλοιο θανόντος.   195
τὸν δ᾽ αὖτε προσέειπε ποδήνεμος ὠκέα Ἶρις·
εὖ νυ καὶ ἡμεῖς ἴδμεν ὅ τοι κλυτὰ τεύχε᾽ ἔχονται·
ἀλλ᾽ αὐτὸς ἐπὶ τάφρον ἰὼν Τρώεσσι φάνηθι,

αἴ κέ σ᾽ ὑποδείσαντες ἀπόσχωνται πολέμοιο
Τρῶες, ἀναπνεύσωσι δ᾽ ἀρήϊοι υἷες Ἀχαιῶν   200
τειρόμενοι: ὀλίγη δέ τ᾽ ἀνάπνευσις πολέμοιο.
ἦ μὲν ἄρ᾽ ὣς εἰποῦσ᾽ ἀπέβη πόδας ὠκέα Ἶρις,
αὐτὰρ Ἀχιλλεὺς ὦρτο Διῒ φίλος: ἀμφὶ δ᾽ Ἀθήνη
ὤμοις ἰφθίμοισι βάλ᾽ αἰγίδα θυσσανόεσσαν,
ἀμφὶ δέ οἱ κεφαλῇ νέφος ἔστεφε δῖα θεάων   205
χρύσεον, ἐκ δ᾽ αὐτοῦ δαῖε φλόγα παμφανόωσαν.
ὡς δ᾽ ὅτε καπνὸς ἰὼν ἐξ ἄστεος αἰθέρ᾽ ἵκηται
τηλόθεν ἐκ νήσου, τὴν δήϊοι ἀμφιμάχωνται,
οἵ τε πανημέριοι στυγερῷ κρίνονται Ἄρηϊ
ἄστεος ἐκ σφετέρου: ἅμα δ᾽ ἠελίῳ καταδύντι   210
πυρσοί τε φλεγέθουσιν ἐπήτριμοι, ὑψόσε δ᾽ αὐγὴ
γίγνεται ἀΐσσουσα περικτιόνεσσιν ἰδέσθαι,
αἴ κέν πως σὺν νηυσὶν ἄρεω ἀλκτῆρες ἵκωνται:
ὣς ἀπ᾽ Ἀχιλλῆος κεφαλῆς σέλας αἰθέρ᾽ ἵκανε:
στῆ δ᾽ ἐπὶ τάφρον ἰὼν ἀπὸ τείχεος, οὐδ᾽ ἐς Ἀχαιοὺς   215
μίσγετο: μητρὸς γὰρ πυκινὴν ὠπίζετ᾽ ἐφετμήν.
ἔνθα στὰς ἤϋσ᾽, ἀπάτερθε δὲ Παλλὰς Ἀθήνη
φθέγξατ᾽: ἀτὰρ Τρώεσσιν ἐν ἄσπετον ὦρσε κυδοιμόν.
ὡς δ᾽ ὅτ᾽ ἀριζήλη φωνή, ὅτε τ᾽ ἴαχε σάλπιγξ
ἄστυ περιπλομένων δηΐων ὕπο θυμοραϊστέων,   220
ὣς τότ᾽ ἀριζήλη φωνὴ γένετ᾽ Αἰακίδαο.
οἱ δ᾽ ὡς οὖν ἄϊον ὄπα χάλκεον Αἰακίδαο,
πᾶσιν ὀρίνθη θυμός: ἀτὰρ καλλίτριχες ἵπποι
ἂψ ὄχεα τρόπεον: ὄσσοντο γὰρ ἄλγεα θυμῷ.
ἡνίοχοι δ᾽ ἔκπληγεν, ἐπεὶ ἴδον ἀκάματον πῦρ   225
δεινὸν ὑπὲρ κεφαλῆς μεγαθύμου Πηλεΐωνος
δαιόμενον: τὸ δὲ δαῖε θεὰ γλαυκῶπις Ἀθήνη.
τρὶς μὲν ὑπὲρ τάφρου μεγάλ᾽ ἴαχε δῖος Ἀχιλλεύς,
τρὶς δὲ κυκήθησαν Τρῶες κλειτοί τ᾽ ἐπίκουροι.
ἔνθα δὲ καὶ τότ᾽ ὄλοντο δυώδεκα φῶτες ἄριστοι   230
ἀμφὶ σφοῖς ὀχέεσσι καὶ ἔγχεσιν. αὐτὰρ Ἀχαιοὶ
ἀσπασίως Πάτροκλον ὑπὲκ βελέων ἐρύσαντες
κάτθεσαν ἐν λεχέεσσι: φίλοι δ᾽ ἀμφέσταν ἑταῖροι
μυρόμενοι: μετὰ δέ σφι ποδώκης εἵπετ᾽ Ἀχιλλεὺς
δάκρυα θερμὰ χέων, ἐπεὶ εἴσιδε πιστὸν ἑταῖρον   235
κείμενον ἐν φέρτρῳ δεδαϊγμένον ὀξέϊ χαλκῷ,
τόν ῥ᾽ ἤτοι μὲν ἔπεμπε σὺν ἵπποισιν καὶ ὄχεσφιν
ἐς πόλεμον, οὐδ᾽ αὖτις ἐδέξατο νοστήσαντα.

Commentary Notes
Iliad 18

The story continues from the end of Book 17. The Greeks are in full retreat, attempting to recover the body of Patroclus, who has been killed by Hector. Antilochus, the son of Nestor, is on his way to Achilles to deliver the unwelcome news of his friend's death.

1–21

Antilochus brings Achilles the news of Patroclus' death. His speech – just four lines long – is inelegant and disjointed, betraying his anxiety and distress at delivering such an unwelcome message to a man so prone to violence.

1

A formulaic line that is often used for a change of scene, being used twice elsewhere in the poem (11.596, 13.673) and once in a slightly altered form (17.366). Here, we are moving from the general scenes of fighting described at the end of Book 17 to the solitary figure Achilles in the Greek camp.

The use of μὲν (1) and δέ (2) emphasizes the change of both scene and subject: 'While the Greeks continued to fight ... Antilochus went as a messenger.'

ὡς – 'so'

μάρναντο – 'they continued to fight'; imperfect tense, with the augment omitted, as is common in Homer.

δέμας – lit. 'in the shape of', i.e. 'like'; adverbial accusative; in Homer, the word is only ever found in this phrase.

2

πόδας ταχὺς – 'swift-footed'; πόδας is an accusative of respect, governed by ταχὺς, lit. 'swift with respect to his feet'. It is usually Achilles who is described as 'swift-footed'; its application to Antilochus here is striking.

Ἀχιλῆϊ – Achilles' name is spelt interchangeably with one or two lambdas throughout the *Iliad*.

3

τὸν – 'him'. In Homer, ὁ, ἡ, τό, is almost always used as a third person pronoun, not
the definite article, as is the case in Attic Greek.

προπάροιθε νεῶν – Achilles watches the fighting from 'in front of his ships', but is
evidently too far away to observe what has happened to Patroclus.

ὀρθοκραιράων – lit. 'with straight or upright horns'. The word is usually used
of oxen, referring to the shape of their horns. Here, it refers to the shape of
Achilles' ships, where prow and stern are turned upright in a kind of crescent
shape.

νεῶν – The Greek camp consists of the several hundred ships which have been
dragged up onto the beach. Achilles currently sits in front of his contingent of
ships, which are located at the very end of the row.

4

τὰ – 'those things'; the antecedent of ἅ.

ἃ τετελεσμένα ἦεν – 'which had already come to pass'; the phrase presumably
refers to Achilles' anxiety regarding the death of Patroclus.

ἦεν = ἦν.

5

ὀχθήσας – ὀχθέω can be used for any emotional disturbance, though it most
commonly refers to irritation or indignation, as here.

ὃν – 'his'.

6

τί τ' ἄρ' – τε ἄρα does not impact the basic meaning of τί and can be left untranslated.

αὖτε – 'again'; the word can convey a sense of impatience or irritation, as here.

This is the second time in the poem that the Greeks have been penned in beside
the ships. The first time had resulted in Patroclus being sent into battle to push the
Trojans back. Achilles now wonders why it is that the Greeks have once again found
themselves in trouble.

κάρη κομόωντες – 'long-haired'. κάρη is an accusative of respect, dependent
on the verb κομόωντες; lit. 'being long-haired with respect to their
heads'.

Readers may notice the additional ὁ in κομόωντες. This is not the uncontracted
form (which would be κομάοντες) but the result of an additional short vowel, a
phenomenon known as diectasis. It is added for metrical reasons and is common in
verbs ending in -αω.

Ἀχαιοί – Homer uses the terms 'Achaeans', 'Argives' and 'Danaans' interchangeably
to refer to the Greeks.

7

νηυσὶν ἔπι – 'beside the ships'; the position of the accent on ἐπί/ἔπι provides an
important clue as to whether we have a preposition (ἐπί), which governs the word
following it, or a postposition (ἔπι), which governs the word preceding it, as here.

κλονέονται = κλονοῦνται; contract verbs in Homer can be left uncontracted for
metrical reasons, as here.

ἀτυζόμενοι πεδίοιο – 'fleeing in terror over the plain'; the word ἀτύζομαι literally means 'driven by ἄτη', where ἄτη = bewilderment, confusion, delusion, etc.; πεδίοιο is genitive of the ground covered, a kind of partitive genitive, hence 'over the plain'.

8

μὴ δή ... τελέσωσι – 'may [the gods] not have fulfilled ...'; the aorist subjunctive here has a past force; Achilles' hope is for something (not) to have happened in the past.

θυμῷ – locative, 'in my heart'.

9

ὥς – explanatory in force, explaining why Achilles is so worried.

μήτηρ – Achilles' mother is the sea-nymph Thetis.

διεπέφραδε – The aorist active and middle of some verbs in Homeric Greek are formed by reduplication; διεπέφραδε is the third person singular aorist indicative active of διαφράζω, 'to declare'.

The prophecy that Achilles now describes – that Patroclus would be killed while Achilles was still alive – has not previously been mentioned in the poem. It appears to have been a common idiom in Greek epic for prophecies to be remembered only after they have already been fulfilled.

ἔειπε = εἶπε.

10

Μυρμιδόνων – The Myrmidons were a tribe from Phthia in an area of northern Greece known as Thessaly. They were called the Myrmidons because they were said to have been created by Zeus from a colony of ants (μύρμηκες).

Μυρμιδόνων τὸν ἄριστον – not Achilles, as we might expect, but Patroclus. Several ancient commentators took issue with this line, remarking that (i) Patroclus was not technically a Myrmidon, since he came from Opuntian Locris, and (ii) the 'best of the Myrmidons' was in any case Achilles, not Patroclus. Even so, there is an obvious poetic justification for the prophecy, which contributes to the pathos of the scene.

ἔτι ζώοντος ἐμεῖο – 'while I am still alive', genitive absolute.

ζώοντος – another example of diectasis. In Attic Greek, we would expect the contracted form ζῶντος. Unlike κομόωντες above (6), where the additional vowel (o) was added before the ώ, here it is added after the ώ. Diectasis can put the short vowel either side of the long one, depending on the metrical pattern required.

11

ὕπο – with instrumental or causal sense, i.e. 'by', 'at the hands of'. On the position of the accent on postpositions, see the note on νηυσὶν ἔπι at line 7.

λείψειν φάος ἠελίοιο – lit. 'to leave the light of the sun', i.e. 'to die'.

12

ἦ μάλα – 'surely'; Achilles surmises from the rout of the Greeks (6–7) and the remembered prophecy (7–11) that Patroclus must have been killed.

Μενοιτίου ... υἱὸς – Patroclus; it is common in Homer to refer to a character only
as 'son of X'.

13

σχέτλιος – 'the fool!'.

ἦ τ' ἐκέλευον – 'and yet I told him ...'. When Achilles agreed that Patroclus could
return to the fighting, he gave him strict instructions to return as soon as he had
driven the Trojans back from the Greek ships. Patroclus had ignored this advice
and pushed on across the plain.

δήϊον πῦρ – the Trojans had been threatening to set fire to the Greek ships,
preventing any retreat and effectively ensuring their complete annihilation.

14

μηδ' Ἕκτορι ἶφι μάχεσθαι – actually, Achilles told Patroclus not to fight against
any of the Trojans after he had pushed them back from the Greek camp; he did
not mention Hector specifically.

ἶφι – 'by force'; Homeric Greek had a separate instrumental case, a role that was
subsumed to the dative case in Attic Greek.

15

εἷος = ἕως, 'while'; the reversal of the length of vowels (known as quantitative
metathesis) is often used for metrical purposes, as here.

κατὰ φρένα καὶ κατὰ θυμόν – the Greeks saw the φρήν as the seat of
thought, whereas the θυμός was the seat of emotions, hence: 'in his mind
and in his heart'.

16

τόφρά – τόφρα simply answers εἷος in the previous line; it need not be translated
in this instance.

οἱ – 'to him', i.e. Achilles.

Νέστορος υἱὸς – Antilochus; on the use of the patronymic in Homer, see note on
12 above.

17

δάκρυα θερμὰ χέων – the Homeric hero seems to have been prone to crying,
although we more often see tears of frustration than tears of sorrow. It is
interesting that the last time these exact words were used (δάκρυα θερμὰ
χέων) was when Patroclus begged Achilles to allow him to return to battle
(16.3).

18

ὤ μοι – 'alas!'; the exclamation highlights Antilochus' own suffering at the dreadful
news, as well as that of Patroclus and Achilles. Most speeches in Homer begin
with a one-line speech-introduction; the lack of one here is both unusual and
striking.

Πηλέος υἱὲ – Achilles.

ἦ μάλα – for this phrase, see note at 12.

λυγρῆς … ἀγγελίης – the harsh enjambment between adjective and noun would have been striking to Greek ears; a lack of fluidity in Antilochus' speech may indicate his anxiety and distress at having to deliver such an unwelcome message to someone so prone to violence.

19

πεύσεαι = πεύσει/πεύσῃ. Instead of the second singular middle ending -ει/-ῃ, Homeric verse generally has a diectasis -εαι. As in Attic prose, πυνθάνομαι takes the genitive of the person or thing learned about.

ἧ – technically, a relative pronoun referring to the 'baneful message' itself, although the sub-clause actually refers to the content of the message, i.e. the fact of Patroclus' death.

ὤφελλε – 'would that …!'; in the aorist, ὀφείλω refers to an impossible wish, i.e. a wish that has not (and will not) come to pass. μὴ is used for the negative.

20

κεῖται Πάτροκλος – the lack of a connecting particle between this and the previous line is striking, further betraying Antilochus' anxiety and distress. Indeed, Antilochus goes on to deliver his entire message as quickly as he can, telling Achilles (i) who has been killed, (ii) what has happened to the body and (iii) what has happened to the armour in just two lines.

The scansion of these two words – five long syllables in a row – may indicate the solemnity with which these words are spoken.

21

γυμνοῦ = 'stripped of his armour', rather than 'naked'. It was customary in Homeric combat for the victorious warrior to attempt to strip the armour from the body of his defeated foe. The stripping of the armour is especially important in this case because Patroclus was wearing Achilles' armour when he was killed.

The positioning of γυμνοῦ in the emphatic runover position is striking: 'They are fighting over his body … which has been stripped of its armour!'.

22–38

Achilles falls to the ground in the agony of grief, covering his head and face in dust, rolling on the floor and tearing his hair. On more than one occasion in the following lines, the description of Achilles seems to be not that of someone in mourning but someone who has actually died.

24

κὰκ κεφαλῆς – 'down over the head'; κὰκ = κατά, which has had the final vowel (ά) 'cut off' (known as apocope) and the final consonant (τ) assimilated to the first letter of the next word – all for metrical reasons.

The image of a face defiled with dust (κόνις) or ash (τέφρα) recurs several times in the *Iliad*, both of those in mourning (e.g. Priam in Book 24) and of those who have died (e.g. Hector in Book 22).

χαρίεν ... ἤσχυνε – the contrast between χαρίεν and ἤσχυνε is striking, as is the contrast between Achilles' 'sweet-smelling tunic' and the 'black ash' with which he defiles himself on the next line.

25

νεκταρέῳ – when used to describe clothing, νεκτάρεος means 'perfumed with fragrant oil', 'sweet-smelling'. However, the word also has divine associations, given its association with νέκταρ ('nectar'), the food of the gods.

26

αὐτός – looks forward to δμῳαὶ δέ on line 28.

μέγας μεγαλωστί – 'great in his greatness'.

26–27

τανυσθεὶς κεῖτο – elsewhere, this phrase is only ever used of a dead body, not someone who is simply lying down, as Achilles is here. Indeed, just six lines previously (20), Antilochus had used the same verb (κεῖμαι) in the same position to describe the dead Patroclus: the parallelism is surely intentional.

27

κόμην ἤσχυνε δαΐζων – 'he disfigured himself, tearing his hear out'; since κόμην is the object of δαΐζων ('tearing his hair out'), ἤσχυνε must here be understood intransitively, e.g. 'he disfigured himself', unlike on line 24, where ἤσχυνε governs a direct object (πρόσωπον).

28

ληΐσσατο – the *Iliad* contains a number of references to the Greeks' raids on cities other than Troy; Achilles himself recalls expeditions with Patroclus at 18.341–2 and 24.7–8. It seems to have been customary on these occasions for the victorious army to carry off the womenfolk, who would work as maidservants and/or concubines in their captors' household.

It may be surprising to the modern reader how cordial the relationship is between Achilles and Patroclus and their enslaved maidservants.

29

θυμόν – accusative of respect, governed by ἀκηχέμεναι.

ἀκηχέμεναι – there is some disagreement as to whether this is the perfect participle of ἀκαχίζομαι ('to be troubled or distressed') or ἄχνυμαι ('to grieve'). However, since ἀκαχίζομαι also means 'to grieve' in the perfect tense, it does not make any difference to the translation.

μεγάλα – adverb, equivalent to μεγάλως, 'greatly', i.e. 'loudly'.

θύραζε – lit. 'to the door', i.e. 'out'.

29–30

ἐκ ... ἔδραμον – Homeric verse occasionally allows the splitting of words into two parts in order to better fit the metre, a phenomenon known as tmesis ('cutting'); translate as a single word, ἐξέδραμον, rather than ἐκ + ἔδραμον.

31

πεπλήγοντο – 'they struck', another aorist formed with reduplication, this time from the verb πλήσσω (cf. διεπέφραδε above, line 9); the beating of one's breast is a typical gesture of mourning for women.

λύθεν = ἐλύθησαν; while λύω is usually used transitively, i.e. to let something go, to release something, it is here used intransitively in the sense 'to buckle'. This is the usual meaning of the verb when found with γυῖα.

ὑπό – adv. 'beneath them, underneath'.

32–5

Ἀντίλοχος δ᾽... ᾤμωξεν – the changes of subject in these four lines are harsh: first Antilochus, then Achilles, then back to Antilochus and finally back to Achilles. The rapid changes of subject may serve to indicate the severity and uncontrollability of Achilles' grief, as well as the concurrency of both men's actions.

34

Antilochus is the subject of δείδιε, while Achilles is the subject of ἀποτμήξειε: 'He (Antilochus) was afraid that he (Achilles) would slash his (Achilles') throat with a knife.'

δείδιε – third person singular pluperfect indicative active of δείδω; the perfect of this verb is often used with present meaning, so the pluperfect can stand for the imperfect, i.e. 'he was afraid'.

γάρ – explains why Antilochus was holding Achilles' hands (χεῖρας ἔχων Ἀχιλῆος) not why Achilles groaned (ὃ δ᾽ ἔστενε κυδάλιμον κῆρ).

σιδήρῳ – probably a 'knife', though σίδηρος can actually denote any tool made of iron. Elsewhere in the poem (4.485), it means 'axe', although chopping one's own head off with an axe is probably beyond even Achilles' remarkable capabilities.

35

σμερδαλέον – adv. 'terribly'.

ᾤμωξεν – subject: Achilles.

36

πατρὶ γέροντι – i.e. Nereus, the Old Man of the Sea.

37

κώκυσέν – it's important to note that Thetis 'shrieks' because she has heard the cries of her son; she has no idea that Patroclus is dead.

ἔπειτα – adv. 'in turn'.

μιν – in Homer, μιν can refer to 'him', 'her' or 'it'; here, it refers to Thetis, so 'her'.

38

Νηρηΐδες – 'Nereids', i.e. the daughters of Nereus, of whom Thetis is one.

Lines 39–49 comprise a long list of the names of the Nereids.

50–64

Thetis hears the cries of her son and speaks of her concerns to her fellow Nereids. At times, she speaks as if Achilles has actually died, reflecting on his youth and upbringing, as well as the fact that she will never welcome him home. By the end of the speech, however, she has turned her attention to Achilles' present suffering and decides to see what the problem is.

50

τῶν … πλῆτο – taken with the genitive, πίμπλημι means 'to fill with', hence: 'was filled with them', where τῶν refers to the Nereids.

καί – καί connects πλῆτο with ἀμφαγέροντο (37); the sentence was interrupted by the list of Nereids, but it is still the same sentence: 'The goddesses gathered round her … and the shining white cave was filled with them'.

51

στήθεα πεπλήγοντο – the Nereids engage in the same symbol of mourning as the δμωαὶ at 31. While the δμωαὶ mourn for Patroclus, however, the Nereids' mourning – like many other details in this scene – evokes the funeral of Achilles.

52

ὄφρ᾽ … εἴδετ᾽ – 'in order that you may know'; ὄφρα of purpose, with the subjunctive εἴδετε; note that εἴδετε is part of οἶδα, not ὁράω.

ἔνι = ἔνεστι; the position of the accent provides an important clue when distinguishing between ἐνί = ἐν and ἔνι = ἔνεστι.

53

εἴδετ᾽ – Attic: εἰδῆτε.

55

ἐπεὶ ἄρ … ἡρώων – the main clause to which ἐπεὶ ought to be subordinated never actually appears; Thetis' sentence trails off as she begins thinking about her son.

56

ἀνέδραμεν – 'he shot up'.

57

φυτὸν ὡς γουνῷ ἀλωῆς – 'like a tree on the slope of an orchard'; this phrase seems to have been proverbial, appearing several other times in the *Iliad*. Modern scholars are still unsure what it actually means. ὡς bears an accent because it refers backwards to φυτὸν.

58

ἐπιπροέηκα – the ἐπι- preposition must mean 'against [the enemy]' rather than 'to [the ships]'.

εἴσω – εἴσω is an adverb, but with the accusative Ἴλιον it has the same effect as if it were the preposition εἰς.

59–60

τὸν δ' οὐχ ... εἴσω – lamenting the lack of homecoming for someone who has died – particularly by or on behalf of one's parents – was a common trope in ancient epic. In this case, there is a slight unease about Thetis' lament that she will never welcome Achilles back to Peleus' house given that she apparently no longer lives there. In any case, Thetis' lament for her son's death is actually premature: it is only with his speech at 98–126 that Achilles announces his decision to return to battle and die in the fighting.

61

ὄφρα – 'while, so long as'.

μοι – 'for me', dative of interest.

ζώει καὶ ὁρᾷ φάος ἠελίοιο – this phrase is only ever used of Achilles.

62

τί οἱ ... χραισμῆσαι – the verb χραισμέω means to be useful to someone (dat.) in something (acc.), hence: 'I am not able to be useful to him (οἱ) in anything at all (τί)'.

64

ὅττί = ὅπερ.

ἀπὸ πτολέμοιο μένοντα – 'having withdrawn from the fighting'; Achilles withdrew from the fighting at the very beginning of the *Iliad* after a quarrel with Agamemnon, the commander-in-chief of the Greek forces.

The participle may have a concessive force, i.e. '*even though* he has withdrawn from the fighting'; what can Achilles possibly have suffered away from the battlefield?

65–77

Thetis makes her way to the Greek camp, accompanied by the Nereids. She asks Achilles why he is weeping, given that the wish he made in Book 1 – the disorderly retreat of the Greek forces – has been accomplished. Just as Thetis began her speech (50–64) by acting as if Achilles had actually died, much of the scene that follows looks like a rehearsal for Achilles' funeral. Achilles himself lies on the ground, his face covered in ash and dust, while Thetis kneels down beside him and cradles his head – a typical gesture for a mourning wife or mother when presented with the corpse of their husband or son. In the background, the Nereids join in the lament, evoking the other womenfolk who would have been in attendance at a Greek funeral.

66

περὶ – adv. 'all around'.

σφισι – 'for them', dative of advantage.

67

ῥήγνυτο – 'divided'; elsewhere in the *Iliad*, the verb used to describe the parting of the sea is λιάζομαι ('to part') or ἀναδύομαι ('to shrink back'); the more violent ῥήγνυμι ('to break open, shatter') gives a sense of Thetis' urgency in getting to Achilles, or perhaps the sheer number of people coming to visit him.

ταὶ – 'they'.

68

ἐπισχερώ – 'in a row'; ἐπισχερώ may refer to the way in which the Nereids land on the beach or the arrangement of the Myrmidons' ships.

ἀλήμεναι – 'to be penned in', from εἴλω.

69

εἴρυντο – pluperfect, 'had been drawn up', i.e. onto the beach. Throughout classical antiquity, it was customary to drag ships onto dry land if they were not going to be used for long periods. This was to prevent the wood from rotting, which could happen if left in the water for too long.

The verb ἐρύω is used to describe the 'dragging' of ships from the water onto dry land, as well as 'dragging' them back into the water again.

70

βαρὺ – adv. 'heavily', 'deeply'.

71

κάρη λάβε – holding the head in the hands was the standard gesture of the chief mourner at a Greek funeral, as we see later in the poem when Achilles holds Patroclus' head (23.136) and Andromache Hector's (24.724). The gesture is also depicted on several Greek vases.

ἑοῖο – 'of her'.

73

σε φρένας ἵκετο – σε and φρένας are both objects of ἵκετο; lit. 'what sorrow comes to you and your heart?', i.e. 'what sorrow comes to your heart?'.

74

τὰ – 'these things', demonstrative pronoun.

τοι = σοι, 'for you', dative of advantage.

75

ἐκ Διός – the position of ἐκ Διός, separated from the rest of the sentence by enjambment, suggests how proud Thetis is of her achievement: 'These things have all been accomplished for you – and by Zeus, no less!'.

Her misjudgement of the situation – the fact that Achilles is devastated, not delighted that everything has come to pass as he has originally requested – is explicable only because she doesn't yet know what has happened to Patroclus.

Achilles ironically repeats Thetis' proud claim at 79.

πρίν – adv. 'previously'.

76

ἀλήμεναι = ἀλῆναι, from εἴλω; this verb has a range of meanings, though here it means 'to crowd together, hem in'.

υἶας Ἀχαιῶν – 'sons of the Achaeans', a standard collocation for 'Achaeans'.

77

σεῦ ἐπιδευομένους – lit. 'with you being wanted'. i.e. 'with your absence being felt [sc. by the Achaeans]'.

This genitive absolute explains the reason for Achilles absenting himself from the fighting: the worse the Greeks performed in his absence from the battle, the more his absence would be felt.

78–93

Achilles tells his mother that Patroclus has been killed in the fighting and vows to take revenge on Hector. The structure of Achilles' first (79–93) and second (97–126) speeches are remarkably similar. Both begin with a statement of grief and Hector's involvement in it (79–84 = 98–103) followed by an impossible wish (84–7 = 104–13) and a return to the present situation with νῦν δέ (88 = 114). Achilles affirms his desire to take revenge on Hector, even if it has a bearing on how long he himself has to live (88–93 = 114–26).

80

ἀλλὰ τί μοι τῶν ἦδος – 'what pleasure in these things is there for me?' Verbs and nouns of desire generally take the genitive case, hence τῶν ἦδος ('pleasure in these things').

τῶν = ταύτων.

81

Πάτροκλος – Achilles places his friend's name in the emphatic runover position. He will go on to place emphatic words at the beginning of lines 83, 89–91 and 93 (δηώσας, παιδός, οἴκαδε, ζώειν, Πατρόκλοιο) to create one of the heaviest-hitting speeches in the whole poem.

περί – 'beyond', 'over and above' (+ gen.).

82

ἶσον ἐμῇ κεφαλῇ – 'equally with my own life'; ἶσον is an adverb; κεφαλή is often used in the broader sense of 'life' or 'self'.

In fact, Achilles values Patroclus *more* than his own life, as his next speech makes clear.

τὸν ἀπώλεσα – the verb ἀπόλλυμι can mean either 'to lose' or 'to destroy', so τὸν ἀπώλεσα can either mean 'I have lost him' or 'I have destroyed him'. Both are equally plausible, and the ambiguity here may be intentional.

Achilles' words are given added emphasis by their position between the main caesura and the so-called bucolic diaeresis, i.e. a word break between the fourth and fifth feet.

83

Θαῦμα ἰδέσθαι – 'a wonder to behold'; ἰδέσθαι is an epexegetic infinitive, an infinitive that clarifies, explains or qualifies a noun or adjective.

85

ἤματι τῷ ... εὐνῇ – the marriage of Peleus and Thetis is one of the central myths in the background of the Trojan War. The most common version stated that Zeus wanted to father a child with Thetis, but learnt that Thetis was destined to bear a son that was greater than his father. Not wanting to give birth to a child that was greater than himself, Zeus forced Thetis to marry the mortal Peleus, which resulted in the birth of Achilles (who was indeed much greater than his father).

The marriage appears not to have been a happy one: by the time of the events of the *Iliad*, it appears that Thetis lives in the sea with her father and sisters, while Peleus lives back in Phthia in Thessaly.

ἔμβαλον – ἐμβάλλω is a verb with a range of meanings; here, it means 'to bring'.

σε – i.e. Thetis.

86

αἴθ᾽ ὄφελες – 'would that you had ...', governs the infinitive.

ἁλίῃσι – substantive use of ἅλιος, 'goddess of the sea'. Interestingly, while Achilles wishes that his father had married a mortal woman instead of a goddess, his wish for his mother is for her to have never been married at all.

87

ἀγαγέσθαι – ἄγω ('to lead, bring') here has the sense of 'to lead to one's home', i.e. 'take as one's wife', 'marry'.

88

νῦν δ᾽ – 'but now', 'as it is', etc. The combination of an imagined situation followed by what has actually happened is highly characteristic of Achilles' thought and language.

This line is highly elliptical, and we must supply several thoughts to complete the sense, including a main clause to govern the result clause. The sense as a whole must be something like this: 'But as it is (νῦν δ᾽) [you married Peleus], so that for you too (ἵνα καὶ σοί) [as well as for me] there should be grief (πένθος ... εἴη) [but in your case it will be] without measure (μυρίον).'

89

παιδὸς ἀποφθιμένοιο – 'for a son who has died'; governed by πένθος ('grief') on the previous line.

89–90

τὸν οὐχ ... νοστήσαντ᾽ – Achilles repeats the words that Thetis had used at 59–60.

90

ἄνωγε – 'commands, bids'; the verb ἄνωγα is perfect in form but present in meaning.

91

οὐδ᾽ ἐμὲ ... μετέμμεναι – οὐδ᾽ ἐμὲ may be read as 'not me either', i.e. 'my heart bids that [because Patroclus has been killed] I should not live either'.

A more straightforward reading would take οὐδε with ζώειν οὐδ᾽ ἀνδρεσσι μετέμμεναι (92): 'My heart bids that I should neither live nor be among men' μετέμμεναι = μετεῖναι.

91

αἴ κε = ἐάν.

92

ὑπὸ ... τυπεὶς, ἀπὸ ... ὀλέσσῃ – two instances of tmesis.

93

ἕλωρα – ἕλωρ means 'prey' for wild beasts or birds; the word ἕλωρα, found only here in the *Iliad*, is abstract, meaning something like 'the compensation due for preying upon someone/something', 'blood-price' is a good translation.

94–6

Thetis replies that if Achilles kills Hector, his own death will follow shortly thereafter. Thetis' speech is remarkably brief given that she is telling her son that he will die young. One scholar implies its brevity is based on its prophetic nature, which were always short so as not to reveal too much detail as to what would happen in the future. Another suggests that Achilles has interrupted his mother before she can finish what she is saying.

The nature of Achilles' fate becomes increasingly clear throughout the poem. In Book 1, we are only told Achilles will have a short life (1.352, 416, 505), while in Book 9, Achilles himself says that he has a choice of two fates (9.411). Now we learn that Achilles will die shortly after Hector. In the books that follow, it is further revealed that Achilles will be killed 'by a god and a man' (19.417), 'under the armed Trojans' wall, by ... Apollo' (21.275), and finally by 'Paris and Apollo ... at the Scaean gate' (22.359).

95

ὠκύμορος – lit. 'swift-fated', i.e. 'doomed to a short life'; the word is only ever used of Achilles in the *Iliad*.

ἔσσεαι = ἔσει (or ἔσῃ); the future tense is important, since it shows that this is the apodosis of a conditional statement (i.e. 'you *will be* doomed to a short life [sc. if you do X]', rather than the statement of a fact.

οἷ᾽ ἀγορεύεις – 'from what you say'. Achilles has said that he will kill Hector (92). This is the condition under which Achilles will be ὠκύμορος.

96

ἔπειτα – 'in that case', i.e. in the case that you kill Hector, not simply 'afterwards', further emphasizing that Achilles' short life is conditional on him killing Hector.

ἑτοῖμος – lit. 'ready', i.e. 'certain to be fulfilled'.

97–126

Achilles replies that he has made up his mind – he will return to battle to avenge the death of Patroclus, even if it means dying himself. In a highly imaginative speech, Achilles offers his thoughts on the nature of both ἔρις ('rivalry') and χόλος ('anger'), before affirming his desire to take revenge on Hector.

98

αὐτίκα – Achilles repeats the word used by Thetis at 96. We may read this as a sign that Achilles' choice has been made, i.e. Thetis: 'If you do as you say, you will die immediately (αὐτίκα) after Hector' (95–6); Achilles: 'Well may I die immediately (αὐτίκα), then!' (98).

It is characteristic of a Homeric hero to choose a short life and glorious death over an inglorious life and death in old age.

οὐκ ἄρ᾽ ἔμελλον – 'it turns out I was not to …', an idiomatic Greek phrase.

99

κτεινομένῳ – a powerful line-beginning.

100

ἔφθιτ᾽ – φθίω tends to suggest a slow decline, rather than being killed in battle. Here, the word is used in a more general sense: 'he died'.

δῆσεν – a doubtful form for ἐδέησεν, 'he needed'; the aorist of δέω is usually ἐδεύσεν; governs the genitive.

ἄρεω ἀλκτῆρα – 'defender against harm'; ἀλκτῆρα refers to ἐμεῖο, but is accusative as the predicate of γενέσθαι.

101

νῦν δ᾽ – a lengthy digression follows this line as Achilles' thoughts turn from his own death to his failure to save Patroclus and the other Greeks (102–6), his thoughts on the nature of ἔρις (107–10) and his renunciation of his quarrel with Agamemnon (111–13). The initial thought is only resumed at 114 with the repetition of νῦν δέ.

For Achilles' use of the phrase νῦν δέ, see 88.

νέομαί – future in sense, i.e. 'I will [not] come'.

102

φάος – lit. 'light', here in the sense of 'saving light'.

103

οἳ δὴ πολέες = 'many of whom'.

δάμεν = ἐδάμησαν, aorist passive.

104

ἄχθος ἀρούρης = 'burden to the earth'.

105

An ancient commentator on this line wrote that Achilles' remarks here are 'boastful and vulgar' (ἀλαζών ... καὶ φορτικός), although he is certainly not alone among the heroes of the *Iliad* to engage in self-praise of this kind.

106

δέ – 'although'.

καὶ ἄλλοι – not simply 'other Greeks', but 'others than those who excel in battle'.

107

ὡς – introducing a wish. This is Achilles' second impossible wish in twenty lines, cf. 86–7.

108

ἐφέηκε – 'causes'; ἐφέηκε is a 'gnomic' aorist (one that describes a general truth) and should be translated using the present tense. The verb governs the infinitive.

ὅς τ' ... ὅς τε – both refer to χόλος.

109

γλυκίων μέλιτος – it is usually words of peace and reconciliation that are 'sweeter than honey', not anger, which gives the comparison special emphasis here. Achilles' admission that anger has an element of pleasure finds support in both ancient writers (e.g. Arist. *Rhet.* 2.2) and modern evolutionary psychology.

καταλειβομένοιο – the image seems to be that of honey 'trickling' down a tree trunk, as happens when wild bees construct their hives in the hollows of dead trees.

110

ἀέξεται – 'mounts up', 'spreads out'.

ἠΰτε καπνός – if the image of 'tricking honey' in the previous line does evoke wild
  bees, the 'smoke' mentioned here might evoke the practice of 'smoking out' bees
  in order to get to their honey.

111
ὡς – 'just as'; Achilles now moves from his general thoughts about χόλος to a
  specific instance of it – his own anger at Agamemnon.

112
ἐάσομεν – Achilles here speaks both for himself and Agamemnon.
προτετύχθαι – 'to be over and done with'.

113
θυμὸν – 'anger'.

114–26
Achilles' speech demonstrates the ring composition that is relatively common in
'set-piece' speeches:

  A I will kill Hector (114–15)
  B and accept death whenever Zeus wills it (115–16)
  C for even Heracles died (117–19)
  B' so I shall die as well (120–1)
  A' but now I shall win great glory (121–5)

114
νῦν δ' – for Achilles' use of this phrase, see 88.
φίλης κεφαλῆς – Achilles' language is ambiguous; his words could refer equally
  to Patroclus ('a life that was dear to me') or to himself ('my own life'). The
  ambiguity may be deliberate, of course. For κεφαλή = 'life', see 82.

117
οὐδὲ γὰρ οὐδὲ – the first οὐδὲ belongs to the whole sentence, connecting it with
  what precedes, while the second belongs to βίη Ἡρακλῆος, hence: 'for neither
  did even'.

βίη Ἡρακλῆος – 'the might of Heracles', periphrasis for 'Heracles'.
The choice of Heracles here is important: in most versions of the myth, Heracles was
granted immortality at the end of his mortal life. If Achilles lives in a world where
'even Heracles died', there really isn't any hope for him.

119
ἀργαλέος χόλος Ἥρης – Hera's 'baneful anger' stems from the fact that Heracles
  was the product of an extramarital relationship between her husband, Zeus, and
  the mortal Alcmene. The χόλος of Hera echoes the χόλος that Achilles spoke
  about at 108–10.

120

ὁμοίη μοῖρα – 'the same fate', i.e. the same as Heracles.

τέτυκται – in the passive voice, the verb τεύχω is used synonymously with εἶναι or γενέσθαι, i.e. 'to be, become, take place'.

121–4

Achilles' long and vivid description of a woman weeping and tearing her cheeks is perhaps a little insensitive given the impact that his own (now inevitable) death will have on his mother, to whom he is speaking.

121

νῦν δ᾽ – Achilles once again returns to the situation at hand with the use of νῦν δε.

κλέος ἐσθλὸν – the acquisition of 'glory' (κλέος) is the raison d'être of the Homeric hero, a set of attitudes referred to by some scholars as the 'heroic code'. Its fullest expression is by Sarpedon in Book 12 (310–28).

ἀροίμην – 'let me win'; a wish, as are the optatives in 124 and 125.

122

βαθυκόλπων – 'deep-breasted', referring either to the deep folds of women's robes or to their cleavage.

124

ἀδινὸν – ἀδινός means 'thick, esp. of things densely crowded and in motion'; the adverb has a broad range of meanings, but here adds emphasis to the verb στοναχῆσαι, i.e. 'to groan *deeply*'.

ἐφείην – for ἐφίημι meaning 'to cause', see 108.

125

γνοῖεν – a wish like the preceding optatives, although its expression of the result of the first wish almost makes it a result clause, i.e. 'may I win good glory ... *so that* they may know ...'.

δηρὸν – while it has been at least two weeks since Achilles withdrew from battle, fighting between the Greeks and Trojans has been ongoing for only three days in that time.

126

οὐδέ με πείσεις – note how the stark three-word summary of Achilles' position contrasts with the longer sentences in most of the rest of his speech.

127–37

Thetis accepts Achilles' decision, but reminds him that he does not have a suit of armour to wear, since Patroclus was wearing his when he was sent out to battle. She vows to go to the blacksmith god, Hephaistos, in order to procure him a new set.

128

ναὶ δὴ ... ἐστι – Thetis' reaction to what Achilles has just said might strike some
readers as being unrealistic: why does she make no effort to dissuade her son
from re-entering the fighting, when doing so means certain death? Indeed, why
does she positively *encourage* his return to the fighting by arranging for a new
suit of armour to be made?

ναὶ δη ταῦτά γε – ταῦτά is used as an exclamation without any strict construction;
here, it is strengthened by ναὶ δὴ, so that the whole phrase means something like
'yes, as you say ...'.

ἐτήτυμον – adv. 'truly', 'indeed', etc.

130

ἔχονται – ἔχονται is passive, with ἔντεα as the subject. While neuter plural nouns
are usually found with a singular verb, a plural may be used when the noun
denotes several distinct objects, as here. In this case, ἔντεα denotes a shield,
breast-plate, helmet and greaves: 'set of armour' might be an appropriate
translation.

μετὰ Τρώεσσιν – 'by the Trojans'; ὑπὸ Τρώων would be the more usual way of
expressing this in Attic prose.

132

ἔχων – 'possessing it', i.e. Achilles' suit of armour.

133

ἐπαγλαΐεῖσθαι – the verb ἐπαγλαΐζομαι ('to pride oneself on a thing') is mostly
found in Greek comedy; Thetis' use of it here suggests a level of contempt for
Hector's undignified behaviour.

134

μή ... καταδύσεο – μή + aorist imperative is relatively rare in Greek literature; the
usual construction for a negative command is μή + subjunctive.

μῶλος Ἄρηος – 'the toil of war'.

135

πρίν ... ἴδηαι – the use of the subjunctive after πρίν instead of the more usual
infinitive emphasizes the certainty of the result.

Homeric Greek omits the ἄν (= κε in Homeric Greek) that we would expect to find
in Attic Greek with πρίν followed by the subjunctive.

ἐν ὀφθαλμοῖσιν – 'before your eyes'.

136

ἠῶθεν – since it is already late in the day, Hephaestus is evidently required to work
on Achilles' new set of armour overnight.

νεῦμαι = νέομαί; future in sense, as at 101.

ἅμ᾽ ἠελίῳ ἀνιόντι – 'with the rising sun'.

137

παρ᾽ Ἡφαίστοιο ἄνακτος – lit. 'from lord Hephaestus', i.e. made by him.

138

πάλιν – here: 'away from' (+ gen.).

141

ὀψόμεναί – the future participle can express purpose without the addition of ὡς (which is regularly found in prose).

143

αἴ κ᾽ ἐθέλῃσιν – 'to see if he would be willing'.

147

ἐνεῖκαι – aorist optative from φέρω.

148–201

Meanwhile the struggle for Patroclus' corpse continues, with Hector fighting furiously against the two Aiantes. Hera sends Iris to rouse Achilles, who will show himself to the Trojans bathed in divine fire.

148–50

Changes of scene in Homer are usually facilitated by the movement or observation of a character. Here, the change is unusually abrupt, coming half-way through the line with the words αὐτὰρ Ἀχαιοί.

150

φεύγοντες – 'driven in flight'.

Ἑλλήσποντον – the Hellespont was the narrow strait of water that linked the Aegean to the Propontis, now known as the Dardanelles.

ἵκοντο – an example of the 'conative' imperfect, implying a *desire* or an *attempt* to do something, i.e. 'The Achaeans were *attempting* to reach …'.

151

οὐδέ κε … ἐρύσαντο – the κε shows that this clause is the apodosis in a conditional; the protasis only appears fifteen lines later with εἰ μὴ … Ἶρις. The sense in full is: 'Nor would the Achaeans have dragged Patroclus' body from the fighting … if Iris had not …'.

περ – the use of περ implies that while the Achaeans could have made it back to the ships, they could not do so while still recovering the corpse of Patroclus.

152

ἐκ βελέων – 'out of range'.

153

τόν – i.e. the corpse of Patroclus.

154

ἀλκήν – accusative of respect; lit. 'like fire' *with respect to his strength*, i.e. 'like fire
   in his strength'.

155

τρὶς μέν ... τρὶς δὲ – this 'three times ...' motif occurs several times in the *Iliad*,
   occasionally with a decisive 'but the fourth time ...'. In this case, the motif
   emphasizes how finely balanced the struggle is between Hector and the Aiantes.
ποδῶν – verbs of touching or holding take the (partitive) genitive.

157

δύ' Αἴαντες – the two 'Aiantes' are Ajax, son of Telamon, and Ajax, son of Oileus;
   when we last saw Patroclus' corpse in Book 17, Menelaus and Meriones were
   carrying the corpse from the battlefield, while the two Aiantes attempted to keep
   the Trojan forces at a distance.
θοῦριν ἐπιειμένοι ἀλκὴν – 'clothed in furious strength'.

158

ὁ δ' – the focus returns to Hector.
πεποιθὼς – the perfect and pluperfect of πείθω can be used to mean 'to put trust
   in', 'depend upon' (+ dat.).

159

ἐπαΐξασκε – forms in -σκον, created from either the present or aorist of a verb,
   are common in Homer as frequentatives, denoting an action that takes place
   repeatedly. ἐπαΐξασκε is a frequentative, as is στάσκε in the following line;
   both emphasize the ceaseless energy of Hector's attack.

160

μέγα ἰάχων – Homer often uses a short form a motif to anticipate an expanded
   form later in the poem. In this case, Hector's war cry anticipates that of Achilles
   at 217.
οὐ ... πάμπαν – 'by no means'.

161–2

One purpose for which the poet uses similes is to describe the 'ordinary' world
   which goes on away from the battlefield where the poem is set.

163

δύω Αἴαντε κορυστὰ – 'the two Aiantes, fully armed'; dual.

167

θωρήσσεσθαι – 'prepare for battle', rather than 'arm oneself'; the word limits the
   sense of ἄγγελος ἦλθε, lit. 'she came as a messenger in order that he should
   prepare for battle', i.e. 'she came to tell him to prepare for battle'.

168

κρύβδα – the gods in the *Iliad* often do things behind each other's backs, both to advance their own schemes and to frustrate those of others. The adverb takes the genitive to describe from whom the secret is being kept.

πρὸ … ἧκέ – tmesis.

169

ἀγχοῦ = ἄγχι.

170

ὄρσεο – 'up now!' Achilles is still lying on his back, as he was when he first heard the news that Patroclus had died. Judging by its other uses in the poem, ὄρσεο appears to have been scornful in tone.

171

οὗ εἵνεκα – 'for whose sake', i.e. Patroclus'; the word ἕνεκα/εἵνεκα is regularly found following the word it governs (postposition).

172–5

οἳ μὲν … οἳ δὲ – the construction here is slightly confusing, since the verb in the οἳ μὲν is a participle (ἀμυνόμενοι), while that in the οἳ δὲ clause is a finite verb (ἐπιθύουσι). The sentence should be translated as if *both* clauses had the same construction, i.e. 'some are defending the body, others are trying to drag it back to the city'.

177

πῆξαι ἀνὰ σκολόπεσσι – 'to impale on a stake'; it is highly unusual for a hero to decapitate a corpse *post mortem*: it happens only once in the whole poem (13.202), although a handful of others claim they are planning on doing so, including both Achilles and Hector.

An ancient commentator on this line claimed that Iris was not telling the truth in order to better rouse Achilles to action. This does not square with the description of Hector at 17.126–7 'pulling [Patroclus' body] away, to cut the head from his shoulders … and drag off the body to give it to the dogs of Troy'.

178

ἄνα = ἀνάστηθι, i.e. 'get up!'.

σέβας δέ σε θυμὸν ἱκέσθω – 'let shame come over your heart'; the word σέβας occurs only here in the *Iliad*.

179

Τρωῇσι κυσὶν μέλπηθρα – 'a plaything for Trojan dogs'; we have already had Iris refer to one form of mutilation in Hector's supposed desire to impale Patroclus' severed head on a spike. Here, we return to a far commoner threat: that of non-burial, such that the body becomes prey for wild dogs and birds. The additional detail that Patroclus will be eaten by *Trojan* dogs is perhaps designed to add insult to injury.

180

σοὶ λώβη – 'shame on you!'.

αἴ κέν ... νέκυς ... ἔλθῃ – a relatively ambiguous phrase, which might mean 'if the body is brought back', 'if the body goes [away]' or 'if he goes to [join] the dead'. In the last case, νέκυς must be taken as accusative plural, rather than nominative singular.

τι ... ᾐσχυμμένος – this refers to the atrocities mentioned at 177 (decapitation) and 179 (body eaten by dogs).

188

ἴω – deliberative subjunctive.

ἐκεῖνοι – i.e. the Trojans; the word ἐκεῖνος suggests dislike.

189

οὐ ... εἴα – 'forbade'.

191

στεῦτο – always used in the sense of 'to declare', either as a boast or a promise, as here.

πάρ' – the position of the accent shows that this is a postposition, governing the word that comes immediately before it (Ἡφαίστοιο).

192

The meaning of this line is relatively clear ('I don't know anyone whose armour I can use'), although the grammar can be a little confusing. Here, τευ = τινός (indefinite) while τεῦ = τίνος (interrogative). We might have expected a relative pronoun (τοῦ or ὅτευ, 'whose') instead of the interrogative, but there are parallels of this admittedly unusual construction in Attic prose (e.g. Xen. *Anab.* 2.1.15, where the interrogative τίς must mean 'of the man who'). The genitive ἄλλου τευ has been attracted from its natural accusative case (as direct object of οἶδα) into the case of the interrogative pronoun (τεῦ).

The ancient commentators on this line make a number of *practical* suggestions as to why Achilles could not simply wear Patroclus' armour (which he must have left behind when he went into battle), although none suggest the obvious *poetic* motive of wanting a grand arming scene before Achilles' final showdown with Hector.

193

Αἴαντός ... σάκος – The shield of Ajax, son of Telamon, was famously large and formidable.

194

ἔλπομ' – 'I suppose', parenthetical.

197

ὅ = ὅτι.

198

αὐτός – 'yourself', 'as you are', i.e. without armour.

ἐπὶ τάφρον – the Greek camp is protected by a rampart and a ditch. While Iris tells Achilles to go ἐπὶ τάφρον, she must mean for him to stand at the top of the rampart 'above the ditch'.

199

αἴ κε = Attic ἐάν, which here has the sense of 'in the hope that'.

202–38

Achilles' appearance enveloped in fire and smoke is enough to scatter the Trojans and allow the recovery of Patroclus' body.

203

αὐτὰρ Ἀχιλλεὺς ὦρτο Διΐ φίλος – Achilles has evidently been lying down since 26. His actions here symbolize the end of his withdrawal from battle, which he had affirmed in his speech at 98–126.

204

ὤμοις – of Achilles.

αἰγίδα – the 'aegis' appears to have been some kind of tasselled shield or cloak that was brandished by the gods in order to strike fear in one's enemies.

206

ἐκ δ᾽ αὐτοῦ – i.e. from the cloud. The flame comes out of the cloud, just as the fire comes out of the smoke in the following simile.

207–14

A simile compares the divine fire that now surrounds Achilles' head to signal beacons from a besieged city. The simile has several points of contact to the narrative: the besieged city suggests Troy and those attacking it, the Greeks, while the signal beacons may represent the razing of Troy once the Greeks have entered the city. Note also that the fighting has gone on 'all day' (πανημέριοι), just as it has done between the Greeks and the Trojans.

207

ἰών – 'rising', rather than simply 'going'.

208

τηλόθεν – a potentially confusing detail; the island on which the city is located is 'far away' only *from the point of view of the poet*. We are to imagine viewing this conflict from some distant point.

ἐκ νήσου – stands in apposition to ἐξ ἄστεος in the previous line, clarifying where the city is located, i.e. 'as when smoke rises from a city, from an island which is far away …'.

One ancient commentator suggested that the mention of an island increases the besieged city's sense of isolation, while their reliance on signal-fires (as opposed to messengers on foot) reflects the Greeks' own reliance on Achilles.

τὴν – relative pronoun; based on its gender, this must refer to the island (νήσου) rather than the city (ἄστεος), though ἀμφιμάχωνται must refer to the enemies surrounding the *city* rather than the island.

209

οἱ δέ – 'the townspeople'.

στυγερῷ κρίνονται Ἄρηϊ – lit. 'they contest [with one another] in hateful war', i.e. 'they fight'. Here, as earlier (134), Ἄρης = 'war, slaughter', not 'Ares'.

ἄστεος ἐκ σφετέρου – i.e. from their walls and towers.

210

ἅμα δ' ἠελίῳ καταδύντι – 'at the setting of the sun'.

211

πυρσοί – 'beacon-fires'; the word occurs only here in Homer.

212

περικτιόνεσσιν ἰδέσθαι – 'for their neighbours to see'.

213

αἴ κέν πως – 'in the hope that …'.

214

ὣς – when ὡς is accented it may (as here) stand for οὕτως, or be a postpositive (cf. φυτὸν ὣς at 57).

215

ἐπὶ τάφρον … ἀπὸ τείχεος – the ditch surrounding the Greek camp has been dug 'at a distance from the wall' (ἀπὸ τείχεος).

216

πυκινὴν – here = 'wise' or 'sagacious'; Thetis had told Achilles not to re-join the fighting until she returned with his new set of armour.

219

ὅτ' … ὅτε – the first ὅτε introduces the general idea ('Achilles cries as when a clear voice [is heard]'), the second adds a specific example ('when a war-trumpet calls').

σάλπιγξ – depending on one's reading of the following line, this 'war-trumpet' may belong either to the defenders of a city or to its attackers.

220

ἄστυ περιπλομένων … θυμοραϊστέων – there is some debate as to the exact meaning of this line. It is possible to see ἄστυ περιπλομένων as being attached to δηΐων ('enemies who are surrounding a city'). Alternatively, ἄστυ περιπλομένων may be taken as going with σάλπιγξ ('the war-trumpet of those surrounding a city'), in which case δηΐων ὕπο θυμοραϊστέων would be taken as an independent phrase. In either case, the expression is unusual, even for a simile.

ὕπο – 'by reason of'.

221

Αἰακίδαο – i.e. Achilles, who is not Aeacus' son, but his grandson.

222

ὄπα χάλκεον – the description of Achilles' voice as 'brazen' may strike readers as unusual. In fact, the word is a surprisingly versatile descriptor in the Homeric poems, being applied elsewhere to the hearts of fighting men, the sleep of a dead warrior and the sky. In this case, the poet may still be thinking of the σάλπιγξ mentioned in 219, which was presumably made of bronze.

Since ὄπα is feminine, the poet must be treating the adjective χάλκεος as if it were of two terminations.

224

ὄσσοντο – i.e. the horses.

225

ἔκπληγεν = ἐξεπλήγησαν.

226

δεινὸν – adv. 'terribly'.

228

τρὶς μὲν ... τρὶς δὲ – for this construction, see note on 155.

231

ἀμφὶ σφοῖς ὀχέεσσι καὶ ἔγχεσιν – scholars have been perturbed by the apparent vagueness of this phrase, which seems to ask a lot of the preposition ἀμφὶ. The general sense is that a disorganized retreat, in which several Trojans are trampled by their own horses, run over by their own chariots or fall on their own weapons.

233

κάτθεσαν = κατέθεσαν.

236

φέρτρῳ – the word φέρτρον appears only here in Homer.

237

ἤτοι – the use of the particle ἤτοι betrays a level of emotion – perhaps Achilles' own? – in the poet's description of Patroclus' death. The particle may be left untranslated.

σὺν ἵπποισιν καὶ ὄχεσφιν – there was no mention of 'horses and chariots' when Achilles sent Patroclus out to fight in Book 16; he had entered the battle on foot.

238

οὐδ᾽ αὖτις … νοστήσαντα – the framing of the death of a hero in terms of them not returning home again is common in the poem. Thetis herself had reflected on Achilles' lack of homecoming in almost exactly the same terms at 59–60.

Vocabulary
Iliad 18

An asterisk * denotes a word in OCR's Defined Vocabulary List for AS.

ἀγάλλω	to glorify, exalt	ἀθάνατος -ον	immortal
Ἀγαμέμνων -ονος, m.	Agamemnon	Ἀθήνη -ης, f.	Athena
		αἴ	= εἰ
ἀγάννιφος -ον	snow-capped	Αἰακίδης -ου, m.	descendent of Aeacus, i.e. Achilles
ἀγαυός -ή -όν	wondrous, illustrious, noble		
ἀγγελίη -ης, f.	message, report	Αἴας -αντος, m.	Ajax; there are two Greek heroes with this name in the *Iliad*: (1) Ajax, son of Telamon ('Greater Ajax'), and (2) Ajax, son of Oileus ('Lesser Ajax'). The plural, Αἴαντες, is used to describe both Ajaxes operating in unison.
*ἄγγελος -ου, m.	messenger		
ἀγλαός -ή -όν	splendid, shining, bright		
ἀγορεύω	to speak, say		
ἀγορή -ῆς, f.	assembly		
ἄγραυλος -ον	dwelling in the field, epithet of shepherds		
ἀγχοῦ, adv.	near, nearby	αἰγίς -ίδος, f.	the aegis
*ἄγω	to bring, lead; (middle) to take as a wife	αἰθαλόεις -όεσσα -όεν	smoky, sooty
ἀδινός -ή -όν	close, thick, esp. of things densely crowded and in motion	αἴθε	(introduces a wish) 'would that...!'
		αἰθήρ -έρος, f.	the upper air, sky
ἀείρομαι	= αἴρομαι	αἴθω	to burn
ἀεκήλιος -ον	unwished for, unwelcome, woeful	αἴθων	shining; (of animals) tawny
		αἰνός -ή -όν	dreadful, horrible, terrible
ἀέξω	to grow, increase	αἰπύς -εῖα -ύ	steep, sheer
ἀθάνατοι -ων, m. pl.	the immortals, i.e. the gods	αἴρομαι	to take up for oneself, i.e. to carry off, win, gain

*αἱρέω	to take with the hand, grasp, seize
ἀίσσω	to shoot, dart, spring, flit
*αἰσχύνω	to disfigure, defile
ἀίω	to hear
ἀκάματος -ον	untiring, unresting, epithet of fire
ἄκοιτις -ιος, f.	wife
*ἀκούω	to hear
*ἀκτή -ῆς, f.	headland, promontory
ἀλαλητός -οῦ, m.	a loud, resounding shout
ἄλγος -εος, n.	pain, grief
ἀλεγεινός, -ή -όν	grievous, painful
ἄλιαι -ίων, f. pl.	the Nereids
ἅλιος -α -ον	of the sea
ἀλκή -ῆς, f.	strength, might
ἄλκιμος -ον	brave, bold
ἀλκτήρ -ῆρος, m.	defender against (+ gen.)
*ἀλλά	but
*ἀλλήλους -α	each other, one another
*ἄλλος -η -ο	other, another
ἄλλοτε ... ἄλλοτε	now ... then, at one moment ... at another moment
ἅλς, ἁλός, m.	the sea
ἀλωή -ῆς, f.	orchard
*ἅμα (+ dat.)	at the same time as, together with
ἅμα, adv.	at once, at the same time
ἀμείβω	to reply, answer
ἀμείνων -ον	better
ἀμύμων -ον	blameless, excellent
*ἀμύνω	to keep off, ward off
ἀμφαγείρομαι	to gather around
*ἀμφί (+ acc.)	around, about
ἀμφί (+ dat.)	around, over, on
ἀμφιζάνω	to settle upon (+ dat.)
ἀμφιμάχομαι	to fight around
ἀμφινέμομαι	to dwell in or around (+ acc.)
ἀμφίστημι	to stand around
*ἀμφότερος -α -ον	both

ἄνα	'up!', 'get up!'
*ἀνά (+ acc.)	in, on
*ἀνάγκη -ης, f.	force, necessity
ἄναξ -ακτος, m.	lord, master
ἀνάπνευσις -εως, f.	respite from something (+ gen.)
ἀναπνέω	to catch one's breath, have a respite
ἀνατρέχω	to run up, shoot up, i.e. to grow quickly (of plants)
ἀνδροφόνος -ον	man-slaying, murderous, epithet of Hector
ἄνειμι	to go up, to rise (of the sun)
ἀνέχω	to hold up, lift up
*ἀνήρ, ἀνδρός, m.	man
*ἄνθρωπος -ου, m. man, (pl.)	mankind
Ἀντίλοχος -ου, m.	Antilochus, son of Nestor
ἄνωγα	(perf. with pres. meaning) to command, order
ἁπαλός -ή -όν	soft to the touch, tender
ἀπαμάω	to cut off, sever
ἀπαμείβομαι	to reply, answer
ἀπάτερθε	apart, aloof
ἀπέχω	to hold from, keep from; (mid.) to keep oneself from, to abstain from (+ gen.)
*ἀπό (+ gen.)	from, away from
ἀποβαίνω	to go away, disembark
ἀποδύω	to strip off (from another)
*ἀπόλλυμι	to lose, destroy; (mid.) perish, die
ἀποστυφελίζω	to drive away by force, knock back (from + gen.)
ἀποτίνω	to pay back
ἀποτμήγομαι	to cut off, sever
ἀποφθίνω	die, perish
ἀπωθέω	to push back
*ἄρα	... then ... (often no recognizable impact on the meaning)
ἀργαλέος -α -ον	painful, baneful, troublesome

ἀργυρόπεζα — silver-footed

ἀργύφεος -η -ον — silver-shining, silver-white

ἀρείων, ἄρειον — better, superior, mightier

ἀρή -ῆς, f. — bane, ruin, destruction

ἀρήιος -α -ον — warlike

Ἄρης -ηος, m. — Ares, the god of war; battle, combat

ἀρίζηλος -ον — conspicuous, clear

ἄριστος -η -ον — best, excellent, noble

ἄρνυμαι — to win, gain

ἄρουρα -ης, f. — earth, ground

ἀσπάσιος -α -ον — welcome, glad, joyful

ἄσπετος -ον — lit. unspeakable, unutterable, i.e. immense, vast, endless

*ἄστυ -εος, n. — town, city

ἀτάρ — and, but

ἀτύζομαι — to flee in terror

αὐγή -ῆς, f. — beam, gleam, glow (esp. of the sun)

αὖθι — right there or then, on the spot (of place or time)

αὐτάρ — and, but

αὖτε, adv. — again; on the other hand, however

*αὐτίκα, adv. — straightaway, immediately

αὖτις — again

*αὐτός -ή -ό — self, myself, yourself, etc. (reflexive pronoun); him, her, it (in oblique cases, used for personal pronoun)

αὔτως, adv. — as it is, even so, nevertheless

αὔω — to cry aloud, shout, call aloud

Ἀχαιοί -ῶν, m. pl. — the Achaeans, i.e. the Greeks

ἀχεύω — to grieve, mourn

ἄχθος -εος, n. — weight, burden

Ἀχιλλεύς -έως, m. — Achilles

ἄχνυμαι — to grieve, mourn

ἄχος -εος, n. — pain, distress

ἄψ, adv. — back, back again

βαθύκολπος — deep-breasted, i.e. with deep folds in the garment

*βάλλω — to throw, cast

*βαρύς -εῖα -ύ — heavy, grievous, severe

βέλος -εος, n. — missile, shot, anything thrown or shot (e.g. arrow, stone)

βένθος -εος, n. — depth (of the sea)

*βίη -ης, f. — bodily strength, force, might

βοῶπις -ιδος — ox-eyed, epithet of Hera

βροτός -οῦ, m. — a mortal man (with or without ἀνήρ)

γαῖα -ης, f. — land

*γάρ — for, since

*γε — at least, at any rate

*γέρων -οντος, m. — old man, (as adjective) old

*γίγνομαι — to come into being, to happen; to be

*γιγνώσκω — to come to know, learn

γλαυκῶπις -ιδος — gleaming-eyed, epithet of Athena

γλυκύς -εῖα -ύ — sweet

γόος -οῦ, m. — weeping, wailing

γουνός -οῦ, m. — rising ground, slope, hill

γυῖα, γυίων, n. pl. — limbs, legs

*γυμνός -ή -όν — stripped of one's armour, naked

δαίζω — to tear, cut through, wound

δαίφρων -ον — warlike; skilful, prudent

δαίω — to kindle, set in a blaze

δάκρυ -ου, n. — tear

δακρυόεις -εσσα -εν — tearful, in tears

δαμάζω — to overcome, overpower, kill

Δαρδανίς, f. — Dardanian woman

*δέ — and, but

δειδίσσομαι — to terrify, scare (away from something, + gen.)

δείδω — to be afraid (that, + μὴ)

δειλός -ή -όν	miserable, wretched
*δεινός -ή -όν	dreadful, terrible
δειρή -ῆς, f.	neck, throat
δέμας (+ gen.)	in the shape of, like
δεῦρο	hither, to here
*δέχομαι	to take, receive, welcome, accept
*δέω	to need a person or a thing (+ gen.)
*δή	(emphasizes preceding word)
δήϊος -η -ον	hostile, destructive; (of fire) burning, consuming; (as noun) enemy
δηιόω	to cut down, slay
δηρός -ά -όν	long, too long (of time)
διαφράζω	to show plainly
*δίδωμι	to give
διίημι	to drive or thrust through a thing
δίομαι	to scare or drive away
δῖος -α -ον	divine
δμωή -ῆς, f.	maidservant, serving-woman
δόμος -ου, m.	house, home
δόρυ, δουρός, n.	spear
δύο, δύω	two
δυσαριστοτόκεια, f.	unhappy mother of the noblest son
δύω	to enter, make one's way into, plunge into; to come upon, take possession of
δυώδεκα	twelve
δῶμα -ατος, n.	house, palace, mansion
*δῶρον -ου, n.	gift, present
ἕ	= οὗ
*ἐάω	to allow, permit someone (acc.) do something (inf.)
ἐγγύθεν, adv.	near
ἔγχος -εος, n.	spear
*ἐγώ, ἐγών	I
*ἐθέλω	to be willing, to want (to do something, inf.)
*εἰ	if
εἶδον	(not used in act. pres.) I saw, perceived
εἴκελος (+ dat.)	like
εἴλω	to crowd together, hem in
*εἰμί	to be
*εἶμι	I shall go
εἶος	= ἕως
εἶπον	I said, spoke
*εἰς (+ acc.)	to, towards
εἰσαναβαίνω	to go up to
εἴσω, ἔσω	towards, into (often following an accusative of destination, e.g. Ἴλιον εἴσω, 'to Troy')
*ἐκ or ἐξ (+ gen.)	out of, from
*ἕκαστος -η -ον	each, every
*ἐκεῖνος -η -ο	that
ἔκπαγλος -ον	terrible, fearful
ἐκπλήσσω	to dismay, terrify
ἐκτελέω	to bring to an end, fulfil, consummate
ἐκτρέχω	to run out
Ἕκτωρ -ορος, m.	Hector
*ἕλκω	to draw, drag
Ἑλλήσποντος -ου, m.	the Hellespont, the narrow strait that links the Propontis to the Aegean Sea; now known as the Dardanelles
ἔλπομαι	to expect, think
ἔλωρα, n. pl.	penalty to be paid, blood-price
ἐμβάλλω	to throw or cast in; to bring (85)
ἐξάρχω	to begin, take the lead in (+ gen.)
ἐξαυδάω	to speak out
ἔξοχος (+ gen.)	standing out from, far above
*ἐμός -ή -όν	my
ἔμπεδος -ον	firm, steadfast
*ἐν (+ dat.)	in, on, onto, among

*ἕνεκα (+ gen.)	on account of, for the sake of, because of	ἑτέρωθεν, adv.	from or on the other side
*ἔνθα, adv.	where, there	ἐτήτυμον, adv.	actually, truly
ἐνί	= ἐν	*ἔτι	still, yet (often with negative)
ἐνόρνυμι	to arouse, stir up in or among (+ dat.)	*ἕτοῖμος -ον	at hand, ready, prepared; (of the future) sure to happen, certain
ἔντεα -έων, n. pl.	amour	ἐτώσιος -ον	useless, fruitless, of no purpose
ἑός, ἑή, ἑόν	his own, her own, its own		
ἐπαγλαΐζομαι	to pride oneself on a thing, glory or exult in it	*εὖ, ἐύ, adv.	well
		εὐκνήμις -ιδος, f.	well-greaved
ἐπαΐσσω	to rush at, assault	εὐνή -ῆς, f.	bed
ἐπακούω	to hear	*εὑρίσκω	to find
ἐπαμύνω	to bring aid to, come to the defence of (+ dat.)	*εὐρύς -εῖα -ύ	broad, wide
		*εὔχομαι	to pray
*ἐπεί	when, after (temporal); since, because (causal)	ἐφετμή -ῆς, f.	command, behest
		ἐφίημι	to send, let fly; to incite someone (acc.) to do something (inf.)
*ἔπειτα	then, afterwards		
ἐπήτριμος -ον	closely woven, thick together, numerous		
		*ἔχω	to have, hold, possess
*ἐπί (+ acc.)	to, towards	*ἕως	while
*ἐπί (+ dat.)	at, to, towards		
ἐπιδεύομαι	to lack, be in need of (+ gen.)	*Ζεύς, Διός, m.	Zeus
ἐπιειμένος -η -ον	clothed in (+ acc.)	ζῶ	to live
ἐπιθύω	to strive vehemently to do a thing (+ inf.)		
ἐπίκουρος -ου, m.	ally	ἦ μάλα	surely
ἐπιπροΐημι	to send forth	ἠδὲ	and
ἐπισχερώ, adv.	in a row, one after another	ἦδος -εος, n.	pleasure, delight
*ἕπομαι	to follow	ἠέλιος, -ου or -οιο, m.	sun
ἔπος -εος, n.	word		
*ἔργον -οῦ, n.	deed, act	ἦμαι	to sit
ἐρίβωλος -ον	fertile, fruitful	ἦμαρ -ατος, n.	day
ἔρις -ιδος, f.	strife, contention, rivalry	ἠνεμόεις -εσσα -εν	windy, breezy
ἔρνος -εος, n.	young sprout, shoot	ἡνίοχος -ου, m.	charioteer
ἐρύκω	to hold back, restrain, detain someone (acc.) from something (gen.)	Ἡρακλῆς -ῆος, m.	Heracles
		Ἥρη -ης, f.	Hera
ἐρύω	to drag, draw; to drag up onto the beach (of ships)	ἥρως, ἥρωος, m.	hero
		ἤτοι	to be sure
*ἔρχομαι	to come, go	ἠύτε	as, like; as when
ἐς	= εἰς	Ἥφαιστος -ου, m.	Hephaestus, the blacksmith god
ἐσθλός -ή -όν	good		
*ἑταῖρος -οῦ, m.	friend, companion	ἠῶθεν, adv.	in the morning

*θάλασσα -ης, f.   sea

θαμέες -ειαί   thick, close-set, densely packed

θαῦμα -ατος, n.   a wonder, marvel

*θεά -ᾶς, f.   goddess

*θεός -οῦ. m.   god

*θεράπων -οντος, m.   attendant, comrade-at-arms

θερμός -ά -όν   warm, hot

θεσπέσιος -α -ον   divine, vast, wondrous

Θέτις -ιδος, f.   Thetis, mother of Achilles

θέω   to run

θνήσκω   to die, be killed; (perfect) be dead

θνητός -ή -όν   mortal

θοῦρις -ιδος, f.   rushing, impetuous, furious, epithet of ἀλκή

θυμοραιστής -οῦ   life-destroying

θυμός -οῦ, m.   heart

θύραζε, adv.   out of doors, out

θυσσανόεις -εσσα -εν   tasselled, fringed

θωρήσσομαι   to prepare oneself for battle, arm oneself

ἰάχω   to cry, shriek, shout

*ἵημι   to send

ἱκάνω   to come to, reach, arrive at

ἱκνέομαι   to come

Ἴλιος -ου, f.   Ilium, the city of Troy

*ἵνα   in order that, so that

*ἵππος -ου, m.   horse; can also denote chariots or charioteers, esp. in contrast to λαός or λαοί ('foot-soldiers')

Ἴρις -ιδος, f.   Iris, the messenger of the gods

*ἴσος -η -ον   equal to, the same as (+ dat.)

*ἵστημι   (transitive) to stand something up, set in place; (intransitive) to place oneself, come to a stand, rise

ἴφθιμος -η -ον   mighty, strong

ἶφι, adv.   by force

*καί   and, even, also

*κακός -ή -όν   bad, evil

καλλίθριξ -τριχος   with beautiful manes (of horses)

*καλός -ή -όν   beautiful

καλύπτω   to cover, conceal, overshadow

καπνός -οῦ, m.   smoke

κάρη κομόωντες   long-haired

κάρη, κάρητος, n.   head

κασιγνήτη -ης, f.   sister

*κατά (+ acc.)   down, according to, by, in, throughout

καταδύω   to go down, set (of the sun)

καταλείβω   to pour down

κατατίθημι   to put or lay down

καταχέω   to let fall down (of tears)

κέ, κέν   = ἄν

*κεῖμαι   to lie down, be dead

*κελεύω   to order, command, tell

κεύθω   to hide, conceal

*κεφαλή -ῆς, f.   head; life

κῆδος -εος, n.   care, anxiety, grief

κήρ, κηρός, f.   doom, fate

κῆρ, κῆρος, f.   heart

κιχάνω   come upon, reach

κλαίω   to cry, lament

κλειτός -ή -όν   celebrated, famous

κλέος, n.   glory

κλονέομαι   to rush wildly, be driven in confusion

κλυτός -ή -όν   famous, illustrious, renowned

κλυτοτέχνης -ου, m.   famous for his art, epithet of Hephaestus

κλύω   to hear

κόλπος -ου, m.   bosom, lap

κόμη -ης, f.   the hair on one's head

κόνις -ιος, f.   dust

κορυθαίολος -ον   with glancing helmet, epithet of Hector

κορυστής -οῦ, m.	helmeted, armed for battle, epithet of the two Aiantes	μεγάθυμος -ον	great-hearted, high-spirited
κορωνίς -ίδος	crook-beaked, curved (of ships)	μεγάλα, adv.	greatly, loudly
		μεγαλήτωρ -ορος	great-hearted, proud
κρατερός -ά -όν	strong, mighty	μεγαλωστί, adv.	greatly, far and wide, over a vast space
κρίνομαι	to get a contest decided, measure oneself (in battle)	*μέγας, μεγάλη, μέγα	great
Κρονίδης -ου, m.	son of Cronus, i.e. Zeus	μέλας -αινα -αν	black
κρύβδα, adv.	in secret from, without the knowledge of (+ gen.)	μέλι -ιτος, n.	honey
κτείνω	to kill, slay	*μέλλω	to be going or about to do something (+ fut. inf.)
κυδάλιμος -ον	glorious, renowned	μέλπηθρον -ου, n.	plaything
κυδοιμός -οῦ, m.	uproar, confusion	μέμαα	(perf. with pres. meaning) to be eager to do something (+ inf.)
κῦδος -εος, n.	glory, renown		
κυδρός -ή -όν	glorious, illustrious, noble	μέμονα	(perf. with pres. meaning) to have in mind, be minded to do something (+ inf.)
κυκάω	to stir up		
κῦμα -ατος, n.	wave, swell (of the sea)		
κύων, κυνός, m.	dog	Μενοίτιος -ου, m.	Menoetius, father of Patroclus
κωκύω	to shriek, wail	*μένω	to remain, wait, hold one's ground
λαιμός -οῦ, m.	throat	μεταυδάω	to speak among
*λαμβάνω	take hold of, seize	*μετά (+ acc.)	after; towards, to, into
λαός -οῦ, m.	the people or men of the army	μετά (+ dat.)	by
λείβω	to pour, pour forth	μέτειμι	to be among, intervene
*λείπω	to leave	μετόπισθε(ν)	from behind
λέχος -εος, n.	funeral couch, bier	*μή	(and compounds) see οὐ
λέων -οντος, m.	lion	*μήτηρ, -έρος or -ρός, f.	mother
ληΐζομαι	to carry off as booty	μίγνυμι	to mix with, come into contact with
λυγρός -ά -όν	baneful, mournful		
*λύω	to loosen, let go; (of one's legs) to weaken, buckle	μιν	him, her, it
λώβη -ης, f.	outrage, insult	μόθος -ου, m.	the tumult or din of battle, battle
		μοῖρα -άς, f.	part, portion; one's lot, destiny, fate
*μακρός -ά -όν	long, tall, high, deep	μυρίος -α -ον	numberless, countless, infinite
*μάλα, adv.	very, exceedingly		
μαρμαίρω	to flash, sparkle, gleam	Μυρμιδόνες -ων, m. pl.	Myrmidons, the Thracian tribe of which Achilles is the leader
μάρναμαι	to fight, do battle with (+ dat.)		
*μάχομαι	to fight	μύρομαι	to melt into tears, shed tears, weep

μῶλος, m. — toil and moil of war

*ναί — yes

ναίω — to dwell, inhabit

*νεκρός -οῦ, m. — corpse

νεκτάρεος -έα -εον — nectarous, fragrant

νέκυς -υος, m. — corpse

νέομαι — to go, come

Νέστωρ -ορος, m. — Nestor, father of Antilochus

νεφέλη -ης, f. — cloud

νέφος -εος, n. — cloud

Νηρηίς -ίδος, f. — a daughter of Nereus, a Nereid

*νῆσος -ου, f. — island

νηῦς, νηός, f. — ship

νοστέω — to return (home)

*νῦν, adv. — now

ὁ, ἡ, τό — he, she, it; who, which; (rarely) the

ὀδύρομαι — to lament, bewail

οἱ μὲν ... οἱ δὲ — some ... others

*οἶδα — to know

*οἴκαδε, adv. — to one's home, homeward

οἰμώζω — to wail aloud, lament

*οἷος, οἵη, οἷον — such, of such a kind

ὄλεθρος -ου, m. — ruin, destruction, death

ὀλέκω — to ruin, destroy, kill

ὀλετήρ -ῆρος, m. — destroyer, murderer

*ὀλίγος -η -ον — little, small

ὄλλυμι — to destroy

ὀλοφύρομαι — to lament, wail

Ὀλύμπιος -ου, m. — the Olympian, i.e. Zeus

Ὄλυμπος -ου, m. — Olympus, a mountain in Thessaly which was the abode of the gods

ὁμιλέω — to associate or go with, to engage (in battle)

*ὁμοῖος -η -ον — like, resembling; the same

ὁμοκλάω — to call or shout to (+ dat.)

ὁμόργνυμι — to wipe, wipe away

*ὀξύς -εῖα -ύ — sharp (of weapons), piercing or shrill (of sounds)

ὀπίζομαι — to regard with awe, to respect

ὀπίσω, adv. — backward, behind

ὁπότε, ὁππότε — whenever, when

*ὁράω — to see, behold, look on

ὀρθόκραιρος -α -ον — with straight or upright horns, (*of ships*) horned, high-horned, high-sterned, etc.

ὀρίνω — to stir, rouse, move

ὁρμαίνω — to ponder, think over (+ acc.)

ὄρνυμι — to arouse, awake, excite; (mid. and perf.) to rouse oneself, arise, spring up

ὅς, ἥ, ὅ — he, this, that (demonstrative pronoun); who, that, which (relative pronoun)

ὅς, ἥ, ὅν — his, her, its

*ὅσος — or ὅσσος, -η, -ον how great, how much, how many, etc.

ὄσσομαι — to see, foresee

*ὅστις, ἥτις, ὅ τι — whoever, whichever, whatever

*ὅτε — when

*οὐ / οὐκ / οὐχ / οὐχί / μή — not

*οὖν — so, then

ὀφείλω — (introduces an impossible wish), e.g. 'would that...!'

*ὀφθαλμός -οῦ, m. — eye

ὄφρα — in order to; while, so long as

ὀχθέω — to be irritated or indignant

ὄχος -εος, n. — chariot

ὄψ, ὀπός, f. — voice

*παῖς or πάϊς, παιδός, c. — child

πάλιν (+ gen.) — away from

Παλλάς -άδος, f. — Pallas, epithet of Athena

πάμπαν, adv.	altogether, entirely	Πηλείων -ωνος, m.	= Πηλείδης
παμφανόων -ωσα	bright-shining, radiant	Πηλεύς -ῆος, m.	Peleus, father of Achilles
πανημέριος -η -ον	all day long	Πηλήϊος -η -ον	of or pertaining to Peleus, father of Achilles
*παρά (+ acc.)	to the side of, unto, to	πίμπλημι	to fill
*παρὰ (+ gen.)	from (a person)	*πιστός -ή -όν	trusty, faithful
*παρὰ (+ dat.)	beside, next to	πλήσσω	to strike, hit, beat
παράκοιτις -ιος, f.	wife	ποδαρκής -ές	swift-footed, epithet of Achilles
παρειαί, παρειάων, f. pl.	the cheeks	ποδήνεμος -ον	wind-swift, epithet of Iris
παρίστημι	to come up to, stand by or near	ποιμήν -ένος, m.	herdsman, shepherd
*πᾶς, πᾶσα, πᾶν	every, all	πόλεμος -ου, m.	war
*πάσχω	to suffer	*πολύς, πολλή, πολύ	many
*πατήρ, πατέρος, m.	father	πολύφρων -ον	thoughtful, ingenious
πάτρη -ης, f.	native land, native country	*ποτέ, adv.	once, one time
*πατρίς -ίδος, f.	native land, native country	ποτί	= πρός
Πάτροκλος -ῆος, m.	Patroclus, son of Menoetius	πότμος -ου, m.	one's fate or destiny (always in a bad sense)
*παύω	to cease, bring to an end; (middle) leave off from, rest from (+ gen.)	πότνια -ης, f.	revered, honourable (usually used as a title of honour for goddesses or ladies)
*πεδίον -ου, n.	plain	*πούς, ποδός, m.	foot
*πείθω	to persuade	Πριαμίδης -ου, m.	son of Priam, i.e. Hector
πεινάω	to be hungry	Πρίαμος -ου, m.	Priam, father of Hector and king of Troy
πελώριος -α -ον	huge, gigantic	*πρίν	before, until
*πέμπω	to send	πρίν, adv.	before, formerly
πένθος -εος, n.	grief, sorrow	*πρό (+ gen.)	before, in front of
πέποιθα	(perf. of πείθω) to put trust in, depend on (+ dat.)	προΐημι	to send on or forward, to send
πέρ	very, at least, even, just	προπάροιθε(ν) (+ gen.)	in front of
περί (+ dat.)	around		
*περί (+ gen.)	above, beyond; about, for, on behalf of	*πρὸς (+ acc.)	to, towards
		προσαυδάω	to speak to, address
περικτίονες -όνων, m. pl.	dwellers around, neighbours	πρόσφημι	to speak to, address
		πρόσωπον -ου, n.	face
περιπέλομαι	to be or go around, surround	προτεύχω	to be past; (perf. pass.) to be over and done with
πήγνυμι	to fix, plant firmly		
Πηλείδης -ου, m.	son of Peleus, i.e. Achilles	πρύμνα -ης, f.	the hindmost part of the ship, the stern

*πρῶτος -η -ον	first, foremost	*σφέτερος -η -ον	their, their own
πτερόεις -εσσα -εν	winged, feathered	σφός	= σφέτερος
		σχέτλιος -α -ον	foolish, headstrong
πτόλεμος	= πόλεμος	*σῶμα -ατος, n.	corpse, carcass
πυκινός -ή -όν	wise, prudent		
πυνθάνομαι	to learn about, hear of someone or something (+ gen)	τάμνω	= τέμνω
		τανύω	to stretch out (on the ground)
*πῦρ, πυρός, n.	fire		
πυρσός -οῦ, m.	torch, beacon	τάφρος -ου, f.	ditch, trench
πω	up to this time, yet (always with a negative)	*ταχὺς -εῖα -ύ	quick, swift, fleet
		*τέ	and
*πῶς	how?	*τέ ... καί	both ... and
*πως	in any way, at all, by any means	τείρω	to oppress, distress, exhaust
		*τεῖχος -εος, n.	wall (of a city or town, or of any fortification)
ῥήγνυμι	to break, burst	τέκνον -ου, n.	child
		τέκος -εος, n.	child
σάκος -εος, n.	shield	Τελαμωνιάδης -ου, m.	son of Telamon, i.e. Ajax
σάλπιγξ -γγος, f.	war-trumpet		
σέβας, n.	shame	τελέω	to complete, fulfill, accomplish
σέλας -αος, n.	brightness, light, gleam	*τέμνω	to cut, cut up
σίδηρος -οῦ, m.	iron, anything made from iron, e.g. a sword or knife	τεῦχος -εος, n.	(mostly in plural, τεύχεα) armour
σκόλοψ -οπος, m.	a sharpened pole or stake	τεύχω	to make, render; (pass.) to be, become, take place
σμερδαλέον, adv.	(of shouting or wailing) terribly		
σπέος -εος, n.	cave, cavern, grotto	τέφρη -ης, f.	ash
στενάχω	to groan, sigh	τηλόθεν	from far away
στένω	to moan, groan	τηλόθι (+ gen.)	far away, far from
στεῦμαι	to promise (to do something, + fut. inf.)	τί	why? how?
		τίκτω	to give birth to
στέφω	to put on as a crown, to crown with something	*τις, τι	someone, something; anyone, anything
στῆθος -εος, n.	breast	τίω	to honour, revere
στοναχέω	to sigh, lament	τοῖος, τοία, τοῖον	such, of such a kind (corresponding to οἷος)
στρέφω	to turn round the other way	*τότε, adv.	at that time, then
στυγερός -ή -όν	hated, abominated, loathsome	τόφρα, adv.	(following ἕως) while ... in that time
*σύ	you	*τρέπω	to turn
*σύν (+ dat.)	with	τρέφω	(of a parent) to bring up, rear (a child)
σφεῖς, σφέων	they, them		

*τρέχω	to run	φλόξ, φλογός, f.	flame, blaze
τρὶς, adv.	three times, thrice	φόνος -ου, m.	murder, slaughter, death
Τροίη -ης, f.	Troy, either the city itself or the surrounding area (also known as the Troad)	φρήν, φρενός, f.	heart, mind
		φρονέω	to think, reflect, consider
		φυλοπις -ιδος, f.	the din of battle
Τρῳάς -άδος, f.	Trojan woman	φυτόν -οῦ, m.	plant, tree
Τρῶες, Τρώων, m. pl.	the Trojans	φωνέω	to speak
*τύπτω	to beat, strike, hit	*φωνή -ῆς, f.	the sound of the voice, voice
		φώς, φωτός, m.	man
*υἱός, υἱοῦ or υἷος, m.	son		
		χάζομαι	to give way, fall back
ὑπέκ, ὑπέξ (+ gen.)	out from under, from beneath, away from	χαλεπαίνω	(of the weather) to be hard, severe; (of persons) to rage, be angry
*ὑπὲρ (+ gen.)	over, above		
*ὑπὸ (+ acc.)	under	χάλκεος -είη -εον	made of bronze
*ὑπὸ (+ dat.)	under; by (a person or thing)	χαλκός -οῦ, m.	bronze
*ὑπὸ (+ gen.)	by or from (a person)	χαλκοχίτων -ωνος	bronze-clad
ὑπὸ, adv.	below, underneath		
ὑποδείδω	to shrink in fear, cower before	χαρίεις -εσσα -εν	graceful, beautiful
		*χείρ, χειρός, f.	hand
ὑποδέχομαι	to receive at home	χέω	to pour, scatter, let fall (of tears)
ὑψίζυγος -ον	high-throned, high-ruling, epithet of Zeus		
		χιτών -ῶνος, m.	tunic
ὑψόσε, adv.	aloft, on high	χόλος -ου, m.	anger
		χολόω	to anger, provoke
φαίδιμος -ον	shining, famous, illustrious	χραισμέω	to be useful to one (+ dat.) in something (+ acc.)
*φαίνω	to show; (mid. and pass.) to come to light, appear		
		χρύσεος -η -ον	golden, made of gold
φάος -εος, n.	light		
φέρτρον, n.	litter, bier for the dead	ὤ μοι	alas!
*φέρω	to carry, bear	ὠκύμορος -ον	lit. 'swift-fated', i.e. soon to die, doomed to a short life, etc.
*φεύγω	to flee from, escape from		
*φημί	to say, speak, declare	ὠκύς, ὠκεῖα, ὠκύ	quick, swift, fleet
φθέγγομαι	to call aloud, cry out	ὦμος -ου, m.	shoulder
φθίω	to decay, wane, dwindle	ὡς, adv.	so, thus
*φίλος -η -ον	one's own; friendly, pleasing; beloved	*ὡς	like, as; so that, in order that; ὡς can also introduce a wish
φλεγέθω	to blaze, glow (of fire)		

Text
Iliad 9

*The Greeks have agreed to send a delegation to Achilles to persuade him to return
to battle. We join the action as the three heroes chosen to lead the delegation –
Odysseus, Phoenix and Ajax – make their way towards Achilles' huts.*

τὼ δὲ βάτην παρὰ θῖνα πολυφλοίσβοιο θαλάσσης
πολλὰ μάλ᾽ εὐχομένω γαιηόχῳ ἐννοσιγαίῳ
ῥηϊδίως πεπιθεῖν μεγάλας φρένας Αἰακίδαο.
Μυρμιδόνων δ᾽ ἐπί τε κλισίας καὶ νῆας ἱκέσθην,   185
τὸν δ᾽ εὗρον φρένα τερπόμενον φόρμιγγι λιγείῃ
καλῇ δαιδαλέῃ, ἐπὶ δ᾽ ἀργύρεον ζυγὸν ἦεν,
τὴν ἄρετ᾽ ἐξ ἐνάρων πόλιν Ἠετίωνος ὀλέσσας:
τῇ ὅ γε θυμὸν ἔτερπεν, ἄειδε δ᾽ ἄρα κλέα ἀνδρῶν.
Πάτροκλος δέ οἱ οἶος ἐναντίος ἧστο σιωπῇ,   190
δέγμενος Αἰακίδην ὁπότε λήξειεν ἀείδων,
τὼ δὲ βάτην προτέρω, ἡγεῖτο δὲ δῖος Ὀδυσσεύς,
στὰν δὲ πρόσθ᾽ αὐτοῖο: ταφὼν δ᾽ ἀνόρουσεν Ἀχιλλεὺς
αὐτῇ σὺν φόρμιγγι λιπὼν ἕδος ἔνθα θάασσεν.
ὣς δ᾽ αὔτως Πάτροκλος, ἐπεὶ ἴδε φῶτας, ἀνέστη.   195
τὼ καὶ δεικνύμενος προσέφη πόδας ὠκὺς Ἀχιλλεύς:
'χαίρετον: ἦ φίλοι ἄνδρες ἱκάνετον ἦ τι μάλα χρεώ,
οἵ μοι σκυζομένῳ περ Ἀχαιῶν φίλτατοί ἐστον.'
ὣς ἄρα φωνήσας προτέρω ἄγε δῖος Ἀχιλλεύς,
εἷσεν δ᾽ ἐν κλισμοῖσι τάπησί τε πορφυρέοισιν.   200
αἶψα δὲ Πάτροκλον προσεφώνεεν ἐγγὺς ἐόντα:
'μείζονα δὴ κρητῆρα Μενοιτίου υἱὲ καθίστα,
ζωρότερον δὲ κέραιε, δέπας δ᾽ ἔντυνον ἑκάστῳ:

οἳ γὰρ φίλτατοι ἄνδρες ἐμῷ ὑπέασι μελάθρῳ.'
ὣς φάτο, Πάτροκλος δὲ φίλῳ ἐπεπείθεθ᾽ ἑταίρῳ.   205
αὐτὰρ ὅ γε κρεῖον μέγα κάββαλεν ἐν πυρὸς αὐγῇ,
ἐν δ᾽ ἄρα νῶτον ἔθηκ᾽ ὄϊος καὶ πίονος αἰγός,
ἐν δὲ συὸς σιάλοιο ῥάχιν τεθαλυῖαν ἀλοιφῇ.
τῷ δ᾽ ἔχεν Αὐτομέδων, τάμνεν δ᾽ ἄρα δῖος Ἀχιλλεύς.
καὶ τὰ μὲν εὖ μίστυλλε καὶ ἀμφ᾽ ὀβελοῖσιν ἔπειρε,   210
πῦρ δὲ Μενοιτιάδης δαῖεν μέγα ἰσόθεος φώς.
αὐτὰρ ἐπεὶ κατὰ πῦρ ἐκάη καὶ φλὸξ ἐμαράνθη,
ἀνθρακιὴν στορέσας ὀβελοὺς ἐφύπερθε τάνυσσε,
πάσσε δ᾽ ἁλὸς θείοιο κρατευτάων ἐπαείρας.
αὐτὰρ ἐπεί ῥ᾽ ὤπτησε καὶ εἰν ἐλεοῖσιν ἔχευε,   215
Πάτροκλος μὲν σῖτον ἑλὼν ἐπένειμε τραπέζῃ
καλοῖς ἐν κανέοισιν, ἀτὰρ κρέα νεῖμεν Ἀχιλλεύς.
αὐτὸς δ᾽ ἀντίον ἷζεν Ὀδυσσῆος θείοιο
τοίχου τοῦ ἑτέροιο, θεοῖσι δὲ θῦσαι ἀνώγει
Πάτροκλον ὃν ἑταῖρον· ὃ δ᾽ ἐν πυρὶ βάλλε θυηλάς.   220
οἳ δ᾽ ἐπ᾽ ὀνείαθ᾽ ἑτοῖμα προκείμενα χεῖρας ἴαλλον.
αὐτὰρ ἐπεὶ πόσιος καὶ ἐδητύος ἐξ ἔρον ἕντο,
νεῦσ᾽ Αἴας Φοίνικι· νόησε δὲ δῖος Ὀδυσσεύς,
πλησάμενος δ᾽ οἴνοιο δέπας δείδεκτ᾽ Ἀχιλῆα·
χαῖρ᾽ Ἀχιλεῦ· δαιτὸς μὲν ἐΐσης οὐκ ἐπιδευεῖς   225
ἠμὲν ἐνὶ κλισίῃ Ἀγαμέμνονος Ἀτρεΐδαο
ἠδὲ καὶ ἐνθάδε νῦν, πάρα γὰρ μενοεικέα πολλὰ
δαίνυσθ᾽· ἀλλ᾽ οὐ δαιτὸς ἐπηράτου ἔργα μέμηλεν,
ἀλλὰ λίην μέγα πῆμα διοτρεφὲς εἰσορόωντες
δείδιμεν· ἐν δοιῇ δὲ σαωσέμεν ἢ ἀπολέσθαι   230
νῆας ἐϋσσέλμους, εἰ μὴ σύ γε δύσεαι ἀλκήν.
ἐγγὺς γὰρ νηῶν καὶ τείχεος αὖλιν ἔθεντο
Τρῶες ὑπέρθυμοι τηλεκλειτοί τ᾽ ἐπίκουροι
κηάμενοι πυρὰ πολλὰ κατὰ στρατόν, οὐδ᾽ ἔτι φασὶ
σχήσεσθ᾽, ἀλλ᾽ ἐν νηυσὶ μελαίνῃσιν πεσέεσθαι.   235
Ζεὺς δέ σφι Κρονίδης ἐνδέξια σήματα φαίνων
ἀστράπτει· Ἕκτωρ δὲ μέγα σθένεϊ βλεμεαίνων
μαίνεται ἐκπάγλως πίσυνος Διί, οὐδέ τι τίει
ἀνέρας οὐδὲ θεούς· κρατερὴ δέ ἑ λύσσα δέδυκεν.
ἀρᾶται δὲ τάχιστα φανήμεναι Ἠῶ δῖαν·   240
στεῦται γὰρ νηῶν ἀποκόψειν ἄκρα κόρυμβα
αὐτάς τ᾽ ἐμπρήσειν μαλεροῦ πυρός, αὐτὰρ Ἀχαιοὺς
δῃώσειν παρὰ τῇσιν ὀρινομένους ὑπὸ καπνοῦ.

ταῦτ᾽ αἰνῶς δείδοικα κατὰ φρένα, μή οἱ ἀπειλὰς
ἐκτελέσωσι θεοί, ἡμῖν δὲ δὴ αἴσιμον εἴη   245
φθίσθαι ἐνὶ Τροίῃ ἑκὰς Ἄργεος ἱπποβότοιο.
ἀλλ᾽ ἄνα εἰ μέμονάς γε καὶ ὀψέ περ υἷας Ἀχαιῶν
τειρομένους ἐρύεσθαι ὑπὸ Τρώων ὀρυμαγδοῦ.
αὐτῷ τοι μετόπισθ᾽ ἄχος ἔσσεται, οὐδέ τι μῆχος
ῥεχθέντος κακοῦ ἔστ᾽ ἄκος εὑρεῖν· ἀλλὰ πολὺ πρὶν   250
φράζευ ὅπως Δαναοῖσιν ἀλεξήσεις κακὸν ἦμαρ.
ὦ πέπον ἦ μὲν σοί γε πατὴρ ἐπετέλλετο Πηλεὺς
ἤματι τῷ ὅτε σ᾽ ἐκ Φθίης Ἀγαμέμνονι πέμπε·
τέκνον ἐμὸν κάρτος μὲν Ἀθηναίη τε καὶ Ἥρη
δώσουσ᾽ αἴ κ᾽ ἐθέλωσι, σὺ δὲ μεγαλήτορα θυμὸν   255
ἴσχειν ἐν στήθεσσι· φιλοφροσύνη γὰρ ἀμείνων·
ληγέμεναι δ᾽ ἔριδος κακομηχάνου, ὄφρά σε μᾶλλον
τίωσ᾽ Ἀργείων ἠμὲν νέοι ἠδὲ γέροντες.
ὣς ἐπέτελλ᾽ ὁ γέρων, σὺ δὲ λήθεαι· ἀλλ᾽ ἔτι καὶ νῦν
παύε᾽, ἔα δὲ χόλον θυμαλγέα· σοὶ δ᾽ Ἀγαμέμνων   260
ἄξια δῶρα δίδωσι μεταλήξαντι χόλοιο.
εἰ δὲ σὺ μέν μευ ἄκουσον, ἐγὼ δέ κέ τοι καταλέξω
ὅσσά τοι ἐν κλισίῃσιν ὑπέσχετο δῶρ᾽ Ἀγαμέμνων·
ἕπτ᾽ ἀπύρους τρίποδας, δέκα δὲ χρυσοῖο τάλαντα,
αἴθωνας δὲ λέβητας ἐείκοσι, δώδεκα δ᾽ ἵππους   265
πηγοὺς ἀθλοφόρους, οἳ ἀέθλια ποσσὶν ἄροντο.
οὔ κεν ἀλήϊος εἴη ἀνὴρ ᾧ τόσσα γένοιτο
οὐδέ κεν ἀκτήμων ἐριτίμοιο χρυσοῖο,
ὅσσ᾽ Ἀγαμέμνονος ἵπποι ἀέθλια ποσσὶν ἄροντο.
δώσει δ᾽ ἑπτὰ γυναῖκας ἀμύμονα ἔργα ἰδυίας   270
Λεσβίδας, ἃς ὅτε Λέσβον ἐϋκτιμένην ἕλες αὐτὸς
ἐξέλεθ᾽, αἳ τότε κάλλει ἐνίκων φῦλα γυναικῶν.
τὰς μέν τοι δώσει, μετὰ δ᾽ ἔσσεται ἣν τότ᾽ ἀπηύρα
κούρη Βρισῆος· ἐπὶ δὲ μέγαν ὅρκον ὀμεῖται
μή ποτε τῆς εὐνῆς ἐπιβήμεναι ἠδὲ μιγῆναι   275
ἣ θέμις ἐστὶν, ἄναξ, ἤτ᾽ ἀνδρῶν ἤτε γυναικῶν.
ταῦτα μὲν αὐτίκα πάντα παρέσσεται· εἰ δέ κεν αὖτε
ἄστυ μέγα Πριάμοιο θεοὶ δώωσ᾽ ἀλαπάξαι,
νῆα ἅλις χρυσοῦ καὶ χαλκοῦ νηήσασθαι
εἰσελθών, ὅτε κεν δατεώμεθα ληΐδ᾽ Ἀχαιοί,   280
Τρωϊάδας δὲ γυναῖκας ἐείκοσιν αὐτὸς ἑλέσθαι,
αἵ κε μετ᾽ Ἀργείην Ἑλένην κάλλισται ἔωσιν.
εἰ δέ κεν Ἄργος ἱκοίμεθ᾽ Ἀχαιϊκὸν οὖθαρ ἀρούρης

γαμβρός κέν οἱ ἔοις: τίσει δέ σε ἶσον Ὀρέστῃ,
ὅς οἱ τηλύγετος τρέφεται θαλίῃ ἔνι πολλῇ.   285
τρεῖς δέ οἵ εἰσι θύγατρες ἐνὶ μεγάρῳ εὐπήκτῳ
Χρυσόθεμις καὶ Λαοδίκη καὶ Ἰφιάνασσα,
τάων ἥν κ᾽ ἐθέλησθα φίλην ἀνάεδνον ἄγεσθαι
πρὸς οἶκον Πηλῆος: ὃ δ᾽ αὖτ᾽ ἐπὶ μείλια δώσει
πολλὰ μάλ᾽, ὅσσ᾽ οὔ πώ τις ἑῇ ἐπέδωκε θυγατρί: 290
ἑπτὰ δέ τοι δώσει εὖ ναιόμενα πτολίεθρα
Καρδαμύλην Ἐνόπην τε καὶ Ἰρὴν ποιήεσσαν
Φηράς τε ζαθέας ἠδ᾽ Ἄνθειαν βαθύλειμον
καλήν τ᾽ Αἴπειαν καὶ Πήδασον ἀμπελόεσσαν.
πᾶσαι δ᾽ ἐγγὺς ἁλός, νέαται Πύλου ἠμαθόεντος: 295
ἐν δ᾽ ἄνδρες ναίουσι πολύρρηνες πολυβοῦται,
οἵ κέ σε δωτίνῃσι θεὸν ὣς τιμήσουσι
καί τοι ὑπὸ σκήπτρῳ λιπαρὰς τελέουσι θέμιστας.
ταῦτά κέ τοι τελέσειε μεταλήξαντι χόλοιο.
εἰ δέ τοι Ἀτρεΐδης μὲν ἀπήχθετο κηρόθι μᾶλλον   300
αὐτὸς καὶ τοῦ δῶρα, σὺ δ᾽ ἄλλους περ Παναχαιοὺς
τειρομένους ἐλέαιρε κατὰ στρατόν, οἵ σε θεὸν ὣς
τίσουσ᾽: ἦ γάρ κέ σφι μάλα μέγα κῦδος ἄροιο:
νῦν γάρ χ᾽ Ἕκτορ᾽ ἕλοις, ἐπεὶ ἂν μάλα τοι σχεδὸν ἔλθοι
λύσσαν ἔχων ὀλοήν, ἐπεὶ οὔ τινά φησιν ὁμοῖον   305
οἷ ἔμεναι Δαναῶν οὓς ἐνθάδε νῆες ἔνεικαν.
τὸν δ᾽ ἀπαμειβόμενος προσέφη πόδας ὠκὺς Ἀχιλλεύς:
᾽διογενὲς Λαερτιάδη πολυμήχαν᾽ Ὀδυσσεῦ
χρὴ μὲν δὴ τὸν μῦθον ἀπηλεγέως ἀποειπεῖν,
ἦ περ δὴ φρονέω τε καὶ ὡς τετελεσμένον ἔσται,   310
ὡς μή μοι τρύζητε παρήμενοι ἄλλοθεν ἄλλος.
ἐχθρὸς γάρ μοι κεῖνος ὁμῶς Ἀΐδαο πύλῃσιν
ὅς χ᾽ ἕτερον μὲν κεύθῃ ἐνὶ φρεσίν, ἄλλο δὲ εἴπῃ.
αὐτὰρ ἐγὼν ἐρέω ὥς μοι δοκεῖ εἶναι ἄριστα:
οὔτ᾽ ἔμεγ᾽ Ἀτρεΐδην Ἀγαμέμνονα πεισέμεν οἴω   315
οὔτ᾽ ἄλλους Δαναούς, ἐπεὶ οὐκ ἄρα τις χάρις ἦεν
μάρνασθαι δηΐοισιν ἐπ᾽ ἀνδράσι νωλεμὲς αἰεί.
ἴση μοῖρα μένοντι καὶ εἰ μάλα τις πολεμίζοι:
ἐν δὲ ἰῇ τιμῇ ἠμὲν κακὸς ἠδὲ καὶ ἐσθλός:
κάτθαν᾽ ὁμῶς ὅ τ᾽ ἀεργὸς ἀνὴρ ὅ τε πολλὰ ἐοργώς.   320
οὐδέ τί μοι περίκειται, ἐπεὶ πάθον ἄλγεα θυμῷ
αἰεὶ ἐμὴν ψυχὴν παραβαλλόμενος πολεμίζειν.
ὡς δ᾽ ὄρνις ἀπτῆσι νεοσσοῖσι προφέρῃσι

μάστακ᾽ ἐπεί κε λάβῃσι, κακῶς δ᾽ ἄρα οἱ πέλει αὐτῇ,
ὣς καὶ ἐγὼ πολλὰς μὲν ἀΰπνους νύκτας ἴαυον,   325
ἤματα δ᾽ αἱματόεντα διέπρησσον πολεμίζων
ἀνδράσι μαρνάμενος ὀάρων ἕνεκα σφετεράων.
δώδεκα δὴ σὺν νηυσὶ πόλεις ἀλάπαξ᾽ ἀνθρώπων,
πεζὸς δ᾽ ἕνδεκά φημι κατὰ Τροίην ἐρίβωλον·
τάων ἐκ πασέων κειμήλια πολλὰ καὶ ἐσθλὰ   330
ἐξελόμην, καὶ πάντα φέρων Ἀγαμέμνονι δόσκον
Ἀτρεΐδῃ· ὃ δ᾽ ὄπισθε μένων παρὰ νηυσὶ θοῇσι
δεξάμενος διὰ παῦρα δασάσκετο, πολλὰ δ᾽ ἔχεσκεν.
ἄλλα δ᾽ ἀριστήεσσι δίδου γέρα καὶ βασιλεῦσι·
τοῖσι μὲν ἔμπεδα κεῖται, ἐμεῦ δ᾽ ἀπὸ μούνου Ἀχαιῶν   335
εἵλετ᾽, ἔχει δ᾽ ἄλοχον θυμαρέα· τῇ παριαύων
τερπέσθω. τί δὲ δεῖ πολεμιζέμεναι Τρώεσσιν
Ἀργείους; τί δὲ λαὸν ἀνήγαγεν ἐνθάδ᾽ ἀγείρας
Ἀτρεΐδης; ἦ οὐχ Ἑλένης ἕνεκ᾽ ἠϋκόμοιο;
ἦ μοῦνοι φιλέουσ᾽ ἀλόχους μερόπων ἀνθρώπων   340
Ἀτρεΐδαι; ἐπεὶ ὅς τις ἀνὴρ ἀγαθὸς καὶ ἐχέφρων
τὴν αὐτοῦ φιλέει καὶ κήδεται, ὡς καὶ ἐγὼ τὴν
ἐκ θυμοῦ φίλεον δουρικτητήν περ ἐοῦσαν.
νῦν δ᾽ ἐπεὶ ἐκ χειρῶν γέρας εἵλετο καί μ᾽ ἀπάτησε
μή μευ πειράτω εὖ εἰδότος· οὐδέ με πείσει.
ἀλλ᾽, Ὀδυσεῦ, σὺν σοί τε καὶ ἄλλοισιν βασιλεῦσι
φραζέσθω νήεσσιν ἀλεξέμεναι δήϊον πῦρ.
ἦ μὲν δὴ μάλα πολλὰ πονήσατο νόσφιν ἐμεῖο,
καὶ δὴ τεῖχος ἔδειμε, καὶ ἤλασε τάφρον ἐπ᾽ αὐτῷ
εὐρεῖαν μεγάλην, ἐν δὲ σκόλοπας κατέπηξεν·   350
ἀλλ᾽ οὐδ᾽ ὣς δύναται σθένος Ἕκτορος ἀνδροφόνοιο
ἴσχειν· ὄφρα δ᾽ ἐγὼ μετ᾽ Ἀχαιοῖσιν πολέμιζον
οὐκ ἐθέλεσκε μάχην ἀπὸ τείχεος ὀρνύμεν Ἕκτωρ,
ἀλλ᾽ ὅσον ἐς Σκαιάς τε πύλας καὶ φηγὸν ἵκανεν·
ἔνθά ποτ᾽ οἶον ἔμιμνε, μόγις δέ μευ ἔκφυγεν ὁρμήν.   355
νῦν δ᾽ ἐπεὶ οὐκ ἐθέλω πολεμιζέμεν Ἕκτορι δίῳ
αὔριον ἱρὰ Διὶ ῥέξας καὶ πᾶσι θεοῖσι
νηήσας εὖ νῆας, ἐπὴν ἅλαδε προερύσσω,
ὄψεαι, αἴ κ᾽ ἐθέλησθα καὶ αἴ κέν τοι τὰ μεμήλῃ,
ἦρι μάλ᾽ Ἑλλήσποντον ἐπ᾽ ἰχθυόεντα πλεούσας   360
νῆας ἐμάς, ἐν δ᾽ ἄνδρας ἐρεσσέμεναι μεμαῶτας·
εἰ δέ κεν εὐπλοίην δώῃ κλυτὸς ἐννοσίγαιος
ἤματί κε τριτάτῳ Φθίην ἐρίβωλον ἱκοίμην.

ἔστι δέ μοι μάλα πολλά, τὰ κάλλιπον ἐνθάδε ἔρρων·
ἄλλον δ᾽ ἐνθένδε χρυσὸν καὶ χαλκὸν ἐρυθρὸν   365
ἠδὲ γυναῖκας ἐϋζώνους πολιόν τε σίδηρον
ἄξομαι, ἅσσ᾽ ἔλαχόν γε· γέρας δέ μοι, ὅς περ ἔδωκεν,
αὖτις ἐφυβρίζων ἕλετο κρείων Ἀγαμέμνων
Ἀτρεΐδης· τῷ πάντ᾽ ἀγορευέμεν ὡς ἐπιτέλλω
ἀμφαδόν, ὄφρα καὶ ἄλλοι ἐπισκύζωνται Ἀχαιοὶ   370
εἴ τινά που Δαναῶν ἔτι ἔλπεται ἐξαπατήσειν
αἰὲν ἀναιδείην ἐπιειμένος· οὐδ᾽ ἂν ἔμοιγε
τετλαίη κύνεός περ ἐὼν εἰς ὦπα ἰδέσθαι·
οὐδέ τί οἱ βουλὰς συμφράσσομαι, οὐδὲ μὲν ἔργον·
ἐκ γὰρ δή μ᾽ ἀπάτησε καὶ ἤλιτεν· οὐδ᾽ ἂν ἔτ᾽ αὖτις   375
ἐξαπάφοιτ᾽ ἐπέεσσιν· ἅλις δέ οἱ· ἀλλὰ ἕκηλος
ἐρρέτω· ἐκ γὰρ εὖ φρένας εἵλετο μητίετα Ζεύς.
ἐχθρὰ δέ μοι τοῦ δῶρα, τίω δέ μιν ἐν καρὸς αἴσῃ.
οὐδ᾽ εἴ μοι δεκάκις τε καὶ εἰκοσάκις τόσα δοίη
ὅσσά τέ οἱ νῦν ἔστι, καὶ εἴ ποθεν ἄλλα γένοιτο,   380
οὐδ᾽ ὅσ᾽ ἐς Ὀρχομενὸν ποτινίσεται, οὐδ᾽ ὅσα Θήβας
Αἰγυπτίας, ὅθι πλεῖστα δόμοις ἐν κτήματα κεῖται,
αἵ θ᾽ ἑκατόμπυλοί εἰσι, διηκόσιοι δ᾽ ἀν᾽ ἑκάστας
ἀνέρες ἐξοιχνεῦσι σὺν ἵπποισιν καὶ ὄχεσφιν·
οὐδ᾽ εἴ μοι τόσα δοίη ὅσα ψάμαθός τε κόνις τε,   385
οὐδέ κεν ὣς ἔτι θυμὸν ἐμὸν πείσει᾽ Ἀγαμέμνων
πρίν γ᾽ ἀπὸ πᾶσαν ἐμοὶ δόμεναι θυμαλγέα λώβην.
κούρην δ᾽ οὐ γαμέω Ἀγαμέμνονος Ἀτρεΐδαο,
οὐδ᾽ εἰ χρυσείῃ Ἀφροδίτῃ κάλλος ἐρίζοι,
ἔργα δ᾽ Ἀθηναίῃ γλαυκώπιδι ἰσοφαρίζοι·   390
οὐδέ μιν ὣς γαμέω· ὃ δ᾽ Ἀχαιῶν ἄλλον ἑλέσθω,
ὅς τις οἷ τ᾽ ἐπέοικε καὶ ὃς βασιλεύτερός ἐστιν.
ἢν γὰρ δή με σαῶσι θεοὶ καὶ οἴκαδ᾽ ἵκωμαι,
Πηλεύς θήν μοι ἔπειτα γυναῖκά γε μάσσεται αὐτός.
πολλαὶ Ἀχαιΐδες εἰσὶν ἀν᾽ Ἑλλάδα τε Φθίην τε   395
κοῦραι ἀριστήων, οἵ τε πτολίεθρα ῥύονται,
τάων ἥν κ᾽ ἐθέλωμι φίλην ποιήσομ᾽ ἄκοιτιν.
ἔνθα δέ μοι μάλα πολλὸν ἐπέσσυτο θυμὸς ἀγήνωρ
γήμαντα μνηστὴν ἄλοχον ἐϊκυῖαν ἄκοιτιν
κτήμασι τέρπεσθαι τὰ γέρων ἐκτήσατο Πηλεύς·   400
οὐ γὰρ ἐμοὶ ψυχῆς ἀντάξιον οὐδ᾽ ὅσα φασὶν
Ἴλιον ἐκτῆσθαι εὖ ναιόμενον πτολίεθρον
τὸ πρὶν ἐπ᾽ εἰρήνης, πρὶν ἐλθεῖν υἷας Ἀχαιῶν,

οὐδ᾽ ὅσα λάϊνος οὐδὸς ἀφήτορος ἐντὸς ἐέργει
Φοίβου Ἀπόλλωνος Πυθοῖ ἔνι πετρηέσσῃ. 405
ληϊστοὶ μὲν γάρ τε βόες καὶ ἴφια μῆλα,
κτητοὶ δὲ τρίποδές τε καὶ ἵππων ξανθὰ κάρηνα,
ἀνδρὸς δὲ ψυχὴ πάλιν ἐλθεῖν οὔτε λεϊστὴ
οὔθ᾽ ἑλετή, ἐπεὶ ἄρ κεν ἀμείψεται ἕρκος ὀδόντων.
μήτηρ γάρ τέ μέ φησι θεὰ Θέτις ἀργυρόπεζα 410
διχθαδίας κῆρας φερέμεν θανάτοιο τέλοσδέ.
εἰ μέν κ᾽ αὖθι μένων Τρώων πόλιν ἀμφιμάχωμαι,
ὤλετο μέν μοι νόστος, ἀτὰρ κλέος ἄφθιτον ἔσται·
εἰ δέ κεν οἴκαδ᾽ ἵκωμι φίλην ἐς πατρίδα γαῖαν,
ὤλετό μοι κλέος ἐσθλόν, ἐπὶ δηρὸν δέ μοι αἰὼν 415
ἔσσεται, οὐδέ κέ μ᾽ ὦκα τέλος θανάτοιο κιχείη.
καὶ δ᾽ ἂν τοῖς ἄλλοισιν ἐγὼ παραμυθησαίμην
οἴκαδ᾽ ἀποπλείειν, ἐπεὶ οὐκέτι δήετε τέκμωρ
Ἰλίου αἰπεινῆς· μάλα γάρ ἕθεν εὐρύοπα Ζεὺς
χεῖρα ἑὴν ὑπερέσχε, τεθαρσήκασι δὲ λαοί. 420
ἀλλ᾽ ὑμεῖς μὲν ἰόντες ἀριστήεσσιν Ἀχαιῶν
ἀγγελίην ἀπόφασθε· τὸ γὰρ γέρας ἐστὶ γερόντων·
ὄφρ᾽ ἄλλην φράζωνται ἐνὶ φρεσὶ μῆτιν ἀμείνω,
ἥ κέ σφιν νῆάς τε σαῷ καὶ λαὸν Ἀχαιῶν
νηυσὶν ἔπι γλαφυρῇς, ἐπεὶ οὔ σφισιν ἥδέ γ᾽ ἑτοίμη 425
ἣν νῦν ἐφράσσαντο ἐμεῦ ἀπομηνίσαντος·
Φοῖνιξ δ᾽ αὖθι παρ᾽ ἄμμι μένων κατακοιμηθήτω,
ὄφρά μοι ἐν νήεσσι φίλην ἐς πατρίδ᾽ ἕπηται
αὔριον ἢν ἐθέλησιν· ἀνάγκῃ δ᾽ οὔ τί μιν ἄξω.᾽
ὣς ἔφαθ᾽, οἱ δ᾽ ἄρα πάντες ἀκὴν ἐγένοντο σιωπῇ 430
μῦθον ἀγασσάμενοι· μάλα γὰρ κρατερῶς ἀπέειπεν·

Commentary Notes
Iliad 9

It is evening after a long and hard day's fighting. The Trojans have been rampant on the battlefield, pushing the Greeks back to their encampment. They eagerly await morning when they can renew their assault – and perhaps annihilate the Greek forces once and for all.

In desperation, Agamemnon sends a delegation to Achilles to try to persuade him to rejoin the fighting. Agamemnon has already outlined the magnificent reparations that he will offer to Achilles to the rest of the Greeks, but now the offer must be presented by Achilles himself. We join the action as the three men chosen to lead the delegation – Odysseus, Ajax and Phoenix – make their way towards Achilles' part of the camp to deliver the news.

182–224

Odysseus, Ajax and Phoenix make their way along to Achilles' part of the camp. On arrival, they are welcomed by Achilles, who offers them food and drink.

182

τὼ δὲ βάτην – the appearance of the dual in this verse and several times over the next eighteen verses is one of the most notorious problems in the *Iliad*. Nestor has just named *three* men to go on the embassy to Achilles – Phoenix, Ajax and Odysseus – but the duals clearly indicate a delegation of just *two* men. The most likely explanation is that the duals have been left over from some previous version of the poem in which the embassy consisted of just two men – though exactly how such a glaring error made it into the final version of the *Iliad* remains a mystery. The aorist is left without its augment, as is common in Homer.

παρὰ θῖνα ... θαλάσσης – The Greek camp consists of several hundred ships which have been dragged up onto the beach and sit in a long line running along the shore. The delegates have just left the huts of Agamemnon, which are located in the middle of the camp, and are now walking 'along the shore' towards the huts of Achilles, which are located at one end of the camp.

183

πολλὰ – adv. 'eagerly', strengthened by the μάλα that follows.

γαιηόχῳ – 'earth-holding', perhaps because the ocean was originally thought of as embracing and supporting the earth, with the land floating on top of it.

ἐννοσιγαίῳ – 'Earth-shaker', i.e. Poseidon. The delegates pray to Poseidon as one of the staunchest supporters of the Greek cause, as well as being the patron god of the sea, beside which they are now walking.

The name 'Earth-shaker' may come from the fact that Poseidon was considered the patron god of earthquakes, or simply because the waves of the sea are considered to be constantly 'beating' the land.

184

πεπιθεῖν – the infinitive describes the intended result of their prayer, 'in order that they might persuade ...'.

μεγάλας φρένας – 'proud heart'; the φρήν (or φρένες) was an internal organ situated in the chest and associated with a wide range of thoughts and emotions. The organ is referred to interchangeably in both the singular and the plural.

Αἰακίδαο – 'grandson of Aeacus', i.e. Achilles. Words in -ίδαο and -ιάδης are usually patronymics, i.e. denoting a father-son relationship, e.g. Λαερτιάδης, 'son of Laertes', Μενοιτιάδης, 'son of Menoetius'. Αἰακίδης, by contrast, is an avonymic, denoting a grandfather-grandson relationship. No reason for this preference is given.

185

Μυρμιδόνων – The Myrmidons were a tribe from Phthia in an area of northern Greece known as Thessaly, so-called because they were said to have been created by Zeus from a colony of ants (Greek: μύρμηκες).

186

τὸν – 'him', i.e. Achilles. In Homer, ὁ, ἡ, τό, is almost always used as a third person pronoun, not the definite article.

φρένα τερπόμενον φόρμιγγι λιγείῃ – This is the only instance in the *Iliad* where we find music in the world of men. Indeed, Achilles is the only character in the *Iliad* to engage in any kind of creative pursuit apart from Helen, who we find in Book 3 'weaving many scenes of the conflict between the horse-taming Trojans and the bronze-clad Achaeans' (3.125–7).

187

ἐπὶ ... ἦεν – in Homer, it is possible for prepositions to become detached from the main verb, a phenomenon known as 'tmesis' ('cutting'). In these cases, students should translate as if the preposition and the verb formed a single word, i.e. ἐπῆεν. ἐπῆεν (= Attic ἐπῆν) is the imperfect of ἔπειμι, which here means 'to be attached [to something]'. The object of the verb, i.e. the lyre, must be understood from the previous line.

ζυγὸν – the crossbar joining the two 'horns' of the lyre, to which the pegs or other fittings that carried the strings were attached.

188

τὴν – 'it', i.e. the lyre; see note on τὸν above, 186.

πόλιν Ἠετίωνος – the 'city of Eëtion' was Thebe, near Troy. The raid that Achilles made on this city is referred to several times throughout the poem. In addition to the lyre that he now plays, other items acquired by Achilles in this raid that are mentioned in the poem include a horse, Pedasus (16.152–4) and a lump of pig iron which Eëtion apparently used as a discus (23.826–7). It was also in this raid that Achilles killed Andromache's father, Eëtion himself, as well as all seven of her brothers (6.414–16, 421–4).

189

ὅ – 'his'.

ἄειδε ... κλέα ἀνδρῶν – 'he was singing about the glorious deeds of men'. Scholars have noted the self-referential (or meta-poetical) nature of Achilles' singing: the *Iliad* is itself a poem about the glorious deeds of men.

190

οἱ – 'him', i.e. Achilles; the pronoun is governed by ἐναντίος, which takes the dative case.

ἧστο – pluperfect, 'had taken a seat'.

σιωπῇ – 'in silence'; from the small number of descriptions that we have of poetic performances of this kind, it seems that the etiquette was for the audience to sit in silence until the poet finished his song.

191

δέγμενος – 'waiting for'.

192

ἡγεῖτο – Odysseus walks in ahead of the others.

193–224

The arrival and reception of guests is a common type-scene in the Homeric poems. As with all type-scenes, the sequence of events is more or less fixed: the host rises and leads his guest(s) to a seat, offers his guest(s) food and drink and only then enquires about the reason for their visit.

193

στὰν – a shorter form of the third person plural ἔστησαν.

αὐτοῖο – i.e. Achilles.

ταφών – the verb τέθηπα ('to be astonished') is perfect in form, but present in meaning.

194

αὐτῇ σὺν φόρμιγγι – 'lyre and all', i.e. with the lyre still in his hand.

ἔνθα – 'where', relative adverb.

θάασσεν – imperfect in the Greek, though we should translate with the pluperfect in English, i.e. 'where he had been sitting'.

196

τὼ – 'them', accusative dual, object of δεικνύμενος.

δεικνύμενος – 'welcoming', perhaps with a wave of the hand. Although the word is related in form and sense to δείκνυμι ('to point at'), it is more directly connected with δειδίσκομαι ('to pledge, greet').

197–8

Achilles' greeting to his friends is a little disjointed, not least because of the insertion of the parenthetical phrase ἦ τι μάλα χρεώ in the middle of the sentence; the οἵ of 198 refers back to φίλοι ἄνδρες in the previous line.

197

ἦ τι μάλα χρεώ – lit. 'indeed there is great need'. Achilles does not state explicitly what there is a need of, though we can assume he means there is need of him. He had spoken explicitly of this need earlier in the poem (χρειὼ ἐμεῖο, 1.341), and Thetis seems to refer to the same thing later on in Book 18 (σεῦ ἐπιδευομένους, 18.77).

198

σκυζομένῳ περ – 'incensed though I am'; the verb σκύζομαι refers to an anger that is particularly deep-felt; the use of περ + participle is the equivalent of the Attic καίπερ + participle.

Ἀχαιῶν φίλτατοί – a curious detail; nothing else in the poem suggests that Achilles was particularly close to either Ajax or Odysseus. In fact, there seems to have been a traditional antipathy between Odysseus and Achilles, a theme which forms the subject of one of Demodocus' songs in the *Odyssey* (8.74ff.). This less-than-friendly relationship between the two men may underlie much of what follows.

ἐστον – This is the final dual in the long sequence that began at 182.

200

εἶσεν – aorist of ἵζω, 'he seated them'.

ἐν κλισμοῖσι ... πορφυρέοισιν – i.e. on chairs with rugs spread over them.

202

κρητῆρα – 'mixing-bowl'; the Greeks of the eighth century BC diluted their wine with water, using a large, deep bowl known as a κρατήρ to mix the two liquids. The presence of the word *ka-ra-te-ra* (i.e. *crater*, mixing bowl) on a Linear B tablet suggests the practice goes back to Mycenaean times.

Μενοιτίου υἱὲ – i.e. Patroclus.

καθίστα – 'set down', present imperative; because of its size and weight, the mixing bowl was most likely set up on the floor, rather than on a table.

203

ζωρότερον δὲ κέραιε – 'mix it stronger', i.e. stronger than usual. We cannot be sure how strong the heroes of the *Iliad* usually took their wine. In Hesiod's *Works and Days* (596), a mixture of three parts water to one of wine is recommended.

204

οἱ – 'these', demonstrative pronoun, as usual in Homer.

ὑπέασι μελάθρῳ – 'under my roof'; technically, the word μέλαθρον referred to the crossbeam of a house, which supported the rafters and the roof. Since the architecture of Achilles' hut is assumed to be rather modest, he must be using the term idiomatically to mean simply 'roof'.

205

Patroclus offers no reply to Achilles, but simply does what has been asked of him, i.e. to prepare the wine and distribute drinking cups to each of the guests. Ancient commentators were touched by Patroclus' silence, seeing it as a sign of his kind and gentle nature.

206–21

Achilles and his companions prepare a meal for their guests in what is the most elaborate non-sacrificial meal in Homer. Unlike other type-scenes (e.g. arming-scenes), where expansion takes place through the elaboration of individual elements, the poet expands the meal-preparation type-scene through the addition of more and more elements.

206

ὅ – 'he', i.e. Achilles.

κρεῖον – 'carving-dish', used for the preparation of meat. It is one of five *hapax legomena* in the next fifteen verses, the others being: ἀνθρακιά ('glowing embers'), ἐλεόν ('side-table'), θυηλαί ('parts burnt as sacrifice') and κρατευταί ('support-blocks').

κάββαλεν = κατέβαλεν, aorist of καταβάλλω.

ἐν πυρὸς αὐγῇ – 'in the light of the fire'; Achilles places the carving-dish next to the fire, presumably so he can see what he is doing. Given that it is now evening in the Greek camp, we can assume that this fire is the only source of light in his hut.

207

ἐν ... ἔθηκε – tmesis; see note on ἐπὶ ... ἦεν at 187. In this case, the verb ἐνέθηκε is the third person singular aorist of ἐντίθημι, which here means 'to place [something] in [something else]'.

νῶτον – 'the back' or 'the chine', a cut of meat containing the backbone; ῥάχις in 209 refers to the same cut of meat. To avoid repetition, students might like to translate νῶτον as 'back' and ῥάχις as 'chine'. They were in any case the best cuts of meat available to the Homeric hero.

208

ἐν – we must supply ἔθηκε from the previous line, resulting in another example of tmesis.

τεθαλυῖαν ἀλοιφῆ – 'smeared with fat'; the ἀλοιφή refers not to the inherent fatness of the hog, but the lard that has been smeared over the surface before roasting.

209
τῷ – 'for him', i.e. Achilles.

ἔχεν – Automedon holds the meat in place while Achilles 'chops' (τάμνεν) it into joints. In the next line, he 'slices' (μίστυλλε) each of the joints into smaller pieces ready to be threaded onto spits and roasted. Note that each of these verbs are imperfect: 'he held', 'he chopped', 'he sliced'.

210
τὰ – 'them', i.e. the large chunks of meat that have just been prepared by Achilles; he now slices them into smaller pieces.

ἀμφι – 'onto'.

212
κατὰ ... ἐκάη – tmesis. The meat is not roasted in the open flame; only the hot embers (ἀνθρακιὴν) are used for roasting, the spits of meat being arranged directly over them.

214
πάσσε δ' ἁλὸς θείοιο – 'sprinkled some salt', partitive genitive; one ancient commentator explained the 'holiness' of the salt on the basis of its preservative power.

κρατευτάων – κρατευταί are the stone or clay blocks placed either side of a fire in order to lay something horizontally above it. It is possible, if a little anachronistic, to translate as 'andirons' or 'firedogs' – although 'blocks' or 'supports' perhaps remains the safest bet.

ἐπαείρας – conveys the idea of lifting something (acc.) up and placing it on something (gen.).

215
εἰν = ἐν.

ἐλεοῖσιν – 'serving-boards'.

216
τραπέζῃ – 'to each table'; the τράπεζα was a small, portable table that would be removed at the end of the meal. Each of the guests has a τράπεζα in front of them.

219
τοίχου τοῦ ἑτέροιο – 'by the opposite wall', genitive of place. Some scholars have taken Achilles' decision to sit directly opposite Odysseus as a sign of his distrust, although it seems to have been standard etiquette to sit opposite one's guest.

220
Πάτροκλον – this is the last mention of Patroclus for exactly four hundred lines.

ὃν – 'his'; ὅς is one of the more versatile words in Homer; it can be used as a demonstrative pronoun ('this', 'that', 'he', 'she'), a relative pronoun ('who', 'which'), as well as a reflexive adjective ('one's own'), as here.

θυηλάς – 'a sacrificial offering'; technically, θυηλή refers to the part of the sacrificial victim that was offered in a burnt-sacrifice, but the simpler 'sacrificial offering' will do here.

222
ἐξ ... ἕντο – tmesis.

223
Ajax nods to Phoenix to start speaking, but it is Odysseus who steps in to make the first speech. It is possible that Ajax has simply made a mistake, forgetting that Odysseus was supposed to make the first speech, although most scholars take this line as indicating that Odysseus has ignored the prearranged order of speakers and decided at the last minute to deliver the first speech himself.

224
δείδεκτ' – 'he pledged [Achilles]'; for the meaning of this word, see the note at 196 above.

225–306

Odysseus makes the first of three speeches aimed at persuading Achilles to return to battle. In a long and well-organized speech, Odysseus informs Achilles of the desperate situation faced by the Achaeans and recounts the extensive list of gifts that have been offered by Agamemnon if he will deliver the Achaeans from destruction. His speech ends with an appeal for Achilles to take pity on his friends and to put a stop of the arrogant and insulting behaviour of Hector.

225
χαῖρ' Ἀχιλεῦ – 'your health, Achilles!'.

δαιτὸς ... ἐΐσης – according to one commentator, the feast is 'equal' because it is one of the rituals by which the hero class affirm their status as equals distinct from (and better than) the community at large.

οὐκ ἐπιδευεῖς – sc. ἐσμέν, 'we are not lacking'; the adjective ἐπιδευής, like all words conveying a want or need of something, governs the genitive case.

226–7
ἠμὲν ... ἠδὲ = 'both ... and'.

226
ἐνὶ κλισίῃ Ἀγαμέμνονος – Immediately before coming to see Achilles, the three delegates to Achilles had been in the hut of Agamemnon, where they had been

treated to a large meal (9.90–2). Ancient commentators complained that it was unrealistic for the heroes to eat twice in the same evening, and suggested emending some of the details so that the delegates only tasted the food Achilles had provided for them. In fact, the primary purpose of the meal is to demonstrate the character of Achilles: angry though he is, he still behaves with exemplary etiquette in the hospitality he provides for his guests.

227

ἠδὲ καί – 'even as'.

πάρα = πάρεστι; the position of the accent on πάρα/παρά provides an important clue as to whether we have a preposition (παρά) or whether πάρα = πάρεστι, as here.

228

δαίνυσθ᾽ – 'for us to dine on'; δαίνυσθαι is used here in a sense that clarifies, explains or qualifies a noun or adjective (known as an epexegetic infinitive).

οὐ ... μέμηλεν – 'are not our concern'; ἡμῖν must be understood.

229

διοτρεφὲς – 'nourished by Zeus'; little does Odysseus know, Achilles had prayed in Zeus in Book 1 to cause the 'very great suffering' (λίην μέγα πῆμα) that Odysseus now describes (1.408–9).

εἰσορόωντες – students may notice the additional ό in this word. This is not because the verb has been left uncontracted (which would be εἰσοράοντες), but the result of the addition of short vowel before the normal contracted ending (-ωντες), a phenomenon known as diectasis.

230

ἐν δοιῇ – 'it is in doubt', ἐστί must be understood.

230–1

σαωσέμεν ... νῆας ἐϋσσέλμους – 'whether we save our well-benched ships or perish'. σαωσέμεν and ἀπολέσθαι are both aorist active infinitives, though only σαωσέμεν is transitive. Despite its position after ἀπολέσθαι, therefore, νῆας must be the object of σαωσέμεν, not ἀπολέσθαι. The technical name for an inversion of word order of this kind is hyperbaton.

231

δύσεαι – 'put on', i.e. as a garment; future tense.

232

τείχεος – i.e. the wall of the Achaeans' camp, not the walls of the city of Troy.

αὖλιν ἔθεντο – 'they have set up camp'; after a day of success in the field, the Trojans have taken the apparently unprecedented step of sleeping outside the walls of the city. The reason for this, as explained by Hector, is to prevent the Achaeans from escaping during the night, adding to the general sense of desperation felt by the Achaeans.

233

ἐπίκουροι – the Trojans are aided in the defence of their city by a range of 'far-famed allies'. Most prominent among them are probably the Lycians, led by Sarpedon and later Glaucus, and the Thracians, led by Rhesus. A full list can be found at 2.819 ff.

234

κηάμενοι … κατὰ στρατόν – the famous description of the hundreds of Trojan campfires lighting up the plain can be found at 8.554–65. κατὰ + accusative can mean 'through', 'throughout'.

234–5

οὐδ᾿ ἔτι φασὶ σχήσεσθ᾿ – 'and they say they will not be held back'; σχήσεσθαι is middle with passive meaning, and the subject is the Trojans, not the Achaeans. As in Attic Greek, οὐ + φημί = 'I say that … not', not 'I do not say …'.

235

ἐν νηυσὶ … πεσέεσθαι – 'to fall upon the ships', i.e. to attack them.

236–7

ἐνδέξια σήματα … ἀστράπτει – the 'signs' (σήματα) referred to here are lightning bolts. The appearance of lightning on the right hand side (ἐνδέξια) was seen to be a favourable omen, as was a clap of thunder (ἀστράπτει). Zeus is favouring Hector and the Trojans.

237

σθένεϊ βλεμεαίνων – 'exulting in his strength'; the same formula is used of Hector by the poet himself at 8.337.

239

λύσσα – the word λύσσα ('rage') has the same root as the Greek word for 'wolf' (λύκος), and perhaps referred originally to the furious rage of a wolf or the madness of a rabid dog. Odysseus is exaggerating Hector's behaviour for rhetorical effect: while Hector was fighting furiously the last time we saw him, there is no sense of him raging like a madman, as stated here.

241

στεῦται – 'he is threatening'; like all verbs of promising and threatening, στεῦμαι governs the future infinitive (ἀποκόψειν).

ἄκρα κόρυμβα – 'the ends of the stern-posts'; in Homer, the ships of the Achaeans are thought of being shaped like the horns of an ox, with both front and back turned upright. Most depictions of these ships indicate that the more prominent upright was at the front, which may have been decorated with simple ornamentation or even a figurehead. It is this ornamentation that we are to imagine Hector 'cutting off' (ἀποκόψειν) here, perhaps to keep as a kind of trophy.

242

αὐτάς, i.e. the ships.

πυρός – 'with fire'; a partitive genitive where the instrumental dative (πυρί) might have been expected.

243

παρὰ τῇσιν – 'beside them', i.e. next to the ships.

ὀρινομένους ὑπὸ καπνοῦ – 'having been roused by the smoke'; the smoke is imagined as coming from the burning ships. One ancient commentator compares the 'smoking out' of the Achaeans to that of wasps from their nest.

244

ταῦτ' – refers to the μή-clause that follows.

οἱ – 'for him'.

245

ἡμῖν δὲ δὴ αἴσιμον εἴη – 'and in that case, our fate would be ...', the optative (εἴη) is used to show that this is a remote fear than the one just mentioned, i.e. that the gods would fulfil Hector's threats.

246

φθίσθαι ... ἑκὰς Ἄργεος ἱπποβότοιο – the motif of 'dying far from home' is frequently employed by the poet as a means of generating pathos for the fallen warrior.

247

ἄνα – 'get up!', 'come on!'.

καὶ ὀψέ περ – 'late though it is'.

248

ἐρύεσθαι – infinitive for imperative; the verb may be taken as the middle infinitive of ἐρύω, 'draw away', or as the active infinitive of ἐρύομαι, 'save'; 'rescue' captures the force of both.

249

τοι = σοι, 'for you'.

249–50

οὐδέ τι ... εὑρεῖν – 'nor will there be any means to find a cure to the disaster when it has happened'. Note the wordplay between ἄχος ('pain, distress') and ἄκος ('cure, remedy').

250

ῥεχθέντος κακοῦ – may be genitive absolute or governed directly by ἄκος; the meaning is the same in both cases.

251

φράζευ = φράζου, imperative, 'take thought'; the word will be echoed by Achilles at 347, φραζέσθω, 'let Agamemnon take thought'.

252–8

Odysseus here recalls the parting words of advice given to Achilles by his father, Peleus.

252

ὦ πέπον – 'my dear friend'; the term is informal, almost colloquial, as well as being potentially patronizing coming from Odysseus. Elsewhere in the poem, the word is only ever used of a superior talking to their inferior, in each case expressing more or less open disapproval.

253

Φθίης – 'Phthia', the city in Thessaly which is home to Achilles and the Myrmidons.

254–8

Odysseus moves from describing Peleus' parting words to Achilles to actually quoting them directly, a rhetorical technique known as prosopopoeia.

254

Ἀθηναίη τε καὶ Ἥρη – like Poseidon, Athena and Hera are both staunch supporters of the Achaean cause.

256

ἴσχειν – 'restrain', infinitive for imperative, as with ληγέμεναι in the next line.

φιλοφροσύνη – 'friendliness', *hapax legomenon*, but cf. Helen's use of the word ἀγανοφροσύνη ('gentleness', 'kindliness') to describe the deceased Hector at 24.772.

257

ληγέμεναι – 'cease from'; the advice is not for Achilles to avoid quarrels (though he should presumably do that as well), but to put an end to them if and when they arise.

κακομηχάνου – lit. 'devising evil', i.e. 'malicious'. This description might bring to mind the goddess Eris' malicious plan to toss a golden apple into the wedding feast of Peleus and Thetis. Alternatively, we might think of Achilles himself as κακομήχανος: in Book 1, he prayed to Zeus to bring death and destruction to his own side.

μᾶλλον – 'so much the more'.

259

ὅ – 'this'.

261

ἄξια – 'valuable, worthy'; the word ἄξιος denotes something that is 'equal in value' to something else. It is implicit in Odysseus' speech that Agamemnon's gifts should be seen as 'equal in value' to his insult of Achilles in Book 1. Achilles, by contrast, considers the gifts as if they are supposed to be 'equal in value' to his own life – which he will decide they are not.

δίδωσι – 'offers'.

262

εἰ – used fairly often in Homer as an exclamation, e.g. 'well then', 'come then'.

κέ τοι καταλέξω – 'I will recount for you …', the aorist subjunctive (καταλέξω) with κέ may be translated as if it were the future tense.

264–99

Odysseus now lists the gifts that Agamemnon will offer to Achilles if he will give up his anger and return to battle. The list is repeated almost verbatim from earlier in the book (122–57), when Agamemnon himself had listed the gifts to the assembled Achaeans.

264

ἀπύρους – 'untouched by fire', i.e. never used.

266

πηγούς – 'strong', lit. 'solidly built', from the verb πήγνυμι.

ἄροντο – 'win', from ἄρνυμαι.

267–9

'He would not be a poor man (οὔ κεν ἀλήϊος εἴη ἀνήρ), nor would he be unpossessed of precious gold (οὐδέ κεν ἀκτήμων ἐριτίμοιο χρυσοῖο), he for whom there was (ᾧ … γένοιτο) as many prizes as the horses of Agamemnon won with their speed' (τόσσα … ὅσσ' Ἀγαμέμνονος ἵπποι ἀέθλια ποσσὶν ἄροντο). The sentence is rather unwieldy, though its meaning is clear: the prizes that Agamemnon's horses have won would amount to a large fortune.

267

ἀλήϊος – 'poor', although the word technically means 'without booty'.

270

ἀμύμονα ἔργα ἰδυίας – lit. 'knowing excellent deeds', i.e. 'skilled in excellent handicraft'.

271

αὐτός – 'you yourself', i.e. Achilles. Agamemnon is in the rather embarrassing situation of compensating Achilles with booty that he himself had won.

272

τότε – i.e. at the time when the spoils of the raid on Lesbos were divided between the Achaean heroes.

κάλλει ἐνίκων φῦλα γυναικῶν – lit. 'who conquered the race of women with their beauty', i.e. who were the most beautiful of those captured during the raid on Lesbos.

273
τοι = σοι, 'to you'.

μετά – 'among them'.

274
κούρη Βρισῆος – i.e. Briseïs, the girl whom Agamemnon confiscated from Achilles in Book 1.

ἐπὶ ... ὀμεῖται – tmesis.

275
μή ποτε – 'that he has never ...', governs the infinitive.

τῆς – 'her', i.e. belonging to Briseïs.

276
ἡ θέμις ... γυναικῶν – 'which is the custom of both men and women', i.e. the activities described in the previous line, rather than the taking of oaths.

277
αὖτε – 'later', 'in the future'; note the antithesis to αὐτίκα earlier in the line.

278
ἄστυ μέγα Πριάμοιο – i.e. the city of Troy.

δώωσ' ἀλαπάξαι – 'grant us to destroy'; the use of δίδωμι + infinitive to mean 'grant', 'allow' is a regular idiom in Attic Greek; δώωσι = δῶσι.

279
χρυσοῦ καὶ χαλκοῦ – genitive after νηήσασθαι, as with all verbs denoting 'filling with' something.

νηήσασθαι – 'to load up', infinitive for imperative, as are ἑλέσθαι (281) and ἄγεσθαι (289).

280
εἰσελθών – most likely refers to 'entering into' the meeting at which the spoils are divided, rather than 'entering into the conquered city'.

283
Ἄργος ... Ἀχαιϊκὸν – i.e. the Peloponnese.

οὖθαρ ἀρούρης – lit. 'udder of the soil', i.e. 'the most fertile of lands'; Note that the noun phrases are next to each other (placed in apposition), so that the quality of fertility adds to our recognition of Argos.

284
οἱ – 'to him', i.e. Agamemnon.

Ὀρέστῃ – Orestes was Agamemnon's only son; he is only mentioned in the *Iliad* here and in the 'mirroring' speech Agamemnon had given earlier, which Odysseus is now relating (almost word for word) to Achilles.

285

θαλίῃ ἔνι πολλῇ – 'amid great abundance'.

287

Χρυσόθεμις καὶ Λαοδίκη καὶ Ἰφιάνασσα – the names of Agamemnon's daughters may be surprising given the (now much more famous) depiction of the children of Agamemnon in later Attic tragedy. There, Agamemnon's daughters were named as Electra and Iphigenia. If Iphianassa is to be identified with Iphigenia, the poet must have been unaware of – or have simply ignored – the tradition in which Iphigenia was sacrificed by her father before the Greeks sailed to Troy.

288

τάων – 'of these', i.e. of three girls just mentioned.

ἐθέλῃσθα – 'you may choose'.

φίλην – 'his own'.

ἀνάεδνον – 'without paying the bride-price'; under ordinary circumstances, the bridegroom would be expected to pay the bride's father on marriage.

289

ἐπὶ ... δώσει – tmesis.

μείλια – 'peace offerings'; the word is connected to μειλίσσω, 'to soften'.

291

εὖ ναιόμενα – 'well-populated'.

292–5

The seven towns mentioned by Agamemnon are surprisingly far south-west of his actual kingdom in and around Mycenae in the north-east Peloponnese (2.569–75). If anything, the cities are actually in the territory of Nestor, even being described at 295 as being located 'at the furthest point of sandy Pylos'. It is unclear how Agamemnon expected to redistribute cities that were outside of his kingdom.

295

νέαται Πύλου ἠμαθόεντος – 'at the furthest point in sandy Pylos', i.e. on the borders of Pylos.

296

πολύρρηνες πολυβοῦται – the two adjectives sit in asyndeton, i.e. without a conjunction between the two words, a relatively common feature in Homeric verse, especially where two adjectives have the same beginning, as here.

297

ὡς – 'like'; the word is accented like this when it *follows* the word it is governing.

298

λιπαρὰς ... θέμιστας – 'rich taxes'.
τελέουσι – 'they will pay', future indicative.

299

μεταλήξαντι χόλοιο – here, as often, the participle has conditional force: 'if you will cease from your anger'.

300–6

In the original speech at 9.122–57, Agamemnon had ended with the extraordinary demand that Achilles should 'take his place below me' (μοι ὑποστήτω, 160) on the grounds that he was both 'more kingly' (βασιλεύτερός, 160) and 'older by birth' (γενεῇ προγενέστερος, 161). It is a detail that Odysseus tactfully omits, returning instead to the desperate situation faced by the Achaean army as a whole and the outrageous behaviour of Hector.

300

ἀπήχθετο ... μᾶλλον – 'he has become too hated', i.e. for you to accept his offer of compensation.
κηρόθι – 'in your heart'; the suffix -θι is locative.

301

σὺ δ' – this begins the main clause after the conditional in the previous line.
ἄλλους περ – 'the others, at any rate'.

303

σφι – 'among them', 'in their eyes'.

304

μάλα τοι σχεδὸν ἔλθοι – lit. 'he would come very close to you', i.e. he would approach you on the battlefield.

306

ἔμεναι = εἶναι.

307–429

Achilles' reply to Odysseus is one of the most powerful speeches in the whole poem. While his speech is not as structured as that of Odysseus, it can be broken into five more or less distinct parts: after a short introduction (308–14), Achilles lists his grievances against Agamemnon (315–45), before describing what has happened and what will happen to the Achaeans in his absence (346–63). After that, Achilles thinks about what life will be like back at home (364–77), before going through exactly what he thinks of the gifts that Agamemnon has offered him (378–416). The speech ends with some advice to the Achaeans and an invitation to Phoenix (417–29).

308
The contrast between the honorific formality of Achilles' addressing of Odysseus and the speech which follows may suggest that Achilles' words are spoken ironically.

309
τὸν μῦθον – 'my will', 'what I am thinking'.

ἀπηλεγέως ἀποειπεῖν – 'to declare forthrightly'; Achilles' speech makes use of a range of aural effects, including assonance and alliteration. The repeated ἀπ- here is the first of several examples.

310
ἦ περ ... ἔσται – lit. 'how I am thinking (ἦ περ δὴ φρονέω) and what shall come to pass (ὡς τετελεσμένον ἔσται)'.

311
τρύζητε – 'murmur', 'mutter'; some scholars have read the word as denoting the 'cooing' of doves (Greek: τρυγόνες), others as the 'croaking' of frogs.

ἄλλοθεν ἄλλος – 'one man after another'; the phrase is obviously also alliterative, cf. ἀπηλεγέως ἀποειπεῖν at 309.

312
κεῖνος = ἐκεῖνος, 'that man'.

ὁμῶς – 'like', governs the dative.

313
χ' = κε; consonants which have an aspirated form employ it when an elision precedes a word with a rough breathing.

ἕτερον ... ἄλλο – 'one thing ... another'.

314
ὥς – 'how', not 'what'; Achilles is referring to how he will deliver his message, i.e. bluntly (ἀπηλεγέως, 309), not what he is planning to say.

315–16
οὔτ' ... οὔτ' ... οὐκ – Achilles' refusal is underlined by the threefold repetition of the negative.

316
ἄρα ... ἦεν – 'it now appears that there is ...', a regular use of the particle ἄρα with the imperfect.

χάρις ... μάρνασθαι – χάρις + inf. = 'gratitude for doing something (+ inf.)'

317
ἐπ᾽ – 'against'.

318
μένοντι – 'for the man who stays behind', i.e. the man who doesn't contribute to the fighting; Attic Greek would have used the definite article here, i.e. τῷ μένοντι, so also with κακὸς and ἐσθλός below (both 319).

319
κακὸς – 'the coward'.
ἐσθλός – 'the brave man'.

320
κάτθαν᾽ – this is a gnomic aorist, expressing a timeless truth, and should thus be translated as if it were in the present tense.
ὅ τ᾽ ἀεργὸς ἀνὴρ ὅ τε πολλὰ ἐοργώς – the use of ὁ, ἡ, τό as a definite article is rare in Homer; its use here has led some scholars to suggest this verse is a late addition to the text.
    The line is highly assonant. Note in particular the balance between the ὅ τ᾽ and ὅ τε, and the words ἀεργὸς and ἐοργώς. If the digamma was still pronounced, the line would have also had the repeated w-sounds in ἀϝεργὸς (= *awergos*) and ϝέϝοργώς (= *weworgōs*).

321
οὐδέ τί μοι περίκειται – lit. 'nor is anything left over for me', i.e. 'nor do I get any advantage'.

322
ἐμὴν ψυχὴν παραβαλλόμενος – 'risking my life'.

πολεμίζειν – infinitive of purpose.

323–4
Achilles utters more similes than any other character in the poem, which may indicate his emotional and rhetorical range. Similes spoken by characters tend to be shorter and more intense compared to those spoken by the poet. It is striking that the warlike Achilles compares himself with a bird feeding its unfledged young.

323
ἀπτῆσι – dative plural of ἀπτήν, 'unfledged'.

324
κακῶς δ᾽ ἄρα οἱ πέλει αὐτῇ – 'and it fares badly for herself'; technically a separate sentence, though the connection with the previous sentence is so strong that we

might choose to translate it as a subordinate clause, e.g. 'even though it fares badly for herself'.

οἱ ... αὐτῇ = ἑαυτῇ.

325

ἀΰπνους νύκτας ἴαυον – 'passed sleepless nights'; the verb ἰαύω usually means 'to sleep', a meaning which would obviously be oxymoronic alongside ἀΰπνους ('sleepless').

327

ὀάρων ἕνεκα σφετεράων – 'for their wives', i.e. the wives of the people Achilles is fighting against, who would form a key part of the spoils from a defeated enemy.

329

πόλεις and ἀλαπάξαι must be understood from the previous line.

330

κειμήλια πολλὰ καὶ ἐσθλά – 'much, good treasure', hendiadys with two words joined by 'and' expressing a single idea.

331

δόσκον – the addition of -σκ- in the middle of the verb indicates that this is a frequentative use of the imperfect, i.e. indicating an action done on multiple occasions, so 'I always gave', rather than simply 'I gave'. So also for δασάσκετο and ἔχεσκεν in 333. The frequentative imperfect never takes an augment.

333

διὰ ... δασάσκετο – tmesis.

334

ἄλλα ... δίδου γέρα – 'Other things he gave as booty ...'.

335

τοῖσι μὲν ἔμπεδα κεῖται – lit. 'for them it lies steadfast', i.e. the booty of the other Achaeans is left untouched once it has been distributed.

336

ἄλοχον – 'my wife', i.e. Briseïs. Briseïs is not Achilles' wife so much as his captured concubine, but the conceit is useful when comparing his own relationship to that of Menelaus and Helen.

336–7

θυμαρέα ... τῇ ... τερπέσθω ... τί ... Τρώεσσιν – The repetition of 't' sounds gives the impression that Achilles is spitting out his words in furious anger, cf. Oedipus' furious response to Tiresias in Sophocles' *Oedipus Tyrannus*: τυφλὸς τά τ' ὦτα τόν τε νοῦν τά τ' ὄμματ' εἶ ('you are blind in your ears, in your mind and in your eyes', 371).

336

τῇ – i.e. Briseïs.

337–9

Note the rhetorical effect of (i) a series of enjambments, (ii) emphatic pauses after the first word of the new line and (iii) the repetition of proper names, especially Ἀτρείδης ('son of Atreus') as the first word. The drama of the lines is heightened by three rhetorical questions.

337

τερπέσθω – 'let him have his pleasure'; we might see Achilles' comments here as a response to Agamemnon's oath (at 274–5) that he has never touched Briseïs.

338

λαὸν – to be understood as the object of both ἀγείρας and ἀνήγαγεν, i.e. 'to assemble an army and lead it here'.

339

ἦ οὐχ – 'was it not ...?'.

341

ἐπεὶ – 'no, for'.

ὅς τις ἀνὴρ – ἐστί must be understood, i.e. 'any man who is ...'.

342

τὴν αὐτοῦ – understand ἄλοχον, i.e. 'his own wife'; this use of the article with the possessive pronoun is unique in Homer.

343

ἐκ θυμοῦ – 'from the heart', i.e. sincerely, deeply.

δουρικτητήν περ – 'even though she was won by my spear'; Briseïs was captured by Achilles during his raid on the town of Lyrnessus.
φίλεον – the use of the past tense is striking.

344

ἀπάτησε – 'cheated', rather than 'deceived'; Agamemnon has cheated Achilles by not rewarding him sufficiently for his efforts in the field. It is a line of argument that Achilles will return to at 371.

345

μή μευ πειράτω εὖ εἰδότος – 'let him not try me: I know him too well'.

347

φραζέσθω – 'let Agamemnon consider how', used with the infinitive; Achilles echoes the φράζευ used by Odysseus at 251.

348

ἦ μὲν – 'for sure'.

νόσφιν ἐμεῖο – lit. 'without me', i.e. 'in my absence'.

The repeated use of the conjunctions καὶ and δὲ, as well as the repetition of δὴ, emphasizes the sarcasm of these lines: 'Oh, I see Agamemnon has been *really* busy in my absence ...'.

349

ἐπ᾽ αὐτῷ – 'in front of it'.

350

μεγάλην – 'deep', since the word here refers to a ditch.

ἐν ... κατέπηξεν – tmesis.

352

ὄφρα – 'as long as'.

μετ᾽ Ἀχαιοῖσιν – 'with the Achaeans', i.e. among them, on their side.

353

ἀπὸ τείχεος – 'away from the wall', i.e. the walls of Troy.

354

ὅσον ἐς – 'only as far as'.

Σκαιάς ... πύλας – the Scaean gate represented one of the two main entrances to the city of the Troy, and the only one that Homer mentions by name.

355

οἶον – refers to Achilles, not Hector.

357

ἱρὰ ... ῥέξας – 'having made a sacrifice'.

358

νηήσας εὖ νῆας – Achilles once again echoes the words of Agamemnon, who said that Achilles could 'pile his ships high with gold and bronze ... if the gods grant us to sack the great city of Priam'. Achilles' words here represent a rejection of that offer: he can pile his ships high with treasure right now and does not need Agamemnon's permission to do so.

ἐπὴν = ἐπεί κε.

359

After the participles ῥέξας (357) and νηήσας (358), we would expect a first person main verb to complete the sentence; instead, Achilles begins a new clause with the words ἐπὴν ἅλα δὲ προερύσσω, 'when I put out to sea'.

361

ἐν δ᾽ – 'and in them', i.e. Achilles' ships; another ὄψεαι must be understood, 'you will see ...'.

364

ἔστι – the position of the accent indicates that this is the 'existential' use of ἔστι, i.e. 'there is/are'.

κάλλιπον = κατέλιπον.

ἔρρων – the verb ἔρρω, which has the basic meaning of 'to go', is strongly pejorative, i.e. 'to go at one's cost, to go with pain or difficulty'; some creativity in translation may be required, e.g. 'when I made this doomed voyage here' (Hammond), 'when I came unluckily here' (Willcock), 'when, to my cost, I came here' (Green), etc.

365–7

Achilles enumerates the booty he will take back home with him in a list that is similar in kind, if not in number, to that of Agamemnon. The implication is clear: Achilles already has precious metals and female slaves – why would he want any more from Agamemnon?

365

ἄλλον – 'besides', i.e. in addition to what I already have at home.

ἐνθένδε – 'from here', i.e. from Troy.

367

ἅσσ᾽ ἔλαχόν γε – 'all the things which I have been allotted', i.e. 'my regular share of the booty', contrasted with γέρας later in the line, 'my special gift of honour'.

ἅσσ᾽ = ἅτινα.

369

ἀγορευέμεν – infinitive for imperative.

372–8

Note the rhetorical effectiveness of the short statements with irregularly placed pauses.

372

ἀναιδείην ἐπιειμένος – 'clothed in shamelessness'.

373

εἰς ὦπα ἰδέσθαι – 'to look me in the eye'; Achilles mocks the fact that Agamemnon didn't have the courage to deliver his message himself, but relied instead upon a delegation.

375

ἐκ ... ἀπάτησε – tmesis.

376

ἅλις δέ οἱ – 'that is enough for him', i.e. let him be content with what he has done.

376–7

ἔκηλος ἐρρέτω – 'let him go to hell at his leisure!', a curse.

377

ἐκ … εἵλετο – tmesis.

εὑ = οὑ, 'his'.

378

τίω δέ μιν ἐν καρὸς αἴσῃ – 'I value him at a splinter's worth'; the word κάρ is thought to have derived from κείρω ('to cut'), thus denoting anything 'cut off', e.g. a scrap, a clipping, or a splinter.

379

τε καὶ – 'or even'.

380

οἱ νῦν ἔστι – i.e. as much as has already been offered.

ποθεν – 'from somewhere else'.

381

οὐδ' ὅσ' – 'not even if he should offer me as much wealth as'; between οὐδε and ὅσα, there must be understood the εἰ τόσα δοίη from 379.

Ὀρχομενὸν … Θήβας – Orchomenus and Thebes were the two great cities of ancient Boeotia, in central Greece.

382

Αἰγυπτίας – the addition of 'Egyptian' at the beginning of the line switches the reference from the Boeotian Thebes to Thebes in Egypt. It is unclear whether this sudden change of geography was in the text all along, or whether 382–3 were later additions to the text. Egypt is not mentioned elsewhere in the whole poem.

ὅθι – 'where'.

ἐν – postposition, governing δόμοις.

383

ἀν' ἑκάστας – 'through each one', i.e. through each gate; πύλας must be understood from the preceding adjective, ἑκατόμπυλοί ('hundred-gated').

387

'until he has paid me back in full for his heart-rending insult'.

ἀπὸ … δόμεναι – tmesis.

388

οὐ γαμέω Ἀγαμέμνονος – there may be a play on words here between οὐ γαμέω ('I will not marry') and Ἀγαμέμνονος ('of Agamemnon').

389

κάλλος – 'in her beauty', accusative of respect, as with ἔργα on the following line.

389–90

ἐρίζοι ... ἰσοφαρίζοι – Greek poets do not use rhyme intentionally, but here the repetition of final syllables gives weight to the statements of impossibility.

392

ἐπέοικε – 'suits'.

βασιλεύτερός – Achilles repeats a word that Agamemnon used at 160, but which Odysseus had prudently not repeated to him.

396

ῥύονται – lit. 'they defend', i.e. 'rule'.

397

τάων ἥν κ᾽ ἐθέλωμι φίλην – Achilles again echoes the language of Agamemnon, cf. τάων ἥν κ᾽ ἐθέλησθα φίλην at 288; the verb ἐθέλω here means 'to choose', rather than its more common meaning of 'to be willing'.

398–400

A complicated sentence, lit. 'My noble heart (μοι ... θυμὸς ἀγήνωρ) bids me (ἐπέσσυτο, sc. με) very much (μάλα πολλὸν), having married (γήμαντα) a regularly courted wife (μνηστὴν ἄλοχον), a well-matched partner (ἐϊκυῖαν ἄκοιτιν), to take pleasure in the possessions (κτήμασι τέρπεσθαι), which the old man Peleus possesses' (τὰ γέρων ἐκτήσατο Πηλεύς).

399

γήμαντα – agrees with the με that must be understood after the main verb.

401–5

The subjects of this sentence are the two ὅσα clauses that start at 401 and 404, respectively; we must also understand an ἐστί to go with ἀντάξιον, which stands as a predicate adjective, lit. 'all the things which they say the city of Troy possesses (ὅσα φασὶν Ἴλιον ἐκτῆσθαι) are not worth the same as my life' (οὐ ... ἐμοὶ ψυχῆς ἀντάξιον [sc. ἐστί]).

402

εὖ ναιόμενον πτολίεθρον – Achilles' words again echo those of Agamemnon, cf. εὖ ναιόμενα πτολίεθρα, 291.

403

τὸ πρὶν – 'beforehand', i.e. before the war, as explained by ἐπ᾽ εἰρήνης ('during peace-time').

404

λάϊνος οὐδὸς ἀφήτορος – 'the stone threshold of the archer', i.e. the whole temple, an example of synecdoche, where the part represents the whole. 'The archer' is a reference to Apollo, named at the start of the next line.

ἐέργει – 'encloses'.

405

Πυθοῖ – Pytho is the older name for the oracle of Apollo at Delphi, located in the foothills of Mount Parnassus in central Greece. The poet of the *Iliad* often talks about the wealth which accumulated in temples and sacred precincts at the site, e.g. 2.549, *Od.* 3.274, *Od.* 12.346.

ἔνι – the position of the accent indicates that this is a postposition, governing the word preceding it.

406–7

ληϊστοὶ μὲν … κτητοὶ δὲ – sc. εἰσί in both cases; ληϊστοὶ refers to booty plundered or stolen during wartime, κτητοὶ to possessions owned legitimately via barter or trade.

407

τρίποδές … ἵππων – tripods and horses were some of the gifts that Agamemnon had offered Achilles (264–5), and he may be thinking particularly of Agamemnon at this point.

ἵππων … κάρηνα – i.e. 'horses', another example of synecdoche, cf. 404.

408

πάλιν ἐλθεῖν – sc. ὥστε, i.e. 'so that it comes back again'.

409

ἀμείψεται ἕρκος ὀδόντων – 'gets past the barrier of his teeth', the dead man's life or soul (ψυχὴ) was thought of as leaving the body via the mouth.

410–16

Achilles here outlines the choice available to him: he can either continue to fight at Troy, die young and win imperishable glory, or he can return home and live a long and peaceful life, but one without glory. This is one of several times in the poem where Achilles talks about his fate, although the choice here outlined is never explicitly mentioned in the poem again.

410

μέ – object of φερέμεν on the following line, with κῆρας (411) the subject of the subordinate clause, i.e. 'that two fates carry me', not 'that I carry two fates'.

413

ὤλετο – 'is lost', aorist with perfect meaning, as at 415; the use of the aorist in the apodosis of a future conditional marks the result as being particularly certain.

κλέος ἄφθιτον ἔσται – 'my glory will be imperishable'; the winning of κλέος, or 'glory', is the fundamental aim of the Homeric hero.

ἔσται – 'there shall be', 'existential' use of εἰμί.

417

καὶ δ' – this is the only time in Homer these two particles are found together; the καὶ indicates an additional thought, the δέ that what follows is distinct from what has preceded, i.e. 'and another thing'.

418–19

οὐκέτι δήετε τέκμωρ Ἰλίου αἰπεινῆς – 'you will no longer find your goal of lofty Troy', i.e. the goal of sacking it.

418

δήετε – present indicative with future sense.

419

ἕθεν = οὗ, reflexive pronoun.

422

τὸ γὰρ γέρας ἐστὶ γερόντων – 'for that is the privilege of the elders'.

424

σαῷ – subjunctive, contracted from σαόῃ.

425

ἥδέ – 'this one', i.e. this plan, with μῆτις understood from 423.

426

ἐμεῦ ἀπομηνίσαντος – 'in my furious absence'; the ἀπο- prefix probably indicates that Achilles' anger has led him to withdraw himself from the rest of the Achaeans. Most translators focus on Achilles' anger rather than his isolation, e.g. 'in the time of my anger' (Hammond), 'because of my implacable anger' (Green).

428

φίλην ἐς πατρίδ' – Achilles' homeland has become the adopted home of Phoenix, who speaks next after Achilles. In his speech, Phoenix explains how he fled from his own home and settled in Phthia where Peleus (Achilles' father) gave him a new life ruling over the Dolopes, a neighbouring tribe, as well as how he helped teach the young Achilles, at times rearing him as if he were his own son.

429

ἀνάγκη δ' οὔ τί μιν ἄξω – 'I will not bring him by force', i.e. I will not force him to come.

430–1

A final couplet describes the stunned reaction to Achilles' astonishing speech.

Vocabulary
Iliad 9

While there is no Defined Vocabulary List for A Level, words in the OCR Defined Vocabulary List for AS are marked with * so that students can quickly see the vocabulary with which they should be particularly familiar.

*ἀγαθός -ή -όν	good, noble, excellent	Αἴας -αντος, ὁ	Ajax
ἄγαμαι	to be amazed, astonished	Ἅιδης -ου, m.	Hades, either the god himself or his realm
Ἀγαμέμνων -ονος, m.	Agamemnon		
		Αἰγύπτιος -α -ον	Egyptian
ἀγγελία -ας, f.	message	αἰεί	= ἀεί
ἀγείρω	to gather together, assemble	αἰέν	= ἀεί
		αἴθων -ωνος	shining, bright
ἀγήνωρ -ορος	bold, proud		
ἄγομαι	to take for oneself, as one's own, esp. to take as one's wife	αἱματόεις -εσσα -εν	bloody, bleeding
		αἰνῶς, adv.	terribly, dreadfully
		αἴξ, αἰγός, m.	goat
ἀγορεύω	to speak, say, declare	Αἴπεια -ας, f.	Aepea, a town in Messenia, belonging to Agamemnon
*ἄγω	to bring, lead		
ἄεθλον -ου, n.	prize		
*ἀεί, adv.	ever, always	αἰπεινός -ή -όν	high, lofty
ἀείρομαι	to take for oneself, i.e. to win	*αἱρέω	to take, grasp; to capture, sack (e.g. a city); (middle) to take for oneself, to choose
ἀεργός -όν	lazy, idle		
Ἀθηναίη -ης, f.	Athena	αἶσα, f.	part
ἀθλοφόρος -ον	prize-winning	αἴσιμον -η -α	decreed by fate
αἴ	= εἰ	αἶψα, adv.	immediately, at once
Αἰακίδης -αο, m.	descendent of Aeacus, i.e. Achilles	αἰών -ῶνος, m.	life, lifetime

ἀκήν, adv. — silently

ἄκοιτις -ιος, f. — wife

ἄκος -εος, n. — cure, remedy

*ἀκούω — to listen

ἄκρον -ου, n. — point

ἀκτήμων — without possession of (+ gen.)

ἄλαδε, adv. — to or towards the sea

ἀλαπάζω — to destroy, sack

ἄλγος -εος, n. — pain, grief

ἀλέξω — to ward off X (acc.) from Y (dat.)

ἀλήιος -ον — without land, i.e. poor

ἅλις, adv. — abundantly, plentifully; enough

ἀλιταίνω — to sin or transgress against

ἀλκή -ῆς, f. — strength, might

*ἀλλά — but

ἄλλοθεν ἄλλος — lit. 'one from one side, another from another', i.e. 'one after another'

*ἄλλος -η -ο — other, another

ἀλοιφή -ῆς, f. — grease, fat

ἄλοχος -ου, f. — wife

ἅλς, ἁλός, f. — the sea

ἀμείβω — to cross, traverse

ἀμείνων -ον — better

ἀμπελόεις, -εσσα, -εν — rich in vines

ἀμύμων -ον — excellent

ἀμφαδόν, adv. — openly

ἀμφί (+ dat.) — around, over, on

ἀμφιμάχομαι — to fight around

*ἄν — would, could indefinite

*ἀνάγκη -ης, f. — force

ἀνά (+ acc.) — up to, up through; in; throughout

ἄνα 'up!' — 'get up!'

*ἀνάγκη -ης, f. — force, necessity

ἀνάγω — to lead

ἀνάεδνος -ον — without bride-price

ἀναίδεια -ας, f. — shamelessness

ἄναξ -ακτος, m. — lord, master

ἀνδροφόνος -ον — man-slaying

*ἀνήρ, ἀνδρός, m. — man

Ἄνθεια -ας, f. — Anthea, a town in Messenia, belonging to Agamemnon

ἀνθρακιά -ιᾶς, f. — glowing coals

*ἄνθρωπος -ου, m. — man, (pl.) mankind

ἀνίστημι — to stand or get up

ἀνορούω — to leap up, spring up

ἀντάξιος -ον — equivalent in value to, worth as much as (+ gen.)

ἀντίον, adv. — opposite (+ gen.)

ἄνωγα — (perf. with pres. meaning) to command, order

*ἄξιος -α -ον — suitable, worthy; of equal value, worth

ἀπαμείβομαι — to answer, reply

ἀπατάω — to cheat, deceive

ἀπαυράω — to take away

ἀπειλή -ῆς, f. — threat, boastful promise

ἀπεῖπον — to refuse

ἀπεχθάνομαι — to incur hatred

ἀπηλεγέως, adv. — bluntly, forthrightly

*ἀπό (+ gen.) — from

ἀποδίδωμι — to atone for

ἀποκόπτω — to chop off

*ἀπόλλυμι — to destroy

Ἀπόλλων -ωνος, m. — Apollo

ἀπομηνίω — to be angry, furious

ἀποπλέω — to sail away, sail home

ἀπόφημι — declare, say clearly

ἀπτήν -ῆνος — unfledged

ἄπυρος -ον — untouched by fire (of kettles or tripods), i.e. unused

*ἄρα — ... then ... (often no recognizable impact on the meaning)

ἀράομαι	to pray	βαθύλειμος -ον	with deep, grassy meadows
Ἀργεῖος -α -ον	of or from Argos, Argive	*βαίνω	to walk
Ἄργος -εος, n.	the city of Argos; (in a wider sense) the whole of Greece	*βάλλω	to throw
		*βασιλεύς -ῆος, m.	king, noble, chief
ἀργύρεος -α -ον	made of silver, silver	βλεμεαίνω	to exult in something (+ dat.)
ἀργυρόπεζα	silver-footed, epithet of Thetis	βοῦς, βοός, m. or f.	ox (m.), cow (f.)
ἀριστεύς -ῆος, m.	chief	Βρισεύς, -έως, m.	Briseus, the father of Briseïs
ἄρνυμαι	to win		
ἄρουρα -ης, f.	only found in the phrase οὖθαρ ἀρούρης, 'the most fertile of land'	γαῖα -ης, f.	land
		γαιήοχος	earth-holding, epithet of Poseidon
ἀστράπτω	to hurl lightning	γαμβρός -οῦ, m.	son-in-law
*ἄστυ -εος, n.	city	*γαμέω	to marry
ἀτὰρ	and, but	*γάρ	for, since
Ἀτρείδης, -αο or -εω, m.	son of Atreus	*γε	at least, at any rate
αὐγή -ῆς, f.	light, glow (of a fire)	γέρας -αος, n.	gift of honour
*αὖθις, adv.	again, back again	*γέρων -οντος, m.	old man
αὖλις -ιδος, f.	encampment	*γίγνομαι	to be, exist
ἄυπνος -ον	sleepless	γλαυκῶπις -ιδος	gleaming-eyed, grey-eyed, epithet of Athena
*αὔριον, adv.	tomorrow		
αὐτὰρ	and, but	γλαφυρός -ή -όν	hollow
αὖτε, adv.	again, on the other hand, however	*γυνή, γυναικός, f.	woman
*αὐτίκα, adv.	straightaway, immediately	δαιδάλεος -α -ον	skilfully made
αὖτις, adv.	= αὖθις	δαίνυμι	to eat
*αὐτός -ή -ό	self, myself, yourself, etc. (reflexive pronoun); him, her, it (in oblique cases, used for personal pronoun)	δαίς -τός, f.	meal
		δαίω	to kindle, light (a fire)
		Δαναοί, -ών, m. pl.	Danaans, i.e. the Greeks
		δατέομαι	to divide up
αὔτως, adv.	in the same way	*δέ	and, but
ἀφήτωρ -ορος, m.	the archer, i.e. Apollo	*δεῖ	it is necessary for X (acc.) to do Y (inf.)
ἄφθιτος -ον	undying, imperishable		
Ἀφροδίτη -ης, f.	Aphrodite	δειδίσκομαι	to greet, welcome
Ἀχαιικός -ή -όν	Achaean	δείδω	to be afraid, fear something
Ἀχαιοί -ών, m. pl.	the Achaeans, i.e. the Greeks		
		δέκα	ten
Ἀχιλλεύς -έως, m.	Achilles	δεκάκις, adv.	ten times
ἄχος -εος, n.	pain, distress	δέμω	to build

δέπας -αος, n. — drinking cup, beaker

δέχομαι — to wait for someone (acc.) until (ὁπότε); to receive, accept

*δή — (emphasizes preceding word)

δήιος -η -ον — hostile

δηιόω — to cut down, slay

δηρός -ά -όν — long, too long (of time)

δήω — to find, meet with

διαπρήσσω — to spend time, pass time

*δίδωμι — to give; to grant, i.e. allow something to happen (+ inf.)

διογενής — Zeus-born, epithet of heroes

δῖος -α -ον — divine, godlike

διοτρεφής -ές — nourished, cherished by Zeus

διχθάδιος -η -ον — double, twofold

δοιή -ῆς, f. — doubt, perplexity; only in the phrase ἐν δοιῇ, 'in doubt'

*δοκέω — to appear, seem (to someone, + dat.)

δόμος -ου, m. — house, home

δορίκτητος -ον — won by the spear

*δύναμαι — to be able (to do something, + inf.)

δύνω — to put on, don (of clothes)

δώδεκα — twelve

*δῶρον -ου, n. — gift

δωτίνη -ης, f. — gift

*ἐάω — to let something go, give it up

*ἐγγύς, adv. — near, nearby

*ἐγγύς (+ gen.) — near to, next to

ἐγκαταπήγνυμι — to thrust firmly in

*ἐγώ, ἐγών — I

ἐδητύς -ύος, f. — food

ἕδος -εος, n. — seat

*ἐθέλω — to be willing, to want (to do something, + inf.); to choose

*εἰ — if; (occasionally used as exclamation) 'well then', 'come now', etc.

εἶδον — (not used in act. pres.) I saw, perceived

εἰκοσάκις, adv. — twenty times

εἴκοσι — twenty

*εἰμί — to be

εἰν (+ dat.) — in, on

*εἰς (+ acc.) — to, towards

εἰσέρχομαι — to enter, go in

εἰσοράω — to look upon

ἔισος -η -ον — epic form of ἴσος, i.e. alike, equal

ἑκάς (+ gen.) — far from

*ἕκαστος -η -ον — each, every

ἑκατόμπυλος — hundred-gated

*ἐκεῖνος -η -ο — that

ἔκηλος, adv. — at one's leisure, freely

ἐκπάγλως, adv. — terribly, exceedingly

ἐκτελέω — to bring to pass, fulfil

Ἕκτωρ -ορος, m. — Hector

*ἐκφεύγω — to flee from, escape from

ἐλαύνω — to lay out, extend

ἐλεαίρω — to take pity on

Ἑλένη -ης, f. — Helen

ἐλεόν -οῦ, n. — side-table

ἐλετός -ή -όν — able to be caught

Ἑλλήσποντος -ου, m. — the Hellespont, the narrow strait that links the Propontis to the Aegean Sea; now known as the Dardanelles

ἔλπω — to hope

*ἐμός -ή -όν — my

ἔμπεδος -ον — firm, immovable

ἐμπρήθω — to kindle, set alight

*ἐν (+ dat.) — in, on, onto, among

*ἐναντίος -α -ον — opposite (someone or something, + dat.)

ἔναρα -ων, n. pl. — spoils, booty

ἕνδεκά	eleven	ἐπιπείθομαι	to obey (+ dat.)
ἐνδέξια, adv.	on the right hand side, from left to right	ἐπισεύω	to want, intend
		ἐπισκύζομαι	to be angry
*ἕνεκα	for the sake of, on account of (+ gen.)	ἐπιτέλλω	to order, command
ἔνθα, adv.	where, there	*ἕπομαι	to follow
*ἐνθάδε, adv.	here	ἐπόμνυμι	to swear (an oath)
*ἐνθένδε, adv.	from here	ἑπτά	seven
Ἐννοσίγαιος -ου, m.	Earth-shaker, i.e. Poseidon	ἔργα -ων, n. pl.	matters, affairs
		ἔργω	to shut in, enclose
Ἐνόπη -ης, f.	Enope, a town in Messenia, belonging to Agamemnon	ἔρδω	to do
		ἐρέσσω	to row (of a boat or ship)
ἐντός, adv.	within	ἐρίβωλος -ον	fertile, fruitful
ἐντύνω	prepare, make ready	ἐρίζω	to compete with, to rival
ἐξαιρέω	to take away for oneself	ἔρις -ιδος, f.	strife
*ἐξαπατάω	to cheat, deceive	ἐρίτιμος -ον	highly prized, precious
ἐξαπαφίσκω	to cheat, deceive	ἕρκος -εος, n.	barrier
ἐξίημι	to let something go, (of desire) to satisfy it	ἔρρω	to go away (pejorative)
		ἐρυθρός -ά -όν	red, ruddy
ἐξοιχνέω	to go forth	ἐρύω	to rescue
ἑός, ἑή, ἑόν	his own, her own, its own	*ἔρχομαι	to come, go
ἐπαείρω	to lift up and place something (acc.) on something (gen.)	ἔρως, ἔρος, m.	desire
		ἐς	= εἰς
		ἐσθλός -ή -όν	good
ἐπεί	when, after (temporal); since, because (causal)	*ἑταῖρος -ου, m.	companion
		ἕτερος -η -ον	other
ἔπειμι	to be on something	ἕτερος μὲν ... ἄλλος δέ	one ... another
ἐπέοικε	(perf. with no pres. in use) to suit someone (+ dat.)		
		*ἔτι	still, yet (often with negative)
ἐπήν	when, after		
ἐπήρατος -ον	lovely, charming	*ἕτοιμος -ον	ready, prepared; (of plans) feasible
*ἐπί (+ acc.)	to, towards		
*ἐπί (+ gen.)	in the time of	εὔζωνος -ον	beautifully girdled
*ἐπί (+ dat.)	at, upon, over	εὔκομος -ον	lovely haired
ἐπιβαίνω	to mount (+ gen.)	ἐυκτίμενος -η -ον	well built
ἐπιδευής -ές	lacking, in need of something (+ gen.)	εὐνή -ῆς, f.	bed
		εὔπηκτος -ον	well built, strong, sturdy
ἐπιδίδωμι	to give as a dowry	εὔπλοια -ας, f.	a good voyage, fair sailing
ἐπιειμένος	clothed in	*εὑρίσκω	to find
ἐπίκουρος -ου, m.	ally		
ἐπινέμω	to distribute		

εὐρύοπα	wide-seeing, epithet of Zeus	θήν, **adv.**	doubtless
*εὐρύς -εῖα -ύ	broad, wide	θίς, θινός, **f.**	shore (of the sea)
εὔσελμος -ον	well-decked (of ships)	θοός -ή -όν	swift
*εὔχομαι	to pray (to someone, + dat.)	*θυγάτηρ, -τέρος, **f.**	daughter
ἐφυβρίζων, **adv.**	insultingly	θυηλαί -ῶν, **f. pl.**	the parts of a sacrificial victim that is burned in a burnt-offering, a sacrificial offering
ἐφύπερθε, **adv.**	above		
ἐχέφρων -ον	sensible, prudent		
*ἐχθρός -ά -όν	hateful	θυμαλγής, -ες	distressing
*ἔχω	to hold, to hold back	θυμαρής -ές	pleasing to the heart, i.e. dear
ζάθεος -η -ον	divine, sacred		
*Ζεύς, Διός, **m.**	Zeus	θυμός -οῦ, **m.**	heart
ζυγόν -οῦ, **n.**	the crossbar of a lyre	*θύω	to make a sacrifice, make a burnt-offering
ζωρός -όν	strong (of wine)		
ἦ, **adv.**	how, as	ἰάλλω	to send out, often used of 'sending out' one's hands towards (e.g.) food, i.e. to reach out for something
ἦ, **adv.**	in truth, surely		
*ἡγέομαι	to lead, lead the way		
ἠδὲ	and		
ἠμαθόεις -εσσα -εν	sandy		
		ἰαύω	to spend (of nights)
ἦμαι	to sit	ἵζω	to sit
ἦμαρ -ατος, **n.**	day	ἱκάνω	to come to
ἠμέν ... ἠδέ	both ... and	ἱκνέομαι	to come, arrive at, reach
ἦρι, **adv.**	early in the morning	Ἴλιος -ου, **f.**	Ilium, the city of Troy
ἦτε ... ἦτε	both ... and	ἱππόβοτος -ον	horse-nourishing
Ἠώς, Ἠοῦς, **f.**	Dawn	*ἵππος -ου, **m.**	horse
θαάσσω	to sit	ἱρά, **n. pl.**	sacrifices
*θάλασσα -ης, **f.**	sea	Ἱρή -ής, **f.**	Ire, a town in Messenia, belonging to Agamemnon
θαλίη -ης, **f.**	abundance		
θάλλω	to abound in, teem with (+ dat.)	ἰσόθεος -ον	godlike, always with φῶς
		ἰσοφαρίζω	to deem oneself equal to someone (acc.) in something (acc.), to rival them
*θάνατος -ου, **m.**	death		
*θαρσέω	to be bold, confident, full of courage		
		*ἵστημι	to stand
θεῖος -α -ον	sacred, holy	ἴσχω	to check, restrain
θέμις, θέμιστος, **f.**	custom; (pl.) tribute, dues	Ἰφιάνασσα, **f.**	Iphianassa, daughter of Agamemnon
*θεός -οῦ, **m.**	god		
		ἴφιος -η -ον	strong, fat, only ever used with μῆλα
Θέτις -ιδος, **f.**	Thetis, mother of Achilles		
Θῆβαι -ῶν, **f. pl.**	Thebes	ἰχθυόεις -εσσα -εν	fishy, full of fish
		*καί	and, even, also

*καθίστημι	to set down	κόνις -ιος, f.	dust
κακομήχανος -ον	malicious	κόρυμβος -ου, m.	stern-post (of a ship)
*κακός -ή -όν	bad, evil, cowardly	κούρη -ης, f.	girl
κάλλος -εος, n.	beauty	κρατερός -ά -όν	strong, mighty, powerful
*καλός -ή -όν	beautiful	κρατευταί -ῶν, m. pl.	stone blocks on which a spit rests
κάνεον -ου, n.	basket, esp. for bread or meat	κρέα, κρεῶν, n. pl.	pieces of meat, meat
καπνός -ού, m.	smoke	κρεῖον -ου, n.	carving dish, for the preparation of meat
Καρδαμύλη -ης, f.	Cardamyle, a town in Messenia belonging to Agamemnon	κρείων -οντος, m.	ruler, lord, master
		κρητήρ -ῆρος, m.	mixing bowl (for wine)
καρός	(gen.) (doubtful word) a whittling, a splinter; only in the phrase τίω σέ μιν ἐν καρὸς αἴσῃ (9.378)	Κρονίδης -ου, m.	son of Cronus, i.e. Zeus
		κτάομαι	to possess
		κτήματα -ων, n. pl.	treasure
κάρτος -εος, n.	might, power		
*κατά (+ acc.)	down, according to, by, in, throughout	κτητός -ή -όν	able to be acquired peacefully, legitimately
καταβάλλω	to put down	κῦδος -εος, n.	glory, renown
καταθνήσκω	to die	κύνεος -α -ον	shameless
κατακαίω	to burn down, burn out	λαγχάνω	to obtain by lot
κατακοιμάω	to sleep	Λαερτιάδης -ου, m.	son of Laertes, i.e. Odysseus
καταλέγω	to list, enumerate, recount		
κέ, κέν	= ἄν	Λάινος -η -ον	of stone
*κεῖμαι	to lie, be placed or situated	λανθάνω	to forget
κειμήλιον -ου, n.	treasure	Λαοδίκη, f.	Laodice, daughter of Agamemnon
κεῖνος -η -ο	= ἐκεῖνος		
κεραίω	to mix	λαοί -ῶν, m. pl.	people, army
κεύθω	to hide	λέβης -ητος, m.	kettle, cauldron
κήδομαι	to be concerned for, care for	*λείπω	to leave
		λεϊστός -ή -όν	= λῃστός
κῆρ, κηρός, f.	doom, fate	Λεσβίς -ίδος, f.	Lesbian woman, i.e. from the island of Lesbos
κῆρ, κῆρος, f.	heart		
κηρόθι, adv.	in one's heart, with all the heart	Λέσβος -ου, f.	the island of Lesbos
		λήγω	to leave off, cease from (+ gen.)
κιχάνω	to catch up with, overtake		
κλέος, n.	glory; (pl.) glorious deeds	λῃίς -ίδος, f.	booty, spoils
κλισίη -ής, f.	hut	λῃστός -ή -όν	able to be plundered, to be carried off as booty or spoils
κλισμός -ού, m.	chair		
κλυτός -ή -όν	famous, illustrious, renowned	λιγύς -εῖα -ύ	clear-toned (of musical instruments)
		λίην, adv.	exceedingly, very much

λιπαρός -ά -όν	rich	μέτειμι	to be among
λύσσα -ης, f.	rage, fury	μετόπισθε, adv.	afterwards, in the future
λώβη -ης, f.	insult, outrage, dishonour	μῆλα -ων, n. pl.	flocks of sheep or goat
μαίνομαι	to rave or rage, like a mad person	μητίετα	counselling, all-wise, epithet of Zeus
μαίομαι	to find	*μή	(and compounds) see οὐ
*μάλα, adv.	very, exceedingly	μῆτις -ιος, f.	plan, strategy
μαλερός -ή -όν	fierce, raging (of fire)	*μήτηρ, -έρος or -ρός, f.	mother
*μᾶλλον, adv.	more, so much the more		
μαραίνω	to die gradually away (of fire)	μῆχος -εος, n.	way, means (of doing something)
μάρναμαι	to fight, do battle	μίγνυμι	to lay with someone, have sex with them
μάσταξ -ακος, f.	a mouthful of food, food	μίμνω	to wait, remain
μεγαλήτωρ -ορα	proud	μιν	him, her, it
μέγαρον -ου, n.	house, home	μιστύλλω	to cut up into small pieces
*μέγας, μεγάλη, μέγα	big, great	μνηστός -ή -όν	wedded
μείλια -ων, f. pl.	peace offerings, goodwill offerings	μόγις, adv.	with difficulty, scarcely
		μοῖρα -ης, f.	part, portion, share
μέλαθρον -ου, n.	roof; hut, dwelling	μοῦνος -η -ον	alone, only
μέλας -αινα -αν	dark, black	μῦθος -ου, m.	request
μέλω	to be an object of care (to someone, dat.)	Μυρμιδόνες -ων, m. pl.	Myrmidons, the Thracian tribe of which Achilles is the leader
μέμαα	(perf. with pres. meaning) to be eager to or eagerly do something (+ inf.)	ναίω	to live, dwell; be situated
		νέατος -η -ον	furthest, outermost
μέμονα	(perf. with pres. meaning) to have in mind, to spare a thought for	νέμω	to deal out, distribute
		νέος -ου, m.	young man
μέν	in truth, indeed, certainly	νεοσσός -οῦ, m.	young bird, nestling, chick
*μέν ... δέ	(marks a contrast)	νεύω	to nod, to give a signal by nodding
μενοεικής -ες	pleasing, satisfying		
Μενοιτιάδης -ου, m.	the son of Menoetius, i.e. Patroclus	νηέω	to load, fill a ship with cargo
Μενοίτιος -ου, m.	Menoetius, father of Patroclus	νηῦς -ός, f.	ship
		*νικάω	to conquer
*μένω	remain, wait	νοέω	to perceive, notice
μέροψ, μέροπος	mortal	νόστος -ου, m.	return home, homecoming
*μετά (+ acc.)	after	νόσφι(ν) (+ gen.)	apart, away from (+ gen.)
*μετά (+ dat.)	with	*νῦν, adv.	now
μεταλήγω	to leave off, cease from (+ gen.)	*νύξ, νυκτός, f.	night
		νωλεμές, adv.	continually, unceasingly

νῶτον -ου, m.	the chine, a cut of meat containing the backbone	*ὅστις, ἥτις, ὅ τι	whoever, whichever, whatever
ξανθός -ή -όν	reddish-yellow, chestnut, sorrel (of horses)	*ὅτε	when
ὁ, ἡ, τό	he, she, it; who, which; (rarely) the	*οὐ / οὐκ / οὐχ / οὐχί / μή	not
ὄαρ -αρος, f.	wife	οὐδός -οῦ, m.	threshold
ὀβελός -οῦ, m.	a spit (for roasting meat)	οὖθαρ -ατος, n.	only found in the phrase οὖθαρ ἀρούρης, 'the most fertile of land'
ὀδούς, ὀδόντος, m.	tooth		
Ὀδυσσεύς -ῆος, m.	Odysseus	οὔποτε / μήποτε	never
ὅθι, adv.	where	*οὗτος, αὕτη, τοῦτο	this
*οἶδα	to know		
*οἴκαδε, adv.	to one's home, homeward	ὄφρα	as long as; in order that, so that
*οἶκος -ου, m.	house, home	ὄχος -εος, n.	chariot
οἶνος -ου, m.	wine	ὀψέ, adv.	late
οἶος -α -ον	alone	Παναχαιοί, m. pl.	the Achaeans
ὄις, ὄιος or οἰός, f.	sheep	πάρα	= πάρεστι
ὀίω	to think, suspect	*παρά (+ acc.)	along, alongside
ὄλλυμι	to destroy, to sack (a town or city)	*παρά (+ dat.)	beside, next to
		παραβάλλω	to risk, stake
ὀλοός -ή -όν	destructive, deadly	παραμυθέομαι	to encourage, exhort someone (+ dat.) to do something (+ inf.)
*ὄμνυμι	to swear (an oath)		
ὁμῶς, adv.	equally as, just as (+ dat.)		
ὀνείατα -ων, n. pl.	food	*πάρειμι	to be present, at hand
*ὄπισθε(ν), adv.	behind	πάρημαι	to sit beside or near
ὀπτάω	to roast	παριαύω	to sleep alongside, next to
ὅπως	how	*πᾶς, πᾶσα, πᾶν	every, all
Ὀρέστης -ου, m.	Orestes, son of Agamemnon	πάσσω	to sprinkle
		*πάσχω	to suffer, experience
ὀρίνω	to stir, rouse (of anger and other emotions)	*πατήρ, πατρός, m.	father
ὅρκος -ου, m.	oath	πατρίς -ίδος, f.	native land, native country
ὁρμή -ῆς, f.	attack, assault	Πάτροκλος -ῆος, m.	Patroclus, son of Menoetius
ὄρνις -ῑθος, m.	bird		
ὄρνυμι	to arouse, awake, excite	παῦρος -ον	little, small; (pl.) few
ὀρυμαγδός -οῦ, m.	loud noise, din, crash, often of crowds of men, esp. in battle	*παύω	cease
		πεζός, adv.	on foot
		*πείθω	to persuade
ὅς, ἥ, ὅν	his, her, its	πειράω	to make trial of, test
ὅσος or ὅσσος, -η, -ον	how great, how much, how many, etc.	πείρω	to pierce, run through

*πέμπω — to send

πέπων -ονος, n. — my dear friend

πέϱ — very, at least, even, just

περίκειμαι — to be an advantage for someone (+ dat.)

πετϱήεις -εσσα -εν — rocky

πηγός -ή -όν — strong, tough

Πήδασος -ου, m. — Pedasus, a town in Messenia, belonging to Agamemnon

Πηλεύς -ῆος, m. — Peleus, father of Achilles

πῆμα -ατος, n. — suffering, woe, harm

πίμπλημι — to fill a vessel or container (acc.) with something (gen.)

*πίπτω — to fall

πίσυνος -ον — trusting in, relying on (+ dat.)

πίων, πίειρα, πῖον — fat

*πλέω — to sail

ποθέν, adv. — from some place, from elsewhere

ποιήεις -εσσα -εν — grassy

πολεμίζω — to fight, wage war

πολιός -ά -όν — grey

*πόλις, -ιος or -ηος, f. — city

πολύ, adv. — much

πολυβούτης -ου, m. — rich in cattle

πολυμήχανος -ον — much-contriving, resourceful, inventive

πολύρρηνος -ον — rich in sheep

πολύς, πολλή, πολύ — many

πολύφλοισβος -ον — loud-roaring

πονέομαι — to toil, work hard

πορφύρεος -η -ον — purple

πόσις -ιος, f. — drink

*ποτέ, adv. — once, one time

ποτινίσσομαι — to go in at, enter

*που — perhaps, possibly, I suppose

πούς, ποδός, m. — foot

Πρίαμος -ου, m. — Priam, father of Hector and king of Troy

πρίν — before someone (+ acc.) did something (+ inf.)

πρίν, adv. — beforehand

προεϱύω — to drag something forward, usu. of ships to the sea, i.e. to launch them

πρόκειμαι — to lie in front of

*πρὸς (+ acc.) — to, towards

πρόσθε(ν), adv. — in front of, before someone (+ gen.)

πρόσφημι — to speak to, address

προσφωνέω — to speak to, address

προτέρω, adv. — forward

προφέρω — to bring

πτολίεθρον -ου, n. — town, city

Πυθώ -οῦς, f. — Pytho, the ancient name for the oracle of Apollo at Delphi

*πύλη -ης, f. — gate

Πύλος, Πύλου, m. — Pylos

*πῦρ, πυρός, n. — fire

πω — up to this time, yet (always with a negative)

ῥάχις -ιος, f. — the chine, a cut of meat containing the backbone

ῥέζω — to do, act; to offer or perform a sacrifice

ῥηιδίως, adv. — easily

ῥύομαι — to defend, i.e. rule

σαόω — to save, preserve

*σῆμα -ατος, n. — sign, signal

σθένος -εος, n. — might, strength

*σῖτος -ου, m. — bread

σιωπῇ, adv. — silently

Σκαιαί -ῶν, f. pl. — (usually with πύλαι) the Scaean Gate, the only gate of the city of Troy that Homer mentions by name

σκῆπτρον -ου, n.	staff, sceptre	τηλύγετος -η -ον	dearly beloved, darling
σκόλοψ -οπος, m.	wooden stake	*τίθημι	to set up
σκύζομαι	to be angry	*τιμάω	to honour
στεῦμαι	to promise, threaten (to do something, + fut. inf.)	τις, τι	someone, something; anyone, anything
στῆθος -εος, n.	breast	τίω	to value, show honour to
στορέννυμι	to spread out	τλάω	to dare, have the courage to do something (+ inf.)
*στρατός -οῦ, m.	army		
*σύ	you	τοῖχος -ου, m.	wall (of a house or enclosure)
συμφράζομαι	to share council with someone (+ dat.)	τόσσος -η -ον	so great, so much, so many
*σύν (+ dat.)	with	*τότε, adv.	at that time, then
σῦς σίαλος, συὸς σιάλοιο, f.	fat hog	τράπεζα -ης, f.	table
		τρεῖς	three
σφεῖς, σφέων	they, them	τρέφω	to raise (of a child)
*σφέτερος -η -ον	their, their own	τρίπος, τρίποδος, m.	tripod
σχεδόν, adv.	near, near to (+ dat.)		
τάλαντον -ου, n.	a talent (a unit of weight for precious metals)	τρίτατος -η -ον	third
τάμνω	to cut up, cut in pieces	Τροίη -ης, f.	Troy, either the city itself or the surrounding area (also known as the Troad)
τανύω	to arrange		
τάπης -ητος, m.	rug or coverlet, laid upon chairs	τρύζω	to mutter or murmur; to coo; to croak
τάφρος -ου, f.	ditch, trench	Τρῳάς -άδος, f.	Trojan woman
τάχιστα, adv.	most quickly, speedily	Τρῶες, Τρώων, m. pl.	the Trojans
τέ	and		
τέ ... καί	both ... and	τῷ	therefore
τέθηπα	(perf. with pres. meaning) to be astonished, amazed	*υἱός, υἱοῦ or υἷος, m.	son
τείρομαι	to be hard-pressed, afflicted	ὕπειμι	to be under
*τεῖχος -εος, n.	wall (of a city or town, or of any fortification)	ὑπερέχω	to hold something (acc.) over something
τέκμωρ, n.	goal, end	ὑπέρθυμος -ον	high-spirited
τέκνον -ου, n.	child, son	ὑπέχω	to possess
τελέω	to fulfil, pay (e.g.) money, tribute, gifts to someone (+ dat.)	*ὑπό (+ gen.)	by, at the hands of
		*ὑπό (+ dat.)	under
*τέλος -εος, n.	end	φαίνω	to reveal, show; mid. to appear
τέρπομαι	to enjoy oneself, take pleasure in (+ dat.)	*φέρω	to carry, bear
		φηγός -οῦ, f.	oak tree
τηλεκλειτός -όν	far-famed	φημί	to say, speak, declare

Φηραί, f. pl. — Pherae, a town in Messenia, belonging to Agamemnon

Φθίη, -ης, f. — Phthia in Thessaly, the home of Achilles

φθίω — to die, perish

*φίλος — beloved, dear, one's own

φιλοφροσύνη -ης, f. — friendliness, kindliness

φλόξ, φλογός, f. — flame

Φοῖβος -ου, m. — Phoebus, another name for Apollo; the expression Φοῖβος Ἀπόλλων ('Phoebus Apollo') is common.

Φοῖνιξ -ικος, m. — Phoenix

φόρμιγξ -ιγγος, f. — lyre

φράζομαι — to consider, think, put one's mind to something

φρήν, φρενός, f. — heart, mind

φρονέω — to have in mind, think, consider

φῦλον -ου, n. — race, tribe

φωνέω — to speak

φώς, φωτός, m. — man

*χαίρω — to be glad, joyful; (as imperative) 'hail!', 'your health!', etc.

χαλκός -οῦ, m. — bronze

χάρις -ιτος, f. — thanks, gratitude; thanks for something (+ inf.)

*χείρ, χειρός, f. — hand

χέω — to pour

χόλος -ου, m. — anger

χρεώ, χρέος, f. — a want or need

*χρή — X (acc.) must do Y (inf.)

χρύσεος -η -ον — golden, made of gold

Χρυσόθεμις, f. — Chrysothemis, daughter of Agamemnon

*χρυσός — gold

ψάμαθος -ου, f. — sand

ψυχή -ῆς, f. — life

ὦκα, adv. — swiftly, quickly

ὠκύς, ὠκεῖα, ὠκύ — swift

ὡς, adv. — so, thus

*ὥς — like, as; so that, in order that

ὤψ, ὠπός, f. — eye, face

Euripides, *Medea*

Introduction, Commentary Notes and
Vocabulary
by Neil Croally

AS: 271–356, 663–758, 869–905
A Level: 214–270, 364–409, 1019–1055,
1136–1230

Introduction

Fifth-century Athens and the dramatic festivals

Fifth-century Athens was a distinctive place; even other contemporary Greeks thought so. The reason was that probably in 508–507 BC the Athenians established an entirely new form of government, or at least the outline of it, called democracy. While early on the Athenians seemed to have called their political experiment *isonomia* (equality before the law), and while there were various additions and reforms to the system during the fifth century, we can still assert with some confidence that fifth-century Athens was a democracy. However, we need to be clear that it was not one like the representative democracies with which we are familiar today. Athens was a *direct* democracy. All citizens – free-born Athenian men over the age of 18 – were entitled to attend the sovereign, legislative assembly (*ekklesia*) and to serve on the annually selected and very large jury body of 6,000. Citizens over the age of 30 could also be elected by lot to serve for a year in the many of the offices of state, but most importantly perhaps in the *boule*, the 500-strong executive body of the city. In the funeral oration that appears in Thucydides, Pericles (the dominant Athenian politician of the 440s and 430s BC) asserts that the citizen who minded his own business had no business in Athens at all (Thucydides 2.46). Athens demanded the political and military involvement of its citizens. It is in this highly civic context that tragedies were performed.

Drama at Athens took place at festivals, that is to say, at city-sponsored events with a religious and civic dimension, which occurred at regular times in the festival or ritual calendar. There were a number of dramatic festivals held in various parts of Attica and established at different times, but the most important dramatic festival was the Great or City Dionysia, which took place in central Athens in March of each year. This festival seems to have been established in the 530s BC under the tyrant Peisistratus but, along with other institutions that pre-existed the democracy, the festival seems to have become part of the collection of institutions of fifth-century Athenian democracy. (Most scholars agree that there is something political about the festival; some argue that we should not see it as distinctively democratic.)

What is clear, though, is that the city of Athens was directly involved in the organization of the Great Dionysia. In the fifth century an official called the *archon eponymos* (a democratic official elected by lot – this is called 'sortitive' election) selected the three tragic poets and the five comic poets whose plays would be performed; he also selected the rich individuals (*choregoi*) who would be asked to pay for the costs of each production (a form of taxation called a *liturgy*). The cost of funding a tragic production was expensive, almost as expensive as the other main liturgy, namely, paying for the upkeep of a trireme for a year. It is also possible that at some point in the fifth century the city of Athens established a special fund (the *theorika*) to subsidize the cost of attending the festival. The council (*boule*) was also involved, organizing the sortitive election of the ten citizens who would judge the contests of both playwrights and actors. The sequence of events is much disputed but it looks as though the festival consisted of a procession with a statue of Dionysus Eleutherios to and back from Eleutheria, some dithyrambic contests, some pre-play ceremonies and the performance of each of the tragedians' three tragedies and one satyr play, and five comedies, each by an individual playwright. (The *dithyramb* is a choral song in honour of Dionysus. *Satyrs* were mythical creatures, partly equine, partly human. They become associated with Dionysus. There is one extant satyr play – Euripides' *Cyclops*. Satyr plays, as far as we can tell, dealt with mythical themes in a more rumbustious, perhaps cruder way than tragedy.)

The ceremonies that preceded the plays and the constitution of the audience demonstrate the political nature of the festival, though evidence is shaky in both cases. It looks as though, before the plays, the generals, the highest officers of the city, made offerings to the gods; crowns were awarded to citizens judged to have contributed importantly to the city; on the stage the tribute from the empire was displayed; there was a procession of new citizens (dressed as hoplites), distinctive because their fathers had died in battle and the city had taken over the cost of their upbringing. The audience watching these ceremonies and then the plays was enormous and mainly made of Athenian citizens. We used to think that as many as 15,000 citizens were in the audience but recent archaeological work has shown that that figure is unlikely: the new estimate is between 4,000 and 7,000. But that it is still very large, given that the citizen population of Athens is estimated to have been between 30,000 and 50,000, and that attendance at the assembly is unlikely to have been more than 6,000. We know that there would have been foreign representatives at the Great Dionysia (they would have brought the tribute), but there is still much debate as to whether women and slaves were present in the audience. The fact remains that there was a very large audience mainly made up of Athenian citizens.

Medea was first performed in 431 BC. This was a significant year for Athens. Pericles, who would die a couple of years later, was arguing that Athens should not concede to Sparta's demands and should be prepared to go to war. The Peloponnesian War was to last off-and-on for twenty-seven years, with Athens losing. Interestingly, Corinth, which is the scene of *Medea*, was an ally of Sparta and an enemy of Athens. We have no evidence as to how this affected the audience's response to the play.

Formal aspects of Athenian tragedy

Stage space, actors and so on

Plays at the Great Dionysia were performed at what is now called the Theatre of Dionysus, which sits underneath the Acropolis at the very heart of Athens. The ruins there now are of a later Roman building. Recent archaeological work shows that in the fifth century, it was likely that the stage and the auditorium were made of wood and were erected each year. The audience was probably seated in a large rectangle, as in the surviving stone theatre at Thorikos in Attica. The plays used four connected but distinct spaces for their performance. The space nearest the audience, and the lowest on the vertical axis, was the *orchestra*, used almost entirely by the chorus. We now think of this as almost circular, but in the fifth century it may have been quadrilateral. Just beyond the orchestra was a slightly raised, shallow platform called the *logeion*, which was the space from where the actors spoke. Behind the *logeion* sat the *skene*, a sort of rectangular hut probably made of wood, decorated but not specifically, which represented offstage space indoors (house, palace, etc.). The top of the *skene*, called the *theologeion*, could be used for appearances of gods. Finally, there was a device, a sort of crane, called the *mechane*, which rose above everything else. Probably originally employed to help with the construction of the stage and auditorium, this too was used for even more striking appearances of the gods (hence the phrase *deus ex machina*). In a coup de théâtre Euripides uses the *mechane* at the end of *Medea* to show Medea with her dead children towering above a distraught Jason. This is a striking use of the possibilities of vertical stage space: has her murder of the children received divine support? Has the murder solved anything?

Actors made their entrances and exits from either side of the *skene*. These passages were called *eisodoi* or *parodoi* and could be used to indicate where a character was entering from, namely, city or elsewhere. Playwrights occasionally used a sort of trolley, the *ekkyklema*, which came out from the *skene* and which allowed dying or dead characters to be displayed on stage, though there seems to be no use of this in *Medea*.

By the time *Medea* was performed the convention was that there were three speaking actors, all of whom were men. *Medea* can be performed with two actors, but that would require the part of Medea to be played by more than one actor. What would the effect of using two rather than three actors be? Given the play shows Medea in a series of confrontations and exchanges, might it be best to give the (stunning, virtuoso) role of Medea to one actor, necessitating the use of two others? There seems to have been no limit on the number of mute performers. All the actors, whichever part they were playing, were masked, and probably in a fairly generic way (older men bearded, younger men not and so on). Costumes, depending on the resources of the *choregos*, were likely to have been splendid. We know this because so much fuss was made about how awful Electra looked in Euripides'play *Electra*.

The chorus is a distinctive part of Attic tragedy. By the time of *Medea*, the chorus would have numbered 15 trained dancers and singers (again, all men, indeed citizens). The chorus (the Greek word for 'dance') had a number of roles. The choral lyrics, which interrupted the dramatic action, were sung and danced (though we know little about the music or the style of dancing), often in highly lyrical metres. They could be used to comment on the events of the play in various ways. Sometimes choruses represent a sort of collectivity (as in *Medea* or Sophocles' *Antigone*); sometimes they do not, and are not much involved in the action; some choruses are important players (*Eumenides* and *Bacchae* are good examples).

Metre

Greek tragedy uses different metres for its various scenes. However, for the most part, the dramatic episodes are conducted in a metre known as the *iambic trimeter*. Indeed, all of the prescribed text is in this metre.

In order to understand how the metre works, it is important to understand the following rules or conventions (note: this is a simplified version of how the metre works):

- Greek metre generally, including the iambic trimeter, distinguishes between short and long syllables;
- there are syllables that are necessarily long because they contain long vowels, such as η and ω and diphthongs (two vowels together forming one vowel sound);
- syllables are also long when a short vowel is followed by two or more consonants, whether those consonants are in the same word or not;
- a double consonant following a short vowel such as ζ, ξ or ψ also makes the syllable long;
- when the second of the two consonants which follow a short vowel in the same word is λ, μ, ν or ϱ, the syllable can be short or long, as the metre requires;
- a short vowel at the end of a word is elided before a word that begins with a vowel (*elision*). Unlike in Latin, this is marked by an apostrophe;
- a short vowel at the beginning of a word is elided when it is preceded by a long vowel (*prodelision*). This is also marked by an apostrophe;
- when two words in sequence have a long vowel at the end of a first word and a long vowel at the beginning of the second word, a single long vowel is formed (*synizesis*).

Modern analysis of the iambic trimeter works on the basis of there being three *metra* in each line. Each metron is made up as follows, where ∪ = a short syllable, and – = a long syllable and × = the so-called *anceps* ('doubtful') where the syllable can be either long or short:

  × – ∪ –

So, a whole line looks as follows:

  × – ∪ – ‖ × – ∪ – ‖ × – ∪ – [though, note, the last syllable can be short]

A *caesura* ('cutting') is a natural word break within the line, normally after the fifth syllable (if there are no *resolutions*; see below), but sometimes after the seventh syllable.

The iambic trimeter is, in theory, a twelve-syllable line. However, because of so-called *resolutions*, the line may have more syllables. Resolutions are when two short syllables replace a single long syllable, that is, in place of the long syllables at positions 2, 4, 6, 8 (and sometimes 10, at least in Euripides).

However, the scheme described above – apparently easy to understand and clear – is not accepted by all scholars. Some prefer a more traditional approach that stresses the 'iambic' rather than the 'trimeter'. In this scheme there are six feet rather than three *metra* (this may be to do with the influence of the *hexameter*, the six-footed line of epic poetry). Below are some of the common metrical units (but in the iambic trimeter the most common are the iamb and the spondee):

Iamb	∪ –
Spondee	– –
Tribrach	∪ ∪ ∪
Dactyl	– ∪ ∪
Trochee	– ∪
Anapaest	∪ ∪ –

Below is iambic trimeter (as understood in the traditional scheme):

1	2	3	4	5	6
∪ –	∪ –	∪ –	∪ –	∪ –	∪ –
– –		– –		– –	∪ ∪
∪ ∪ ∪	∪ ∪ ∪	∪ ∪ ∪	∪ ∪ ∪		
– ∪ ∪	– ∪ ∪				
∪ ∪ –					

It is sometimes argued that the iambic trimeter is the metre most like prose. Certainly, it allows for conversation that sounds natural. As with all metres, a poet can use the scheme to achieve certain effects, but it should be said that there is not much metrical variation in *Medea*. Of the play's 1030 iambic lines there are 75 in which a unit other than an iamb or a spondee is used. There are no anapaests in *Medea*'s iambic trimeters.

Language and style

Euripidean language does not always follow the rules taught to twenty-first-century pupils about ancient Greek. Below are listed some grammatical usages that are rarely found in prose (if at all):

- omission of the article, where it would be expected in prose (as in line 220);
- alternative dative plural forms, i.e. -αισι(ν) and -οισι(ν);

- *crasis* (the joining of two words to make one word, where the first word is either the article or καὶ) is fairly common (e.g. οὑμὸς at 229);
- placing the preposition after the noun it governs (as at line 217);
- different pronoun forms: accusative plural (394: σφε); dative plural (399: σφιν);
- non-compound forms of verbs that would normally be compounds in prose (e.g. κτενῶ in line 394).

Below are some common features of tragic language:

- asyndeton – the lack of connection – can be used for stylisic effect, as Greek prose normally insists on clear connection between every sentence;
- in stichomythia – an exchange between two actors where each actor speaks one line – the syntax can be interrupted by the other speaker, or the syntax of one speaker's line might be completed by the other speaker, or by the first speaker in their next line;
- ἐστί is often omitted (as at line 345);
- while there is occasional enjambement, most lines have some form of punctuation at the end of the line;
- word order – flexible in Greek prose – is even more varied in verse.

A brief note on technical terms

Some commentaries and introductions to tragedy like to make not inconsiderable use of technical terms. This author's view is that it is perfectly possible to respond to *Medea* in an interesting and sophisticated way without persistent recourse to such terms. However, there is one term that does appear several times, namely, *metonymy* (a form of metaphor in which one term is used for another). In *Medea* this is most common with the various words for 'bed' (explanations are given in the commentary).

aphorism	a principle or precept expressed pithily.
hendiadys	a stylistic feature whereby a single idea is expressed by two words joined by a conjunction.
litotes	understatement, sometimes by the use of a double negative.
metaphor	non-literal language.
metonymy	a form of metaphor, in which one term stands for another, e.g. 'Downing Street announced today'.
tautology	repetition or saying the same thing twice.

Medea – the myth

With a small number of notable exceptions, tragedy took its stories from existing bodies of myth. *Medea* is no exception to this rule. But, as is often the case with other tragedies, we do not have a full treatment of the various parts of the Medea myth before Euripides' play. We think that an earlier epic poet called Eumelus may have written an extensive treatment in a lost epic poem, *Corinthiaca*, and there seems to have been another lost epic, *Naupactia* (no author known), which dealt with the Medea myth. There are allusions to various parts of the story in Homer, Hesiod and Pindar, but we have no full account of the expedition of the Argonauts until Apollonius Rhodius' epic of the third century BC. From Apollonius the story of Jason and the Argonauts runs as follows. Jason's father, Aeson, had his kingship of Iolcus in Thessaly usurped by his half-brother, Pelias. When Jason, on reaching adulthood, tried to claim the kingdom as his birthright, Pelias demanded that Jason first fetch the Golden Fleece from Colchis on the Black Sea. Pelias expected that the task would be impossible. Jason and his comrades built the first ship, the Argo, sailed to Colchis and secured the Golden Fleece with the help of Medea, the daughter of the king of Colchis, Aeetes. To delay her father's pursuit, Medea killed her brother. When she and Jason returned to Iolcus, Medea persuaded the daughters of Pelias to cut up their father and boil him in order to restore his youth. Following Pelias' not unexpected death, Jason and Medea fled to Corinth.

The important thing to remember is that authors were free to vary the details of the myth (Euripides, for instance, wrote a play in which Helen was never in Troy at all), and were also free to concentrate on one particular section of the story. As with most myths, there is a considerable variety in the different versions, in relation to, for instance, how Medea murders her brother, where Jason and Medea live, the number of children they have and how and by whom the children are killed (in one version it is the Corinthians rather than Medea who murder the children). That said, allusion is made in the play to the Argonauts' expedition, where Jason was charged to get hold of the Golden Fleece, and also the help that Medea gave Jason to acquire the fleece, including the murder of her brother, Apsyrtus, possibly to slow down Medea's father as he pursues Jason. Euripides' play, though, refers to killing Apsyrtus 'at the hearth' (line 1334): killing a relative in their home is particularly horrible. Reference is also made to Medea causing the death of Pelias (see lines 9, 486–7, 504–8): it was the usurper Pelias who asked Jason to take on what he thought was the impossible task of fetching the Golden Fleece.

There is some fragmentary evidence that there was a *Medea* written by an earlier tragedian called Neophron. It is even claimed that Euripides based his play on Neophron's, or even passed off Neophron's play as his own. There is a very careful consideration of this in the introduction to Mastronarde's commentary (Mastronarde 2002: pp. 57–64). While accepting that debate about Neophron's play is likely to continue, Mastronarde concludes that the fragments we have are likely to come from a play written after Euripides' version.

In fact, based on the allusions to the myth that occur in earlier authors, it looks as though Euripides may have provided the following innovations: the character of Glauke, Jason's marriage to her, Aegeus' involvement, the use of a poisoned robe to kill Creon and his daughter, Medea's deliberate murder of the children, Medea's escape in a chariot given to her by her grandfather, the Sun. However, we should not be confident that each of these were Euripidean innovations: we simply lack the evidence to demonstrate that.

Medea – the play

Medea is a very powerful play, which has inspired both an extensive body of scholarly work and a large number of modern theatrical productions. This short introduction cannot do justice to the variety of critical approaches (please see the 'Suggestions for further reading'), but it does try to deal with the structure of the play, some of its important themes, the staging of the play and the reception of the play both in antiquity and in modern times.

The play's structure

Medea is organized to create as much dramatic and emotional impact as possible. At first, even though she plans a murderous revenge, Medea has the chorus (and the audience in modern productions, at least) on her side. To be able to achieve the revenge she has actually planned, Medea needs to be confident she has a sanctuary after she has committed the murders. This explains the Aegeus scene (even though some scholars have found the plotting unsatisfactory). It is only after this scene that the chorus realize what Medea actually plans to do. The Aegeus scene is surrounded by two contrasting encounters between Jason and Medea. In the first she tells (what she believes to be) the truth about Jason's treatment of her, and achieves nothing, confronted by Jason's complacent misogyny. After the Aegeus scene, she has a very different meeting with Jason, where she pretends to be reconciled to his new marriage, and where she offers presents, through which she hopes to secure the deaths of Glauke and Creon. Once news reaches Medea that she has been successful, the play relentlessly leads to the murder of the children, and to her triumph over Jason. The play's structure is often analysed in rather a technical way, but understanding the structure can also help with understanding plot, theme and character. The following description of the structure is borrowed from Mastronarde's commentary. To make sense of it, the following technical terms will be useful:

> *parodos* entry of the chorus
>
> *episode* spoken scene between actors
>
> *stasimon* sung choral lyric
>
> *exodos* the last scene of the play (literally: the going out)

Prologue (1–130)

- Nurse's monologue (1–48)
- dialogue between the Nurse and the tutor (49–95)
- anapaestic exchange between the Nurse and Medea indoors (96–130)

Parodos (131–213)

  anapaests of Nurse and Medea, with some choral song

First episode (214–409)

- Medea's monologue with brief comment from the chorus (214–70)
- dialogue between Medea and Creon (271–356)
- Medea and the chorus (357–409)

First stasimon (chorus) (410–45)

Second episode (446–626)

    debate between Medea and Jason

Second stasimon (627–62)

Third episode (663–823)

- dialogue between Medea and Aegeus (663–763)
- Medea and chorus (764–823)

Third stasimon (824–65)

Fourth episode (866–75)

- dialogue between Medea and Jason, with the children brought out by the tutor

Fourth stasimon (976–1001)

Fifth episode (1002–80)

- dialogue between Medea and the tutor (1002–20)
- Medea's great monologue (1021–80)

Anapaestic interlude, in place of a chorus (1081–1115)

Sixth episode (1116–1250)

- dialogue between Medea and the messenger (1116–35)
- messenger speech (1136–1230)
- Medea and the chorus (1231–50)

Fifth stasimon (1251–92)

Exodos (1293–1419)

- dialogue of Jason and chorus (1293–1316)
- iambic dialogue between Medea and Jason (1317–88)
- anapaestic dialogue between Medea and Jason (1389–1414)
- chorus' summary (1415–19)

Themes

Medea is a very rich and sophisticated play, organized around Medea's revenge on Jason for his betrayal (revenge is not uncommon as a motivating device in tragedy). It shows an acute interest in Medea's psychology; it represents Medea as a powerful 'other' figure, both as barbarian and as woman; key interests of the play are rhetorical efficacy, sexual politics and religious propriety. The imagery used in the play – naval, medical, animal, military – serves to deepen and sharpen the play's concerns as listed above (Mastronarde 2002: 34–6 is good but concise on the imagery in the play).

To achieve her revenge Medea has to overcome a number of obstacles. First, she has to overcome her own despair, which dominates the opening of the play; second, she needs someone on her side and looks here for the chorus' sisterly support; third, she needs a little extra time and manages to persuade Creon to give her a day; fourth, she needs sanctuary once she has committed the murders, and she succeeds in persuading Aegeus to give her a home in Athens; fifth, she needs to win Jason round so that the lethal gifts can be delivered to Glauke and Creon; finally, she needs to overcome her own psychological difficulties.

It is most especially in relation to the killing of the children that Euripides' complex portrait of a woman divided against herself is seen. This is best demonstrated in her famous monologue (1019–80), where her veering back and forth between preparing to murder her children to shouting the impossibility of such an act for a mother is passionate, powerful and realistic. At the same time, Euripides' psychological interest is also apparent in the way that the wildly despairing Medea of the early part of the play can become an acute analyst of sexual inequality, a powerful orator arguing against misogyny and unfair dealing, an extremely skilful manipulator of men and – finally – the extreme and extremely vengeful and violent figure whom we see at the end of the play. The portrait, in its compelling variety, is powerful and complex.

One of the reasons for Medea's acute sense of betrayal is that Jason swore an oath to her, made by joining right hands. Oaths – and the breaking of them – pervade the play (see, for instance, 160ff., 209, 412–13, 439, 492–5, 659–92, 698, 731ff., 745ff., 1352, 1364). Hands are important in relation to oaths (496–8), and as a sign of familial connection (see 899, 1069–73), but they are also important in supplication (e.g. 324ff.) and, more troublingly, as the agents of violence (e.g. 857, 864, 1055, 1239, 1244, 1254, 1279, 1283, 1309, 1322, 1365). This pervasive reference to oaths and supplication, and thereby to Greek gods and religious institutions, demonstrates the complicated relationship that the barbarian Medea has to Greek *mores*.

It is in the various representations of Medea as 'other' – as a woman, as a barbarian, as a barbarian with special magical powers and as a woman whose grandfather is the Sun – that *Medea* is most extraordinary and most threatening. Commonly described as frightening (e.g. 38ff., 271, 282, 316), as difficult (525), as different (579), both Jason and Medea agree that there is something about Medea's barbarian origins that marks her out, though there is nothing in the way she speaks Greek or in her attitudes to, say, Greek religious practice that substantiates that view. However, Jason argues that had he not brought Medea to Greece from her barbarian land, she would not be enjoying the rule of law guaranteed by Greek civilization (536–8), so the distinction between Greek and barbarian remains important ideologically. Medea thinks that Jason finds having a barbarian wife no longer respectable (591–2). She also claims to Aegeus that she has a special knowledge of drugs (717–18). Medea seems in many ways special but it is in her confronting of male supremacy that her challenge, her threat is most obvious.

We first hear Medea lamenting from inside the house. Nearly her first words when she appears on stage are 'I have come out of the house' (214). Thus she begins her appropriation of what in fifth-century Athenian ideological terms was supposed to be the exclusive possession of men, namely, engaging in rhetoric and violence outside the house (women were supposed to confine themselves inside, and to keep quiet: see the note on 214–15). In her first great speech (214ff.), Medea decries how badly the institution of marriage treats women (though it is not clear she is married to Jason – note, however, line 910 where Jason himself *implies* that they are married – and the institution she describes looks very fifth-century and very Athenian). At lines 248–51, she offers a direct challenge to male supremacy based on men's participation in war. She manipulates Creon successfully, even though he is wary, and she makes a passionate though unsuccessful case against Jason in their first debate (i.e. Jason is not persuaded of her case, though the chorus are). She manipulates Aegeus to secure sanctuary in Athens. She manages to keep the chorus complicit, even when they realize that she plans to murder her children. She persuades Jason to take the children bearing presents to Glauke. She brings about the deaths of Glauke and Creon, and manages to kill her own children. Her achievements in persuasion, manipulation and violence are remarkable. In a series of confrontations with (mainly) men, who are characterized as variously fearful (Creon), complacent and unpleasant (Jason) or easily manipulated (Aegeus), she for the most part wins.

Why is Medea such a threat? First of all, it is because she so dominantly and successfully does what men claim they do (that's the rhetoric and the violence). Second, it is whom she chooses to kill. By killing Glauke, she destroys one part of Jason's future and one way in which, in a patrilineal society, he can secure his legacy. By killing her own children, she destroys another part of his future. In short, her attack is one against patriarchy itself. No wonder the play may have been perceived as shocking in 431 BC; no surprise that the early twentieth-century suffragettes took up the play as a rallying cry.

It is a typically Euripidean irony, though, that a play seen by many as proto-feminist is one in which a mother kills her own children.

Staging

The *skene* – the rectangular hut at the back of the stage – represents the house where Medea and Jason have been living in Corinth. It does not quite seem to be in the centre of the city. One of the exits leads to the centre of the city, where Creon's palace is situated; the other leads to the gates at the city walls. Interestingly, all the characters except Aegeus enter and exit using the city side, though it is not clear whether the chorus entered from both sides. There are few props required for the play: some mark of royalty, such as a sceptre, for Creon and Aegeus; perhaps some weapons for Creon's attendants; Medea's gifts to Glauke.

Tragedy at the time of *Medea* used three male actors. It is likely that the lead actor – the protagonist, who competed in the protagonists' competition – would have taken the part of Medea. The second actor could perhaps have played the parts of the Nurse, Creon and Jason, while the third could have been the tutor, Aegeus and the Messenger. There are a number of silent parts: the attendants of Creon and Aegeus, and possibly for Jason as well, and, of course, the children.

The masks and costumes of the actors are likely to have been conventional. So Creon would have been bearded but perhaps greying, while Aegeus and Jason would have been bearded but without grey. Costume may have been used to distinguish the free (and indeed noble) from the slaves. Most discussion in this area has centred around Medea herself. The Nurse in the prologue describes her as not eating and as crying continually. It is not clear whether that was reflected in her mask but there is some reason to doubt that it was: appearances that departed from convention are normally commented on in the texts themselves, as in the case of Electra's rags in *Electra* and Orestes' wild hair in *Orestes*. More interesting is whether Medea was costumed in an overtly non-Greek way, as iconographic depictions of Medea produced after 431 BC have her wearing elaborate eastern robes of various sorts (this is not the case with iconographic representations produced before 431 BC). Another way that Medea's otherness may have been indicated was by the colour of her skin (Herodotus 2.104 says that the Colchians were dark-skinned like the Egyptians), but no iconographic depiction has her with anything other than light skin.

As already mentioned, the most stunning theatrical effect of *Medea* is the use of the *mechane* at the end of the play. This piece of theatre kit allowed characters to appear way above the acting space. What is shocking about the use of it in *Medea* is that the *mechane* is normally reserved for gods (in the play the *mechane* is explicitly said to be the chariot belonging to her divine grandfather, the Sun). Yet here we see a mother with the corpses of the children she has murdered. At the same time, the use of the device visually represents her superiority over Jason but perhaps also the fact that she has left the human realm.

Reception

It seems fairly clear that Euripides' *Medea*, though it did not win the first prize in 431 BC, had become, by some time in the fourth century, if not earlier, something of a 'classic'. Certainly, there seem to have been a number of literary treatments in the fourth century BC, and there is a good collection of iconographic representations of Medea from the fourth century BC which seem to show an interest in Euripides' version. What is particularly fascinating is how Medea is so often represented in a chariot and also so often in non-Greek clothing (for an interesting online discussion, with images of the vase paintings, please go to 'The Underworld Painter and the Corinthian adventures of Medea: An interpretation of the crater in Munich' by Ludovico Rebaudo, which can be accessed at http://www.engramma.it/eOS2/index.php?id_articolo=1380).

The play proved popular among the Romans as well, with adaptations written by Ennius, Accius, Ovid, Seneca the Younger and Hosidius Geta. In the modern era one of the most celebrated of productions was the 1907 production at the Savoy Theatre, using Gilbert Murray's translation. This is sometimes referred to as the 'votes-for-women' production, during which mass arrests of women activists were made. After the Second World War, the French playwright Jean Anouilh translated the play in 1946 and there was a highly popular production on Broadway directed by Robinson Jeffers in 1947. There is a magnificent film released in 1969, directed by Pier Paolo Pasolini, and starring the great opera singer Maria Callas as Medea. The German novelist Christa Wolf published a novel *Medea* in 1996 (translated as *Medea: A Modern Retelling* by John Cullen). Recent years have seen some famous productions in London: Diana Rigg starred as Medea in 1993, and Fiona Shaw played the role in 2001. In 2014, Helen McCrory played the part, and in 2015, in another modern retelling by writer Rachel Cusk, Medea was played by Kate Fleetwood.

Clearly, the play retains its power.

Euripides – a brief note

Euripides, born probably in the 480s BC, was one of the three great Athenian tragedians of the fifth century. We have seventeen tragedies in more or less complete form written by Euripides, compared to seven each for Aeschylus and Sophocles. The first sure date of his life is 455 BC, the date of his first production at the Great Dionysia. The earliest play that we have is *Alcestis* (438 BC). *Medea* is, in fact, the second of the plays that we have, performed in 431 BC. Euripides died in 406 BC, and two of his surviving plays (*Iphigeneia at Aulis* and *Bacchae*) were performed posthumously between 405 and 400 BC.

Euripides had a distinctive reputation in antiquity; he still does. One view – backed up by the fact that he won only four first prizes in the dramatic competition at the Great Dionysia, compared with Aeschylus' 13 and Sophocles' possible 20 – was that Euripides was not popular with the Athenian audience. However, the fact that he was granted entry to the dramatic festival on at least twenty occasions (there is evidence that Euripides had 92 plays performed) would suggest otherwise. One common critical response to his relative lack of success in the dramatic competition is to argue that there is something about the plays themselves that the audience found troubling or even scandalous.

One area where this may have been true was the shocking representation of women – and *Medea* certainly seems to fit into that category. (The plot of Aristophanes' *Thesmophoriazusae* is based on the hostility of the women of Athens to Euripides because of the dramatic female figures he created.) Another area – again much satirized in Aristophanes – is the pervasiveness in his plays of sophistic thought and rhetoric, used to challenge and even subvert some of fifth-century Athens' most cherished values. The picture of Euripides as a transgressive, subversive iconoclast is not new; that does not mean, though, that it is not true.

However, we probably do need to provide a slightly more nuanced picture. Aristophanes' *Frogs*, produced a year or so after Euripides' death, confirms that Euripides was already seen as one of the three great tragedians. Challenging and subversive though his plays can be, Euripides can also be seen as an innovative practitioner who contributed to changes in and the development of tragic convention. Certainly, his popularity increased after his death, and his literary influence is significant, not only on the New Comedy of the fourth century but also on authors as different as Ovid and Seneca.

Suggestions for further reading

The critical literature on *Medea* is vast and still expanding. Below are a few items. Many articles from scholarly journals are now available online at JSTOR.

Commentaries

Elliott, Alan (ed.) *Euripides Medea* (Oxford: Oxford University Press, 1969).
Mastronarde, Donald J. (ed.) *Euripides: Medea* (Cambridge: Cambridge University Press, 2002).
Mossman, J. (ed.) *Euripides: Medea* (Oxford: Aris and Phillips, 2011) (with facing translation).
Page, D.L. (ed.) *Euripides: Medea* (Oxford: Oxford University Press, 1938).

Translations

Harrison, J. (ed.) *Euripides Medea*. Translated by Judith Affleck (Cambridge: Cambridge University Press, 1999).
Kovacs, David. *Euripides Volume I* (Cambridge, MA: Harvard University Press, 1994).
Morwood, James. *Euripides: Medea and Other Plays* (Oxford: Oxford University Press, 2008).
Rutherford, Richard B. (ed.) *Medea and Other Plays*. Translated by John Davie (London: Penguin, 2003).
Vellacott, P. *Euripides: Medea/Hecabe/Electra/Heracles* (London: Penguin, 1963).

Critical treatments

Allan, W. *Euripides: Medea* (London: Duckworth, 2002).
Barlow, S.A. 'Stereotype and reversal in Euripides' *Medea*', *Greece and Rome* 36 (1989): pp. 158–71.
Clauss, J.J. and Johnston, S.I. (eds.) *Medea: Essays on Medea in Myth, Literature, Philosophy and Art* (Princeton, NJ: Princeton University Press, 1997).
Easterling, P.E. 'The infanticide in Euripides' *Medea*', *Yale Classical Studies* 25 (1977): pp. 177–91.
Foley, H.P. 'Medea's divided self', *Classical Antiquity* 8 (1989): pp. 61–85.
Knox, B.M.W. 'The *Medea* of Euripides', *Yale Classical Studies* 25 (1977): pp. 193–225.
McDermott, E. *Euripides' Medea: The Incarnation of Disorder* (Pennsylvania, 1989).
The text is from Diggle, J. *Euripidis Fabulae. Tomus 1* (Oxford: Oxford University Press, 1984).

Text

Μή.   Κορίνθιαι γυναῖκες, ἐξῆλθον δόμων
μή μοί τι μέμψησθ᾽· οἶδα γὰρ πολλοὺς βροτῶν   215
σεμνοὺς γεγῶτας, τοὺς μὲν ὀμμάτων ἄπο,
τοὺς δ᾽ ἐν θυραίοις· οἱ δ᾽ ἀφ᾽ ἡσύχου ποδὸς
δύσκλειαν ἐκτήσαντο καὶ ῥᾳθυμίαν.
δίκη γὰρ οὐκ ἔνεστ᾽ ἐν ὀφθαλμοῖς βροτῶν,
ὅστις πρὶν ἀνδρὸς σπλάγχνον ἐκμαθεῖν σαφῶς   220
στυγεῖ δεδορκώς, οὐδὲν ἠδικημένος.
χρὴ δὲ ξένον μὲν κάρτα προσχωρεῖν πόλει·
οὐδ᾽ ἀστὸν ᾔνεσ᾽ ὅστις αὐθάδης γεγὼς
πικρὸς πολίταις ἐστὶν ἀμαθίας ὕπο.
ἐμοὶ δ᾽ ἄελπτον πρᾶγμα προσπεσὸν τόδε   225
ψυχὴν διέφθαρκ᾽· οἴχομαι δὲ καὶ βίου
χάριν μεθεῖσα κατθανεῖν χρῄζω, φίλαι.
ἐν ᾧ γὰρ ἦν μοι πάντα, γιγνώσκω καλῶς,
κάκιστος ἀνδρῶν ἐκβέβηχ᾽ οὑμὸς πόσις.
πάντων δ᾽ ὅσ᾽ ἔστ᾽ ἔμψυχα καὶ γνώμην ἔχει   230
γυναῖκές ἐσμεν ἀθλιώτατον φυτόν·
ἃς πρῶτα μὲν δεῖ χρημάτων ὑπερβολῇ
πόσιν πρίασθαι δεσπότην τε σώματος
λαβεῖν· κακοῦ γὰρ τοῦτ᾽ ἔτ᾽ ἄλγιον κακόν.
κἂν τῷδ᾽ ἀγὼν μέγιστος, ἢ κακὸν λαβεῖν   235
ἢ χρηστόν· οὐ γὰρ εὐκλεεῖς ἀπαλλαγαὶ
γυναιξὶν οὐδ᾽ οἷόν τ᾽ ἀνήνασθαι πόσιν.
ἐς καινὰ δ᾽ ἤθη καὶ νόμους ἀφιγμένην
δεῖ μάντιν εἶναι, μὴ μαθοῦσαν οἴκοθεν,

οἵῳ μάλιστα χρήσεται ξυνευνέτῃ.   240
κἂν μὲν τάδ᾽ ἡμῖν ἐκπονουμέναισιν εὖ
πόσις ξυνοικῇ μὴ βίᾳ φέρων ζυγόν,
ζηλωτὸς αἰών· εἰ δὲ μή, θανεῖν χρεών.
ἀνὴρ δ᾽, ὅταν τοῖς ἔνδον ἄχθηται ξυνών,
ἔξω μολὼν ἔπαυσε καρδίαν ἄσης   245
ἢ πρὸς φίλον τιν᾽ ἢ πρὸς ἥλικα τραπείς·
ἡμῖν δ᾽ ἀνάγκη πρὸς μίαν ψυχὴν βλέπειν.
λέγουσι δ᾽ ἡμᾶς ὡς ἀκίνδυνον βίον
ζῶμεν κατ᾽ οἴκους, οἱ δὲ μάρνανται δορί,
κακῶς φρονοῦντες· ὡς τρὶς ἂν παρ᾽ ἀσπίδα   250
στῆναι θέλοιμ᾽ ἂν μᾶλλον ἢ τεκεῖν ἅπαξ.
ἀλλ᾽ οὐ γὰρ αὑτὸς πρὸς σὲ κἄμ᾽ ἥκει λόγος·
σοὶ μὲν πόλις θ᾽ ἥδ᾽ ἐστὶ καὶ πατρὸς δόμοι
βίου τ᾽ ὄνησις καὶ φίλων συνουσία,
ἐγὼ δ᾽ ἔρημος ἄπολις οὖσ᾽ ὑβρίζομαι   255
πρὸς ἀνδρός, ἐκ γῆς βαρβάρου λελῃσμένη,
οὐ μητέρ᾽, οὐκ ἀδελφόν, οὐχὶ συγγενῆ
μεθορμίσασθαι τῆσδ᾽ ἔχουσα συμφορᾶς.
τοσοῦτον οὖν σου τυγχάνειν βουλήσομαι,
ἤν μοι πόρος τις μηχανή τ᾽ ἐξευρεθῇ   260
πόσιν δίκην τῶνδ᾽ ἀντιτείσασθαι κακῶν
τὸν δόντα τ᾽ αὐτῷ θυγατέρ᾽ ἥν τ᾽ ἐγήματο,
σιγᾶν. γυνὴ γὰρ τἄλλα μὲν φόβου πλέα
κακή τ᾽ ἐς ἀλκὴν καὶ σίδηρον εἰσορᾶν·
ὅταν δ᾽ ἐς εὐνὴν ἠδικημένη κυρῇ,   265
οὐκ ἔστιν ἄλλη φρὴν μιαιφονωτέρα.
Χο.   δράσω τάδ᾽· ἐνδίκως γὰρ ἐκτείσῃ πόσιν,
Μήδεια. πενθεῖν δ᾽ οὔ σε θαυμάζω τύχας.
ὁρῶ δὲ καὶ Κρέοντα, τῆσδ᾽ ἄνακτα γῆς,
στείχοντα, καινῶν ἄγγελον βουλευμάτων.   270

Κρ.   σὲ τὴν σκυθρωπὸν καὶ πόσει θυμουμένην,
       Μήδει᾽, ἀνεῖπον τῆσδε γῆς ἔξω περᾶν
       φυγάδα, λαβοῦσαν δισσὰ σὺν σαυτῇ τέκνα,
       καὶ μή τι μέλλειν· ὡς ἐγὼ βραβεὺς λόγου
       τοῦδ᾽ εἰμί, κοὐκ ἄπειμι πρὸς δόμους πάλιν   275
       πρὶν ἄν σε γαίας τερμόνων ἔξω βάλω.
       αἰαῖ· πανώλης ἡ τάλαιν᾽ ἀπόλλυμαι·
Μή.   ἐχθροὶ γὰρ ἐξιᾶσι πάντα δὴ κάλων,
       κοὐκ ἔστιν ἄτης εὐπρόσοιστος ἔκβασις.
       ἐρήσομαι δὲ καὶ κακῶς πάσχουσ᾽ ὅμως·   280
       τίνος μ᾽ ἕκατι γῆς ἀποστέλλεις, Κρέον;
Κρ.   δέδοικά σ᾽, οὐδὲν δεῖ παραμπίσχειν λόγους,
       μή μοί τι δράσῃς παῖδ᾽ ἀνήκεστον κακόν.
       συμβάλλεται δὲ πολλὰ τοῦδε δείγματα·
       σοφὴ πέφυκας καὶ κακῶν πολλῶν ἴδρις,   285
       λυπῇ δὲ λέκτρων ἀνδρὸς ἐστερημένη.
       κλύω δ᾽ ἀπειλεῖν σ᾽, ὡς ἀπαγγέλλουσί μοι,
       τὸν δόντα καὶ γήμαντα καὶ γαμουμένην
       δράσειν τι. ταῦτ᾽ οὖν πρὶν παθεῖν φυλάξομαι.
       κρεῖσσον δέ μοι νῦν πρός σ᾽ ἀπεχθέσθαι, γύναι,   290
       ἢ μαλθακισθένθ᾽ ὕστερον μεταστένειν.
Μή.   φεῦ φεῦ.
       οὐ νῦν με πρῶτον ἀλλὰ πολλάκις, Κρέον,
       ἔβλαψε δόξα μεγάλα τ᾽ εἴργασται κακά.
       χρὴ δ᾽ οὔποθ᾽ ὅστις ἀρτίφρων πέφυκ᾽ ἀνὴρ
       παῖδας περισσῶς ἐκδιδάσκεσθαι σοφούς·   295
       χωρὶς γὰρ ἄλλης ἧς ἔχουσιν ἀργίας
       φθόνον πρὸς ἀστῶν ἀλφάνουσι δυσμενῆ.
       σκαιοῖσι μὲν γὰρ καινὰ προσφέρων σοφὰ
       δόξεις ἀχρεῖος κοὐ σοφὸς πεφυκέναι·
       τῶν δ᾽ αὖ δοκούντων εἰδέναι τι ποικίλον   300
       κρείσσων νομισθεὶς ἐν πόλει λυπρὸς φανῇ.
       ἐγὼ δὲ καὐτὴ τῆσδε κοινωνῶ τύχης·
       σοφὴ γὰρ οὖσα, τοῖς μέν εἰμ᾽ ἐπίφθονος,
       τοῖς δ᾽ ἡσυχαία, τοῖς δὲ θατέρου τρόπου,
       τοῖς δ᾽ αὖ προσάντης· εἰμὶ δ᾽ οὐκ ἄγαν σοφή,   305
       σὺ δ᾽ αὖ φοβῇ με· μὴ τί πλημμελὲς πάθῃς;
       οὐχ ὧδ᾽ ἔχει μοι, μὴ τρέσῃς ἡμᾶς, Κρέον,
       ὥστ᾽ ἐς τυράννους ἄνδρας ἐξαμαρτάνειν.
       σὺ γὰρ τί μ᾽ ἠδίκηκας; ἐξέδου κόρην

ὅτῳ σε θυμὸς ἦγεν. ἀλλ᾽ ἐμὸν πόσιν 310
μισῶ· σὺ δ᾽, οἶμαι, σωφρονῶν ἔδρας τάδε.
καὶ νῦν τὸ μὲν σὸν οὐ φθονῶ καλῶς ἔχειν·
νυμφεύετ᾽, εὖ πράσσοιτε· τήνδε δὲ χθόνα
ἐᾶτέ μ᾽ οἰκεῖν. καὶ γὰρ ἠδικημένοι
σιγησόμεσθα, κρεισσόνων νικώμενοι. 315

Κρ. λέγεις ἀκοῦσαι μαλθάκ᾽, ἀλλ᾽ ἔσω φρενῶν
ὀρρωδία μοι μή τι βουλεύῃς κακόν.
τοσῷδε δ᾽ ἧσσον ἢ πάρος πέποιθά σοι·
γυνὴ γὰρ ὀξύθυμος, ὡς δ᾽ αὔτως ἀνήρ,
ῥᾴων φυλάσσειν ἢ σιωπηλὸς σοφή. 320
ἀλλ᾽ ἔξιθ᾽ ὡς τάχιστα, μὴ λόγους λέγε·
ὡς ταῦτ᾽ ἄραρε, κοὐκ ἔχεις τέχνην ὅπως
μενεῖς παρ᾽ ἡμῖν οὖσα δυσμενὴς ἐμοί.

Μή. μή, πρός σε γονάτων τῆς τε νεογάμου κόρης.
Κρ. λόγους ἀναλοῖς· οὐ γὰρ ἂν πείσαις ποτέ. 325
Μή. ἀλλ᾽ ἐξελᾷς με κοὐδὲν αἰδέσῃ λιτάς;
Κρ. φιλῶ γὰρ οὐ σὲ μᾶλλον ἢ δόμους ἐμούς.
Μή. ὦ πατρίς, ὥς σου κάρτα νῦν μνείαν ἔχω.
Κρ. πλὴν γὰρ τέκνων ἔμοιγε φίλτατον πολύ.
Μή. φεῦ φεῦ, βροτοῖς ἔρωτες ὡς κακὸν μέγα. 330
Κρ. ὅπως ἄν, οἶμαι, καὶ παραστῶσιν τύχαι.
Μή. Ζεῦ, μὴ λάθοι σε τῶνδ᾽ ὃς αἴτιος κακῶν.
Κρ. ἕρπ᾽, ὦ ματαία, καί μ᾽ ἀπάλλαξον πόνων.
Μή. πονοῦμεν ἡμεῖς κοὐ πόνων κεχρήμεθα.
Κρ. τάχ᾽ ἐξ ὀπαδῶν χειρὸς ὠσθήσῃ βίᾳ. 335
Μή. μὴ δῆτα τοῦτό γ᾽, ἀλλά σ᾽ ἄντομαι, Κρέον.
Κρ. ὄχλον παρέξεις, ὡς ἔοικας, ὦ γύναι.
Μή. φευξούμεθ᾽· οὐ τοῦθ᾽ ἱκέτευσα σοῦ τυχεῖν.
Κρ. τί δ᾽ αὖ βιάζῃ κοὐκ ἀπαλλάσσῃ χερός;
Μή. μίαν με μεῖναι τήνδ᾽ ἔασον ἡμέραν 340
καὶ ξυμπερᾶναι φροντίδ᾽ ᾗ φευξούμεθα,
παισίν τ᾽ ἀφορμὴν τοῖς ἐμοῖς, ἐπεὶ πατὴρ
οὐδὲν προτιμᾷ μηχανήσασθαί τέκνοις.
οἴκτιρε δ᾽ αὐτούς· καὶ σύ τοι παίδων πατὴρ
πέφυκας· εἰκὸς δέ σφιν εὔνοιάν σ᾽ ἔχειν. 345
τοὐμοῦ γὰρ οὔ μοι φροντίς, εἰ φευξούμεθα,
κείνους δὲ κλαίω συμφορᾷ κεχρημένους.
Κρ. ἥκιστα τοὐμὸν λῆμ᾽ ἔφυ τυραννικόν,
αἰδούμενος δὲ πολλὰ δὴ διέφθορα·

καὶ νῦν ὁρῶ μὲν ἐξαμαρτάνων, γύναι,   350
ὅμως δὲ τεύξῃ τοῦδε. προυννέπω δέ σοι,
εἴ σ᾽ ἡ 'πιοῦσα λαμπὰς ὄψεται θεοῦ
καὶ παῖδας ἐντὸς τῆσδε τερμόνων χθονός,
θανῇ· λέλεκται μῦθος ἀψευδὴς ὅδε.
νῦν δ᾽, εἰ μένειν δεῖ, μίμν᾽ ἐφ᾽ ἡμέραν μίαν·   355
οὐ γάρ τι δράσεις δεινὸν ὧν φόβος μ᾽ ἔχει.

357–63: *This is a short response from the chorus, which sympathizes with Medea, but also wonders what Medea can do in the circumstances she finds herself in.*

Μή. κακῶς πέπρακται πανταχῆ· τίς ἀντερεῖ;
       ἀλλ᾽ οὔτι ταύτῃ ταῦτα, μὴ δοκεῖτέ πω.   365
       ἔτ᾽ εἴσ᾽ ἀγῶνες τοῖς νεωστὶ νυμφίοις
       καὶ τοῖσι κηδεύσασιν οὐ σμικροὶ πόνοι.
       δοκεῖς γὰρ ἄν με τόνδε θωπεῦσαί ποτε
       εἰ μή τι κερδαίνουσαν ἢ τεχνωμένην;
       οὐδ᾽ ἂν προσεῖπον οὐδ᾽ ἂν ἡψάμην χεροῖν.   370
       ὁ δ᾽ ἐς τοσοῦτον μωρίας ἀφίκετο
       ὥστ᾽, ἐξὸν αὐτῷ τἄμ᾽ ἑλεῖν βουλεύματα
       γῆς ἐκβαλόντι, τήνδ᾽ ἐφῆκεν ἡμέραν
       μεῖναί μ᾽, ἐν ᾗ τρεῖς τῶν ἐμῶν ἐχθρῶν νεκροὺς
       θήσω, πατέρα τε καὶ κόρην πόσιν τ᾽ ἐμόν.   375
       πολλὰς δ᾽ ἔχουσα θανασίμους αὐτοῖς ὁδούς,
       οὐκ οἶδ᾽ ὁποίᾳ πρῶτον ἐγχειρῶ, φίλαι·
       πότερον ὑφάψω δῶμα νυμφικὸν πυρί,
       ἢ θηκτὸν ὤσω φάσγανον δι᾽ ἥπατος,
       σιγῇ δόμους ἐσβᾶσ᾽, ἵν᾽ ἔστρωται λέχος.   380
       ἀλλ᾽ ἕν τί μοι πρόσαντες· εἰ ληφθήσομαι
       δόμους ὑπερβαίνουσα καὶ τεχνωμένη,
       θανοῦσα θήσω τοῖς ἐμοῖς ἐχθροῖς γέλων.
       κράτιστα τὴν εὐθεῖαν, ᾗ πεφύκαμεν
       σοφοὶ μάλιστα, φαρμάκοις αὐτοὺς ἑλεῖν.   385
       εἶέν· καὶ δὴ τεθνᾶσι· τίς με δέξεται πόλις;
       τίς γῆν ἄσυλον καὶ δόμους ἐχεγγύους
       ξένος παρασχὼν ῥύσεται τοὐμὸν δέμας;
       οὐκ ἔστι. μείνασ᾽ οὖν ἔτι σμικρὸν χρόνον,
       ἢν μέν τις ἡμῖν πύργος ἀσφαλὴς φανῇ,   390
       δόλῳ μέτειμι τόνδε καὶ σιγῇ φόνον·
       ἢν δ᾽ ἐξελαύνῃ ξυμφορά μ᾽ ἀμήχανος,
       αὐτὴ ξίφος λαβοῦσα, κεἰ μέλλω θανεῖν,
       κτενῶ σφε, τόλμης δ᾽ εἶμι πρὸς τὸ καρτερόν.
       οὐ γὰρ μὰ τὴν δέσποιναν ἣν ἐγὼ σέβω   395
       μάλιστα πάντων καὶ ξυνεργὸν εἱλόμην,
       Ἑκάτην, μυχοῖς ναίουσαν ἑστίας ἐμῆς,
       χαίρων τις αὐτῶν τοὐμὸν ἀλγυνεῖ κέαρ.
       πικροὺς δ᾽ ἐγώ σφιν καὶ λυγροὺς θήσω γάμους,
       πικρὸν δὲ κῆδος καὶ φυγὰς ἐμὰς χθονός.   400

ἀλλ᾽ εἶα φείδου μηδὲν ὧν ἐπίστασαι,
Μήδεια, βουλεύουσα καὶ τεχνωμένη·
ἕρπ᾽ ἐς τὸ δεινόν· νῦν ἀγὼν εὐψυχίας.
ὁρᾷς ἃ πάσχεις; οὐ γέλωτα δεῖ σ᾽ ὀφλεῖν
τοῖς Σισυφείοις τοῖσδ᾽ Ἰάσονος γάμοις,   405
γεγῶσαν ἐσθλοῦ πατρὸς Ἡλίου τ᾽ ἄπο.
ἐπίστασαι δέ· πρὸς δὲ καὶ πεφύκαμεν
γυναῖκες, ἐς μὲν ἔσθλ᾽ ἀμηχανώταται,
κακῶν δὲ πάντων τέκτονες σοφώταται.

410–662: *Following Medea's speech there is a famous chorus, often referred to as the 'New Song', in which the members of the chorus announce that now everything has changed. At last there can be a poetry that praises and celebrates women, and criticizes men.*

Following the chorus there is the first argument between Medea and Jason, in which Medea is sharply critical of Jason, and in which Jason is complacent about what he is about to do.

Before this scene the chorus reflect on the nature of love, specifically on both its good and destructive effects. The chorus also, as a way of understanding Medea's plight, ask never to be made homeless and stateless.

Aegeus arrives having come from the oracle at Delphi, where he has been asking about whether he will ever be able to have children.

**A
Level**

Αἰ.	Μήδεια, χαῖρε· τοῦδε γὰρ προοίμιον	
	κάλλιον οὐδεὶς οἶδε προσφωνεῖν φίλους.	
Μή.	ὦ χαῖρε καὶ σύ, παῖ σοφοῦ Πανδίονος,	665
	Αἰγεῦ. πόθεν γῆς τῆσδ᾽ ἐπιστρωφᾷ πέδον;	
Αἰ.	Φοίβου παλαιὸν ἐκλιπὼν χρηστήριον.	
Μή.	τί δ᾽ ὀμφαλὸν γῆς θεσπιῳδὸν ἐστάλης;	
Αἰ.	παίδων ἐρευνῶν σπέρμ᾽ ὅπως γένοιτό μοι.	
Μή.	πρὸς θεῶν, ἄπαις γὰρ δεῦρ᾽ ἀεὶ τείνεις βίον;	670
Αἰ.	ἄπαιδές ἐσμεν δαίμονός τινος τύχῃ.	
Μή.	δάμαρτος οὔσης ἢ λέχους ἄπειρος ὤν;	
Αἰ.	οὐκ ἐσμὲν εὐνῆς ἄζυγες γαμηλίου.	
Μή.	τί δῆτα Φοῖβος εἶπέ σοι παίδων πέρι;	
Αἰ.	σοφώτερ᾽ ἢ κατ᾽ ἄνδρα συμβαλεῖν ἔπη.	675
Μή.	θέμις μὲν ἡμᾶς χρησμὸν εἰδέναι θεοῦ;	
Αἰ.	μάλιστ᾽, ἐπεί τοι καὶ σοφῆς δεῖται φρενός.	
Μή.	τί δῆτ᾽ ἔχρησε; λέξον, εἰ θέμις κλύειν.	
Αἰ.	ἀσκοῦ με τὸν προύχοντα μὴ λῦσαι πόδα ...	
Μή.	πρὶν ἂν τί δράσῃς ἢ τίν᾽ ἐξίκῃ χθόνα;	680
Αἰ.	πρὶν ἂν πατρῴαν αὖθις ἑστίαν μόλω.	
Μή.	σὺ δ᾽ ὡς τί χρῄζων τήνδε ναυστολεῖς χθόνα;	
Αἰ.	Πιτθεύς τις ἔστι, γῆς ἄναξ Τροζηνίας.	
Μή.	παῖς, ὡς λέγουσι, Πέλοπος, εὐσεβέστατος.	
Αἰ.	τούτῳ θεοῦ μάντευμα κοινῶσαι θέλω.	685
Μή.	σοφὸς γὰρ ἁνὴρ καὶ τρίβων τὰ τοιάδε.	
Αἰ.	κἀμοί γε πάντων φίλτατος δορυξένων.	
Μή.	ἀλλ᾽ εὐτυχοίης καὶ τύχοις ὅσων ἐρᾷς.	
Αἰ.	τί γὰρ σὸν ὄμμα χρώς τε συντέτηχ᾽ ὅδε;	
Μή.	Αἰγεῦ, κάκιστός ἐστί μοι πάντων πόσις.	690
Αἰ.	τί φής; σαφῶς μοι σὰς φράσον δυσθυμίας.	
Μή.	ἀδικεῖ μ᾽ Ἰάσων οὐδὲν ἐξ ἐμοῦ παθών.	
Αἰ.	τί χρῆμα δράσας; φράζε μοι σαφέστερον.	
Μή.	γυναῖκ᾽ ἐφ᾽ ἡμῖν δεσπότιν δόμων ἔχει.	
Αἰ.	οὔ που τετόλμηκ᾽ ἔργον αἴσχιστον τόδε;	695
Μή.	σάφ᾽ ἴσθ᾽· ἄτιμοι δ᾽ ἐσμὲν οἱ πρὸ τοῦ φίλοι.	
Αἰ.	πότερον ἐρασθεὶς ἢ σὸν ἐχθαίρων λέχος;	
Μή.	μέγαν γ᾽ ἔρωτα· πιστὸς οὐκ ἔφυ φίλοις.	
Αἰ.	ἴτω νυν, εἴπερ, ὡς λέγεις, ἐστὶν κακός.	
Μή.	ἀνδρῶν τυράννων κῆδος ἠράσθη λαβεῖν.	700
Αἰ.	δίδωσι δ᾽ αὐτῷ τίς; πέραινέ μοι λόγον.	
Μή.	Κρέων, ὃς ἄρχει τῆσδε γῆς Κορινθίας.	

Αἰ.   συγγνωστὰ μεντἄρ᾽ ἦν σε λυπεῖσθαι, γύναι.
Μή.   ὄλωλα· καὶ πρός γ᾽ ἐξελαύνομαι χθονός.
Αἰ.   πρὸς τοῦ; τόδ᾽ ἄλλο καινὸν αὖ λέγεις κακόν.   705
Μή.   Κρέων μ᾽ ἐλαύνει φυγάδα γῆς Κορινθίας.
Αἰ.   ἐᾷ δ᾽ Ἰάσων; οὐδὲ ταῦτ᾽ ἐπήνεσα.
Μή.   λόγῳ μὲν οὐχί, καρτερεῖν δὲ βούλεται.
        ἀλλ᾽ ἄντομαί σε τῆσδε πρὸς γενειάδος
        γονάτων τε τῶν σῶν ἱκεσία τε γίγνομαι,   710
        οἴκτιρον οἴκτιρόν με τὴν δυσδαίμονα
        καὶ μή μ᾽ ἔρημον ἐκπεσοῦσαν εἰσίδης,
        δέξαι δὲ χώρᾳ καὶ δόμοις ἐφέστιον.
        οὕτως ἔρως σοὶ πρὸς θεῶν τελεσφόρος
        γένοιτο παίδων καὐτὸς ὄλβιος θάνοις.   715
        εὕρημα δ᾽ οὐκ οἶσθ᾽ οἷον ηὕρηκας τόδε·
        παύσω γέ σ᾽ ὄντ᾽ ἄπαιδα καὶ παίδων γονὰς
        σπεῖραί σε θήσω· τοιάδ᾽ οἶδα φάρμακα.
Αἰ.   πολλῶν ἕκατι τήνδε σοι δοῦναι χάριν,
        γύναι, πρόθυμός εἰμι, πρῶτα μὲν θεῶν,   720
        ἔπειτα παίδων ὧν ἐπαγγέλλη γονάς·
        ἐς τοῦτο γὰρ δὴ φροῦδός εἰμι πᾶς ἐγώ.
        οὕτω δ᾽ ἔχει μοι· σοῦ μὲν ἐλθούσης χθόνα,
        πειράσομαί σου προξενεῖν δίκαιος ὤν.
        τοσόνδε μέντοι σοι προσημαίνω, γύναι·   725
        ἐκ τῆσδε μὲν γῆς οὔ σ᾽ ἄγειν βουλήσομαι,   726
        ἐκ τῆσδε δ᾽ αὐτὴ γῆς ἀπαλλάσσου πόδα·   729
        αὐτὴ δ᾽ ἐάνπερ εἰς ἐμοὺς ἔλθης δόμους,   727
        μενεῖς ἄσυλος κοὔ σε μὴ μεθῶ τινι.   728
        ἀναίτιος γὰρ καὶ ξένοις εἶναι θέλω.   730
Μή.   ἔσται τάδ᾽· ἀλλὰ πίστις εἰ γένοιτό μοι
        τούτων, ἔχοιμ᾽ ἂν πάντα πρὸς σέθεν καλῶς.
Αἰ.   μῶν οὐ πέποιθας; ἢ τί σοι τὸ δυσχερές;
Μή.   πέποιθα· Πελίου δ᾽ ἐχθρός ἐστί μοι δόμος
        Κρέων τε. τούτοις δ᾽ ὁρκίοισι μὲν ζυγεὶς   735
        ἄγουσιν οὐ μεθεῖ᾽ ἂν ἐκ γαίας ἐμέ·
        λόγοις δὲ συμβὰς καὶ θεῶν ἀνώμοτος
        φίλος γένοι᾽ ἂν κἀπικηρυκεύμασιν
        τάχ᾽ ἂν πίθοιο· τἀμὰ μὲν γὰρ ἀσθενῆ,
        τοῖς δ᾽ ὄλβος ἐστὶ καὶ δόμος τυραννικός.   740
Αἰ.   πολλὴν ἔδειξας ἐν λόγοις προμηθίαν·
        ἀλλ᾽, εἰ δοκεῖ σοι, δρᾶν τάδ᾽ οὐκ ἀφίσταμαι.

ἐμοί τε γὰρ τάδ᾽ ἐστὶν ἀσφαλέστερα,
σκῆψίν τιν᾽ ἐχθροῖς σοῖς ἔχοντα δεικνύναι,
τὸ σόν τ᾽ ἄραρε μᾶλλον. ἐξηγοῦ θεούς.   745

Μή.   ὄμνυ πέδον Γῆς πατέρα θ᾽ Ἥλιον πατρὸς
τοὐμοῦ θεῶν τε συντιθεὶς ἅπαν γένος.

Αἰ.   τί χρῆμα δράσειν ἢ τί μὴ δράσειν; λέγε.

Μή.   μήτ᾽ αὐτὸς ἐκ γῆς σῆς ἔμ᾽ ἐκβαλεῖν ποτε,
μήτ᾽, ἄλλος ἤν τις τῶν ἐμῶν ἐχθρῶν ἄγειν   750
χρῄζῃ, μεθήσειν ζῶν ἑκουσίῳ τρόπῳ.

Αἰ.   ὄμνυμι Γαῖαν φῶς τε λαμπρὸν Ἡλίου
θεούς τε πάντας ἐμμενεῖν ἅ σου κλύω.

Μή.   ἀρκεῖ· τί δ᾽ ὅρκῳ τῷδε μὴ ᾽μμένων πάθοις;

Αἰ.   ἃ τοῖσι δυσσεβοῦσι γίγνεται βροτῶν.   755

Μή.   χαίρων πορεύου· πάντα γὰρ καλῶς ἔχει.
κἀγὼ πόλιν σὴν ὡς τάχιστ᾽ ἀφίξομαι,
πράξασ᾽ ἃ μέλλω καὶ τυχοῦσ᾽ ἃ βούλομαι.

759–868: *Once Medea has secured the agreement of Aegeus that she can settle in Athens, she first of all celebrates the likelihood of her vengeance being effective. But she also announces – to the chorus – that she will kill her own children. The chorus beg her not to do that, but Medea is keen to cause as much hurt as possible to Jason.*

    The chorus then sing a beautiful lyric in praise of Athens and beg Medea to change her mind. At this point Jason, as requested by Medea, enters.

Μή.   Ἰᾶσον, αἰτοῦμαί σε τῶν εἰρημένων
συγγνώμον᾽ εἶναι· τὰς δ᾽ ἐμὰς ὀργὰς φέρειν   870
εἰκός σ᾽, ἐπεὶ νῷν πόλλ᾽ ὑπείργασται φίλα.
ἐγὼ δ᾽ ἐμαυτῇ διὰ λόγων ἀφικόμην
κἀλοιδόρησα· Σχετλία, τί μαίνομαι
καὶ δυσμεναίνω τοῖσι βουλεύουσιν εὖ,
ἐχθρὰ δὲ γαίας κοιράνοις καθίσταμαι   875
πόσει θ᾽, ὃς ἡμῖν δρᾷ τὰ συμφορώτατα,
γήμας τύραννον καὶ κασιγνήτους τέκνοις
ἐμοῖς φυτεύων; οὐκ ἀπαλλαχθήσομαι
θυμοῦ; τί πάσχω, θεῶν ποριζόντων καλῶς;
οὐκ εἰσὶ μέν μοι παῖδες, οἶδα δὲ χθόνα   880
φεύγοντας ἡμᾶς καὶ σπανίζοντας φίλων;
ταῦτ᾽ ἐννοηθεῖσ᾽ ᾐσθόμην ἀβουλίαν
πολλὴν ἔχουσα καὶ μάτην θυμουμένη.
νῦν οὖν ἐπαινῶ σωφρονεῖν τέ μοι δοκεῖς

κῆδος τόδ᾽ ἡμῖν προσλαβών, ἐγὼ δ᾽ ἄφρων,　　　　　885
ἣ χρῆν μετεῖναι τῶνδε τῶν βουλευμάτων
καὶ ξυμπεραίνειν καὶ παρεστάναι λέχει
νύμφην τε κηδεύουσαν ἥδεσθαι σέθεν.
ἀλλ᾽ ἐσμὲν οἷόν ἐσμεν, οὐκ ἐρῶ κακόν,
γυναῖκες· οὔκουν χρῆν σ᾽ ὁμοιοῦσθαι κακοῖς,　　　890
οὐδ᾽ ἀντιτείνειν νήπι᾽ ἀντὶ νηπίων.
παριέμεσθα, καί φαμεν κακῶς φρονεῖν
τότ᾽, ἀλλ᾽ ἄμεινον νῦν βεβούλευμαι τάδε.
ὦ τέκνα τέκνα, δεῦρο, λείπετε στέγας,
ἐξέλθετ᾽, ἀσπάσασθε καὶ προσείπατε　　　　　895
πατέρα μεθ᾽ ἡμῶν καὶ διαλλάχθηθ᾽ ἅμα
τῆς πρόσθεν ἔχθρας ἐς φίλους μητρὸς μέτα·
σπονδαὶ γὰρ ἡμῖν καὶ μεθέστηκεν χόλος.
λάβεσθε χειρὸς δεξιᾶς· οἴμοι, κακῶν
ὡς ἐννοοῦμαι δή τι τῶν κεκρυμμένων.　　　　　900
ἆρ᾽, ὦ τέκν᾽, οὕτω καὶ πολὺν ζῶντες χρόνον
φίλην ὀρέξετ᾽ ὠλένην; τάλαιν᾽ ἐγώ,
ὡς ἀρτίδακρύς εἰμι καὶ φόβου πλέα.
χρόνῳ δὲ νεῖκος πατρὸς ἐξαιρουμένη
ὄψιν τέρειναν τήνδ᾽ ἔπλησα δακρύων.　　　　　905

906–1018: *The chorus respond with relief and hope that Medea has indeed changed her plans. Jason also commends Medea on her change of heart, and asks his sons to grow into strong and loyal young men.*

An exchange between Medea and Jason follows, in which Medea asks Jason to ask Creon to allow her children to stay. In order to bring Creon round Medea sends the children off with Jason with presents (a dress and a golden crown) for his bride-to-be.

The chorus sing an ode in which they sing of the certain death of the children, and of Glauke, and of the ignorance of Jason.

The children's tutor returns with the children to tell Medea that the children's banishment has been cancelled and cannot understand Medea's distraught response.

Μή.	δράσω τάδ᾽. ἀλλὰ βαῖνε δωμάτων ἔσω	
	καὶ παισὶ πόρσυν᾽ οἷα χρὴ καθ᾽ ἡμέραν.	1020
	ὦ τέκνα τέκνα, σφῷν μὲν ἔστι δὴ πόλις	
	καὶ δῶμ᾽, ἐν ᾧ λιπόντες ἀθλίαν ἐμὲ	
	οἰκήσετ᾽ αἰεὶ μητρὸς ἐστερημένοι·	
	ἐγὼ δ᾽ ἐς ἄλλην γαῖαν εἶμι δὴ φυγάς,	
	πρὶν σφῷν ὀνάσθαι κἀπιδεῖν εὐδαίμονας,	1025
	πρὶν λουτρὰ καὶ γυναῖκα καὶ γαμηλίους	
	εὐνὰς ἀγῆλαι λαμπάδας τ᾽ ἀνασχεθεῖν.	
	ὦ δυστάλαινα τῆς ἐμῆς αὐθαδίας.	
	ἄλλως ἄρ᾽ ὑμᾶς, ὦ τέκν᾽, ἐξεθρεψάμην,	
	ἄλλως δ᾽ ἐμόχθουν καὶ κατεξάνθην πόνοις,	1030
	στερρὰς ἐνεγκοῦσ᾽ ἐν τόκοις ἀλγηδόνας.	
	ἦ μήν ποθ᾽ ἡ δύστηνος εἶχον ἐλπίδας	
	πολλὰς ἐν ὑμῖν, γηροβοσκήσειν τ᾽ ἐμὲ	
	καὶ κατθανοῦσαν χερσὶν εὖ περιστελεῖν,	
	ζηλωτὸν ἀνθρώποισι· νῦν δ᾽ ὄλωλε δὴ	1035
	γλυκεῖα φροντίς. σφῷν γὰρ ἐστερημένη	
	λυπρὸν διάξω βίοτον ἀλγεινόν τ᾽ ἐμοί·	
	ὑμεῖς δὲ μητέρ᾽ οὐκέτ᾽ ὄμμασιν φίλοις	
	ὄψεσθ᾽, ἐς ἄλλο σχῆμ᾽ ἀποστάντες βίου.	
	φεῦ φεῦ· τί προσδέρκεσθέ μ᾽ ὄμμασιν, τέκνα;	1040
	τί προσγελᾶτε τὸν πανύστατον γέλων;	
	αἰαῖ· τί δράσω; καρδία γὰρ οἴχεται,	
	γυναῖκες, ὄμμα φαιδρὸν ὡς εἶδον τέκνων.	
	οὐκ ἂν δυναίμην· χαιρέτω βουλεύματα	
	τὰ πρόσθεν· ἄξω παῖδας ἐκ γαίας ἐμούς.	1045
	τί δεῖ με πατέρα τῶνδε τοῖς τούτων κακοῖς	
	λυποῦσαν αὐτὴν δὶς τόσα κτᾶσθαι κακά;	

A Level

οὐ δῆτ᾽ ἔγωγε· χαιρέτω βουλεύματα.
καίτοι τί πάσχω; βούλομαι γέλωτ᾽ ὀφλεῖν
ἐχθροὺς μεθεῖσα τοὺς ἐμοὺς ἀζημίους;   1050
τολμητέον τάδ᾽· ἀλλὰ τῆς ἐμῆς κάκης
τὸ καὶ προσέσθαι μαλθακοὺς λόγους φρενί.
χωρεῖτε, παῖδες, ἐς δόμους. ὅτῳ δὲ μὴ
θέμις παρεῖναι τοῖς ἐμοῖσι θύμασιν,
αὐτῷ μελήσει· χεῖρα δ᾽ οὐ διαφθερῶ.   1055

*1056–1135: Medea continues her monologue, changing her mind a number of times.
The chorus sing an ode about what it means to have children.*

*Then a messenger brings news of what has happened at the palace. The
messenger is horrified; Medea is exultant.*

Ἄγγ.   ἐπεὶ τέκνων σῶν ἦλθε δίπτυχος γονὴ
σὺν πατρί, καὶ παρῆλθε νυμφικοὺς δόμους,
ἥσθημεν οἵπερ σοῖς ἐκάμνομεν κακοῖς
δμῶες· δι᾽ ὤτων δ᾽ εὐθὺς ἦν πολὺς λόγος
σὲ καὶ πόσιν σὸν νεῖκος ἐσπεῖσθαι τὸ πρίν.   1140
κυνεῖ δ᾽ ὁ μέν τις χεῖρ᾽, ὁ δὲ ξανθὸν κάρα
παίδων· ἐγὼ δὲ καὐτὸς ἡδονῆς ὕπο
στέγας γυναικῶν σὺν τέκνοις ἅμ᾽ ἑσπόμην.
δέσποινα δ᾽ ἣν νῦν ἀντὶ σοῦ θαυμάζομεν,
πρὶν μὲν τέκνων σῶν εἰσιδεῖν ξυνωρίδα,   1145
πρόθυμον εἶχ᾽ ὀφθαλμὸν εἰς Ἰάσονα·
ἔπειτα μέντοι προυκαλύψατ᾽ ὄμματα
λευκήν τ᾽ ἀπέστρεψ᾽ ἔμπαλιν παρηίδα,
παίδων μυσαχθεῖσ᾽ εἰσόδους. πόσις δὲ σὸς
ὀργάς τ᾽ ἀφήρει καὶ χόλον νεάνιδος,   1150
λέγων τάδ᾽· Οὐ μὴ δυσμενὴς ἔσῃ φίλοις,
παύσῃ δὲ θυμοῦ καὶ πάλιν στρέψεις κάρα,
φίλους νομίζουσ᾽ οὕσπερ ἂν πόσις σέθεν,
δέξῃ δὲ δῶρα καὶ παραιτήσῃ πατρὸς
φυγὰς ἀφεῖναι παισὶ τοῖσδ᾽ ἐμὴν χάριν;   1155
ἡ δ᾽, ὡς ἐσεῖδε κόσμον, οὐκ ἠνέσχετο,
ἀλλ᾽ ἤνεσ᾽ ἀνδρὶ πάντα, καὶ πρὶν ἐκ δόμων
μακρὰν ἀπεῖναι πατέρα καὶ παῖδας σέθεν
λαβοῦσα πέπλους ποικίλους ἠμπέσχετο,
χρυσοῦν τε θεῖσα στέφανον ἀμφὶ βοστρύχοις   1160
λαμπρῷ κατόπτρῳ σχηματίζεται κόμην,

**A
Level**

ἄψυχον εἰκὼ προσγελῶσα σώματος.
κἄπειτ᾽ ἀναστᾶσ᾽ ἐκ θρόνων διέρχεται
στέγας, ἁβρὸν βαίνουσα παλλεύκῳ ποδί,
δώροις ὑπερχαίρουσα, πολλὰ πολλάκις   1165
τένοντ᾽ ἐς ὀρθὸν ὄμμασι σκοπουμένη.
τοὐνθένδε μέντοι δεινὸν ἦν θέαμ᾽ ἰδεῖν·
χροιὰν γὰρ ἀλλάξασα λεχρία πάλιν
χωρεῖ τρέμουσα κῶλα καὶ μόλις φθάνει
θρόνοισιν ἐμπεσοῦσα μὴ χαμαὶ πεσεῖν.   1170
καί τις γεραιὰ προσπόλων, δόξασά που
ἢ Πανὸς ὀργὰς ἤ τινος θεῶν μολεῖν,
ἀνωλόλυξε, πρίν γ᾽ ὁρᾷ διὰ στόμα
χωροῦντα λευκὸν ἀφρόν, ὀμμάτων τ᾽ ἄπο
κόρας στρέφουσαν, αἷμά τ᾽ οὐκ ἐνὸν χροΐ·   1175
εἶτ᾽ ἀντίμολπον ἧκεν ὀλολυγῆς μέγαν
κωκυτόν. εὐθὺς δ᾽ ἡ μὲν ἐς πατρὸς δόμους
ὥρμησεν, ἡ δὲ πρὸς τὸν ἀρτίως πόσιν,
φράσουσα νύμφης συμφοράν· ἅπασα δὲ
στέγη πυκνοῖσιν ἐκτύπει δραμήμασιν.   1180
ἤδη δ᾽ ἀνελθὼν κῶλον ἐκπλέθρου δρόμου
ταχὺς βαδιστὴς τερμόνων ἂν ἥπτετο·
ἡ δ᾽ ἐξ ἀναύδου καὶ μύσαντος ὄμματος
δεινὸν στενάξασ᾽ ἡ τάλαιν᾽ ἠγείρετο.
διπλοῦν γὰρ αὐτῇ πῆμ᾽ ἐπεστρατεύετο·   1185
χρυσοῦς μὲν ἀμφὶ κρατὶ κείμενος πλόκος
θαυμαστὸν ἵει νᾶμα παμφάγου πυρός,
πέπλοι δὲ λεπτοί, σῶν τέκνων δωρήματα,
λευκὴν ἔδαπτον σάρκα τῆς δυσδαίμονος.
φεύγει δ᾽ ἀναστᾶσ᾽ ἐκ θρόνων πυρουμένη,   1190
σείουσα χαίτην κρᾶτά τ᾽ ἄλλοτ᾽ ἄλλοσε,
ῥῖψαι θέλουσα στέφανον· ἀλλ᾽ ἀραρότως
σύνδεσμα χρυσὸς εἶχε, πῦρ δ᾽, ἐπεὶ κόμην
ἔσεισε, μᾶλλον δὶς τόσως ἐλάμπετο.
πίτνει δ᾽ ἐς οὖδας συμφορᾷ νικωμένη,   1195
πλὴν τῷ τεκόντι κάρτα δυσμαθὴς ἰδεῖν·
οὔτ᾽ ὀμμάτων γὰρ δῆλος ἦν κατάστασις
οὔτ᾽ εὐφυὲς πρόσωπον, αἷμα δ᾽ ἐξ ἄκρου
ἔσταζε κρατὸς συμπεφυρμένον πυρί,
σάρκες δ᾽ ἀπ᾽ ὀστέων ὥστε πεύκινον δάκρυ   1200
γνάθοις ἀδήλοις φαρμάκων ἀπέρρεον,

δεινὸν θέαμα· πᾶσι δ᾽ ἦν φόβος θιγεῖν
νεκροῦ·τύχην γὰρ εἴχομεν διδάσκαλον.
πατὴρ δ᾽ ὁ τλήμων συμφορᾶς ἀγνωσίᾳ
ἄφνω παρελθὼν δῶμα προσπίτνει νεκρῷ.   1205
ᾤμωξε δ᾽ εὐθὺς καὶ περιπτύξας χέρας
κυνεῖ προσαυδῶν τοιάδ᾽· "Ὦ" δύστηνε παῖ,
τίς σ᾽ ὧδ᾽ ἀτίμως δαιμόνων ἀπώλεσεν;
τίς τὸν γέροντα τύμβον ὀρφανὸν σέθεν
τίθησιν; οἴμοι, συνθάνοιμί σοι, τέκνον.   1210
ἐπεὶ δὲ θρήνων καὶ γόων ἐπαύσατο,
χρῄζων γεραιὸν ἐξαναστῆσαι δέμας
προσείχεθ᾽ ὥστε κισσὸς ἔρνεσιν δάφνης
λεπτοῖσι πέπλοις, δεινὰ δ᾽ ἦν παλαίσματα·
ὁ μὲν γὰρ ἤθελ᾽ ἐξαναστῆσαι γόνυ,   1215
ἡ δ᾽ ἀντελάζυτ᾽· εἰ δὲ πρὸς βίαν ἄγοι,
σάρκας γεραιὰς ἐσπάρασσ᾽ ἀπ᾽ ὀστέων.
χρόνῳ δ᾽ ἀπέστη καὶ μεθῆχ᾽ ὁ δύσμορος
ψυχήν· κακοῦ γὰρ οὐκέτ᾽ ἦν ὑπέρτερος.
κεῖνται δὲ νεκροὶ παῖς τε καὶ γέρων πατὴρ   1220
πέλας, ποθεινὴ δακρύοισι συμφορά.
καί μοι τὸ μὲν σὸν ἐκποδὼν ἔστω λόγου·
γνώσῃ γὰρ αὐτὴ ζημίας ἐπιστροφήν.
τὰ θνητὰ δ᾽ οὐ νῦν πρῶτον ἡγοῦμαι σκιάν,
οὐδ᾽ ἂν τρέσας εἴποιμι τοὺς σοφοὺς βροτῶν   1225
δοκοῦντας εἶναι καὶ μεριμνητὰς λόγων
τούτους μεγίστην μωρίαν ὀφλισκάνειν.
θνητῶν γὰρ οὐδείς ἐστιν εὐδαίμων ἀνήρ·
ὄλβου δ᾽ ἐπιρρυέντος εὐτυχέστερος
ἄλλου γένοιτ᾽ ἂν ἄλλος, εὐδαίμων δ᾽ ἂν οὔ.   1230

**A
Level**

Commentary Notes

The prologue is delivered by the Nurse. At the very beginning of the play she laments that Jason ever launched the Argo in order to secure the Golden Fleece. She describes how Jason on his return, after many years with Medea, has decided to leave her and marry Glauke, the daughter of Creon, the king of Corinth. She also describes the extreme emotional effect this 'betrayal' has had on Medea.

After the prologue Medea's children enter with their tutor and, in the exchange between the tutor and the Nurse that follows, the tutor reveals that the rumour is that Creon plans to banish Medea and her children.

We then hear Medea lamenting and complaining from inside the house – represented on stage by the skene – as well as the Nurse's and the chorus' responses to Medea's fevered and violent language.

214–66

Medea's speech, in its calmness at least, contrasts with what we have heard from her so far. However, it should be noted that tragedy does not require the consistency and development of character that it is so much a feature of modern European drama and prose. The 'rhetoric of the situation' (to use A.M. Dale's phrase) is arguably a more important determinant of how a character behaves and presents herself. Medea, while apparently more rational than she has been while still inside the house, utters a speech in which the thought is not always clear. On Medea's costume and appearance, and on whether she is accompanied by (silent) attendants, see the Introduction 4: Staging.

214–15

Κοϱίνθιαι γυναῖκες: The address to the Corinthian women, the chorus, is important in the sense that the solidarity between Medea and chorus in their shared outrage at Jason's behaviour is a characteristic of the first part of the play. That solidarity makes the chorus' later change of opinion all the more dramatic.

Medea also uses a very formal address, stressing the Κοϱίνθιαι, thereby also
highlighting her own non-Corinthian status. ἐξῆλθον δόμων: this works as
a sort of stage direction ('Here is Medea'), but it is also interesting from an
ideological point of view. If, at the level of ideology, women were supposed to
stay inside the house (see, e.g., Xenophon *Oeconomicus* 7.30), then this is a
bold opening statement, and anticipates the dramatic acts of persuasion and
violence that Medea performs in the remainder of the play in the outside space
ordinarily reserved for men. μή μοί τι μέμψησθ': Medea directly seeks support.
μή + subjunctive need not follow a verb of fearing; it can be used when there is
any sense of apprehension.

215–27
These lines are a reflection on what it means to be an outsider, whether that is
because one is perceived as haughty ('σεμνούς'), as distant or aloof ('ἀφ'
ἡσύχου ποδὸς': literally 'from a quiet foot') or as a foreigner (ξένον).

216
ὀμμάτων ἄπο means literally 'away from eyes', i.e. 'out of sight'.

217
ἐν θυϱαίοις means literally 'in doorways', though it is often used to mean 'outside'.
The contrast is surely between being out of sight on the one hand and being in
public on the other. Still, 'in doorways' is perhaps a strange way to talk of being
in public and may reflect the liminality of women's position in fifth-century
Athens. ἀφ' ἡσύχου ποδὸς is an intriguing metaphor (even a metonymy) and
probably means something like 'quiet life'.

218
There is hendiadys in this line: 'they have acquired a bad reputation and laziness' =
'a bad reputation *for* laziness'.

219–21
βϱοτῶν is the antecedent of ὅστις. These lines are a generalized complaint about
prejudice. σπλάγχνον must mean here something like 'real character' but is
often used metaphorically to refer to the seat of emotions (especially violent or
extreme ones such as anger).

222
πϱοσχωϱεῖν is used metaphorically here, i.e. 'conform' or 'comply'. It is no surprise
that Medea brings up the problem of being a foreigner so quickly (ξένον), for
her outsider status is at the very core of her problem.

223–4
ἤνεσ' = ἤνεσα = 'I approve'. We might expect a present tense, but the tense here has
been described as a 'dramatic' aorist. The effect of using an aorist has produced a
variety of answers. Is it polite? Or tentative? Or, by contrast, is it emphatic? The
foreigner's status is contrasted with that of a bolshy local (ἀστὸν is not quite

citizen – πολίτης) and can be used to refer to women, who were not citizens in any Greek *polis*). There are a lot of negatives in this couplet: αὐθάδης means 'headstrong' or 'stubborn' (and is ironically a quality often associated with heroes); πικρός – bitter; ἀμαθίας – ignorance or irrationality.

225–9

There is pathos in these lines. What has happened to Medea has been unexpected (ἄελπτον), but has still destroyed her (διέφθαρκ'). She sees and addresses the chorus as friends (φίλαι), but at the moment she pleonastically confirms that she wants to die (I depart - οἴχομαι; letting go the delight of life - βίου χάριν μεθεῖσα; I want to die - κατθανεῖν χρῄζω). The cause of her problem is the man on whom she depended for everything (πάντα): she confesses her new understanding (γιγνώσκω καλῶς) that he has turned out (ἐκβέβηχ') to be the worst of men (κάκιστος ἀνδρῶν). These are very powerful lines: the πάντα is emphatic, as is the contrast between the adverb καλῶς at the end of 228 and the superlative adjective κάκιστος at the beginning of 229. Note also how the actual identification – οὑμὸς πόσις – is left until the end (οὑμὸς = ὁ ἐμός; this joining together of words is called *crasis*). It is important, anyway, to note how important the theme of marriage (and Jason's behaviour as a husband) is in the play.

230–66

This is an extended and celebrated reflection on the status and experience of women in the ancient world, as true of the world of the fifth-century Athenian audience as of any other Greek city or time. Medea deals with the inequities of getting married, of the experience of marriage and childbirth for a woman, of the contrasting and freer experience of a husband. She ends with an appeal to the chorus for support in her efforts to take vengeance on Jason.

230–1

Medea starts with a generalization and an extreme one (note πάντων and the superlative adjective ἀθλιώτατον). φυτόν refers to anything that has grown; it could be said to be not a very positive word for women ('creature' perhaps). At Homer *Iliad* 16.446–7 Zeus says nothing is more wretched than a man; Medea thinks that women are even more wretched.

232–4

Medea describes the economic process of getting married. The description is highly rhetorical: a husband is bought (πόσιν πρίασθαι) for an extravagant sum (χρημάτων ὑπερβολῇ), when what one is really buying is a master of one's body (δεσπότην σώματος). The dowry system described is a feature more of the classical period than of the world described in myth. Women in classical Athens possessed almost no rights, and certainly would not have possessed the assets to pay a dowry; that normally came from the father of the bride. Line 234 is a good summary of why getting married is such a bad deal for women.

A
Level

235–7

A woman's experience in marriage is here contrasted with that of a man. The implication is that marriages are arranged – that is why women will not know whether their husband is good or bad until they are married. The problem is again described in extreme terms (ἀγὼν μέγιστος). In addition, Medea claims that respectable divorces are not possible for women (it was possible but very rare in fifth-century Athens), and that denying husbands (presumably sexual favours) is not possible. The description is stark and perhaps exaggerated, but that is no reason to think it unrealistic, broadly speaking. Women could return to their father's house, citing their husband's unreasonable behaviour, but they might not be welcome.

238–40

Medea now moves to her more specific problems as a foreign wife. The strangeness and dislocation of the experience is emphasized in the adjective καινά (new), as well as in the care in which both ἤθη and νόμους are mentioned. In this context, where both words are used, the former probably refers to cultural practices at the individual or familial level, the latter to broader cultural practices (including laws). Medea's description of how difficult it is for a foreign wife is economically expressed in the three-word phrase 'it is necessary to be a seer' (δεῖ μάντιν εἶναι). Some irony here, perhaps, as Medea is (in)famous for her own magical powers. 'To be a seer' is followed by the indirect question of line 240: the thing that needs to be divined is how to manage one's bed-partner. οἵῳ is in the dative agreeing with ξυνευνέτη, which is itself dependent on χρήσεται. The line can be translated: 'with what sort of man she will have to deal as a husband'. Sex, its successes and failures, will be important when Jason and Medea first argue.

241–3

Even the positive side of marriage is expressed conditionally (crasis: κἂν = καὶ ἐάν), emphasizing the hard work that is necessary to achieve a reasonably good outcome: ἐκπονουμέναισιν; μὴ βίᾳ φέρων ζυγόν. The latter phrase refers to a husband's experience of marriage but in an interesting way. It is normally women who are said to be under the yoke in marriage.

243

The only alternative to a (reasonably) positive experience of marriage is death, baldly expressed (θανεῖν χρεών).

244–5

Men's experience of marriage is different: they can seek comfort elsewhere. Note the contrast between being bored indoors (ἔνδον) and being able to go outside (ἔξω μολών). The τοῖς of τοῖς ἔνδον is masculine plural in the conventional Greek way, but the phrase clearly refers to women. Mastronarde thinks that the phrase, though plural, refers to the man's wife; others think it can refer to the household as a whole. ἔπαυσε is an example of what is called a gnomic aorist, that is to say, an aorist used in a proverbial or generalized way. ξυνών can have a sexual connotation.

246

This line is interesting in two ways: first, the metre is odd (the alpha of ἥλικα should be long but, for various reasons, it must be short); second, the idea that a husband might be consoling himself with other *women* is qualified.

247

Women's experience in marriage is necessarily (ἀνάγκη) tied to one person. A concise and powerful line.

248-51

These are celebrated lines. Medea confronts male-dominated ideology, in which it is said that women leading domestic lives (ζῶμεν κατ᾽ οἴκους) experience no danger (ἀκίνδυνον βίον), while men, by contrast, because of their need to fight in battle (οἱ δὲ μάρνανται δορί), deserve power and wealth. Medea addresses the most basic division of labour – women produce children; men fight – and states that the different rewards based on that division are entirely wrong. If pain and risk are the criteria by which political and economic power is secured, then women should have that power. This is one of the most direct challenges to patriarchy as exists in Athenian tragedy. Note how Medea expresses this belief in patriarchy as common (λέγουσι), but concisely says that the belief is wrong (κακῶς φρονοῦντες). In lines 250–1, note also how the phrase is enveloped by the contrasting numbers (τρὶς ... ἅπαξ). ἡμᾶς in line 248 is what is known as a proleptic object, that is, one that anticipates the subject of the dependent clause ὡς ἀκίνδυνον βίον ζῶμεν κατ᾽ οἴκους.

252-8

Medea now contrasts her situation with that of the (Greek) chorus.

252

The situation for Medea and the Greek women of the chorus is different. The use of ἀλλά... γὰρ marks a change in Medea's train of thought. λόγος here must mean something like 'argument' or 'reasoning'. αὐτὸς ... κἄμ᾽: crasis of ὁ αὐτός ... καὶ ἔμ᾽. In this episode it is likely that Medea will be talking to one of the chorus, hence the singular σὲ (the same pronoun is singular in 259).

253-8

It is in these lines that the contrasts between Medea's and the chorus' situations are most explicitly expressed. In lines 253–4, Medea claims that the chorus possess four positive things: a *polis*, a father's home (πατρὸς δόμοι), enjoyment of life (βίου ... ὄνησις) and the company of friends (φίλων συνουσία). In lines 255–8, Medea claims her life is in explicit contrast: she is not only *apolis* (to be citiless was a disaster in the classical world: one had no rights or protections) but abandoned (ἔρημος – note the emphatic asyndeton as well; note also that

A Level

ἔϱημος and βαϱβάϱος are both dual termination adjectives, i.e., the masculine
and feminine endings are the same); she has been violated by her husband
(ὑβϱίζομαι πϱὸς ἀνδϱός); using very strong vocabulary she claims that she was
taken as plunder (λελησμένη); and she now lacks all familial support (listed
for emphasis οὐ μητέϱ᾽, οὐκ ἀδελφόν, οὐχὶ συγγενῆ). The extremity of her
condition is confirmed in the final word – συμφοϱᾶς (in the genitive case after
the infinitive μεθοϱμίσασθαι, which is used epexegetically, i.e. as an added
explanation).

259–63

Because of her parlous situation, Medea turns to the chorus for help. The chorus,
however, must be viewed as thinking the same way. The individual chorus
member talking to Medea is a representative of the chorus as a whole. The future
tense – βουλήσομαι – is probably an idiomatic use, making the request a little
more polite ('I would like …'). In lines 260–1 Medea confirms that she wishes
to take vengeance on Jason (δίκην πόσιν … ἀντιτείσασθαι: δίκην πόσιν is
a double accusative), but makes it conditional (see line 260). It is a reasonable
question to ask how advanced and detailed her plans are, especially when we
look at line 262. The first word of line 263 makes clear what Medea wants of the
chorus: silence. But there is an irony in that. Silence is the condition prescribed
for women in classical Athens (see Pericles in the Funeral Oration: Thucydides
2.45.1). Yet, as Medea launches her attack on Jason (and on patriarchy), it is
precisely that male-prescribed female quality that Medea wants. Since the chorus
is on the stage most of the time, there are sometimes good dramatic reasons for
actors to ask for the chorus to be silent.

263–6

Medea concludes her remarkable speech with a generalization about female
psychology. In lines 263–4 Medea casts women as fearful in the conventional
male realms of war and fighting. There is some irony here, as Medea will
move into the outside world of women where she will perform several acts
of horrific violence. The claim in line 265 that what really provokes a woman
into bloody and violent action is something going wrong with the bed (εὐνὴν)
is one that is repeated by Jason at lines 569–72. The various words for bed
are used metonymically throughout the play to stand for marriage, desire and
reproduction. One commentator – Mastronarde – notes interestingly that
these lines raise the problem of misogynistic statements put into the mouths of
women. He notes the following possible interpretations: the represented female
has internalized the ideology of the dominant group; it is a representation of real
women who have accepted male dominance as the status quo; either the speaker
or the audience is aware of the incongruity. Dramatically, Medea is trying to
persuade the chorus to be on her side and may, for that reason, be simplifying
her situation.

267–8

The chorus respond. They are on Medea's side and will do as she asks (δϱάσω
τάδ᾽); they think her vengeance is just (ἐνδίκως; and they should be aware

**A
Level**

that it is going to be bloody, as Medea had ended her speech with the bloody adjective μιαιφονωτέρα); they empathize with her misfortune (πενθεῖν δ᾽ οὔ σε θαυμάζω τύχας [indirect speech after θαυμάζω is rare]). At this point in the play, Medea seems clearly to be the wronged party. The chorus' sympathy is normally felt by audiences as well – at least this far in the play. Medea's rhetoric – normally an area for male achievement – has been successful.

269–70

Tragedy had no written stage directions. This is one of those couplets that acts as such. Creon is coming (and he should, by his costume and the number of attendants, obviously be important). There is something ominous in the adjective καινῶν: new decisions can be bad for Medea.

A
Level

271–356

Creon, the ruler of Corinth, has just entered, probably with attendants (see line 335). Medea awaits his ruling. Creon means to stamp his authority on the situation as quickly as possible.

271–2

Opening with σε shows how abrupt and direct Creon wants to be (the other two men to appear, Jason and Aegeus, will be similarly abrupt); two negative adjectives in these lines, related to Medea's attitude to Jason (σκυθρωπὸν καὶ πόσει θυμουμένην), precede Creon's address to Medea.

272–3

Creon's edict is given very briefly. Note the tense of ἀνεῖπον: one might expect a present tense; perhaps the aorist signifies Creon's view that there can be no argument that the decision has been made. An alternative view is that such aorists are normally deemed to be polite, and that therefore Creon is mixing brusque authority with a more polite and diffident approach. The edict confirms the tutor's view earlier (70–2) that Medea is to be exiled with her two children. One could reasonably speculate as to why Creon needs to banish the children, given that they are the children of his soon-to-be son-in-law. Note how the two children frame 'with yourself' (δισσὰ σὺν σαυτῇ τέκνα).

274–6

An interesting use of μέλλειν here, meaning something like 'hesitate' or 'delay'. βραβεὺς may originally have been an umpire of an athletic contest. In these lines there is further emphasis of Creon's determination to be rid of Medea. All three verbs are first person singular, and the first person pronoun sits at the beginning of the clause.

277

Medea responds with extreme negativity: all the words but the definite article stress that (αἰαῖ ... πανώλης ... etc.).

278–9

κάλων is the accusative singular of κάλως, which – broadly – means 'sail'. More specifically, the word refers to lines at the bottom of sails which could travel up the surface of a sail (these are known as 'brails'). Letting out the brails exposes the whole sail to the wind and therefore increases speed. (Nautical imagery pervades the play, perhaps unsurprisingly given Jason's launch of the Argo; see, e.g., 258.) The metaphor – making the biggest possible effort – may be said to be appropriate: Medea needed refuge when she escaped with Jason; she claims not to have such a haven now. εὐπρόσοιστος = 'easy to approach', and may continue the nautical imagery, especially as ἔκβασις can mean a 'landing place'.

280–1

Medea, though badly treated (she claims), asks Creon why she is to be expelled.

282–3

Creon's answer is surprising but concise. He even justifies his plain-speaking (παραμπίσχειν means 'cover up the meaning'). There is some dramatic irony in his fear. Creon is already onto the idea that Medea may harm his daughter.

284

πολλὰ ... δείγματα ('many pieces of evidence') is the subject, followed (here at least) by a genitive; συμβάλλεται means something like 'come together'.

285–6

Creon briefly characterizes Medea: σοφὴ (clever), κακῶν πολλῶν ἴδρις (skilled in many harms) and grieving because deprived (literally) of her husband's bed (λυπῇ = second person singular; ἐστερημένη is the perfect participle passive of στερέω). It is important to note here how throughout the play various words for bed (λέκτρων here) stand for marriage, sex and reproduction.

287–9

Creon explains that he has heard that Medea has threatened not only Jason but also his daughter and himself. δράσειν is dependent on ἀπειλεῖν. τὸν δόντα refers to Creon, γήμαντα to Jason and γαμουμένην to Glauke. In ancient Greece, when men marry, the verb is active; when women marry, it is middle.

289–91

For Creon it's all about self-defence, though he might be exhibiting some anxiety that he is acting pre-emptively. ἔστι needs to be supplied with κρεῖσσον. Note the contrast between νῦν and ὕστερον. μαλθακισθένθ᾽ is from μαλθακίζομαι, a rare verb. φεῦ φεῦ: this exclamation stands outside the metre. In 291 note the compound verb μεταστένειν: the *meta* stresses how the lamentation will occur later, or afterwards.

292–315

Famous lines, these, in which Medea describes the problems of being thought clever by other people. Also, Medea refers to the gender politics that pervade the play.

292–3

οὐ νῦν με πρῶτον ἀλλὰ πολλάκις: highly rhetorical. Medea cleverly does not launch a direct criticism of Creon. Both με and κακά are the objects of εἴργασται.

294–5

Rather proverbial. ἀρτίφρων (of sound mind) and σοφούς are both part of the vocabulary of cleverness. ἐκδιδάσκεσθαι is a good example of the middle voice: it means 'have one's children taught'.

AS

296–7

ἧς is genitive by attraction. 296 should be translated: 'Apart from the other disadvantage, namely, idleness …' There are lots of negative words in this couple: ἀργίας (idleness or uselessness), φθόνον (envy) and δυσμενῆ (difficult). ἀλφάνουσι, though familiar in epic, is rare in tragedy.

298–9

Parodied at Aristophanes *Thesmophoriazusae* 1130ff., these lines once again describe the dangers of appearing too clever, especially to the stupid (σκαιοῖσι). The paradoxical quality – bringing wise things (σοφὰ) but not appearing wise (σοφὸς) – is typical of Euripides. Note also the crasis of κοὐ = καὶ οὐ.

300–1

Take ἐν πόλει with νομισθεὶς in line 301. τῶν … δοκούντων is comparative genitive after κρείσσων.

302

Medea confirms that she is in the position she has been describing. Note the emphasis of ἐγὼ δὲ καὐτὴ (and note the *crasis*).

303–5

Grammatical gender returns. When Medea had been talking generally, she used the masculine form of σοφὸς (line 299) and λυπρὸς (line 301). Now that he is talking specifically about herself she is σοφή. Many commentators have found these lines, and especially 304, baffling (note the similarity of line 304 to line 808). Medea's argument seems to be as follows: because I am clever, some are jealous of me, others think I am quiet, others that I am of an other nature, others again that I am useless. Commentators have found some of the descriptions redundant. However, a case could easily be made that Medea's sense of how she is perceived need not be entirely logical or concise. She is perceived as clever and that, in her opinion, causes her several problems. 303 and 305 start and end with the same word – σοφή. Cleverness is central to Medea's self-definition, and to the way she thinks others perceive her.

But then she says 'I am not too clever'. What does she mean? She could be starting to try to convince Creon that he has nothing to fear. She could be obliquely commenting on the irony of her situation: how does a clever person come to be on the point of being exiled? There could also be some (dramatic) irony: her *sophia* will be used to devastating effect later in the play.

306

The μὴ continues syntactically from the verb of fearing in the first part of the line.

307–8

The opening phrase uses ἔχει with an adverb to mean 'That is not how it is for me'. Note the direct address to Creon as part of the parenthetical 'don't fear me' and the acceptance of the realities of power in line 308.

AS

309

The τί here is probably better translated 'how?', though the more normal 'why' is also possible. Note the contrast between σὺ and μ᾽.

309–11

ἐξέδου is second person singular aorist indicative middle ('you gave your daughter in marriage for your own interests'). Creon is even complimented: he has acted in a sensible manner (σωφρονῶν – a participle).

312

τὸ … σὸν – literally 'your thing'; so, your interests, welfare, happiness.

313

An imperative (νυμφεύετ᾽) followed by an optative expressing a wish for the future (πράσσοιτε), both in the plural. That the first is the plural is more confusing, as νυμφεύετ᾽ surely refers to Creon marrying his daughter to Jason; some confusion may persist with εὖ πράσσοιτε: is Medea including Jason in this group she hopes will prosper?

313–15

First of all a direct appeal, using an imperative (ἐᾶτέ). Then a concessive use of a participle (ἠδικημένοι – though wronged), then (arguably) a causal one explaining her promise of silence (νικώμενοι – because we have been defeated). Line 315 perhaps sums up the position of women in fifth-century classical Athens: we will be silent, conquered by those who are more powerful.

316–23

Creon's reply.

316–18

The adjective Creon uses – μαλθάκ᾽ – picks up the participle he used in 291. ἀκοῦσαι is an epexegetic infinitive ('you say words that are soothing *to hear*'). ὀρρωδία – uncommon in tragedy – introduces the syntax used with a verb of fearing, even though it is a noun.

319–20

Creon seems to suggest that Medea is not ὀξύθυμος and *not* like a man, and more like (a dangerous) quiet clever woman (σιωπηλὸς σοφή). Medea can be seen by the audience or reader as both ὀξύθυμος and σιωπηλὸς σοφή: that is why she is so dangerous. Creon has not quite grasped this.

321

Firm: an imperative with a superlative and a prohibition – don't talk (useless) words!

322–3

Creon once again reveals how much he fears Medea's cleverness (the word here is τέχνην). ἄραρε is the perfect tense of ἀραρίσκω used intransitively, i.e. 'be firmly fixed'. κοὐκ ἔχεις τέχνην ὅπως = 'and you have no device by which'; the ὅπως-clause, with its indicative verb, may, according to Mastronarde, 'be classed with the normal object clauses with verbs of effort and striving' (Mastronarde, *ad loc.*).

324–39

Stichomythia, i.e. line-by-line dialogue.

324

Medea appeals (formally by Creon's knees) and – rhetorically interesting, this – by his daughter, described as 'newly married'. There are two resolutions in line 324, i.e. where two short syllables take the place of one long syllable. Might this stress the earnestness of Medea's appeal?

325

An incomplete conditional here: *even if you were to try*, you would never persuade me.

326

Medea tries to appeal to Creon's sense of shame (αἰδέση), which is often adduced as the correct attitude to hold towards the gods and rituals that invoke them, such as oaths and supplication.

327

Creon makes clear that he loves his own household more than Medea.

328

At first, it is not clear which country Medea refers to when she addresses ὦ πατρίς. Most commentators assume that it is her homeland of Colchis. But there is no reason – given that she is about to be expelled and has been living in Corinth for some years – to think that she is not referring to Corinth. It may be true that the apostrophe marks the end of Medea's attempt to converse with Creon.

329

An oddly pious line from Creon (only my children are more important to me than my fatherland). Does he understand what Medea is saying? In stichomythia, by using the particle γάρ, a speaker assents to what has been said in the line before.

330

A proverbial line from Medea. The 'loves' (ἔρωτες) that cause trouble surely refer to Medea and Jason, but do they also refer to Jason and his new bride-to-be.

331

Creon – prosaically – continues Medea's line: '[that depends], I suppose, on how the fortunes stand by'.

332

Medea, in her desperation, now calls on Zeus.

333

Creon, rudely, reminds Medea that he must go.

334

Medea uses both πονοῦμεν and πόνων – she understands what trouble is. This can be seen as quite a sharp response to the king, someone she needs something from (κεχρήμεθα meaning 'need' or 'be in want of' takes the genitive).

335

A real threat from Creon here – note the use of βία (violence). Note also that the reference to attendants (ὀπαδῶν) allows for non-speaking actors to be on stage. ὠσθήσῃ is the future passive of ὠθέω.

336

The opening of this line – μὴ δῆτα τοῦτό γ᾿ – is 'No, not *that*.' δῆτα stresses the plea Medea is making; the γ᾿ emphasizes the thing she wishes to avoid.

337

The noun ὄχλον is interesting. Often it means 'mob' or 'crowd'; here it must mean something like 'nuisance' or 'trouble'.

338–9

οὐ τοῦθ᾿ ἱκέτευσα σοῦ τυχεῖν = 'it was not to get this from you that I begged [you]'. σοῦ is 'from you'. Medea accepts that she will be leaving. Creon is confused about what she therefore wants. βιάζῃ = second person singular (why are you acting violently?). The fact that Medea has made physical contact in her supplication makes it ritually more difficult to deny.

340–7

Medea makes a direct appeal to Creon, both for herself (allow me to stay for one day) and for her children. For the latter appeal, Medea refers to the fact that Creon is a father as well. An actor could make something of the many 'm' and 'p' sounds.

341

ξυμπερᾶναι = 'bring to full completion'; ἢ φευξούμεθα is an indirect question dependent on ξυμπερᾶναι.

342

ἀφορμὴν is best taken as an object of the phrase ξυμπερᾶναι φροντίδ᾿ ('complete my plans for resources for my children').

343

προτιμᾷ has the sense of 'give priority to'.

AS

344

The opening of this line is a direct, brief appeal. The following lines stress the hardship the children will face.

345

Medea appeals to Creon's reasonableness, at least in relation to his (soon-to-be) grandchildren (supply ἐστί with εἰκὸς).

348–56

Creon's response to Medea's supplication.

348–9

Creon states that he is not excessively tyrannical (τυϱαννικόν), and does possess tact or a sense of shame (αἰδούμενος). πολλὰ δὴ διέφθοϱα means 'I have made a mess of many things'.

350

There is a pathos in Creon's confession of fallibility here (ἐξαμαϱτάνων). And in 351 he grants her wish for an extra day.

351–4

A certain firmness returns here, reiterating the terms of the exile and confirming that the consequence of not abiding by the terms will be death (θανῇ). Line 352 is a rather tortuous and solemn way of saying 'tomorrow'. The solemnity continues in the final words of 354.

355–6

Some scholars argue that the reasoning of these lines is absurd. However, there is strong irony in these lines in the apparent confidence of Creon's assertion.

AS

357–63: This is a short response from the chorus, which sympathizes with Medea, but also wonders what Medea can do in the circumstances she finds herself in.

364–7

These lines from Medea could be construed as quite aggressive. The phrases are short and curt; there is some plosive alliteration in lines 364 and 365. There is the rhetorical question at the end of 364 and the imperative at the end of 365. There are also the threats of 366 (to the newly-weds) and in 367 to other family members. Note the litotes as well: the struggles for the family will be οὐ σμικροὶ (this form of adjective is archaic and poetic).

368–9

The τόνδε refers to Creon. Medea characterizes herself as seeking advantage (κερδαίνουσαν) and as scheming (τεχνωμένην). Her question to the chorus is rhetorical and is stated in conditional form. (Normally, when participles are used in the protasis, the εἰ is omitted.)

370

Medea confirms that the only way she would have addressed or touched Creon was because she needed something from him. χεροῖν is dative dual plural.

371–5

The idiom of the result clause in 371–2 is very Greek (he has arrived at so great a level of stupidity that ...); ἐξὸν is accusative absolute; ἑλεῖν would ordinarily mean 'capture', but better here 'control' or even 'thwart'. βουλεύματα and its cognates appear very frequently as words referring to Medea's plans for revenge (except perhaps at lines 1078–9). Understand 'me' (i.e. Medea) as the object of ἐκβαλόντι. The day's grace granted by Creon is going to allow Medea to complete her revenge which she describes in these lines as the murder of Creon, Glauke and Jason (described as 'my husband', with the ἐμόν emphatically placed at the end of the line). No mention is made of the children at this early point.

376–7

To use roads in this sort of metaphorical way was as common in ancient Greek literature as it is in ours. Medea stresses how many options she has. ἐγχειρῶ is a deliberative subjunctive ('should I put my hands to'). Note how the chorus are addressed as 'friends': at this point in the play Medea seems to need agreement that she has been wronged and friendly support for her plans to take vengeance.

378–80

Medea runs through some of her options: arson in 378 and then a stealthy (σιγῇ) murder in the bedroom in 379–90. The liver is often seen in ancient Greek literature as the seat of life or the emotions (cf. 'heart'). Various words for bed – it is λέχος here – are used throughout the play to refer metonymically to the site of sexual desire, the place where children are conceived and even to marriage itself. ἔστρωται is the perfect passive of the verb στόρνυμι ('I spread').

A
Level

381–3

ἕν τί means 'one unspecified thing'. τί, though accented, is still enclitic. πρόσαντες continues the road metaphor of 376, meaning something like 'obstruction'. ὑπερβαίνουσα means here 'crossing over [the threshold] into' and τεχνωμένη means not just 'planning' but 'doing the thing I planned to do', hence Vellacott's 'in the act'. Note how τεχνωμένη picks up the same participle in 369. Line 383 is important for the characterization of Medea: she hates the idea of being mocked or being a laughing stock to her enemies. That is a common characteristic of heroes (note especially Sophocles' Ajax). The line means that we should not hesitate to think of Medea as a (tragic) hero in the manner of an Ajax. Note also how the world is already being divided up into friends (e.g. the chorus) and enemies (Creon, Glauke and Jason).

384–5

Medea comes to a conclusion about the best method, namely, poison (φαρμάκοις). However, it is the way that Medea talks about this and what her way of talking says about herself that is interesting. One needs to supply the word for 'road' with εὐθεῖαν (i.e. it's best to take the straight way) so once again the road metaphor (begun in line 376) continues. Note also that Medea says that poison has the advantage of being where her natural abilities lie (ᾗ πεφύκαμεν/σοφαὶ μάλιστα; ἑλεῖν here means not just 'take' but 'kill'). This ability as a poisoner, who is clever (σοφοὶ – the masculine form is used here), is precisely what Creon fears. But Medea is emerging as an extremely distinctive figure: barbarian, heroic, clever.

386

εἶέν: this little stand-alone exclamation indicates a pause in Medea's thinking.

386–9

Now the planning for after the revenge has taken place starts (καὶ δὴ τεθνᾶσι – the perfect tense has the sense of something like 'Suppose that they are dead'). Medea is wise enough to realize that there are unlikely to be any cities (line 386) or any individuals (387–8) who will give sanctuary to a murderer. The two adjectives in 387 (ἄσυλον ... ἐχεγγύους) are both to do with security. The impossibility of any city or friend coming to her aid is starkly expressed in 389 (οὐκ ἔστι = 'there is none').

389–91

The first alternative (ἢν μέν) is discussed, namely, that someone may appear who could offer her refuge. That there may be some optimism in this hope is perhaps expressed by the fact that Medea says she will only have to wait a small time (389: σμικρὸν χρόνον) and that her rescuer will be a tower (πύργος: a common metaphor in Greek and one which we use as well, e.g. 'tower of strength'). But Medea's hope is expressed as a condition; what follows from that condition being fulfilled is a murder carried out with cunning and in silence (δόλῳ ... καὶ σιγῇ). This is another piece of important self-characterization.

A Level

392–4

The second alternative (ἢν δ᾽) is rehearsed: there is no help forthcoming. Here Medea imagines using a sword rather than poison, direct face-to-face violence rather than cunning. ἀμήχανος in line 392 grammatically describes ξυμφορά, but it is really Medea who will be resourceless (so this is a sort of transferred epithet). Medea is prepared to take this action even if she is to die (the aorist infinitive is sometimes used after μέλλω). In 394, Medea says she will kill them (σφε) but she does not say who exactly or how many. (In line 375 she had listed the father – Creon –, his daughter – Glauke – and her husband, Jason.) The final phrase of 394 is an elegant variation on the more normal 'to this point of daring'.

395–8

Medea invokes Hecate. Hecate is a pre-Olympian goddess, associated with all that is magical and mysterious. She is also invoked by Thessalian witches. Medea therefore characterizes herself as a witch, though this is the only such reference in the play. There is something interesting in the way Medea describes Hecate spatially, that is, as occupying the innermost recesses of her hearth. In classical Athens, altars to Hecate stood outside houses and outside the gates of the city, and at crossroads. Medea seems to associate Hecate with – for men – the dangerous powers of the inside of the house. Note the emphatic position of the 'no' or 'not' at the beginning of 395. χαίρων in line 398 literally means 'rejoicing' or 'being happy' but has the sense, as Elliot says, of 'getting away with it'.

399–400

Medea promises the violence to come. Three things are mentioned: the marriage, the joining of families by marriage (κῆδος) and Medea's exile. In all three cases Creon et al. will have a bitter experience: note the repetition of the adjective – πικροὺς and πικρὸν – both placed emphatically at the beginning of their lines.

401–2

Medea addresses herself. (ἀλλ᾽ εἶα is common in Euripides and means something like 'but come on'.) It is notable that three attributes of intellectual capacity are stressed (ἐπίστασαι, βουλεύουσα … τεχνωμένη): her ability to scheme (τεχνωμένη) has already been described in lines 369 and 382, using the same word. Perhaps even more interestingly is the way that Medea explicitly addresses herself. First, her hold on herself, on who she is and what she is doing will become increasingly uncertain as the play progresses. Second, for Greeks there was always something in a name. Medea's is related to μήδομαι and μῆδος, both to do with scheming and planning.

403–7

Medea continues to address herself and to demand that she be extreme and bold. Note the shortness of the first three phrases, with an imperative beginning the first, νῦν the second. This second half of 403 seems to invoke exhortation before battle; this sits interestingly with what Medea said at lines 249–51 about preferring to stand in the hoplite phalanx rather than give birth. In lines 404–6, Medea again repeats the (heroic) idea that mockery must be avoided (see line 383)

A
Level

but here with the added context of her royal and divine lineage. Line 405 needs
some explanation. Literally it must mean 'this Sisyphean marriage of Jason'.
Sisyphus, a figure with various reputations in myth, was the founder of Corinth
so, by metonymy (common in Greek literature), Sisyphean means 'Corinthian'.
But it could also be more critical, in that one of Sisyphus' reputations was as a
trickster and oath-breaker. The beginning of 407 refers back to 401 (i.e. 'know').

407–9

ἐπίστασαι in 407 means 'you have the knowledge'. πρός here is adverbial ('in
    addition'). Medea ends with an aphorism about the nature of women. The lines
    are nothing if not hyperbolic: note the two superlatives. Note also how the
    one that is negative (ἀμηχανώταται) is related to good things (ἐσθλ᾽), while
    the one that is (ambivalently) positive (σοφώταται) is related to bad things
    (κακῶν), indeed all (πάντων) bad things. It is reasonable to ask whether the
    chorus agree with this scathing generalization about women.

        Overall, Medea's is a fascinating self-presentation. She is prepared to take
    vengeance (though she does not yet reveal her plans for her own children, or for
    where she will find sanctuary); she is prepared to scheme and plan; she is clever;
    she hates the idea of being mocked; she is fully aware of her ambivalent social
    status – non-Greek but divine and royal.

*410-662: Following Medea's speech there is a famous chorus, often referred to as
the 'New Song', in which the members of the chorus announce that now everything
has changed. At last there can be a poetry that praises and celebrates women, and
criticizes men. Perhaps we should be alert to the irony: is this – Euripides' Medea –
the first instance of the new poetry? Does a play in which a mother will kill her own
children celebrate women?*

*   Following the chorus there is the first argument between Medea and Jason, in
which Medea is sharply critical of Jason, and in which Jason is complacent about
what he is about to do. From Medea's point of view, the argument goes nowhere
(even though the chorus are in obvious support).*

*   Before this scene the chorus reflect on the nature of love, specifically on both its
good and destructive effects. The chorus also, as a way of understanding Medea's
plight, ask never to be made homeless and stateless.*

*   Aegeus arrives having come from the oracle at Delphi, where he has been asking
about whether he will ever be able to have children.*

**A
Level**

663–4

Aegeus, the king of Athens (and the soon-to-be father of Theseus), arrives onstage (with silent attendants to mark his status). Remarkably, Aegeus' greeting is very brief and very uninformative. Some critics see his unexplained arrival as a clumsy piece of plotting. However, Corinth is on the route between Delphi and Troezen (a city on the north of the Peloponnese that belonged to Athens). To that extent, there is nothing unusual about Aegeus' appearance. His arrival is important not only in terms of plot – Aegeus will provide the sanctuary Medea needs – but also in terms of the theme of fathers and children. Also, Aegeus seems to know Medea already, but there is no way from the extant myths to explain that. Still, it is important that Aegeus, like Medea, sees the world in terms of friends (and, presumably, enemies).

665–6

Medea responds in a similarly friendly fashion, with a little flattery (παῖ σοφοῦ Πανδίονος). πέδον in 666 goes with γῆς τῆσδ᾿, i.e. the ground of this land (it's a little pleonastic).

667–707

This sort of exchange between two actors, where each speaks a line, is called *stichomythia*.

667ff.

Aegeus tells Medea that he has been to the oracle at Delphi to ask about his prospects of having children.

668

Medea interestingly casts Delphi as the centre of the earth (ὀμφαλὸν = literally navel). One myth, as narrated by Pindar, has Zeus releasing two eagles, one from the east, one from the west. He observed where the two eagles met; that place was Delphi. Delphi as the centre of the earth is important for the spatial interests of the play (Medea, remember, comes from the edges of the earth).

669–74

ὅπως γένοιτό μοι can be seen as either a purpose clause or an indirect question but, either way, the sense ('how there might be for me') is clear. Medea and Aegeus exchange information about his trip to Delphi and about the god's answers to his queries about children. Note the use by Medea of λέχους in line 672 to refer metonymically to marriage. Aegeus responds, perhaps rather pompously, that he is not unyoked (ἄζυγες – litotes) of a bed (εὐνῆς). There are two participles in line 672: the first is a genitive absolute; the second is in the nominative agreeing with Aegeus.

675–8

In response to Medea's question about what the oracle says, Aegeus replies that (a) it is too clever (σοφώτερ᾿), and (b) he needs someone with Medea's sort of mind to

AS

interpret it (σοφῆς picks up the earlier comparative). The oracle was notorious
for providing opaque or ambiguous answers. κατ᾽ ἄνδρα means 'in accordance
with the nature of a human being' or, more briefly, 'by human standards'. That
Aegeus thinks Medea capable of interpreting the answer is another sign of her
unusual cleverness. But that cleverness, because she is a woman, is perceived by
some as dangerous.

679–88

Line 679 reads oddly for a modern audience: literally it means 'don't loose the
projecting foot of the wineskin'. Animal hides were used to hold wine, but the
meaning of the oracle – which, interestingly, Medea does not interpret – seems
to be that Aegeus will conceive a child the next time he has sexual intercourse,
but that he should not have sexual intercourse before returning to Athens.
However, in Troezen Aegeus slept with the daughter of Pittheus (mentioned in
683) named Aithra, by whom he had a son, Theseus. Note how the stichomythia
allows for the exchange between Medea and Aegeus to be lively and dramatic:
there is interruption, anticipation and all the usual features of conversation. 680
continues the syntax of 679: this often happens in stichomythia. 683: Pittheus
is only known by his family connection to Theseus. 684: Medea seems to know
a number of Greeks, at least by reputation (ὡς λέγουσι), and she likes the
characteristic of wisdom (686: σοφὸς used predicatively, that is, the man is
wise; note also the crasis of ἀνήρ). It is not clear in which war Aegeus fought
with Pittheus (line 687), but Medea anyway in line 688 offers just good wishes
(and no interpretation of the oracle). ὅσων is in the genitive case after τύχοις.
By a process known as attraction, it remains in the genitive case even though it
is the object of ἐρᾷς.

689–708

Aegeus sees that Medea is troubled, asks her why, receives her explanation and
offers his opinion on Jason's behaviour.

689

συντέτηχ᾽ is the perfect of συντήκω used intransitively ('has wasted away'). ὅδε
means 'this [skin] of yours'.

690

Medea is very emphatic about Jason: he is the worst of all men (κάκιστός …
πάντων).

691–2

Aegeus asks for a clear answer as to the cause of Medea's low spirits (δυσθυμίας).
Medea's response emphasizes that Jason has wronged her: the verb ἀδικεῖ starts
the sentence; Medea also stresses that she has done nothing wrong to Jason.

AS

693–6

Aegeus is at first unsure what he has heard, as he asks Medea in line 693 to explain to him more clearly (σαφέστερον picks up σαφῶς in line 691). Medea explains that Jason has another woman (or wife – γυναῖκ᾽ can mean either) whom he has installed as Medea's mistress (ἐφ᾽ ἡμῖν δεσπότιν). The superlative αἴσχιστον in line 696 shows us that Aegeus is shocked by this news; οὔ που expresses an incredulity. 696 is further confirmation of Medea's changed situation: she used to be φίλοι (friends) with Jason; now she is ἄτιμοι (lacking honour).

697–9

Aegeus' question in 697 suggests that, in some circumstances, a husband taking another lover might just be acceptable, though it is not clear from the alternatives given by Aegeus which is worse, falling in love with another woman or falling out of love with one's wife. Once again the word λέχος is used, but because it is juxtaposed with ἐρασθείς, which normally refers to sexual desire, it seems here that 'bed' is used as a shorthand for sex. Medea's response in 698 is perhaps sarcastic – 'Oh yes (γ᾽), he's very much (μέγαν) in love (ἔρωτα: this word is in the accusative, the object of ἐρασθείς, continuing the syntax from line 697)'. The words ἐρασθείς and ἔρωτα point to sexual desire rather than to the family relations normally described with verbs and other words related to *philos*. She also describes Jason as disloyal to his friends: another instance where the world is viewed as made up of friends and enemies. Aegeus in 699 picks up on this very basic offence to Greek morality – if he is bad, let him go (ἴτω). Note, though, that the Athenian is not yet fully committed to Medea's story (εἴπερ, ὡς λέγεις – if, as you say …).

700–3

In this exchange Medea reveals that Jason has fallen for the king of Corinth's daughter. κῆδος is used to refer to family connection; τυράννων here means 'royal', and it is not clear whether the word in this context is pejorative. 701 shows that now Aegeus is intrigued. 702 is simply factual. 703 shows that Aegeus sees the seriousness of the situation. Note the crasis of μέντοι and ἄρα. ἦν with ἄρα shows that Aegeus knew that something was true all along: 'it was pardonable [and it always was] that you were grieving'. συγγνωστά is neuter plural.

704–8

704: Medea expresses her feelings of abandonment in one word (ὄλωλα is used intransitively, and the perfect tense has the force of a present) and then adds (πρός γ᾽; πρός is used adverbially – 'in addition') that she is to be exiled. Aegeus' response in 705 is one of shock: this is most obvious in the phrase καινὸν αὖ λέγεις κακόν. πρὸς with the genitive means 'at the hands of'; τοῦ is an alternative form of the interrogative pronoun τίνος. Medea in 706 is again factual and to the point. Aegeus in 707 is again shocked, asking an incredulous question (ἐᾶ δ᾽ Ἰάσων;) and expressing his disapproval (οὐδὲ ταῦτ᾽ ἐπήνεσα; note the aorist, used instead of the present tense would expect). In 708 Medea answers Aegeus' question, but it is difficult to translate or to settle on the tone.

AS

Some commentators see the line as sarcastic, i.e. he says that he doesn't like it,
but he is willing to endure it; others see some recognition on Medea's part that
Jason has or may have tried to limit harm to Medea.

709–18

Medea now begins to supplicate Aegeus (ἱκεσία ... γίγνομαι), hoping for sanctuary
in Athens. She does so formally, by touching both his beard (γενειάδος) and his
knees (γονάτων). Supplication is an appeal with a religious dimension; to turn down
a formal supplication such as this might have very serious consequences. However, it
is not clear whether we should see Medea as kneeling before Aegeus.

711–13

Medea begs for pity, repeating the imperative at the beginning of line 711. She also
stresses the wretchedness of her situation (711: δυσδαίμονα; 712: ἔρημον) and
asks quite explicitly in 713 for a home in Athens (note the tautological emphasis
of χώρᾳ καὶ δόμοις). ἐφέστιον ('a guest at one's hearth') seems in the context
of supplication to point to more than the ordinary responsibilities a host has to
a guest; it is also a dual-form adjective, like ἔρημον in the line before.

714–18

These are important lines for the understanding of Medea's character. The opening
couplet seems at first rather bland in expressing hopes that Aegeus will have
children, though 'may your desire be end-bringing' (ἔρως ... τελεσφόρος) is
a striking phrase. Line 716 marks a sort of change: what is this discovery that
Aegeus has been unaware of (and note the cognate accusative of εὕρημα ...
ηὕρηκας)? Line 717–18: it is Medea herself, who with her potions (φάρμακα)
will ensure that Aegeus has children (note how in lines 717–18 she repeats the
idea: I will stop you being childless and will cause you to have children). We
should note that Medea actually has no role in Aegeus becoming a father.

719–22

Aegeus' response seems at first straightforward. He is eager (πρόθυμός) to grant
the favour (χάριν), because of the gods (πρῶτα μὲν θεῶν) and because of
Medea's promise to help him have children, an area in which he confesses he
is completely 'useless' or 'utterly undone' (φροῦδός εἰμι πᾶς ἐγώ). Both θεῶν
and παίδων are in the genitive case dependent on ἔκατι; ὧν is in the genitive
dependent on γονάς.

723–8

Aegeus' offer of help is, however, conditional. He will give sanctuary to Medea but
only if she can get to Athens herself and without his help. Should she manage
this, he promises to keep her protected (ἄσυλος; note that Medea had been
worried about this; see line 387) and not hand her over to anyone. There has
been some discussion about the sequence of the lines. Mastronarde follows

AS

Diggle in placing 729 before 727. There is detailed discussion at Mastronarde *ad loc.* That 726 and 729 effectively repeat the same idea is not necessarily a reason to remove one of the lines: Aegeus is clearly concerned that he is not to be the one to take Medea to Athens. And there is a perfectly reasonable connection between 729 and 730 – You must get yourself out of Corinth, because I do not want to give any reasons to criticize to my (Corinthian) hosts. In 728 note the use of οὐ μή + subjunctive to express a strong future statement ('I *will* not give you up').

729–30

Aegeus first reiterates that Medea must organize her own departure (using a distinctive Greek idiom: release your foot from this land) and then explains that there is a politics to this: he does not want to be seen as blameworthy by his Corinthian hosts.

731–3

Medea agrees to Aegeus' terms but wants the further guarantee of an oath (does this mean that Medea is aware of the revulsion her murders will cause?). Aegeus is surprised at first not to be trusted (μῶν οὐ πέποιθας = 'surely you do not doubt what I say'; note also the perfect tense used where we might expect a present).

734–5

Medea explains that she has enemies – first the house of Pelias and then Creon. Pelias was the king of Iolcus who asked Jason to get the Golden Fleece, thinking that Jason would fail (Jason had a right to the throne of Iolcus). Having secured the fleece and returned to Iolcus, Medea persuades Pelias' daughters to chop him up and boil him, claiming that he would in this way be rejuvenated. The enmity of the house of Pelias is therefore not a surprise.

734–40

Medea explains why a sworn oath is so important. Though a friend of Aegeus', she does not believe promises not backed up by sworn oaths will truly bind him (note ζυγεὶς). She also continues to see the world in terms of the friend/enemy polarity (line 738) and in terms of power (lines 739–40). τούτοις agrees with ἄγουσιν (which is a participle used conditionally); ὁρκίοισι depends on ζυγεὶς; μεθεῖ = μεθεῖο, which is a second singular aorist middle optative, i.e. 'let go of'; κἀπικηρυκεύμασιν means 'demands' (and is another example of crasis).

741–5

Aegeus takes Medea's demands for a sworn oath either with aplomb or with a degree of exasperation ('great indeed is the foresight you have shown ...'). He goes on to explain how swearing an oath makes political sense for him. Again – see especially line 744 – the world is seen in terms of friends and enemies. (744 means 'having some excuse to show to your enemies'.)

AS

746–7

Medea names the gods by whom Aegeus must swear. Her grandfather, the Sun, is included, but then so is the whole race of gods (θεῶν … ἅπαν γένος).

748–55

The business of the oath is carried out. Aegeus asks what he should swear (748: note the two future infinitives – δράσειν), Medea gives the detail (749–51: note the repetition of μήτ' – Medea is keen to stress what Aegeus must not do; ἤν in 750 means 'if'). Aegeus swears by all the gods that Medea had named (752–3). Medea is satisfied but asks about the penalty for breaking the oath (754 – note the optative πάθοις: used without ἄν it must be a main verb, and therefore must be a wish – 'What are you going to wish to suffer …?'). μὴ 'μμένων in 754 is prodelision from μὴ ἐμμένων. Aegeus gives a standard answer (755).

756–8

Tragedy has no stage directions. Here is an example of a character saying something that amounts to a stage direction: Aegeus is going to exit. Medea's description of what she plans to do before arriving in Athens is neutral; alternatively, we could see her statement as one that betrays no doubt at all.

759-865: Once Medea has secured the agreement of Aegeus that she can settle in Athens, she first of all celebrates the likelihood of her vengeance being effective. But she also announces – to the chorus – that she will kill her own children (children are an important theme, of course, especially in the Aegeus scene). The chorus beg her not to do that, but Medea is keen to cause as much hurt as possible to Jason.

The chorus then sing a beautiful lyric in praise of Athens, but one which wonders how even Athens can harbour a murderess like Medea (hence her insistence on the oath). The chorus continue to beg Medea to change her mind. At this point Jason, as requested by Medea, enters.

This is the second encounter between Jason and Medea. Medea acts in a very different way, emollient and charming rather than critical and aggressive, appealing to Jason's vanity and repeating the sorts of positions he adopts. In her earlier exchange with Jason she had – arguably at least – told the truth, won the argument (in principle), but had achieved nothing. Here she lies and achieves what she wants. This is a sophisticated and typically Euripidean approach to the strengths and weaknesses of rhetoric. Jason enters, presumably with the slave sent to fetch him.

866–8

Jason is brusque, but says that he will listen. In fact, he presents himself in a positive way. The participle in line 866 is used concessively: 'although you are hostile'. In 867 τοῦδέ γ' is dependent on οὔ … ἁμάρτοις ('you would not fail to get this', i.e. my coming at your request).

869–71

Medea addresses Jason directly. Note that the verb for beg (αἰτοῦμαί) is brought near the beginning of the sentence, and Medea is clear to ask for forgiveness (συγγνώμον'). Her appeal is based on their earlier loving relationship (νῷν πόλλ' ... φίλα: νῷν is first person dual pronoun and is dative of agent – 'by us two'). ἐστί is to be understood after εἰκός.

872–8

Medea describes her internal dialogue, and she does so in extreme rhetorical terms. She has castigated herself (κἀλοιδόρησα); she addresses herself as foolish or perverse (Σχετλία); she accuses herself of being mad and resentful (μαίνομαι καὶ δυσμεναίνω), and of being hostile to Creon and Jason (ἐχθρὰ δὲ γαίας κοιράνοις καθίσταμαι πόσει θ',). And all this is contrasted with a new image of Jason as planning things well (τοῖσι βουλεύουσιν εὖ), and of doing only what is most advantageous for the family (τὰ συμφορώτατα). The marriage into the royal family is not now seen as an affront but as a benefit, as are future royal siblings for Medea's children.

878–9

Medea asks herself two rhetorical questions. Anger (θυμοῦ) is an important part of Medea's heroic character, but here she asks whether she should get rid of it.

880–1

More rhetorical questions, again reinforcing the ideas of (a) exile and (b) lack of friends.

882–3

Medea confesses directly here that she was foolish and absurdly angry before. Note the use of θυμουμένη, which picks up the noun θυμοῦ in 879.

884–5

Medea moves from castigating herself to praising Jason (this is a pretty complete rhetorical performance). He is praised for being sensible (σωφρονεῖν), contrasted with Medea's silliness (ἄφρων). Once again the new family connection is commended (κῆδος); προσλαβών has the sense of 'taking on in addition'.

886–8

These lines are a little disturbing as Medea suggests that not only should she have helped with Jason's plans; she should also take pleasure (ἥδεσθαι) in tending to the bride (νύμφην) and standing by the marriage bed (παρεστάναι λέχει).

889–90

Medea concludes this little passage with a pithy generalization about the nature of women. Note how γυναῖκες emphatically starts line 890.

890–1

On the basis of women's inferior nature, Medea asks Jason not to imitate women and not to be drawn into a competition of foolishness (ἀντιτείνειν νήπι' ἀντὶ νηπίων).

AS

892–3

The section of the speech addressed to Jason reaches its conclusion, uttered directly and briefly (verbs dominate the couplet). παριέμεσθα is the middle of παρίημι, meaning 'I ask for pardon.' The vocabulary picks up earlier parts of the speech: κακῶς φρονεῖν echoes the σωφρονεῖν and ἄφρων of lines 884–5; βεβούλευμαι is related to Jason's plans in 886 (τῶνδε τῶν βουλευμάτων).

894–9

Medea addresses the children, repeating τέκνα: the effect is pathetic. She also repeats her instruction to come outside (λείπετε στέγας, ἐξέλθετ'); this is another stage direction. Some scholars think the children enter with their tutor. Further imperatives ask the children to embrace and speak to their father. 897 contrasts friends and enemies again, abandoning previous hostile relations (πρόσθεν ἔχθρας) towards friends (ἐς φίλους). In 896–7 take μητρὸς μέτα with the imperative διαλλάχθηθ', i.e. be released along with your mother from ... 898 uses the formal, technical term for a treaty (σπονδαὶ) for Medea's claimed new relationship with Jason. The verb 'to be' has to be understood in the first part of the line; the subject of the second part of the line comes at the end, so that the line is framed by σπονδαὶ at the beginning and χόλος at the end. μεθέστηκεν in 898 is the perfect of μεθίστηι, used intransitively (i.e. 'has gone'). 899 has Medea asking the children to take their father's right hand: that would be a sign of détente.

899–900

The ὡς is there to explain why Medea has suddenly exclaimed οἴμοι. There is dramatic irony in what she says: the audience (and the chorus) will think that the 'hidden evils' refer to the planned murder of the children. It is not clear what Jason thinks they refer to.

901–2

οὕτω should be taken with ὀρέξετ'. Again, the dramatic irony is sharp: if Medea goes through with her plan, the children will not live for a long time.

902–3

ἀρτίδακρύς must mean something like 'ready to cry'.

904–5

νεῖκος πατρὸς translates as 'quarrel with your father'. ὄψιν is a metonymy, not 'sight' itself but the thing that does the seeing, i.e. the face. τήνδ', agreeing with ὄψιν, suggests that Medea is referring to the face of one of her children.

AS

906-1018: The chorus respond with relief and hope that Medea has indeed changed her plans. Jason also commends Medea on her change of heart and asks his sons to grow into strong and loyal young men.

An exchange between Medea and Jason follows, in which Medea asks Jason to ask Creon to allow her children to stay. In order to bring Creon round Medea sends the children off with Jason with presents (a dress and a golden crown) for his bride-to-be.

The chorus sing an ode in which they sing of the certain death of the children, and of Glauke, and of the ignorance of Jason.

The children's tutor returns with the children to tell Medea that the children's banishment has been cancelled and cannot understand Medea's distraught response.

1019–20

When Medea says 'I will do these things' she refers to the tutor's advice not to grieve so violently. There is pathos in these lines as well: if Medea kills the children, they won't have any daily needs (οἶα χρὴ καθ᾽ ἡμέραν). The very ordinariness of the lines is in contrast to the awful violence that Medea plans.

1021–39

Medea reflects on the future and how hopeless and desolate it will be for her.

1021–3

Again a double pathetic address to the children (note σφῷν, which is the second person dual pronoun). The children will now have both a city (πόλις) and a house (δῶμ᾽), and Medea will be left wretched (ἀθλίαν), the children deprived of their mother (μητρὸς ἐστερημένοι) – though she is more likely to be talking of her own deprivation (because she knows they are to die).

1024–7

Here Medea stresses her exile (φυγάς) and how that will mean she cannot partake in the various rituals associated with boys growing up, principally those to do with marriage (note here especially lines 1026–7, where she mentions water, wives, marriage beds and torches). The word for water (λουτρά) is an emendation. The manuscripts have λέκτρα, meaning beds. Some editors have found the tautology (with λέκτρα and εὐνάς) too much. But using two words for bed, given the various things they can metaphorically stand for, does not seem odd. And one could note line 1338 in this play, where the phrase εὐνῆς ἕκατι καὶ λέχους appears. No subject is stated in the πρὶν clauses, as the subject is the same as that of the main verb in 1024 (i.e. ἐγώ). ἀγῆλαι is the aorist infinitive of ἀγάλλω (adorn).

1028–31

αὐθαδίας is in the genitive as it gives the reason for Medea feeling so wretched. The noun and its related adjective are rarely used in Euripides, but, meaning 'stubbornness' or 'being headstrong', they are very appropriate for Medea. Lines 1029 and 1030 both begin with the adverb ἄλλως. This repetition, technically anaphora as the repeated words both start their clauses, stresses the uselessness

A
Level

of her nurture of the children and the pain she suffered in giving birth to them. πόνοις is regularly used to refer to labour in childbirth, and the idea of pain in childbirth is explicitly picked up in the phrase στεϱϱὰς ... ἀλγηδόνας (cruel pains). The metaphor of κατεξάνθην is striking and extreme. The verb καταξαίνεσθαι refers to the practice of combing out impurities in wool with an instrument something like a comb with very sharp points. However, the verb can also mean 'to be tortured', as when people's bodies were dragged over a sharp-toothed object, causing severe lacerations and bleeding.

1032–6
In 1032 Medea uses another adjective from the extensive Greek vocabulary of suffering (δύστηνος). Overall, the lines induce a sense of pathos, as Medea lists her (rather conventional) hopes she had for her children (i.e. that they would look after her in her old age, would bury her when the time came, would be a source of envy). Medea concludes with an economically expressed statement that her hopes have gone (note how the verb 'has died' has moved into an early position in the clause). ζηλωτὸν ἀνθϱώποισι: ζηλωτὸν is neuter in apposition to the preceding phrase. This phrase means something like 'a thing wanted/admired/envied by [all] men'.

1036–7
Medea gives a contrasting account of what her future will actually hold. ἐστεϱημένη is a perfect passive participle. In 1037 she describes her future life as both anguished (λυπϱὸν) and painful (ἀλγεινόν).

1038–9
The children will no longer see their mother. The explanation Medea gives of this in 1039 ('having moved away into another condition of life') is a rather disturbing euphemism (though it could be seen as a reiteration of the Greek religious idea that the dead continued to dwell somewhere). Dramatically, however, it is important that the children do not know what is going to happen to them.

1040ff.
One of the reasons *Medea* is so celebrated and has been so attractive for modern directors and actors is because of the complicated psychological portrait delivered by Euripides in these lines.

1040–1
The children look at their mother (another stage direction, this) with the same eyes that few lines ago were no longer going to look at her. If they are indeed laughing, as 1041 suggests, that is sharply inappropriate, and Medea's adjective πανύστατον (last of all) is ominous, and in tragedy is used to describe the last action before death. γέλων is a cognate accusative ('why do you smile your last smile?').

1042–3
She starts with another exclamation meaning 'alas', picking up the φεῦ φεῦ from two lines before. δϱάσω is a deliberative subjunctive (what should I do?). The

image of her heart departing is a touching one, and she once more is addressing the chorus. The reason for her change of heart is, again, the very sight of her children. εἶδον is aorist, but we translate as present.

1044–5

In 1044 δυναίμην is optative because it is part of a conditional sentence in which the 'if' clause is omitted e.g (if you were to ask or force me to do it, I couldn't). χαιρέτω is a third person singular imperative, meaning here 'let it (bouleumata) be done with'. βουλεύματα clearly here refers to the plans to kill the children; in line 1079 the very same noun will refer to some sort of rational faculty which would stop Medea killing her children. This whole scene presents Medea as under intense psychological pressure. In line 1045 she emphatically changes her plans.

1046–7

Medea notes the irrationality of her plans to kill the children: making her children suffer (τοῖς τούτων κακοῖς – κακοῖς is an instrumental dative) to hurt their father and thereby suffer twice as much herself. Unusually, τῶνδε and τούτων both refer to the children. No doubt an actor could make something of all the 't' and 'k' sounds in these lines.

1048

οὐ δῆτ᾽ ἔγωγε is a very emphatic phrase. Medea then repeats the last two words of line 1044. This looks like certainty but could connote the very opposite.

1049–50

Medea veers back sharply to her earlier views. Again, as at line 383, Medea hates the idea of being a figure of ridicule (γέλωτ᾽ ὀφλεῖν) and of allowing (μεθεῖσα here) her enemies to go unpunished. The world continues to be seen by Medea in those polarized friend/enemy terms.

1051–2

τολμητέον: verbal adjective indicating obligation (like a gerundive in Latin); the verb ἐστί is understood; τάδ᾽ most obviously refers to the plan to kill the children. κάκης is in the genitive because it explains why she has admitted 'soft words' into her heart. κάκης – from the noun κάκη – should here be translated 'cowardice'. προσέσθαι is from προσίημι, which means 'admit' or 'allow into'. In exclamations, such as this, an infinitive is sometimes used (with or without the article; here the article is used). So, the sentence means: 'but it is as a result of my cowardice, the admission of soft words into my heart'.

1053–5

Medea instructs the children to enter the house, a stage direction with an ominous quality. In tragedy, women often commit violence inside the house. θύμασιν means 'sacrifices'. One editor dismisses the idea that Medea is using this metaphor in order to divest herself of personal responsibility for the killings. However, casting murders as sacrifices is relatively common in tragedy. In

A Level

Medea's case, we know that the killings will have a religious dimension as, at the end of the play, she will appear in a chariot given to her by her grandfather, the Sun. There is also the possibility that Medea, in accordance with what she says in lines 1046–7, sees the killings as a sort of self-sacrifice. διαφθερῶ is future tense and would ordinarily mean 'I shall destroy.' Other suggestions for here are 'I shall weaken.' χεῖρα, literally 'hand', is often used metonymically to refer to violence.

1056–1135: Medea continues her monologue, changing her mind a number of times. She ends with a famous couplet that means something like 'I understand that what I am about to do is wrong. But my spirit/anger (thumos) is more powerful than my moral/rational faculties (bouleumaton).

The chorus sing an ode about what it means to have children.

Then a messenger brings news of what has happened at the palace. The messenger is horrified; Medea is exultant.

Messenger speeches are common in tragedy. The sorts of actions which we expect to see on stage and in films – fights, violence, worse – tend to be reported in these (to us) rather long narratives. But, given the pre-eminence of Homer and the pervasiveness of epic narrative, it is perhaps no surprise that tragedy should include narratives of these sorts.

This messenger speech contrasts the initially happy scenes at the palace with what happens once the presents are opened and the dress is put on.

1136–40

δίπτυχος literally means 'two-folded' but here just means 'two'. The messenger – one of the δμῶες (attendants) – is clearly on the side of the royal family. He stresses that the house entered is νυμφικούς (bridal). The attendants' pleasure (ἥσθημεν) is contrasted with their sympathy for Medea's plight (σοῖς ἐκάμνομεν κακοῖς). δι᾽ ὤτων literally means 'through our ears', but the whole phrase must mean something like 'a lot of talk buzzed through our ears'. This is followed by an indirect statement – that's why ἐσπεῖσθαι, from σπένδω, is in the infinitive (in the perfect tense: the sense is 'to have reached a truce').

1141–3

The positive feelings arising from the end of the quarrel between Medea and Jason continue in these lovely images of one of the attendants kissing one of the boys' hand and another their blond hair. The messenger notes his own pleasure.

1144–6

ξυνωρίδα means 'pair'. Arguably, it is at least insensitive of the messenger to say that he and the other attendants now admire their new mistress, and how she has only eyes for Jason (πρόθυμον … ὀφθαλμόν).

1147–9

Lines 1147–8 describe an apparently shy, awkward young girl. On seeing the boys, she hides her eyes and turns away (or perhaps there is some bitterness?).

A
Level

μυσαχθεῖσ᾽ is from μυσάττομαι, used here for the only time in tragedy: it is easiest to translate it as 'dislike'.

1149–50

These are just about the first positive words said about Jason (apart from by Jason himself, of course). ἀφῄρει is imperfect (and the phrase is similar to line 456) and has the sense of 'he kept trying to take away'. Note how the messenger stresses the youth of the bride (νεάνιδος).

1151–5

The messenger reports what Jason said to Glauke. Οὐ μὴ … ἔσῃ: one editor notes that the future indicative used in this way indicates a vehement instruction ('You will not …'). These lines also see the world in terms of friends (and enemies). After instructing Glauke to stop being angry (παύσῃ δὲ θυμοῦ), to turn around, to judge the friends of her husband as her own, he moves quickly in lines 1154–5 to ask Glauke to ask her father to revoke his children's exile. This is a little confusing, as the children's tutor had said at 1002 that the exile had been revoked.

1156–62

These lines describe the pleasure before the pain. It is a lovely portrait of a young, happy, in-love girl, delighted with her gifts. ἠνέσχετο – from the verb ἀνέχω – is what is called a doubly augmented form. The same is true of ἠμπέσχετο from ἀμπέχω. μακρὰν is adverbial – a long way away. βοστρύχοις translates as 'curls'. The little mirror scene (1161–2) is perhaps a little disturbing, mainly in the juxtaposition between Glauke's laughter (προσγελῶσα) at her lifeless form (ἄψυχον). She soon will be lifeless, and not in a reflection.

1163–6

This little pen portrait shows the princess' delight in her new robe and crown. Again, it will be a contrast to the awful violence that starts in just a few lines. ἀναστᾶσ᾽ translates as 'standing up'; ἁβρὸν is used adverbially ('daintily'); πολλὰ πολλάκις means 'many, many times'. τένοντ᾽ refers to the thick tendon in the back of the leg (she may be looking at the tendon as she stretches her leg to see how the dress hangs).

1167–70

The horror begins (a terrible sight to behold – δεινὸν … θέαμ᾽ ἰδεῖν). The next three lines are dominated by verbs, because things start happening and changing so quickly: her skin colour changes; she starts moving sideways (λεχρία), shaking, barely able to sit down. The language is quite difficult: κῶλα is an accusative of respect ('shaking as to her limbs'); μόλις φθάνει/θρόνοισιν ἐμπεσοῦσα μὴ χαμαὶ πεσεῖν is a difficult phrase, which means literally 'she barely anticipates falling on her chair so as not to fall on the ground' (μὴ χαμαὶ πεσεῖν includes an epexegetic infinitive). The sense is clear: she just reaches her chair.

A
Level

1171–5

The narrative zooms out, including the perspectives of others who have not really been mentioned thus far. An old attendant thinks that something divine is causing what is happening to Glauke. The choice of Pan is perhaps not surprising, as he is a god often associated with madness. ἀνωλόλυξε refers to the ritual wailing women engaged in during certain religious rituals. But the old attendant sees foam coming from Glauke's mouth (διὰ στόμα χωροῦντα λευκὸν ἀφρόν), her pupils disappearing (ὀμμάτων τ᾽ ἄπο κόρας στρέφουσαν = 'twisting the pupils away from the eyes') and no blood in her skin.

1176–7

Difficult to translate, but this means 'she let out (ἧκεν is from ἵημι) a great wail (κωκυτόν) sounding against (ἀντίμολπον) the ὀλολυγῆς'.

1177–80

These lines describe the frenetic action, as attendants react to Glauke's predicament. Note ἡ μὲν ... ἡ δὲ; note also that it is the (authoritative) male figures – father and husband – who need to be informed. Lines 1179–80 emphasize all the running about (πυκνοῖσιν ... δραμήμασιν) and the noise it makes (ἐκτύπει).

1181–4

The opening couplet is difficult: by now (ἤδη), having gone along the leg (κῶλον) of the full track (ἐκπλέθρου δρόμου: ἐκπλέθρου means six *plethora*; a *plethron* is a sixth of a stade; ἐκπλέθρου therefore means a *stade*, i.e. 200 yards), a quick runner (ταχὺς βαδιστὴς) would have touched the finish (τερμόνων ἂν ἥπτετο). There is much scholarly discussion about how far exactly the runner is supposed to have run: but this is an adverbial clause that really means 'quickly'. ἐξ ἀναύδου means 'from non-speaking', i.e. 'after some silence'. μύσαντος is from μύω, which means 'I am shut'.

1185–9

In 1185 διπλοῦν means 'double'; ἐπεστρατεύετο is a military metaphor. In lines 1186–7 the fantastic effects (θαυμαστὸν) of Medea's magic is made clear: a stream of all-consuming fire (νᾶμα παμφάγου πυρός) issues from the crown; at the same time the finely wrought robe (πέπλοι δὲ λεπτοί) beings to eat away the princess' flesh (note the imperfect: ἔδαπτον).

1190–4

In these distressing lines the princess tries to escape, to throw the crown from her head. She is still on fire (πυρουμένη), shaking hair and head this way and that (line 1191). Horribly, the crown stays firmly (ἀραρότως) in place, and the more she shakes her hair, the more the fire burns.

1195–203

This is a very extreme description of Glauke's physical demise. 1195 stresses how overwhelmed she is: πίτνει begins the line; νικωμένη ends it. She

A Level

is unrecognizable except to her father (δυσμαθὴς ἰδεῖν). κατάστασις means 'condition': her facial features are no longer clear. ἔσταζε is from στάζω meaning 'drop'. Fire and blood, now mixed, pour from her head. Perhaps the nastiest image is of the way her flesh comes away from her bones, compared here (ὥστε = like) to pine resin dropping (πεύκινον δάκρυ), because of the unseen jaws (γνάθοις ἀδήλοις) of Medea's potions (φαρμάκων). There is a lot of metaphor to unpack in these lines. The whole thing is summed up briefly in 1202: it is a terrible sight. 1202–3: the princess is now dead (νεκροῦ): all are scared to touch her; what they have witnessed – τύχην unusually means 'what has happened' here – is lesson enough (διδάσκαλον).

1204–21

These lines describe the entry and death of Creon. They are full of pathos. He is wretched (τλήμων), ignorant at first of what has happened to his daughter (συμφορᾶς ἀγνωσίᾳ), but as soon as he sees her dead on the floor, falls next to her (προσπίτνει), wails, embraces her, kisses her and speaks (1206–7).

1207–10

Creon addresses his dead daughter, mainly by asking a series of questions, which express his incomprehension. His grief is palpable, most especially when using the optative he states that he would prefer to die with her (συνθάνοιμί). There is possibly a colloquial usage in 1209: τὸν γέροντα τύμβον should mean 'the old man who is a grave'; presumably, it means 'the old man close to the grave'.

1211–21

Creon's death is described pathetically. He stops lamenting and wailing, and then tries to get up. But, in another ghastly simile, his useless efforts to disentangle himself from his daughter – and her finely wrought robe (λεπτοῖσι πέπλοις – the same phrase as at 1188) – are compared to the way that ivy clings to the branches of laurel (κισσὸς ἔρνεσιν δάφνης). Just as the earlier sight was terrible, so is this struggle (δεινὰ δ᾽ ἦν παλαίσματα). And, just as Glauke's earlier struggles with the crown caused things to get worse, the same happens here with Creon. The more he tries to get up, the more he is held down. The vocabulary of pathos is pervasive: σάρκας ... ἀπ᾽ ὀστέων (the same as Glauke); ὁ δύσμορος; he is no longer to win the struggle (κακοῦ γὰρ οὐκέτ᾽ ἦν ὑπέρτερος). As the corpses lie together, line 1220 pairs the child and her father in the order of the words (παῖς τε καὶ γέρων πατήρ). Line 1221 has caused editors some trouble. πέλας could be comprehensible, going with the line before. And the last three words might mean 'a disaster [causing] a longing for tears' (although most editors think this is doubtful).

1222–3

The messenger addresses Medea briefly, mainly in order to say he has nothing more to say, and wants no part of her affairs (τὸ σὸν – literally 'your thing').

A Level

1224–30

The messenger ends with a series of general observations. This is not uncommon in Euripides: see, e.g., *Andromache* 1161ff.; *Bacchae* 1150ff.; *Helen* 1617ff.; *Supplices* 726ff.

The idea that mortal life is a shadow is a fairly common idea in Greek literature (see, e.g., Sophocles *Ajax* 126). οὐδ᾽ ἂν τρέσας εἴποιμι means 'I can confidently say.' The view that those who seem clever are actually the most stupid is also not uncommon (τούτους in 1227 picks up τοὺς σοφοὺς βροτῶν, etc. in 1225–6). The final three lines of the speech are also conventional. No mortal is happy, even if they seem so. The final couplet works as follows: with wealth flowing in (genitive absolute: ὄλβου δ᾽ ἐπιρρυέντος), one man might seem more fortunate than another (εὐτυχέστερος ἄλλου γένοιτ᾽ ἂν ἄλλος), but he is not happy (εὐδαίμων δ᾽ ἂν οὔ).

Following the messenger speech, Medea goes inside the house and kills her children. Their shrieks are reported by the chorus, who also reflect on Ino, another mother who killed her children.

Jason arrives on stage, angry and suffering because of the deaths of Glauke and Creon. He has to be informed that his children are dead as well. He demands to see Medea.

She appears, but not on stage, but with the dead children in the mechane, the sort of fireman's lift usually used for appearances of gods (note: deus ex machina). The mechane represents the chariot lent to her by her grandfather, the Sun. Jason and Medea exchange angry words, and Medea refuses to let Jason touch or bury the children. As Medea leaves, Jason reflects on his disastrous situation.

**A
Level**

Vocabulary

An asterisk * denotes a word in OCR's Defined Vocabulary List for AS.

ἅ	the	*αἱρέω	I take
ᾇ	the	*αἰσθάνομαι	I perceive
ἀβουλία, ἡ	thoughtlessness	*αἰσχρός	shameful, disgraceful
ἁβρός	delicate, luxurious	*αἴτιος	responsible
*ἄγαν	too much	αἰτοῦμαί	I beg
*ἄγγελος	messenger	αἰών	age, period
*ἄγω	I lead, bring	ἀκίνδυνος	not dangerous, riskless
ἀγάλλω (aor. infinitive ἀγῆλαι)	I honour, adorn	*ἀκούω	I hear
		*ἄκρος	top (of)
ἀγνωσία	ignorance, unawareness	ἀλγεινός	painful
*ἀγών	contest, trial	ἀλγηδών (irregular neuter comparative = ἄλγιον)	pain, grief
*ἀδελφός	brother		
ἄδηλος	unknown		
*ἀδικέω	I wrong, injure	ἀλγύνω	I feel pain, grieve
*ἀεί	always	ἀλκή	strength, force
ἄελπτος	unhoped for	*ἀλλά	but
ἀζήμιος	unpunished	ἀλλάσσω	I exchange
ἄζυγής	unyoked, unmarried	*ἄλλος	other, another
ἄθλιος	wretched	ἄλλοσε	to another place
αἰαῖ	alas	ἄλλοτε	at another time, at other times
Αἰγεύς	Aegeus		
*αἰδέομαι	I feel shame, respect	ἄλλως	otherwise
αἰεί	always	ἀλφάνω	I acquire, incure
*αἷμά (n.)	blood	*ἅμα	at the same time
αἰνέω (aor. = ᾔνεσ')	I praise	ἀμαθία	ignorance, irrationality

*ἁμαρτάνω	I make a mistake, fail	ἀνώμοτος	unsworn
ἄμεινον (iregular neuter comparative of *ἀγαθός)	better	ἀπαγγέλλω	I report
		ἄπαις	childless
ἀμήχανος	without resources, impossible	ἀπαλλαγή	divorce
		ἀπαλλάσσω	I remove from, escape from, take away
ἀμπέχω (3rd sing. aor. middle = ἠμπέσχετο)	I put on (clothes)		
		ἄπαξ	once
		*ἅπας	all
*ἀμφὶ + acc.	around, about	*ἀπειλέω	I threaten
*ἄν	would, could *indefinite*	ἄπειμι	I am absent
*ἀνάγκη	necessity	ἄπειρος	unused to, ignorant of
ἀναινομαι (infinitive = ἀνήνασθαι)	I reject, refuse	ἀπορρέω	I flow or fall away from
		ἀποστρέφω	I turn back or aside
ἀναίτιος	blameless, not responsible	ἀπέχθομαι	I am hated
ἀναλίσχω (2nd pers. sing. = ἀναλοῖς)	I waste	*ἄπο + gen.	away from, from
		ἄπολις	cityless, stateless
ἄναξ	lord	*ἀπόλλυμι	I destroy, lose, die (middle)
ἀναύδος	speechless		
ἀνέρχομαι	I go up	ἀποστέλλω	I send away, despatch
ἀνέχω (poetic aorist infinitive = ἀνασχεθεῖν)	I hold up, support	*ἅπτομαι (1st sing. aor. = ἡψάμην)	I bind, grasp
		*ἄρα	then (or introduces a question)
ἀνέχω (3rd sing. aor. middle = ἠνέσχετο)	I continue, persist	ἀραρίσκω (intransitive perfect 3rd person = ἄραρε)	I am firmly fixed
ἀνήκεστος	incurable		
*ἀνήρ	man	ἀραρότως	closely, strongly
*ἄνθρωπος	man, human being	ἀργία	idleness
ἀνίστημι (aor. participle ἀναστᾶσ᾽)	I stand up	ἀρκέω	I am sufficient, ward off
		ἀρτίδακρύς	ready to cry
*ἀντὶ + genitive	instead of, in return for	ἀρτίφρων	of sound mind, intelligent
ἀντιλάζομαι	I receive in return	ἀρτίως	just, recently
ἀντιλέγω	I gainsay, speak against	*ἄρχω + gen.	I rule
ἀντίμολπος	different in sound from	ἄση	pain, distress
ἀντιτείνω	I offer in return, pay	*ἀσθενής	weak
ἀντιτίνω (aor. middle infinitive = ἀντιτείσασθαι)	I exact a penalty	ἀσκός	wine skin
		ἀσπάζομαι	I welcome, embrace
ἄντομαί	I meet, entreat	*ἀσπίς	shield
ἀνολολύζω	I cry aloud, wail	ἀστός	townsperson

ἄσυλος	unharmed	*βούλομαι	I want
*ἀσφαλὴς	safe	βραβεὺς	judge
ἄτη	madness, fury, delusion	βρότος	mortal
ἄτιμος	unhonoured	γαῖα	earth, land
*αὖ	again	γαμέω (aor.	I marry
αὐθάδης	headstrong, stubborn	participle = γήμας)	
αὐθαδία	stubbornness	γαμήλιος	bridal
*αὖθις	again	γάμος	marriage
*αὐτὸς	self, same, him, her, it, them	*γέ	at least
		*γελάω	I laugh (at), mock
αὕτως	similarly	γενειάς	beard
ἀφίημι (aor. infinitive = ἀφεῖναι)	I let go	*γένος (n.)	type, family, race
		γεραιός	old
ἀφαιρέω	I take away	*γέρων	old man
*ἀφικνέομαι	I arrive	γηροβοσκέω	I look after in old age
*ἀφίσταμαι	I revolt	*γῆ	land, earth
ἀφίστημι	I cause to revolt	*γίγνομαι	I become, happen
ἄφνω	suddenly	*γιγνώσκω	I know, understand
ἀφορμή	haven, place of safety	γλυκύς	sweet
ἄφρων	mindless	γνάθος	jaw
ἄχθομαι	I am burdened, vexed	*γνώμη	opinion, judgement
ἀχρεῖος	useless, unprofitable	γονὴ	offspring, family
ἀψευδὴς	truthful	γόνυ	knee
ἄψυχος	lifeless	γόος	wailing
βαδιστὴς	a runner	*γυνὴ	woman, wife
*βαίνω	I go	δαίμων	god, spirit
*βάλλω	I throw	δάκρυον	tear
*βάρβαρος	barbarian	*δακρύω	I shed tears
βιάζω	I force	δάμαρ	wife
*βία	force, violence	δάπτω	I devour, tear
*βίος	life	δάφνη	laurel
βίοτος	life	*δέ	and, but
*βλάπτω	I harm, injure	δέδοικά	I fear
*βλέπω	I see	δεδορκώς	having seen, having sight
βλώσκω (infinitive μολεῖν)	I go	*δεῖ + acc.	it is necessary
		δεῖγμα	sample, evidence
βόστρυχος	hair	δείκνυμι	I show
βούλευμα	plan, decision	*δεινός	terrible, clever, strange

δέμας	body	δύσκλεια	dishonour
δέχομαι	I receive	δυσμαθής	hard to learn, difficult
δεξιά	right hand	δυσμεναίνω	I bear ill-will
*δέομαι	I need, ask	δυσμενής	hostile
δέσποινα	mistress	δύσμορος	ill-fated
*δεσπότης	master	δυσσεβέω	I act impiously
*δεῦρο	hither	δυστάλαινα	very miserable
*δή	indeed (stresses the previous word)	δύστηνος	wretched
		δυσχερές	annoying, troublesome
*δῆλος	clear, certain	δῶμα	home, house
*δῆτα	of course, certainly	*δῶρον	gift
*διὰ + acc.	because of, on account of	*ἐάω	I allow
*διὰ + gen.	through	ἐάνπερ	if
διαλλάσσω	I change, exchange	ἐγείρω	I wake, rouse
διάγω	I pass time	ἐγχειρέω	I take in hand, undertake, attempt
*διαφθείρω	I destroy		
διδάσκαλος	teacher	*ἐγώ	I
*δίδωμι	I give	*ἔγωγε	I at least
διέρχομαι	I go, pass through	*ἐθέλω	I want
*δίκαιος	just, fair	*εἰ	if
*δίκη	justice	εἶα	Well now!
διπλόος	double	εἰέν	well
δίπτυχος	double, twofold	εἰκός	likely, probable, reasonable
δίς	two times, twice		
δισσός	double, twofold	εἰκών	image, likeness
δμῶες	attendants	εἰμι	I am
*δοκεῖ + dat.	it seems good	εἶμι	I shall go
*δόλος	trick, stratagem	ἐργάζομαι	I work, make
δόμος	house, home	*εἰς + accus.	to, towards
*δόξα	opinion, glory	εἰς (fem. accus. singular = μίαν)	one
δόρυ	spear		
δορύξενος	ally	εἰσβαίνω	I go into
δραμημα	course, race	εἴσοδος	entrance
δράω	I do	εἰσοράω	I look at
δρόμος	course, race	εἴτε ... εἴτε	whether ... or
*δύναμαι	I can	*ἐκ or ἐξ + genitive	out of
δυσδαίμων	ill-starred, unhappy	Ἑκάτη	Hecate
δυσθυμία	despondency, anxiety	ἕκατι + gen.	on account of
		ἐκβάλλω	I throw out

ἔκβασις	exit	ἔξειμι (present imperative = ἔξιθ’)	I go out
ἐκδιδάσκομαι	I have someone taught		
ἐκδίδωμι (aor. middle 2nd sing. = ἐξέδου)	I give in marriage	ἐξίημι	I let out, loosen
		ἐξικνέομαι	I reach, arrive at
		*ἔξεστι + dat.	it is possible
ἐκλείπω	I desert, abandon	ἔξω	outside
ἐκμανθάνω	I learn	ἔοικα	I am like
ἑκούσιος	voluntary, willing	ἐπαγγέλλομαι	I promise
ἐκπίπτω	I fall out, lose	*ἐπαινέω	I praise
ἔκπλεθρος	six *plethra* long	*ἐπεί	when
ἐκποδὼν	out of the way	ἔπειμι (prodelision of participle = 'πιοῦσα)	I come
ἐκπονέομαι	I work through		
ἐκτίνομαι (future middle ἐκτείση)	I take vengeance on		
		*ἔπειτα	then
*ἐλαύνω	I drive	ἐπικηρύκευμα	demand (by a herald)
ἐλπίς	hope	ἐπιστρατεύομαι	I wage war on
ἐμαυτοῦ	of myself, my own	ἔπος (n.)	word
ἐμμένω	I abide, stand fast	ἐπιρρέω	I flow
*ἐμός	my	*ἐπίσταμαι	I know
ἔμπαλιν	backwards, again	ἐπιστροφή	reaction, recoil
ἐμπίπτω	I fall upon	ἐπιστρωφάω	I come to
ἔμψυχα	alive	ἐπίφθονος	envious, jealous
*ἐν + dat.	in, on	*ἕπομαι + dat.	I follow
ἐνδίκως	justly	ἐράω	I love, desire
ἔνδον	inside	*ἔργον	work, task, deed
ἔνειμι	I am in	ἐρευνάω	I seek, search, explore
ἐννοοῦμαι	I consider, reflect	*ἔρημος	deserted, abandoned
ἐντός	inside	ἔρνος (n.)	shoot (of a plant)
ἐξαιρέομαι	I remove	ἕρπω	I go, come
ἐξαμαρτάνω	I fail, make a mistake	*ἔρχομαι	I go
ἐξανίστημι (aor. infinitive = ἐξαναστῆσαι)	I raise up, stand up	ἔρως	love, desire
		ἐς + acc.	to, towards
ἐκτρέφω (aor. ἐξεθρεψάμην	I raise, nurture	ἐσθλός	good, decent, honourable
		ἑστία	hearth
ἐξελαύνω	I drive out	ἔσω	within
ἐξέρχομαι	I go out	*ἔτι	still, yet
ἐξευρίσκω	I find out, discover	*εὐ	well
ἐξηγέομαι	I dictate, name	εὐδαίμων	fortunate, prosperous

εὐθύς (feminine acc. = εὐθεῖαν) — straight

*εὐθὺς — immediately

εὐκλεής — of good reputation

εὐνή — bed (marriage)

εὔνοια — goodwill, kindness

εὐπρόσοιστος — attainable, easy

εὔρημα — discovery, gain

*εὐσεβής — pious

*εὐτυχής — fortunate

εὐτυχέω — I am fortunate

εὐφυής — graceful

εὐψυχία — good courage

*ἐπί + acc. — against, onto, on, at

*ἐπί + dat. — on

*εὑρίσκω (2nd sing. perfect = ηὕρηκας) — I find

ἐφέστιος — by one's hearth

ἐφίημι (3rd person aor. = ἐφῆκεν) — I allow

ἐφοράω — I look on

ἐχεγγύους — responsible, trustworthy

ἐχθαίρω — I hate

*ἐχθρός — hostile

*ἔχω — I have, hold, + adverb 'be', + infinitive 'can'

*ζάω — I live

ζεύγνυμι (aor. passive participle = ζυγείς) — I yoke, bind

*Ζεύς — Zeus

ζηλωτὸς — enviable

ζημία — punishment, penalty

ζυγόν — yoke (of marriage)

*ἤ — or

*ἡγέομαι — I lead (+ dat.), consider

*ἤδη — now, already

*ἥδομαι (aor. = ἥσθημεν) — I enjoy, am glad

ἡδονή — pleasure

ἦθος (n.) — custom

*ἥκιστα — least, not at all

*ἥκω — I have come

ἥλικα — as big as

Ἥλιος — The sun

*ἡμεῖς — we (us)

*ἡμέρα — day

ἧπαρ — liver

ἥσσων — weaker, inferior

ἡσυχαῖος — quiet

ἥσυχος — quiet

θανάσιμος — deathly, fatal

θάτερος — other

*θαυμάζω — I am amazed, admire

θαυμαστός — amazing, marvellous

θέαμα (n.) — sight, spectacle

θέλω — I want

θέμις — lawful, just

*θεός — god

θεσπιῳδός — prophetic

θηκτός — sharpened

θιγγάνω (aor. infin. = θιγεῖν) — I touch

θνήσκω — I die

θνητά — mortal

θρῆνος — wailing, lamentation

θρόνος — throne, chair

*θυγάτηρ — daughter

θῦμα — sacrifice

θυμὸς — spirit, anger

θυμόομαι — I am angry

θυραῖος — outside, outdoors

θωπεύω — I flatter

Ἰάσων — Jason

ἴδρις — experienced, skilful

ἵημι (3rd sing. present = ἵει) — I send out

ἱκέσιος — suppliant, supplicating

ἱκετεύω — I supplicate, entreat

*ἵνα	so that, in order to	*κελεύω	I order
κἀγώ = καί ἐγώ	and I	κερδαίνω	I gain, profit
*καθίσταμαι	I am appointed, get into a state	κηδεύω	I care for, marry
*καί	and, even, also, actually	κῆδος	care, concern, marriage
καινός	new	κισσὸς	ivy
*καίτοι	and yet	κλαίω	I lament, wail
*κακός	bad, wicked, cowardly	κλύω	I hear
κἀλοιδόρησα = καί ἐλοιδόρησα (see λοιδορ-έω)	and I rebuked	κοινωνέω	I have a share in
		κοίρανος	ruler, leader
κάλως	rope, cable	κόμη	hair
κἄμ᾽ = καί ἐμέ	and me	κόρη	girl
		Κορίνθιαι	Corinthian women
*κάμνω	I toil, am weary	κόσμος	good order, decoration
κἀμοί = καί ἐμοί	and to/for me	κοὐ = καί οὐ	and not
κἀν = καί ἐν	and in	κοὐδὲν = καί οὐδὲν	and nothing
κἄπειτ᾽ = καί ἔπειτα	and then	κρᾶς	head
		κράτιστος	most powerful, best
κἀπιδεῖν = καί ἐπιδεῖν (see ἐφοράω)	and to look on	κρείσσων	more powerful
		Κρέων	Creon
κἀπικηρυκεύμασιν = καί ἐπικηρύκευμασιν	and by their demands	*κρύπτω	I hide (something)
		*κτάομαι	I obtain, acquire
κάρα	head	κτείνω	I kill
καρδία	heart	κτυπέω	I ring, resound
κάρτα	very, very much	κυνέω	I kiss, entreat
καρτερέω	I endure, persevere	κυρέω	I am, meet
καρτερός	utmost verge, strongest point	κωκυτός	wailing
		κῶλον	limb
κασίγνητος	brother	*λαμβάνω	I take, capture
κατά + acc.	in, according to	*λανθάνω	I escape the notice of
κατάστασις	institution	λαμπὰς	torch
καταξαίνω	I comb, tear to pieces	λάμπομαι	I shine
καταθνήσκω	I die	λαμπρός	bright
κάτοπτρον	mirror	*λέγω (future = ἐρήσομαι)	I say, tell, speak
καὐτὸς = καί	and you yourself		
κέαρ	heart	*λείπω	I leave behind, abandon
κεἰ = καί εἰ	and if	λέκτρον	bed (marriage) – often in plural
κεῖνος	that		
*κεῖμαι	I lie, am situated	ληίζομαι (perfect passive participle = λελησμένη)	I am seized as plunder

λεπτός	delicate, fine, subtle	*μένω	I stay, remain
λευκός	white	μέλεω	I am an object of care, concern
λέχος (n.)	bed		
λεχρίος	slanting, oblique	*μέλλω	I intend, hesitate
λῆμα	character, spirit	μέμφομαι	I blame
λιτή	prayer, entreaty	*μέν	on the one hand
*λόγος	word, account, reason, story, argument, speech	μέντἄρ' = μέντοι ἄρα	truly
λοιδορ-έω	I rebuke, scold	*μέντοι	however, certainly
λουτρόν	bath, libation	μεριμνητής	someone who is careful about . . .
λυγρός	gloomy, miserable		
λυπέομαι	I am grieved, distressed	*μέτα + gen.	with
λυπρός	wretched, distressed	μεταστένω	I lament afterwards
*λύω	I loosen, release	μέτειμι	I will go about
μὰ	by (Zeus!)	*μή	not
μαίνομαι	I am mad	Μήδεια	Medea
*μακρός	long, big	*μηδὲν	nothing
μαλθακίζω	I soften	μήν	indeed
μαλθάκός	soft, weak, effeminate	*μήτε . . . μήτε	neither . . . nor
*μάλιστα	very much, especially	*μήτηρ	mother
*μᾶλλον	more	*μηχανή	device, plan
μάντευμα (n.)	an oracle	μηχανάομαι	I contrive, devise
*μάντις	prophet	μιαίφονος	bloodthirsty, murderous
μάρναμαι	I fight, struggle	μίμνω	I remain, wait
μάταιος	idle, foolish, vain	*μισέω	I hate
*μάτην	in vain	μνεία	memory
*μέγας	big	*μόλις	scarcely, with difficulty
μεθίημι (aor. participle = μεθεῖσα; aorist indic. = μεθῆχ'; aor. subjunctive = μεθῶ; μεθεῖο, which is a second singular aorist middle optative; future infin. = μεθήσειν)	I let go	μοχθέω	I am weary
		μῦθος	story, speaking
		μυσάττομαι (aor. participle is μυσαχθεῖσα)	I feel disgust
		μυχός	recess
		μύω	I am shut, closed
		μῶν = μή οὖν	not therefore
		μωρία	stupidity
μεθίστημι (3rd sing. perfect = μεθέστηκεν)	I go	ναίω	I dwell
		νᾶμα	stream
		ναυστολέω	I sail
μεθορμίζω	I find refuge	νεᾶνις	girl

νεῖκος	quarrel, strife	ὄλβιος	happy, wealthy
*νεκρός	corpse	ὄλβος	happiness, wealth
νεογάμου	newly married	ὀλολυγή	loud crying (of joy or lamentation)
νεωστὶ	just now, recently		
νήπιος	childish, foolish	ὄμμα (n.)	eye
*νικάω	I defeat, beat	*ὄμνυμι	I swear
*νομίζω	I think, calculate, reckon	ὁμοιόομαι	I become like
*νόμος	law, custom, convention	ὀμφαλός	centre
νυμφεύω	I betroth	*ὅμως	nevertheless
νύμφη	bride	ὀνίνημι (infin. = ὀνάσθαι)	I profit, benefit
νυμφικός	bridal, nuptial		
νυμφίος	newly wedded, bridal	ὄνησις	profit, benefit
*νῦν	now	ὀξύθυμος	quick to anger, passionate
νῶν	us two	ὀπηδός (gen.pl. = ὀπαδῶν)	attendant
ξανθός	yellow		
*ξένος	stranger, foreigner	ὁποῖος	of what sort
*ξίφος (n.)	sword	*ὅπως	so that, how
ξυμπεραίνω	I accomplish jointly	ὁράω (future = ὄψεται)	I see
ξυμφορά or συμφορά	disaster, event, misfortune		
		*ὀργή	anger
ξύνειμι	I live with	ὀρέγομαι	I aim, desire
ξυνεργὸς	partner, associate	*ὀρθός	straight, correct
ξυνευνέτης	bed-partner	ὅρκιος	bound by oath
ξυνοικέω	I live together	*ὅρκος	oath
ξυνωρίς	pair	ὁρμάω	I set out for
ὁ	the	ὀρρωδία	shuddering
*ὅδε	this	ὀρφανός	bereft
*ὁδός (f.)	road, way	*ὅς	who
*οἶδα	I know	*ὅσος	as much, as big
*οἰκέω	I live in, inhabit	ὀστέον	bone
οἴκοθεν	from home	*ὅστις	who, whoever
*οἶκος	house, home	*ὅταν	whenever
*οἰκτείρω	I pity	οὐ or οὐκ or οὐχ or οὐχὶ	not
οἶμαι	I think		
οἴμοι	alas	οὖδας (n.)	ground
οἰμώζω (aor. = ᾤμωξε)	I wail, groan	*οὐδὲ	and not, nor, not even
		*οὐδείς	no one
		οὐδὲν	nothing
*οἷος	such as	*οὐκέτι	no longer
οἴχομαι	I depart	*οὔκουν	not

ούμὸς = ὁ ἐμός	mine	*πατρίς	fatherland
*οὖν	and so, therefore	πατρῷος	belonging to one's father
οὖς (gen. plur. = ὤτων)	ear	*παύω	I stop
		πέδον	ground
οὔτε . . . οὔτε	neither . . . nor	*πείθω (1st person perfect = πέποιθά)	I persuade
οὔτω or οὔτως	thus, so		
*ὀφθαλμός	eye	*πειράομαι	I try
ὀφλισκάνω (aor. infin. = ὀφλεῖν)	I owe, incur	πέλας	near
		Πελίης	Pelias
ὄχλος	nusiance, trouble	Πέλοψ	Pelops
ὄψις	sight	πενθέω	I lament, mourn
*παῖς	child	πέπλοι	clothes
*παλαιός	former, ancient	περαίνω	accomplish, finish
πάλαισμα	struggle	περάω	I go, I go across
*πάλιν	back, again	*πέρι + gen.	about, concerning
πάλλευκος	all white	περιπτύσσω	I embrace
παμφάγος	all-devouring, voracious	περισσῶς	excessively
Πανδίων	Pandion	περιστέλλω	I wrap up, cloak, cover
Πάν	Pan	πεύκινος	made of pine- or fir-wood
πανταχῆ	in every way	πῆμα (n.)	misery, calamity
πανύστατος	last of all	πικρὸς	bitter, harsh
πανώλης	utterly ruined	πίμπλημι (aor. indicative = ἔπλησα)	I fill up with
*παρά + acc.	against		
*παρά + dat,	with, beside	*πίπτω (alternative form = πίτνω)	I fall
παραιτέομαι	I beg, ask for a favour		
παραμπίσχω	I clothe, disguise	πίστις	faith, pledge
παρίστημι (aor. subjunctive = παραστῶσιν; perfect infin. = παρεστάναι)	I stand by	*πιστὸς	reliable, faithful, trustworthy
		Πιτθεύς	Pitheus
		πλημμελὲς	faulty, unpleasant
πάρειμι	I am present	*πλὴν + gen.	except
παρέρχομαι	I enter	πλόκος	hair
*παρέχω	I provide, cause, produce	πούς	foot
παρηίς	cheek	ποθεινός	desiring, calling for
παρίημι	I concede, give up	πόθεν	from where
πάρος	before, formerly	ποικίλος	many coloured, varied
*πᾶς	all, every	*πόλις	city
*πάσχω	I suffer	*πολίτης	citizen
*πατὴρ	father		

*πολλάκις	often	προσφέρω	I use, apply
*πολὺς	much, many	προσφωνέω	I address, speak to
*πόνος	toil, labour	προσχωρέω	I approach
*πονέω	I toil, suffer	πρόσωπον	face
*πορεύομαι	I go, march	προτιμάω	I take heed of
πορίζω	I provide	προκαλύπτω	I veil, cover
πόρος	means, way	προυννέπω	I proclaim, announce
πορσύνω	I prepare, provide	προέχω	I jut out
πόσις	husband	*πρῶτον	first
*ποτε	when, at some time	πυκνός	dense, crowded
*πότερον . . . ἤ	whether . . . or	*πῦρ (n.)	fire
*που	where?	πύργος	tower, bulwark
*που	I suppose	πυρόομαι	I am on fire
*πρᾶγμα (n.)	thing, matter	πω	at all
*πράσσω	I do, fare, manage	ῥάδιος (comparative = ῥάων)	easy
πρίαμαι	I buy		
*πρίν	before, until	ῥᾳθυμία	meaning, i.e. laziness, carelessness
*πρὸ + gen.	in front of, before		
*πρόθυμός	eager, ready	*ῥίπτω	I throw
προμήθεια	forethought	ῥύομαι	I rescue, defend
προξενέω	I am a protector or patron	σάρξ	flesh
		*σαφής	clear
προοίμιον	introduction (especially of a speech)	σέβω	I honour, worship
		σέθεν	your
*πρός + acc.	to, towards, against	σείω	I shake
πρός + gen.	out of, from	σεμνός	haughty, proud
προσάντης	arduous, unpleasant	*σιγάω	I am silent
προσαυδάω	I address	*σιγή	silence
προσγελάω	I smile at	σίδηρος	iron
προσδέρκομαι	I look at	Σισυφείοις	Sisyphean (i.e. Corinthian)
προσείχομαι	I am held firm		
προσημαίνω	I foretell, announce	σιωπηλὸς	silent
προσίημι (infinitive = προσέσθαι)	I admit, allow into	σκαιός	stupid
		σκῆφις	excuse, pretence
*πρόσθεν	before	σκιά	shadow
προσλαμβάνω	I gain	σκοπέομαι	I consider, examine
προσλέγω	I address, speak to	σκυθρωπός	sullen
προσπίπτω	I fall upon, embrace	σμικρός	small
πρόσπολος	attendant	*σὸς	your

*σοφὸς	wise	συνουσία	company
στάζω	I drip	συντήκω (perfect = συντέτηχ')	I waste away
σπανίζω	I lack		
σπαράσσω	I tear, rend	συντίθημι	I put together
στέλλω	I make a journey	*σφε	them
σπένδω (infinitive = ἐσπεῖσθαι)	I make up (a quarrel)	σχετλίος	hard-hearted, cruel
		σχῆμα	form, type
στερέω (perfect passive participle = ἐστερημένη)	I deprive	σχηματίζομαι	I arrange (hair)
		*σῶμα	body
σπείρω	I sow, beget	σωφρονέω	I am sensible
σπέρμα	seed	τάλας (feminine form = τάλαινα)	wretched, long-suffering
σπλάγχνον	heart (seat of the emotions), real character	τἄλλα = τά ἄλλα	other things
		τἀμὰ = τά ἐμά	my
σπονδαὶ	agreement, treaty	τἂν = τοι ἄν	would, could
στέγη	house	*τάχα	quickly
στείχω	I walk, go	*ταχὺς	quick
στενάζω	I groan	*τε . . . καί	both . . . and
στερρός	hard, harsh	τείνω	I stretch
στέφανος	crown	τίκτω (aor. infinitive = τεκεῖν)	I give birth to
στόμα	mouth, speech		
στόρνυμι (perfect passive = ἔστρωται)	I spread out	τέκνον	child
		τέκτων	craftsman
		τελεσφόρος	bringing fulfillment
στρέφω	I turn	τέρην	tender
στυγέω	I hate	τέρμων	boundary
*σύ	you	*τέχνη	craft, skill
*συγγενής	related, kin	τεχνάομαι	I contrive
συγγνώμων	indulgent, disposed to forgive	τίθημι (fem. aor. participle = θεῖσα)	I place, make
συγγνωστός	forgiveable	*τις, τι	a certain . . ., somewhat
συμβάλλομαι	I contribute	*τίς, τί	who? what?
συμβαίνω	I come to an agreement	τλήμων	wretched, long-suffering
συμφύρω (perfect participle = συμπεφυρμένον)	I knead together	*τοι	I assure you
		τοιάδε	such as
σύμφορος	advantageous	τόκος	child
σὺν + dat.	with	*τολμάω	I dare
σύνδεσμος	a binding, fastening	τόλμα	daring
συνθνήσκω	I die together	τοσόνδε	to such an extent

*τοσοῦτος	so great, so many	φείδομαι	I spare
τόσος	so great	*φέρω	I carry, bear, endure
τόσως	so much, as much as	φεῦ	alas
*τότε	then, at that time	*φεύγω	I flee
τοὐμὸν = τό ἐμόν	mine	*φημί	I say
τοὐνθένδε = τό ἐνθένδε	from here	*φθάνω	I do something first
		*φθόνος	grudge, envy
τρεῖς	three	φθονέω	I grudge
τρέμω	I tremble	*φίλος	friend
*τρέπω (aor. passive participle = τραπείς)	I turn	*φιλέω	I like, love
		*φοβέομαι	I fear
τρέω	I fear	*φόβος	fear
τρίβω	I spend, waste (time)	Φοῖβος	Phoebus (Apollo)
τρὶς	three times	φόνος	murder, slaughter
Τροζηνίος	Trozenian	φράζω	I speak, declare
*τρόπος	way, manner	φρὴν	mind
*τυγχάνω (2nd person future = τεύξῃ)	I happen to be + participle, I get + gen.	φρονέω	I think, understand
		φροντίς	thought, reflection
		φροῦδός	gone, departed
τύμβον	tomb	φυγὰς	an exile
τυραννικός	royal	*φυλάσσω	I guard
τύραννος	king	φυτεύω	I produce, plant
*τύχη	chance, luck, fortune	φυτόν	creature
ὑβρίζομαι	I am violated	φύω	I am
*ὑμεῖς	you	φῶς (n.)	light
ὑπεργάζομαι	I perform (a service)	*χαίρω (imperative = χαῖρε)	I rejoice (imperative = 'Hello!' or 'Goodbye')
ὑπερβαίνω	I step over		
ὑπερβολή	extravagance	χαίτη	hair
ὑπέρτερος	superior to	χαμαὶ	on the ground
ὑπερχαίρω	I am exceedingly happy	χάρις	favour, sake
*ὕπο + gen.	through, with	*χείρ (note the acc. plural χέρας)	hand
*ὕστερον	later		
ὑφάπτω (aor. subjunctive = ὑφάψω)	I set on fire from underneath	χθών	land
		χόλος	anger
φαιδρός	radiant, bright	*χράομαι + dat. (fut. = χρήσεται)	I use, treat
*φαίνομαι	I appear		
φάρμακον	drug, potion, remedy	χράω	I prophesy
φάσγανον	sword	*χρὴ (or χρῆν or χρεών)	it is necessary

χρῄζω	I desire, need	χωρὶς + gen.	without, apart from
*χρῆμα (n.)	thing, property	ψυχὴ	soul, mind, life
χρησμός	an oracular response	ὤ	O!
χρηστήριον	oracle	*ὧδε	thus
χρηστός	good, useful	ὠθέω (future = ὤσω; 2nd sing. future passive = ὠσθήσῃ)	I push
χροιά	skin		
*χρόνος	time		
*χρυσός	gold	ὠλένη	arm
*χρυσοῦς	golden	*ὡς	as, when, that, because, how
χρώς	skin		
*χώρα	land, place, country	*ὥστε	so that (result)
*χωρέω	I go		

Aristophanes, *Peace*

Introduction, Commentary Notes and
Vocabulary by Charlie Paterson

A Level: 1–10, 13–61, 180–336

Introduction

The opening of Aristophanes' *Peace* is a remarkable introduction to the wild imagination and fierce wit of Athens' most popular and successful comic playwright. Furthermore, the play as a whole is a window onto life in Athens at a crucial moment in its history: as Aristophanes prepared *Peace* for the stage in 421 BC, Athens and Sparta were the closest they had ever been to securing peace since the outbreak of the Peloponnesian War in 431. After a decade of fighting and the deaths of prominent leaders on both sides, negotiations were a tense and lengthy process. Perhaps only a few weeks after the performance of *Peace* in Athens, terms were agreed and the Peace of Nicias came into effect. Instead of celebrating the farcical solution of a problem that was, in reality, too complex to solve without the magic and imagination of theatre, *Peace* presented a problem that was as close to being solved as it had ever been before. Although far from a simple celebration of the peace negotiations between Athens and Sparta, this play abounds in optimism and festivity and as such is unique among the plays of Aristophanes.

This introduction provides an overview of the Peloponnesian War before looking at the life of Aristophanes, the performance context of the play and concerns with its staging and direction, the main themes and motifs of the play and the style and metre of the Greek. Suggestions for further reading, much of which is the basis of this introduction and commentary, are also provided to help candidates further their studies of Aristophanes, Greek comedy and the Peloponnesian Wars. This is by no means an exhaustive introduction; rather, it aims to provide students with enough understanding of the author, his times, his genre and the structure of the play to encourage them to develop their own personal responses to the literature and take on further research.

Plot and structure of *Peace*

It is useful to begin with an outline of the plot and structure of the play. Scholarly analysis of Aristophanic comedy has revealed that comedies had a loose structure made up of a range of component parts, which could be manipulated according to the needs of the plot. These structural elements are highlighted below in italics.

Prologue – an introduction to the theme and hero of the play, as well as an opportunity to warm the audience up for what is to come.

Lines 1–81: After leaving the audience in uncertainty for a time, two slaves eventually explain that they are making cakes out of dung to feed a giant dung beetle which their master has obtained in order to fly to Zeus and have it out with him over the years of wars that the Greeks have suffered.

82–172: Trygaeus, the hero, flies over the stage on a giant beetle and explains his plan. He ignores his daughters' concern for him and continues on his journey to Zeus. The beetle is easily distracted by the smell of excrement in the streets below, which makes for a rather bumpy journey. Trygaeus presents himself as Bellerophon, the hero of a recent Euripidean tragedy.

173–235: Trygaeus arrives at the house of Zeus. Hermes, playing the role of a rather rude doorkeeper, is at first rather unhelpful. After he is given some sacrificial meat, he becomes more amenable and tells Trygaeus that the gods have become so fed up with mortals causing war that they have moved away to the highest point of the heavens. War is housesitting for them and has trapped Peace in a cave blocked up with boulders. Hermes also reveals that War is planning to use a pestle and mortar to make a savoury paste using the cities of Greece as his ingredients.

236–88: War comes out to make his paste and lists off the cities as he puts ingredients into a large mortar. His slave, named Uproar, is sent to find a pestle but there are none in the house and both Athens and Sparta have lost theirs. It is clear that these pestles are meant to be Cleon and Brasidas, the Athenian and Spartan leaders respectively, who sought to continue the war before both died in the previous summer. War is forced to go back inside to make a pestle himself.

Parodos – the chorus enters the theatre from the sides to sing and dance.

289–360: While the coast is clear, Trygaeus calls on all Greeks to help him free Peace. The chorus are unable to contain their joy; they sing about their previous sufferings and the joy that peace will bring. They call on Trygaeus to lead them in rescuing Peace.

361–424: Hermes re-enters and stops Trygaeus as he is about to approach the rocks covering Peace. He warns that Zeus has threatened death to those who help Peace. Trygaeus shows his cunning and wins Hermes over with flattery and deception. He suggests that the gods of the Persians, Moon and Sun, have been plotting against the Greek gods. Trygaeus promises Hermes additional festivals in his honour and offers him a golden libation bowl.

425–59: Trygaeus and Hermes pour a libation and pray for divine blessing on their endeavour. They pray for peace and for those who strive to stop peace to be cursed.

460–519: The chorus heave on the ropes as they try to pull Peace out of the cave. It is hard to get the group of Greeks to pull together: the Boeotians don't pull properly, an Athenian warmonger is accused of getting in the way, the Argives sit at the back and mock, some of the Spartans don't pull properly, the Megarians are so weak they can't pull and the Athenians are in the wrong place. Finally, the Athenian farmers alone are successful in pulling Peace onto the stage with her two attendants, Opora ('Vintage') and Theoria ('Festival-Goer'). As Peace returns, she brings with her the things that war stole from the Athenians: good wine and festivals held in the countryside.

520–600: Trygaeus, delighted at the return of Peace, surveys the audience with Hermes and comments on the peacetime occupations of the spectators. The chorus gather as an army of farmers, holding agricultural tools, and make a prayer to Peace in which they make clear how important she is for those in the countryside.

Agon – usually a conflict set out as two contrasting speeches with some comments from the chorus. This is a deeply unusual agon in that everyone agrees with Hermes: Peace has returned and so there is no conflict.

601–56: Trygaeus wonders why Peace has been absent for so long. Hermes is able to explain the reason and so presents the origins of the wars. He first links Pericles to a scandal with Pheidias, the sculptor of the Parthenon who stood accused of misappropriating some of the gold and ivory intended for the great statue of Athena. Hermes suggests that Pericles started the war to divert public attention away from the scandal, a rumour which is likely to have been invented to give the effect of a god providing a detail that had so far been unknown by mortals. He also lists the Megarian decree, the fear of the allied states in the face of increasing tribute demands, the appeal of turning to Sparta and the lust for profit as causes of war. He moves on to the devastating effect war has had on the farmers and rural life of Athens before he comes to a cutting depiction of the politician Cleon as a greedy lover of war, hater of the farmers and abuser of the law courts.

657–733: Peace, represented on stage by a statue, is presented by Hermes as too angry to speak to the audience because of their treatment of her. Hermes claims she is whispering into his ear, mainly asking questions. She wants to know who her biggest supporter and worst enemy were, who is currently in power and what has changed during her absence. Hermes suggests that Trygaeus take Opora, one of Peace's attendants, as his wife and that he lead Theoria to the Council.

First Parabasis – the stage clears of actors and the chorus come forward to recite and sing an interlude in which Aristophanes can reflect on his efforts and the effect of his writing. There is a second parabasis on a different topic later in the play.

734–818: The chorus remove their masks and step out of character to address the audience as the poet himself. They present Aristophanes as a great benefactor of Athens who has turned the genre of comedy into a tool for attacking the monsters of the democracy, particularly Cleon. They suggest he should be rewarded for his innovative approach and courage in the face of adversity. They go on to mock his bald head and celebrate the return of Peace.

819–908: Trygaeus returns to the stage leading Opora and Theoria. He has now returned to his own house and enters into an exchange with his slave about what he saw on his journey. He sends Opora inside for a bath and orders wedding preparations to begin. While the girl is inside, the chrous and Trygaeus have an exchange about his happiness and upcoming marriage. Trygaeus then reveals Theoria to the slave and the audience, whom he characterizes as the Council. He describes the return of sex and festivities that Theoria brings to Athens and the chairman eagerly accepts her.

909–73: The chorus praise Trygaeus. He initiates the installation of Peace and prepares, with his slave, to sacrifice a sheep.

974–1015: Trygaeus and the chorus pray to Peace so that she might accept their sacrifice and reveal herself to them fully. They call on her to put an end to fighting and to restore a wide range of good foods to the marketplace.

1016–51: The slave takes the sheep inside for slaughter and Trygaeus arranges a fire to cook the meat. Hierocles, an oracle-collector, is attracted by the smell of the cooking meat, but Trygaeus is concerned that he will make some objection to peace, presumably as the real Hierocles had recently done in Athens. He thus decides to pretend not to see him.

1052–126: Hierocles starts to give advice on how to share out the meat. When he realizes the purpose of the sacrifice, he is quick to give prophecies against peace. Trygaeus calls Hierocles a fraud and chases him away.

Second Parabasis

1127–90: The chorus rejoice that Peace has returned and celebrate the rustic life she has brought back with her. They present a dialogue between neighbouring farmers who have finished the sowing and plan to eat and drink lavishly to demonstrate their delight that god has sent down rain for their land. The chorus then criticizes the military leaders and details the harm they have done to the people of Athens, contrasting the joys of peace with the difficulties of war.

1191–269: A man who crafts hooks for pruning the vines and a potter come with gifts for Trygaeus. The first man praises him as peace has led to his businesses returning to health. By contrast, an arms-dealer, helmet-maker and spear-maker are upset because their businesses are ruined without war. Trygaeus mocks them and suggests ridiculous new uses for their merchandise.

1270–304: Two boys appear on stage and practise the songs they wish to sing at the wedding party. The first boy is only able to sing lines about war and amusingly turns out to be the son of Lamachus, the Athenian general known for his fervour for war. The second boy turns out to be the son of Cleonymus, a man who brought shame upon himself by throwing away his shield and fleeing from battle in 424. This boy sings the beginning of a song written by the poet Archilochus, which describes a man throwing his shield away.

Exodos – the final scene of the play and the exit of the chorus to music.

1305–59: Trygaeus and the chorus turn to the food that has been left by the sickle-maker and potter and start the wedding celebrations in earnest. They celebrate the return of rural life and the gifts that Peace provides for all Greeks.

The Peloponnesian Wars

To understand Trygaeus' mission to restore peace to Athens and the other Greek states, we need to look at the forces uniting and separating the Greeks in the decades preceding the performance of the play. The Persian Wars of 490 and 480–479 were a unifying force among the squabbling Greek states. Sparta led an effective but uneasy alliance in opposition to the eastern invaders and Athens made a significant contribution to the resistance. As the Spartans and their Peloponnesian allies started to withdraw after much success but increasing unpopularity, a new alliance developed against the Persians. This Delian League, so known because it was established on the island of Delos, sought to remove the Persians from the Aegean. Each member of the league made a contribution, known as tribute, and had a vote in any council called by the league. However, Athens was quick to take a dominant role: neutral states were forced to join and pay tribute, original members were prevented from leaving or forced to pay more tribute and Athens held executive power. In essence, Athens was exercising hegemony over the other states under the guise of promoting a united front against the Persian empire. During this time, Sparta and its allies were not part of the league but remained distant observers.

Meanwhile in Athens, the constitution was a direct democracy: all male citizens over a certain age were considered politically equal in that they could all participate in the functioning of the democracy. The Assembly, the main decision-making body, met around forty times each year and any male citizen over the age of 20 could speak on issues and vote by raising their hand. Although such a process ensured a large demographic of people could take part in the political machinations of the state, charismatic men emerged and started to dominate politics by proposing popular motions and vying for the power that the support of the common people could give them. From 461, the political scene in Athens changed dramatically with the exile of Cimon, a previous ambassador to Sparta, who had sought a peaceful relationship between the two states. When he sent troops to Sparta in the mid 460s to help quell the rebellion of their subject peoples, the helots, the Athenian troops caused offence; they were sent home and Cimon was ostracized (a form of exile lasting ten years), making way for reforms that led to greater power in the hands of the people coupled with an anti-Spartan foreign policy. Athens was then quick to make treaties with anti-Spartan states: Thessaly, Argos and Megara.

Athenian hostility towards Sparta and overweening dominance over its subordinates in the Delian League was not a way to promote unity among the Greeks. Soon Athens became embroiled in clashes with Corinth, a powerful ally of Sparta, in what has become known as the First Peloponnesian War. Meanwhile, Athenian forces started to push into mainland Greece and gain some significant territory. At the same time, although the threat of Persia had all but vanished from the Aegean, Athens nevertheless retained a tight grip on the Delian League, even moving the League's treasury to Athens in 454. However, such abuse of power was not sustainable, and the Athenian empire was soon rocked by rebellions against Athenian hegemony in Euboea and Megara. Since Athens was distracted with their efforts to quell these rebellions, King Pleistoanax of Sparta chose this moment to lead an army against Attica, the greater region of Athens. This threat was short-lived: Pleistoanax turned back before reaching the city itself, perhaps after receiving a bribe from Pericles. However, such events demonstrated the extent of the tension between the two states and their allies. This period of instability in mainland Greece was finally concluded with the establishment of a thirty-year peace treaty in 445: Athens gave up its power on the mainland but retained power over the Delian League.

Thirty years proved to be too optimistic a timeframe and soon war became inevitable. Thucydides suggests two major events that led to the breakdown of the peace treaty: those at Corcyra and Potidaea. As the Athenians turned their attentions away from mainland Greece and to the area around the Black Sea and the south of Italy, they took an interest in Corcyra, a Corinthian colony with a large fleet and important coastal position which they had to keep away from the Corinthians if they were to ensure their control of the sea. As Corinth and the Corcyrans came to blows over Epidamus, a Corcyran colony, Corcyra sought support from Athens and received some limited help from them. Athens also sought to force Potidaea, another Corinthian colony, to join the Delian League but this led to Corinth backing an anti-Athenian rebellion in the region. Another major factor for war came in 433/2 when the Athenians imposed extremely strict trade sanctions on pro-Spartan Megara and its citizens, which would have been economically crippling as well as politically humiliating. Sparta, persuaded by Corinth that the Athenians had broken the terms of the peace treaty, and in fear at the growing power of Athens, declared war. It can be argued that Athens may not have broken the letter of the law as found in the treaty, but broke the spirit of it. It is very likely that the treaty was simply not adequate for the complex situation between the many Greek states and so war inevitably returned.

War proper broke out in 431 and lasted, with a short period of relative peace from 421 to 414, until the defeat of Athens in 404. The long first ten years of the war, which lead to 421 and the peace treaty anticipated in Aristophanes' *Peace*, dragged on as the two sides were badly matched: Sparta and her allies were land powers, while Athens was a sea power with influence over a huge number of the islands in the Aegean. As a result, there was rarely the chance for anything that could be called a decisive victory. The Spartan king Archidamus initiated yearly invasions of Attica to entice the Athenians out to battle and to weaken them by disrupting their rural economy and food supply; the first ten years of the war are now referred to as the Archidamian War. The Athenian general and politician, Pericles, responded with a defensive strategy to avoid the otherwise inevitable defeat at the hands of a greater hoplite force. The Athenians in the countryside were forced to move into the Long Walls, which connected the city of Athens to its harbour, the Piraeus. Although this meant that the countryside of Attica was lost to the Spartans, the Athenians still had access to the sea and their empire.

When Pericles died in 429, to some extent this defensive policy died with him. Cleon, a popular demagogue who rose to power in the democracy as a fierce critic and rival of Pericles, gained huge influence in Athens and pursued a more offensive strategy. He kept control over the empire, quelling rebellions in Miletus and Lesbos with harsh punishments, sent generals to lead naval raids along the coast near Sparta and fortified key posts around the Peloponnese. It is worth noting at this point that the picture we receive of Cleon is a difficult one to interpret. Both Thucydides and Aristophanes seem to agree that he was a fierce warmonger and rabble-rouser who had excessive power over the democratic institutions of Athens. However, there may be reasons for Thucydides and Aristophanes to present him in this light. He supported the commercial or working class of Athens: he notably increased the pay for jurymen to ensure greater representation in the juries. This popular appeal is a clear target in satire and history written by conservatives. It is also possible that both authors held a grudge against him: Thucydides' exile from Athens may have been strongly supported by Cleon and Aristophanes may have been prosecuted by Cleon for his negative presentation of the Athenian empire, as discussed later in this introduction. There may be more social snobbery and personal enmity behind the presentation of Cleon than historical fact.

Nevertheless, it was the case that the state of Athens was as its most bellicose at this time. The conditions at home were terrible and a clear source of the discontent found in *Peace*. Although manufacturers of weapons and those in leadership roles had much to gain in terms of wealth and prestige, the majority of other citizens, particularly those who came from the countryside, suffered greatly. The farmers and agricultural workers lost their incomes as their homes and land were destroyed by the annual Spartan invasions. As Athens quickly used up its vast resources building ships, training soldiers and importing food, huge levies were put in place for wealthy citizens who then became embittered at their personal loss. The overcrowding of the city and land within the Long Walls, as well as the increased contact between the states of the empire, led to the outbreak of a devastating plague that may have killed up to half of the population. Furthermore, Athenian men could be called up at any time on expedition and as the population reduced through disease and military failure, men with insufficient training or expertise were sent as both basic soldiers and senior leaders.

The year 425 could be considered a turning point in the war. Demosthenes, an Athenian general, fortified Pylos, a peninsula on the coast of Messenia near Sparta. A threat so close to home alarmed the Spartans, who were quick to end their invasion of Attica and send a fleet to Pylos. Despite being greatly outnumbered, clever strategy on the part of the Athenians and some weaknesses on the Spartan side led to defeat for the Spartans and a group of some 300 hoplites becoming trapped on the nearby island of Sphacteria. These men were to be a fantastic bargaining chip for the Athenians and the threat to kill these men was certainly enough for Sparta to put an end to all invasions of Attica. The Spartans sent multiple embassies to Athens to seek peace terms but they were rejected each time. The Athenians took the opportunity to garrison Pylos and gave the territory to local Messenians to launch attacks against Sparta. Thucydides saw this as a sign of Athenian arrogance: his Spartan ambassadors made it clear that the Athenians were missing the best possible peace treaty and channelling their hopes into an uncertain outcome. Cleon was certainly an influential voice for the continuation of war.

Cleon's opposite number in Sparta was Brasidas. He was a distinguished solider and leader, having played an influential role in rescuing Methone from Athens in 431 and fought bravely at Pylos; he strongly supported the continuation of war. In 424, he led an army to support Perdiccas, king of Macedonia in the Chalcidic peninsula, where several cities were revolting against the Athenians. Perdiccas had been at odds with Athens since Athenian colonists founded Amphipolis on the River Strymon, which posed a threat to the stability of his own country. The city of Amphipolis, which controlled the crossing of the river, was a major producer of timber and ran several local silver mines. In a run of success in the area, Perdiccas and Brasidas took control of Amphipolis, which was a significant loss for the Athenians and a contributing factor to a one-year peace treaty established in 423. This was also a significant moment for our understanding of this time period as Thucydides was sent by the Athenians to save Amphipolis but arrived too late. He was exiled as punishment and as a result of this had access to information from both sides of the war, which allowed him to write his vital history of the period.

During this supposed peace, Brasidas was still making progress in the north of Greece. He took control of Skione and went on to attack Mende and Potidaea. In response, Cleon proposed death for all inhabitants of Skione and sent out troops. As soon as the year of peace finished, Cleon was quick to raise a large force to take back Amphipolis; however, he suffered a serious defeat at the hands of Brasidas. The defeat for Athens was of such enormity that peace was the only sensible response. Furthermore, both Brasidas and Cleon, the two men who had most ardently sought war, were both killed in the fighting. The Athenian general, Nicias, and Spartan king, Pleistoanax, were eager to make peace and the eventual treaty, known as the Peace of Nicias, was confirmed in the spring of 421. It was designed to last fifty years but it was troubled from the start. Negotiations were by no means simple: Athens still held the Spartan troops captured on Sphacteria and wanted the return of Plataea and Amphipolis, while Sparta continued to threaten Athens with invasions of Attica unless Megara's port was freed. The terms set out a return to the status quo of 431, but Amphipolis was never truly returned to the Athenians. The allies were not in agreement about peace: Corinth and Thebes, both Spartan allies, voted against the treaty. Meanwhile in Athens, Alcibiades, another popular politician, was trying to disrupt the peace by seeking connections with disillusioned Spartan allies, Corinth and Sparta.

Therefore, the Athenians who took their seats in the theatre to watch *Peace* in the spring of 421 would have been men who had been hugely affected by the last decade of war. Every member of the audience would have lost multiple relatives to both the plague and warfare. Many, particularly those who came from the countryside, would also have lost their homes and livelihoods. Anyone who had been to the Council or Assembly in recent months would have been aware of the loss of Cleon's fierce rhetoric for war, as well as the tense negotiations that were still ongoing and the fragile peace that they might create for the Greek states. It is under these circumstances that they came face to face with Trygaeus' solution to war and celebration of peace.

Aristophanes

The surviving plays of Aristophanes, the father of Old Comedy, demonstrate his skill for writing absurd fantasy, sharp satire, filthy jokes and all the song and dance you would expect at a festival. These elements of his plays are now considered the key traits of the earliest form of comedy. He was also the most popular comic playwright, as shown by the wealth of his work that has survived from antiquity: we have eleven of his plays as well as around thirty-two potential titles and nearly 1,000 short fragments which survive either on papyrus or as citations in the works of other authors. Such an impressive survival rate is due to demand for his work in antiquity: ancient scholars were quick to produce commentaries on the majority of his works and Quintilian, the Roman rhetorician of the first century AD, encouraged his readers to study Aristophanes' writing as a golden example of the grandeur of Attic Greek. By contrast, of the fifty or so other comic dramatists writing at the same time, no single complete play has survived.

However, it is very difficult to make many certain statements about the man behind the plays. Little information has survived about him other than what we have in his plays, the ancient summaries of them, known as hypotheses, and the ancient commentaries, referred to as scholia, that were written about the plays. As you might expect, caution is needed when dealing with this evidence. The *parabasis*, an extended speech by the chorus, in which the chorus seems to speak on behalf of the playwright, provides some information on his motive for writing and small personal details, such as his baldness. However, it is impossible to confirm whether we see a true picture of the playwright. The ancient scholars, known as scholiasts, who wrote summaries and commentaries on the plays were writing from a great distance, both temporally and geographically, and cannot be relied upon not to embroider the truth. We also have depictions of Aristophanes in literary texts, most notably the Aristophanes that appears as a character in Plato's *Symposium*, where he gives a brilliant speech on love and sexuality. However, his character here seems to be based more on his role as a comic poet than a representation of his genuine beliefs: the story he tells is a farcical allegory, much like the plots of his plays, and his drunken behaviour and hiccoughing are the telltale characteristics of a vulgar comic character.

Nevertheless, we can make a few relatively certain statements about the playwright. The scholia on the *Clouds* suggests he felt too young to produce a play in 427 BC, the year in which his first play *Banqueters* was produced, and so we can suppose that he was born in the middle of the fifth century, around 445–450. His father was a certain Philippus and his family must have been relatively affluent as he was taught to read and write to a very high level, as demonstrated by the remarkable versatility of his writing. He certainly had a keen interest in the workings of the democracy and its key players, and perhaps served as a councillor. He fathered three sons who continued in their father's footsteps by becoming comic playwrights and producers. The date of his death is uncertain but best placed in the 380s.

By contrast, we are able to say a good deal about Aristophanes' career, which got off to a very promising start: his first play was produced in 427 and received second prize at the City Dionysia festival. It only took another year before he was awarded the first prize at the City Dionysia for his *Babylonians*. It is recorded that his depiction of the subjects of the Athenian empire as Babylonian slaves in this play led to his prosecution by Cleon, which was potentially the source of Aristophanes' fiercely negative presentation of the politician in his plays. We also know that a man named Callistratos produced his first three plays and that producers were also employed for many of this later plays. It could perhaps be concluded that

Aristophanes preferred the role of playwright to the managerial one of organizing the actors, chorus and staging. He continued writing up to 388, the year in which his son Araros produced two of his plays: *Aiolosikon* and *Cocalus,* neither of which survive. During his very successful career, he was awarded first prize at least six times. *Frogs* was such a popular play that it was given the extraordinary honour of being re-performed in Athens. For our purposes here, it should be noted that by the time of the performance of *Peace* in 421, Aristophanes was a well-established and successful playwright: at least eight of his plays had already been produced, two of which had taken the top prize.

Performance context

When reading *Peace* it is important to bear in mind its performance context. Comic performances were staged in a competition that formed part of state religious festivals in honour of Dionysus. This meant they were not frequent but nevertheless held a central position in the Athenian calendar. Moreover, the plays were performed among symbolic civic and religious rituals, which must have influenced the way in which the audience responded to the drama, which was often highly critical of the state and its politicians. In the city there were two major festivals each year: the Great or City Dionysia at the end of March and the Lenaea, a smaller festival which took place in January and had a greater focus on comedy. There were also Rural Dionysia, which took place in December and gave the opportunity to those who lived in the countryside to hear some of the performances from the City Dionysia.

    Peace was performed at the City Dionysia. It is noteworthy that the religious rituals and celebrations of fertility, agriculture and merriment found in the play are found in the introductory events of the festival. It started with a procession, mainly of men carrying large wooden phalluses as symbols of fertility, to the precinct of Dionysus. A sacrifice was made to Dionysus and a celebration was held which included the dithyrambic competition in which choirs competed in dancing and singing hymns in honour of Dionysus. The majority of the festival, which lasted for several days, was given over to drama competitions. Three tragic trilogies were performed, each trilogy accompanied by the performance of a satyr play. Comedy was added to the festival in 486 and originally five comedies were performed; however, this went down to three during the war. It is unclear whether the comedies were performed on one day or divided between the trilogies. There were prizes for best tragedy and best comedy, which were awarded by the panel of ten judges, all selected by lot from a shortlist compiled by the Athenian Council. Winning poets were awarded a crown of ivy and paraded through the streets of Athens. There was fierce rivalry between poets and Aristophanes often ridicules his opponents in his writing. To take an example from *Peace*, the word for dung beetle could at first be confused for Cantharos, a comic playwright who had seen recent success and whom Aristophanes might have wanted to depict eating excrement.

    The performance of the play was introduced by a series of rituals: during the war years, the generals made libations in the theatre; the allies of the Athenians brought in their annual tribute and piled it up in the centre of the theatre; men who had greatly benefited the city were named and awarded honours; children orphaned by the wars were paraded into the theatre, given armour and promised support by the state. This was not only a festival in honour of the god of wine, fertility and theatre but also a presentation of Athens' democratic leaders and the might of the state Not only is the audience encouraged to admire the might of Athens but they are also encouraged to do their duty for the state as the state does its duty to the orphans and those who have given their time and wealth to Athens. However, to go from such civic rituals to watching the fantasy world of comedy in which politicians are harshly ridiculed, absurd solutions to current woes are depicted and lavatorial humour abounds must have had a strong effect on the audience. Through the license allowed to comic playwrights, the spectators are invited to step up as good citizens and to ponder the difficulties and ambiguities within the state.

It is also worth considering the size and demographic of the audience. The Theatre of Dionysus Eleuthereus had a capacity of 15,000–20,000 people. The audience would have mainly consisted of wealthy Athenian citizens along with senior magistrates of the democracy, such as archons and generals. The politician Pericles did introduce a fund to make a day at the theatre affordable for the poorest and to ensure more representation; for some this may have allowed a day off work but many of the poorest would still have been unable to attend. There is disagreement in the surviving sources as to the presence of women in the theatre, but it is possible and it is certainly the case that the priestess of Dionysus was present. There were a number of non-Athenians present as well: metics, who were resident aliens in Athens and worked as artisans or businessmen, as well as dignitaries of allied states, many of which were Ionian islands, who would have been encouraged to admire the might of Athens. In *Peace,* Trygaeus characterizes the audience as farmers, merchants, carpenters, craftsmen, immigrants, foreigners and islanders (296–8) and the slaves who open the play mimic an Ionian Greek in the audience (lines 45–9). This suggests that the audience was at least imagined to be more than just the wealthy city slickers of Athens: it represented the whole state and its empire.

Staging comedy

Actors were male and comedies were usually restricted to a cast of three, although there are several plays that required four. For *Peace,* there must have been three main actors for the major characters (Trygaeus, Slaves A and B, Hermes, Uproar, Arms-Merchant, Hierocles, Sickle-Maker), perhaps two additional actors from the chorus for small parts (Trygaeus' daughters, Boys) and several silent actors (Attendants, Opora and Theoria, Potter, Spear-Maker, Helmet-Maker). Actors wore masks that depicted their character in one, often grotesque, facial expression and a costume befitting their character. For many characters these must have made clear their identity long before they were named either by themselves or by another character. In *Peace,* Hermes provides a good example of a character who must have had an obvious costume and so does not need to be named in the script at his first appearance. All actors playing male characters would also have worn a large artificial penis and possibly padded suits that gave them fat bellies and large bottoms.

To recreate the first performance of *Peace* is very difficult, as the original copies of the play did not mark how the lines were divided by characters and provided no stage directions. The surviving manuscripts do indicate the speaker in places but these are based on the assumptions of the early scholiasts and critics. Even these later interpretations are sometimes difficult to follow as the scribes used a small symbol to indicate a change in speaker, not necessarily indicating the name of the character. Modern editors have established the speakers and stage directions presented in this commentary using the same methods as ancient commentators: what makes the best sense given the context and the restrictions of the theatre. It is interesting to think about this as you read the play and to consider how the lines could be attributed differently when there are two or three actors on stage and at which points actors could enter or leave the stage for varying effects.

When it comes to picturing the staging of the play, we have some notes from the scholiasts but mainly have to rely on interpretation of the text. Before discussing this in more detail, it is important to have a clear picture of the theatre of Dionysus in your mind. At the centre of the theatre was the orchestra, a circular space from which the rows of seating rose upwards around just over half of the circumference. At either side of the orchestra there were two sizeable entry passageways known as *parodoi* and at the back of the orchestra was the *skene*, which would have been a simple wooden building of two stories. The second storey could be reached by the actors from the back and the flat roof allowed them to appear before the audience at a height. It is unlikely that there was a high stage in front of the skene as both comedy and tragedy required freedom of movement between the actors and the chorus. The skene is likely to have had three doors: one larger central door and smaller doors on each side of this. There is also some evidence to suggest that movable sets were being used at this time to help set the scene. Two further devices were in use at the time of Aristophanes. The first was the crane, which was used to fly characters across the orchestra. The actors were suspended on a rope and the crane was most likely mounted onto the roof of the skene. The second was the *ekkyklema*, a platform which was fitted with scenery and then wheeled through the central doors of the skene.

The theatre came with several constraints that limited the possibilities for theatrical illusions. Firstly, the plays were performed during daylight and so characters simply stated if it was meant to be dark in the play. Secondly, as the skene represented the transition between inside and outside, all action that was seen by the audience and not hidden by the skene was assumed to be happening in an outside setting. For this reason, the vast majority of the drama had to be depicted as if it were happening in the open air. In *Peace*, for example, War has to come outside to make his paste out of the Greek cities, when it would have made better sense if he were to make it inside. Perhaps for the Athenians, who spent much of their time outside, this would not have seemed so unusual. Furthermore, as there were no curtains, stagehands would have been visible to the audience throughout. However, in the world of comedy, there was no need to hide the mechanics and limitations of the theatre. Characters often draw attention to the theatrical world in which they exist and break the fourth wall. For example, the slaves in the prologue speak about the audience and their understanding of the play so far (lines 43–61) and Trygaeus calls upon the crane operator to pay attention as he controls the beetle (line 174).

In the original performance of *Peace*, it is likely that all three doors on the skene were used. The central doors led into the cave where Peace was held prisoner and the side doors were used for the house of Trygaeus and the house of Zeus. The crane was used for the giant dung beetle, which must have been a real visual treat for the audience. When Trygaeus mounts the beetle and appears in the air at line 82, his flight takes him across the stage from one door to the other. Although Hermes pretends that Peace speaks in the play, she does not have any lines and a note in the scholia tells us she was a statue. In fact, Aristophanes' rivals mocked him for using a statue to play the main character in his comedy and it might be for this reason that he only won the second prize. Her rescue is likely to have been the chorus hauling the statue out of the central doors on the ekkyklema. Either the doors were already open and the chorus removed fake rocks from the platform to reveal the goddess or the doors of the skene were made to look rocky and were opened to reveal the statue. It is likely that the ekkyklema then remained on the stage throughout the rest of the play and Peace became a prominent image on the stage throughout the final episodes.

Another important element of comedy was the chorus, which provided singing, dancing and a collective voice to comment on the action of the play. The traditional chorus was made up of twenty-four male Athenian citizens who were not professional actors. They sang and danced to choral odes that were set to music. A leader commanded the chorus and took part in dialogue with the main actors. Although the character or size of a comic chorus was not entirely fixed within a play, the chorus of *Peace* stands out as rather fluid in its identity. The chorus in *Peace* arrives as *Panhellenes* (line 302), men from across the Greek states, and Trygaeus call on them as *Hellenes*, men of Greece as opposed to specifically Athenian men (line 292). However, the chorus sing of themselves in particularly Athenian terms by line 464, where they promise not to be fierce or badly tempered jurymen in the democracy when Peace has returned. When it comes to the final big pull to free Peace, however, they are Panhellenes again as the various groups of Greeks are accused of not putting their backs into it (lines 464–507). By line 508 all the members of the chorus appear to be farmers and peasants from the Athenian countryside. It appears to be the case that Aristophanes adapts the chorus to suit the drama on stage. As Trygaeus sets out for a truly panhellenic peace, the chorus help to demonstrate the struggle it is to get the Greek states to pull together; as Trygaeus celebrates the return of peace, the effect of this on the rural life of Athens becomes the key focus. The most important element of the chorus, which must not be forgotten as you read the text, is the rhythm, sound and movement they brought to the performance and the festival atmosphere they created.

The play

The play follows much the same structure as other early Aristophanic comedies: a free Athenian citizen, the hero of the play, focuses on a key problem in the state which can only be solved through comic and farcical means. The solution is achieved, a variety of scenes are presented to show the results of the change and then a celebration is held in honour of the hero. In *Peace*, Trygaeus represents, as is shown by his name and profession, an Athenian farmer who seeks peace to ensure a return to the old country life that existed before the war. Unusually, the aim of the hero is actually about to be met in the real world and *Peace* stands out from other comedies for presenting an outcome that is in fact achievable. However, the act of recovering peace in the play requires all the Greeks to, quite literally, pull together, which the chorus show to be an incredibly difficult task. The chances of the Athenian farmers being the driving force for panhellenic peace were not high. Furthermore, the peace that is celebrated in the play is presented as the peace of the Golden Age, as first depicted by Hesiod, in which men live a godlike and rustic existence of festivals and leisure, free from care and toil. This is, of course, far from the very tense and fragile peace that was possible in 421. Thus, although the play is closely connected to the contemporary reality – it is certainly more optimistic than any other comedy – it is still far from a simple celebration of the new Peace of Nicias.

Within the play, the obstacles to peace and the return of the rustic lifestyle are apparently insurmountable. At first Trygaeus, a mere mortal, has to get to heaven in order to call Zeus to account for the sufferings in Greece. His untrusty steed, a rather picky, demanding and foul-smelling dung beetle, only just gets Trygaeus to Zeus' home. Furthermore, the gods have moved as far away from mortals as possible and the personified god, War, has now taken control of mortal matters. Peace has also been trapped inside a deep cavern, piled over with rocks, and Zeus has vowed death and destruction to anyone who tries to save her. Not only are the obstacles to peace enormous but also the world in which the Greeks live is one abandoned by the gods. Other than Hermes, the traditional pantheon of gods are not seen and never return to their original home. In fact, Hierocles, the oracle-collector, is the only character to argue that the gods pay attention to mortal affairs, yet he is chased off the stage by Trygaeus for being a con artist. The situation for the Athenians and the Greeks as a whole is made to seem dire.

However, this godless world is as optimistic as it is pessimistic: in this world without gods it is the actions of mortals that matter and so if mortals can continue to create war without any action from the gods, they can surely stop it as well. The power of human action comes across strongly. Although war is presented in personified form, he is far from a god of the pantheon. In fact, he is quickly shown to represent the human condition: he intends to use mortals, Cleon and Brasidas, as the pestles that are to crush the Greek states. Furthermore, Hermes provides a remarkable speech on the origins of the war in which the key forces are entirely mortal. The selfishness and greediness of men are presented as the root of the Peloponnesian War: he presents Pericles as provoking war to avoid public scrutiny over a financial scandal; the subjects of Athens are presented as avaricious and treacherous men who use war to their advantage; demagogic politicians are attacked for manipulating poor Athenian farmers for their own political and financial benefit. Although it is a positive thought that human actions, not the gods, are what control the war, Hermes presents a damning attack on human nature and the selfishness that is in the way of the peace Trygaeus desperately wants. Given the civic rituals that surrounded the performance of the play, the audience must have done more than laugh. They are perhaps encouraged to question their role in the state and the stability of their democracy.

The festive joys of the second half of the play provide a vivid picture of all the good that will come to those who have in the past been manipulated to think that war is in their own interest. These depictions of joy present the strongest possible argument against the arguments that Aristophanes associated with Cleon. It is hard to get to the end of the play and think that anything other than peace is in the interests of a rural Athenian. Furthermore, the many obstacles that stand in Trygaeus' way swiftly vanish in the face of determination. Although revolting, the beetle does get Trygaeus to Zeus' house; although he is unpleasant at first, Hermes is quickly persuaded to join Trygaeus and the chorus; the chorus of Athenian farmers prove themselves to be strong enough to save Peace without divine intervention. The play provides a glorious representation of the power of human endeavour and suggests that the men of Athens can secure peace if they look out for their own collective interests rather than being manipulated by self-serving politicians. By human endeavour, Trygaeus turns slaves toiling with excrement and war feasting on Greek cities into peaceful leisure and a wedding feast.

Style

A range of techniques or devices which are common in Old Comedy are found in *Peace*. The following list provides some key features of the text set for examination.

- **Surrealism and allegorical imagery:** Aristophanes' imagination brings the abstract to life and confronts the audience with it in comic ways. The fantasy nature of the plot is seen from the opening when we find out that a giant dung beetle has been obtained so that the master can reach the gods. Trygaeus decides to fly on a beetle because it is the only creature in Aesop's fables that is able to fly up to the gods. Thus, there is some absurd logic to this choice of beetle: Trygaeus takes the fable to be true and so a giant beetle is found which he can ride on. Setting a scene at the house of Zeus and the other gods is also surreal and the comedy is heightened by the characterization of Hermes as a doorkeeper and slave of Zeus. The fact that the gods have moved with most of their belongings but have left behind a random selection of knick-knacks is also amusing. Further abstract ideas are taken by Aristophanes and made concrete in an entertaining fashion: Trygaeus' trip to heaven with meat, which he gives to Hermes, is an absurd depiction of a sacrifice; War mixing together a paste out of the Greek states is an extended culinary metaphor for war taking over and feeding on the Greeks.

- **Anticlimax:** as with other comedies, the conflict of the agon is quickly resolved and the dramatic tension of the plot is eased early in the play. *Peace* is unusual in that the speeches of the agon are not particularly antagonistic: there would certainly have been members of the audience who disagreed with the arguments given by Hermes, but Trygaeus and the chorus simply agree with him. Such swift resolution of a weighty topic is farcical and the lack of conflict here perhaps suggests how obvious the route of peace should be to the Athenians. Such early resolution also allows the play plenty of time to portray the festivity fitting for a comedy at a religious festival. The episodes that follow the main drama of the play allow for humour and jokes as well as a cheerful ending.

- **Paratragedy**: Aristophanes plays with tragedy in two ways: paratragedy and tragic parody. The first term refers to general parody of the style and conventions of tragedy. Aristophanes likes to contrast high tragic lines with lowly comic devices. Much vocabulary and diction is taken from the grand style of tragedy for comic effect: the words sound overblown when contrasted with the ridiculous situations in which they are used. For example, Trygaeus' pathetic outburst at the end of his flight on the beetle is tragic, but he instantly calls on the crane operator, breaking the fourth wall and returning to the world of comedy (lines 154–77). At line 235, the 'θυείας φθέγμα πολεμιστηρίας' ('the voice of the martial mortar') contains in it a stark contrast between the tragic φθέγμα and the purely comic πολεμιστηρίας.

- **Tragic parody**: the second way in which Aristophanes uses tragedy is his parody of specific plays. This can be subtle: we first hear Trygaeus shouting from inside as a slave on the outside worries about his madness, much like Medea and the Nurse in Euripides' *Medea*. His parody can also be much more substantial. The most extended use of a tragedy in *Peace* is found in the flight of the beetle which parodies Euripides' *Bellerophon*. This tragedy only survives in twenty-eight fragments and a few incomplete ancient summaries; however, it is likely that it presented the audience with the hero Bellerophon who has been reduced to a state of poverty. He decries the gods as undeserving of sacrifices from mortals and goes on to fly to heaven on Pegasus, the mythical flying horse, in order to confront the gods; however, he is thrown off during the flight and soon dies. As ever, the tragic hero learns an important lesson: humans may never understand the working of the gods, but must respect them. The parallels with the comic plot of *Peace* are clear. Although so little of the Euripides' play remains, there are certainly three verbal allusions to Euripides' script and there are several references to the beetle as Pegasus. Trygaeus' daughter even warns him not to slip off the beetle in case he should provide Euripides with a plot for one of his tragedies (lines 146–8). The parody itself is amusing and stops the mission of the hero from seeming too serious. There is also some drama here as it is not clear until he lands if Trygaeus will make it or become a second Bellerophon. This is also a form of generic one-upmanship: Comedy can reach the places that Tragedy cannot.

- **Other theatrical parody**: as well as tragedy, satyr plays – tragicomic burlesques that followed tragic trilogies – are also parodied. A common scene in satyr seems to have been the hauling of a cult object from obscurity. In Aeschylus' *Dictyulci*, for example, a chest in which Danae is trapped is dragged out of the sea by the chorus of satyrs. The similarities to the dragging of Peace from the cave are clear. As well as parody of different genres, there is also parody of the conventions of the theatre: the slaves at the start of the play address and mock the audience (lines 43–9, for example), while Trygaeus calls on the crane operator to make sure he doesn't fall off (line 174).

- **Poetic versatility and use of other genres:** Aristophanes was a very versatile and skilled poet and he plays with the meaning not only of words but also metre and genre. For example, he produces beautiful lines of choral lyrics (e.g. lines 775–96 and 797–818). When the two boys sing, he writes epic hexameters in the mouth of the first boy (lines 1270–97). The hexameters are martial poetry and are no longer appropriate in the world of peace, whereas the lyric lines provide an excellent vehicle for a joyful celebration of peace. To add humour he quotes Archilochus for the second boy (lines 1298–9), providing the opening lines of a famous elegiac poem about a man throwing away his shield. This provides a dig at the Athenian Cleonymus, who did just that in battle and is named as the father of the boy. There is also parody of a range of poetic genres beyond tragedy. For example, the hero of the comedy is very much a mock epic hero: his great adventure and cunning plans are a comic reworking of Homer's *Odyssey*.

- **Innovation:** Aristophanes was an innovator with language, genre and theatrical conventions. There are many coinages of his own that are designed to amuse, such as ἱπποκάνθαρος (line 181) to describe the beetle as a new Pegasus and πολλοδεκάκις (line 243), which helps to bring out the excessively aggressive nature of War.

- **Political and topical satire:** as the chorus says in the first *parabasis*, Aristophanes uses comedy to leave the average citizen alone and 'attack the monsters' (lines 752–3). He brings real issues facing the Athenians to life in a farcical manner and while doing so is able to lampoon key figures of the day. Aristophanes' satirical style must have put many noses out of joint and one particular enmity can be found in both his plays and the accompanying scholia: the *Babylonians,* which was produced at the City Dionysia of 426, led to a prosecution of Aristophanes by Cleon. Although the play does not survive, it seems to have attacked the magistrates of the democracy and Cleon felt it embarrassed the state of Athens in front of the foreign guests present at the performance. Although there is no evidence that the case was successful, there is plenty for Aristophanes' resulting anger: Cleon is most unflatteringly caricatured in *Knights* of 424 and *Wasps* of 422. Savage derision of Cleon is also found in *Peace*, a year after the politician's death. In fact, there is more abuse directed at Cleon in *Peace* than at any other contemporary politician. He is depicted as a warmonger and demagogue: at the beginning of the play, the slaves suggest an audience member will think the beetle is an allusion to Cleon eating shit in the underworld (lines 45–8); he is a potential pestle for smashing the Greek states together (line 270); he is also Cerberus in the underworld (line 313). This comparison to the guard dog of the Underworld is surely mocking his claim to be the watchdog of the people of Athens, and the blustering bark of the dog refers to his rabble-rousing style in the Assembly. Lamachus, an Athenian general, is also presented disparagingly as a lover of war and it is his son at the end of the play who can only recite military verses (line 1290).

- **Teasing and abuse:** although the most stinging attacks are aimed at political figures, there is plenty of abuse hurled at contemporary celebrities, Athenian officials and others. In *Peace*, the audience comes in for some abuse when the slave mockingly describes the different statuses of the audience members (lines 50–3). There is also the opportunity to mock foreigners as the slaves mimic an Ionian (lines 45–9), Hermes plays a Spartan (lines 212–14) and Trygaeus recalls a song sung by Datis the Mede in terrible Greek (lines 289–91). Furthermore, there is Hierocles, a real collector of oracles, who most likely opposed peace in Athens and thus made himself a prime target for abuse.

- **Sexual and scatological jokes:** bawdy humour is found throughout comedy and helps to create a relaxed, festive atmosphere. Scatological humour is frequent: the opening scene builds to an irreverent pun on a cultic title of Zeus (line 42), translated masterfully by Sommerstein as 'Lord of the Thunder-Crap'; Trygaeus nearly loses control of his bowels on the beetle (lines 175–6); the chorus fart with carefree joy (line 335); Trygaeus turns a breastplate into a potty (lines 1224–39). Sexual jokes are also frequent, such as the presentation of Datis as a sexually frustrated slave masturbating during his afternoon rest (lines 289–91).

Speaking, chanting and singing

It is important not to forget the rhythm and musicality of *Peace* as you read it. The actors mostly spoke their lines but also chanted and sang a few. Iambic trimeter is the metre commonly used for spoken lines. It is made up of three iambic metra, each of which is made up of two, two-syllable feet. In a basic iambic metron, the first syllable can be either long or short (represented by ×), the second and fourth are long (represented by –) and the third is short (represented by ∪). This provides the fundamental structure:

× – ∪ – × – ∪ – × – ∪ –

This simple form of the metre could easily become rather tedious, so the poet had various ways in which these metra could be varied: a long syllable could be replaced by two short syllables (∪∪) and an anapaest (∪∪ –) could be used in place of any foot but the last. The many variations available here mean that iambic trimeter can closely create the sounds and rhythms of natural, conversational speech. The vast majority of the text set for examination in Greek is written in this meter.

The chorus sang or chanted many lines, which are written in a wide variety of Greek metres and designed to be accompanied by music and dance moves. Within the text set for examination, the chorus enters to free Peace at line 299 with lines of trochaic tetrameters, the basic form of which is:

– ∪ – × – ∪ – × – ∪ – × – ∪ – ×

As with the iambic trimeter above, the author can vary this basic form to avoid monotony. Trochaic tetrameters are often used to create a real sense of speed and thus excitement. At line 299 this is particularly fitting and the sense of speed is further emphasized by the fact the metre shifts suddenly in the middle of a sentence. Other metres also bring with them a particular feeling or meaning. Dactylic hexameter, the metre of Homer's epics, brings with it a sense of military achievement. It is seen towards the end of the play when the two boys are rehearsing to sing at the wedding but are unable to sing anything other than militaristic epic lines. A complete lack of metre, for example the extra-metrical shouting in line 60, also provides important variation and highlights key moments in the plot.

Sommerstein's commentary, found in the further reading listed below, is particularly useful in highlighting the changes in metre during the play.

Questions

The following questions are designed help to develop discussions on individual scenes as well as the whole play.

For individual scenes:

- What scenery might be visible at this time?
- What costumes would we expect for each character? What props do characters carry and how do they use them for comic effect?
- What demands are being made on the actors and the theatre?
- What is the significance of the name of each character? How is each character presented? Do they live up to their name?
- What makes a scene funny? What is the balance between satire, physical comedy and coarse, scatological humour?

For the play as a whole:

- What knowledge does the play demand of its audience? What can we learn about the audience from the play?
- Does this play have any meaning for Athenians who do not live in the countryside?
- How seriously do you think Aristophanes mocks individuals? How seriously do you think he mocks Athenian citizens as a body?
- Does the play present peace as a comic impossibility or an achievable situation? Do you think the audience would consider Trygaeus to be mad as the slaves do at the start? Are the celebrations at the end justified?
- What is the relationship between tragedy and comedy? What use of tragedy does comedy make? What use of other genres does Aristophanes make?

- What picture of the Athenian democracy does Aristophanes present?
- In what ways, if any, can this comedy be considered serious?
- To what extent is the play a window onto the realities of Athenian politics? Can the play be read as a historical source?

Further reading

This brief bibliography provides the two most useful commentaries, on which this introduction and commentary heavily rely, as well as good translations of *Peace* and other comedies. There are also some suggestions for accessible secondary reading on Aristophanes, Greek comedy, *Peace* and the Peloponnesian Wars.

Primary reading

Olson, S.D. *Aristophanes: Peace* (Oxford: OUP, 1998).
Sommerstein, A.H. *Aristophanes: Peace* (Oxford: Aris & Phillips, 2005).
Barrett, D. (ed.) *Aristophanes: The Birds and Other Plays* (London: Penguin Books, 2003).

Secondary reading

Bowie, A.M. *Aristophanes: Myth, Ritual and Comedy* (Cambridge: CUP, 1993).
de Ste Croix, G.E.M. *The Origins of the Peloponnesian War* (London: Bloomsbury, 1972).
Dover, K.J. *Aristophanic Comedy* (London: B.T. Batsford Ltd., 1972).
Goldhill, S. 'The Great Dionysia and Civic Ideology', in J. Winkler and F. Zeitlin (eds.), *Nothing to Do with Dionysus* (Princeton, NJ: Princeton University Press, 1990).
Kagan, D. *The Archidamian War* (Ithaca: Cornell University Press, 1990).
MacDowell, D.M. *Aristophanes and Athens: An Introduction to the Plays* (Oxford: OUP, 1995).
Newiger, H. 'War and Peace in the Comedy of Aristophanes', in E. Segal (ed.), *Oxford Readings in Aristophanes* (Oxford: OUP, 1996).
Rhodes, P.J. *A History of the Classical Greek World* (Oxford: Blackwell Publishing, 2006).
Silk, M.S. *Aristophanes and the Definition of Comedy* (Oxford: OUP, 2000).

Text

Οἰκέτης Α
    αἶϱ᾽ αἶϱε μᾶζαν ὡς τάχος τῷ κανθάϱῳ.

Οἰκέτης Β
    ἰδού. δὸς αὐτῷ, τῷ κάκιστ᾽ ἀπολουμένῳ·
    καὶ μήποτ᾽ αὐτῆς μᾶζαν ἡδίω φάγοι.

Οἰ. Α   δὸς μᾶζαν ἑτέϱαν, ἐξ ὀνίδων πεπλασμένην.

Οἰ. Β   ἰδοὺ μάλ᾽ αὖθις. ποῦ γὰϱ ἦν νῦν δὴ ᾽φεϱες;   5
    ἢ κατέφαγεν;

Οἰ. Α   μὰ τὸν Δί᾽, ἀλλ᾽ ἐξαϱπάσας
    ὅλην ἐνέκαψε πεϱικυλίσας τοῖν ποδοῖν.
    ἀλλ᾽ ὡς τάχιστα τϱῖβε πολλὰς καὶ πυκνάς.

Οἰ. Β   ἄνδϱες κοπϱολόγοι, πϱοσλάβεσθε πϱὸς θεῶν,
    εἰ μή με βούλεσθ᾽ ἀποπνιγέντα πεϱιδεῖν.   10

Lines 11–12: Slave A demands a cake made from the excrement of a young male prostitute and makes a crude joke. More information on these lines can be found in the commentary.

Οἰ. Β   ἑνὸς μέν, ὦνδϱες, ἀπολελύσθαι μοι δοκῶ·
    οὐδεὶς γὰϱ ἂν φαίη με μάττοντ᾽ ἐσθίειν.

Οἰ. Α   αἰβοῖ, φέϱ᾽ ἄλλην χἀτέϱαν μοι χἀτέϱαν,   15
    καὶ τϱῖβ᾽ <ἔθ᾽> ἑτέϱας.

Οἰ. Β   μὰ τὸν Ἀπόλλω ᾽γὼ μὲν οὔ
   οὐ γὰρ ἔθ᾽ οἷός τ᾽ εἴμ᾽ ὑπερέχειν τῆς ἀντλίας.

Οἰ. Α   αὐτὴν ἄρ᾽ οἴσω συλλαβὼν τὴν ἀντλίαν.

Οἰ. Β   νὴ τὸν Δί᾽ ἐς κόρακάς γε, καὶ σαυτόν γε πρός.
   ὑμῶν δέ γ᾽ εἴ τις οἶδέ μοι κατειπάτω   20
   πόθεν ἂν πριαίμην ῥῖνα μὴ τετρημένην.
   οὐδὲν γὰρ ἔργον ἦν ἄρ᾽ ἀθλιώτερον
   ἢ κανθάρῳ μάττοντα παρέχειν ἐσθίειν.
   ὗς μὲν γάρ, ὥσπερ ἂν χέσῃ τις, ἢ κύων
   φαύλως ἐρείδει· τοῦτο δ᾽ ὑπὸ φρονήματος   25
   βρενθύεταί τε καὶ φαγεῖν οὐκ ἀξιοῖ,
   ἢν μὴ παραθῶ τρίψας δι᾽ ἡμέρας ὅλης
   ὥσπερ γυναικὶ γογγύλην μεμαγμένην.
   ἀλλ᾽ εἰ πέπαυται τῆς ἐδωδῆς σκέψομαι
   τῃδὶ παροίξας τῆς θύρας, ἵνα μή μ᾽ ἴδῃ.   30
   ἔρειδε, μὴ παύσαιο μηδέποτ᾽ ἐσθίων
   τέως ἕως σαυτὸν λάθῃς διαρραγείς.
   οἷον δὲ κύψας ὁ κατάρατος ἐσθίει,
   ὥσπερ παλαιστής, παραβαλὼν τοὺς γομφίους,
   καὶ ταῦτα τὴν κεφαλήν τε καὶ τὼ χεῖρέ πως   35
   ὡδὶ περιάγων, ὥσπερ οἱ τὰ σχοινία
   τὰ παχέα συμβάλλοντες εἰς τὰς ὁλκάδας.

Οἰ. Α   μιαρὸν τὸ χρῆμα καὶ κάκοσμον καὶ βορόν·
   χὤτου ποτ᾽ ἐστὶ δαιμόνων ἡ προσβολὴ
   οὐκ οἶδ᾽. Ἀφροδίτης μὲν γὰρ οὔ μοι φαίνεται,   40
   οὐ μὴν Χαρίτων γε.

Οἰ. Β   τοῦ γάρ ἐστ᾽;

Οἰ. Α   οὐκ ἔσθ᾽ ὅπως
   οὐκ ἔστι τὸ τέρας τοῦ Διὸς σκαταιβάτου.

Οἰ. Β   οὐκοῦν ἂν ἤδη τῶν θεατῶν τις λέγοι
   νεανίας δοκησίσοφος, ᾽τόδε πρᾶγμα τί;
   ὁ κάνθαρος δὲ πρὸς τί᾽;

Οἰ. Α   κᾆτ᾽ αὐτῷ γ᾽ ἀνὴρ   45
   Ἰωνικός τίς φησι παρακαθήμενος·

'δοκέω μέν, ἐς Κλέωνα τοῦτ' αἰνίσσεται,
ὡς κεῖνος ἐν Ἀΐδεω σπατίλην ἐσθίει.'
ἀλλ' εἰσιὼν τῷ κανθάρῳ δώσω πιεῖν.

Οἰ. Β ἐγὼ δὲ τὸν λόγον γε τοῖσι παιδίοις   50
   καὶ τοῖσιν ἀνδρίοισι καὶ τοῖς ἀνδράσι
   καὶ τοῖς ὑπερτάτοισιν ἀνδράσιν φράσω
   καὶ τοῖς ὑπερηνορέουσιν ἔτι τούτοις μάλα.
   ὁ δεσπότης μου μαίνεται καινὸν τρόπον,
   οὐχ ὅνπερ ὑμεῖς, ἀλλ' ἕτερον καινὸν πάνυ.   55
   δι' ἡμέρας γὰρ εἰς τὸν οὐρανὸν βλέπων
   ὡδὶ κεχηνὼς λοιδορεῖται τῷ Διὶ
   καί φησιν, 'ὦ Ζεῦ, τί ποτε βουλεύει ποιεῖν;
   κατάθου τὸ κόρημα· μὴ 'κκόρει τὴν Ἑλλάδα.'
   ἔα ἔα·   60
   σιγήσαθ', ὡς φωνῆς ἀκούειν μοι δοκῶ.

*Lines 62–179: The Slave reveals the purpose of the dung beetle and soon Trygaeus
appears flying on the back of it. His daughters come out to stop him from going on
his mission; he does not listen but sets out like Euripides' Bellerophon. The beetle
is easily distracted by food below and so the journey is rough, but Trygaeus finally
makes it to the home of Zeus. For a more detailed summary of these lines, see the
commentary.*

Ἑρμῆς
   πόθεν βροτοῦ με προσέβαλ' – ; ὦναξ Ἡράκλεις,   180
   τουτὶ τί ἐστι τὸ κακόν;

Τρυγαῖος
       ἱπποκάνθαρος.

Ἑρ. ὦ μιαρὲ καὶ τόλμηρε κἀναίσχυντε σὺ
   καὶ μιαρὲ καὶ παμμίαρε καὶ μιαρώτατε,
   πῶς δεῦρ' ἀνῆλθες, ὦ μιαρῶν μιαρώτατε;
   τί σοί ποτ' ἔστ' ὄνομ'; οὐκ ἐρεῖς;

Τρ.   μιαρώτατος.   185

Ἑρ. πατὴρ δέ σοι τίς ἐστιν;

Τρ.   ἐμοί; μιαρώτατος.   187

Ἑρ.   ποδαπὸς τὸ γένος δ᾽ εἶ; φράζε μοι.

Τρ.   μιαρώτατος.   186

Ἑρ.   οὔτοι μὰ τὴν γῆν ἔσθ᾽ ὅπως οὐκ ἀποθανεῖ,
        εἰ μὴ κατερεῖς μοι τοὔνομ᾽ ὅ τι ποτ᾽ ἐστί σοι.

Τρ.   Τρυγαῖος Ἀθμονεύς, ἀμπελουργὸς δεξιός,   190
        οὐ συκοφάντης οὐδ᾽ ἐραστὴς πραγμάτων.

Ἑρ.   ἥκεις δὲ κατὰ τί;

Τρ.   τὰ κρέα ταυτί σοι φέρων.

Ἑρ.   ὦ δειλακρίων, πῶς ἦλθες;

Τρ.   ὦ γλίσχρων, ὁρᾷς
        ὡς οὐκέτ᾽ εἶναί σοι δοκῶ μιαρώτατος;
        ἴθι νυν κάλεσόν μοι τὸν Δί᾽.

Ἑρ.   ἰὴ ἰὴ ἰὴ,   195
        ὅτ᾽ οὐδὲ μέλλεις ἐγγὺς εἶναι τῶν θεῶν·
        φροῦδοι γάρ· ἐχθές εἰσιν ἐξῳκισμένοι.

Τρ.   ποῖ γῆς;

Ἑρ.   ἰδοὺ γῆς.

Τρ.   ἀλλὰ ποῖ;

Ἑρ.   πόρρω πάνυ,
        ὑπ᾽ αὐτὸν ἀτεχνῶς τοὐρανοῦ τὸν κύτταρον.

Τρ.   πῶς οὖν σὺ δῆτ᾽ ἐνταῦθα κατελείφθης μόνος;   200

Ἑρ.   τὰ λοιπὰ τηρῶ σκευάρια τὰ τῶν θεῶν,
        χυτρίδια καὶ σανίδια κἀμφορείδια.

Τρ.   ἐξῳκίσαντο δ᾽ οἱ θεοὶ τίνος οὕνεκα;

Ἑρ.   Ἕλλησιν ὀργισθέντες. εἶτ᾽ ἐνταῦθα μέν,
      ἵν᾽ ἦσαν αὐτοί, τὸν Πόλεμον κατῴκισαν,   205
      ὑμᾶς παραδόντες δρᾶν ἀτεχνῶς ὅ τι βούλεται·
      αὐτοὶ δ᾽ ἀνῳκίσανθ᾽ ὅπως ἀνωτάτω,
      ἵνα μὴ βλέποιεν μαχομένους ὑμᾶς ἔτι
      μηδ᾽ ἀντιβολούντων μηδὲν αἰσθανοίατο.

Τρ.   τοῦ δ᾽ οὕνεχ᾽ ἡμᾶς ταῦτ᾽ ἔδρασαν; εἰπέ μοι.   210

Ἑρ.   ὅτιὴ πολεμεῖν ᾑρεῖσθ᾽, ἐκείνων πολλάκις
      σπονδὰς ποιούντων· κεἰ μὲν οἱ Λακωνικοὶ
      ὑπερβάλοιντο μικρόν, ἔλεγον ἂν ταδί·
      'ναὶ τὼ σιὼ νῦν Ὠττικίων δωσεῖ δίκαν.'
      εἰ δ᾽ αὖ τι πράξαιτ᾽ ἀγαθόν, Ἀττικωνικοί,   215
      κἄλθοιεν οἱ Λάκωνες εἰρήνης πέρι,
      ἐλέγετ᾽ ἂν ὑμεῖς εὐθύς· 'ἐξαπατώμεθα
      νὴ τὴν Ἀθηνᾶν'. – 'νὴ Δί᾽, οὐχὶ πειστέον.
      ἥξουσι καὖθις, ἢν ἔχωμεν τὴν Πύλον.'

Τρ.   ὁ γοῦν χαρακτὴρ ἡμεδαπὸς τῶν ῥημάτων.   220

Ἑρ.   ὧν οὕνεκ᾽ οὐκ οἶδ᾽ εἴ ποτ᾽ Εἰρήνην ἔτι
      τὸ λοιπὸν ὄψεσθ᾽.

Τρ.   ἀλλὰ ποῖ γὰρ οἴχεται;

Ἑρ.   ὁ Πόλεμος αὐτὴν ἐνέβαλ᾽ εἰς ἄντρον βαθύ.

Τρ.   εἰς ποῖον;

Ἑρ.   εἰς τουτὶ τὸ κάτω, κἄπειθ᾽ ὁρᾷς

      ὅσους ἄνωθεν ἐπεφόρησε τῶν λίθων,   225
      ἵνα μὴ λάβητε μηδέποτ᾽ αὐτήν.

Τρ.   εἰπέ μοι,
      ἡμᾶς δὲ δὴ τί δρᾶν παρασκευάζεται;

Ἑρ.   οὐκ οἶδα πλὴν ἕν, ὅτι θυείαν ἑσπέρας
      ὑπερφυᾶ τὸ μέγεθος εἰσηνέγκατο.

Τρ.   τί δῆτα ταύτῃ τῇ θυείᾳ χρήσεται;   230

Ἑρ.　τρίβειν ἐν αὐτῇ τὰς πόλεις βουλεύεται.
　　　ἀλλ᾽ εἶμι· καὶ γὰρ ἐξιέναι, γνώμην ἐμήν,
　　　μέλλει· θορυβεῖ γοῦν ἔνδοθεν.

Τρ.　　　　　　　　　　　　　　　οἴμοι δείλαιος.
　　　φέρ᾽ αὐτὸν ἀποδρῶ· καὶ γὰρ ὥσπερ ᾐσθόμην
　　　καὐτὸς θυείας φθέγμα πολεμιστηρίας.　　　　　　235

Πόλεμος
　　　ἰὼ βροτοὶ βροτοὶ βροτοὶ πολυτλήμονες,
　　　ὡς αὐτίκα μάλα τὰς γνάθους ἀλγήσετε.

Τρ.　ὦναξ Ἄπολλον, τῆς θυείας τοῦ πλάτους –
　　　ὅσον κακόν – καὶ τοῦ Πολέμου τοῦ βλέμματος.
　　　ἆρ᾽ οὗτός ἐστ᾽ ἐκεῖνος ὃν καὶ φεύγομεν,　　　　240
　　　ὁ δεινός, ὁ ταλαύρινος, ὁ κατὰ τοῖν σκελοῖν;

Πό.　ἰὼ Πρασιαὶ τρὶς ἄθλιαι καὶ πεντάκις
　　　καὶ πολλοδεκάκις, ὡς ἀπολεῖσθε τήμερον.

Τρ.　τουτὶ μέν, ἄνδρες, οὐδὲν ἡμῖν πρᾶγμά πω·
　　　τὸ γὰρ κακὸν τοῦτ᾽ ἐστὶ τῆς Λακωνικῆς.　　　　245

Πό.　ὦ Μέγαρα Μέγαρ᾽, ὡς ἐπιτετρίψεσθ᾽ αὐτίκα
　　　ἁπαξάπαντα καταμεμυττωτευμένα.

Τρ.　βαβαὶ βαβαιάξ, ὡς μεγάλα καὶ δριμέα
　　　τοῖσιν Μεγαρεῦσιν ἐνέβαλεν τὰ κλαύματα.

Πό.　ἰὼ Σικελία, καὶ σὺ δ᾽ ὡς ἀπόλλυσαι.　　　　　250

Τρ.　οἵα πόλις τάλαινα διακναισθήσεται.

Πό.　φέρ᾽ ἐπιχέω καὶ τὸ μέλι τουτὶ τἀττικόν.

Τρ.　οὗτος, παραινῶ σοι μέλιτι χρῆσθαι 'τέρῳ.
　　　τετρώβολον τοῦτ᾽ ἐστί· φείδου τἀττικοῦ.

Πό.　παῖ παῖ Κυδοιμέ.

Κύδοιμος
　　　　　　τί με καλεῖς;

Πό.   κλαύσει μακρά.   255
ἕστηκας ἀργός; οὑτοσί σοι κόνδυλος.

Τρ.   ὡς δριμύς.

Κύ.   οἴμοι μοι τάλας, ὦ δέσποτα.

Τρ.   μῶν τῶν σκορόδων ἐνέβαλες εἰς τὸν κόνδυλον;

Πό.   οἴσεις ἀλετρίβανον τρέχων;

Κύ.   ἀλλ᾿, ὦ μέλε,
οὐκ ἔστιν ἡμῖν· ἐχθὲς εἰσῳκίσμεθα.   260

Πό.   οὔκουν παρ᾿ Ἀθηναίων μεταθρέξει ταχὺ <πάνυ>;

Κύ.   ἔγωγε νὴ Δί᾿· εἰ δὲ μή γε, κλαύσομαι.

Τρ.   ἄγε δή, τί δρῶμεν, ὦ πόνηρ᾿ ἀνθρώπια;
ὁρᾶτε τὸν κίνδυνον ἡμῖν ὡς μέγας·
εἴπερ γὰρ ἥξει τὸν ἀλετρίβανον φέρων,   265
τούτῳ ταράξει τὰς πόλεις καθήμενος.
ἀλλ᾿, ὦ Διόνυσ᾿, ἀπόλοιτο καὶ μὴ ᾿λθοι φέρων.

Κύ.   οὗτος.

Πό.   τί ἐστιν; οὐ φέρεις;

Κύ.   τὸ δεῖνα γὰρ,
ἀπόλωλ᾿ Ἀθηναίοισιν ἀλετρίβανος,
ὁ βυρσοπώλης, ὃς ἐκύκα τὴν Ἑλλάδα.   270

Τρ.   εὖ γ᾿, ὦ πότνια δέσποιν᾿ Ἀθηναία, ποιῶν
ἀπόλωλ᾿ ἐκεῖνος κἂν δέοντι τῇ πόλει.
ἢ πρίν γε τὸν μυττωτὸν ἡμῖν ἐγχέαι.

Πό.   οὔκουν ἕτερον δῆτ᾿ ἐκ Λακεδαίμονος μέτει
ἀνύσας τι;

Κύ.   ταῦτ᾿, ὦ δέσποθ᾿.

Πό.   ἥκέ νυν ταχύ.   275

Τϱ. ὦνδϱες, τι πεισόμεσθα; νῦν ἀγὼν μέγας.
     ἀλλ᾿ εἴ τις ὑμῶν ἐν Σαμοθϱάκῃ τυγχάνει
     μεμυημένος, νῦν ἐστιν εὔξασθαι καλὸν
     ἀποστϱαφῆναι τοῦ μετιόντος τὼ πόδε.

Κύ. οἴμοι τάλας, οἴμοι γε κᾷτ᾿ οἴμοι μάλα.   280

Πό. τί ἐστι; μῶν οὐκ αὖ φέϱεις;

Κύ.   ἀπόλωλε γὰϱ
     καὶ τοῖς Λακεδαιμονίοισιν ἀλετϱίβανος.

Πό. πῶς, ὦ πανοῦϱγ᾿;

Κύ.   εἰς τἀπὶ Θϱάκης χωϱία
     χϱήσαντες ἑτέϱοις αὐτὸν εἶτ᾿ ἀπώλεσαν.

Τϱ. εὖ γ᾿ εὖ γε ποιήσαντες, ὦ Διοσκόϱω.   285
     ἴσως ἂν εὖ γένοιτο· θαϱϱεῖτ᾿, ὦ βϱοτοί.

Πό. ἀπόφεϱε τὰ σκεύη λαβὼν ταυτὶ πάλιν·
     ἐγὼ δὲ δοίδυκ᾿ εἰσιὼν ποιήσομαι.

Τϱ. νῦν τοῦτ᾿ ἐκεῖν᾿· ἥκει τὸ Δάτιδος μέλος,
     ὃ δεφόμενός ποτ᾿ ᾖδε τῆς μεσημβϱίας,   290
     ‘ὡς ἥδομαι καὶ χαίϱομαι κεὐφϱαίνομαι.’
     νῦν ἐστιν ὑμῖν, ὦνδϱες Ἕλληνες, καλὸν
     ἀπαλλαγεῖσι πϱαγμάτων τε καὶ μαχῶν
     ἐξελκύσαι τὴν πᾶσιν Εἰϱήνην φίλην,
     πϱὶν ἕτεϱον αὖ δοίδυκα κωλῦσαί τινα.   295
     ἀλλ᾿, ὦ γεωϱγοὶ κἄμποϱοι καὶ τέκτονες
     καὶ δημιουϱγοὶ καὶ μέτοικοι καὶ ξένοι
     καὶ νησιῶται, δεῦϱ᾿ ἴτ᾿, ὦ πάντες λεῴ,
     ὡς τάχιστ᾿ ἅμας λαβόντες καὶ μοχλοὺς καὶ σχοινία·
     νῦν γὰϱ ἡμῖν αὖ σπάσαι πάϱεστιν ἀγαθοῦ δαίμονος.   300

Χοϱός
     δεῦϱο πᾶς χώϱει πϱοθύμως εὐθὺ τῆς σωτηϱίας.
     ὦ Πανέλληνες, βοηθήσωμεν, εἴπεϱ πώποτε,
     τάξεων ἀπαλλαγέντες καὶ κακῶν φοινικίδων·
     ἡμέϱα γὰϱ ἐξέλαμψεν ἥδε μισολάμαχος.
     πϱὸς τάδ᾿ ἡμῖν, εἴ τι χϱὴ δϱᾶν, φϱάζε κἀϱχιτεκτόνει·   305

οὐ γὰρ ἔσθ᾽ ὅπως ἀπειπεῖν ἂν δοκῶ μοι τήμερον,
πρὶν μοχλοῖς καὶ μηχαναῖσιν εἰς τὸ φῶς ἀνελκύσαι
τὴν θεῶν πασῶν μεγίστην καὶ φιλαμπελωτάτην.

Τρ. οὐ σιωπήσεσθ᾽, ὅπως μὴ περιχαρεῖς τῷ πράγματι
τὸν Πόλεμον ἐκζωπυρήσετ᾽ ἔνδοθεν κεκραγότες; 310

Χο. ἀλλ᾽ ἀκούσαντες τοιούτου χαίρομεν κηρύγματος.
οὐ γὰρ ἦν ἔχοντας ἥκειν σιτί᾽ ἡμερῶν τριῶν.

Τρ. εὐλαβεῖσθέ νυν ἐκεῖνον τὸν κάτωθεν Κέρβερον,
μὴ παφλάζων καὶ κεκραγώς, ὥσπερ ἡνίκ᾽ ἐνθάδ᾽ ἦν,
ἐμποδὼν ἡμῖν γένηται τὴν θεὸν μὴ ᾽ξελκύσαι. 315

Χο. οὔτι νῦν γ᾽ ἔτ᾽ ἔστιν αὐτὴν ὅστις ἐξαιρήσεται,
ἣν ἅπαξ εἰς χεῖρας ἔλθῃ τὰς ἐμάς. ἰοὶ ἰοί.

Τρ. ἐξολεῖτέ μ᾽, ὦνδρες, εἰ μὴ τῆς βοῆς ἀνήσετε·
ἐκδραμὼν γὰρ πάντα ταυτὶ συνταράξει τοῖν ποδοῖν.

Χο. † ὡς κυκάτω καὶ πατείτω πάντα καὶ ταραττέτω, 320
οὐ γὰρ ἂν χαίροντες ἡμεῖς τήμερον παυσαίμεθ᾽ ἄν.

Τρ. τί τὸ κακόν; τί πάσχετ᾽, ὦνδρες; μηδαμῶς πρὸς τῶν θεῶν,
πρᾶγμα κάλλιστον διαφθείρητε διὰ τὰ σχήματα.

Χο. ἀλλ᾽ ἔγωγ᾽ οὐ σχηματίζειν βούλομ᾽, ἀλλ᾽ ὑφ᾽ ἡδονῆς
οὐκ ἐμοῦ κινοῦντος αὐτὼ τὼ σκέλει χορεύετον. 325

Τρ. μή τί μοι νυνί γ᾽ ἔτ᾽, ἀλλὰ παῦε παῦ᾽ ὀρχούμενος.

Χο. ἢν ἰδού· καὶ δὴ πέπαυμαι.

Τρ.   φής γε, παύει δ᾽ οὐδέπω.

Χο. ἓν μὲν οὖν τουτί μ᾽ ἔασον ἑλκύσαι, καὶ μηκέτι.

Τρ. τοῦτό νυν, καὶ μηκέτ᾽ ἄλλο· μηδὲν ὀρχήσησθ᾽ ἔτι.

Χο. οὐκ ἂν ὀρχησαίμεθ᾽, εἴπερ ὠφελήσομέν τί σε. 330

Τρ. ἀλλ᾽, ὁρᾶτ᾽, οὔπω πέπαυσθε.

Χο.   τουτογὶ νὴ τὸν Δία
τὸ σκέλος ῥίψαντες ἤδη λήγομεν τὸ δεξιόν.

Τρ.   ἐπιδίδωμι τοῦτό γ᾽ ὑμῖν, ὥστε μὴ λυπεῖν ἔτι.

Χο.   ἀλλὰ καὶ τἀριστερόν τοί μ᾽ ἐστ᾽ ἀναγκαίως ἔχον.
ἥδομαι γὰρ καὶ γέγηθα καὶ πέπορδα καὶ γελῶ   335
μᾶλλον ἢ τὸ γῆρας ἐκδὺς ἐκφυγὼν τὴν ἀσπίδα.

Commentary Notes

Lines 1–42

The play begins with an anonymous man (Slave B) dressed in the scruffy attire of a slave kneading round cakes in a large mixing bowl. As he kneads, he presumably makes clear his disgust at his task. A second anonymous slave (Slave A) comes out of one of the side doors of the stage, which represents the door to an Athenian house, and frantically calls out to his companion. In the opening exchange between the slaves it quickly becomes apparent that the cakes being kneaded are made of dung and have to be produced at a fast rate in order to satisfy a greedy and rather fussy dung beetle, which is hidden behind the door of the house.

This is a hugely engaging opening scene as it remains unclear for a long time why there is such a dung beetle and who the free Athenian hero of the comedy will be. It is also not clear for several lines whether this is a real beetle or an extended joke at the expense of another playwright or contemporary politician. As well as keeping the audience guessing, this scene also provides an entertaining contrast between the two slaves: Slave A is terrified by the voracity of the beetle and the speed at which cakes need to be produced to sate the beast, while Slave B wallows in self-pity at his wretched role kneading the stinking dung into cakes. Their exchange varies in speed as it contains a variety of distichomythia (two lines per character), stichomythia (one line per character) and hemistichomythia (half lines per character), as well as a longer speech in which Slave B laments his task. The bawdy nature of the scene, with multiple references to excrement, opportunities for physical comedy and an extended joke at the expense of Zeus himself, is sure to have set the audience laughing from the start.

1

αἶρ᾽: the sense of the verb is 'pick up and hand over'.

μᾶζαν: a cake made of roasted barley flour mixed with a liquid such as milk or wine to form a paste that was kneaded into shape. This sweet delicacy was known for its moist, dense texture.

ὡς τάχος = ὡς τάχιστα.

τῷ κανθάρῳ: with the introduction of the dung beetle, a creature that gathers and eats dung, Slave B's signs of disgust must start to make sense and it becomes clear that the cakes are not the delicious delicacy their name would initially suggest. As the giant dung beetle remains hidden offstage at this point, the audience remains unsure as to whether these cakes are for a man who is being called a dung beetle and thus presented as a 'shit eater', a common term of abuse in Greek comedy, or for a real dung beetle. Sommerstein suggests the audience may initially think of the comic poet Kantharos who was victorious in the City Dionysia of the previous year, 422 BC, and a clear rival of Aristophanes. Given the author's reputation for fiercely mocking the politician Cleon, some might suspect a reference to him.

2

ἰδού: 'there you go'.

τῷ κάκιστ᾽ ἀπολουμένῳ: 'to the one about to perish most terribly' is best translated as a general curse, e.g. 'that abominable creature'. Consider how you can most effectively bring out the slave's anger in your translation.

3

μήποτ᾽... φάγοι: a negative wish for the future using the optative. The slave curses the beetle with the wish that he never taste anything better than dung. However, this shows the slave to be rather foolish: the beetle would love nothing more than to eat only dung!

αὐτῆς: genitive of comparison, assume μᾶζης.

ἡδίω = ἡδίονα.

4

ἐξ ὀνίδων: Ass dung would have been a common sight and smell in the streets of Athens. It is amusing that the beetle is picky about the type of dung it eats.

5

ποῦ ... ἦν: 'where is the cake which' – a condensed direct question followed by a relative clause for which the antecedent has to be understood.

γὰρ: often used to strengthen a question.

νῦν δὴ: 'just now' – δὴ is often used to give greater exactness to adverbs.

6

ἢ κατέφαγεν: the slave can't believe that the beetle has eaten the first cake so quickly.

μὰ τὸν Δί᾽: 'no by Zeus' – this oath is understood as negative by context. Slave A responds in this way not because Slave B was wrong but because his wording was insufficient to describe the greediness of the beetle: it didn't just eat the cake, it devoured the whole lot.

ἐξαρπάσας: the compound strengthens the meaning of the verb and so brings out the bad manners of the beetle.

7

ἐνέκαψε: 'it gulped down' – a much stronger verb than Slave B's κατέφαγεν.

περικυλίσας τοῖν ποδοῖν: τοῖν ποδοῖν is in the dual dative form. The slave provides a realistic description of dung beetles, which use their front legs to roll dung and gather it into a ball. It is at this point that it becomes clear to the audience that the slaves are dealing with a real dung beetle.

8

τρῖβε: as the tense of imperatives is based on aspect, the present form here suggests that the slave must keep on kneading over a long period.

πυκνάς: a good μᾶζα was dense in texture. It is amusing that even though made of dung, the cakes need to be made well. It is likely that Slave A returns inside at this point. Given there are no surviving stage directions, it is interesting to consider when actors enter and exit the stage and the effect this could have on the drama.

9

ἄνδρες κοπρολόγοι: the slave speaks out to the audience members, who are often the butt of jokes in comedy, and amusingly characterizes at least some of those watching as dung-collectors. There were indeed men who collected dung in the city and removed it to the countryside where it was sold. This was presumably a rather humble and easily mocked profession. He calls upon dung-collectors as they are more used to the terrible smell than he is.

10

εἰ μή: 'unless' – the negative μή is used in the protasis (if clause) of conditionals.

11–12: These lines have not been included in the prescription for examination. Slave A returns to the stage and requests another dung-cake, this time made from the excrement of a young male prostitute. This gives the opportunity for a coarse sexual joke of the sort that is common in Old Comedy, particularly from the mouths of characters of low status. Although these two lines are not essential for our understanding of the play, they do add to the bawdy nature of this opening scene and to the humorous warm-up act that these hapless slaves provide. These lines also further the characterization of the beetle as picky and demanding. Once Slave B provides the dung-cake, Slave A presumably returns inside.

13

ἑνὸς ... ἀπολελύσθαι: 'to be found not guilty of one charge' – ἀπολύμαι takes a genitive of the crime. ἀπολελύσθαι is a perfect passive infinitive – the perfect tense describes a current state caused by a past action and is thus best translated as the present.

ὦνδρες = ὦ ἄνδρες.

μοι δοκῶ: 'I think' – followed by an indirect statement using the infinitive construction.

14

οὐδείς. ... ἂν φαίη: 'no one can say' – a negative potential optative with ἄν creates a strong assertion.

με μάττοντ᾽ ἐσθίειν: μάττοντα is in agreement with με and should be translated temporally – 'while kneading'. It was a common complaint among Athenians that slaves pilfered from the household stores but at least this slave can't be accused of stealing dung.

15

αἰβοῖ: a cry of both panic and despair as the slave feels the pressure of supplying enough dung-cakes to satisfy the beetle.

ἄλλην: assume μᾶζαν for all the adjectives in this line.

χἀτέραν = καὶ ἑτέραν.

16

<ἔθ᾽>: these angular brackets show that the editor has added this form of ἔτι to the text. This line, as preserved in the manuscripts of the play, required one more syllable to be metrically complete.

μὰ τὸν Ἀπόλλω: 'no by Apollo' – the negative nature of this oath is made clear by the following οὔ.

'γὼ μὲν οὔ: 'I will not' – a future tense form of the previous verb should be assumed.

17

ὑπερέχειν: 'to keep my head above' – followed by the genitive.

τῆς ἀντλίας: bilge water is the filthy liquid that collects at the bottom of a ship. The slave uses the metaphor of being unable to keep his head above the water while bailing out a ship to vividly portray his inability to keep up with the excessive demands of the beetle. The fact that bilge water is filthy and unpleasant makes it a perfect comparison for the dung the slave is kneading.

18

αὐτὴν... ἀντλίαν: Slave A repeats the word used by Slave B but amusingly appears to have misunderstood his partner's use of it. Slave B uses a metaphor to show how he is overwhelmed by demand but Slave B does not understand it and thinks his partner is overwhelmed by the smell of the dung in the mixing bowl.

ἄρ᾽: 'in that case'.

οἴσω συλλαβών: 'I shall pick it up and take it with me' – note here the common use of a finite verb and participle in Greek when English would use two finite verbs joined by a conjunction.

19

νὴ τὸν Δί᾽: 'yes by Zeus' – a strong positive assertion.

ἐς κόρακάς: 'carry it to hell' – the imperative form of φέρω has to be assumed from what Slave A has just said. This phrase takes its force from the fact that ravens feed on carrion and so to go to the crows implies you are denied burial and left to be eaten by the birds.

γε … γε: repetition puts emphasis on the καί. The assumed imperative needs to be repeated.

πρός: 'as well'.

20

ὑμῶν δέ … τις: 'one of you' – an example of a partitive genitive.

κατειπάτω: 'let him say' – third person imperative which introduces an indirect question.

21

ἂν πριαίμην: 'I might buy' – potential optative in an indirect question.

μὴ τετρημένην: 'of the sort that has no openings' – using μή rather than οὐ gives the participle a generic force: it describes a particular type of nose.

22

ἦν ἄρ': 'it turns out that' – the imperfect tense is used with ἄρα to highlight that a past truth that is still true has just been recognized. It is best translated with the present tense.

23

μάττοντα: this participle is the accusative subject of the infinitive παρέχειν.

ἐσθίειν: infinitive of purpose.

24

ὗς … κύων: pigs and dogs were common animals in Athens and are likely to have lived on leftovers and dung. They are also considered to be slaves to their own bodily desires and lacking in self-control.

ὥσπερ + ἄν + subjunctive = 'as soon as'.

χέσῃ: crude vocabulary commonly found in comedy. The implication here is that dogs and pigs do not need the excrement to be kneaded into shape for them; they eat it as it comes.

25

φαύλως: 'greedily'.

ἐρείδει: 'gets to work on', i.e. 'devours'.

26

βρενθύεταί: a βρένθος is a type of waterbird and so the origin of this verb for behaving arrogantly is likely to be the proud pluming of feathers carried out by birds. One might note the amusing contrast between the beauty of a pluming bird and the voracious appetite of the dung beetle.

27

ἢν μὴ παραθῶ = ἐάν + subjunctive, forming the protasis (if clause) of a future open conditional. This is accompanied by a present tense apodosis to show how characteristic this behaviour is of the beetle – 'if I don't do X … he does Y'.

μή is the usual negative for a protasis. παραθῶ is the active aorist subjunctive from παρατίθημι and αὐτῷ, referring to the beetle, should be assumed as the indirect object.

τρίψας: aorist active participle of τρίβω.

28

μεμαγμένην: perfect passive participle of μάττω.

ὥσπερ γυναικὶ: the dative is used here as the contrast is to the assumed dative on line 27 (see note above). This dig shows the Athenian gender stereotype of women being very particular about the way in which their food is prepared; it was common in comedy to associate women with extravagance and prissiness. It is humorous that we are yet to meet a human hero, but an insect being compared to a human.

29

εἰ: 'whether' – an indirect question is introduced by the verb σκέψομαι.

πέπαυται τῆς ἐδωδῆς: παύω takes the genitive. ἐδωδή is mainly used to refer to the food of animals and so brings with it connotations of uncivilized, unrestrained eating.

30

τηδὶ: 'in this way'. If the slave wishes not to be seen by the beetle within, he presumably opens the door inwards. This must also be the best way to delay the revelation of the beetle to the audience while also exciting them with the prospect of seeing it.

παροίξας τῆς θύρας: aorist active participle of παροίγνυμι, which takes a genitive.

ἵνα μή ... ἴδῃ: negative purpose clause. ἴδῃ is the aorist active subjunctive of ὁράω. μ᾽ = με.

31

ἔρειδε: present imperative of ἐρείδω. The slave repeats the vocabulary he used in line 25 (see note above).

μὴ παύσαιο μηδέποτ᾽: 'may you never stop' – μή + optative is used for a negative wish for the future. If a compound negative, such as μηδέποτ᾽, follows another negative, it forcefully confirms the negative (unlike in English where they cancel each other out).

ἐσθίων: παύω is followed by a participle.

32

τέως ἕως: 'until'.

σαυτὸν λάθῃς διαρραγείς: this subjunctive, commonly found in a relative clause after a potential optative, is best translated in the present tense in English. λανθάνω + accusative + participle = I escape the notice of X in doing Y. It is often best to translate the participle as the main verb: I do Y without X noticing. διαρραγείς is the aorist passive participle of διαρρήγνυμι, which is very commonly used in curses.

33

οἷον: 'how'.

κύψας: 'head down' – the aorist active participle of κύπτω. This image of the beetle standing with his head down is the beginning of the comparison of the beetle to a wrestler. Wrestling was a key part of an Athenian boy's education and the audience would have easily understood this image. This is the second time that the dung beetle has been described as a human.

κατάρατος: 'accursed'.

34

παραβαλὼν τοὺς γομφίους: 'moving its mandibles from side to side'. The γομφίους are the large appendages around the beetle's mouth that are used to gather and soften food. Here they are likened to the arms of a wrestler moving from side to side as he engages in a bout.

35

καὶ ταῦτα: 'and furthermore' – the slave turns to a second description of the beetle.

τὼ χεῖρέ: accusative dual form. This must refer to the front legs of the beetle.

πως: 'rather'.

36

ὡδί: 'like this' – this emphatic form of ὧδε suggests that the slave does an impression of the beetle, making the most of an opportunity for some physical comedy.

τὰ σχοινία: 'ropes' – in particular, thin ropes which were often plaited together for greater strength and longevity.

37

συμβάλλοντες εἰς τὰς ὁλκάδας: the second image employed by the slave to describe the beetle is that of workers who create thick ropes used to hold and tow the heavy cargo ships that transported supplies across the Mediterranean. To create ropes, thinner ropes are plaited together using a crank. The workers' hands must have turned in circles to work the crank and their heads must have moved from side to side as they assessed their work. Given the naval strength of the Athenians, it is likely that the audience would have pictured this easily.

38

μιαρὸν ... βορόν: ἐστί has been omitted from this tricolon of adjectives. It is unclear in the surviving manuscripts how the lines at this point are divided between the two slaves. It could be an interesting activity to experiment with the different ways of dividing the lines between them and the effects this would have on the drama.

μιαρόν: 'filthy', which is an understandable description given what the beetle eats; however, this word also has the strongly pejorative sense 'polluted' which is the polar opposite of 'sacred' and used to refer to any destabilizing element in society.

τὸ χρῆμα: 'the creature'.

39

χὤτου ... ἡ προσβολὴ: the syntax of this indirect question is complex – 'of whichever of the gods the attack is', i.e. 'which of the gods is attacking us'. χὤτου = καὶ ὅτου – a genitive of possession. δαιμόνων is a partitive genitive. The slaves consider the beetle so terrible that they assume it has been sent as a form of divine retribution.

ποτέ: used to strengthen the indefinite nature of ὅστις in the question and as such is not needed in the English translation.

ἡ προσβολὴ: 'attack' – the use of this military word brings out the threat the slave feels from the beetle.

40

οἶδ' = οἶδα, which introduces the indirect question on the previous line.

Ἀφροδίτης ... φαίνεται: ἡ προσβολὴ remains the nominative. The use of the genitive Ἀφροδίτης follows the pattern of the previous line, with εἶναί supplied to follow φαίνεται – 'does not appear to be of Aphrodite'. The slave provides two examples of goddesses that cannot have sent the beetle in order to bring out the hideous nature of the creature. Aphrodite, the goddess of beauty, provides a stark contrast with the ugliness and repulsive smell of the beetle.

41

οὐ μὴν: = 'not indeed'.

Χαρίτων: the three Graces (Aglaia, Euphrosyne and Thalia) were the daughters of Zeus and Eurynome and became the attendants of Aphrodite. As with Aphrodite above, such images of beauty could not have produced such a horrible creature.

γε: marks out the importance of the Graces within the sentence and as such does not require translation.

τοῦ = τίνος

οὐκ ἔσθ' ὅπως: 'there is no way in which' or 'it cannot be that'.

42

Διὸς σκαταιβάτου: Aristophanes has forged a new word here by adding the letter sigma to the beginning of a traditional cult title for Zeus (καταιβάτης = descending with a thunderbolt). In doing so, the prefix for down (κατα-) forms the stem of σκῶρ (σκατ-), which means 'excrement' or 'shit'. This comic wordplay should come across in your translation. Sommerstein translates the phrase as 'Zeus, Lord of the Thunder-crap' but there are many creative ways in which to translate this. There is no response to this joke in the script. In fact, Slave B quickly moves on to asking what the point of the whole opening scene has been. There is something highly amusing about building up to such witty wordplay and instantly moving on without comment.

Lines 43–61

After the intriguing opening of the play, the slaves now begin to explain what the audience have seen. After a brief joke at the expense of the recently deceased politician

Cleon, Slave A returns into the house. Slave B explains that his master, suffering from madness, openly shows his anger at Zeus. The slaves both speak directly to the audience in an insolent tone and have several opportunities for mimicry and physical comedy.

43

ἂν ... λέγοι: 'may say' – a potential optative.

τῶν θεατῶν: a partitive genitive following τις.

44

δοκησίσοφος: 'who thinks he is wise' – a rather grand compound adjective, the tone of which is surely mocking the young men of the audience who have been trained in sophistry.

τόδε πρᾶγμα τί: 'what's happening here?' – the verb ἐστί has been omitted.

45

ὁ κάνθαρος δὲ πρὸς τί: the question word comes at the end of the clause. The clause is best reordered in English: 'what has the beetle got to do with anything?'

κᾆτ' = καὶ εἶτα.

γ': this particle is often found with pronouns to give them emphasis but is not necessary in your English translation.

46

ἀνὴρ Ἰωνικός τίς: τίς is the indefinite pronoun – 'a certain'. It has an accent because the word that follows is an enclitic and so leans on the previous word and passes its own accent up the sentence. Representatives of the subject cities (many of which were Ionian) brought their tribute to the City Dionysia, carrying it into the theatre and placing it on display. The Athenians mocked the Ionians for their effeminate ways and the dialect of Greek they used. The introduction of this anonymous Ionian gives a perfect opportunity for a comic impression.

47–8

δοκέω ... ἐς ... αἰνίσσεται ... κεῖνος: direct speech allows the actor to mimic an Ionian for comic effect. These forms are all Ionic in dialect.

ἐς Κλέωνα: the Ionian interprets the beetle as an allusion to Cleon, now dead, eating excrement in the Underworld. The reason this bitter comment about Cleon is put into the mouth of an Ionian may be to do with tribute. In 425, tribute was raised to its highest level and this was probably still in effect in 421 when *Peace* was first performed. Cleon was held responsible for this rise in taxation and so the Ionians are unlikely to have held him in much regard.

ἐν Ἀΐδεω: supply δόμοις to make sense of the genitive Ἀΐδεω.

σπατίλην: a rare and unpleasant word – not only is Cleon depicted as eating excrement, he is eating the runniest, smelliest sort.

49

εἰσιὼν ... δώσω: Greek uses a participle and finite verb where English would use two finite verbs connected with a conjunction.

πιεῖν: 'something to drink' – infinitive of purpose. The implication is that the slave will urinate and give it to the beetle as a drink. Slave A now leaves the stage and never returns.

50

τοῖσι: poetic form of τοῖς found throughout the play either with or without a final ν, depending on the start of the following word.

παιδίοις: diminutive form. The slave sets off on an ascending list of audience members, which is overblown and irreverent given that he is merely a slave speaking to the mainly free Athenian audience. His diminutives are gently mocking.

51

ἀνδρίοισι: diminutive and poetic form.

52

τοῖς ὑπερτάτοισιν ἀνδράσιν: these men of high positions are likely to be the magistrates of Athens who had reserved seating in the theatre.

53

καὶ ... ἔτι ... μάλα: 'and also, especially ...'.

τοῖς ὑπερηνορέουσιν: this adjective is almost exclusively found in the epic poetry of Homer where it conveys excessive arrogance in purely negative terms (e.g. the suitors of Penelope in the Odyssey). Thus the word is perhaps purposefully chosen to be double-edged: at first it sounds like a grand epic word for the most important men in the theatre, but its true meaning is far from complimentary. The men being referred to are likely to be the most senior of those who have reserved seating in the theatre: the highest magistrates, state priests and the generals of the Athenian navy.

τούτοις: the deictic pronoun suggests that the actor is pointing at these men.

54

ὁ δεσπότης: this refers to Trygaeus who is as yet unnamed. At last there is mention of an Athenian citizen who could be the hero of the play.

μαίνεται: implies a powerful and violent madness.

καινὸν τρόπον: 'in a new way'.

55

οὐχ ὅνπερ ὑμεῖς: 'not in the way you are (mad)' – ὅνπερ refers back to τρόπον and a form of the verb from the previous line should be assumed to follow ὑμεῖς (μαίνεσθε). It is common for characters in comedy to abuse the audience.

ἕτερον καινόν: supply τρόπον.

56

δι᾽ ἡμέρας: 'all day'.

57

ὡδί: the actor clearly mimics his master.

κεχηνώς: 'with his mouth wide open' – perfect active participle of χάσκω.

λοιδορεῖται: this verb is followed by a dative and suggests quite forceful abusive behaviour towards Zeus. The master's madness is becoming clear as he is described as adopting a standard position of prayer but then hurling abuse at the king of the gods whom he is meant to placate.

58

τί ποτε βουλεύει ποιεῖν: direct speech again allows for some comic mimicry.

59

κατάθου: aorist imperative of κατατίθεμαι. The master impudently presents Zeus not as a war bringer but as a slave doing the sweeping.

μὴ 'κκόρει = μὴ ἐκκόρει. There is wordplay here as 'don't sweep away' also contains the word for children (κόρος/κόρη) and so can be interpreted as 'don't make childless'.

τὴν Ἑλλάδα: this refers to all the Greek-speaking states in the Mediterranean and Near East, highlighting the extent of the troubles that they have faced in recent years.

60

ἔα ἔα: 'wait a second, listen up' – the metre of the poetry is lost for a line as the slave notices something and draws the audience's attention to it.

61

σιγήσαθ' = σιγήσατε. This seems to imply that the audience could become noisy at times and may here be responding to the rather poignant prayer of the master that was just reported by the slave.

ὡς ... δοκῶ: causal clause. δοκῶ introduces an indirect statement using the infinitive construction. The main nominative (I) is also the subject of the infinitive in the indirect statement.

φωνῆς ἀκούειν: here ἀκούειν takes the genitive of the noise that is heard.

62–179: The voice of Trygaeus, whose name is not yet known by the audience, is heard calling on Zeus from within the house. The slave goes on to explain how his master's madness developed: at first, he wanted to reach Zeus by making little ladders but he fell down, then by going out and getting an enormous beetle on which he could fly. The slave looks inside one more time and is shocked to find his master now riding the huge insect like a horse and starting to fly into the air.

Trygaeus then appears by means of the theatrical crane, sitting on a giant dung beetle. The slave calls him mad and asks where he is going. The master replies that his slave should support him on his journey and stop men on the earth shitting, so that the beetle is not distracted from its true purpose by the smell of food. Trygaeus makes clear that he aims to fly up to Zeus so that he can ask him about his plans for the Greeks.

The slave calls into the house for the master's children and they come out to beseech him not to go. However, their constant wheedling at their father, who presumably has struggled to feed them due to the poverty caused by wartime conditions, has meant that he no longer cares for them. One daughter asks how he intends to reach Zeus and he describes his beetle as a winged horse in words that are very likely to have been taken from or based on lines from Euripides' Bellerophon. Trygaeus thus begins to present himself as the parody of a tragic hero.

The daughter asks a series of questions intended to put her father off his mission. She asks why he did not use Pegasus so as to look more like Bellerophon in the eyes of the gods and so gain their favour. Trygaeus explains that he could not afford to feed himself and a horse; however, he can feed himself and provide excrement for the beetle. When the daughter asks what will happen if he falls into the sea, he suggests the beetle can also be a boat and raises his comic phallus as an oar. When asked which harbour he would seek, he amusingly suggests the Beetle Harbour, a common term for the Peiraeus, the main port of Athens. Finally, the daughter begs him not to fail and thus provide a real plot for Euripides to use.

Trygaeus says farewell to the girls and sets off. As he flies, Trygaeus sings an anapaestic chorus, the opening lines of which do parody a passage from Euripides' Bellerophon, in which Bellerophon seeks to calm his flying steed, Pegasus. It becomes clear that the beetle is distracted by alleyways, which are a good source of dirt and shit. The rough journey almost becomes too much and Trygaeus calls upon the crane operator to pay attention otherwise he will shit himself with fear (providing another meal for the beetle!). As the journey becomes smoother, he catches sight of the house of Zeus and starts to head back towards the stage.

Lines 180–235

During the flight, Trygaeus and the beetle move across the stage from one side to the other. There is room for some silent comic acting as the beetle lands: the hero now tries to disembark and prepares himself both emotionally and physically to knock on the door of the gods. A voice from inside is heard and then the door opens and Hermes, the messenger god, comes out. Although he is not named until line 365, his mask and costume, presumably wings and a wand, make his identity clear to the audience. Trygaeus receives a gruff reception and quickly becomes sarcastic and impudent.

Hermes turns out not to be as fierce as his initial introduction suggests; in fact, he is easily pleased with a gift of meat and starts to provide some information. We find out that the gods have moved house, leaving behind a few household items, to be as far away from the warmongering Greeks as possible. Hermes also tells us that War has moved into the house of the gods and, having trapped Peace in a deep cavern, he intends to pound the Greek states together with his pestle and mortar into a savoury paste.

The scene is entertaining in the way it presents the gods as normal Athenian men: Zeus lives in an ordinary house but is wealthy enough to have a slave (Hermes) who watches the door and is open to bribes for information. The gods even leave some essential household items behind in their rush to leave. Furthermore, this section sets up the comic depiction of the war among the Greek states as the anthropomorphic god War pounding the states together, which will allow for the use of entertaining props and an extended culinary metaphor when the god appears on stage.

180

πόθεν βροτοῦ με προσέβαλ': Hermes is so struck by the sight of the beetle that he is unable to finish his sentence. We should assume 'voice' as the nominative to go with the genitive βροτοῦ. There is a certain grandeur to these opening words from the god: βροτοῦ is a word mainly used in the high genres of epic and tragedy, and the structure of the sentence is in the style of tragedy.

ὦναξ Ἡράκλεις: an expression of surprise.

181

τουτὶ: emphatic form of τοῦτο.

τὸ κακόν: 'evil' – an adjective and article used to create a noun.

ἱπποκάνθαρος: an Aristophanic coinage, which merges the words for horse and beetle to create a mythical creature. The prefix ἱππο- can be used to give a sense of enormity, which is fitting for the giant beetle that has just been flying around the stage. However, comparing the beetle to a horse also continues the comparison of the beetle to Pegasus and so Trygaeus is presenting himself as a perverse version of Bellerophon (see summary of lines 62–179). Despite talking to a god, Trygaeus is clearly not taking the situation seriously.

182

μιαρὲ: see note on line 38. All the following adjectives are in the vocative. The excessive repetition of various compound or superlative forms of μιαρός shows how Hermes is overcome with anger to the extent he is almost speechless.

κἀναίσχυντε = καὶ ἀναίσχυντε.

184

πῶς δεῦρ' ἀνῆλθες: note that the beetle is likely to be sitting on the stage at this point, so this is likely to be a sign of surprise or disbelief rather than a genuine question.

μιαρῶν: partitive genitive following μιαρώτατε.

185

ἔστ' ὄνομ' = ἔστιν ὄνομα. Hermes asks a series of three questions which ask for information by which an Athenian citizen can be identified.

οὐκ ἐρεῖς: ἐρῶ is the future tense of λέγω. It is clear that Trygaeus is taking his time to respond to Hermes by and the god's impatience is starting to show. Trygaeus mocks Hermes by simply repeating what he has called him rather than giving his real name.

187

ἐμοί: 'my father?' – Trygaeus follows the syntax of Hermes' question in using the dative here. By repeating the dative he is surely teasing the questioner. The line numbers on the text adhere to the original line numbers of the manuscripts but not the order in which they are preserved. It is clear that 186 and 187 were copied in the wrong order as it makes more sense for the questions to go from name to father and then to country, particularly given the increasingly ridiculous answers. The confusion is likely to be a result of three lines ending in the same word: a scribe copying at speed could easily glance away, look back at the text and return to the wrong line, missing out a section and then reinserting it in the wrong place.

186

τὸ γένος: 'by birth' – an accusative of respect.
φράζε μοι: the imperative brings out Hermes' impatience.

188

οὔτοι ... ἔσθ' ὅπως οὐκ: 'there is no way that you will not ...', which is best translated 'you will most certainly ...'. See note on line 41.
ἀποθανεῖ: the future tense of ἀποθνῄσκω is the contract middle form ἀποθανοῦμαι. The use of the simple future tense in both the protasis and apodosis of this conditional makes it a stronger threat.

189

εἰ μὴ κατερεῖς: κατερῶ is commonly used as the future form of καταγορεύω.
τοὔνομ' = τὸ ὄνομα.
τοὔνομ' ὅ τι ποτ' ἔστι σοι: literally 'your name, whatever it is to you' but best translated 'what your name is'. The noun here is placed in the main clause of the sentence and not in the indirect question where we might expect it to be. This is called prolepsis and is common in conversational speech. σοι is a dative of possession.

190

Τρυγαῖος: the audience (and Hermes) finally discover the hero's name. As usual in Aristophanic comedy, his name is appropriate to his role: the root of the name is τρυγάω 'I gather crops or fruit' which not only fits his profession as a vine-dresser but also his role as defender of the Athenian countryside.
Ἀθμονεύς: a deme or political region about six miles outside of Athens. By giving Trygaeus this deme, Aristophanes presents him as a man from the country.
ἀμπελουργὸς δεξιός: 'vine-dresser' – a man who is skilled in pruning vines but likely to also mean an all-round viticulturist.

191

συκοφάντης: the sycophants of Athens were people who took others to court not for the public good, as was expected in the democracy, but out of a desire for personal gain. Given the danger they represented in Athenian society, they can be presented as villainous characters. Trygaeus contrasts himself with these figures and presents himself as a humble defender of the democracy in order to gain access to Zeus.
πραγμάτων: 'legal disputes'. ἐραστὴς πραγμάτων and συκοφάντης are essentially the same in meaning.

192

κατὰ τί: 'for what reason' or 'why'.

τὰ κρέα ταυτί σοι φέρων: the sense of the verb in the question is assumed in the answer – '<I have come> bringing ...'. After an animal was sacrificed, the Athenians burned the fat, bones and some meat. The gods were thought to eat the meat by inhaling the smoke. Trygaeus' trip up to the gods to physically hand the meat over is a comic reinterpretation of a traditional sacrifice.

193

πῶς ἦλθες: 'is that really why you came?' – this is a dramatic exclamation as opposed to a genuine question. Note how Hermes, originally unwelcoming, has quickly changed his tune on receiving the sacrificial meat.

ὦ γλίσχρων: formed from the adjective γλίσχρος (sticky, sweaty) to vividly convey Hermes' greed. The noun is formed to complement Hermes' δειλακρίων and thus mock his sudden change in tone.

193–4

ὁρᾶς ὡς: indirect statement using ὡς is a poetic version of the ὅτι construction.

195

ἴθι νυν: 'come on now' – frequently used before a second imperative.

κάλεσόν: aorist imperative. Trygaeus acts like he is speaking to a slave rather than a god.

ἰηῦ ἰηῦ ἰηῦ: 'ha ha ha!' – Hermes responds to Trygaeus' request with mocking laughter.

196

ὅτ' = ὅτι – a causal clause.

οὐδὲ μέλλεις: 'you have no chance of'.

τῶν θεῶν: ἐγγύς takes the genitive.

197

φροῦδοι γὰρ: assume εἰσί(ν).

εἰσιν ἐξῳκισμένοι: the perfect tense is formed here using the perfect passive participle and part of εἰμί. Note that the middle form ἐξοικίζομαι is used here.

198

ποῖ γῆς: 'where on earth (have they moved) to?' – assume the verb from the previous line. γῆς is a partitive genitive, literally translated 'to where of land'.

ἰδοὺ γῆς: 'on earth indeed!' – ἰδοὺ is used when repeating someone else's words in a dismissive manner.

πόρρω πάνυ: 'a long, long way away!'.

199

αὐτὸν ... κύτταρον: 'the very pinnacle' – κύτταρον is found in Greek literature to refer to a range of hollow, dome-shaped objects: in particular, the cells of a wasps' nest and the cup of an acorn. They provide a comically small comparison for the dome of the sky. It appears that the gods have moved as far away from mortals as they can to the very top of the dome.

ἀτεχνῶς: 'to put it simply'.

τοὐρανοῦ: τοῦ οὐρανοῦ.

200

κατελείφθης: aorist passive of καταλείπω.

201

σκευάρια: these tend to be small household items. We soon learn that War is unable to find a suitable pestle, which suggests that the gods have taken most of their belongings with them. It is comic to present the gods as humans who leave knick-knacks around the house.

202

χυτρίδια: 'small earthenware pots'.

σανίδια: perhaps 'chopping boards', but can simply be 'planks of wood'.

κἀμφορείδια = καὶ ἀμφορίδια – 'small jars'. Note that all three of these nouns are diminutives: the gods have only left behind the small non-essentials.

203

τίνος οὕνεκα: 'why' – genitive + οὕνεκα.

204

Ἕλλησιν ὀργισθέντες: translate the participle as a causal clause – 'because they had become angry …'. ὀργίζομαι is followed by the dative.

εἶτ' = εἶτα.

205

ἵν' = ἵνα – 'where', not to be confused with a purpose clause.

τὸν Πόλεμον: war is personified as the new tenant of Zeus' house. The audience may remember the personification of war in Aristophanes' *Acharnians*, which was produced in 425. In this earlier comedy, War was presented as a drunken party animal.

206

παραδόντες: aorist active participle of παραδίδωμι.

δρᾶν: present active infinitive of δράω.

ὅ τι βούλεται: 'whatever he wants' – ὅστις can introduce an indefinite clause with the indicative rather than the usual indefinite construction.

207

ἀνῳκίσανθ': the prefix makes it clear that the gods have moved upwards to keep away from mortals. Note the contrast with κατῴκισαν in line 205.

ὅπως + superlative adverb = as X as possible.

208

ἵνα μὴ βλέποιεν: negative purpose clause. βλέποιεν is in the optative rather than the subjunctive because it follows a historic main verb; this makes no difference to the translation.

209

μηδ᾽ ... αἰσθανοίατο: the purpose clause continues with μη and another optative verb. αἰσθανοίατο is a poetic form of the third person plural present optative.

ἀντιβολούντων μηδὲν: assume ὑμῶν with ἀντιβολούντων, which are in the genitive following αἰσθανοίατο.

210

τοῦ = τίνος.

οὕνεχ᾽ = οὕνεκα – see note on line 203.

εἰπέ: aorist active imperative of λέγω. Trygaeus is becoming increasingly impatient and worried.

211

ᾑρεῖσθ᾽ = ᾑρεῖσθε – imperfect tense of αἱρέομαι. The imperfect tense implies that mortals repeatedly got in the way of peace treaties by opting to wage war.

211–12

ἐκείνων ... ποιούντων: 'although ...' – a concessive genitive absolute. ἐκείνων refers to the gods. Since it is clear that peace did not work, translate the participle as conative: 'trying to make peace treaties'. Hermes is saying that mortals have blocked divine attempts to make peace rather than the other way around.

212

κεἰ = καὶ εἰ.

οἱ Λακωνικοὶ: a comic term for the Spartans, which draws attention to their region in the Peloponnese rather than stating their city.

213

ὑπερβάλοιντο ... ἔλεγον ἂν: 'if they ever ..., they would always ...' – this is a past general condition made up of a protasis of εἰ + optative and an apodosis of the imperfect indicative + ἂν. It is likely that this refers to 430 when the Athenians, now weakened by plague and threatened by the Spartan invasions of Attica, sought a peace treaty in vain.

μικρόν: 'by a small amount' or 'a little'.

ταδί = τάδε which is best translated 'the following'.

214

ναὶ τὼ σιὼ = νὴ τὼ θεώ in Spartan, Doric dialect. The dual form τὼ σιὼ refers to Castor and Pollux who grew up in Sparta and were common in Spartan oaths. Once again, direct speech offers the opportunity to mimic a Spartan for comic effect.

Ὠττικίων = ὁ Ἀττικίων – a condescending Spartan form for 'the little Attic man'. The singular is being used to represent their enemy as one.

δωσεῖ δίκαν: 'will pay the penalty'. δίκαν is also in the Doric dialect.

215

εἰ δ': a second past general conditional. See note on line 213.

τι πράξαιτ' ἀγαθόν: literally 'you do something good' but best translated 'achieve some success'. πράξαιτε is second person plural. This refers to the Athenian occupation of Pylos, as confirmed on line 219. Note that although both Athenians and Spartans are depicted as getting in the way of peace, the Spartans are presented in a worse light: Spartan weakness is mentioned first and only the Spartans are described as seeking peace in an embarrassing state of weakness.

δ' αὖ: 'on the other hand'.

Ἀττικωνικοί: a comic term for the Athenians which echoes οἱ Λακωνικοί on line 212. It refers to their region rather than their city. Here it is vocative following πράξαιτε.

216

κἄλθοιεν = καὶ ἔλθοιεν – the protasis of the past general condition continues.

οἱ Λάκωνες: another term for the Spartans.

εἰρήνης πέρι: genitive + πέρι = 'concerning'.

217

ἐλέγετ' ἄν: apodosis of the past general conditional. See note on line 213.

ἐξαπατώμεθα: Thucydides reports in Book 4 of his *History of the Peloponnesian War* that when the Spartan embassies reached Athens seeking the release of the Spartan hoplites trapped on the island of Sphacteria, the Assembly was misled by their leaders, in this case Cleon, into rejecting the Spartan offer of peace. Cleon is depicted as telling the Athenians that the Spartans had bad intentions so that the Assembly would vote against peace and continue the war. His motivation is said to be greed.

218

νὴ τὴν Ἀθηνᾶν: Athena was the patron goddess of Athens. She is used for the stereotypical oath of the Athenians just as Castor and Pollux are for the Spartans in line 214.

οὐχὶ = οὐ.

πειστέον: the gerundive of πείθω in an impersonal neuter form – 'we must not be persuaded'.

219

καὖθις = καὶ αὖθις.

ἢν ἔχωμεν: ἢν = ἐάν and introduces the protasis of a future open conditional – ἐάν + subjunctive = 'if we ..., they will ...'. The apodosis comes before the protasis. Here ἔχω has the sense 'keep hold of' or 'continue to occupy'.

τὴν Πύλον: it is now made explicitly clear that Aristophanes is alluding to the Athenian occupation of Pylos in 425. See note on line 215.

220

γοῦν: 'at any rate' or 'after all' – here showing support for what Hermes has said.

χαρακτὴρ ... τῶν ῥημάτων: ἐστίν needs to be understood here and the adjective taken predicatively; translate in the following order – ὁ χαρακτὴρ τῶν ῥημάτων <ἐστίν> ἡμεδαπὸς – before refining your translation. The word χαρακτὴρ is used for the design punched onto a coin during the minting process and helps to convey how Trygaeus considers these words to be distinctively Athenian.

221

ὧν οὕνεκ᾿: 'therefore' – ὧν refers back to all that has just been said about Spartans and Athenians blocking peace.

οἶδ᾿ = οἶδα.

ποτ᾿ ... ἔτι: 'ever again'.

Εἰρήνην: given that this was performed and not read, it is not immediately clear that peace is personified in the way that War has been until Trygaeus asks his question on the next line.

222

τὸ λοιπὸν: 'in the future'.

ὄψεσθ᾿ = ὄψεσθε – future tense of ὁράω.

γὰρ: strengthens the question but difficult to translate other than in tone.

223

αὐτὴν: 'her' – refers to Εἰρήνην.

224

ποῖον: understand ἄντρον.

εἰς τουτὶ = εἰς τοῦτο – the deictic pronoun implies that Hermes is now pointing at the cave in which Peace has been trapped. It is most likely that he points to the central doors of the stage. τὸ κάτω implies that Hermes points downwards towards the doors.

κἄπειθ᾿ = καὶ ἔπειτα.

225

ὅσους ... λίθων: accusative ὅσους is the object of ὁρᾷς on the previous line. λίθων is a partitive genitive – 'how many (of) rocks'.

ἄνωθεν: 'from above'. It is difficult to tell exactly how this was staged. We are initially led to picture a cave but here the entrance seems to be piled up from above as if it is a hole in the ground.

226

ἵνα μὴ λάβητε μηδέποτ᾿: negative purpose clause. The two negatives work together to strengthen the negative meaning; therefore, it is best to omit the first when translating.

αὐτήν: 'her' – refers to Εἰρήνην.

εἰπέ μοι: see note on line 210.

227
ἡμᾶς ... δρᾶν: 'to do to us'.
δὲ δὴ: marks a surprised tone.

228
πλὴν ἕν: 'except for one thing' – πλὴν is used adverbially with a single word when a negative precedes it. It is possible to imagine that a second οἶδα is missing: 'I don't know except *I know* one thing.' This expression is common in tragedy and otherwise not found in Aristophanes. Hermes is clearly speaking in a grand manner as he toys with Trygaeus. Hermes must know exactly what is planned but is enjoying his dominant role in the exchange.
ἑσπέρας: genitive of time.

229
ὑπερφυᾶ τὸ μέγεθος: 'monstrous in size' – ὑπερφυᾶ is the accusative singular form in agreement with θυείαν. τὸ μέγεθος is an accusative of respect.
εἰσηνέγκατο: aorist of εἰσφέρω.

230
ταύτῃ τῇ θυείᾳ: dative following χράομαι.

231
τὰς πόλεις: the cities of Greece.
βουλεύεται: from βουλεύομαι not βούλομαι. As the exchange becomes more terrifying for Trygaeus there is some hope in the fact that War is still only planning.

232
καὶ γὰρ: 'for in fact'.
ἐξιέναι: infinitive of ἔξειμι following μέλλει on line 233.
γνώμην ἐμὴν: 'in my opinion'.

233
θορυβεῖ: a strong verb to use here as it often describes the noise of crowds in confusion.
ἔνδοθεν: 'inside'.
οἴμοι δείλαιος: a tragic exclamation as Trygaeus realizes that the noise he hears means that War is about to appear. Trygaeus starts to move off towards the side of the stage where he will hide when War arrives.

234
φέρ'= φέρε – the imperative provides a sense of urgency.
ἀποδρῶ: iussive subjunctive of ἀποδιδράσκω – 'let me escape!'.
καὶ γὰρ: 'for in fact'.
ὥσπερ ᾐσθόμην: by repeating the verb the sense becomes clear – 'I heard ... as if I heard it'. A clearer translation would therefore be 'I think I heard'.

235

καὐτός = καὶ αὐτός – 'also I'.

θυείας φθέγμα πολεμιστηρίας: this phrase is a peculiar mix of comic and tragic vocabulary: φθέγμα is often found in tragedy but πολεμιστηρίας is only found in comedy. The idea of a speaking warrior mortar is also hugely comic and one might guess at words that would be more fitting here: the sound of a trumpet or the shout of a leader. It is a moment of high emotion but only so much as comedy will allow. Such a line provides a perfect transition into the next scene and the appearance of War.

Lines 236–88

After making a lot of noise offstage, War appears carrying a huge mortar and a selection of ingredients. He is preparing to make a savoury paste, commonly used to accompany fish or meat, out of certain Greek cities which all have a connection to a foodstuff commonly used in Greek cookery. As he names each city he presumably picks up the ingredient each one is associated with and shows it to the audience. Once the ingredients are in the mortar he sends his slave, appropriately named Uproar, to find a pestle, since there is not one in the house. Uproar first goes to Athens to use Cleon as a pestle, a man known to have pursued war rather than peace, and then to Sparta for Brasidas, a similar warmonger. As both men are now dead, War is left without a pestle and so is forced to go inside to make one himself.

236

βροτοὶ πολυτλήμονες: both words bring an epic tone and, along with repetition of βροτοὶ and the dramatic ἰώ, make this a powerful opening line for War.

237

ὡς: introduces either an exclamation ('how …!') or a strong assertion ('… let me tell you!').

τὰς γνάθους: accusative of respect. This suggests that mortals are going to be metaphorically punched in the face. War is characterized as a vicious brawler.

238

ὦναξ Ἄπολλον: Apollo was associated with poetry, music, prophecy and medicine. The call to him here may have been provoked by the threat of physical harm and the potential need for medical assistance in the future. However, it is also likely that Apollo was commonly used at moments of shock or surprise.

τοῦ πλάτους: genitive of exclamation – a colloquial usage. The joke is that the mortar must be enormous if all the cities of Greece are to fit inside it.

239

ὅσον κακόν: supply ἐστί to form an exclamation – 'what an evil it is'.

τοῦ βλέμματος: another genitive of exclamation.

240–1

ἆρ᾽ ... σκελοῖν: this question shows Trygaeus' astonishment at coming face to face with War, a figure that causes such terror in the mortal world.

240

καὶ: used here to draw attention to the new information provided in the relative clause but does not need translation.

241

ὁ δεινός, ὁ ταλαύρινος: both adjectives are used by Homer to describe Ares, the god of war.

τοῖν σκελοῖν: genitive dual form following κατά. 'The one down your legs' can be interpreted in two ways: War is so terrifying that it either turns legs to jelly or sends excrement down legs as soldiers lose control of their bowels. The second interpretation seems far more fitting given the tone of comedy and the many scatological references found in the opening of the play.

242

Πρασιαί: War has begun to make a paste in the mortar using the cities of Greece as his ingredients. Prasiae was a town located on the coast of Laconia. It was attacked by the Athenians in 430 during their summer campaign along the coast. Prasiae has been chosen here because it recalls the inability of the Greeks to make peace by recounting key events in the last decade of the Peloponnesian War but also its name is similar to πράσα (leeks) and so it makes a good ingredient for a savoury paste. War holds up some leeks to the audience before throwing them into the mortar.

243

πολλοδεκάκις: a word coined by Aristophanes to create this hyperbolic description.

ὡς: introducing an exclamation.

ἀπολεῖσθε: future tense of ἀπόλλυμαι.

244

τουτὶ = τοῦτο.

ἄνδρες: Trygaeus addresses the audience.

οὐδὲν ἡμῖν πρᾶγμά: supply ἐστί to make sense of this – 'it is no bother for us'.

245

τῆς Λακωνικῆς: genitive of possession. Trygaeus does not show much concern as he hears of the fate of Prasiae. His lack of interest here will contrast dramatically with his response when Attica is mentioned in line 252.

246

ὦ Μέγαρα Μέγαρ᾽: Megara was located on the Isthmus of Corinth and became an ally of Sparta during the Peloponnesian Wars. The Megarian Decree of *c.* 432, which essentially banned Megarians from harbours and markets across the Athenian empire as a punishment for cultivating sacred land and showing disrespect to the Athenians, was an important catalyst for war. From 431,

Athens invaded Megara twice annually until 424. It was a key exporter of garlic and a head of garlic is likely to be held up by War before he throws it into the mortar.

ἐπιτετρίψεσθ': future tense of ἐπιτρίβομαι. An amusing double meaning is found here as the verb can suggest the act of destroying something like a city but also the act of crushing garlic for cooking.

247

καταμεμυττωτευμένα: 'beaten into a paste'. A μυττωτός is a garlic-based paste used to flavour cooked meat or fish.

248

βαβαὶ βαβαιάξ: a sound to show shock or horror. Trygaeus is not necessarily sympathetic to such a great enemy of Athens, but is surely surprised by the terrible treatment they are about to receive. However, this could also be the response of someone whose eyes are caused to water by the chopping of garlic.

ὡς: introduces an exclamation.

μεγάλα καὶ δριμέα: these adjectives describe τὰ κλαύματα in the following line. δριμέα is often used to describe something with a strong taste like garlic and so is very fitting in this extended cookery scene.

249

τὰ κλαύματα: the audience might have expected the word 'garlic' given what has come before and so is surprised by 'wailings'.

250

Σικελία: Sicily had been in turmoil as Syracuse and other Dorian cities fought against Leontini and the Ionian cities. Athens had supported Leontini, using both warfare and diplomacy to try to encourage more cities to support the Ionians against Syracuse. Sicily was famous for its cheese and so War must hold up a chunk before throwing it into the mortar.

ὡς: introduces an exclamation.

ἀπόλλυσαι: present tense rather than future suggests that there is nothing that can be done to protect Sicily. Notice that the distichomythia turns to stichomythia as the pace increases towards the dramatic introduction of Attica to the mortar.

251

πόλις: this must refer to the territory of Sicily rather than a specific city.

διακναισθήσεται: the future passive of διακναίω. This vocabulary further develops the culinary theme ('will be grated') as well as that of warfare ('will be destroyed').

252

φέρ': see note on line 234. War suddenly deviates from the pattern he has established for introducing cities for the mortar. Attica is placed in a particularly emphatic position at the end of the line.

ἐπιχέω: iussive subjunctive – 'let me pour over'.

καὶ: 'also'.

τουτὶ: τοῦτο.

τἀττικόν = τὸ Ἀττικόν. The honey produced on Mt. Hymettos was famous across the Greek world.

253

οὗτος: 'oi you!'.

'τέρῳ = ἑτέρῳ – the dative follows χρῆσθαι.

254

τετρώβολον: the point being made is that the honey is expensive due to its quality and perhaps also due to the limitations that war has put on its production.

φείδου: imperative of φείδομαι, which takes a genitive.

τἀττικοῦ: see note on line 252.

255

παῖ: vocative – War calls for his slave boy.

Κυδοιμέ: the slave's name is 'din of battle', 'uproar' or 'hubbub'. Translators tend to translate his name into an English form; for example, Sommerstein calls him 'Hurlyburly'. The boy emerges from Zeus' house and must be wearing the shabby clothes of a slave. A war demon of the same name appears in Homer's *Iliad*.

256

ἕστηκας: the perfect tense of ἵστημι is used for a present state – 'you are standing'.

οὑτοσί = οὗτος – assume ἐστί – 'here is …'.

257

ὡς δριμύς: ὡς introduces an exclamation. δριμύς describes κόνδυλος in the previous line.

οἴμοι μοι τάλας: common tragic exclamation of grief and horror.

258

τῶν σκορόδων: 'some of the garlic' – the accusative 'some' has to be assumed to go with this partitive genitive.

259

οἴσεις … τρέχων: as seen previously, the finite verb and participle are best translated as two finite verbs joined by a conjunction in English. You may also wish to consider an adverbial phrase for τρέχων – 'at a run'. A question in the future tense can often be translated as an imperative – 'get!'.

260

οὐκ ἔστιν ἡμῖν: a dative of possession with the pestle as the nominative. It is amusing to note that in their hurry to leave, the gods left the mortar but took the pestle.

261

παρ' Ἀθηναίων: παρά + genitive = 'from'.

μεταθρέξει: μεταθρέξομαι is the future tense of μεταθρέχω.

ταχὺ <πάνυ>: the angular brackets show that πάνυ has been suggested as an addition to this line. The textual critic Dobree put forward this suggestion in order to complete the line, which was otherwise un-metrical. The phrase ταχὺ πάνυ is found elsewhere in Aristophanes and makes good sense here.

262

ἔγωγε: 'I will'. The tense is assumed from μεταθρέξει on the previous line.

εἰ ... κλαύσομαι: a future open conditional. The protasis is condensed into εἰ δὲ μή and the verb needs to be assumed – 'if I don't (do this)'.

263

ἄγε δή: 'come on then'. Although Trygaeus is speaking to the audience, the colloquial imperative ἄγε remains in the singular form.

τί δρῶμεν: the subjunctive is used to make this a deliberative question.

ἀνθρώπια: a diminutive form is used to show his sympathy for the people.

264

τὸν κίνδυνον ἡμῖν ὡς μέγας: the noun here is placed in the main clause of the sentence and not in the indirect question in order to mimic the style of conversational speech. ἡμῖν is a possessive dative. Assume ἐστί for sense – 'how great the danger is for us'.

265

φέρων: 'with'.

266

τούτῳ: the pestle.

ταράξει: not only a verb for mixing, and thus appropriate for the extended cookery metaphor, but also very frequently used with the sense of creating political turmoil.

267

ὦ Διόνυσ': Trygaeus turns to Dionysus in this personal prayer for several reasons. As a vine-dresser, Trygaeus is likely to pray to this god of viticulture frequently. The god of harvest and agriculture is also very fitting for a man on a mission to protect the Athenian countryside. Dionysus Eleuthereus ('the deliverer') is also an appropriate god to free the Greeks from their current grief and sorrow. Finally, as the play is performed at the City Dionysia, it is possible that there is a statue of Dionysus Eleuthereus on stage for Trygaeus to turn to as he prays.

ἀπόλοιτο: optative wish for the future.

μὴ 'λθοι: ἔλθοι is a second optative wish for the future. μὴ is the negative form used with the optative.

268

οὗτος: 'here I am' – used in a vocative sense to gain the attention of someone.
τὸ δεῖνα γὰρ: 'um, well ...' – mumbled interjections to delay giving the news.

269

ἀπόλωλ᾽= ἀπόλωλε.
Ἀθηναίοισιν: dative of possession.

270

ὁ βυρσοπώλης: the pestle must be Cleon who had inherited wealth from his family's
tanning and leather-working business and had recently died at Amphipolis. A
pestle is an object that creates destruction by smashing and mixing ingredients;
for this reason, it is a suitable description of a demagogue who did the same
in politics. In fact, Aristophanes had already compared Cleon to a pestle in his
Knights.
ἐκύκα: imperfect tense of the contract verb κυκάω. This is a verb commonly found
describing the actions of demagogues in Athens.

271–2

εὖ γ᾽ ... ποιῶν ἀπόλωλ᾽: literally 'doing well he died' which comes to mean 'he did
us a good service by dying'.

272

ἐκεῖνος: Cleon.
κἀν δέοντι = καὶ ἐν δέοντι – 'and just at the right time'.
τῇ πόλει: dative of advantage – 'for the city'.

273

ἢ ... ἐγχέαι: 'or before he pours out the paste for us'. πρίν is followed by an
infinitive. The sense of this line is uncertain because it is not clear why the paste
is poured out for the Athenians when they have already been included in the
ingredients for it. Furthermore, the nominative of the previous line is Cleon, but
this line can only be read with a sudden shift to War as the unnamed subject of
ἐγχέαι.

274

μέτει: another future question used as an imperative.

275

ἀνύσας τι: 'quickly'.
ταῦτ᾽= ταῦτα – assume a verb like δράσω to take this accusative.
δέσποθ᾽= δέσποτα – the vocative form.
ἧκέ: imperative.

276

πεισόμεσθα: πείσομαι is the future tense of πάσχω.

νῦν ἀγὼν μέγας: assume ἐστί here – 'now this is ...'.

277

ὑμῶν: partitive genitive.

Σαμοθρᾴκη: Samothrace, an island in the north of the Aegean Sea, was home to a well-known mystery cult. Little is known about mystery cults, but it is clear that initiates called upon the gods of the cult to protect them at times of crisis.

τυγχάνει: τυγχάνω is followed by a participle to give the meaning 'I happen to be ...'. It is often best to translate the participle as the main verb and τυγχάνω as an adverbial phrase: 'I X by chance'.

278

νῦν ... καλὸν: 'now it is a good time to ...' – ἐστιν + neuter adjective + infinitive is a common construction for 'it is X to do Y'.

279

ἀποστραφῆναι ... πόδε: an indirect statement using the infinitive construction following the introductory verb εὔξασθαι on the previous line. The genitive participle, τοῦ μετιόντος, is best translated as a noun: 'the errand-boy'. τὼ πόδε is in the accusative dual form. The use of ἀποστραφῆναι creates a pun: it can mean 'to turn away' when talking about danger or bad luck, but also 'to twist back' when used to describe the torture of a person. So at first it sounds to the audience like a prayer for protection but by the end of the line it is clearly a prayer for injury.

280

κἆτ' ... μάλα = καὶ ἔτι ... μάλα – 'and yet again ...'.

281

μῶν οὐκ: 'surely' – a double negative that requires a positive answer.

282

τοῖς Λακεδαιμονίοισιν: a dative of possession.

283

τἀπὶ ... χωρία = τὰ ἐπὶ ... χωρία. ἐπὶ + genitive = 'towards' or 'in the direction of'. The plural χωρία implies a range of places along the very northern coast of the Aegean Sea.

αὐτὸν: the Spartan pestle is the general Brasidas who died at Amphipolis in 422 as Cleon and the Athenians sought to recapture the town. Cleon died in the same battle. For several years Brasidas had been in the regions near Thrace providing support to the towns that were revolting against Athens. Because of his military success and increasing influence, he was considered to have opposed peace and is thus a very suitable pestle.

284

ἑτέροις: 'to other people' – the people he supported include the towns around Chalcis and King Perdiccas of Macedon.

285

εὖ ... ποιήσαντες: see note on line 271. Assume ἀπώλεσαν from the previous line as the main verb in this sentence too.

ὦ Διοσκόρω: for Castor and Pollux, see the note on line 214. The noun is in the dual vocative form.

286

ἂν εὖ γένοιτο: ἴσως is often followed by ἂν and a potential optative to express a cautious hope for the future.

θαρρεῖτ᾿: imperative.

287

ἀπόφερε ... λαβών: translate both verbs as imperatives – 'pick up and take back'.

ταυτὶ = ταῦτα – this agrees with τὰ σκεύη.

288

δοίδυκ᾿ = δοίδυκα.

εἰσιὼν ποιήσομαι: translate both as finite future verbs. See note on line 18.

Lines 289–336

Trygaeus is delighted that War has so far been unable to make his paste. With War safely back in the house, Trygaeus calls the chorus and audience together to free Peace from the cave. The metre shifts from iambics to fast trochaics as the chorus join and celebrate the promise of a peaceful future. However, the demands of the plot and the demands of the genre clash: as the chorus is needed to help free Peace and avoid War's attention, they are unable to stop singing and dancing. Trygaeus quickly loses his temper with the chorus in a scene that must have been full of movement and sound.

289

τοῦτ᾿ ἐκεῖν᾿ = τοῦτο ἐκεῖνο – 'this is it'!' The sense here is that Trygaeus has found a time for which Datis' song is fitting.

Δάτιδος: Datis the Mede commanded the Persian campaign into Greece, which ended at Marathon.

290

ὃ: accusative neuter relative pronoun referring back to τὸ μέλος.

δεφόμενός: this is a colloquial word and rather crude: 'wanking'. It is important not to fear the use of such coarse language when translating Greek comedy. The Athenians seemed to associate afternoon masturbation with men from the

East, as demonstrated by the surviving phrase 'a Lydian at noon'. This is likely to be because many slaves were from the East and their only chance for sexual pleasure may have been during their afternoon break when masters would take a nap. Therefore, this image of Datis not only presents him in an embarrassing act but also in the role of a sexually frustrated slave.

ᾖδε: imperfect tense of ἀείδω.

τῆς μεσημβρίας: genitive of time.

291

χαίρομαι: this appears to be an error, as χαίρω would be the correct form to use here. Confusing the correct voice of verbs is also found in Timotheus' *Persians* to show a Phrygian struggling with the Greek language. This short piece of direct speech is therefore designed not only to show Trygaeus' delight at the opportunity he now has to stop War but also to gain a few laughs by mocking a Persian.

κεὐφραίνομαι = καὶ εὐφραίνομαι.

292

νῦν ... καλὸν: see note on line 278. The infinitive following this construction is ἐξελκύσαι on line 294.

Ἕλληνες: using 'Greeks' as opposed to 'Athenians' encourages the audience to look beyond state rivalries and see the significance of the message of the play for all the Greek states.

293

ἀπαλλαγεῖσι: aorist participle of ἀπαλλάσσομαι agreeing with ὑμῖν on the previous line.

πραγμάτων ... μαχῶν: genitives following ἀπαλλάσσομαι.

294

πᾶσιν: dative follows φίλην – 'beloved by us all'.

295

πρὶν ... κωλῦσαί: πρὶν + infinitive = 'before'.

ἕτερον ... δοίδυκα ... τινα: accusative subject of the infinitive κωλῦσαί.

296

κἄμποροι = καὶ ἔμποροι.

297

μέτοικοι: 'metics' were foreigners in Athens who had limited citizenship. They could not own land and were subject to heavy taxes; nevertheless, they had the right to remain in Athens, set up businesses and access the Athenian legal system. There were a large number of metics in Athens at this time and many of them had become very wealthy.

ξένοι: there would have been a large number of foreign visitors at the City Dionysia.

298

νησιῶται: this must refer to the men from the islands of the Aegean Sea which were part of the Athenian empire. They were not citizens of Athens but were from allied states.

ἴτ' = ἴτε – imperative.

ὦ πάντες λεῴ: the vocabulary used here is that of a herald making a solemn announcement. From this point the metre of the poetry changes from iambic trimeters to trochaic tetrameters, which give a greater sense of speed and excitement as Trygaeus calls together the chorus and audience. The metre remains trochaic tetrameters until just beyond the examination prescription.

299

λαβόντες: this aorist participle is best translated in the present tense.

300

ἡμῖν ... πάρεστιν: 'it is possible for us ...' – followed by the infinitive σπάσαι.

σπάσαι: there is an amusing pun here: 'to pull' and 'to drink'. Trygaeus is calling on them to both pull Peace out of the cave and drink a libation to the Good Spirit.

ἀγαθοῦ δαίμονος: supply 'a libation' – a drink was poured to the Good Spirit at the end of a meal to mark the beginning of drinking and entertainment. This is a call to make the most of this opportunity and move on to the fun that can follow if Peace is rescued.

301

χώρει: imperative of χωρέω.

εὐθὺ τῆς σωτηρίας: εὐθὺ + genitive = 'straight to ...'.

302

ὦ Πανέλληνες: a particularly inclusive term for all Greeks. The members of the chorus are encouraging each other but also all those in the audience to play their part in ensuring peace.

βοηθήσωμεν: iussive subjunctive.

εἴπερ πώποτε: 'if ever' – the chorus suggests this is a now or never moment.

303

τάξεων ... κακῶν φοινικίδων: the genitives follow ἀπαλλαγέντες. φοινικίδων were part of the uniform of officers in the Athenian army. With peace back, there will be no need for military knowledge or regalia.

304

ἡμέρα ... ἥδε μισολάμαχος: as it is a compound adjective, μισολάμαχος is two-termination (i.e. the masculine and feminine endings are the same). Here it is feminine nominative singular in agreement with ἡμέρα. Lamachus was an Athenian soldier who rose to the high position of general on several occasions, including during the Sicilian expedition. He is found in Aristophanes as a model soldier but also as a man eager to continue the war for financial gain. Thus, the day on which Peace is saved would certainly be hostile to him.

305

πρὸς τάδ᾽: 'therefore'.

κἀρχιτεκτόνει = καὶ ἀρχιτεκτόνει – imperative of ἀρχιτεκτονέω.

306

οὐ γὰρ ἔσθ᾽ ὅπως: see note on line 41.

ἂν δοκῶ μοι: 'I intend to …'. ἂν + subjunctive is commonly found after ὅπως in this construction and has no effect on the otherwise obvious translation.

307

πρὶν … ἀνελκύσαι: πρὶν + infinitive = 'before'.

μηχαναῖσιν: poetic dative plural ending for μηχαναῖς.

308

θεῶν πασῶν: partitive genitive.

φιλαμπελωτάτην: Peace is described in such a way because it was common during an invasion to destroy the crops and farms of the enemy. Vineyards were an essential part of the Athenian rural economy and so were frequently destroyed during Spartan invasions of Attica to weaken the wealth and power of Athens.

309

οὐ σιωπήσεσθ᾽: a question in the future tense is used as an imperative.

ὅπως μὴ: a negative purpose clause using the future tense (ἐκζωπυρήσετ᾽ on line 310) rather than a subjunctive.

τῷ πράγματι: the dative follows περιχαρεῖς.

310

ἐκζωπυρήσετ᾽ ἔνδοθεν: there is a double meaning here. The chorus could either enrage War *who is inside*, or they could inflame him *from the inside*, much like a fire that has burnt down so that there are no flames but there is a hot core ready to be rekindled.

κεκραγότες: perfect participle of κράζω agreeing with the second person plural nominative.

311

τοιούτου … κηρύγματος: the genitive follows ἀκούσαντες. κήρυγμα is normally used for public proclamations and reminds us of the official vocabulary used on line 298. Trygaeus' words are being taken as an official proclamation.

312

οὐ γὰρ ἦν … ἥκειν: 'for it was not …', introduces an indirect command with the infinitive as the chorus explains what they were not told to do in the proclamation.

ἔχοντας σιτί᾽ ἡμερῶν τριῶν: 'with food rations for three days'. These were the usual orders when calling together soldiers for an expedition. The chorus are delighted to be called together for something other than military duty.

313

τὸν κάτωθεν Κέρβερον: Cerberus was the enormous three-headed dog that guarded the entrance to the Underworld. This is another allusion to Cleon who is thought to have described himself as the watchdog of the people of Athens. Aristophanes takes his words and turns them against him. This is a particularly fitting comparison now that Cleon is himself dead and in the Underworld.

314

μὴ: in place of ἵνα μή to create a negative purpose clause with the subjunctive γένηται on line 315.

παφλάζων καὶ κεκραγὼς: Cleon's loud voice is frequently commented on in Aristophanic comedy. Having a loud voice to rouse a crowd is surely a mark of his demagoguery.

315

ἐμποδὼν ... μὴ 'ξελκύσαι: μὴ + infinitive here follows a verb of prevention.

316–17

οὔτι ... ἐμάς: these lines are modelled on lines 976–7 of Euripides' *Children of Heracles*. They are the words of Alcmene, Heracles' mother, as she prepares to have Eurystheus, the terrible king of Argos who has brought great suffering to her son and grandchildren, killed. They are words of passion and conviction in the face of great suffering and so add a moment of grandeur to the comic scene.

οὔτι νῦν γ᾽ ἔτ᾽ ἔστιν: 'there is no longer anyone ...'.

αὐτὴν: refers to Peace.

ἐξαιρήσεται: irregular future of ἐξαιρέω.

ἢν ἅπαξ ... ἔλθῃ: 'once she has come' – ἢν + subjunctive is technically the protasis of an open future conditional to go with the apodosis on the previous line.

ἰοὶ ἰοὶ: loud cheers of joy and celebration.

318

ἐξολεῖτέ ... ἀνήσετε: future open conditional starting with the apodosis. ἐξολεῖτέ is the irregular future tense of ἐξόλλυμι.

τῆς βοῆς ἀνήσετε: the genitive follows ἀνίημι, here found in the future tense.

319

ταυτὶ = ταῦτα.

συνταράξει: see note on line 266. The nominative is unclear here: it could be War or Cleon. It is likely that Aristophanes has left this vague on purpose in order to highlight their similarities.

τοῖν ποδοῖν: dual dative.

320

ὡς ... ταραττέτω: the use of ὡς here is unusual and probably corrupt. As such, the editor has used an obelus (or dagger) to mark this. It is best ignored when translating this line. All three verbs in this line are third person singular imperatives – 'let him ...'. See note on line 270 for use of κυκάτω. This line echoes line 995 of Aeschylus' *Prometheus Bound* where the central character directs these commands at Zeus.

321

χαίροντες ἡμεῖς ... παυσαίμεθ᾽ ἄν: the optative and ἄν found here form the apodosis of a remote future conditional for which the protasis needs to be assumed: '(even if he did all these things), we would not ...'.

322

τί τὸ κακόν: 'what is this madness?'
τί πάσχετ᾽: 'what's the matter with you?'

323

διαφθείρητε: μηδαμῶς + subjunctive creates a negative command.

324

βούλομ᾽ = βούλομαι.
ὑφ᾽ = ὑπὸ + genitive.

325

οὐκ ἐμοῦ κινοῦντος: 'without me moving them' – a genitive absolute.
αὐτὼ τὼ σκέλει: the dual accusative form. αὐτὼ is best translated 'by themselves'.
χορευέτον: a gerundive which here takes an agent in the accusative – 'my legs feel the need to dance'.

326

μή τί μοι νυνί γ᾽ ἔτ᾽: 'not any more now, thank you very much'. μοι is an ethic dative which shows the emotional involvement of the speaker and is often translated as 'please' or 'goodness me'. Here, a sarcastic 'thank you very much' has been suggested but there are many ways to translate this.
ὀρχούμενος: παῦε is followed by a participle.

327

ἦν ἰδού: 'see, look'.

328

τουτί = τοῦτο in agreement with ἕν.
ἔασον: imperative.

329

τοῦτό: 'that's it'.

καὶ μηκέτ᾽ ἄλλο: a subjunctive verb to follow μηκέτ᾽ needs to be supplied here to create a negative command – e.g. 'and don't <make> another <move>.'

μηδὲν ὀρχήσησθ᾽: μη + subjunctive = negative command.

330

ἂν ὀρχησαίμεθ᾽: the optative + ἂν here should be translated as a future tense to match the future tense of the protasis.

τί: 'in any way' – the indefinite article has an accent due to the following enclitic. See note on line 46.

331

ὁρᾶτ᾽: either indicative or imperative.

τουτογὶ = τοῦτο – here best translated as 'we'll do this' or 'yes.'

332

ἤδη λήγομεν: the present tense emphasizes their intention to stop.

333

ὥστε μὴ λυπεῖν ἔτι: 'as long as you don't …' – result clause construction of ὥστε + infinitive. Assume με as the object after λυπεῖν.

334

τἀριστερόν = τὸ ἀριστερόν.

μ᾽ ἐστ᾽ ἀναγκαίως ἔχον: 'it is necessary for me …' – supply 'to throw out' for sense.

335

γέγηθα: perfect tense of γηθέω.

πέπορδα: perfect tense of πέρδομαι. Farting is often a sign of joy and satisfaction.

336

τὸ γῆρας ἐκδὺς: the metaphorical language here presents the feeling of being young again as the taking off of old age like it is a piece of clothing.

ἐκφυγὼν τὴν ἀσπίδα: the shield represents military service.

Vocabulary

While there is no Defined Vocabulary List for A Level, words in the OCR Defined Vocabulary List for AS are marked with * so that students can quickly see the vocabulary with which they should be particularly familiar.

*ἀγαθός -ή -όν	good	ἀμπελουργός -οῦ, m.	vine-grower
*ἀγών -ῶνος, m.	struggle, contest, crisis	ἀμφορείδιον -ου, n.	small jar
ἀείδω, imp. ἦδον	to sing	*ἄν	particle used to make clause indefinite/potential (e.g. would, could)
Ἀθηνᾶ -ᾶς, f.	Athena		
Ἀθηναία -ᾶς, f.	Athena		
Ἀθηναῖος -α -ον	Athenian	ἀναγκαῖος -α -ον	necessary
ἄθλιος -α -ον	wretched, miserable	ἀναίσχυντος -ον	shameless
Ἀθμονεύς	of Athmonum (a region of Attica)	ἄναξ ἄνακτος, m.	lord
		ἀνδρίον -ου, n.	inferior man, little man
αἰβοῖ	bah! (exclamation of disgust or astonishment)	*ἀνέλκω, aor. inf. ἀνελκύσαι	to drag up
Ἀΐδης -εω, m.	Hades, the Underworld	*ἀνέρχομαι, aor. ἀνῆλθον	to come up
αἰνίσσομαι	to hint at, allude to	*ἀνήρ, ἀνδρός, m.	man
*αἱρέομαι	to choose	ἀνθρώπιον -ου, n.	poor little person
*αἴρω	lift up, give	ἀνίημι, fut. ἀνήσω	(+ gen.) to cease from
*αἰσθάνομαι, aor. ἠσθόμην	(+ gen.) to hear	ἀνοικίζω	to move upwards, move to safety
*ἀκούω	(+ gen.) to hear		
ἀλγέω	to be in pain, suffer	ἀντιβολέω	to entreat, supplicate
ἀλετρίβανος -ου, m.	pestle	ἀντλία -ας, f.	bilge-water, filth
*ἀλλά	but	ἄντρον -ου, n.	cave
*ἄλλος -η -ο	other, another	ἀνύω	to do quickly
ἄμη -ης, f.	shovel	ἄνω	on high

ἄνωθεν — from above

*ἀξιόω — to deign, see fit

ἀπαλλάσσομαι, aor. ἀπηλλάχθην — (+ gen.) to be free from

ἅπαξ — once

ἀπαξάπας -ασα -αν — all at once, entirely

ἀπεῖπον — to be worn out, give up from exhaustion

ἀποδιδράσκω, aor. ἐπέδρα — to run away, escape

*ἀποθνήσκω, fut. ἀποθανοῦμαι — to die

*ἀπόλλυμι, fut. mid. ἀπολοῦμαι — to destroy, lose; (middle) die

Ἀπόλλων -ωνος, m. — Apollo

ἀπολύω, perf. pass. inf. ἀπολελύσθαι — (+ gen.) to acquit of, be found not guilty of

ἀποπνίγω — to choke, suffocate

ἀποστρέφω, aor. pass. ἀπεστράφην — to turn away, twist back

ἀποφέρω — to carry off

*ἄρα — then, in that case

*ἄρα — *particle introducing a question*

ἀργός -όν — idle, lazy

*ἀριστερός -ή -όν — left

ἀρχιτεκτονέω — to be chief architect

*ἀσπίς -ίδος, f. — shield

ἀτεχνῶς — simply

Ἀττικίων — little Athenian

Ἀττικός -ή -όν — Attic

Ἀττικωνικοί -ῶν, m. — men of Attica

*αὖ — on the other hand

*αὖθις — again

*αὐτίκα — at once, very shortly

*αὐτός -ή -ό — himself, herself, itself; (not in nom.) him, her, it

*Ἀφροδίτη -ης, f. — Aphrodite

βαβαί βαβαιάξ — goodness me!

*βαθύς, βαθεῖα, βαθύ — deep

βλέμμα -ατος, n. — expression, look

*βλέπω — to look

*βοή -ῆς, f. — shout, shouting

*βοηθέω — (+ dat.) to help

βορός -ά -όν — greedy

*βουλεύομαι — (+ inf.) to resolve to, plan to

*βούλομαι — to want, to wish

βρενθύομαι — to act haughtily, behave arrogantly

βροτός -οῦ, m. — mortal

βυρσοπώλης -ου, m. — leather-seller

*γάρ — for

*γε — at least

*γελάω — to laugh

*γένος -ους, n. — family, birth

γεωργός -οῦ, m. — farmer, peasant

*γῆ -ῆς, f — land

γηθέω, perf. γέγηθα — to rejoice

γῆρας -αος, n. — old age

*γίγνομαι, aor. ἐγενόμην — to become, happen, be

γλίσχρων -ονος, m. — greedy one, niggard, miser

γνάθος -ου, f. — jaw

*γνώμη -ης, f. — opinion

γογγύλος -η -ον — round

γομφίος -ου, m. — molar, tooth

*γοῦν — at any rate

*γυνή γυναικός, f. — woman

δαίμων -ονος, m./f. — divine power, god, goddess

Δᾶτις -ιδος, m. — Datis

*δέ — and, but

δείλαιος -α -ον — wretched

δειλακρίων -ωνος, m. — poor little creature

δεῖνα -ος, n. — a certain thing, (here) the thing is

*δεινός -ή -όν — terrible, fearful

*δεξιός -ά -όν — skilled, right

δέον -οντος, n. — the right time

*δέσποινα -ας, f.	mistress	*εἷς, μία, ἕν	one
*δεσπότης -ου, m.	master	*εἴσειμι	to enter
*δεῦρο	here	εἰσοικίζομαι	to move in
δέφομαι	to masturbate, wank	*εἰσφέρω, aor. εἰσήνεγκα	to carry in
*δή	in truth, indeed, then	*εἶτα	then
δημιουργός -οῦ, m.	craftsman	*ἐκ/ἐξ	(+ gen.) from, out of
*δῆτα	(in a question) then	ἐκδύω, aor. ἐξέδυν	to take off, be rid of
*διά	(+ acc.) because of	*ἐκεῖνος -η -ο	that, (pl.) those
	(+ gen.) for, through(out)	ἐκζωπυρέω	to rekindle
διακναίω, fut. pass. διακναισθήσομαι	to grate, tear into pieces	ἐκκορέω	to sweep clean
διαρρήγνυμι, aor. pass. part. διαρραγείς	to break; (passive) to burst	*ἐκλάμπω, aor. ἐξέλαμψα	to shine forth
*διαφθείρω	to destroy, ruin	*ἐκτρέχω, aor. ἐξέδραμον	to run out
*δίδωμι, fut. δώσω	to give, pay	*ἐκφεύγω, aor. ἐξέφυγον	to escape
*δίκη -ης, f.	punishment, penalty	*ἕλκω	to drag, (here) dance
Διόνυσος -ου, m.	Dionysus	*Ἑλλάς -άδος, f.	Greece
Διόσκοροι -ων, m.	the Sons of Zeus, Castor and Pollux	*Ἕλληνες -ων, m. pl.	Greeks
δοῖδυξ -υκος, m.	pestle	*ἐμβάλλω, aor. ἐνέβαλον	to throw into
*δοκέω	to seem, think	*ἐμός -ή -όν	my, mine
δοκησίσοφος -ον	considering oneself wise	ἐμποδών	in the way
*δράω, aor. ἔδρασα	to do	ἔμπορος -ου, m.	traveller
δριμύς -εῖα -ύ	bitter, fierce	ἔνδοθεν	from inside
ἔα	whoa!	*ἐνταῦθα	here
*ἐάω, aor. εἴασα	to allow	*ἐξαιρέω, fut. ἐξαιρήσομαι	to take away
*ἐγγύς	(+ gen.) near	ἐξαπατάω	to deceive, trick
ἐγκάπτω, aor. ἐνέκαψα	to gulp down greedily	ἐξαρπάζω, aor. ἐξήρπασα	to snatch away
ἐγχέω, aor. ἐνέχεα	to pour into a vessel	*ἔξειμι	to come out
*ἐγώ	I	*ἐξέλκω, aor. inf. ἐξελκύσαι	to drag out, (here) rescue
ἐδωδή -ῆς, f.	food, meal	ἐξοικίζομαι	to move out
*εἰ	if	ἐξόλλυμι	to destroy utterly
*εἰμί, imp. ἦ(ν)	to be	*ἔπειτα	then
*εἶμι, imp. ἴθι	to go	*ἐπί	(+ acc.) towards
εἴπερ	if indeed	ἐπιδίδωμι	to give, bestow, make a gift of
*εἰρήνη -ης, f.	peace		
*εἰς	(+ acc.) into, to		

ἐπιτρίβομαι, fut. ἐπιτετρίψομαι	to be rubbed out, be crushed	Θρᾴκη -ης, f.	Thrace
ἐπιφορέω	to pile upon	θυεία -ας, f.	mortar, bowl (for grinding herbs, etc.)
ἐπιχέω	to pour over	*θύρα -ας, f.	door
*ἔργον -ου, n.	task, function	ἰδού	behold, there you go
ἐρείδω	to lean on, set to work on	ἰηῦ ἰηῦ ἰηῦ	ha ha ha!
*ἔρχομαι, aor. ἦλθον	to go, come	*ἵνα	there, where; so that, in order that
*ἐσθίω, aor. ἔφαγον	to eat		
*ἑσπέρα -ας, f.	evening	ἰοί	*a cry of joy*
*ἕτερος -α -ον	the other of two, another	ἱπποκάνθαρος -ου, m.	horse-beetle
*ἔτι	still, further, in addition	*ἵστημι, perf. intrans. ἕστηκα	to set up, stand
*εὖ	well		
*εὐθύς	at once, immediately	*ἴσως	perhaps
εὐθύς -εῖα -ύ	straight, direct	ἰώ	oh! alas!
εὐλαβέομαι	to beware of	Ἰωνικός -ή -όν	Ionian, from Ionia
εὐφραίνομαι	to make merry, be elated	κάθημαι	to sit down, be seated
εὔχομαι, aor. ηὐξάμην	to pray	*καί	and, even, also
		καινός -ή -όν	new, strange
ἐχθές	yesterday	*κακός -ή -όν	bad, evil
*ἔχω	to have	κάκοσμος -ον	smelly
*ἕως	until	*καλέω	to summon
*Ζεύς Διός, m.	Zeus	καλός -ή -όν	fine
*ἤ	than	κάνθαρος -ου, m.	dung-beetle
ἦ	surely... not?	*κατά	(+ acc.) concerning, about
*ἤδη	already, by now		(+ gen.) down
*ἥδομαι	to be pleased, be delighted	*καταγορεύω, aor. κατεῖπον	to tell
ἡδονή -ῆς, f.	pleasure, delight	καταλείπω, aor. pass. κατελείφθην	to leave behind
*ἡδύς ἡδεῖα ἡδύ	sweet to taste		
*ἥκω, fut. ἥξω	to have come	καταμυττωτεύω	to make mincemeat of
ἡμεδαπός -ή -όν	of our land	κατάρατος -ον	accursed, abominable
*ἡμέρα -ας, f.	day	*κατατίθεμαι, imp. κατάθου	to lay aside, put down
ἤν	if; look!		
ἡνίκα	when	κατεσθίω, aor. κατέφαγον	to eat up, devour
Ἡρακλῆς Ἡρακλέους, m.	Heracles		
		κατοικίζω	to settle in residence, establish, place
θαρρέω	to have courage, be bold		
θεατής -οῦ, m.	spectator	κάτω	below
*θεός -οῦ, m./f.	god	κάτωθεν	from below
θορυβέω	to make noise	Κέρβερος -ου, m.	Cerberus

κεφαλή -ῆς, f	head	*λοιπόν -οῦ, n.	the future
κήρυγμα -ατος, n.	proclamation, announcement	*λοιπός -ή -όν	left over, remaining
*κινέω	to move	*λυπέω	to vex, cause pain, be a nuisance
κλαίω, fut. κλαύσομαι	to cry, wail	μὰ	(+ acc.) by X, for X's sake (often referring to a god)
κλαῦμα -ατος, n.	(pl.) weeping, wailing, misfortunes	μᾶζα -ης, f.	cake, barley-cake
Κλέων -ωνος, m.	Cleon	μαίνομαι	to be mad
κόνδυλος -ου, m.	knuckle, a punch	*μακρός -ά -όν	long
κοπρολόγος -ου, m.	dung-gatherer	*μάλα	especially, as much as any
κόραξ -ακος, m.	raven, crow	*μᾶλλον	more
κόρημα -ατος, n.	broom	μάττω, perf. μέμαγμαι	to knead, mould
κράζω, perf. ἐκέκραξα	to shout, shriek	μάχη -ης, f.	battle
κρέας κρέως, n.	meat	*μάχομαι	to fight
κυδοιμός -οῦ, m.	uproar	Μέγαρα -ων, n.	Megara
κυκάω	to stir up, throw into confusion	Μεγαρεύς -έως, m.	citizen of Megara
κύπτω, aor. part. κύψας	to stoop, to put one's head down	*μέγας, μεγάλη, μέγα	big
κύτταρος -ου, m.	pinnacle	μέγεθος -εος, n.	size
κύων κυνος, m./f.	dog	μέλε	(vocative) master
*κωλύω, aor. ἐκώλυσα	to hinder, get in the way	μέλι -ιτος, n.	honey
*Λακεδαιμόνιος -α -ον	Spartan	*μέλλω	to be destined to, be about to
Λακεδαίμων -ονος, f.	Laconia, Sparta	μέλος -εος, n.	song
Λάκων -ωνος, m.	a Spartan	μέν	indeed
Λακωνική -ῆς, f.	Laconia, Sparta	*μέν ...δέ ...	on the one hand ...on the other ...
Λακωνικός -ή -όν	Spartan	μεσημβρία -ας, f.	midday, noon
*λανθάνω	to do (+ participle) without (+ accusative) realizing	μετατρέχω, fut. μεταθρέξομαι	to run and fetch
*λέγω, fut. ἐρῶ, aor. εἶπον	to speak, say	μέτειμι	to go to fetch
λεώς -ώ, m.	people	μέτοικος -ου, m.	immigrant
λήγω	to stop	*μή	not
*λίθος -ου, m.	stone	*μηδαμῶς	in no way
*λόγος -ου, m.	word, plot	*μηδέ	and not
λοιδορέομαι + dat.	to hurl abuse at	*μηδείς, μηδεμία, μηδέν	no one, nothing
		*μηδέποτε	never
		*μηκέτι	no longer
		μήν	truly, indeed

*μήποτε	never
μηχανή -ῆς, f.	machine, crane
μιαρός -ή -όν	filthy
*μικρός -ά -όν	small, little
μισολάμαχος -ον	hostile to Lamachos
*μόνος -η -ον	alone
μοχλός -οῦ, m.	crowbar
μυέομαι, perf. pass. part. μεμυημένος	to be initiated (into a mystery cult)
μυττωτός -οῦ, m.	a savoury paste
μῶν	surely not ...?
*ναί	(+ acc.) yes by X (often referring to a god)
*νεανίας -ου, m.	young man
νή τὸν Δία	(+ acc.) yes by Zeus (strong affirmation)
νησιώτης -ου, m.	islander
*νῦν	now, just now
*ξένος -ου, m.	foreigner
*ὅδε, ἥδε, τόδε	this
*οἶδα, plup. ᾔδη	to know
οἰκέτης -ου, m.	house-slave, slave
οἴμοι	alas!
οἷον	how
*οἷος -α -ον	what sort of
*οἷος τ'εἰμί	to be able
οἴχομαι	to go
ὁλκάς -άδος, f.	cargo ship
ὅλος -η -ον	whole, entire
ὀνίς -ίδος, f.	the dung of an ass
*ὄνομα -ατος, n.	name
ὅπως	in such a manner as; (+ superlative adverb) as X as possible; so that
*ὁράω, fut. ὄψομαι, aor. εἶδον	to see
*ὀργίζομαι, aor. ὠργίσθην	(+ dat.) to grow angry with
ὀρχέομαι, aor. ὠρχησάμην	to dance

*ὅς, ἥ, ὅ	who, which
*ὅσος -η -ον	how much; (pl.) how many
ὅσπερ, ἥπερ, ὅπερ	who, which
*ὅστις, ἥτις, ὅ τι	whoever, whatever
ὅτε	when, since
*ὅτι	that
ὁτιή	because
*οὐ (οὐκ, οὐχ)	not
*οὐδέ	and not
*οὐδείς, οὐδεμία, οὐδέν	no one, nothing
οὐδέπω	not yet
*οὐκέτι	no longer
*οὔκουν	(impatient question) not
*οὐκοῦν	surely
οὕνεκα	(+ gen.) on account of
*οὐρανός -οῦ, m.	sky, heaven
οὔτι	by no means, not at all
οὔτοι	indeed not
*οὗτος, αὕτη, τοῦτο	this, (pl.) these
*παῖς, παιδός, m.	child
παλαιστής -οῦ, m.	wrestler
*πάλιν	back, again
παμμίαρος -ον	utterly vile
Πανέλληνες -ων, m. pl.	all the Greeks
πανοῦργος -ον	wicked, villainous
πάνυ	altogether, completely
*παρά	(+ gen.) from
παραβάλλω, aor. παρέβαλον	to throw to the side, move sideways
παραδίδωμι	to hand over, betray
παραινέω	to advise, recommend
παρακάθημαι	to sit beside
παρασκευάζομαι	to get ready
παρατίθημι, aor. subj. παραθῶ	to serve
*πάρεστι(ν)	it is possible
*παρέχω	to provide

παροίγνυμι	to open a little	πολυτλήμων -ονος, m/f.	much enduring
*πᾶς, πᾶσα, πᾶν	all, the whole	πονηρός -ά -όν	poor, wretched
*πάσχω, fut. πείσομαι	to suffer, endure	πόρρω	far away
πατέω	to trample on	*ποτέ	ever
*πατήρ -τρός, m.	father	πότνια -ας, f.	mistress, lady
*παύω, perf. πέπαυμαι	to stop	*ποῦ	where?
παφλάζω	to splutter	*πούς ποδός, m.	foot
παχύς -εῖα -ύ	thick	*πρᾶγμα -ατος, n.	matter, affair, trouble
*πείθω	to persuade	Πρασιαί -ῶν, f.	Prasiae
πεντάκις	five times	*πράττω, aor. ἔπραξα	to achieve, accomplish
*πέρδομαι	to fart	πρίαμαι	to buy
*περί	(+ gen.) about	*πρίν	(+ inf.) before
περιάγω	to turn in a circle	*πρόθυμως	eagerly
περικυλινδέω, aor. περιεκύλισα	to roll around	*πρός	(+ gen.) by
περιοράω, aor. περιεῖδον	to overlook, allow		(+ acc.) concerned with, to do with
			(adverb) as well, besides
περιχαρής -ές	joyful	*προσβάλλω, aor. προσέβαλον	to strike, reach
*πίνω, inf. πιεῖν	to drink	προσβολή -ῆς, f.	attack, assault
πλάσσω, perf. πέπλασμαι	to form, mould	προσλαμβάνω, aor. προσέλαβον	to lend a hand, help
πλάτος -εος, n.	breadth, width		
*πλήν	(adverb) except, save	πυκνός -ή -όν	dense, firm, solid
ποδαπός -ή -όν	from what country?	Πύλος -ου, f.	Pylos
πόθεν	from where?	πω	yet
*ποῖ	to where?	πώποτε	ever
*ποιέω, fut. ποιήσω	to do, make	πως	somehow, rather
*ποῖος -α -ον	what kind of?, which?	πῶς	how?
*πολεμέω	to wage war	ῥῆμα -ατος, n.	word
πολεμιστήριος -α -ον	of a warrior, martial	*ῥίπτω	to throw
*Πόλεμος -ου, m.	war	ῥίς ῥινός, f.	nose
*πόλις -εως, f.	city	Σαμοθράκη -ης, f.	Samothrace
*πολλάκις	many times, often	σανίδιον -ου, n.	board, plank
πολλοδεκάκις	many tens of times, umpteen times	*σεαυτόν, σεαυτήν/ σαυτόν, σαυτήν	yourself
		*σιγάω	to be quiet
*πολύς, πολλή, πολύ	much, many	Σικελία -ας, f.	Sicily
		σιός -οῦ, m.	god (in Spartan dialect)

σιτίον -ου, n.	corn, food
σιωπάω, fut. σιωπήσομαι	be quiet
σκαταιβάτης -ου, m.	descending in a storm of shit
σκέλος -εος, n.	leg
σκέπτομαι, fut. σκέψομαι	to look
σκευάριον -ου, n.	utensils, small household items
σκεῦος -εος, n.	stuff, items, household utensils
σκόροδον -ου, n.	garlic
σπατίλη -ης, f.	diarrhoea
σπάω, aor. ἔσπασα	to draw in, drink
σπονδαί -ῶν, f.	treaty, truce
*σύ	you (sg.)
συκοφάντης -ου, m.	lover, malicious accuser
συλλαμβάνω, aor. συνέλαβον	to gather together, carry off
συμβάλλω	to twist together
συνταράσσω, fut. συνταράξω	to throw into disorder
σχῆμα -ατος, n.	gesture, dance, dancing
σχηματίζω	to dance
σχοινίον -ου, n.	rope
*σωτηρία -ας, f.	safely, salvation
τάλας τάλαινα τάλαν	wretched
ταλαύρινος -η -ον	shield-bearing
τάξις -εως, f.	military formation
ταράσσω, fut. ταράξω	to throw into disorder, stir up
*ταχύς -εῖα -ύ	quick
*τε ...καί ...	both ... and ...
τέκτων -ονος, m.	carpenter
τέρας -ατος, n.	divine sign, monster
τετραίνω, perf. τέτρημαι	to perforate, pierce holes into
τετρώβολος -ον	costs 4 obols
τέως	so long
τῃδί	in this way, in this direction
τήμερον	today
τηρέω	to watch over, look after
*τις, τις, τι	someone, something
τοι	in truth, indeed
*τοιοῦτος -αύτη -οῦτο	such
τολμηρός -ά -όν	audacious
*τρεῖς, τρία	three
τρίβω, aor. ἔτριψα	to knead, pound
*τρίς	three times, thrice
*τρόπος -ου, m.	way, manner
*τυγχάνω	(+ participle) to happen to be
*ὑμεῖς	you (pl.)
ὑπερβάλλω, aor. ὑπερέβαλον	to prevail, gain the advantage
ὑπερέχω	(+ gen.) to stay above
ὑπερηνορέων -οντος, m.	superman, an overbearing man
ὑπέρτατος -η -ον	of the highest rank
ὑπερφυής -ές	enormous, monstrous
*ὑπό	(+ acc.) under, beneath
	(+ gen.) by, out of, because of
ὑς ὑός, m.	pig
*φαίνομαι, aor. ἐφάνην	(+ inf.) to appear to be, to seem
φαύλως	simply, without a second thought
φείδομαι	(+ gen.) to be sparing with
*φέρω, fut. οἴσω	to carry
*φεύγω	to flee
*φημί	to say
φθέγμα -ατος, n.	voice
φιλάμπελος -ον	vine-loving
φίλος -η -ον	dear, beloved
φοινικίδιον -ου, n.	a little Phoenician, crimson robe
φράζω, fut. φράσω	to declare, explain

φρόνημα -ατος, n.	pride, arrogance	*χράω, aor. ἔχρησα	to lend
φροῦδος -η -ον	gone away	*χρή	(+ inf.) it is necessary
*φωνή -ῆς, f.	voice	*χρῆμα -ατος, n.	thing, creature
φῶς φωτός, n.	light	χυτρίδιον -ου, n.	small pot
*χαίρω	to rejoice	*χωρέω	to come
χαρακτήρ -ῆρος, m.	character	χωρίον -ου, n.	place, district, region
Χάριτες -ων, f. pl.	the Graces	ὦ	(+ voc.) o (addressing someone)
χάσκω, per. part. κεχηνώς	to gape, hold one's mouth open	ὡδί	in this way
χέζω, aor. ἔχεσον	to shit	*ὡς	as, since, that, how
*χείρ χειρός, f.	hand	*ὡς τάχιστα	as quickly as possible
χορεύω	to dance	ὡς τάχος	as quickly as possible
*χράομαι, fut. χρήσομαι	(+ dat.) to make use of	*ὥσπερ	as if, just as, as soon as
		ὠφελέω	to help